# Natural Law and Practical Reason

# NATURAL LAW and PRACTICAL REASON

## *A Thomist View of Moral Autonomy*

MARTIN RHONHEIMER

Translated from the German by Gerald Malsbary

FORDHAM UNIVERSITY PRESS
New York

Moral Philosophy and Moral Theology, No. 1
ISSN 1527-523X

Library of Congress Cataloging-in-Publication Data

Rhonheimer, Martin, 1950–
[Natur als Grundlage der Moral. English]
Natural law and practical reason : a Thomist view of moral autonomy / Martin Rhonheimer ; English translation from the German original by Gerald Malsbary.—1st ed.
p. cm.—(Moral philosophy and moral theology ; no. 1)
Includes bibliographical references (p. ).
ISBN 0-8232-1978-X (hc.)—ISBN 0-8232-1979-8 (pbk.)
1. Christian ethics—Catholic authors. 2. Natural law.
3. Thomas, Aquinas, Saint, 1225?–1274—Ethics. I. Title.
II. Series.
BJ1249.R4713 2000
171'.2—dc21 99-089242

Printed in the United States of America
06 5
First Edition

# CONTENTS

Preface to the English Edition vii

Abbreviations Used for the Citation of Thomas's Works xii

Introduction xiii

PART I
THE LAW OF THE PRACTICAL REASON: METHODOLOGY AND CONCEPTUAL FOUNDATIONS

1 Natural Law and the Practical Reason as the Subject of Philosophical Ethics 3

2 The Concept of the Natural Law in Thomas Aquinas: A Theory of the Practical Reason 58

PART II
PERSONAL AUTONOMY, NATURAL LAW, AND MORAL OBJECTIVITY: IN-DEPTH STUDIES

Preliminary Note 179

3 The Model of "Autonomous Morality" 181

4 The Concept of Autonomy 195

5 Participated Autonomy: Toward a Metaphysics and Anthropology of the Natural Law 234

6 Natural Dynamics of the Reason: The Epistemological Structure of the Natural Law 257

7 The Normative Function of the Reason and Its Fulfillment in Moral Virtue 307

8 "Teleological Ethics" (I): Utilitarianism and the Deontology/Teleology Distinction 351

9 "Teleological Ethics" (II): Physicalism and Hidden Deontology 382

10 The Objectivity of Human Action: The Object of Action and the Practical Reason 410

11 The Objectivity of Human Action: Detailed Treatment of Some Classic Problems 452

12 The Objectivity of Human Action: The Object of Action and the Natural Law 491

13 Some Philosophical Conclusions—and an Orientation for Moral Theology 534

Author's Postscript to the English Edition 555

Bibliography 593

Bibliographical Supplement 611

Index 617

# PREFACE TO THE ENGLISH EDITION

When the original edition of this book appeared in 1987, I never would have dreamed it would one day be published in English. That this is now occurring is, obviously, for me a moment of joy and gratitude.

During the last two decades the academic debate about natural law has been very intense, and English-writing authors have furnished the most remarkable contributions to the subject. Nonetheless, I presume that with this book I am not carrying coals to Newcastle. I hope that it will be of some help, contributing in a useful way to this discussion. This hope is nourished by my personal conviction that the views put forward in these pages cannot easily be attached to one of the well-known sides of the debate. Moreover, the subject has certainly acquired new and increased interest since the appearance in 1993 of the encyclical *Veritatis Splendor.*

The original motivation in writing this book was to discuss critically and to overcome 1) misunderstandings in the traditional neothomistic view of natural law and 2) the unjustified claims of some recent currents in Roman Catholic moral theology, which try to found, upon what I deem a rather unfaithful reading of Aquinas's teaching on natural law, a new yet problematic understanding of moral autonomy.

I shall challenge this reading from an exclusively philosophical standpoint, as well as the corresponding conception of moral autonomy, closely connected with the adoption, by the same moral theologians, of consequentialism and proportionalism. I shall do that by systematically exploring Aquinas's doctrine on natural law, putting into evidence both its coherency and its connection with other features of Aquinas's teaching on human action, namely his conception of the moral object and some related questions.

Rejecting a certain neothomistic, rather naturalistic understanding of natural law, I shall explain how natural law is to be called not a law of nature as such, but properly a law of practical reason, yet completely natural to humankind because reason obviously is an essential part of human nature. Moreover, I shall argue that the position rooted in a revisionist reading of Aquinas, leading to a deeply flawed conception of moral autonomy, derives part of its plausibility from what I think to be widespread traditional prejudices, as, for example, the idea of severing "reason" from "nature"—and vice versa—opposing one to the other, and a "physicalist' misconception of what constitutes the moral object of a human act. This will be further explained in the introduction.

I am convinced that a discourse on natural law is a discourse on practical reason. What distinguishes a natural-law doctrine from any other kind of theory about practical reason, however, is that it contains a view of practical reason as embedded in specific natural inclinations of the human person. Nevertheless, a doctrine of natural law is not a doctrine about natural inclinations but precisely one about practical reason, which is shown to be practical insofar as it works in a context determined by natural inclinations. Being so tightly bound up with practical reason, any conception of natural law necessarily includes an understanding of moral autonomy. Autonomy is rooted in reason. Only a reasonable being—that is, a being acting on reasons, on the grounds of its own insight into the good—can be called "autonomous." Curiously enough, the currents of Catholic moral theology criticized here have opted for autonomy not so much understood as the human person's capacity of acquiring knowledge of his or her proper good and therefore acquiring mastery over him- and herself, but as the capacity of determining this good in a "creative" way, independently of any preconceived standard. According to this conception, natural law is reduced to humankind's capacity of rationally "creating" conceptions about the good and the corresponding moral norms. I shall challenge this view, showing its inner contradictions and shortcomings, its lack of textual faithfulness—insofar as it claims to be a thomistic view—and develop an alternative view of moral autonomy that does justice to the human person's cognitive autonomy in grasping and establishing the fundamental standards of the human good, as well as the dependence of these standards on preconditions that are not at humankind's disposal. Therefore, practical reason, even though not simply "receptive," may not properly be called a morally "creative" power, but rather a power that is constitutive of the human good.

As the reader will notice, in the course of the following exposition I will pay special attention to the question of contraception. This is not because contraception is meant to be a major subject of this book but because this problem, in the past, was the one that provoked the emergence of the views here criticized. As is well known, in Roman Catholic moral theology the question of contraception has become something like a test-case for different understandings of natural law and for the corresponding arguments based on it. The excursus about contraception is meant to show how the view of natural law developed in this book would apply to this question.

Since the publication of the original edition of this book there has been much development in moral philosophy and natural-law theory, but for this English edition I have preferred not to alter the original text. The only change consists in having, for technical reasons, split the original's sections 6 and 7 of part 2 into several smaller sections. The original bibliography has likewise been included without modification; yet it is followed by a new bibliographical supplement indicating relevant publications since 1987. The excursus about contraception has also remained unchanged, although I later (1989) published a more developed account of my view in *The Linacre Quarterly.* At the end of the main text I have added an extensive and completely new postscript that relates the original context and concerns of the book and its reception in the academic world. There I also respond to some of the most important criticisms put forward so far.

Considering my subsequent work on the subject, in the postscript's last section I also indicate some issues toward which I have slightly changed my approach and some questions that I have treated more fully in some articles and especially in two other books, both published in 1994: *Praktische Vernunft und Vernunftigkeit der Praxis,* which shows how Aquinas's doctrine on natural law is a theory of moral principles required by and being a complement of Aristotelian virtue ethics centered in prudence; and *La prospettiva della morale,* which systematically develops the philosophical part of a virtue ethics on thomistic grounds, stressing the importance of the intentional understanding of human acts, the nexus between natural-law principles and the virtues, mainly prudence, and proposing on these grounds a thorough criticism of consequentialism. So even if the present book is a book about natural law, it must be read in the context of an approach centered in the virtues. That is why I deem extremely valuable, also as a complement to the present exposition of my own views, Pamela M. Hall's *Narrative and the Natural Law: An Interpretation of Thomistic Ethics* (Notre Dame, Ind.: University of Notre Dame Press, 1994), unfortunately unknown to me before concluding the manuscript.

As usual, I will not be able to do justice to all the people to whose previous work I am deeply indebted. Without Wolfgang Kluxen's pioneer work on Aquinas's moral philosophy and Germain Grisez's well-known article "First Principle of Practical Reason," I would have remained in substantial errors and misunderstandings concerning Aquinas's thinking. Very enlightening for me also was Theo. G. Belman's work on Aquinas's conception of the "moral object," John Finnis's approach to natural law, although never fully adopted by me, and Giuseppe Abba's very rich scolarship. I have also profited from Ralph McInerny's writings on thomistic ethical theory; his sympathy for my work was for me an encouragement I remember thankfully. The work of G. E. M. Anscombe and discussions with her were important for my understanding of the central features of action theory. Moreover, I am grateful for helpful discussions about several topics related to my work with Tadeusz Styczen, Josef Seifert, Fernando Inciarte, Otfried Höffe, Germain Grisez, John Finnis, Romanus Cessario, Russell Hittinger, David M. Gallagher, Robert A. Gahl, Werner Wolbert, Servais Pinckaers, Livio Melina, A. Laun, and many others. I owe much to Angel Rodríguez Luño, the person by whom I was most encouraged, stimulated, and assisted in committing myself to this work on philosophical ethical theory. I also remember gratefully the late Ramón García de Haro, a most remarkable teacher of moral theology, through whom I also became familiar with the enriching views of the already mentioned Servais Pinckaers. Most of these people were decisive, in one or the other way, in helping me find my own stand.

Moreover, support by Wolfgang Kluxen has been important for realizing the original German edition of this book. And so was the financial aid given by the German Bishop's Conference, the Archdiocese of Cologne and its archbishop, the late Cardinal Joseph Hoffner, and the Lindenthal Institute, Cologne. I think it is fair to repeat here this expression of my gratitude.

As to this English edition, I feel in a very special way indebted to Romanus Cessario, who, besides the friendship he offered me, is the person whose interest, generosity, and commitment made it possible to plan and realize this English edition. In this respect I also thank John Finnis and Russell Hittinger for their support and encouraging interest in my work, as well as Deal Hudson from Fordham University for having equally contributed in an important and decisive way to rendering this English edition possible. Gerald Malsbary has translated the German text faithfully and, as far as I am able to judge, in a really excellent way, improving considerably its readability by substituting the many Latin quotations of the original with English translations of the texts. Not only for this reason, I would not be surprised if the English version reads better than its German predecessor.

Finally, I want to express special thanks to the editorial staff of Fordham University Press for having so nicely edited the book, generously tolerating one of its main defects: its rather excessive size. European and especially German philosophers will always admire authors from the Anglo-Saxon world for their ability to say important things in few words.

Martin Rhonheimer
June 1996

# ABBREVIATIONS USED FOR THE CITATION OF THOMAS'S WORKS

(All works are cited according to the Marietti edition (Turin); the only exception is the Commentary on the Sentences, which is cited according to the edition used in the *Index Thomisticus: S. Thomae Aquinatis Opera Omnia,* vol. 1, ed. R. Busa, Stuttgart, 1980)

| | |
|---|---|
| *In Sent.* | *In Quattuor Libros Sententiarum Petri Lombardi ("Commentary on the Sentences")* |
| *C.G.* | *Summa contra Gentiles* |
| *I* | *Summa Theologiae, Prima pars* |
| *I-II* | *Summa Theologiae, Prima secundae* |
| *II-II* | *Summa Theologiae, Secunda secundae* |
| *III* | *Summa Theologiae, Tertia pars* |
| *Comp. Theol.* | *Compendium Theologiae ad fratrem Reginaldum (Opuscula Theologica, vol. I)* |
| *In Ethic.* | *In Decem libros Ethicorum Aristotelis ad Nicomachum expositio (In I Ethic.—Commentary on the First Book of Aristotle's Nicomachean Ethics)* |
| *In de Anima* | *In Aristotelis librum de Anima commentarium* |
| *In Phys.* | *In ocio libros physicorum Aristotelis expositio* |
| *In Met.* | *In duodecim libros Metaphysicorum Aristotelis expositio* |
| *In Post. Anal.* | *In Aristotelis libros Posteriorium Analyticorum expositio* |
| *In de Div. Nom.* | *In librum beati Dionysii de Divinis Nominibus expositio* |

| | |
|---|---|
| *In de Causis* | *In librum (pseudo-)Aristotelis de expositione bonitatis purae seu Librum de Causis expositio* |
| *Super Joannem* | *Super Evangelium S. Joannis Lectura* |
| *Ad Rom.* | *Super Epistolam S. Pauli ad Romanos Lectura* |
| *Ad I (II) Cor.* | *Super primam (secundam) epistolam S. Pauli ad Corinthios Lectura* |
| *In duo Praecepta* | *In duo praecepta caritalis et in decem Legis praecepta expositio (Opuscula Theologica, vol. II)* |
| *De Verit.* | *Quaestiones disputatae De Veritate* |
| *De Malo* | *Quaestiones disputatae de Malo* |
| *De Pol.* | *Quaestiones disputatae de Potentia* |
| *De Anima* | *Quaestiones disputatae de Anima* |
| *De Virt.* | *Quaestiones disputatae de Virtutibus in communi* |
| *De Virt. Card.* | *Quaestiones disputatae de Virtutibus cardinalibus* |
| *De Caritate* | *Quaestiones disputatae de Carilate* |
| *Quaestio Quodlibet* | *Quaestiones Quodlibetales* |

# INTRODUCTION

In recent years, many Catholic moral theologians have tried to develop new philosophical bases and modes of argument for the establishment of ethical norms, and they have done so with the intention of doing justice to the individual responsibility of the human person. It is maintained as an established and notorious truth that the traditional moral theology—with its so-called natural law basis for moral demands upon human behavior—has not only lost its power to convince but also is equivalent to an abstract "legalism" that neglects the individual and his moral independence.

Accordingly, in recent decades[1] there has emerged within the field of moral theology a new interpretation of the Thomist[2] doctrine of the natural law (*lex naturalis*). This interpretation places special emphasis on the idea that, according to Thomas Aquinas, the natural law is a law of *reason* and not of *nature*. This emphasis, though quite promising at the outset, has unfortunately led to a historically inaccurate interpretation of Thomas. It has become the starting point (and to a large extent the justification) for what is called "autonomous morality" and, often in close connection, for "teleological ethics," the latter being largely identical with the "consequentialism" and "proportionalism" of the English-speaking world.

This attempt to overcome the naturalistic interpretation of the natural law and the "physicalistic" foundation of moral norms through recourse to Thomas Aquinas has failed. Those who support a morality of "theonomous autonomy" only fall victim to a new physicalism, this time with clearly spiritualistic traits: a dualism, in fact, between "nature" and "reason" or between "nature" and "person." What is particularly lacking in this interpretation is an adequate understanding of the *practical reason*, and of its independence from the theoretical reason.

The purpose of the present study is to show that the fallacies of this distorted Thomism (and of the new modes for establishing moral norms that have been based upon it) can be explained by the points of departure taken by its champions. While many neo-scholastic interpreters have tended to present a version of the Thomistic concept of the natural law that in important respects is incorrect (i.e., "naturalistic"), on the other hand, the leading critics of this so-called "traditional" viewpoint have not in fact succeeded in overcoming its faults. Such criticism is based, at decisive places, on analogous misconceptions and is, in the truest sense, a "system-immanent" critique of a "normative ethics" that has long neglected the independence and autonomy of moral experience as well as the normative-constitutive function of the practical reason within that experience. It is a critique that, to a large extent, draws its plausibility—and its legitimacy as the "only alternative"—from a repetition of precisely the same errors and omissions.

Such misinterpretations have also to do with understanding the *objective* meaning of human actions. Currently, there is a widespread belief that it is impossible to make moral judgments upon human actions independently of the concrete intentions of the performer of the action or of the whole complex of its consequences. This belief will here be shown to be the end result of a falsified and "naturalistic" view of the *object of the action*, that is, of the objective dimension of human actions. "Teleological ethics" is the fruit of this often unnoticed connection. For despite its innovative intention, it is fettered, like "autonomous morality," to very deep-seated prejudices of an educational tradition that had treated phenomena like "moral norms," "law," and "commandment" as the fundamental themes of moral theology. The "rebellion" of recent years against such a legalistic "norm ethics," though legitimate in itself, has remained for the most part within the orbit of the presuppositions that the movement had from its beginning; according to these presuppositions, the morally relevant, practically objective goods of human actions, were reduced to "natural givens." The attempt to overcome this "naturalism" (above all through the introduction of the concept of "premoral" goods or evils) has led contemporary moral theology into modes of argumentation that (under close analysis, especially of their anthropological implications) exhibit certain dualistic and spiritualistic traits.

We are concerned here not with an "ethical naturalism" in the classical sense, but rather with what one might term "*methodic naturalism*" (or "methodic physicalism"). To be sure, no moral theologian today would still derive moral normativity immediately from "nature" as such (understood as the naturally "given" and "presented"); "methodic naturalism" consists, rather, in taking over from ethical naturalism its own (physicalistic) interpretation of the objects of human actions, in order to seek out a new way to establish the moral "ought." Yet this is only "to pour new wine into old skins."

Nevertheless, one must affirm and take seriously the good intention of a moral theology that has taken such a path. It has been formulated in an atmosphere of criticism (often historically and technically unsophisticated criticism) of a certain kind of morality—one in which the responsibility of the person and his fundamental self-determination, as well as the inner-personal character of the morally good and its obligating dimension (the appearance of the good as "ought"), all appear to have been fully subordinated to absolutely valid "norms" that are imposed from without, independently of every opinion and of the concrete needs of individuals. Moral action, according to such a conception, would be a mere "consequence" or "application" of norms or laws, one of which would be the "law of nature." We must leave as an open question the extent to which the traditional moral theology has thus been unfairly caricatured as moral positivism. What matters is to understand that models of moral theory, like those of "autonomous morality" or the "teleological weighing of goods," are pleading for a rediscovery of the personal dimension of moral responsibility and decision, or in other words, for a truly *human* morality.

The question, then, is whether the above-mentioned models are capable of such a task. The answer is "no." This is not only in virtue of the fact that such approaches are one-dimensional and lack the depth necessary for anything but a superficial encounter with the complex and multilevel moral theological tradition, but also because of their methodic naturalism, which in a paradoxical way impedes a departure from that tradition at the very points where a departure would seem both necessary and fruitful.

Certain fundamental considerations are central to an adequate understanding of the human person as a moral subject, of his moral autonomy and responsibility—including the definition of what is proper to ethics, moral action as personal accomplishment, and the theonomous determination of human morality—and yet all such considerations are slighted or omitted by "autonomous morality" and its special method of the "teleological weighing of goods." This moral theological *via nova*, which is insufficient from both the theologian's and the philosopher's point of view, is also internally inconsistent.

The present study is meant as a sketch, taken from texts of Thomas Aquinas, of central aspects of the personal structure of the natural law (*lex naturalis*) and of moral "objectivity." At the same time, it will attempt to correct traditional "naturalistic" misunderstandings, which survive in present-day moral theology with an influence greater than ever before. It will pursue at once a *systematic* and a *critical* goal. What is meant when we speak of human nature as the foundation of moral normativity? What are the methodological principles for a normative ethics that makes use of natural law arguments? The key to answering these questions, it will be maintained, can be found by attending to the personal structure of the natural law—a structure that becomes clear in Thomas only in the context of a theory of the practical reason. The natural law will be shown to be the *law of the practical reason,* and this is why a theory of the *lex naturalis* is precisely a theory of the practical reason. Furthermore, the independence of the practical reason vis-à-vis the theoretical reason must be established, and it must be shown how the practical reason can be a subject of ethics at all.[3]

Such a concept of the natural law will also have clear anthropological implications: a personal anthropology is assumed, in contrast to the dualistic or spiritualistic one that characterizes (often unintentionally) many of today's approaches. Accordingly, special attention will be given to the anthropology and ethics of married life.

In the following pages, concrete applications of actual moral theological questions will be developed, such as, what does it mean for a type of behavior to violate the natural law? to be "unnatural"? An instructive example of the correct application of such statements will be presented in detail in the case of contraception.

The actual plan of the work is as follows: part I contains, in chapter 1, a methodological critique of the traditional derivation of moral norms from a "natural metaphysics," or the "essentialistic" interpretation of the natural law; this is followed by a proposal for a new methodology of ethics as a theory of the practical reason. The independence (autonomy) and underivability of moral experience as guided by the practical reason is treated, as well as the relationship of such experience to ethics, for which it provides the subject matter. This leaves the path clear for a theory of the natural law as a law of the practical reason.

Chapter 2 offers a "reconstruction" of the basic elements of the Thomistic doctrine of the personal structure of the *lex naturalis,* in response to the representatives of "autonomous morality." The result is a conception of the natural law as "the law of the practical reason" that underlies an *objective* moral normativity of circumscribed content. In this way, it can be shown why "unnatural" or "un-natural-lawful" behavior is always also "antirational" behavior, and why it violates in principle the specifically human basis of our actions. In addition, the natural law will be shown to be a law that operates in the context of human freedom, a law that in fact grounds this freedom as responsible and specifically *human.*

Part II contains more extensive analyses of certain aspects touched upon in part I. First, the model of "autonomous morality" is treated. The concept of autonomy at its basis is explored, certain distinctions and clarifications are made, and "personal autonomy" is expounded as the fundamental characteristic of human behavior (chapters 3 and 4). The disclosure of the *lex naturalis* as a participation of the eternal law (*lex aeterna*)—and thereby the disclosure of the *participative* structure of human autonomy—is taken in steps, with analyses of the metaphysics and anthropology of the natural law (chapter 5), of the natural law's epistemological structure (chapter 6), and finally, with an exposition of the fundamentally normative ("standard-making") function of human reason and its fulfillment in moral virtue (chapter 7). In the course of the argument it is shown how and why the concept of a "creative reason" is untenable and to what degree such a conception ignores reason's moral *standard-making* function.

On this foundation is then built a detailed analysis of so-called "teleological" (or "proportionalist" or "consequentialist") ethics" that brings out its fundamentally naturalistic (or "physicalistic") presuppositions and modes of argumentation (chapter 8). This critique leads to a concluding, summary analysis of the concept of the "moral object"; I want to show that the *object of action* is what provides the subject matter for the *practical reason*, and is the truly *objective* moral content of human behavior; further, that this practical–rational objectivity is related to the *lex naturalis*—indeed, that it is the fundamental and universally constitutive foundation of that law.

The result should show that the legitimate demands of moral autonomy for "self-legislation" are fully satisfied by the *participative autonomy* of moral experience and by the conception of a natural law that is constituted through the practical reason. The consequences of this corrected conception of autonomy for the relationship between human ethics, on the one hand, and Christian morality, revelation, and the Church's magisterium, on the other, are essentially different from those of so-called "autonomous morality."

The following study is fundamentally *philosophical* in nature, despite a few specifically theological reference points. Philosophical reflection, based on a truly *philosophical* ethics, is an especially urgent need for serious moral theological query in the contemporary world. In this regard one could call the present contribution a kind of "philosophical–ethical propaedeutic" for moral theological discussion. It is precisely the *philosophical* study of the ethics of St. Thomas that can perform so indispensable a service to moral theology in the present day. This is not only because so many philosophically questionable forms of moral theology, trying to gain legitimacy by way of being "a new interpretation of Thomas," do in fact deserve to be subjected to a philosophical analysis in the light of Thomas, but also because the Second Vatican Council has held up St. Thomas as "the Master" of theological research and training (see *Optatam Totius* 16), and has called him "exemplary" for the understanding of "how faith and reason meet in the one Truth" (see *Gravissimun Educationis* 10). A merely re-edited or "warmed over" school Thomism would not be in accord with the Council's intention. What is really needed is an exacting study of definite doctrines of St. Thomas that is oriented toward the original texts; we must go to school with *him* (and not his compilers), and then go independently, in relation to new questions and problems, along the same path he took. "Thomist" philosophy and theology provide a completely *open* realm of reflection for their actualization and supplementation through contact with contemporary thought. Consequently, the following study is indebted, both in methodology and in content, to philosophical work done in ethical personalism, the phenomenology of values, and Anglo-American philosophy, as well as more recent Aristotelian research.

Last, but not least, the present work should be of help to teachers and students of moral theology in their task of gaining a solid and well-considered position in relation to widespread philosophical "renewal movements" in moral theology that are only superficially reflective; it can help facilitate personal judgments in relation to theological fashions that often seek an intellectual monopoly. In this regard as well, it is to be hoped that what follows contributes to a genuine and lasting renewal of moral theology.

Of course, many questions can be touched upon only briefly; my purpose is to present a basic outline and sketch the principal features, not to provide a full and "watertight" description. This may suffice for the present, since "if a general sketch of a subject is first presented . . . then each person can work further on his own and articulate it with details—for this, time is a good explorer and helper" (Aristotle, *Nichomachean Ethics*, 1,7).

## Notes

1. It probably began even before the Second Vatican Council with S. Pinckaers' exemplary attempt to overcome some of the "physicalistic" or "naturalistic" arguments long endemic to the so-called "Thomistic" school; see his collection of essays from the 1950s and early 1960s, the tendency of which is clear in the title: *Le Renouveau de la morale: Études*

*pour une morale fidèle à ses sources et à sa mission présente* (Tournai, 1964); see especially the essay "Le rôle de la fin de l'action morale selon St. Thomas" (1961), pp. 114–143.

2. Unless the context indicates otherwise, the term "Thomist," in accordance with an international and popular convention, will be used to signify the person of Thomas Aquinas himself, and not the "Thomist (or "Thomistic") school."

3. In this I am especially indebted to the study (generally recognized as pioneering) by W. Kluxen, *Philosophische Ethik bei Thomas von Aquin* (1964; 2nd ed., Hamburg, 1980), whose results will find here not only new confirmation, but also (in some areas) wider application.

# Part I

# The Law of the Practical Reason: Methodology and Conceptual Foundations

# 1

# Natural Law and Practical Reason as the Subject of Philosophical Ethics

## Why a "Reconstruction" of the Concept of Natural Law Is Necessary

In recent years it has become widely believed that the philosophical justification for the natural basis of moral behavior, as treated by so-called "traditional Catholic moral theology," is seriously defective. In the context of pressing moral theological disputes—above all, in the controversy about contraception, which worked as a catalyst—the neo-scholastic doctrine of natural law has, to all intents and purposes, been declared bankrupt by a whole series of representative Catholic moral theologians who describe it as *physicalism, biologism,* or *essentialism.*

That this criticism is in some respects justified does not alter the fact that the really decisive issue has been customarily neglected—an unsolved problem that is now all the more difficult to solve. This concerns the question "What is the importance of the practical reason for the constitution of the *lex naturalis*?" The "renovated" understanding of the concept of the natural law as "the creative reason," and the placement of this within the context of a "theonomous autonomy," is obtained from a very questionable, textually selective, and one-sided reading of Thomas. The bankruptcy of the neo-Thomistic doctrine is shared in by its opponents, and has only been disguised.

From this standpoint, the contemporary effort to renew the principles of moral theology (or fundamental morality) through a theory of norm derivation known as "autonomous ethics" or "an ethics oriented toward salvation history" appears unconvincing. Now that moral theology has attacked the neo-scholastic philosophy of the natural law, there is a pressing need for a philosophical analysis of that attack, which began as an attempt to find a new philosophical basis for moral theology. In fact the actual *legitimacy* of the attempt can largely be disputed, to the extent that it is claimed to be a *necessary consequence* of the uncertainties and restrictions of traditional arguments about the establishment of norms.[1]

In today's situation, the new criticism that is needed must be constructive, which is to say it cannot submit to the temptation to wage an "apologetic" battle. Above all, it must lay bare, and seek to overcome, the defects of neo-Thomistic moral philosophy, and it must do so by way of a renewed and nonselective encounter with the texts of St. Thomas. The astonishingly free use of sources, characteristic of the ideologically motivated treatment of Thomas in recent years, is historically unprecedented and without any methodological justification. One does not work from the text but only "with texts," often carefully extricated from the larger context of Thomas's *quaestiones*: the result is a "Thomism" tailor-made to one's own liking, with which to legitimize a completely new theological approach.

A constructive criticism of these claims would also reflect today's growing interest in an authentic philosophical ethics. Such interest has grown articulate about a *theological ethics*, which is not only increasingly cavalier about its theology but also is quite questionable in its philosophy, which moves ever more fully into the tracks of utilitarianism[2] and falls prey to an anthropological dualism[3] according to which "anything goes" as long as one has goodwill.

The critical questioning of what lies behind these tendencies, even in the context of moral theological concerns, clearly remains the task of unprejudiced philosophical reflection, which will be of service to theology precisely to the extent that it remains true to its own philosophical method.

The following studies are intended primarily to take farther and deeper the numerous attempts of recent years to discover a method of *philosophical* ethics in St. Thomas; the result can be of decisive importance for a philosophical–ethical theory of the establishment of norms, as well as for understanding the Thomist concept of the natural law.

Since the concept of a philosophical ethics is closely connected with the concept of the practical reason, this chapter and chapter 2 will concentrate on showing how the practical reason is the subject of philosophical ethics; once that is done, why and how the concept of the natural law is part of a theory of the practical reason will begin to make sense.

## "Physicalism": The Practical Reason, Misunderstood

The leading objection to the "traditional" doctrine of the natural moral law is that it constitutes *physicalism* (or *naturalism*): it means that one attempts to derive ethical norms from laws—especially biological laws—that are in accord with being and belong to the premoral sphere. Such an attempt, it is maintained, is improper for two reasons: (1) because moral norms cannot be inferred from premoral ("ontic," physical, or biological) laws or values, and (2) because in principle no *ought* can ever be derived from an *is*.

There does exist, within the neo-Thomistic tradition of natural law doctrine, and especially in the German speaking world, a definite school of essentialistic and physicalistic interpretation of the concept of the natural law. Nevertheless, most critics of this school have become victims of the same tradition: far from overcoming its central presuppositions, they have instead only constructed a new theory for grounding morality upon some of the same faulty premises.

The mistake of both sides here is the inability to conceive of the *constitutive role* played by the practical reason in the recognition of moral values. This means that, within the perspective of certain academic trends (in which a large number of contemporary moral theologians have been educated), the natural law is frequently understood as an object of knowledge that lies, somehow, in the nature of things, over against the practical reason; in this way, however, one overlooks the role of the practical reason in actually *constituting* the natural law. For St. Thomas this is a decisive point: for him, the natural law is not simply "discovered" by the reason, but rather "constituted" by the reason for an act of *practical* understanding. Thomas understands the natural practical reason as a *law-giver* and not simply as an executor of the law.

In close connection with this foreshortened conception of the natural law can be found a derivation of moral norms from a naturally ("physicalistically") understood reality (i.e., of "ontic," premoral value). Despite the praiseworthy attempt of many contemporary moral theologians to prove that such a derivation is impossible or (at least) implausible, the attempt becomes questionable precisely because it implies a dualistic dissociation of reason and morality, on one side, against nature and the order of existence, on the other; in the end, the naturalistic interpretation of the objects of human actions as premoral, ontic givens is retained—and yet this was exactly what should have been rejected.

This retained dualism, which sets "being" and "nature" against the "creative reason" (now the emancipated, but also "natureless" neo-scholastic reason), then becomes the starting point for a utilitarian teleologism, which conceives of the practical reason as a calculus for the maximization of benefits through the comparison of goods. The so-called "naturalistic fallacy" becomes superfluous and is overcome to a degree; what unfortunately remains in place is naturalism itself, which makes this solution a nonsolution. It should occasion no surprise (as I hope to demonstrate) that the "naturalistic fallacy" reappears in "teleological ethics" by returning, as it were, through the back door.[4]

Physicalism or naturalism, whether in its traditional form or in newer variants, depends on the failure to recognize the constitutive function of the practical reason as the *evaluating factor* of human behavior. This morally evaluating reason is what must be rediscovered today; an understanding of it is closely connected with the reason's most basic function: the establishment of an order, since "*it is the task of the reason to put into order*" (*rationis est ordinare*).[5] Unless this function of the reason is first understood, it will be difficult to conceive that the natural law is an *ordering of the reason* (*ordinatio rationis*), or that moral virtue is an *order of the reason* (*ordo rationis*).

Without meaning to slight the achievements of neo-Thomist studies of the natural law, it cannot be disputed that many of them have overlooked the special character of the practical reason.[6] One sees it all too frequently mistaken for a combination of theoretical–metaphysical apprehension plus will.[7] This is a result of identifying the *lex naturalis*—in the sense of a modern scientific law—with a natural order that lies in the being of things; it means understanding the concept of a "natural order" (*ordo naturalis*) that lies beneath the "ought" in such a way that the reason is reduced to an organ that merely "reads off" what "is" and prescribes what "ought" to be. Formulas like "Fulfill your essence!" or "Become what you are!" are commonplace in this kind of natural law theory.[8]

## Statements about the Natural Law by the Magisterium and by Moral Theologians

### *The Nontechnical Language Used by the Magisterium*

The Church has never claimed to make philosophically discursive argumentation the subject of her official teaching, not even in regard to the moral requirements of the natural law. The magisterium proclaims the existence of the natural law and its implications in a language used for revelation, a language that is intelligible to all and that appeals to the common experience of mankind. Even when philosophical and theological terms are used in magisterial pronouncements, they are not intended to provide an instruction in philosophy or theology; rather, they are employed as a means of proclaiming and informatively presenting the contents of faith, which either have not been discursively reasoned out or are simply incapable of being so reasoned.

In the normal pastoral language, as well as in daily communication, there exist terms for the natural law that one may designate as a kind of "shorthand" or "abbreviation." Such formulations are indispensable, but they do not make the lineaments of a philosophical theory of the *lex naturalis* very clear. "Shorthand" formulations are not for analysis but for communication. This relative indifference of magisterial expression toward theological and philosophical reflection can be found in all areas of Church doctrine—it likes sharp and clear boundaries, and includes only what is absolutely essential.

The essentialistic variant of natural law theory has been overly dependent on the intuitive certainty of such abbreviated language. Although it has satisfied some of the demands for clarification of the *lex naturalis*, it has come into conflict with some other interests. What is needed for correction is not so much a "paradigm shift" as a "return to the sources" (*ressourcissement*), in order to obtain a deeper and more nuanced understanding—in other words, there is need for a more careful and thorough study of St. Thomas himself.

If, then, we speak in abbreviated fashion about an "objective moral order" that is "rooted in the being of man" and that can be discovered through the light of reason, we still have not decided how such an order is to be understood. Furthermore, it is still unclear how morality is connected with the being or the nature of man: How are we to understand the kind of reason that is involved? How does it fulfill its function in practice?

If we begin this way, and say that "nature" is the norm of morality—as *mensura* (measure) or *regula* (rule)—then an unreliably premature decision has been made in our theory: we will now have to search for moral norms and natural law in the so-called essence or *natura metaphysica*, and derive them from it. Furthermore, we have disoriented ourselves in gaining access to the texts of St. Thomas, in which one searches in vain for a statement that nature is the measure of what is good. Such a philosophical theory of the *lex naturalis* would run the risk of getting involved with problems that would otherwise not exist. For example: how do you acquire a knowledge of human nature from which the moral good could be deduced?

### *Problematic Moral Theological Interpretations*

This calls for a brief review of earlier interpretations. Josef Fuchs systematized the formulations by the magisterium on the topic of the natural law in his standard work, *Natural Law: A Theological Investigation*,[9] and he noted that there were two series of formulations: one referring to its "ontological aspect," and the other having to do with the "noetic aspect of natural law, the fact that it is written in the heart of man, and therefore naturally evident to him."[10] To the former series belong such formulations as that marriage is monogamous by "nature," that this trait follows from the "nature of man" himself, that ownership of private property is given "by nature," that the order of values results "from the nature of things" and so on.

What is really known at this point? Only that the moral order has a natural foundation. *How* this natural foundation and rule become operative is not explained. Fuchs nevertheless interprets in this way: "In these [texts concerned with the ontological aspect] the being, the very essence or nature of man as composed of body-and-spirit, appears as a norm of moral behavior and of law." This conclusion goes much too far. One could, it is true, allow it to stand as an "abbreviated" manner of speaking, but then it would be transformed, in the hands of a moral theologian, into a much more comprehensive, analytic statement: nature is the norm and measure of the morally good: or the moral order is reduced to the natural order.

When Fuchs then goes on to speak of the second series of formulations (i.e., that the natural law is written in the heart of man and can be known naturally), this second aspect can be interpreted only in harmony with the first, and that means that a decision about possible interpretations has already been made. To quote Fuchs: "The reality of being implies an objective assertion of the moral and juridical order. Subjectively this consists in the affirmation that rational knowledge is determined by real being; *reason reads the natural law in the nature of all things and particularly in the nature of man.* To say that reason is able to read the law written in the heart of man means simply that reason is able to grasp the law of nature from the ontological reality of man and of all things."

All such formulations can hold good to a certain extent in the abbreviated language of everyday speech and in preaching, but if one tries to build a systematic analysis upon their foundation, one meets with the unpleasant consequence of a hasty decision: an inescapable schematism that conceives the natural law as the "objective" order of nature, which the reason "subjectively" recognizes, or "reads off."

But such a schema does not provide a fair account of the position of "traditional Catholic moral theology,"[11] something that can easily be seen by a glance at some of the "traditional" handbooks of moral theology, let alone the many systematic monographs that have been devoted to this theme. In the classic manual by Merkelbach, for example, the schema in question is not to be found: the manual keeps very close to the formulations of St. Thomas and to his characterization of the *lex naturalis* as an "ordering of the reason" (*ordinatio rationis*) and a "prescription established by the reason" (*dictamen ratione constitutum*).[12] If we turn to the handbook by D. Prümmer, we find a less clear account of the natural law. However, Prümmer limits himself in practice to his definition of the law as "the participation of the eternal law in the rational creature," the schema of an "objective" natural law as the order of nature and of a "subjective" one as the knowledge of this order by the reason, is entirely absent.[13]

The case is very different with the well-known manual by Mausbach and Ermecke, which declares, "The natural law comprises the physical (*lex naturalis physica*) and the moral natural law (*lex naturalis ethica*). By this law, we understand the totality of all those moral norms that man can recognize as morally binding in nature, thanks to his natural reason. . . . The natural reason or conscience of man is the *knowing organ* for the natural law, and *not* its essence; the natural law is *object*, an ideal subject matter of human knowing.[14]

It is not so much a matter of "traditional Catholic moral theology" as it is a matter of various schools and tendencies within the tradition, by which a very definite and, it seems to me, distorted perspective on the *lex naturalis* has been handed down. Unfortunately, for the most part our moral theologians have come to know "Catholic moral theology" only through the filter of distinct school traditions, to the neglect of the study of the great masters and the Church Fathers. In this way, the view of "traditional Catholic moral theology" held by many moral theologians reveals, in fundamental features, the stamp of doctrines representing only one or other school tradition or another.

Just such a doctrine is that of the distinction between an "objective" natural law as "the order of nature," and a "subjective" knowledge of this order, by means of the reason, as of an essential order of things that is ultimately "obliging" and that, so understood, allows the derivation of the "ought" from the "is." But what completely escapes notice in such a doctrine is the practical reason, insofar as it constitutes the *lex naturalis* in its own act of knowing; in other words, it remains unacknowledged and forgotten that the practical reason has a *natural* way of knowing that belongs to the nature of man and contributes to the formulation of the natural law. We are discussing here the natural act of the practical reason, which belongs of course to the "nature of man," but at the same time, because it is nature, does not stand "over against" the act of the practical reason, *but instead is itself this act, or the order established through it* (*ordinatio rationis*). The natural law, therefore, is not simply "read off" from nature by the reason, but rather is constituted by the reason itself in its natural act of practical knowing.

### *A "Forgotten" Text of Leo XIII and the Teaching of Vatican II*

There does exist a formulation of the magisterium, in which this aspect is precisely addressed. It is the encyclical letter *Libertas Praestantissimum* of Leo XIII, which appeared in 1888. What makes this text so significant is not merely that it assumes some understanding of the natural law in the context of concrete problems, but rather that it has the natural law itself as its special theme, *ex professo*. Curiously enough, Fuchs refers to this text only obliquely and in passing. This is probably because the doctrine of the encyclical belongs to neither of his two "series," owing to its more comprehensive and fundamental bearing on the question.[15]

The text reads as follows:

> [The most fundamental of all laws is the *lex naturalis*] . . . which has been written and carved into the individual souls of all human beings, because it is *itself the human reason insofar as it commands the carrying out of right action and forbids wrongdoing*. Now this *prescription* of the human *reason* could not have the power of law, unless it were the voice and interpreter of a higher reason, to which our mind and our freedom ought to be subject. . . . It therefore follows that the law of nature is the very *eternal law* implanted in those who have the use of reason, inclining them to a right action and goal, and it is also the eternal reason of God, the Creator and Governor of the whole universe.[16]

In this formulation there is no notion of a natural law as the "objective natural order," that would then be known (subjectively) by the reason. That the natural law has been engraved in the soul of the human being follows from the fact, explicitly brought out in the text, that the natural law is "itself the human reason, insofar as it commands the carrying out of right action and forbids wrong-doing." In this way the natural law retains its adequate definition as a "prescription of the reason" (*praescriptio rationis*), which means the same thing as an "ordering of the reason" (*ordinatio rationis*)—a point that will become clearer in what follows. The natural law thus has its basis in an act of the practical reason; the natural law is itself this *praescriptio*, and not a known order of nature. The power of the law (*vis legis)* lies not in nature but rather in a prescriptive act of the reason, which, because it is a natural act (*impressum* or *insculptum in anima)*, constitutes a natural law.

The binding, legal power comes to the reason (this is the second point made in the text) not by way of the "natural order," to be "read off" from the nature of things, but rather by way of the divine reason, or the "eternal law" (*lex aeterna*), which is founded, or "born," in the human reason. The natural law is therefore objective and fundamental, and its contents are not the "order of nature" but rather the *eternal law itself* (*ipsa lex aeterna*), insofar as it is "present" to our reason, or is participated in by the reason; a law that "inclines us to the right action and goal" (*inclinans ad debitum actum et finem*).

These expressions speak the language of St. Thomas, and they open up an entirely new perspective. And yet we are considering here "only" a magisterial outline: we may possibly be raising more problems than can be solved.

The formula that makes the natural law become the objective order of nature and the subjective knowledge of the same, provides a possible escape from such problems. However, a price must be paid if that escape route is taken: one must sacrifice this grand vista of the natural law, consisting essentially in the *praescriptio* of the human reason, as a formal, conscious, intelligent, free, and responsible partaking in the power and wisdom of the divine reason, and thereby also a "sharing" as well in the divine providence and governance of the universe. In order to escape the problems entailed by this view, one must have recourse to another model of the natural law: that of the naturalistic–stoic position. It would not be possible, however, to maintain that such a model is at the basis of the statements of the magisterium.[17] It seems much more to be the case that the purported naturalistic (or "biologistic") character of magisterial texts appears only in the interpretations of some critics.

It may appear that the only possible "liberating" alternative to the mistaken naturalistic interpretation of the concept of the natural law is a reason that, instead of "reading off" a natural order from things, is endowed with the "creative" task of forming the moral order. "Nature" then remains as a premoral substratum in respect to which man must "behave responsibly," and with that the ethical relevance of nature seems to be exhausted. Once again, a mistaken dualism of reason and nature has been permitted to enter the picture. The practical reason is itself a part of that human nature, which is the basis of the moral order. And this is why there also emerges, as a *praescriptio* of this reason—or to be precise, of the *natural* reason (*ratio naturalis*)—a *natural* law of human behavior.

This position, as introduced by the text of Leo XIII (a text with apparently very limited influence and scarcely studied today), will undergo a thorough confirmation in the present researches on the concept of the natural law. One such confirmation can be found in the impressive statements of the Second Vatican Council, which refer in other terms to the natural law of the practical reason:

> In the depth of his conscience man discovers a law that he has not given to himself, but which he must obey, and the voice of which sounds when it must in the ear of his heart, urging him always to love and carry out what is good and to avoid what is bad: do this, avoid that. For man has a law written in his heart by God, to obey which is his very dignity, and according to which he will one day be judged. The conscience is the most secret center and sanctum of a man, in which he is alone with God, whose voice resounds within him. By conscience is revealed in a marvelous way that law which is fulfilled by the love of God and neighbor.[18]

In this text there is an implied distinction between "conscience" and "law": the conscience of man discovers the law as something given beforehand, as a normative truth, in which God speaks to man and through which the human person feels obliged as a moral subject. The moral law gives rise to a truth claim, concerning which the conscience can do nothing, but to which it is subordinated in its knowing. The act of the conscience does not consist in a positing of truth, but rather in a finding or discovery.[19]

Nevertheless, it must be emphasized—and will be clearly shown in what follows—that the same law, to which the conscience is obliged, has its cognitive origin precisely in the human person as moral subject. Not to acknowledge this would amount to a moral positivism, and would miss the truth that, at the basis of any recognition of or obedience to the moral "ought" or good, there exists, and must always exist, a *person's own insight* into the moral "ought" or good. Thus in its fundamental aspects the moral law cannot be understood as being brought in "from outside" (even if such a possibility is present, in the form of advice, instruction, and preaching, a possibility that neither contradicts nor removes the need for one's own insight into the moral "ought"); the law emerges, rather, from what we will later clarify more fully as an *autonomy* of the moral experience of the subject himself. This is based on the fact that the human person, through participation, *bears in himself* "the eternal, objective, and universal divine law, by means of which God orders, leads, and governs the whole world and the ways of the human community, according to the counsel of His wisdom and love"[20]—and this law truly belongs to man. "God made man a partaker in His law, so that under the gentle guidance of divine Providence, man might be more and more able to discover the unchanging truth."[21]

Now the real question—for which an answer has hardly been sketched—is the following: How is a moral "ought" constituted that originates from the individual and therefore autonomous insight of the subject (as a true participation in the divine law), and that at the same time presents an indispensable truth to which the conscience is obligated? In brief: How is it possible to harmonize the *autonomy* of insight into the moral good or "ought" (without which no truly moral behavior can ever take place) with the *theonomy* and noetic indispensability of the same moral "ought"? An "essentialistic" conception of the natural law would provide us with an inadequate methodology for answering this question: we must therefore first show *why* this is so, before turning to a positive methodological exposition of philosophical ethics, in order to clear a path for understanding the natural law as the law of the practical reason.

## A Critique of the Essentialistic Interpretation of the "*Lex Naturalis*"

The Thomist conception of the natural law can be understood only in reference to a reality that Thomas calls the "order of reason" (*ordo rationalis*).[22] This concept provides the key to Thomist ethics. But some representatives of neo-Thomism, especially in the German-speaking world, have tended to distort this "order of reason" into an "order of nature" (*ordo naturae* or *ordo naturalis*): while retaining the element of "order," they have in fact undermined it by neglecting the element of "reason."

### *Reason or Nature?*

In question 18, article 5, of the Prima Secundae (*Summa Theologiae*, I–II), the following well-known statement appears: "*in actibus autem humanis bonum et malum dicitur per comparationem ad rationem*" (in human actions, however, good and bad are said to be through comparison with the reason). The confusion about the concept of the *lex naturalis* appears to arise from a failure to take Thomas at his word, both here and in a great number of similar passages. What Thomas says is that the *ratio*, or reason, is *mensura* and *regula* (measuring stick and rule) for all willing, striving, and morality in general. Indeed, the leading theme of ethics from Augustine to Thomas is the "good will," which implies intending the good, wanting to do the good (or choose it, *eligere*), and not being indifferent about carrying it out effectively. The good will then forms a unity of intention and responsibility. The measure and rule of this will, the constitutive principle of its very "goodness," Thomas says, is the reason—and this is not only as the rule of "subjective" morality but also as an "objective" measure. This is because reason is not only the measuring and regulating "factor," in the sense of the *application* of a measure; rather, reason is the *measure itself*, and thereby the norm of morality.

The first and most important question is whether Thomas means to be taken literally in this. The sad truth of the matter is that he has not always been so taken. The problem is not whether the *ratio*, as a *mensura* that belongs to created reality, is still to be referred to a transcendent "remote standard" (*regula remota*), such as the mind of the Creator: that is unquestionably true for Thomas. The problem is only whether the reason has, or does not have, this role in the ordering of human behavior. For there cannot be two measures at the same level, or they would interfere with one another.

The choice that is now before us was brought out very clearly in the controversy among P. Elter, V. Cathrein, and L. Lehu. It took place in the 1920s but is still instructive. The first two[23] were of the opinion that the regulatory function of the reason must be referred to the "nature considered as a whole" (*natura complete spectata*); a rule, their argument goes, is really a nature, and the reason only recognizes and applies this "rule." Lehu, on the other hand, appears to me to be one of the few scholars to have taken Thomas at his word, and his judgment on the matter, though in need of some supplements, remains valid today.[24]

In retrospect it has become obvious that a consistent interpretation of Thomas has not held the field. The consequences can be seen in the neo-Thomist concept of the natural law.

### *Why the Moral Order Cannot Be Reduced to the Natural Order*

An example of this inconsistency can be seen in Michael Wittmann's interpretation[25] that calls for a "middle way" as an attempt to satisfy both sides: while this appears at first to be well considered, on closer view it actually closes the door to a precise understanding of Thomas. In Wittmann's view, "Lehu took a good idea and pressed it too far and too one-sidedly,"[26] and with that, the whole issue was decided. The very point of Lehu's interpretation—and of Thomas's moral theory—lay precisely in this "one-sidedness."

Wittmann wanted to emphasize that the order of morality has its foundation in being, and St. Thomas would never have disputed that; not only because human reason is itself a component of the order of being, but also because every knowing is always something that is "measured by things" (*mensuratum a rebus*; see *I–II,* q. 64, a. 7). Furthermore, it is clear that for Thomas, created reality (*res creatae*) is itself the cognitive rule for the reason (*I–II,* q. 74, a. 7). But Thomas is not speaking here of any "essential nature" as a "rule," nor does he maintain that "created things" (*res creatae*) are already the measure of *morality.*

Thus Wittmann came to a misleading conclusion, reducing the moral ordering of the reason to the order of nature: "The moral order arises, according to Thomas, from the world of things, or objective reality, and has the character of the order of being or nature that lies in things."[27]

It is simply impossible to find the moral order in the "world of things": in that world, for example, can be found neither justice nor friendship nor virtue; nor can one find matrimony or anything similar. If you are married in a civil ceremony, you follow a law that has been written down beforehand, and you can say that this marriage corresponds to paragraph *x* in the state's code of law. But you can never find a corresponding law in "nature" or in the "world of things," by following which, a marriage can be said to be contracted. The "naturalness" or "natural law character" of marriage must be explained in some other way.

Even if you define morality as fulfillment (according to nature), you must ask yourself, "Is not the fulfillment of things created along with them?" But what has not yet been created cannot be deduced from the order of nature.

### *A False Methodology*

With such questions, I believe, we encounter closed doors. It is really only a matter of taking Thomas at his word. Someone may object that what something should be—its perfection or fulfillment—can be "read" from its nature. Every entity possesses an essence and the powers that go along with it, and the former, as the foundation of the latter, qualifies them as good or bad, since "action follows being" (*operari sequitur esse*).

While that cannot be disputed, it could help us only if we were able to know the created reality with the eyes of the Creator, that is, in the light of the *lex aeterna.* On the contrary, we know the essences of created things by their acts.[28] What is "first in the order of being" (*primum in essendo*) remains the "last in the order of knowing" (*ultimum in cognoscendo*). The human being, unlike other created beings, is not subject in his behavior to a "single determination" (*determinatio ad unum*), which is to say that his actions are free, and can therefore be carried out "according to nature" or "not according to nature"—that is, they can be good or bad, in accordance with or opposed to a virtue, and thus, in respect to their indeterminacy, they are morally *not yet qualifiable*, even if certain modes of behavior are supposed to be the "norm" or the "rule" among people living at a certain period of time or in a certain society.

A purely empirical grasp of what people actually do is never enough for an accurate understanding of human behavior. But even the metaphysical understanding of the "nature of man" cannot provide the point of departure, at least in this matter, because a metaphysics or anthropology that is relevant for ethics must presuppose a concept of human action that is *specific* for human action as such and not merely an empirical–factual notion of it.

With the appeal to the "essence" or "nature" as the basis for judging the goodness of actions, one arrives *methodologically* at a dead end. In other words, we are concerned with a question of method, and a mode of knowing, that respects the peculiar demands of the subject matter—here, the human being, who, as will be shown in due course, is not a *res naturalis*, not a "natural thing." Man, insofar as he is a morally acting entity, transcends what is natural through his reason. The distinctiveness of this transcendence cannot be derived from a concept of human nature. Rather, it is through the analysis of moral behavior that the essence of man can be revealed and clarified.

## *The "Morally Good" Cannot Be Derived from the* "Essentia"

There are still other reasons why, in the context of Thomist metaphysics, the derivation of the morally good from the so-called "essential nature" is problematic.

Such a derivation rests on the assumption that the essence and nature of things, including that of man, provide a goal, and therefore a measure of their excellence and perfection. This, for instance, is what Heinrich Rommen[29] and Josef Pieper[30] maintain, the latter using the formula "Become what you are!" This is a beautiful saying, of course, but it is a useless principle for analysis. For the question arises, "How can I *become* what I am, when I already *am* what I am?" What meaning can it have to say that one is what one is only when one "becomes" it? The intended meaning, of course, is simply that man fulfills his human nature only through moral behavior, and only in that way does he become human in the full sense of the word. But the maxim assumes that the word "man" (or "human," if you will) is being used in two different senses. First, the sense of "the specific nature of man" is intended, but second, the sense understood is man "in the mode of perfection," and this latter meaning says that man is *not only* what he is, namely, simply a man.

Metaphysical arguments of this kind justify themselves with a corresponding conceptual system for ontology: the "essence" exists first in its unspecificity as imperfection. Only through morally good behavior does it succeed to a perfected mode of existence. The essence is therefore to be understood as the goal of the perfecting process.[31] Such a metaphysics is essentialist and therefore quite different from that of St. Thomas.[32]

On closer inspection it becomes apparent that someone who argues this way is "sawing the branch out from under himself." It means first of all that one can deduce the measure of the good (i.e., good *actions*) from the essential nature of the entity, but then it is suddenly postulated that this essential nature comes into existence only at the end of the perfecting process. That in turn implies that the measure is not derived from that which is, but rather from the knowledge of what should be. The normative–practical posing of the question is given a certain priority and autonomy over against the knowledge of that which is. With that, practical knowing is divorced from the purely metaphysical, and an internal contradiction appears within this essentialistic epistemology of norm derivation. Sentences like "Become what you are!" or, "Whatever is, should also be!" are methodologically useless.

The contradiction is only disguised if you pretend that the knowledge of the perfected entity—that is to say, virtue—is a purely metaphysical knowledge of the order of being or of the "essential nature," or that it is a deduction from a *natura metaphysica.* We find ourselves again in that familiar circle where one "reads" from nature only what has already been put there, in anticipation of the knowledge of the perfection corresponding to the nature. Such a circle seems to be unavoidable in a theory of the natural law that is constructed on the lines of a metaphysics that takes the "essence" as the "fullness of being" (*plenitudo essendi*)—and that is very unlike the metaphysics of St. Thomas.[33]

That the entity—or, to be more precise, the *forma substantialis*—and thus the "nature," is a "goal," is doubtless clear to Thomas, who knew the Aristotelian doctrine well from the second book of the *Physics*: "the form is an end" (*forma est finis*). But this does not mean that the nature or the substantial form (i.e., the principles that constitute a definite *natura*) provide the goal of the process of *perfection*; rather, it is the *goal of the coming-into-being* (*finis generationis*) of a natural thing.[34]

In his *Politics,* Aristotle also used the axiom that "the nature is a goal," but this was in the context of describing the coming-into-being—the "genesis"—of the polis from its components: persons and households.[35] But all this has nothing to do with the relation between nature and the morally good: rather, both Aristotle and St. Thomas maintain that this good comes into being by habitual practice, as a virtue or, in other words, as a "second nature." It is the business of ethics to investigate the interrelationship and connection between nature and perfection, but the two are not deducible one from the other.

## *The Inconvertibility of* "Esse Morale" *and* "Esse Essentiale"

For Thomas, "moral goodness" (*bonitas moralis)* is a "fullness of the essence" (*plenitudo essendi),* the ultimate perfection of something through its actions; it is precisely the area that goes beyond the nature, beyond the principles of the *essentia* (see *De veritate*, q. 21, a. 5). In order to respect a metaphysical principle, it should be emphasized in this context that the convertibility of the morally good with being is a convertibility with *moral* being (*esse morale)* and not with substantial, "essential" being *(esse essentiale).*

Whereas in the natural process of coming-to-be (*generatio simpliciter),* it is a "substantial being" (*esse substantiale*) that acquires reality, Thomas calls the process of moral perfection a "coming-to-be in relation to something" (*generatio secundum quid*), from which "accidental being" (*esse accidentale*) arises; this is "moral being" (*esse morale*), an accidental existence, that comes in as *an addition to* the principles of the essence. Even so, it is still "goodness as such" (*bonitas simpliciter*): "This is because something is called 'an entity' (or 'a being') insofar as it is considered absolutely, but it is called 'good' in relation to something else. In itself, for the purposes of its own subsistence, something is perfected according to the principles of its essence; but in order for it to be in a proper relation with what is outside of itself, it can become perfected exclusively through accidents, which are added to the essence. . . . Only in God are wisdom, justice, courage, and so on (which is to say, every perfection) identical with His essence; in us they are super-added to the essence *(essentiae superadditae),* as virtues. Moral perfection *(bonitas absoluta* or *simpliciter)* occurs in God together with His essence; in us, however, moral perfection is considered *as among those things which are added to the essence (secundum ea quae superadduntur essentiae.* (ibid.).

The cherished axiom that "being is convertible with the good" (*ens et bonum convertuntur*) need not be understood to imply the convertibility of the *bonum morale* with the *esse essentiale.* Thomas expressly disputes such an identification and insists that the order of operative perfection (morality) goes beyond the order of nature.

The statement that "every ought is based on an is" becomes problematic if being is equated with the *essentia*; in fact, the human nature or "essence" gives rise to powers, which, though not identical with that essence, are suited to it; these powers in turn give rise to actions, widening the field of the "natural" entity. While the *essentia* is what is metaphysically necessary for constituting a human being, the field of actions forms what goes beyond what is necessary for constituting a human being, and this is the region of *freedom.* Such an entity, situated in freedom, cannot be *derived* from its metaphysically necessary constitution; it can only be *founded* in it. Human freedom is a metaphysically conditioned freedom, to be sure, but it is still freedom all the same. One simply cannot "derive" through compelling logic the good (i.e., moral good) that is executed freely, in the sense of being accomplished with rational deliberation and deliberate purpose.

It needs to be shown how the orientation of the will toward the good is in origin not an insight into an essence, but rather a matter of *practical* experience. To be sure, the nature of man finds expression in such experience, but since the orientation of the will consists in the practical reason's statement "This is good" or "I should do this," it is not derivable from an insight into an essence. Practical reasoning is founded in human nature, and therefore makes possible in the first place any metaphysical insight into that nature.

An essentialistic analysis of the moral "ought" is inadequate because it requires that practical insight, *as derived from metaphysics,* be put in the place of practical insight, *as naturally founded.* The *esse morale* really needs a special mode of knowing to be adequately understood: a mode that brings into play a discipline and method that, though not independent of metaphysics, are still distinct from it.

## Practical Reason and Philosophical Ethics

### *The First Question*

The starting point for an investigation in ethics is not a question about the theoretical knowledge of an essence or nature, because ethics does not originate from wondering what a man *is*, but rather from, "*How should he behave?*" and "*What fulfillment is properly his?*" The question "*What is man?*" only comes after this, and is founded upon it.

The initial impulse for an ethical question is not an awe-inspiring confrontation with being itself, but rather practical experience: "Every art and every inquiry, and likewise every action and every decision, appears to aim after some good, so that the good has been aptly named to be that toward which all things aim." This is the first sentence of Aristotle's *Nicomachean Ethics*.

The statement reveals the starting point of any science of human affairs: the experience of intentionally striving after a goal that accompanies every human action; the object of the striving—the goal—is called the "good." This basic experience leads to the discovery of the practical reason, and becomes thereby the subject matter of ethics; or, to be more precise, it leads to several questions: What is the real, and not just the apparent, good? What is the highest, most self-sufficient good? In what consists the "aptitude"—the *aretê*—that is, the "virtue" of man that corresponds to the fulfillment, in his action, of this good?

Such questions require a normative answer that moves within the logic of the "ought." Further, a great number of answers to these questions are already available, and even as we ask them, we are already involved in the particular ethos we are living.[36] The question about the "ought" does not answer to the experience of being, but rather to the experience—the subjective experience—of the goal-directed nature of our striving, choosing, and doing. Moral philosophy, or philosophical ethics, arises from systematic reflection upon this experience.

The question about virtue is not, however, a question of the practical reason *as such*; it corresponds, rather, to the mode of knowing, which reflects upon the *activity* of the practical reason. All the same, it can still be maintained that such judgments as "All striving is guided to some goal" and "That toward which everything strives we call the good," are not derived from metaphysics, but represent an original experience that is *sui generis*.

We are concerned, therefore, with an experience that can, and indeed must, eventually become a topic of metaphysical analysis, because within its purview lies an aspect of human *being*—its incompleteness and (hence) its perfectibility. Metaphysics attains thereby an understanding of the dynamic aspect of being. The experience of intentionality in actions ("practical" intentionality) is experience of being—as all experience is in some way experience of being—but it is not as such derived from the *theoria* of metaphysics; it is original. It is situated in front of metaphysics, as it were—conditioning it, and ultimately leading into its *theoria*. At the same time, however, the experience gives rise to another question that is not intended to look at the experience ontologically, but instead wishes to investigate its own logic—the "logic" of intentionality: What is actually good? What is virtue?

This original intuition (or experience) of the good as the goal of striving, choosing, and doing forms the starting point for the activity of the practical reason. And the reflection upon this starting point is the beginning of moral philosophy.

*The Unity of the Intellect and Its "*Extensio*"*

In this context, the first question to arise concerns the difference between the speculative and the practical reason. It appears that two different aspects of the question are not always sufficiently distinguished: namely, whether the speculative and the practical reasons belong to two different *powers* of the soul, on the one hand, and on the other hand, the completely different topic of the difference between the speculative and practical *modes of knowing*, that is, the difference between speculative (theoretical) and practical *judgments*. While Thomas keeps to the *unity of the power*, at the same time he emphasizes a *fundamental difference between theoretical and practical judgments*, upon which is based the difference between theoretical and practical knowledge.

In the *Summa Theologiae, Prima Pars* (hereafter referred to as *I)* q. 79, a. 11, Thomas appears to treat only the first aspect. The question, indeed, is "Whether the speculative and practical intellects are different powers."[37] Thomas denies the existence of two different powers, citing the authority of Aristotle, the *De anima* (III, ch. 10): "But opposed to this is what is said in the third book of the *De anima*, that the speculative intellect becomes practical through an extension" (*Sed contra est quod dicitur in III De Anima, quod intellectus speculativus per extensionem fit practicus*). The act of the practical intellect is only a "stretching out" (*extensio)* of its speculative act through an "application to a task" (*ordinatio ad opus*) that comes into play.

This precise wording, with *extensio*, is not found in Aristotle's text, which is quoted precisely by Thomas later, in the body of the article: "The speculative intellect differs from the practical by its end [*fine*]."[38] The concept of an *extensio* is really a paraphrase, and appears to be justified by the fact that Thomas is here showing that both acts belong to the same power. It is only by reason of two different kind of actions, which differ only in their goal, that one may speak of the speculative as opposed to the practical intellect. This "extending" or "becoming-practical" [*Praktischwerden*] of the speculative act of the intellect is meant to indicate that both speculative and practical knowing are accomplished through the same power. The power and, to be more exact, the "agent intellect" (*intellectus agens*) as "light" (*lumen*), are *one*. Its action—an "intellective apprehending" (*apprehensio intellectualis*)—is in essence and always speculative, because the intellect is like a spiritual light and eye that both illuminates and sees.[39] This natural activity is also at the basis of practical judgments, in its "application to a task" (*ordinatio ad opus*); no other power is needed (see also *Summa Theologiae, Prima Secundae*—hereafter referred to as *I–II*—q. 64, a. 3).

*The Difference Between the Speculative and the Practical Reason*

What does it mean to say that the speculative and practical intellects are distinguished only by their goal or end (*fine, τέλει*)? The goal of the intellect, of its speculative *apprehensio*, is the making visible of the intelligible truth that is contained within sense experience. Is not the practical intellect directed to truth as well?

Thomas emphasizes that it is, since the good, toward which the practical intellect is oriented, is a "truth"; otherwise, it would not be intelligible, as *I–II*, q. 64, a. 3 states. The object of the practical reason is the good that can be ordered to action, and the good as considered under the aspect of truth.[40] Accordingly, we have here to do with a *speculatio*, with a "making visible" of an intelligible truth. But how are we to understand what has also been said, namely, that the practical and speculative intellects differ in their ends? This is not much clarified by the concept of *extensio*, which was brought in to preserve the unity of the power in view of its different acts.

In fact, the statement of Aristotle that the practical intellect differs from the speculative by its goal or end is found in a context of Aristotle's writings quite different from the context of the *quaestio* of Thomas we are now considering. It was not a question about the unity of the power, but rather about the evidence for a difference in structure and character between theoretical and practical *judgments*. Putting aside, then, the fact that the intellect is always speculative by nature—for *speculatio* is the kind of apprehension that is peculiar to the intellect as distinct from the senses, since it "sees" what the senses do not (namely, the *intelligible* truth)—putting aside, that is, the nature of the power itself, it is a question here of the different ends that the conscious subject pursues when using the intellect in a theoretical manner at one time and in a practical manner at another. Despite the persisting speculative character of the power, the cognitive intentions of the acts of knowing differ from one another. In one case, this intention or goal is theoretical (mere knowing, for the sake of knowing, of that which exists); in the other, it is practical (the determination of the practical good, of that which should be done). Theoretical judgments belong to the first mode, and practical judgments to the second (see *De Anima,* III, 10, 433a15). While it can be said that practical judgments are an "extension" of the speculative *act* of the reason, they are not to be considered as an "extension" of its theoretical *judgments,* but rather a distinct kind of judgments.

Thomas's commentary on the *De Anima* clearly shows that he did not overlook the distinctive structure of practical judgments. It is evident that the *extensio* of the intellect can in no way be understood as a mere "willing" of the content of theoretical judgments, through the intervention of some act of the will, so that this content becomes related to the sphere of action. An entity that has been apprehended by a metaphysical–theoretical act of knowing need not be (in fact, cannot be) "willed" in this sense, because it already exists. The will can direct itself lovingly to what exists, of course, but that is the affective fulfillment of contemplation. The objects in nature for human *theoria* are practical objects only for God, Who creatively wills them into existence.

The relationship between the practical intellect and the will (or love) is the other way around: whereas *theoria* begins with a wondering–questioning orientation of the intellect toward the truth, and confirms the truth with an expression of the Creator's love ("and God saw that everything was very good"), the principle of the practical intellect is the "seekable" (*appetibile*), the object of a striving. The "application to a task" (*extensio ad opus*) rests on a moving power (*motio*), which belongs to practical judgments by their own principle. This principle is the *appetibile,* or practical good, which "moves without being moved" and is the "first thing considered by the practical intellect" (*primum consideratum ab intellectu practico; In III De Anima,* lect. *15*). As unmoved and yet moving principle, it is the starting point for the *consideratio* of the practical intellect, which thereby obtains its moving power, its *extensio.* As Thomas points out, "The practical intellect is said 'to move' for this reason, that its principle, the *appetibile* [or 'thing sought-after'] moves it."[41]

*The "Appetitive" Condition of the Practical Reason*

So much, then, seems clear: for Thomas, the act of the practical reason—the making of practical judgments—arises neither from the willing of what is theoretically known nor from a metamorphosis of theoretical judgments into practical ones. On the contrary, the practical reason possesses at the outset a different relationship to "seeking" or "striving": it is embedded in this "seeking" and depends upon it. The *appetibile*, the principle of the practical reason (its *primum consideratum*), is not just any kind of good, but must be a *practical* good. Practical goods are not such as emerge in the necessary structure of being as "givens," or as "things" that one strives after or considers in action.[42] Rather, they are at the basis of the contingency of action and thereby, of striving. For a thief, the "practical good" that is striven for is not "money" but rather the *possession* or *use* of the money. Money as such is no practical object; it exists independently of all actions, and its possession or its use comes about through action. In order for it to become an object of action, it needs a "striving" organized by the practical reason: a "seeking" or appetition that is formed on the basis of a practical judgment: "this (i.e., not the money but the use or possession of the money) is good."

What necessarily exists can be willed (loved) to the extent that it exists. An act of the will that has to do, for example, with the contents of a safe is practically irrelevant, or undetermined as such. It can consist in the mere recognition of, or pleasure in, the ownership or success of others. Practical goods, however, "are" only to the extent that they are "sought after" or "willed" or "loved," and they "are" any of these only on account of a practical judgment of the reason, and that is why they can be one way or another. They can also not exist at all, and are thus contingent. They are contingent, too, because they can be realized in concrete actions in various ways, and thus can be otherwise.[43] The practical intellect is the "light" embedded in this intentional structure of seeking and doing the practical good that makes possible the separation of the seeming good from the real good (the special task of intellectual *speculatio*) and the determination of what is good until the stage of choice (*electio*) is reached (see *In III De Anima*, lect. 15, no. 827).

Now in all of this, the principle that "nothing is willed that has not first been known" (*nihil volitum nisi praecognitum*) has not in any way been violated. Practical seeking (the intention and the *electio* that depends upon it and makes it concrete) always rests upon a judgment of the practical reason. And the first act of knowing obtains its information from a reality (*res*) that is present to it.[44] This reality is in each case something previously given to the intellect, providing a natural field for its *apprehensio*. In the case of theoretical knowledge, the field is that of being itself; in the case of practical knowledge, the *primum consideratum* is an *appetibile*, which, since it is first, must be a "naturally sought" (*naturaliter appetibile*) to which a natural inclination (*naturalis inclinatio*) corresponds.

The object of the *inclinatio naturalis* is, from the outset, practical (a goal); it presents a "naturally known" (*naturaliter cognitum*) in an act of the natural reason, and as such is understood as a practical good and a human good (*bonum humanum*).[45] This original act of the "natural reason" (*ratio naturalis*) is the starting point of all practical judgments. Such judgments are incapable of derivation or reconstruction from judgments of metaphysical theory—just as incapable, in fact, as the first principles of the practical reason are of being derived or reconstructed from the first principles of the theoretical reason. Both possess a character of originality, and each has its own "rights."

Again, it should be made clear that the practical intellect does not lose its fundamental character of intellectual "light" (*lumen*). It is only that the speculative (or intellective) *apprehensio* is directed to a "seekable" (*appetibile*), to a practical judgment. The original *speculatio* is integrated into the intentional dynamic of seeking (*inclinatio naturalis—intentio—electio*) through the appetitive condition of this kind of *apprehensio*: an *extensio* toward the "doable" (*operabile*) has taken place.

### *The Reflexive Widening of Acts of Knowing*

Knowledge of the truth, for Thomas, is attained when the intellect reflects on its own judgment (see *De Veritate* q.1, a. 9). This reflexive "return" (*reditio*) of the intellect upon its own act is of great significance, because it makes possible an understanding of the fact of moral consciousness as well as the practical normativity that results from the act of the practical reason. Thomas even sees the possibility of freedom as rooted in this ability to reflect, an ability that has its source in the spiritual nature of the intellect.[46]

As for the truth of judgment in general, which consists in a "making equal of thing and understanding" (*adaequatio rei et intellectus*), Thomas emphasizes that knowledge of truth requires not only an *adaequatio* but also the consciousness of it by reflection. This is possible because the intellect—in contrast with the sensitive powers of apprehension—is able to reflect on its own act. For such reflection, it is not enough only to recognize one's act: that would be merely the consciousness of one's own knowing. In addition, the "proportion" (*proportio*) of the act to the known reality must also be known. This in turn is possible only when the nature of the act itself is understood, which once more presupposes the recognition of the nature of the active principle, or the power, that lies at the basis of the act. Through this, one achieves at last a "complete return" (*reditio completa*) to the knowledge of the *essentia*, which lies at the basis of this power, as its cause. Only then is knowledge of truth complete.[47]

The same doctrine of the reflexive "return" (*reditio*) is applied by Thomas to the practical reason in regard to virtues and their acts.[48] Without going into this matter in great detail, the following should be said: every act of the intellect provokes, as it were spontaneously, a reflection of the same intellect upon its own action, by which we become conscious of the act itself as well as of its object and, finally, of the power that is at the basis of the act. In this way we reach, more or less explicitly, the nature of the human soul. Interpretation and analysis of this reflective experience of the self can be extremely productive and can extend in many directions.

Such reflection can first of all consist in phenomenological analysis of the consciousness of the acting person,[49] an analysis that, if it appears in Thomas at all, is only as hints or beginnings.[50] A second possibility involves pursuing this reflection in a theoretical–metaphysical fashion: in this way one would arrive at a metaphysics of knowledge and the fundamental elements of a philosophical anthropology. A third possibility would involve systematic reflection on the act of the practical reason as such, and then we would find ourselves in the area of moral philosophy or philosophic ethics.

### *Epistemological Priority of the Act of the Practical Reason*

It should now be clear that while the oft-recalled axiom *agere sequitur esse* (doing follows being) provides a fundamental principle of *being*, it is precisely for this reason not a principle for *knowing*. The order of knowing is the reverse of that of being. The nature is disclosed by the acts, and not the other way around. What man is, is revealed by his actions, and for the interpretation of these actions, self-reflective experience is indispensable.[51] For experience of the self is the *only* gateway to the spiritual nature of the acts of the human soul and its freedom. The way to the metaphysical understanding of man—that is, to a philosophical anthropology—really passes *through* the practical experience of the self as practical judging, seeking, willing, and acting. To maintain that these aspects of human existence are *originally* to be disclosed by a metaphysical insight into an essence implies a reversal of the order of knowing, and amounts to a methodological blunder.[52]

Since the *agere* or the *operari* cannot be derived from being, neither can the "ought" be derived from the "is." The act is the "first known" (*primum cognitum*) for the knowing intellect. If we inquire into its foundation in being, we have posed a metaphysical question. If, on the other hand, we inquire into its normative–practical content—and this would concern "seeking" acts of the practical reason in general, and willed acts in particular, together with external actions—we find ourselves in the area of philosophical ethics.

It should not be forgotten at this point that the "ought"—the preceptive character of this act—does not need any derivation, and does not have to be "added" to the act. Rather, these acts of the practical reason are already a subject of ethics because of their appetitive condition. They are already preceptive acts. The act of the practical reason—the practical judgment—already, by its origin, moves within the "logic" of the "instruction" or "precept" (*praeceptum*) and the "command" (*imperium*). This does not compromise the truth that the experience of the "ought" or of duty, or of the normative in general, finds its fulfillment in the reflection of the intellect on its own act.

There is also a certain autonomy of the act of the practical reason that corresponds to its epistemological priority. It is not possible to derive the preceptive structure of practical judgments from mere statements about reality, nor can one reduce them to such. This is because practical judgments are a "command to pursue or avoid" (*dictamen prosecutionis* or *fugae*); this corresponds to a "yes" answer of the will to the good (a *prosecutio*) or a "no" answer to an evil (a *fuga*).[53]

We are concerned here with a natural and fundamental relationship, the conscious experience of which takes place in the self-reflection of the intellect; it is only through such reflection that the relationship—which has by nature a preceptive, moving character—is also known as a *praeceptum*, as a "norm" or an "ought," and can be reflectively stated in the form of a statement: "the good is to be sought" [*bonum est prosequendum*], and "the evil is to be avoided" [*malum est vitandum*]. Preceptive (or "ought") statements, then, are in this way derivable from intelligible *acts of the will* because they are included in them. And either their object is universal (for example, the first principle of the practical reason), or they are singular and concrete in relation to a definite action "here and now" (*hic et nunc*).

### *The Underivability of the First Principle of the Practical Reason*

A deeper analysis shows that the *normative* character of the first principle of the practical reason is just as underivable and unprovable as the *foundational* character of the first principle of the theoretical reason, the principle of contradiction. In other words, it is impossible to derive the normative value of the judgment "good is to be sought and done, evil is to be avoided" (*bonum est prosequendum et faciendum, malum est vitandum*) from the natural and fundamental relation between *bonum* and its "pursuit" (*prosecutio*), since the judgment in question can be neither derived nor proved, but is simply present in experience. If the attempt is made, the most one can come up with is an "empty formula" or tautology, or a structural principle of formal logic.[54]

To do this is to try to prove the unprovable, which is to misunderstand the very nature of this principle. What is under consideration here is not an expressed judgment, but rather the structure of a rationally-conditioned act of seeking that has been brought to expression by reflection. This act of seeking in itself—or the first practical judgment that underlies it—is the first principle of the practical reason. The structure of this practical judgment does not depend on the connection of two terms (subject and predicate), as is the case with a statement (*enuntiatio*), but rather upon the relation between the "seeking principle" (*appetitus*) and the "seekable" (*appetibile*). The relation is not a cognitive connection, such as expressed in the copula *est* or *non est*; it consists, rather, in the *prosecutio* or the *fuga*, which may be called the "practical copula."[55]

It is only by reflection upon this act of the practical reason (integrated as it is with a "seeking") that we can obtain a linguistically formulated version of this *praeceptum* in the form of a *statement*: "good is to be pursued . . ." (*bonum est prosequendum . . .*). This is a judgment in the usual sense of the word, but one that cannot be derived from any other judgment or premises; it comes about only as a confirmation, which has become conscious by reflection, of the first act of the practical reason. Instead of an "empty formula" or "tautology" or "ethical thought-principle" of formal logic, we have here to do with an original appetitive relationship—and at the same time, an intellective intuition—that constitutes the intellect as practical and makes possible its *extensio*.

Everything that is either recognized in a universal sense as good (by way of the "natural reason") or that is concretely determined to be done *hic et nunc* (in a *iudicium electionis*, through prudence) is formulated under the controlling power of this first principle, as a "direction" or "precept" (*praeceptum*) of the practical reason: in the former case, it is a precept of the natural law (*lex naturalis*); in the latter, it is a precept of prudence.[56]

### *The Subject of Philosophic Ethics: the* Ordo Rationis

Once philosophical ethics is defined as scientific reflection upon the activity of the practical reason, it then becomes important to define more closely just what kind of activity this is. Thomas has expressed his understanding in a very precise fashion in his commentary on the *Nichomachean Ethics*. It will be well worth our trouble to consider what he says.

First, he declares, the practical reason does not have the task of considering an order of being that is independent of it, such as the order of things in nature (*ordo quem ratio non facit, sed solum considerat, sicut est ordo rerum naturalium; In Ethic.*, lect. 1). This is, rather, the task of natural science and metaphysics (ibid.). The practical reason is concerned, rather, with an order that the reason itself creates consciously among the acts of the will (*ordo quem ratio considerando facit in operationibus voluntatis*; ibid.). This *ordinare*, or *ordinatio*, accurately describes the preceptive or imperative character of the practical reason. The *ordo*, which is not the "order of natural things" (*ordo rerum naturalium*), but rather an "order of reason" (*ordo rationis*) that is created by the reason in the acts of the will, is the subject matter of moral philosophy (*moralis philosophia*).

The reflective character of philosophical ethics, which has been repeatedly mentioned, comes clearly to the fore, and Thomas formulates it under various aspects.[57] The subject matter of *philosophia moralis* is the "order of voluntary acts" (*ordo actionum voluntarium*), or "human operations, insofar as they are ordered in relation to one another and toward an end" (*operationes humanae, secundum quod sunt ordinatae ad invicem et ad finem; In I Ethic.*, lect. 1).

Thomas makes a further precision: ethics has to do with actions that arise from the will in accordance with the ordering of reason: that is, with "human actions" (*actus humani*) or with "human action ordered to an end" (*operatio humana ordinata in finem*), or simply with "man insofar as he acts voluntarily for the sake of an end" (*homo prout est voluntarie agens propter finem*; ibid.).

This last formulation points out that the analysis of the practical reason is always an investigation about the human being, and from the very distinct point of view of actions. To this extent, ethics becomes anthropology, or is already part of anthropology, without having to be derived directly from metaphysical–anthropological statements. Ethics possesses at the very outset an inner connection with the subject area of anthropology. From this it can be inferred that a more extensive anthropological foundation need not be foreign to the subject of ethics. And it is also true that ethics can contribute to the improvement of anthropology.

*Ethics and Philosophical Anthropology*

While the enriching and perfecting of anthropology through ethics can be left aside for the purposes of the present context, nevertheless the idea of providing an anthropological foundation for ethics needs more refinement. It is still to be emphasized—in the face of possible misunderstandings—that we are concerned not with the relation of morality to human nature but with a methodological question about the relation of ethics as a *science* of moral behavior to anthropology as a philosophical doctrine of man.

It has already been stressed that reflection on one's own act is the starting point not only for any metaphysical doctrine about the soul or about man in general, but also for that experience of the self that gives moral philosophy its subject matter. This reflective experience of the self is that by which the intellect moves in a "complete return" (*reditio completa)* from its acts to the more or less explicitly conceived nature of the spiritual power that (together with the senses) underlies these acts, and by which it finally comes up against the nature of the soul itself—it is an experience that belongs to the inner, reality-grasping structure of spiritual–intellectual consciousness. As such, it cannot be derived from metaphysics or anthropology. On the contrary, metaphysics and anthropology, as well as knowledge of man in his full (i.e., not only corporeal and empirico-phenomenalistic) being, are not even possible without this experience and its systematic exploration.

This reflective experience of the soul belongs not only to the metaphysics of human existence but also to the practical reason; it does not make for a "foreign" theoretical basis or a mere "supplement," but rather pertains to self-revelation, to the "hermeneutic" of its own act. While the practical reason experiences itself and knows itself as ordering reason, it also opens itself up to this reflective experience of the self in the *reditio completa*—and yet it is nevertheless always one and the same power that is concerned in every activity of the reason.

Therefore, questions such as the following are not strange to the practical reason: "What is reason and what is its relation to other powers of the soul? What is the soul?" Or, to be more precise, such questions are not strange to the *human person* as he or she knows and acts practically, for these questions about the soul and the ordering of its powers arise from an original and spontaneous, prescientific and fundamental experience that is common to both the theoretical and the practical reason.[58]

As long as one understands that there is a basic experience of the knowing subject—of the person, that is to say—that forms a starting point common to both ethics and metaphysics and that gives rise to questions about the soul and the ordering of its powers, then it should also be apparent that moral philosophy, in virtue of its subject matter, possesses an inner, necessary, and indissoluble connection to anthropology and metaphysics.[59] To force a separation of them from ethics for the sake of an improperly conceived methodological autonomy would amount to falsifying the subject matter of practical philosophy.

Consequently, cooperation between metaphysical anthropology and philosophical ethics—without losing, to be sure, their methodological distinctiveness and their fundamental, mutual underivability—is not only a possibility: it is practically unavoidable.[60] This is because ethics will not be permitted to close itself off from a metaphysical–anthropological knowledge of the soul when such knowledge illuminates a basic experience that is also inherent in the practical reason. On the other hand, a separation from metaphysics would lead unavoidably, as has been often seen, to a focus on the social or historical conditions of human behavior. That such experiences must be taken into account in ethics is not to be doubted; however, they are not *fundamental,* and they do not constitute the subject matter of ethics. Even when they are only implicitly considered as fundamental, they lead to a misunderstanding and distortion of the personal structure of human behavior.

In such a cooperative effort we are not to deduce ethics from anthropology, nor to subordinate the former to the latter. Rather, we seek an inner, mutually illuminating relationship that is made possible by the unity of their subject matter. A metaphysics that refused to consider the basic experience of the practical reason would be just as false as an ethic that refused to consider any metaphysical clarification of the question about the soul, although that question may arise within the reflective experience of the practical reason. In any case, whatever belongs to the most intimate nature of man, when it becomes the subject matter of human knowledge, naturally becomes compartmentalized into sciences that vary in their methodological structure.[61]

### *The Aristotelian Paradigm for the Relationship Between Ethics and Anthropology*

The methodology for an anthropological illumination of an ethical problem can be developed on the basis of Aristotle's *Nichomachean Ethics*. The starting point—as already mentioned—is the basic experience of the practical reason, which pursues all seeking and action for a goal, which we called the "good" (*NE,* I, ch. 1). Second, it is shown that all human beings strive after a final, complete, self-sufficing good, the attainment of which we can call happiness.[62] Finally, after considering various possibilities for a fundamental orientation of life (ibid., I, ch. 3), the many opinions about the nature of the good (ch. 4), and the certainty that the highest, most complete good must have the character of self-sufficiency and be a *finis ultimus* (ch. 5), the ethical inquiry poses a question that originates from a fundamental interest of the reason in its search for the concrete form of the "good to be done" (*bonum faciendum*): it is here that the criterion is to be found for determining the human good in general—its excellence or virtue.[63]

Man sees himself surrounded by various ways of life, each of which has its own "specific activity" (*ergon idion*), the fufillment or "entelechy" of which is the excellence of each mode of life.[64] The personal experience of the human being (and the internal logic of the self-reflecting reason) recognizes his own proper activity as activity that is in accordance with the reason-endowed part of his soul (*NE,* I, ch. 7; 1098a4). There can be further distinguished a plurality of powers in the soul: there is one part "that obeys the reason, and another part that possesses reason and thinks" (ibid.). Thus the "peculiar task" or "special function" of man consists in "activity of the soul that is reasonable, or not without reason"; human excellence (or virtue) is activity that is according to reason, and happiness consists in a life lived with virtue (1098a7–18).

In this brief sketch, reason has been shown to be the measure of morality, and this has been done through an anthropological treatment of the reflective experience of the practical reason. But nothing has yet been decided about precisely what makes for virtuous activity. We still don't know what Aristotle means by "right reason" (*orthos logos*). That will become clear only through further study of the practical reason and its activity.

To make such a study possible, an additional anthropological clarification is needed: virtue has been pointed out as the special concern of ethics, but virtue is an excellence of the soul and not of the body (*NE,* I, ch. 13; 1102a16). We have still not gone beyond the bounds of self-reflective experience, if the question concerns the hierarchical ordering of the various powers or parts of the soul. For the consciousness of the manifold powers of the soul and of the struggle between the reason and the senses is itself an authentic experience.

The study of the soul is the subject matter of philosophical psychology, and thus part of anthropology. Aristotle refers to this, even when he does not refer specifically to his treatise *De Anima*: "Enough has been said about the soul in the exoteric works, and can be of use [*chresteón*] here" (1102a26). In other words, there will be a "use" made, an "application" made, of further anthropological knowledge for the special field of the reflective experience of the practical reason, which is itself the starting point and subject matter of the anthropology that is to be drawn upon here.

In this way Aristotle arrives at his doctrine about the "natural mastery" of the reason over the sensitive part of the soul, which latter participates, through virtue, in the rationality of the dominant part.[65] In fact, it is precisely in this "ordering of the soul"—an *ordo rationis*—that moral virtue consists. Bringing this order into play, and making it effective in actions, is the function of the practical reason, and how it does this will be studied in detail. The practical reason thereby becomes *orthos logos* (or *recta ratio*) and evolves a virtue (prudence) that facilitates this function (see *NE* VI, ch. 13).

This is not the place for a complete exposition of the Aristotelian theory of virtue and of St. Thomas's treatment of "right reason." My purpose has been only to show how a combined effort of ethics and anthropology that preserved the integrity of both methods was not only possible but also necessary. In other words, anthropology can make ethically relevant observations that ethical philosophy cannot do without. On the other hand, ethics can contribute to anthropology.[66]

*Integration of Ethics into a Metaphysics of Actions*

Apart from anthropology, which has its own bearing on metaphysics, philosophical ethics has yet another special relation to the latter, and still on the level of reflection on the act of the practical reason. Every human act (*actus*)—a special kind of *operatio*—can and must, insofar as it is a being (*ens qua ens*), be treated from the special point of view of metaphysics, which considers the structure of being. Accordingly there exists what has been called a "metaphysics of actions."[67] It is not necessary to repeat here what W. Kluxen said on this matter decades ago.[68]

In any case, such a metaphysics of actions can provide indispensable illumination upon the subject matter of philosophical ethics. It makes possible, above all, an integration of the practical reason into the structure of created existence, and thereby enables us to understand the ultimate meaning of moral behavior in its dimension of "personal autonomy" (see chs. 3–5). The practical reason only answers the question "What ought we to do?" It does not ask the question "Why *ought* we at all?" and yet this question does belong to ethics.[69]

Just such a metaphysics of action, with a clarification of the meaning and ultimate purposefulness of all action and of life in general, can be found in Aristotle. He saw it in realizing the possibility of contemplating truth, in a life according to the "intellect" (*nous*), which is like a "god in us" (*Protreptikos*, frg. 110)—an anticipation of the apotheosis of the human spirit. While the young Aristotle was still under the influence of the Platonic Academy, he made, for a time, a radical demand for a single meaning of earthly human existence: "And so one must either philosophize or quit living and take one's leave of this existence; everything else seems like a foolish waste of time and empty babbling" (ibid., frg. 108). Afterward, however, Aristotle conceived another ideal—less perfect, perhaps, but more widely accessible—in the life of the polis, the "complete community" (*communitas perfecta*) of human social life, wherein life led according to the highest wisdom (the contemplation of truth) remained the norm, though actually possible only for the few.

This "metaphysics of actions" that is associated with Aristotelian ethics is not abandoned when Christian moral theology (and here enters Thomas, in view of his whole moral theory) can speak of a wisdom that is founded on the understanding of faith (*intellectus fidei*) and is accessible to *all* persons, and of a life that corresponds to that wisdom, which may be identified with a new, more exalted polis: the "city of God" (*civitas Dei*), a *communitas perfecta* to which all mankind is called. This is of course outside the purview of philosophical ethics and is not the concern of the present discussion, but the consequence of such a theological perspective is not "to quit living and take leave of this existence," rather, it is to realize human life in its full meaning, which goes beyond human nature. And if the theory of this kind of life—moral theology—is unwilling "to take leave of this existence," then philosophical ethics will have its own indispensable contribution to make to theology, since it deals with the life of man.

### *Toward Establishing the Normative Function of Reason*

The Aristotelian doctrine of virtue and a "metaphysics of actions" make it possible for St. Thomas to determine the normative principle of moral behavior. Since Thomas derives the practical reason—as the "proper function" (*operatio propria*, the Aristotelian *ergon idion*) of man—from man's specific nature (*In I Ethic.,* lect. 10), the determination is formulated as follows: "The good of each thing lies in this, that its operation is in accordance with its form. The peculiar form of man is that he is a rational animal. Whence it is fitting that the function [*operatio*] of man is good, insofar as it is in accordance with right reason, for perversity of the reason goes against the nature of reason" (*perversitas enim rationis repugnat naturae rationis*; *In I Ethic.,* lect. 2).

On the basis of this formulation it becomes apparent that Thomas uses this reference to the soul, the "substantial form" (*forma substantialis*), just as Aristotle did, in order to determine the formal principle of human (i.e., moral) actions, *but not* in order to maintain that the *forma substantialis*—the essential nature of man—is the measure of the goodness of an *operatio*. The reference to the soul is used, rather, to show the criterion for discovering this measure; and this can only be the *ratio*, and indeed, *ratio recta*.[70]

The concept of right reason (*ratio recta*) is not just another term for the *forma substantialis*, but rather indicates the rectitude (*rectitudo*) of a spiritual power or its acts. The standard for this is the judgment of reason that possesses such rectitude as a practical truth, a "statement of right reason" (*dictamen rationis rectae*).[71] It would not make sense otherwise for Thomas to speak in the passage about a "perversion of the reason" (*perversitas rationis*) that would contradict not only *recta ratio,* but also the nature of the reason itself. Such a perversion would affect only the power and its operation, not the substantial form.

That this is the correct interpretation of the passage can be confirmed by Thomas himself, who indicates that the *recta ratio* corresponds to an intellectual virtue (prudence) that will be discussed in the sixth book of Aristotle's treatise (see *In II Ethic.,* lect. 2). This is what grounds the normative function of the reason: "The difference between good and evil in the moral sense can accordingly be specified only when it results from recourse to the principle of human actions, and this principle is the reason"[72]—and not the "essential nature" or *natura metaphysica.*

What has now been established, in the light of a metaphysics of actions, is what the practical reason itself already experienced in carrying out its own activity. In order for the practical reason (that is, the practically judging person) to become conscious of this "measuring" function, and to exercise it, no previous metaphysical deduction or derivation of the function is necessary: that would be absurd, and would mean that moral–practical knowledge is reserved for the professional philosopher. The possibility of moral-practical knowledge is grounded not in metaphysics but in the natural light of the *ratio naturalis.*[73] The establishment through reflection (*demonstratio*) of the measure-providing function of the reason by recourse to the substantial form—the human soul—originates from reflection after the fact, in the sense of a *reditio completa.*

These observations are crucial for the correct interpretation of

*I–II*, q. 18, a. 5, where Thomas writes as follows: "It is clear, then, that the difference between good and evil, considered with regard to an object, is a difference that essentially (*per se*) arises in relation to the reason: namely, whether the object matches it or not" (*Patet ergo quod differentia boni et mali circa obiectum considerata, comparatur per se ad rationem: scilicet secundum quod obiectum est ei conveniens vel non conveniens*). It is not the "nature of the soul" that is meant to be the terminus ad quem for this "matching" (see *conveniens*): the "nature of the soul" is only the basis for the certainty that the reason itself is the terminus; the moral specification of objects comes about with respect to the reason and its practical judgments.

What Thomas had just said beforehand should not be forgotten: just as the form gives the species to a natural thing, so the object constitutes the species of an action (*actio habet speciem ex obiecto*; *I–II,* q. 18, a. 2). The object is thus the "form" of the action, and as such is a conception of the reason (*conceptio rationis*): "just as the species of natural things arise from natural forms [*constituuntur ex naturalibus formis*], so the species of moral actions arise from forms [*constituuntur ex formis*] as they are conceived by the reason" (*prout sunt a ratione conceptae*; ibid., a. 10). In this way Thomas clearly distinguishes between, on the one side, a "natural form" (*forma naturalis),* which as substantial form constitutes an entity within a definite mode of existence (*modus essendi*), and, on the other side, "a form conceived by the reason" (*forma a ratione concepta*), which is nothing other than the "object," which gives the *moral specification* to an action—or, ultimately, its goodness (*bonitas*) or its badness (*malitia*).[74]

These remarks are not intended to present something new or hitherto unobserved. Lehu's monograph is as important today as ever: apart from some polemical features relative to its time, it has not become obsolete. If, since 1930, his work had been taken more seriously (instead of being "neutralized" by school traditions), beneficial effects could have resulted for the understanding of the Thomist doctrine of the objectivity of moral acts and of the *lex naturalis.* Time and again there have been reversals and confusions between two levels—between the *forma naturalis* (the *genus naturae*), on the one hand, and the *forma a ratione concepta* (the object on the level of the *genus moris*), on the other; between, again, the *ordo naturalis* and the *ordo rationis* (which commonly occurs in the interpretation of Thomas that tends to naturalism). All this has led, in the end, to dubious interpretations of the *lex naturalis*. And this kind of misinterpretation frequently appears *not* to have been surmounted, even in authors of the present day who are providing "new interpretations" of Thomas.

To be sure, it appears that these scholars have recognized anew that the real measure of morality is the reason, and that the natural law cannot be equated with a natural order that is only to be "read off" from "the nature of things." Nevertheless, they have not yet found their way back to the Thomist concept of the natural law, since the newly crafted concept of "the creative reason" is still based on a dualism between "the natural order" and "reason." This dualism includes an underlying assumption about the "physicalistic" derivation of norms, which misses the fact that the objectivity of action rests upon a *conceptio rationis*, which has for its part been formed by an act of the *ratio naturalis*. Consequently, the reason is not only the *measuring* principle (a *mensurans*), it is also the natural *measure* or *rule* (*mensura, regula*) of what is moral, and that is why its actions formulate the *lex naturalis*.

From this perspective, the path is clearer to a better understanding of the Thomist concept of natural law. This law is truly a law of the practical reason, a "work of the reason" (*opus rationis*; *I-II*, q. 94, a. 1), "something constituted by way of the reason" (*aliquid per rationem constitutum*; ibid.) This means that a theory of the natural law can ultimately become part of a theory of the practical reason.

## Notes

1. See, for example, A. Auer, "Hat die autonome Moral eine Chance in der Kirche?" in G. Veit, ed., *Moral begründen—Moral verkünden* , Innsbruck and Vienna, 1985, p.12: "In the discussion about contraception [in the mid-1960s], the failure of the traditional argumentation to convince became so obvious that a new mode of argumentation, which was long waiting in the wings, pressed its way forward without the backing of any fine pedigree."

2. For an explanation of this criticism see R. Spaemann, "Über die

Unmöglichkeit einer universalteleologischen Ethik," in *Philosophisches Jahrbuch* 88 (1981): 70–89.

3. See Germain Grisez, "Dualism and the New Morality," in M. Zalba, ed., *L'agire morale,* vol. 5 of *Tomasso d'Aquino nel suo settimo centenario,* (Naples, 1974), pp. 323–330.

4. The term 'naturalistic fallacy' apparently comes from G. E. Moore, *Principia Ethica* (1903; rep. Cambridge, 1984). Exactly what such a naturalistic error might be is not completely clear from Moore's account because he never succeeds in showing what he means when he calls 'the good' a 'non-natural property.' On the other hand, Moore seems, in my opinion, to have had a correct intuition (although he never succeeds in expressing it in exact metaphysical terms): the moral 'good' (and therewith the 'ought') possesses a peculiar ontological and epistemological status that can not be reduced to, identified with, or derived from, the 'is.' In a subtle analysis Moore shows that even the hedonistic utilitarianism of J. S. Mill rests on a 'naturalistic fallacy' (*Principia Ethica,* pp. 64–81). And the same would hold, according to Moore, for the method of 'naturalistic ethics' (p. 40): "This method consists in substituting for 'good' some one property of a natural object or of a collection of natural objects." The critique of so-called 'teleological ethics' that appears later in the present study (chapter 2, section "The Moral Object and How It Is Constituted" and especially chapter 8) will reveal just such a 'naturalistic method.' To be precise: the view that the morally good can result from the optimizing of 'premoral,' 'ontic,' 'physical' goods through a process of comparison of goods, is itself the product of a naturalistic method. To be sure, this is not what Moore would call a substitution of the moral good for 'some one property of a natural object,' but it is indeed a substitution for 'a collection of natural objects.' The calculus comparison of '*premoral*' goods can determine nothing about the '*moral* good.' It can appear possible only when one is under the spell of the naturalistic fallacy. Moore's position rests directly on the tradition of David Hume, who was the first to speak of the underivability of the 'ought' from the 'is' (see *A Treatise of Human Nature,* III.I.i; see also D. D. Raphael, *British Moralists,* II, Oxford, 1969), p. 19, no. 490). In his attack on the purely metaphysical–essentialistic determination of the moral good (in the tradition of Gabriel Vásquez, Francisco Suárez, and Hugo Grotius) that he found in Samuel Clark's *A Discourse of Natural Religion* (1706), Hume overlooked the special nature of the *practical* reason, and his oversight was very influential. For Hume, the reason has no practical significance whatsoever: "reason is perfectly inert, and can never either prevent or produce any action or affection" (*Treatise,* p. 9, no. 490 in Raphael). 'Passions,' 'volitions', and 'actions' can be neither

true nor false, can neither agree nor disagree with the reason. "Reason . . . cannot be the source of moral good and evil . . . actions can be laudable or blameable; but they cannot be reasonable or unreasonable. . . . Moral distinctions, therefore, are not the offspring of reason. Reason is wholly inactive, and can never be the source of so active a principle as conscience, or a sense of morals" (*Treatise,* pp. 9–10, no. 490 in Raphael). A useful confrontation of Hume with Aristotle can be found in T. H. Irwin, "Aristotle on Reason, Desire and Virtue," *The Journal of Philosophy* 72 (1975): 567–578.

5. Thomas Aquinas, *Summa Theologiae*, I–IIae, q. 90, a. 1.

6. A well-annotated survey of neo-Thomist interpretations of the natural law and more recent articles by contemporary moral theologians can be found in A. Laun, *Die naturrechtliche Begründung der Ethik in der neueren katholischen Moraltheologie* (Vienna, 1973). Unfortunately, the study is virtually confined to the German speaking world, and the "Wesensethik" and "Seinsethik" that predominate there. The picture of Thomism it provides is not sufficiently differentiated. One should also mention H. D. Schelauske, *Naturrechtsdiskussion in Deutschland*, (Cologne, 1968).

7. In making this criticism I am following in many points the study of Germain Grisez, "The First Principle of Practical Reason," in A. Kenny, ed., *Aquinas. A Collection of Critical Essays* (London, 1969), pp. 340–382. All the same, a few objections seem pertinent, such as those of Ralph McInerny; see his "The Principles of Natural Law," *American Journal of Jurisprudence* 25 (1980): 1–15; and further: *Ethica Thomistica. The Moral Philosophy of Thomas Aquinas* (Washington, D.C.), 1982, pp. 48ff. Indispensable help has been provided by Wolfgang Kluxen, *Philosophische Ethik bei Thomas von Aquin,* 2nd ed. (Hamburg 1980). In this connection Jacques Maritain should be mentioned, especially his *Neuf leçons sur les notions premières de la philosophie morale* (Paris, 1951), English trans. by Cornelia Borgerhoff as *An Introduction to the Basic Problems of Moral Philosophy* (Petersham, Mass., Publications, 1990). Despite his problematic conception of the relationship between ethical philosophy and moral theology (and between philosophy and theology in general), it seems to me that he has understood in an excellent way the distinction between speculative and practical knowing, as well as the epistemological situation of philosophic ethics. Reference should also be made to John M. Finnis, *Natural Law and Natural Rights*, (Oxford, 1980), and *Fundamentals of Ethics*, (Oxford and New York, 1983). Through his excellent analyses Finnis reaches conclusions largely similar to those of the present study.

8. See some of the earlier "classics" of natural law thought such as

Heinrich Rommen, *Die ewige Wiederkehr des Naturrechts,* (Munich, 1947); Josef Pieper, *Die Wirklichkeit und das Gute*, 7th ed. (Munich 1963), and in English translation by Stella Lange as *Living the Truth* (San Francisco, 1989); Gallus M. Manser, *Das Naturrecht in thomistischer Beleuchtung*, (Freiburg, Switzerland, 1944). The concept of the "essential nature" (*Wesensnatur*) of man, which has so long been in use, is very questionable. I am not sure to what term it corresponds in Thomas. It involves the ever-present risk that the polyvalent and analogous term *natura* will become reduced to *essentia.* No more fortunate is the term *natura metaphysica,* which was long central to Josef Fuchs's attempt to establish a concept of natural law, as in his *Lex naturae. Zur Theologie des Naturrechts,* (Düsseldorf, 1955). Built on the same foundation of rationalistic essentialism is the well-known critique of Karl Rahner, "Bemerkungen über das Naturgesetz und seine Erkennbarkeit," in *Orientierung* 19 (1955): 239–243 (English translation); although Rahner did recognize the weakness of this position, he nevertheless concluded by exalting the metaphysical rationalism represented by Josef Fuchs, with his plea for a "transcendental deduction."

9. Translated by Helmut Reckter, S.J., and John Dowling (New York, 1965); the original is *Lex naturae. Zur Theologie des Naturrechts* (Düsseldorf, 1955).

10. The various quotations from Fuchs's book here are taken from pp. 6–9 of the translation.

11. As, for instance, B. B. Schüller, "Zur theologischen Diskussion über die lex naturalis," in *Theologie und Philosophie* 4 (1966): 490, who states: "Catholic theology has thereby come to the conclusion that the subjective basis of the lex naturalis is reason, and its objective basis of the law is the 'nature' of man. That nature is the objective basis means in this case that it is negative: the lex naturalis cannot receive its 'being there' and its 'being-thus' [*Dasein* and *Sosein*] through the free disposition of the human being; when positive, it means that man comprehends the lex naturalis insofar as he understands his own pre-givenness [*Vorgegebenheit*] as his responsibility [*Aufgegebenheit*], his own being (given to him without his cooperation) as his unconditional 'ought.' "

12. See B. H. Merkelbach, *Summa Theologiae Moralis,* vol. 1, 2nd ed. (Paris 1935), p. 225 (n. 245).

13. See D. F. Prümmer, *Manuale Theologiae Moralis,* 9th ed., vol. 1 (Freiburg im Breisgau, 1940, pp.105ff. (nn. 151,152). When Prümmer distinguishes the "*objective*" and "*subjective*" *considerata* of the *lex naturalis,* it means something other than the schema we are discussing. It has to do, rather, with the objective or subjective consideration of the participation of the *ordinatio* of the eternal law. Insofar as man, by his creation,

is subject to this *ordinatio*—without any reference to *my* consciousness of it—one can speak of a natural law in an "objective" sense; insofar as the natural law is constituted in *my* acts of practical reason and is operative in my behavior, one can speak of the natural law in the "subjective" sense. This simply means that the *ordinatio* of the *lex naturalis* (the moral order) exists independently of the human subject, but *not* in the "order of nature"; rather, it is in the participative and *created* relationship of the human reason to the divine reason; one could, of course, identify this relationship with the "order of nature," but in an entirely different sense: not as an order that stands "over against" the human reason and is known by it, but rather as an "order of nature" that is *in* the human reason itself.

14. J. Mausbach and G. Ermecke, *Katholische Moraltheologie,* vol. 1, *Die allgemeine Moral,* 9th edition, Münster, 1959. This handbook, like B. Häring, *Das Gesetz Christi*, 6th ed. (1961), was influenced by Scheler's philosophy of values, as well as by its moral theological reception by F. Tillmann and T. Steinbüchel.

15. In Prümmer, however, the text is introduced without any consequences being drawn from it. It should be mentioned here that the moral theological handbooks of the past, due to a one-sided "apologetic" stance against "indifferentism," "relativism," "subjectivism," and so on, were more interested in asserting the *existence* of the natural law than in a clarification of its nature. Teaching about the latter topic is not the duty of the magisterium, but of moral theology. To that extent one must appreciate the useful service rendered by Fuchs, who in the context of his times attempted to present just such a moral theological treatment of the issue.

16. Denzinger and Schön. n. 3247: "Quae scripta est et insculpta in hominum animis singulorum, quia ipsa est humana ratio recte facere iubens et peccare vetans. Ista vero humanae rationis praescriptio vim habere legis non potest, nisi quia altioris est vox atque interpres rationis, cui mentem libertatemque nostram subiectam esse oporteat. . . . Ergo consequitur, ut naturae lex sit ipsa lex aeterna insita in iis qui ratione utuntur, eosque inclinans ad debitum actum et finem, eaque est ipsa aeterna ratio Creatoris universumque mundum gubernantis Dei."

17. This view has been represented in connection with the debate over *Humanae Vitae* by L. Oeing-Hanhoff, "Der Mensch: Natur oder Geschichte? Die Grundlagen und Kriterien sittlicher Normen im Licht der philosophischen Tradition," in F. Heinrich, ed., *Naturgesetz und christliche Ethik. Zur wissenschaftlichen Diskussion nach Humanae Vitae* (Munich, 1970), pp. 13–47. See likewise H. Welzel, *Naturrecht und materiale Gerechtigkeit,* 4th ed. (Göttingen, 1980), esp. pp. 60–61. The rather su-

perficial treatment by Welzel is based on the mistaken procedure of imposing upon St. Thomas a certain methodology—precisely that of deriving "practical knowledge" from metaphysics. As the present study intends to show, what for Thomas is "according to nature" is the content of an underived and freestanding (autonomous) practical knowledge of the good; what is in accord with nature is not originally or primarily the subject of metaphysics, but rather the subject matter and content of *moral practical experience* that has been guided and formed by the reason.

18. "In imo conscientiae legem homo detegit, quam ipse sibi non dat, sed cui obedire debet, et cuius vox, semper ad bonum amandum et faciendum ac malum vitandum eum advocans, ubi oportet auribus cordis sonat: fac hoc, illud devita. Nam homo legem in corde suo a Deo inscriptam habet, cui parere ipsa dignitas eius est et secundum quam ipse iudicabitur. Conscientia est nucleus secretissimus atque sacrarium hominis, in quo solus est cum Deo, cuius vox sonat in intimo eius. Conscientia modo mirabili illa lex innotescit, quae in Dei et proximi dilectione adimpletur." Pastoral Constitution *Gaudium et Spes,* n. 16.

19. See also the analysis by T. Styczeń, "Das Gewissen—Quelle der Freiheit oder der Knechtung?" *Archiv für Religionspsychologie* 17 (1986):130–147.

20. Second Vatican Council, Declaration on Religious Freedom, *Dignitatis humanae,* n. 3.

21. Ibid.

22. On this see Vernon J. Bourke, "Right Reason as the Basis for Moral Action" in M. Zalba, ed., *L'agire morale,* vol. 5 of *Tommaso d'Aquino nel suo settimo Centenario* (Naples, 1974), pp. 122–127; and the same author's *St. Thomas and the Greek Moralists* (Milwaukee, Wisc., 1947), esp. pp. 21–29; Frank J. Yartz, "Order and Right Reason in Aquinas' Ethics," *Mediaeval Studies* 37 (1975): 407–418.

23. P. Elter, "Norma honestatis ad mentem Divi Thomae," *Gregorianum* 8 (1927): 337 ff.; V. Cathrein, "Quo sensu secundum S. Thomam ratio sit regula actuum humanorum?" *Gregorianum* 5 (1924): 584ff.

24. See above all L. Lehu, *La Raison—Règle de la moralité d'après Saint Thomas* (Paris, 1930). See also in this connection J. Tonneau, "Le Volontaire en *esse naturae* et en *esse moris*" in *Thomistica Morum Principia,* (Rome, 1960), pp. 196–203.

25. M. Wittmann, *Die Ethik des Hl. Thomas von Aquin* (Munich, 1933).

26. Ibid., p. 285.

27. Ibid., p. 286. To be fair to Wittmann, it must be said that he does indeed refer to the "rational character" of the natural law; thus he recognizes that in Thomas the natural law "as an order of being is to be

sought not so much in finite things as in divine providence" (p. 345). We will return to this point. The problem with Wittmann's exegesis is that he includes all the different aspects without showing how they are synthesized by Thomas. It appears that Wittmann depends too one-sidedly on the Stoic and Neoplatonic elements in Thomas's thought; thus he says in passing that "there is no sign of Aristotelian influence."

28. See St. Thomas, *De Veritate*, q. 10, a. 1: "Quia vero rerum essentiae sunt nobis ignotae, virtutes autem earum innotescunt nobis per actus, utimur frequenter nominibus virtutum vel potentiarum ad essentias significandas." (Because the essences of things are unknown to us, but their virtues are known to us because of their actions, we frequently use the names of virtues or potencies to signify essences.) See also the following words of K. Wojtyla: "Because the 'operari' follows from the 'esse,' the way to understand the 'esse' is in the other direction. We have here a gnoseological dependence. We create from the human 'operari' *not only the knowledge that the human being is 'subject' of his own behavior, but also who he is, as subject of his behavior.* ("Person: Subjekt und Gemeinschaft," in K. Wojtyla, A. Szostek, and T. Styczen, *Der Streit um den Menschen. Personaler Anspruch des Sittlichen,* ed. by von J. Kardinal Höffner (Kevelaer, 1979), p. 20. Also published in English in *Review of Metaphysics,* 33 (1979): 273–308; quoted passage at p. 275.

29. Rommen, *Die ewige Wiederkehr des Naturrechts*, p. 185: "The ontological order becomes a moral order for man, who has free will."

30. J. Pieper, *Living the Truth,* translation of *Wahrheit der Dinge* by Lothar Krauth and of *Die Wirklichkeit und das Gute* by Stella Lange (San Francisco, 1989) pp. 161–162: "The natural law demands of rational creatures first of all the affirmation, the imperative carrying out, and the preservation of the natural order of the world. Secondly and essentially, it demands that man must place himself under the obligation of the sentence, "Become what you are, a statement in which the inherent direction of all reality is expressed." What seems to require criticism here is not so much the content—one understands what is meant—but rather the style of the argument.

31. See Rommen, *Die ewige Wiederkehr des Naturrechts*, p. 52: "The good is what corresponds to the essential nature. The essence of a thing exhibits as well its purpose within the created order, and in its completed perfection it is also the goal of its growth and becoming. The essential nature is thus the measure." See also J. Pieper, *Living the Truth,* p. 160: "The good is nothing else than this goal and end of the movement of being, the realization of the essence [Sosein]."

32. Following a Thomist metaphysics, one would say, "Every entity is constituted according to a definite 'species,' in terms of which its

'essence' or 'nature' can be ascertained. In addition, each entity desires through its action a second perfection that is related to the first perfection [*actus primus*] as the goal of the former. The essence is not the goal and the perfection, but through actions a perfection can be attained that is the *goal of the 'essence.'* It is only on the condition that there is a *determinatio ad unum* of the corresponding operative powers that such a perfection can be derived from the essence."

33. See Pieper, *Living the Truth*, p. 160.

34. Aristotle, *Physics,* II, chs. 2 and 8; see also Thomas's *In II Phys.*, lect. 4: "Set natura quae est forma, est finis materiae."

35. Aristotle, *Politics,* I, ch. 2, 1252b–1254b: "For the state is in relation to them as the goal toward which they strive, and that is nature. For the character that each thing has at the end of its development (*genesis)*, we call the nature of that thing."

36. Aristotle begins with an analysis of various ways of life and opinions about the good life, using the method of the *Topica.* On this see G. Bien, "Die menschlichen Meinungen und das Gute. Die Lösung des Normproblems in der aristotelischen Ethik," in M. Riedel, ed., *Rehabilitierung der praktischen Philosophie,* vol. 1, Freiburg im Breisgau, 1972), pp. 345–371. Evidence of this method of proof treatment can be found in the second *quaestio* of the *Prima Secundae* (of Thomas's *Summa Theologiae*), which is not so un-Aristotelian in structure as has been claimed from time to time.

37. "Utrum intellectus speculativus et practicus sint diversae potentiae."

38. Aristotle, *De Anima,* III, 10, 433a15. As quoted by Thomas in Latin translation: "speculativus differt a practico fine."

39. This is treated in more detail in chapter 6, section "The 'Light of Natural Reason.' "

40. "et bonum est quoddam verum, alioquin non esset intelligibile . . . ita obiectum intellectus practici est bonum ordinabile ad opus sub ratione veri." (I, q. 79, a. 11, ad 2).

41. "propter hoc dicitur intellectus practicus movere, quia scilicet eius principium, quod est appetibile, movet," *In III De Anima,* lect. 15. This has been rightly seen by G. E. M. Anscombe, *Intention* (Oxford, 1958), p. vii: "The starting point for a piece of practical reasoning is something wanted, and the first premise mentions something wanted." An important criticism of a divergent interpretation of Aristotle (A. Kenny, *Will, Freedom, and Power* [Oxford, 1975]) can be found in J. Finnis, *Fundamentals of Ethics* (Oxford and New York, 1983) p.30ff.

42. For the concept of the "practical good" (τὸ πρακτὸν ἀγαθόν), see Aristotle *De Anima,* III. For Thomas, such objects of action are not

things; for instance, "money" is not the object of an action, but rather the "possession" of money. Objects of action are always objects of the will, and as such involve in each case an 'operation' and an 'actus exterior.' T. G. Belmans, *Le sens objectif de l'agir humain,* pp. 175–185, is very good on this point. A reified conception of the objects of action as 'premoral goods' is a typical feature of so-called 'teleological ethics'; such goods are then placed against moral values. More on this topic can be found in chapters 8 and 9.

43. See K. Hedwig, "Circa particularia. Klugheit und Notwendigkeit im Aufbau des ethischen Actes bei Thomas von Aquin," in *The Ethics of Thomas Aquinas,* Proceedings of the Third Symposium of St. Thomas Aquinas' Philosophy (Rolduc, 1983), ed. L. J. Elders and K. Hedwig, Studi Thomistici 25, pp. 161–187.

44. One cannot simply translate *res* with the word "thing" even if "things" are *res. Res* has a wider range of meaning, and indeed the sense of "*re*ality" in general. Useful observations on this can be found in Belmans, *Le sens . . .* , pp. 164ff. Thomas uses the term '*res*' especially to characterize objects of action that are really '*operationes*'; thus the object of '*electio*' is the '*res volita*' (*In III Sent.*, d. 39, q. 1, a. 2) even though Thomas maintains that "choice is always about human actions" (*electio semper est humanorum actuum*: *I–II,* q. 14, a. 3).

45. Even here Thomas speaks of an '*apprehensio*'; see *I–II,* q. 94, a. 2. That the understanding of these human goods is always an understanding of *intelligible* goods is especially emphasized by J. Finnis, *Fundamentals of Ethics*, pp. 26–55.

46. "Iudicium autem est in potestate iudicantis secundum quod potest de suo iudicio iudicare: de eo enim quod est in nostra potestate, possumus iudicare. Iudicare autem de iudicio suo est solius rationis, quae super actum suum reflectitur, et cognoscit habitudines rerum de quibus iudicat, et per quas iudicat: unde totius libertatis radix est in ratione constituta." (Judgment, however, is in the power of the one who judges to the extent that he is able to judge about his own judgment: for we are able to judge about whatever is in our power. Now it is only the reason that can judge about its own judgment, which it does when it reflects on its own act, and when it considers the nature of things about which it judges, and by which it judges. And that is why the root of all freedom is constituted in the reason.) *De Veritate*, q. 24, a. 2.

47. *De Veritate*, q. 1, a. 9. The doctrine of the *reditio completa* was developed by Thomas in dependence on Proclus; see *In Lib. De Causis Expositio*, prop. XV (lect. 15). W. Kluxen also refers to its significance in the present connection (*Philosophische Ethik*, p. 189).

48. *De Veritate*, q. 10, a. 9. See also *Summa Theologiae,* I, q. 87, a. 4:

"actus voluntatis intelligitur ab intellectu, et inquantum aliquis percipit se velle, et in quantum aliquis cognoscit naturam huius actus, et per consequens naturam eius principii, quod est habitus vel potentia." (The act of the will is understood by the intellect, and it does this insofar as someone perceives that he wills, and insofar as he recognizes the nature of this act, and consequently the nature of its principle, which is a habitus or power.)

49. See also the analysis by K. Wojtyla, *The Acting Person*, trans Andrzej Potocki (Dordrecht, Holland, and Boston, 1979), which the author states emphatically to be not 'phenomenalistic' but only supplementary to the classical theory of the '*actus humanus*.'

50. As can be found. e.g., in the tract on the conscience in *De Veritate*, q. 17, a. 1.

51. See K. Wojtyla, "The Person: Subject and Community" *Review of Metaphysics* 33 (1979): 273–308: "The experience of one's personal subjectivity is nothing other than a full actualization of everything contained virtually in the human subject (*suppositum humanum*), in metaphysical subjectivity. It is a full and fundamental revelation both of this and of the being in this experience. This seems to be the philosophical sense of the old adage, 'to act follows upon being' (*operari sequitur esse*). The human subject (*suppositum humanum*) and the human self are two poles of one and the same human experience" (pp. 283–284). See also Finnis, *Fundamentals of Ethics*, ch. 1.

52. Kluxen is concerned precisely with this: not, that is, with an "emancipation" of ethics from metaphysics, but rather with showing that the foundation of ethics in metaphysics and in corresponding "derivations" is only known *afterward*, in reflection. "To the contrary, one must say that knowledge of the foundational essence only comes to fruition when the experience of what is founded, that is, the experience of the moral realm, is given. Here we must remind ourselves of the maxim, that a power is always known from its operation: this primary relationship controls the Thomistic teaching on the self-consciousness of the soul in such a way, that it is primarily associated with the character of a reflection, that only follows an actual knowing. . . . If one inquires only about the basis of morality, it is no otherwise. As the mere power of providing a basis, the basis is first to be recognized in the coming-into-being of the basis, and the logical process must afterwards move itself into the shape of a reflection . . . the result is the metaphysical 'grounding' or 'derivation' of morality. But it must be decisively stated, that this 'grounding' or 'derivation' is essentially *after the fact* of knowledge." To a certain extent this also agrees with the criticism by D. von Hildebrand of the derivation of moral values from 'nature' (in his *Ethics* [Chicago,

1953], pp. 185–186). The priority, postulated by Hildebrand, of the knowledge of the 'morally good' to the knowledge of the 'naturalness' of this good, really exists. Nevertheless, with his statement that "Thus our understanding of moral goodness is by no means dependent on the analysis of the nature of man" (p. 186), Hildebrand seems to me to have gone too far; it reveals the one-sidedness of the philosophy of values approach. An analytical clarification of the morally good can indeed result from anthropology (as will be shown more precisely later), but only *after* an anthropology has been "entered into" through *original,* and thus underived, moral experience.

53. See *De Malo*, q. 10, a. 1 :"Est autem considerandum, quod appetitivae virtutis est obiectum bonum et malum; sicut obiecta intellectus sunt verum et falsum. Omnes autem actus appetitivae virtutis ad duo communia reducuntur, scilicet ad prosecutionem et fugam; sicut et actus intellectivae virtutis referuntur ad affirmationem et negationem; ut hoc sit prosecutio in appetitu quod affirmatio in intellectu, et hoc sit fuga in appetitu quod negatio in intellectu." (It must be considered that good and evil are the objects of the appetitive virtue, just as the objects of the intellect are the true and the false. Now all the objects of an act of appetitive virtue are reduced to two common ones, namely, to pursuance or avoidance, just as the acts of the intellective virtue are reduced to affirmation and negation, so that what is pursuance in the *appetitus* is affirmation in the intellect, and what is avoidance in the *appetitus* is negation in the intellect.) This is how the difference between the first principles of the theoretical and practical reason is to be understood. The first principle of the theoretical reason (one cannot both affirm and deny at the same time) "is founded on being and non-being" (*fundatur supra rationem entis et non entis)*; that of the practical reason (good is to be pursued and evil avoided) "is founded on the good, since 'good is what all things seek' " *(fundatur supra rationem boni, quae est 'Bonum est quod omnia appetunt'*) (*Summa Theologiae, I–II,* q. 94, a. 2). More will be said about this below.

54. This is the mistake that F. Böckle seems to me to have made; see "Natur als Norm in der Moraltheologie," in F. Heinrich, ed., *Naturgesetz und christliche Ethik* (Munich, 1970), p. 80: "Man is so molded by his rationality, that he cannot otherwise think—in the realm of logic—than on the basis of the principle of contradiction, and—in the realm of ethics—otherwise than from the basic principle of morality: *bonum faciendum, malum vitandum* . . . in any case one must observe that this idea of 'good' is thought formally as an idea and is not related to concrete goods." Böckle has apparently missed, among other things, the fundamental difference between 'thinking' and 'acting.'

55. See the text of the *De Malo*, cited in note 53 above. It should not be forgotten that such practical judgments possess the structure of a '*iudicium ex inclinatione*'; an excellent, but unfortunately hard to obtain study on this dimension of practical judgments is R. T. Caldera, *Le Jugement par inclination chez Saint Thomas d'Aquin* (diss., Univ. of Freiburg [Switzerland], 1974).

56. A formulation with the same parallelism as this can be found at *Summa Theologiae, I–II* q. 96, a. 1, ad 2: "Ad singulares enim actus dirigendos dantur singularia praecepta prudentium; sed lex est praeceptum commune. (For the direction of single actions, the single precepts of prudent persons are in question, but the law is a general precept.)

57. See also In III *De Anima*, lect. 14: "Aliquando autem intellectus considerat aliquid agibile, non tamen practice, sed speculative, quia considerat ipsum in universali, et non secundum quod est principium particularis operis . . . manifestum est quod intellectus speculative considerando aliquid agibile non movet. Ex quo patet, quod intellectus speculativus nullo modo movet aliquid." (Sometimes, however, the intellect considers some action, not in a practical way, but theoretically, because it considers it in a general fashion, and not as if it were the principle of some particular deed to be done . . . it is clear that when the intellect considers something in a speculative way it does not set into motion any action. And from this it is clear that the theoretical intellect does not in any way move something.) The difference between the two points of view consists not only in the difference between the universal and the particular, but also in the fact that in the former case, the principle or *primum consideratum* is not an *appetibile,* but rather an act of the practical reason that has become the subject of reflection.

58. In the first book of the *Nichomachean Ethics,* Aristotle points out that the person who does not try to live by his reason, but follows his passions, is an unfit student of the subject, "but for those who order their desires and actions in accordance with reason, such a science can be very useful" (1095a10). And one may complete his observation as follows: only in this way can there be an openness to an authentic experience of the practical reason. While the expositions by J. Fuchs on the relation of ethics and metaphysics are in some respects completely correct, they nevertheless require clarification in view of the certainty that both ethics and metaphysics are rooted in a *common* experience. ("Autonome Moral und Glaubensethik" in D. Mieth and F. Compagnon, eds., *Ethik im Kontext des Glaubens* [Freiburg and Vienna, 1978], esp. pp. 53–59). Fuchs arrives at a much too undifferentiated conception of the difference between ethics and metaphysics (p. 58). The bond between the two disciplines is ruptured by the assumption that moral expe-

rience is ultimately inaccessible to rational (metaphysical) exploration. The resulting subjectivism and ethical solipsism are obvious. Fuchs's conception of metaphysics is all too rationalistic ("aprioristic"): he overlooks the fact that the starting point of a metaphysical anthropology has the same experiential content as that upon which ethics is based.

59. This is also connected to the fact that, in the history of philosophy, the classical teaching of Socrates and Plato about the soul grew out of the posing of practical–ethical questions. E. Voegelin has analyzed this very well in his *The New Science of Politics*, (Chicago and London, 1952), pp. 61–70. Such a theory "rather is an attempt at formulating the meaning of existence by explicating the content of a definite class of experiences" (p. 64).

60. On the essential questions here I am in agreement with T. Styczeń, "Zur Frage einer unabhängigen Ethik," in *Der Streit um den Menschen*, pp. 161 f.: "We are concerned here not with the connection between, on the one side, an autonomously conceived subject of ethics and of ethics itself and, on the other, separated and independent philosophical disciplines (such as philosophical anthropology and metaphysics); instead, we are concerned with the continuity of a theory, the requirements and character of which are determined by the questions that this subject itself provokes. In other words, we are not concerned with an external connection of ethics with any other theory, but rather with a balanced construction of a theory of its own subject matter in its own area." See also H. Juros and T. Styczen, "Methodologische Ansätze ethischen Denkens und ihre Folgen für die theologische Ethik," in *Theologische Berichte,* vol. 4 (Zurich, 1974), pp. 89–108.

61. Only in the divine knowledge, and consequently in theology, does such a division *not* exist. "Unde in scientiis philosophicis alia sit speculativa et alia practica, sacra tamen doctrina comprehendit sub se utramque; sicut et Deus eadem scientia se cognoscit, et ea quae facit." (Wherefore in the philosophic disciplines speculative knowledge is distinct from practical, but sacred doctrine comprehends both in itself, just as God knows Himself with the same knowledge with which he knows what He makes.) *Summa Theologiae, I,* q. 1, a. 4. Accordingly, a "theological ethic" is really impossible. The concept already contains a contradiction: as ethics, it must give up its theological character. Moral theology, on the other hand, is true theology. At any rate, in the past, the error has often been made of using theological categories to solve problems that are soluble only by a philosophic method. The opposite mistake consists in using philosophical methods to solve specifically moral theological problems in a "theological ethics." Theological expressions then increasingly contain an "ideological" character to justify

certain philosophical positions that have been inadequately grounded or reflected upon at the philosophical level.

62. *Nichomachean Ethics*, I, ch. 2. The eudaemonistic ethic is founded on the thought that happiness depends on the good; the attainment of the good is precisely happiness. Eudaemonism has often been misunderstood, ever since Kant confused it with hedonistic utilitarianism, which in fact signifies the opposite: that the good depends on happiness, or, in other words, whatever is perceived as happiness (satisfaction of desire) is good. On this see A. Lambertino, "Eudaemonologia tomista e critica kantiana all'eudaemonismo" in *L'Agire morale*, pp. 261–269. An inadequate idea of Aristotelian eudaemonism seems to be at work in J. Seifert's comment that eudaimonism intends to ground moral values with the concept of "true happiness"; in reality, the concept of happiness presupposes the determination of moral values, so that one is faced with circular reasoning (as in his differentiated and very sensitive study, "Was ist und was motiviert eine sittliche Handlung?" [Salzburg and Munich, 1976], p. 33). Against this it can be maintained that even Aristotle determines "true happiness" through an analysis of the morally good, i.e., *eupraxia* (good action, the moral virtue). From the concept of happiness *as such* nothing can be derived, even in Aristotle's view. The constitutive conditions of happiness must really be demonstrated *through* an analysis of good action and of virtue—the "moral value," that is. In addition, the Aristotelian understanding of the means-end relation must be correctly understood; just as the means is generally an (operative) concretizing of the end, so also *eupraxia* is nothing other than the operative concretizing of happiness. See also J. D. Monan, *Moral Knowledge and Its Methodology in Aristotle* (Oxford, 1968), p. 60ff.; T. Ando, *Aristotle's Theory of Practical Cognition*, 3rd ed. (The Hague, 1971), esp. p. 244; T. Engberg-Pedersen, *Aristotle's Theory of Moral Insight* (Oxford, 1983), pp. 175, 193, 203. There is also a very widely used but, it appears to me, faulty interpretation of this matter in P. Aubenque, *La prudence chez Aristote* (Paris, 1963).

63. "And yet saying that happiness is the highest good is perhaps to say something everyone would agree with; what is needed is a clearer account of what it is" (*Nichomachean Ethics,* I, ch. 6, 1097b22–23).

64. This teaching is Platonic in origin (see *Republic* I, 352d-353b). R. A. Gauthier comments as follows on the underlying idea: "The *ergon* of an entity, its function or proper task, is the operation for which it was made, and which, since it is its purpose, defines as well its essence. Every being which has a task to accomplish exists, in effect, for this task" (R. A. Gauthier and J. Y. Jolif, *L'Ethique à Nichomaque*, 2nd ed. [Löwen and Paris, 1970], vol. 2, 1, p. 54).

65. This method does not involve the subalternation of ethics under

anthropology, as Kluxen has rightly established (*Philosophische Ethik*, p. 55).

66. For instance, it can enable anthropology to make normative statements, and become "normative anthropology."

67. (*Metaphysik der Handlung*): it is justified by the fact that "Metaphysics takes into account actions as well, insofar as actions exist, and orders them within the total order of "being as a whole," which is based on God as the principle of all being" (W. Kluxen, *Philosophische Ethik*, p. 93).

68. As far as I can understand, Kluxen had the same concern as the present work: to show how false it is to conceive of philosophical ethics as a derivation from metaphysics. Many must have become accustomed to doing just this, it seems to me, and the studies of Kluxen must have been variously misunderstood and misused, for an "autonomy of morality in respect to metaphysics" to be created (thus A. Auer, "Die Autonomie des Sittlichen nach Thomas von Aquin," in K. Demmer and B. Schüller, eds., *Christlich Glauben und Handlung* [Düsseldorf, 1977], p.37). One gets the impression that Auer and others did not correctly understand Kluxen; the latter speaks, first of all, of "underivability" and not of "autonomy"; second, he is not concerned with the relation between metaphysics and morality, but rather with that between metaphysics (as a science) and philosophical ethics (as a science). Auer nevertheless draws the conclusion that the order of actions (the subject of ethics) is autonomous in relation to the order of being (the subject of metaphysics). One can hardly cite Kluxen in support of such an "Autonomie des Sittlichen gegenüber der Naturordnung" ("autonomy of morality from the order of nature") (Auer, p. 36); see the quotation in note 67. More on this can be found in chs. 3–5.

69. We are concerned here with a specifically *philosophical* problem whose solution is already contained in systematic moral theology. Moral theology assumes revelation and faith as its proper methodological principle; through the faithful acceptance of revelation, the question "Why *ought* I at all?" is already answered. The question does not exist as a "basis problem." But it is otherwise in philosophical ethics: "Ethics cannot ignore any questions that emerge spontaneously upon the basis of moral experience, and that make their decisive claim only after the construction of an ethical theory with its methodological features. . . . The clarification of questions of this kind requires a necessary connection of normative theses (which means the conclusions of ethics) with descriptive statements of philosophical anthropology as well as metaphysics, and this is because morality as the subject of ethics presents us with a normative interpersonal relationship" (H. Juros and T. Styczeń, "Methodologische Ansätze," p. 100).

70. See also *Summa Theologiae, I–II,* q. 71, a. 2; on which see Kluxen, pp. 188–195.

71. That by *regula rationis* Thomas means *ratio* as *dictamen* has been convincingly shown by L. Lehu, *La Raison—Règle de la moralité d'après Saint Thomas.*

72. W. Kluxen, *Philosophische Ethik*, p. 84.

73. The constitutive meaning of the *ratio naturalis* is overlooked by all those who try to make Thomas into a teacher of "autonomous morality." The misinterpretation of the *ratio naturalis* by J. Th. C. Arntz ("Die Entwicklung des naturrechtlichen Denkens innerhalb des Thomismus," in F. Böckle, ed., *Das Naturrecht im Disput* [Düsseldorf, 1966], pp. 87–120), which took it to be purely formal knowledge—without any relation to the *inclinationes naturales*—was then accepted and put into wider circulation by F. Böckle. The latter (see, in the volume just cited, his "Rückblick und Ausblick," p. 122) reinterprets the *ratio naturalis* as the "nature of the human knowing faculty" (*Natur des menschlichen Erkennvermögens*) and the "inborn part of human knowledge" (*das Angeborene in der menschlichen Erkenntnis*). This combination of a transcendental emphasis with the rationalistic thesis of an inborn *a priori* of reason enables him to conceive the natural law as the formal–logical consistency of moral judgments—independent, that is, of any material objectivity of the natural inclinations. Just how inadequate such an interpretation of Thomas is, should become clear in what follows.

74. This point was also correctly seen by L. Lehu: "La moralité est une forme qui se trouve dans l'acte humain et dans les vertus morales; l'objet est appelé moral en tant seulement qu'il est cause de la moralité de l'acte" (p. 111). "D'après S. Thomas, la règle de la moralité de l'objet, c'est la raison." (p. 115).

# 2

# The Concept of the Natural Law in Thomas Aquinas: A Theory of the Practical Reason

## Distinguishing Between the Preceptive–Practical and Descriptive-Reflective Levels

In chapter 1, we distinguished two levels of practical knowing, or knowing concerned with behavior: on the one hand, the level on which the practical judgments of the reason are carried out, and on the other, the level of reflection upon these acts of the practical reason. This second level, insofar as it becomes scientific reflection, is the level of moral philosophy. Even though it shares in the practical interests of reason, moral philosophy retains its theoretical character, since it aspires to statements that are universal and extend beyond the concrete *operabile.*

For an adequate understanding of the concept of the *lex naturalis,* it is of the utmost importance to keep these two levels distinct. This will help to make clear how the acts of the practical reason itself do *not* have the natural law for their object, because they in fact *constitute* the natural law. The object of the practical reason is instead the good that is within the field of action—the *bonum operabile*—under the aspect of practical truth, that is, insofar as it agrees with a right will. It is precisely this good (*bonum*) that is the object of the practical reason, and is also the object of what Thomas calls a precept (*praeceptum*) of the natural law.

The discovery of this natural law in man—its cognitive objectification, one might say—occurs only on the level of reflection, where the order of precepts of the natural law is recognized as an order of right actions established by the practical reason. The reflective and habitual knowledge that is appropriate to this ordering is the *habitus* of moral knowing (*scientia moralis*), and the scientific and systematic reflection that corresponds to this is moral philosophy. In the course of moral philosophical reflection, the natural law is recognized to be nothing other than the preceptive activity of the practical reason, as it constitutes the order of the virtues (*ordo virtutum*) and as it constitutes the content of this order—itself an *ordo rationis*.

Once this distinction between the two levels is recognized, a few problems can immediately be addressed that from this standpoint turn out to be pseudoproblems. For instance, it should now be clearer how a *normative statement* such as "good is to be done" (*bonum est faciendum*) or "evil is to be avoided" (*malum est vitandum*) is not a statement made by the practical reason at the level where it actually *makes* such "precepts" or commands, but rather is a statement of *reflection upon* this preceptive act of the practical reason. The object of the practical reason, rather, is the "good" itself that is in question; the practical reason does not produce a statement but rather a *prosecutio*, and this takes the form of either an intention or an *electio,* from which an action immediately follows. The practical reason constitutes the command (*praeceptum*) and not a "normative statement": the latter is a "statement" (*enuntiatio*) in a prescriptive or "ought" mode, and not a precept.

For this reason, it is not "commands," "duties," "obligations" or "norms" that are the object of the practical reason, but rather the *good*. In the (practical) objectification of the good the practical reason *constitutes* commands, norms, duties, and so on under the aspect of the good, that is, it forms statements in the form of "ought" or "should." The practical good becomes objectified as commandment, norm, or duty only in reflection—and then a *normative statement* arises such as "good is to be pursued" (*bonum prosequendum est*).[1]

Again, it is only in the application (*applicatio*) of this normative knowing to concrete behavior—which is to say, to the level of the preceptive act of the practical reason—that such practical imperatives as "this is my duty" or "I should do or avoid doing that" or "I shouldn't have done that" come into play. Such practical imperatives are really acts of the conscience (*con-scientia,* "knowing-along with") that are not acts of the practical reason in the proper sense, but rather an "application of knowledge" (*applicatio scientiae*) to concrete, preceptive acts of the practical reason and the actions that follow therefrom.[2]

Now, it could not be maintained that this distinction between the practical and reflective levels is explicitly drawn by Thomas; indeed, it is everywhere only implicit,[3] and yet to neglect the distinction would create difficulties.[4] That Thomas does distinguish the two levels is shown in his teaching on the reflective nature of the apprehension of truth. And the situation is the same with the apprehension of practical truth or "normativity." Under close inspection, then, Thomas's treatise on the natural law appears as a reflection upon the act of the practical reason, insofar as it constitutes a moral law. What is more, the treatise is also a reflection on virtue, on the *actus humanus* in general, and on the place of the sensual drives or *passiones* in the context of moral behavior. In various treatises, in fact, the field of the natural law is always present in the background, as an "ordering of the reason" (*ordo rationis*) in regard to both structure and content. What specifically characterizes the treatise on the law is the explication of this *ordo rationis*: that it has the character of law, which is at the same time a participation in the eternal law of divine providence.

It appears, then, that we cannot avoid making a distinction between, on the one hand, the *praeceptum* as an act of the practical reason and, on the other hand, the reflective consideration of this act (including description, normative statements, moral science, general and habitual moral knowledge, moral philosophical theory). One important outcome of this distinction is a clearly defined conception of the conscience as an *application* of moral science: moral science is a *habitus* consisting of precepts formulated as normative statements—a normative knowledge, that is to say—which again *becomes practical* when applied to concrete willing (intending, choosing, and doing).

The problem of "deriving" preceptive judgments or normative statements from descriptive statements is thus an apparent problem only. All "descriptions" and statements of moral philosophy (or of an anthropology considered in the context of ethics) arise in fact from reflection upon the practical reason and remain in relation to it. *The* praeceptum *of the practical reason is not the outcome of ethics, but its very subject matter.* Similarly, any anthropological clarification or any integration into a "metaphysics of action" is merely an expansion, fuller statement, or particular justification at the level of description or theory ("descriptive" statements), and it is made without leaving behind the starting point, which is the practical reason (the subject matter of all this theorizing) and its peculiar preceptive structure; only in this sense can philosophical ethics begin to be "normative anthropology."

The distinction we are making is of utmost importance for a moral philosophical theory of the *lex naturalis*. For the natural law is not primarily and per se a collection of normative statements that the practical reason simply finds "already there" to "follow": instead, it is the first, immediate, *result* of the practical reason's preceptive acts. The natural law, in fact, could be called the "preceptive subject matter" of the human reason. In a theory of the natural law, then (and indeed in terms of any ethical theory), the natural law becomes "descriptive subject matter" to the extent that the reason reflects upon its own acts. In an analogous way, it is also objectified in the *habitus* of "moral science" in the form of prescriptive statements.[5] This science (or "knowledge") becomes, in turn, practical again—that is, preceptive—only when it is applied to concrete acts by judgments of the conscience.

## The Natural Law as a Work of the Reason (*Opus Rationis*)

For Thomas, every law is essentially something that "belongs to the reason" (*aliquid pertinens ad rationem*; *I–II*, q. 90, a. 1) as well as "a work of the reason" (*opus rationis*; *I–II*, Q. 94, a.1) Therefore, wherever reason is absent, as in the subrational forms of life and nonliving nature, there are no laws in the strict sense. One can speak of laws in this sense only *per similitudinem*, on the basis of a certain similarity (*I–II*, q. 91, a. 2, ad 2um). In this realm of being there are no law-giving acts, but only acts that correspond to a law, that are accomplished "according to law." Nonrational creatures do not "act" (*non agunt*) but rather "are acted" (*sed magis aguntur*); they are the objects of a norm that they contain and follow, but do not themselves constitute.[6]

Using an etymological analysis—and whether it is historically accurate does not matter in this case—Thomas characterizes law as "a certain rule and measure of acts, according to which someone is induced to do something, or is restrained from doing something; for law [*lex*] gets its name from binding [*ligando*] because it binds to doing."[7]

Thomas here assumes, as something well known and established, that the first principle of human actions, insofar as they are human, is the reason, which he consequently presents as a "rule" and "measure." In actions the first thing is the end, and the task of the reason is precisely to order actions to their end. Now, since law is characterized by being a rule of actions or a measure, its rational character thereby becomes obvious: an act of reason corresponds to law, and reason itself has a law-giving function. In this way, Thomas is able to reduce the concept of law to a concept of "ordering of the reason" (*ordinatio rationis*).[8]

"Law" is neither a power, nor a habit, nor a simple act of the reason as such (see the second objection to the first article of *I–II,* q. 90), but rather "something constituted through an act of this kind" (*aliquid per huiusmodi actum constitutum*; ibid., ad 2um). It therefore involves "universal judgments of the practical reason, ordered to actions" (*propositiones universales rationis practicae ordinatae ad actiones*), and is thus analogous to an *enuntiatio* of the theoretical reason (ibid.).

The term *propositio*, to which Thomas ascribes the essential character of law (*ratio legis*) in calling it "something constituted through the reason" (*aliquid per rationem constitutum*), may cause some surprise at first, but the reason for it is as follows: *propositio* is not used here in the grammatical sense (sentence or statement), which would correspond to the *enuntiatio* of the theoretical reason. *Propositio* is, rather, a "judgment" in a logical sense, because judgments are called "propositions" in logic. The *enuntiatio* of the speculative reason is one specific type of *propositio*. When it comes to law, on the other hand, there is a *propositio* of the practical reason. It is not a "statement" but rather a "command" or "precept" (*praeceptum*).

This becomes clearer in q. 92, where Thomas speaks not simply of a *propositio*, but rather of a *dictamen rationis*. This would be a judgment in any case, whether of the theoretical or the practical reason: "Just as enunciation is a statement of the reason [*dictamen rationis*] in the mode of declaration [*per modum enuntiandi*], so also is law, but in the mode of commanding [*per modum praecipiendi*]."

The law, then, as an "ordering of the reason" is a "command" or "precept" (*praeceptum* or *imperium*) spoken by the practical reason.[9] Thomas thus defines law as the "preceptive subject matter" of the reason—or as a "product" (*aliquid constitutum*) of the practical reason. And yet this product must not be thought of in a reified fashion: as preceptive subject matter of the reason (or "object" of the practical reason), it cannot be considered in isolation from the reason's ordering act. Rather, *as subject matter* [*Gegenstand*], it is really the *content* of this act.[10]

This *praeceptum* as such is, strictly speaking, inexpressible in language, at least in its unique character as a practical *judgment* (*in actu exercito*); at the most, it can be expressed only as a command: "Do that!" The adequate expression of the practical judgment as *praeceptum* appears only to be *an act of the will itself* that has been stamped by the preceptive content of this judgment (the *prosecutio* or *fuga* at the level of the *intentio* or *electio*) or *the action itself* thus willed. The intersubjectively encountered "language" of the preceptive act of the reason is, finally, *behavior itself.* The act of the practical reason is therefore immediately experienced in its *accomplishment*, and it is only at the level of reflection (already spontaneously present[11] *in* the accomplishing of the action it accompanies) that the linguistic formulation of the *praeceptum* is possible: "This must be pursued and done," and so on. At this stage we have arrived at a normative statement at the level of reflection. It is an *enuntiatio* with normative content, which again becomes practical in the application that occurs with a judgment of the conscience.

We can now place in its proper context one of Thomas's oft-quoted but seldom understood statements: "The natural law is something constituted by the reason, just as the *propositio* is a work of the reason." (*Lex naturalis est aliquid per rationem constitutum; sicut etiam propositio est quoddam opus rationis*; *I–II*, q. 94, a.1). The meaning of this sentence is apparently the following: the natural law, like every law, is neither a *habitus*, nor a power, nor any mere act of the reason, but rather something that is constituted through the practical reason, namely, a *praeceptum* of the practical reason—in fact, a "universal precept" (*praeceptum universale*).[12]

For not a few interpreters, this sentence has become a kind of liberating formula that establishes the "autonomy" of the natural law in contradistinction to the so-called "natural order." Apart from its unsuitability to the context, such an interpretation blinds one to the fact that the quest for an autonomy of this kind depends upon a naturalistic reduction of the concept of "nature." It will be shown more fully below how the natural reason (*ratio naturalis*) which grounds this precept both in its content and in its effect, *itself belongs to "nature."* A full metaphysical disjunction between nature and reason (and also between free will and nature) makes sense in a Kantian, but not a Thomistic, context.[13] A dualistic anthropology like this, which leads inevitably to an ethics of a spiritualistic character, and to a radical "disposability" of the natural, has its ultimate origin in an attempt to *oppose* reason to a thoroughly naturalistic ("physicalistic") interpretation of the "order of nature"; such a reason would have the character of unlimited freedom vis à vis the natural.[14] This would indeed remove the whole problem that is presently under discussion: the constitution of a natural law through the practical reason. For on the basis of an innovative interpretation of the natural law as a foundation for a "theonomous autonomy," a completely different paradigm has been constructed for the establishment of norms: the teleological/utilitarian, which is discussed in detail in chapter 8.[15]

## The Natural Law as Participation in the Eternal Law

Thomas says next that the natural law is a "participation in the eternal law by the rational creature" (*participatio legis aeternae in rationali creatura; I–II*, q. 91, a. 2). "Now there is no small disagreement about the weight and significance that should be given to this definition within the framework of a philosophical theory of the natural law. For many scholars, this connection of the *lex naturalis* with the *lex aeterna* represents a metaphysical or theological "addition" that is really outside the interest of a philosophical ethics, since it does not contribute anything essential to an understanding of St. Thomas's conception of natural law.[16]

This would hold true to the extent that the *knowledge* of the participative foundation of the *lex naturalis* in the *lex aeterna* does not constitute either the preceptive act of the practical reason or the reflective experience of this act as law. But another question remains: Is it possible, without such an acknowledgment, to know the binding character of the law? Or, more precisely, to be conscious of the *ordinatio* of the preceptive act of the practical reason *as* law? There is something analogous at the level of the knowledge of being: being is at first knowable in its purposive structure without recourse to the *causa prima* (subsistent being, *esse subsistens*); nevertheless, this finality, as a *constitutive* feature of experienced being, can be known and understood in its positive intelligibility only when it is conceived as a participation in subsisting being by way of a connection (*resolutio*) to the *causa prima.*

In any case, it is from just such a metaphysical *resolutio* that the connection of the *lex naturalis* to the *lex aeterna* has its origin, and therefore is "a last stage in knowing" (*ultimum in cognoscendo*) that presents no further problems for an integration of ethics into a metaphysics of action.

However, aside from the question of moral duty, the participative context of *lex naturalis* and *lex aeterna* holds further significance: if this context is understood, the concept of the natural law can be illuminated at some decisive points.[17]

## *The Constitution of the* Lex Naturalis *Through the* Lex Aeterna

Law in general can be defined as "a statement of the practical reason in the leader of state"; now, *assuming* that the world is governed by God's providence, it is possible to call the "plan" of the divine governance of the world (*ratio gubernationis rerum in Deo*) a "law." This plan or law is a "conception" (*conceptum*) of the divine reason (*ratio divina*), and is thus eternal: it is an eternal law (see *I-II*, q. 91, a.1).

Now the natural law is not something "different from the eternal law" (*aliquid diversum a lege aeterna*), but rather a "certain participation of it" (*quaedam participatio eius*; ibid., a. 2, ad 1um). It is important to emphasize this, because the "space" in which the human reason is efficacious as lawgiver is not to be thought of as "free space" within which, somehow, nothing has been foreseen or ordained, so that this "space" would not itself be subject to any law. This is the error—based on a misunderstanding of the nature of divine providence—that forms the basis of the concept of "theonomous autonomy."

On the contrary—and this is something that must be emphasized to counter the naturalistic fallacy—this law that pertains to human behavior exists only in the mind of God, and not in created nature. This order (established through the *lex aeterna* and constituted, for the realm of human actions, through the *lex naturalis*) is not at all a "natural order," but rather an "order of the reason" (*ordo rationis*) that exists from eternity in God, and which is then constituted, by the mediation of the human reason, in acts of the will and in particular actions.[18]

The connection of the *lex naturalis* with a *lex aeterna* that transcends nature itself is possible only in a metaphysics of created being and shows the Thomistic doctrine of the natural law, despite all possible parallels, to be the only real alternative to the Stoic concept of the natural law and its principle of "living in accordance with nature" (*secundum naturam vivere*). On the level of the creature—which is a *causa secunda*—the order of the natural law is actually a work of the reason (*aliquid per rationem constitutum*), and thereby is formally an order of the reason (*ordo rationis*); it is not a "natural order," as Stoic teaching and a naturalistic doctrine would have it: an order that the reason must "discover" in order to live in accordance with it. The philosophers of the Stoa did, it is true, discover the *lex aeterna*, and this explains the great attraction of their doctrine, which has always exerted influence on philosophies of Christian inspiration. But Stoicism also identifies the *lex aeterna* with the natural order of being, and the Stoic natural law becomes a rational participation in the necessity of the order of being, while freedom becomes an "insight into necessity," to use the formula of Hegel, a modern "Stoic." The problem that results from this identification is the circularly reasoned, concrete-material determination of the content of such a natural law.[19]

### *Man's Double Participation in the Eternal Law*

We come now to a problem posed in all its sharpness by Thomas: How is the order of the eternal law communicated to the level of the creature, and made transparent and effective there? The fact that this can take place through direct revelation or divine legislation of a positive nature (see q. 19, a. 4, ad 3um) is not at issue for the concept of the *lex naturalis*. In answering the question, Thomas brings precision to his concept of the natural law.

He returns to his earlier definition of the law in general as a *regula* or *mensura*. Since all creatures are subordinated to divine providence, and thereby to the eternal law, the rule or measure that corresponds to it must somehow be contained within creation. In the first place, all created being, everything that has existence, has been formed according to a definite species, and thus possesses a determinate mode of existence, which one may call its "essence." Consequently, all existing things are already "measured" and "ruled" in their existence by the creative reason of God. This passive participation in the *lex aeterna* is expressed in "the inclination to the proper operations and ends" (*inclinatio in proprios actus et fines*) of each species (see I–II, q. 91, a. 2). All creatures—including man—possess this passive *impressio* of the eternal law in their very being, expressing itself in their natural inclinations to specific actions and goals.[20]

Accordingly, the *naturalis inclinatio* is the appetitive foundation, anchored in being and nature, of all actions and all goal-directedness.[21] This does not, however, provide an adequate order of action (*ordo operationis*) for human beings; in subrational forms of life, natural inclinations are directed in turn by natural ordering principles (such as instincts) to their actions and toward the ends that suit them (*fines debiti*; see *In IV Sent.*, dist. 33, q. 1, a. 1). This orientation toward the "suitable" or "right" (*debitum*) is also necessary, because the natural inclination as such is merely the existential foundation upon which and within which the order of actions unfolds.

However, man, as Thomas emphasizes, possesses a higher kind of participation in the eternal law—namely, a participation in the eternal reason itself—whereby he possesses a natural inclination to his proper act and end (*naturalis inclinatio ad debitum actum et finem*).[22] The nonrational creature does not have this kind of *inclinatio* to the *debitum*, though it does possess a natural *determinatio* of its inclinations. But *inclinatio* and *determinatio* are not the same: whereas all nonrational living things possess in their instincts—or whatever else one chooses to call their normatively operational ordering principle—the purely passive *determinatio* or *regulatio* of their natural inclinations (a *mensuratio*, in fact), man, on the other hand, is equipped with a different, active and cognitive ordering principle for his determination and orientation toward the *debitum* (or good); this is a *naturalis inclinatio* at a new level, which arises from his natural reason (*ratio naturalis*) as a participation in, or image (*imago*) of, the divine reason (*ratio divina*).[23]

Through this, the eternal law is transparent to us. In human beings, it is a light (*lumen*) that comes from an "impression of the divine light upon us" (*impressio divini luminis in nobis*). This light makes it possible for us to distinguish between good and evil, and herein lie the function and efficacy of the *lex naturalis*, by which man becomes a "sharer in Providence, looking out for himself and others" (*providentiae particeps, sibi ipsi et aliis providens*; *I–II*, q. 91, a. 2). Through the natural law, man himself becomes a participating and responsible interpreter of the divine providence, is coworker and coexecutive of the divine government of the world in relation to himself and others.[24] "The rational creature therefore partakes of the divine providence not only in being governed, but also in governing . . . the governing aspect of human actions, insofar as they are personal actions, belongs to divine providence" (*Summa Contra Gentiles*, III, c. 113).

If, in the case of man, the natural law consists essentially in this active, rational participation in the eternal law, it must not be forgotten that man is also subject, in his being and in the natural inclinations of his being, to a passive "measurement" (*mensuratio*) that lies at the basis of this higher participation. Students of Thomas who think they find a "creative reason" in his doctrine have no textual support for their neglect of the twofold nature of participation.[25]

## *Natural Reason as a* "Mensura Mensurata"

To recapitulate, we can now say the following: man possesses, as every creature does, a multiplicity of naturally given inclinations, which tend in each case to their appropriate (*proprii*) actions and ends, and yet this is still not "the good" in the moral sense (*actus et finis debitus*)—the good, that is, in the operative sense, with regard to an operative concretizing in the context of the ordering of the practical reason. For this further orientation toward the *bonum operabile* (which is more than the *bonum proprium* of the *inclinatio*), man, unlike the nonrational creation, does not have merely a *determinatio* or *regulatio* of natural inclinations, but instead—in the form of a natural inclination at a higher level—has his own active and cognitive principle of *determinatio* or *mensuratio*: the natural reason, an "intellectual light" (*lumen intellectuale*), the principle of "self-determination" toward the good (freedom) and the principle of order for the natural inclinations. This ordering, which is not a "natural order" in the same sense as the ordering of inclinations toward their specific *actus proprii*, is an ordering of the reason (*ordo rationis*) that is not simply "there," but must be created; it has the character of *providence* in regard to one's own actions and is "something constituted by the reason" (*aliquid per rationem constitutum*).[26] It is an order that is not there "by nature" (*a natura*); rather, it is "in accord with nature" (*secundum naturam*), since it establishes itself, and it does this to the extent that it is *secundum naturam*.[27]

All natural inclinations, insofar as they exist "by nature" (*a natura*), are also "measured" (*mensuratae*). Therefore even the natural inclination of the *ratio naturalis* for the *debitum*—the good, under the intelligible aspect of truth—is something "measured" (*mensuratum*) "by nature" (*a natura*). The other natural inclinations, when ordered, are something "measured" (*mensuratum*) "by reason" (*a ratione*), and the reason in relation to them is a "measurer" (*mensurans*). It is this especially in regard to the will, which is a "willing in the reason" (*appetitus in ratione*), in the act of which man experiences his "self-autonomy," his freedom, his mastery over himself, his inclinations, and his acts.[28] The will is the moving principle of all the other powers in man, insofar as these powers are active in the context of a "human act" (*actus humanus*). The object of the will—its goal—is communicated to the will only by way of the reason: it is a "good of the reason" (*bonum rationis*), and that reveals how the reason is not only a *mensurans*, a "measure-giving principle," but also is itself the *mensura*, the adequate measure or standard for a human action (see *I–II*, q. 1, a. 1).

In this way, we can gain a clearer understanding of the constitution of the objects of actions: the "moral object" (*objectum morale*), which as an analogue of the *lex naturalis* is "something constituted by the reason" (*aliquid per rationem constitutum*), will be discussed later. At present we have established the following: all natural inclinations belong to the natural law; as such, however, they still do not have the character of a law.[29] Instead, they form the natural basis upon which the law is constituted.[30] The law, which becomes established as an *ordo ad debitum actum et finem* in the acts of the will, in sensitive urges, and in external behavior, is not just a "measurer" (*mensurans*), but is at the same time a "measure" (*mensura*): it is not just something that "scans" or "reads off" or "applies" a measure that is there in nature, but is itself the measure and rule.[31] The "autonomistic" interpretation of Thomas has largely neglected this decisive point: it correctly criticizes a conception of the practical reason as a mere "reading organ," only to raise it to the status of a "creatively" determining principle. Such an interpretation misses the fact, however, that reason is a "standard" or "measuring stick" [*Maßstab*] that belongs to the nature of man. The same error is made by A. Auer when he calls the practical reason "the organ that discovers human possibilities, and therefore moral obligations."[32] In this case the reason no longer merely "reads off," but instead makes "new discoveries" possible—but its standard-providing nature is forgotten in the process.

## The Constitution of the Natural Law Through the *Ratio Naturalis*

The constitution of the natural law through the natural reason was never made the subject of a distinct *quaestio* or systematic analysis by St. Thomas; but he did treat various aspects of the question in a variety of contexts. The central one is the much-analyzed second article of *quaestio* 94 of the *Prima Secundae*. In this article the question posed is very narrow: it is intended to show that the natural law does not contain only a single command, but many. We should avoid the mistake of expecting too much from this one article: it must be supplemented by other contexts. Nevertheless, it does include the decisive indication of how the natural law is constituted in man by "his natural inclination to his proper end and act" (*inclinatio naturalis ad debitum finem et actum*) or *ratio naturalis*.

### *The First Principle of the Practical Reason and the Natural Law*

"Just as in the speculative reason," the second article of *quaestio* 94 begins, "there are also in the practical reason primary, underivable, and universally known judgments (*propositiones per se notae communiter omnibus*). These are judgments whose terms are known to all (*quarum termini sunt omnibus noti*). The terms for practical judgments of this kind consist in each case of a good (*bonum*: from the most universal *bonum communissimum* to the concrete *bonum operabile*) and a practical predicate, "to be pursued" or "to be avoided" (*prosequendum* or *fugiendum*). Such a description of practical judgments—as "normative statements"—is in any case meaningful only in reflection on the act of the practical reason—on the level, that is, where practical judgments are capable of a linguistic formulation. At the level of their original execution they are not accessible to such formulation, since they then involve either an appetitive–preceptive *affirmatio* of what is recognized as "good" (*prosecutio*) or a corresponding *negatio* (*fuga*).

Here, too, it appears, Thomas places himself as usual at the level that is suited to moral science: that of the reflective description (*in actu signato*) of spiritual processes. One must always be careful to keep this in mind, in order to avoid equating the preceptive act of the practical reason with a "normative statement" (*enuntiatio*): to do so would be to distort or lose sight of the very subject matter of the description.[33]

When Thomas says, then, that the first principle of the practical reason is based on the "nature of the good" (*ratio boni*), which is that "good is what all things seek" (*bonum est quod omnia appetunt*), he does not mean that the practical reason is based on this "sentence," rather, it is based upon a fact that is only reflectively formulated and grasped in it, and this is the fact of the "seekable" (or "striven-for," "sought-after," *appetibile*) that is constantly objectified as the reason's goal. Now the *appetibile is* either a true or a seeming good, and even the truly good must still "seem" good (*phainomenon agathon*), though its goodness must go beyond appearance by being good in respect to truth as well. (For this reason, when the virtuous man does what *seems to him* to be good, he spontaneously does what is truly good—hence the "efficiency" of moral virtue.)

The "nature of the good" (*ratio boni*) is therefore nothing other than what we experience as "good"—the *appetibile*, the actuality of the practical object that is experienced in willing, as willing's own object. The practical reason objectifies this as "good" (*bonum*) on the basis of an intellectual act, to which the appetitive response of the *prosecutio* follows. To be precise, the response does not *follow*, but rather *rests upon* it, since the *prosecutio* has already been stated in the judgment itself. In reflection upon this process, the first principle of the practical reason can be formulated: "Good is to be pursued and done, evil is to be avoided" (*bonum est prosequendum et faciendum, malum vitandum*).

*The Imperative (or Preceptive) Character of the First Principle*

It has already been shown how this first principle appears as an "empty formula" or tautology only when its true (practical) nature is not understood. Even at the level of reflection, when treated only as a normative "statement," it seems to say nothing, because it is too general and too fundamental. Treated in this way, one cannot "derive" anything of practical significance from it.

And yet this first principle does not need to "say" anything. As a "precept," it really has a completely different function: that of commanding or requesting. What Thomas says about the *imperium* in another context pertains as well to this act of the reason: that "it is nothing other than an act of the reason ordering, with a certain motion, that something be done" (*nihil aliud est quam actus rationis ordinantis, cum quadam motione, aliquid ad agendum*; *I–II*, q. 17, a. 5). The first principle of the practical reason has the task of drawing a primary practical conclusion from the experienced fact of willing or striving for any *appetibile*, and this consists in ordering *this* willing or striving (which always means the naturally willing or striving *person*) toward action, and in moving it toward that action.[34] Without this first principle, which exists in the context of "the will as nature" (*voluntas ut natura*), there could be no other actions of the practical reason and no action at all: it explains the "reaching out to a task" (*extensio ad opus*) of the practical reason in general.

This first principle and its "ordering movement" (*ordinatio motiva*) are constantly present in all other principles of the practical reason. As Thomas says, it is the foundation of all other "precepts" of the natural law. In the first principle of the practical reason, the "natural inclination to what is fitting" (*inclinatio naturalis ad debitum*)—the "natural reason" (*ratio naturalis*)—has already set down its first determinative (though still universal) act; it is followed by the (likewise first and universal) "ordering toward the suitable" or "good" (*ordinatio ad debitum* or *bonum*). If there are further "goods" (*bona*), which the natural reason spontaneously grasps as such in an analogous way, then these, too, are judged by the reason to be *prosequenda* and *facienda* on the basis of the first principle.

In the article we are speaking of, Thomas provides for the existence of such "further" *bona* (which he will afterward discuss more thoroughly) when he draws the following inference from the first principle: "that is to say, that all those things to be done or avoided pertain to the precepts of the natural law, which the practical reason naturally understands to be human goods" (*ut scilicet omnia illa facienda vel vitanda pertineant ad praecepta legis naturae, quae ratio naturaliter apprehendit esse bona*); the demonstration of such a plurality of human goods, or of a multiplicity of natural law commandments pertaining to these goods, is precisely the aim of the article. Nevertheless, it should not be understood that the other self-evident principles of the natural law (the practical reason) are only deductive conclusions from the first and most fundamental, since they would not then be self-evident (*per se notae*).

It is important to note that the first principle, "*bonum est prosequendum . . .*" (or, to be exact, the judgment of the *prosecutio boni* as such) cannot arise or become known in isolation from any further content. It is not otherwise with the theoretical knowledge of being, where the contradiction of "being" (*ens*) and "not-being" (*non ens*) does not arise as such, in its pure formality. It is always experienced in concrete being, and it is in this fundamental characteristic of being (in its concrete state) that the principle of contradiction *reveals itself* as the first principle of the knowledge of being.

It must likewise be emphasized that the first principle of the practical reason always reveals itself only in the materially determined areas of the *prosecutio*; it appears as somehow compartmentalized into distinct areas that are naturally present to the natural reason as it makes its evaluations. And because it is "the ordering and moving principle" (*principium ordinans et motivum*), it is here that it develops its efficacy as the foundation of actions.

*The Spontaneous Comprehension of Fundamental Human Values* (Bona Humana)

The "areas" in question belong, for Thomas, to the natural inclinations and are, in a way, marked out by them. Since they are natural and not acquired tendencies, they are directed by natural necessity—by a *determinatio ad unum*—toward a good that is proper (*proprium*) to them. The natural aim of these tendencies has not yet reached the realm of the *debitum* of the practical reason, but this occurs as soon as the natural reason comprehends these goals as practical goods, as "seekable" (*appetibile*), in order to make them its own goals, which it does spontaneously and naturally. The goals of natural inclinations are *natural* objects (*appetibilia*) of the natural reason. The latter does not "lord" it over these inclinations: it can neither bring them into existence nor even become "free" of their dynamism without completely forfeiting the possibility of a fundamental and specifically human practical knowledge, because the natural inclinations are rooted in the essential constitution of the person. And yet, on this ontic level, they are still not *bona rationis*. This is why Thomas calls *the inclinations* that exist "by nature" (*a natura*) "general rules or measures for everything that man must do—and of these things [that is, *actions*] the natural reason is the measure, even though the natural reason is not the measure of the things that are by nature [that is, the *inclinations*])."[35] This means that the natural inclinations in themselves are only an "indirect" rule or standard, or in other words, they form the basis of the standard; they still do not have the power to govern actions. They are, rather, a standard and rule for the natural reason, which in turn is the rule and standard for actions through "its causing of order (*ordinatio*) in the natural inclinations."

Therefore, Thomas concludes, the natural reason understands everything toward which a natural inclination of man is directed to be a human good. The order of the commands of the natural law thus corresponds to the order of the natural inclinations (*I–II,*

q. 94, a. 2), and this demonstrates the plurality of those commands, completing the task of this particular article. What remains unclarified—because it was not part of the original question—is the nature of the relationship between *inclinatio* and *praeceptum*, or between the "fitting act" (*actus proprius*) of the natural inclination and the "right act" (*debitum*) that is commanded in the act of the practical reason.

In this classic passage, Thomas speaks of natural inclinations on three levels. First are those that belong to every entity on the basis of its substantiality, or the inclinations that belong to the "conservation of one's own being, according to one's nature" (*conservatio sui esse secundum suam naturam*). On the next level are those inclinations that man has in common with all living things, for which Thomas gives the examples of "the inclination toward the joining of male and female" (*coniunctionem maris et feminae*) and "the rearing of children" (*educationem liberorum*). Finally, there are specifically human tendencies that follow from the nature of the reason itself, such as the *inclinatio* toward knowing the truth, toward living in a community with others, and so on. Out of all these inclinations there arise corresponding precepts of the natural law that order these inclinations (and the acts and ends that go with them) in accordance with reason. A more detailed understanding of this is not to be had from the body of the article, since the question asked at the outset of the article has been sufficiently answered.

### *The Integration of Fundamental Human Values into the Structure of Human Action*

Now what does it mean to say that the *ratio naturalis* "understands" (*apprehendit*) the goals of the natural inclinations as "goods" (*bona*), or as *bona humana*, or even as "acts to be pursued" (*opera prosequenda*)? It must first of all be emphasized that these goals are not "goods" in the same way for the natural reason as they are for the various natural appetites (*appetitus naturales*) that belong to the natural inclinations. The reason apprehends these inclinations in an intellective manner: the *bona* to which they are oriented are not objectified by the natural reason as *sensibilia*, but rather as *intelligibilia*, and thereby they are objectified within the context of a total ordering of the "human good" (*bonum humanum*), and the "human good" as such is the "good of the reason" (*bonum rationis*).[36]

At this point it should be recalled that this *apprehensio*, though a speculative act, is nevertheless not a speculative *judgment*, because it emerges from a *naturalis inclinatio ad debitum actum et finem* whose cognitive content has been stamped by the "light of the natural reason" (*lumen rationis naturalis*); the bearer of the inclination is the "will as nature" (*voluntas ut natura*), or the act of the will (see *I–II,* q. 10, a. 1) that has been naturally directed toward fundamental human goods. The judgment that results from this is a practical, preceptive judgment.

The will, which is an intellective or rational "seeking power" (or appetitive power, *appetitus*) seeks not only its own good (the *bonum rationis*) but also the good of all the other powers, of all that belongs to man in his totality (see *I–II*, q. 9, a. 1). The *apprehensio* and *prosecutio* of the goals of the natural inclinations are not to be conceived of as a purely speculative judgment and insight, or as the "confirmation by" or "subordination to" the reason of such goals. On the contrary, once they have been apprehended as natural inclinations that belong to the person, they are brought into (that is, integrated within) reason's own order by the reason, and thereby become the object of the will's intellective "seeking."[37] And only as such are they in each case the content of a *praeceptum* and a *prosequendum* and belong to the natural law. "All inclinations of any part of human nature, that is, both of the concupiscible and irascible parts, belong to the natural law [*pertinent ad legem naturalem*] *insofar as* they are regulated by the reason" (*I–II,* q. 94, a. 2, ad 2um). This is because reason is "the ordering principle of everything that has to do with human beings" (*ordinativa omnium quae ad homines spectant*; ibid., ad 3um).

To avoid a naturalistic interpretation of *I–II*, q. 94, a. 2, it is crucial to note that the *praeceptum* (or *prosecutio*) that results from the apprehension of the natural inclinations and their goals is *already* a *praeceptum* of the practical reason and *as such* does not arise from the natural inclination itself, but rather from a motion (*motio*) of the intellective appetite or will; otherwise, a preceptive act of this kind would not imply a voluntary act, or an *actus humanus.*

Without going any deeper into the interplay of intellect and will, it is possible to grasp a structure in the constitution of the natural law that is entirely characteristic of the practical reason: the goal of any natural inclination—an *appetibile*—becomes an object of the will by the *ratio naturalis*; the will, for its part, moves the reason to a "command" (*imperium*), a preceptive–ordinative act; and this act, so long as its content is universal, is a command of the natural law.

The structure of the constitution of objects of the will and of objects of action can be described in the same manner, to show how such a structure can indicate "moral quality" (the *genus moris*). The most precise formulation, which Thomas offers for it in another context, should be quoted in full: "The good is represented to the will as an object; and insofar as it belongs to the order of reason, it pertains to moral matter (*genus moris*), and causes moral goodness in the act of the will. For reason is the principle of human and moral acts" (*I–II,* q. 19, a. 1, ad 3um).

This means that the will grasps each object through the reason (*I–II,* q. 19, a. 3); the will can be moved only by a *bonum rationis* and not by a *bonum sensibile* as such. Consequently, only the goals of the *ratio naturalis*—those of the "third" level—are always adequate objects for the will, and not those of the other levels. "But sensible or imaginable good [*bonum sensibile, bonum imaginarium*] is not proportioned to the will but to the sensitive appetite [*proportionatum . . . appetitui sensitivo*]" (ibid., a. 1, ad 3um). Such objects are adequate for the will only insofar as they have been objectified through the natural reason. The will depends on its object exactly to the extent that it depends on the reason (ibid.). Here Thomas is stressing the fact that every "seeking for a proper end" (*appetitus finis debiti*), every right apprehension and striving after an end, implies a work of the reason.[38]

What has been said gains further confirmation by Thomas's exposition of the morality of the "exterior action" (*actus exterior, actus imperatus a voluntate*).[39] Every goal of a natural inclination that becomes an object of the will is also pursued by that inclination in an act "commanded by the will" (*imperatus a voluntate*), and thus within the order of reason. What is true for every *actus exterior* (or *actus imperatus*) is true here as well: that it is "an object of the will to the extent that it is proposed to the will by the reason [*proponitur voluntati a ratione*] as a good that has been apprehended and ordered by the reason [*quoddam bonum apprehensum et ordinatum a ratione*]" (*I–II*, q. 20, a. 1, ad 1um).

This cognitive integration of a *bonum* into the context of the *bonum rationis* is already implied by the concept of "human good" (*bonum humanum*), which is analogous to the concept of "human act" (*actus humanus*). When Thomas says, in *I–II*, q. 94, a. 2, that the reason "naturally apprehends as goods" (*naturaliter apprehendit ut bona*) the ends of the natural inclinations, there is already signified in such cases a *bonum* in its human and personal intelligibility, and thus the *bonum humanum*, since an intellective *apprehensio* is at work. This is why everything "that the practical reason naturally apprehends to be human goods" belongs to the natural law (ibid). That Thomas understands the *regulatio rationis* to be implicit in such apprehension is expressly stated in the *ad secundum:* (*secundum quod regulentur ratione*).

In order, then, for the ends of the natural inclinations to become objects of the will—and thereby the subject matter of a preceptive act of the practical reason (a *praeceptum* of the *lex naturalis*)—it is first of all necessary that there be an intellective *apprehensio* and *ordinatio* of them; in this way, they become adequate objects of the will as *bona humana* (or *bona rationis*), and then, through an *imperium* of the will, they can be effectively pursued within this order. And yet the reason has nothing to say about the existence itself of these natural inclinations, or of their ends, which form the very foundation and the "naturally given principles" (*principia a natura*) for this process; on the contrary, it is really thanks to these inclinations that the reason is able to be a practical reason, as a principle of freedom. The knowing human person experiences these inclinations as belonging to his own being, as inherent in it (*impressae; principia ei indita*). He cannot put himself out of their reach without contradicting the very conditions of his human existence, including his reason and all orientation toward freedom—a God-created freedom that is naturally limited and conditioned. Without reason, the natural inclinations would be merely blind, natural urges; on the other hand, without the natural inclinations and an orientation toward them, the practical reason would be just as blind, and would be incapable of telling man what is of most importance in his behavior.

### *The Subject Matter of the Natural Law: The* Ordo Ad Finem

We are now in a position to make some precisions: the "ordering" (*ordinatio*) of the natural law is *teleologically* carried out by the whole ensemble of goals laid out by the natural inclinations; all the same, it actually covers the "ordering to the end" (*ordo ad finem*) that corresponds to a given goal, which is at the same time an "order of operation" (*ordo operationis*) and thus a "right [or "suitable"] act" (*actus debitus*). A law is "something that pertains to the reason" (*aliquid ad rationem pertinens*), because it pertains to the reason to establish an order to an end in the acts of the will and in behavior (*rationis est ordinare ad finem; I–II,* q. 90, a. 1). Such a perspective appears to suggest Thomas's concept of the natural law in his early *Commentary on the Sentences.*[40] There he writes: "To all things are assigned certain principles, through which they not only are able to perform actions proper to themselves [*operationes propriae*], but also make them suitable for their ends" (*In IV Sent.*, d. 33, q. 1, a. 1). Thomas distinguishes three levels where this rule is realized, depending on whether a merely natural thing, or a nonrational animal, or a human being is in question.

With regard to the first, where the activity is based on natural necessity (*ex necessitate naturae*), the "natural" or substantial form is itself the principle of the activity, through which the specific acts, being adjusted to the goal at the same time, take place with an ordering to this end. And yet this is not true for man, despite what a naturalistic conception of the natural law would tend to maintain. For all animals—man included—possess a *cognitive* principle, so that the principle of their activity is apprehension (whether sensitive or intellective is not of concern at this stage) and appetition.[41] For this reason it is necessary "that there be a natural act of knowing [*naturalis conceptio*] and (in the power to "strive after" or "seek") a natural inclination, through which the activity proper to the *genus* or *species* takes place in accordance with the goal."

The *naturalis conceptio* and the *naturalis inclinatio* are what in animals is called "natural judgment" (*naturalis aestimatio*); it is a natural instinct, which is itself determined. This determination is not merely due to a "necessity of the end" (*necessitas finis*), which man has, too, and which not only is compatible with freedom but also provides the very foundation of freedom in a creature; it is also due to a "single determination" (*determinatio ad unum*) in regard to the activity itself. Thomas explains that nonrational living things behave "so that they do not regulate their own activity through their own judgment, but rather are compelled, by the power of nature, to accomplish suitable actions." Man differs from them in that he grasps the "meaning of the end" (*ratio finis*) as well as the relationship or *proportio* of the single actions to the end.[42] Therefore, he concludes, the *naturalis conceptio* which has been given to man, and by which he is guided to act properly, is the *lex naturalis* or *ius naturale.*

The natural law is here revealed to be identical with the light of the natural reason,[43] which, moved by the natural inclination of the will to the good, makes it possible for the human being to accomplish the special actions of his natural inclinations with his own judgment, in a way that is suited to the ends of these inclinations. It must not be forgotten that because of the spiritual nature that belongs to the will, and thereby to all the human inclinations, there exists an openness for a multiplicity of possible actions, which become specified to a concrete action in each case only through the act of the "free will" (*liberum arbitrium*) or "choice" (*electio*).[44]

This *ordo* of human actions is the subject matter, and the work, of the natural law: "something constituted by the reason" (*aliquid a ratione constitutum*). It is the *ordo ad finem,* in which the *finis* means the human good that a natural inclination tends toward in the order of reason. Thomas further maintains that an *ordo virtutis* corresponds to this *ordo rationis*; thus moral virtue is the expression of the *ordo rationis* and a work of the natural law.[45]

## The Natural Law and Virtue

The third article of *quaestio* 94 of the *Prima Secundae* has been "overlooked" by not a few writers on Thomas. And yet this article really makes possible a conclusive explanation of the concept of the natural law. It takes up the question of whether all acts of the virtues belong to the natural law (*utrum omnes actus virtutum sint de lege naturae*). The answer of St. Thomas is in essence the following: insofar as any action can have the character (*ratio*) of moral virtue, so all virtuous actions belong to the natural law; for the natural law constitutes, in a universal way, that which makes a virtuous act virtuous—although this must be understood in relation to its objectively specific determination, and not merely in its character as an act of a *habitus* (*I–II*. q. 94, a. 3).

### *The Identity of the* Ordo Rationis *with the* Ordo Virtutis

The justification for this at first only recalls something familiar: it rests upon the existence of a "natural inclination that man act in accordance with reason" (*naturalis inclinatio quod agat secundum rationem*; ibid.). This tendency corresponds to the specifically human (i.e., rational) part of the soul (ibid.). Such rationally guided action is really nothing other than an "action in accordance with virtue." Therefore action that is virtuously carried out corresponds (in the same way as the natural law) to a "dictate of the natural reason" (*dictamen rationis naturalis*).[46]

What it means to identify the *ordo rationis* (constituted by the natural law) with the *ordo virtutis* (see *I–II,* q. 100, a. 2 ) becomes clear as soon as one considers what moral virtue really involves. The virtue of each "seeking" or "striving" (*appetitus*) does not consist in the attainment of the natural end as such (*finis naturalis*) of this *appetitus*, but rather in its participation in the reason, in its subordination to the reason.[47] This applies as well to the will, or intellective appetition, as to sensitive appetition. "A moral disposition [*habitus*] possesses the character of human virtue to the extent that it agrees with the reason" (*I–II,* q. 58, a. 2). Moral virtue "is nothing other than a certain participation of right reason in the appetitive part [of the soul]" (see *De Virtutibus*, a. 12, ad 16um; *I–II*, q. 61, a. 2; *II–II,* q. 141, a. 6).

The "good" of man (*bonum hominis*) toward which moral virtue is directed consists in this: "that the reason sufficiently recognize the truth, and that the lower urges be ordered in accordance with the rule of the reason" (*De Virtutibus*, a. 9). The human being is not a purely spiritual being whose action and willing are exclusively of a spiritual nature. By nature, man is an "animal"—he not only *has* a body, he *is* one[48]—a body that is informed and animated by a rational soul. As body and *anim-al* he possesses knowledge through the senses and sensitive appetite, certain possibilities and needs that are bound up with the body, but that are not "subhuman," "alien," or "confining natural phenomena." Instead, such needs and possibilities are integrated into his very being; they represent the foundations of human existence, and help constitute his human personhood. In just the same way, all the human *natural inclinations* provide the basic patterns in accordance with which human life and action are *human*. Although these tendencies must be ordered by the reason, they already possess a human meaning simply in virtue of their belonging to the essence of man, as part of the human *suppositum*. In this sense, they do not need to be "humanized" or "spiritualized" before they can tell us anything about human nature.[49]

This leads us to oppose decisively the essentially *dualistic* position of many contemporary moral theologians who represent the natural inclinations (even those of the *natura animalis*) as merely so much "raw material"—a realm of "subhuman" existence—as if these inclinations were not already human goods simply by being included in human nature, but rather can become such only after an integration into the sphere of the human. That such is not the case can be readily seen in regard to the most fundamental of human tendencies, which man has in common with all subsisting beings: the tendency toward self-preservation (*conservatio sui esse*). It would make no sense to say that this *esse* is not already a *bonum humanum* by nature, and that it must be "made into" one.

One must avoid confusing two "integrations": on the one hand, the existential integration of these inclinations in the context of the person (which, because it is always present, and makes a human being human, in this sense is not something to be "achieved"), and on the other, the practical–cognitive and operative integration that takes place through the *ratio naturalis* and moral virtue. Man does not have to humanize these inclinations in the first or existential sense, since they are human tendencies to begin with. Nevertheless, they must still be ordered (in the second sense) *practically* and *cognitively* in their human meaning and properly followed. The inclinations will not accomplish this by themselves. At this point, it is worthwhile to recall the injunction "Become what you are!"; it was criticized earlier, but now can be seen to have a certain clear but limited meaning.

And yet a position that holds that the natural inclinations would be "human" only to the extent that they have been comprehended by the reason would mean that only through such comprehension can man existentially endow the inclinations with any human meaning. Such a position would be spiritualistic or dualistic, and would likewise imply that man possesses, over the nature *that he himself is,* a "right to control" or a "power to determine meaning" that this same human nature does not more specifically determine.

At the same time, the naturalistic position must be opposed. According to this, man is *merely* a complex of natural inclinations that would already be normative without any further "cognitive integration," and would already, as such, have the character of a morally meaningful natural law. The fundamental unity of the human soul as a *forma substantialis* stands opposed to a plurality of parts of the soul and natural inclinations to go with them. Equally opposed to such a position are the substantial unity of body and soul and, finally, the unity of the person and action: the *suppositum humanum.* This unity makes it possible for all the natural inclinations to have a relation of value to the whole: a value that is not immediately "read off" from the end of each inclination, but that results from the inclinations' relationship to the specifically human, to the rational part of the soul.

On the basis of an empirical assessment of natural inclinations *alone,* relatively little of a normative nature can be stated about moral behavior. On the other hand, such normative statements will be possible only when these inclinations are respected as *human* tendencies, as goods of the human person (*bona humana*). Without such respect, there would be neither moral philosophy nor moral theology, since both would be only remotely able to say anything true.[50]

### *Moral Virtue as the Integration of Natural Inclinations into the Ordering of the Reason*

Now the ontic/natural orientation of every inclination toward its "proper good" (*bonum proprium*) must be brought into the orientation of each inclination toward its specifically human "moral good" (*bonum debitum*), which is the "good of the reason" (*bonum rationis*), and which in its turn formally constitutes moral virtue.[51] Only in such a case does the fully human meaning of each one of these natural ends become clear, in the totality of the human person. This second, "vertical" *ordo*, which corresponds to the hierarchy of parts of the soul, shows, for example, that the natural inclination toward self-preservation (*ad conservationem sui esse*) in man is not simply an inclination to hold on to a "mere existence." Such a "will to be" (or *conatus*), though fundamental (it comes to be "by nature," *a natura*) does not express the *bonum humanum* of "remaining in existence" in its fully human specificity and meaning.

In stating this, Thomas takes up once more an Aristotelian idea: "One considers the existence of man above all in relation to the intellect. Thus it is the virtuous man—the one who lives most fully in accordance with intellect and virtue—who wants to live and exist in the highest degree. This is because he wants to 'live' and 'be' in accordance with what is permanent in him. He who primarily wants to 'live' and 'be' in accordance with the body, which changes, does not truly want to live and be" (*In IX Ethic.*, lect. 4).

Every natural tendency has a fundamental nature. While belonging to man, and already a *bonum humanum*, any inclination will reveal and actualize its specifically human meaning only in the context of being ordered within the *ordo rationis*, which is nothing other than the *ordo virtutis*.[52] This "conformity to the reason"—the constitutive and formal element of moral virtue—reveals the true character of the natural inclinations; a character we could never appreciate without respecting at the outset the importance of the natural inclinations as the very conditions for constituting the human *suppositum*, and for constituting morality.

The process of forming moral virtue is correlated with this vertical order of the parts of the soul and its powers: the mind, which knows through the *intellectus agens*, and which grasps the *bonum appetibile* of a natural inclination in its human meaning, puts into motion the intellective "seeking power," or the will. Only a good that has been recognized intellectively is capable of moving the will. The will, in turn, moves the sensitive appetitive power—an "act commanded by the will" (*actus imperatus a voluntate*)—in accordance with the ordering of the reason, through which the *bonum appetibile* of the will is objectified. In this way we transfer the *ordinatio rationis* (the *ordo rationis*) to the natural inclinations. Through the "command" (*imperium*) of the will, the lower powers of the soul "obey" the reason, as their position within the structure of the person requires. The habitual orientation of these urgings according to the *ordinatio rationis* is known as moral virtue. Therefore Thomas concludes: "Virtue of the appetitive part (that is, moral virtue) is nothing other than a certain disposition or form, stamped and pressed upon the appetitive power by the reason." (*Virtus appetitivae partis nihil est aliud quam quaedam dispositio sive forma, sigillata et impressa in vi appetitiva a ratione; De Virtutibus,* a. 9).

### *The Natural Inclinations as "Seeds of the Virtues"* (Semina Virtutum)

Thomas shows once more how distant he is from any form of naturalism by emphasizing that only natural things (*res naturales*) possess the "determination" (*determinatio*) of their inclinations through a natural form (*forma naturalis*); the natural inclination of natural things is therefore due to a *forma* that is *a natura*—it is an "inclination to a single thing" (*inclinatio ad unum*). In this case the meaning of every natural inclination is exhausted in itself.

This is not the case, however, with man. Like all living things, man possesses a "seeking power" (*vis appetitiva*) that is not determined to a single thing; this *vis appetitiva* can function in opposed ways in relation to an object, that is, as a "pursuing" (*prosecutio*) or as a "fleeing" (*fuga*). As already explained, in subrational living things, the action of the appetitive power in relation to its objects (under the aspect of the *debitum*) is governed by a further principle that naturally determines it toward a single thing: the *aestimatio naturalis*. In man this governing principle is the reason. Reason is what gives form and a determination to the "seeking" (or *appetitus*), and a habit (*habitus*) of this is called moral virtue, which is formed as a "second nature"—"as if it were a form, tending to a single thing in a natural way" (*quasi quaedam forma per modum naturae tendens in unum*)—namely, toward the "good of the reason" (*bonum rationis*) or the "human good" (*bonum humanum*).[53] Now this "good" is itself many-sided: it is a multiplicity that is possible only because of the determination of reason, and this, of course, must in each case be understood to be a *forma a ratione concepta*, in accordance with the earlier characterization of the objects of actions. It leaves many possibilities open for different persons in different situations, within the framework of the field marked out by the natural inclinations. For this reason, the natural law does not regulate all the acts of a virtue one by one; they are determined, rather, by prudence in conformity with the "universal precept" (*praeceptum universale*) of the natural law as well as other norms or laws, which for their part can never be in contradiction to the natural law.[54]

Here the Stoic doctrine that the natural inclinations are "seeds of the virtues" (*semina virtutum*) finds confirmation by Thomas, albeit with modification: Thomas says that the natural inclinations "belong to the natural law," since they, too, correspond to an *impressio* of the eternal law in man. Nevertheless, it is important to stress the fact that as such they are *not yet* the natural law—no more so than the *actus proprius* of a natural inclination can be regarded as an act of virtue. If the natural inclination has not been governed by the reason, it can, in its natural spontaneity as a so-called "natural virtue," lead to *inhuman* consequences. This is seen in the human will when it is not oriented through the virtue of justice to the good of others: this is what happens when the will, naturally and in principle, only seeks its own good as the only good, or even experiences the good of others as evil, which is envy or jealousy. But the natural law comes into existence in the rational government of the natural inclinations. This is consequently not merely a "natural ordering" (*ordinatio naturalis*); it is also an "ordering" of the natural inclinations, an "ordering of the reason" (*ordo rationis*) *amid* the natural inclinations. This is also true for the inclination "to the good of the reason" (*inclinatio ad bonum rationis*): the human will, which does not possess, in its merely natural orientation to the good, an adequate basis for pursuing the good of another (*bonum alterius*); it also needs regulation by the reason and by a virtue—the virtue of justice.[55]

Just like the natural law, moral virtue is the perfection of natural inclinations through conformity to the reason (*conformitas ad rationem*). This is why Thomas can also say, "The habits of the virtues pre-exist in us in certain natural inclinations, which are the beginnings of the virtues (*virtutum inchoationes*)."[56] A natural inclination is a "beginning" in two senses: (1) as a "habitual disposition" (*dispositio habitualis*), in the case of a natural inclination, it is a "beginning" that is "by nature" (*a natura*), and in the case of virtue, it is a "beginning" acquired through the repetition of rationally-guided and (above all) *internal* acts of the will directed toward action (*electiones*)—through this acquisition it becomes *stamped* (*impressa*) upon the appetitive power; (2) virtue is a "consummation" of the "beginning" represented by the natural inclination (that is, virtue "completes" what the inclination "begins") because it integrates the inclination into the *bonum rationis*.

## The Moral Object, and How It Is Constituted

In order to understand what follows, it would seem helpful at this point to interject a few provisional and summary remarks on the concept of the moral object (*obiectum morale*), even though this is a theme that must be treated more comprehensively in a later context (chapter 4). There is a far-reaching analogy or parallelism between the constitution of the natural law and that of the moral object; in fact, if one looks closely, it is really one and the same phenomenon, studied under two aspects and—in part—on two different levels: the two aspects mutually complement and illuminate one another.

### *Abstract (Ontic) and Moral-Practical Objectification—and a New Version of the Naturalistic Fallacy*

The "proper goods" (*bona propria*) toward which the natural inclinations tend are abstract/ontic; that is, at the level of their "physical nature" (*genus naturae*) and abstracted from their integration within the *suppositum*, they are not yet moral values of immediate relevance to action. Nevertheless, they cannot be called "premoral" goods, such as the dualistic thesis maintains. At the level of the *genus naturae*, to be sure, no moral judgment can be undertaken. But to maintain that they were "premoral" goods would make sense only in an ethical method that must always take into account the context of the *suppositum* in order to be ethical. In other words, to treat the goals of these natural inclinations as if they were premoral goods would mean that they possessed no intrinsic *proportio ad rationem* at all; that they would be, to use Thomas's expression "indifferent in respect to their species." This is to say that they would be without intrinsic moral significance even in the context of the *suppositum* and not only when *abstractly considered* (that is in their *genus naturae*); that they would acquire such significance only through further circumstances or intentions of the person who acts.

However, the abstract/ontological treatment of the natural inclinations and their ends is inadequate from the point of view of anthropology as well as of ethics, since it cannot lead to a judgment that is morally qualitative—such as, in fact, the position that holds them to be "indifferent" or "premoral" goods.[57] It is not the ends of these inclinations that is premoral, but rather the abstract manner of treatment, and that is not only "pre-" but also "nonmoral." As an abstraction of these natural inclinations, such analysis involves a separation of them from the context of the person, from the *suppositum*—the mere objectifying of their *genus naturae*.[58]

To characterize the goals of the natural inclinations as "premoral" goods would mean endowing them with a moral qualification (or really, disqualification) on the basis of their *genus naturae*. But this would be an impermissible *transgressio in aliud genus*, which can easily be recognized as a variant of the "naturalistic fallacy." It results from the failure to observe that the *genus naturae* and the *genus moris* are not simply "derived" from one another. On the level of the *genus naturae*, no morally qualifying predications are allowable. "Morally indifferent," however, is just such a predication.

An ethics that is structurally spiritualistic and dualistic necessarily has its basis in a abstract/ontological method of treating the objects of actions. In ethics this is a fundamental error, an *error in principiis*. It is a naturalistic interpretation of the objects of actions, based upon the illegitimate derivation of objective (and *specific*) *indifference* from what is abstractly considered: the *genus naturae* of the natural inclinations that have been separated out from the whole context of the human *suppositum*. What follows—to take the example of "teleological ethics"—is that such "premoral" and ethically indifferent goods must eventually be re-integrated into an ethical context, in order to overcome the naturalistic starting point. But an ethical theory of this kind is no longer capable of adequately reconstructing the whole context of the human person, and in order to reach norms of action, must become "universally teleological," and that means *utilitarian* (see chapter 8).

In reality, these *bona propria*—the *bona particularia* of the natural inclinations—can by no means become objectified by the practical reason in their *genus naturae*, even in moral philosophical reflection. As mentioned above, the ontic/natural aspect of these goods or goals is an abstraction, a dislodgment from their context, and therefore a reduction of their intelligibility. The human being, as the subject of practical (self-)experience, is never a mere collection of diverse natural inclinations that somehow offer themselves to this experience apart from any context. He is, rather, a *person*, a definite kind of *suppositum*, in which "animal nature" (*natura animalis*) as well as "rational nature" (*natura rationalis*) are integrated: he is body, sensation, and spirit. Above all, every experience and consciousness of such natural inclinations is an achievement of the person as a whole, who experiences these inclinations as "my *own*," as "belonging to me." Such experience takes place existentially, and not abstractly. Every inclination and its good are always experienced as *my* experience, and not as something "foreign," such as the surrounding nature: they are always related to a personal context.[59] This kind of experience is only the result of the original existential (or anthropological) integration of the various natural levels in the *suppositum*. On the basis of this *suppositum* (which helps clarify such an experience), it becomes evident that every natural inclination possesses, by nature and within the context of the person, a significant orientation that always transcends the mere *genus naturae*, and that would be distorted and disturbed in its intelligibility through a merely abstract mode of treatment. In a moral examination, the natural meaning of natural inclinations is a *personal* meaning, not to be identified with the "physical nature" (*genus naturae*) of the inclination.

The achievement of the natural reason, the acts of which are acts of the person, consists precisely in grasping the transcendence of these *bona particularia* on the basis of their integration within the *suppositum*. The natural act of the practical reason represents a "natural inclination toward virtue" or "toward living in accordance with reason" (*vivere secundum rationem*): every such act comprehends these *bona particularia* as *bona humana*, and thus as moral goods of the whole person. This process is the moral objectification of goods or values. The object of the practical reason is constituted in it, and becomes the object of the will, which thereby obtains its moral quality. By way of the will, this moral content is transferred to the actions carried out and "commanded" by the will; such acts are *actus humani*, human and moral actions, because they originate from an "intellective seeking" (*appetitus intellectivus*), and ultimately from a "deliberate willing" (*voluntas deliberata*).

### *The Object of Action: A* 'Forma a Ratione Concepta"

The statement that the goals of the natural inclinations are transcendent in view of their integration within the *suppositum* is only another expression of the truth that the *objective value* or moral content (that is,, the *objectum actus in genere moris*) is constituted through a "proportion to the reason" (*proportio ad rationem*). We cannot reify the concept of the "moral object" without risking its reduction to the *genus naturae.*[60] A great deal of the plausibility of "teleological ethics"—as will be shown later in this study—is due to the fact that it has attacked just such a naturalistic (or "physicalistic") misunderstanding of the *moralitas ex obiecto;* "teleological ethics" does this, however, while ignoring the principal weakness—the misunderstanding of the practical reason—and thereby falls victim to a regrettable naturalism.

St. Thomas states, as already noted, that "the species of moral acts are constituted by forms, as they are conceived by the reason" (*species moralium actuum constituuntur ex formis, prout sunt a ratione conceptae; I–II,* q. 18, a. 10). This "form conceived by the reason" (*forma a ratione concepta*) is nothing other than the object of an action in its "moral quality" (*genus moris*). For this reason Thomas underlines the fact that this object is not a matter "out of which" (*materia ex qua*), such as would underlie a natural process of generation as a coprinciple with the *forma substantialis* without which the matter could not be defined, and that, as *materia prima,* is pure potentiality. Objects of action, by contrast, are called matter "concerning which" (*materia circa quam*): this is not an indeterminate coprinciple of the whole object, but rather the object itself, considered with respect to its material determinateness. It is already configured by the practical reason itself, and thus (in direct contrast to the *materia ex qua*) "it has, in a way, the character of form, to the extent that it gives the act its species" (*habet quodammodo rationem formae inquantum dat speciem*).[61] In the *Commentary on the Sentences,* Thomas calls the *materia circa quam* the "end of the act" (*finis actus*), which is nothing other than its "object" (*obiectum*).[62]

This equivalence between moral object (that is, object of the practical reason, *actus exterior ordinatus a ratione*, and as such, set before the will as an object proportioned to the goal of its striving) and the *materia circa quam* may be confusing at times. The confusion ceases when one realizes that for Thomas a formal and material aspect can be seen in every object (as in every "good" in general);[63] they do not amount to two "things," nor do they stand in relation to one another as hylomorphic coprinciples, but rather, to use the appropriate metaphor, they are related as color to light.[64] The *materia circa quam,* objectified by the *ratio,* is not an "unformed matter" (*materia informis*); rather, it is already an ordered material that has been stamped with the reason. As Thomas says, it is a "proper matter" (*materia debita*, or *materia commensurata a ratione*), because of the "reason's goal" (*finis rationis*); without the formal light of the *ordo rationis* (which is an *ordo ad finem*), even the *materia circa quam* cannot be thought of (see *Contra Gentiles* III, 9).

## *The Object as the Goal of the Will*

The will, when it extends to an act outside of itself (an *actus imperatus*), is not itself the cause of the moral goodness of this act, in the sense of a "purpose of the agent" (*finis operantis*), which would endow a premoral, "exterior event" with the moral quality of an intention.[65] The goal of the will is, first of all, the *materia circa quam* that has been offered to its command by the reason, as the will's *materia debita.* The error we are concerned with results from a reversal of the order of qualification (*ordo specificationis*) and the order of execution (*ordo executionis*). As Thomas says, the moral goodness of an external action does not come from the will but from the reason, because of the *materia debita* and *circumstantiae debitae*.[66] The external act is the object of the will only to the extent that it is set before the will as a good that has been comprehended and ordered by the reason. In this order of morally objective *specification*, the "good of the reason" (*bonum rationis*) *precedes* the "good of the will" (*bonum voluntatis*). In the order of the *execution* of an action, the reverse is true: here the goodness of the exterior act is really effected by the will; for the will, as soon as it has been specified by the reason, conveys its *bonitas* to the externally willed action, which now possesses a moral quality to the extent that it is willed (*volitum*); the moral quality of an action is thus, from this point of view, a *consequence* of the inner (elective and intentional) act of the will.[67]

Here, then, is the mistake in reasoning committed by L. Janssens and those who follow him. First, they overlook the difference between the order of specification and the order of execution. Second, they overlook the constitutive ordering function that the reason has in regard to the *materia debita*, or the object; it is not seen that the object of the will must always be "something apprehended and ordered by the reason" (*apprehensum et ordinatum a ratione*), and therefore already possesses a moral specification, and as "premoral" good could never be willed at all.[68] Third, the *actus exterior* as object and as goal (*finis*) of the will is systematically confused with an "end that the agent sets for himself" (*finis quem agens sibi praestituit*, or a mere *finis operantis*); what escapes notice is that it is not only the *intentio* that has a *finis* to aim toward, but also the *electio*, which is what is presently in question.[69]

Whenever Thomas speaks of a "goal" or "end" (*finis*), Janssens reads "end of an agent" (*finis operantis*), and does not observe that the object of the external action of the will is itself a *finis*, but not a *finis quem agens sibi praestituit* (an end that the agent provides for himself). Rather, it is that which Thomas occasionally calls a *finis operis*, which specifies an action within the total context of the human person.[70]

Now this *species* is precisely what a human act acquires "from the object, as related to the principle of human acts, which is the reason" (*ab obiecto relato ad principium humanorum actuum, quod est ratio*).[71] The *finis operis* is nothing other than the object of the *electio,* which is itself the reason-stamped act of the will; if we are not prepared to disintegrate the structure of the *actus humanus,* then we may not reduce the moral quality that comes from the object (*moralitas ex obiecto, moralitas ex fine*) to the object (or goal) of the intention or the *finis operantis.* To do so, one cannot call on the authority of Thomas—it would be necessary to go back at least as far as Abelard.

### *On the Concept of the "Objectivity" of the Natural Law and of Moral Behavior*

It can be held provisionally, then, that there is a parallelism between the constitution of the objects of action (as moral objects) and the constitution of objects of natural law precepts. In both cases there is a "seekable apprehended and ordered by the reason" (*appetibile apprehensum et ordinatum per rationem*). The precept (*praeceptum*) of the natural law and the object of a concrete action (which is the object of the similarly preceptive act of *electio*) are both "something constituted by the reason" (*aliquid a ratione constitutum*) and have their origin in an *ordinatio rationis.* This *objective* (and that means "rationally ordered") content of natural inclinations is expressed as a universal (*in universali*) through the natural law (*lex naturalis*). And here, to be "objective" means to be integrated into the natural intentionality of the *ratio naturalis,* and thereby to be ordered, measured, and regulated by the same. "Objective" also means to be integrated into the context of the whole person and the *suppositum,* and into the purposive structure of human existence.[72]

This same characteristic marks the objective content of a concrete *operabile,* the subject matter of a choice (*electio*), which in turn, if it is the choice of a person with virtue, has been informed by a precept of prudence. This "precept" is not universal, but of a singular and concrete nature. But prudence, as "the right reason of performable actions" (*recta ratio agibilium*), does not consist in man by nature alone. It draws its formal "rectitude" from the precept of the natural law, because "the natural law is that according to which the reason has its rectitude" (*lex naturalis est secundum quam ratio recta est*).[73]

## Beyond Naturalism and Dualism: The Problem of the So-Called "Sin Against Nature" ("*Peccatum Contra Naturam*")

The preceding analysis has shown how the natural law comprises elements of both nature and reason: there is not only that which is "from nature" (*a natura*); but there is also an "ordering of the reason" (*ordinatio rationis*) in relation to it, which makes what is begun by nature to be carried out in accordance with reason, and thereby in a human manner. It is important to note, however, that this ordering act of the natural reason (*ratio naturalis*) and the orientation toward the good that is peculiar to it (the *bonum rationis*) are themselves "natural" (*a natura*): the good of the reason is fundamentally something that is "naturally known" (*naturaliter cognitum*).[74]

It follows, then, that every disordered act (*peccatum*) disturbs the order of reason. And yet in certain contexts Thomas speaks of a "sin against nature" (*peccatum contra naturam*). But given the ordering role of the reason, such a thing could not exist if we wanted to speak precisely. We seem to be faced with inconsistent terminology.

It is no solution to the problem to say that whatever goes against the reason also goes against human nature. That is true, of course, and Thomas never tires of saying so. Nevertheless, he does distinguish "contra *rationem* agere" from a morally insufficient "contra *naturam* agere." It is crucial to study this distinction carefully, and it should be possible in the light of the foregoing analysis—in fact, a solution has already been implied and only needs to be drawn out more distinctly.

Thomas clarifies the terminology of "*peccatum contra naturam*" through a distinction between "two natures" of the human being: the *natura rationalis* and the *natura animalis*. Of course this is a purely analytical distinction between two levels or aspects of a single human nature. If one considers man specifically—that is, in view of the nature "that is proper to man" (*quae est propria hom-*

*ini*)—all sins whatsoever go against the order of reason, and are thus "against nature." On the other hand, if one considers nature as distinct from the reason and as what is common to the other *animalia*, then one would understand the *peccatum contra naturam* in a more limited sense (see *I–II*, q. 94, a. 3, ad 2um).

### *Personal Anthropology: A Prerequisite for Understanding*

Let us recapitulate what has been said: insofar as the human being, as a creature of God, has been constituted according to a specific essence (or "mode of being," *modus essendi*), through his natural inclinations he participates as a "measured" entity (*mensuratus*) in the eternal law. These natural inclinations make a man be what he *is* before he *does* anything whatsoever. They each tend toward their "proper good" (*bonum proprium*), to their "proper act and goal" (*ad proprium actum et finem*), and the *proprium* of the reason is the "right" or "good" (*debitum*). Through the ordering that comes from the "natural inclination of the reason toward the right act and end" (*inclinatio naturalis ad debitum actum et finem*), the whole complex of natural inclinations is carried out in accordance with their integration within the whole context of the person. The "rational ordering" (*ordinatio rationalis*) that effects all of this is called the "natural law" (*lex naturalis*); it is the formal participation (formal because rational, actively measuring, and legislative) of the rational creature in the "eternal law" (*lex aeterna*).

The natural inclinations that belong to the human soul are multiple, since the human soul, by nature, is the form of a body. They range from the inclination toward the conservation of one's own being (*inclinatio ad conservationem sui esse*), through the drives to feed oneself and secure individual survival, as well as the inclination toward the joining of male and female (*inclinatio ad coniunctionem maris et feminae*), which is directed to the well-being and survival of the species, all the way to the inclinations that are exclusively human, such as toward finding out truth, especially the truth about God (the *bonum commune* of the whole universe), as well as for living in common with others, and all the demands of justice that such life implies.

This, then, is a rough sketch of what man discovers, in himself and in the context of society with his fellow human beings, as the naturally given foundations for his life and actions. He experiences himself immediately as an entity in a material world that is constituted by bodiliness or corporeality, and all that goes with it. It is especially in his actions that he experiences himself as a body.[75] Nevertheless, he experiences his animal nature—his sensual drives and inclinations, and the dynamism that accompanies them—as a *passio* of the soul. Even at this level he grasps their meaningful coherence within the context of the whole human species: man feels a certain natural solidarity in terms of what Thomas calls the "common good of nature" (*bonum commune naturae*).[76] Such solidarity reveals itself most of all in the inclination toward handing on human life. Thereby, one is placed within a community of the human species ("humanity") that transcends the individual; one's acts possess an orientation toward this *bonum commune naturae*, even apart from the fact that they also attain a very special and human quality within the context of the person.

Finally, the human being has a unique position amid all other forms of life because of his spiritual soul, which has been created "in the image of" (*ad imaginem*) the divine nature. Through the possession of this divine likeness, man has the ability to recognize truth, to love, and to live in community with his fellow human beings, so that friendship is nothing other than seeking the good of another as if it were one's own. The spiritual nature of man is the basis for his freedom, as well as for the power to determine his own actions (personal autonomy), and especially for a certain capability in relation to the natural inclinations: those tendencies, that is, that while not following from the "law of the spirit," nevertheless, because of their existential integration in the *suppositum*, are constitutive and meaningful elements of the whole person, and therefore must be integrated in actions. To these inclinations man has the capacity of giving "the law of the spirit," and of carrying them out in a way that is fully human and suited to the spirit. And that means through understanding their coherence in the context of the person and subordinating them to the moving command of the will—the *appetitus intellectivus*—in the form of human love.

### *The Model of Married Love*

To illustrate the comprehensive personal structure of human willing or loving, the natural inclination toward the "joining of male and female" can serve as an example, despite the inevitable displeasure we will incur from those who consider it a scandal to refer to this natural inclination as "that which nature has taught every animal" (*quod natura omnia animalia docuit*).[77]

This natural inclination, when it is the basis for a man and woman's joining with one another for the sake of handing on human life (in a naturally given orientation toward the "common good of nature" and the survival of the species), points far beyond the "animal" context. It does not, to be sure, become an "incarnation" of human love, as it is sometimes said—no more so, in fact, than the human being is an "incarnate spirit." The term "incarnate spirit" would better describe an incarnate *angel* (or an incarnate *divine person*). Man, on the contrary, is a bodily entity that is "ensouled" and endowed with reason, according to the classical and precise formulation: *animal rationale.*

Married love, therefore (not just *love,* but rather in its specific difference as *married* love between man and woman), is neither something that has only secondarily become "incarnate" nor some originally purely spiritual phenomenon. Rather, it arises fundamentally and originally out of the natural inclination of the animal nature of man, and yet, because of its existential integration in the *suppositum*, reveals itself as something new: as human love between husband and wife, which then, thanks to the specific dignity of man as a spiritual creature, possesses the character of married love.[78]

Even the finality of procreation itself (as well as the *bonum commune naturae*) contains a new, higher dimension within the context of the *suppositum* "man." This is because it is no longer oriented toward the "good of the species" alone, but directly toward the *bonum* of a new spiritual *individual*, of a person with his or her own individuality, who also bears the *imago Dei*; an individuality that, thanks to the spirituality of the human soul, implies immortality (and incorruptibility), and transcends the species.[79] We are concerned, therefore, not only with the mere handing on of life at the level where the *naturalis inclinatio* takes its rise, but also with the handing on of *human* life, which is ultimately to "hand on the image of God from one human being to another."[80]

There is a still further degree of interpenetration of this act with the love from which it takes its rise, and it becomes clear even without moving to the theological level: when one considers how the beginning of each human life is accompanied by God's direct act of creation of the human soul, human procreation can be recognized as a direct sharing in the divine creativity.[81] And this makes something else apparent, which can be mentioned here only in passing: that the transmission of human life (as human life in general) presents a complete anomaly within the sum total of phenomena met with in nature. The transmission of human life does not possess merely the autonomy of a *causa secunda,* which belongs to all natural phenomena; it is much rather a cooperation between the creaturely action of the human being (*causa secunda*) and the creative action of God; with regard to the creation of the soul (and indeed, with that, to human life as a whole) the *causa secunda* becomes a kind of "instrumental cause." This is the decisive point of departure for understanding the limited power of the human being to have control over human life, whether that life be one's neighbor's or one's own.[82] The immediately creative operation of God at the origin of every human life is ultimately the reason why one can speak of the *sacredness* of this life. For human life is not *only* a natural phenomenon; it is the single phenomenon of the corporeal world that transcends nature by its constitutive principles, both at its origin and in its subsistence.

## *Integral Anthropology or Spiritualism?*

To understand the "joining of male and female" (*coniunctio maris et feminae*) simply as a "material field" for the "incarnation" or for the "expression" of human love, would mean falling prey again to a spiritualistic interpretation of man. It is really the other way around. The love between man and woman in the form of married love is there only because of the *inclinatio naturalis* that lies at its basis. Married love, as a specific form of human love, is founded *in* this natural tendency: it comes into existence through the carrying out of the inclination, but in a human manner. And that means in a rationally ordered manner, corresponding to the *lex naturalis,* and conducted by the *appetitus intellectualis,* or the will, which is human love (*dilectio,* and through grace, *caritas*). When we consider this love in the context of natural inclination, we cannot miss its unity of sensuality and spirituality, which reveals as well its mutuality and permanence.

It is necessary to add, however, that the *inclinatio naturalis ad coniunctionem maris et feminae* becomes married love only to the extent that it is carried out in a human fashion, that is, in correspondence with the natural law, within the order of reason (by way of an *ordinatio rationis*). In other words, it can also be carried out in a not fully human fashion: outside the bounds, that is, of faithful married love between *one* man and *one* woman.[83] Or even within marriage it can be distorted by irresponsibility and licentiousness. This is because the human person participates with his intellect in the *lex aeterna*, and is consequently called to exercise this "sharing" in the Creator's plan in a responsible manner; he is an "interpreter of the Creator's love," providing for himself and others (*sibi ipsi et aliis providens*). Parenthood must also be exercised in a responsible manner, and this is determined both by the generosity of love and by personal and external circumstances, which can lead a person to a wise moderation that does not impair the meaning of his love.

At this point it seems fitting to answer the question about the "object" of human love and of the marital act in particular. If the starting point of our consideration is an ontologically abstract treatment of the "physical nature" (*genus naturae*) of the human procreative act as an act of "generative power," then we would have to conclude that the "natural" object of this act is procreation, but that the same act can contain, as a "second end," the expression of the love of the spouses.[84]

But this appears to me to be an unsatisfactory way to frame the question. We have seen how the love between a man and a woman comes from a "natural inclination for a male and female to be joined" (*naturalis inclinatio ad coniunctionem maris et feminae*). Now this natural inclination, with its naturally given procreative purposiveness at the level of "that which nature has taught all animals" (*quod natura omnia animalia docuit*), becomes an *actus humanus* in the human being in the full sense of the term only in the case of married love. The love between man and woman in its unitive character (the bodily and voluntary joining) lies at the basis of the phenomenon. It is not the "object" or *finis operis* of an act of "generative power" (*potentia generativa*), but rather an act of human love *that springs from the natural inclination and is ordered by the reason*, which reaches its *consummatio* and *ultima perfectio* in the "joining of the flesh" (*copula carnalis*).[85] The marital act is thus seen not as an act of the power of procreation, which still "serves" in addition as an expression of love; rather, it is the complete and *personal* act of a love that in its origin aims toward the transmission of life and that, as an *actus humanus*, is *voluntary* and *responsible*.

Consequently, when we inquire into the "object" of the marital act, we inquire into the object or "objective significance" of the love between husband and wife, and not into the "natural end" (*finis naturalis*) of the procreative power. Nevertheless, at the same time we hold firmly to the fact that this love, the significance of which we are trying to assess, is still based upon a natural inclination that is essentially procreative. Because of this indissoluble connection between "human procreation" and "love between husband and wife," we can identify the "object" (or significance) of the marital act as the loving (bodily) union of husband and wife; the procreative character of this act belongs essentially with the "object" or *finis operis*. This character lies, as has been already stated, in the basis of the phenomenon "love between husband and wife," and defines or constitutes this love as a specific kind of human love. For this love to have its meaning, actual physiological and biological fruitfulness of the procreative capacity is not required, but only the openness of *the will* to such fruitfulness, a will to be fruitful, which in man is always exercised in the context of responsibility, and which is also the foundation for what is known as "responsible parenthood" (see chapter 10).

It is not simply upon the naturally procreative purposiveness of the bodily union between man and wife that we can base the (morally) *objective* and fundamental connection between married love and human procreation; the moral context is grasped more fully when we recognize that the only form of life transmission suited to human dignity is simply such as to have its origin in love between two human persons and in their loving union as a participation in the love of the Creator. Thus the love between husband and wife, and its consummation in the *commixtio carnalis*, is much more than a mere "means" of procreation, on the one hand, or an "expression" of love on the other. The "object" or moral significance of loving union is this bodily union *itself* as a personal act and in its dimension as love, which serves for the procreation of human life. This love and its *ultima perfectio* or *consummatio* in marital unity is thus the personal act or *actus humanus* in which new human life has its origin: thus a life that is oriented toward love originates in love as befitting human dignity; and the love from which such life arises involves (on the natural plane) a cooperation with the divine, creative love, and becomes (on the supernatural plane) an image of the redeeming love of Christ for His Church and (through Her) for all human persons. The loving union of spouses possesses this significance whether or not the act is biologically fruitful in this or that instance. Only the human will can disturb the meaning of the act in regard to its fruitfulness, by disturbing the meaning of love; the actual biological and physiological condition of the procreative power could not do this.

When we speak of the "nature of the marital act," we do not mean the "nature of the actualization of sexual capability" (Fuchs) at the level of its physical nature (*genus naturae*), but rather the "nature of a personal act," which is finally the nature of the love itself between man and woman, insofar as it arises from a natural inclination, and which is carried out "according to the order of reason" (*ordinatio rationis*).[86] The personal nature of the marital act causes it to be essentially oriented toward the transmission of human life, for the love between man and woman is the only form of the transmission of human life that is worthy of the human person: as a personal act, it is at the same time always an act of human responsibility.

Once one is freed from a naturalistic perspective, some very apt statements of Pope Pius XII can be understood in their true meaning: "The marital act within its natural context is a personal action, a simultaneous and immediate cooperation of the spouses, something in accordance with the essence of those doing the action and with the nature of the act itself, an expression of mutual self-giving that effects the 'becoming one flesh' as the words of Scripture state. This is much more than the joining of two gametes, which could also take place by artificial methods, and without the natural act of the spouses. The marital act, as nature has ordained it, is a personal cooperation, to which the spouses have given each other the right with their marriage vows."[87]

In view of these considerations, it is possible to speak of a *pecca-*

*tum contra naturam*, which in a certain way always "denatures" the foundations of human willing, loving, and moral/practical valuation. Such a *peccatum contra naturam* would be a "perversion," caused by man himself, of a *naturalis inclinatio* that does not, by its nature, arise directly from the *ratio*. It is not a "disordering" (*deordinatio*) of an *actus debitus*, which would be a disruption of the *ordo rationis*; it is a disordering in a more fundamental way, in relation to an *actus proprius*, which is a disruption of the *ordo naturae* (for the distinction between the *actus proprius* and the *actus debitus*, see above, section "The Spontaneous Comprehension of Fundamental Human Valuesm" subsection "The Constitution of the Natural Law Through the *Ratio Naturalis*").

Understanding how such a perversion in the second sense would be a moral evil at all, is possible—to say it once again—only on the basis of a personal and comprehensive view of the human person, and in an anthropology of the *animal rationale*. This comprehensive or integrative point of view alone is capable of forming an ethics of love and sensuality:[88] otherwise, one will tend toward a spiritualistic interpretation of human nature based on dualistic arguments. By "spiritualism" is meant an anthropology and ethics in which bodiliness and sensuality are granted no constitutive moral significance in the context of human actions; instead, through the dualistic antithesis of "person" and "nature," *all* human acts are viewed as *originally* spiritual phenomena. Such phenomena are only subsequently allowed to "express" or "incarnate" bodiliness and sensuality on a plane that is itself "subhuman" or "subpersonal," and indifferent toward such acts; this plane of "expressive behavior" is a "material" field for the soul, and lacks any proper moral significance; upon this field its shaping force can be "disposed."[89]

The personal and integral anthropology and ethics of St. Thomas offer a different perspective: spiritual acts, to be sure, are understood to be those that cause specification and that ultimately provide significance and order. At the same time, however, it is recognized that bodiliness and sensation are the *foundation* for all spiritual acts. And so, just as the soul needs no bodily organs for its spiritual acts, nevertheless these acts are oriented to the body for their full execution. This applies to all acts of intellective knowledge, which would remain objectless without a *phantasma* or a *conversio ad phantasmata.* For by nature the soul is the form of a body, and the separation of the two goes against its nature, is *contra naturam.*

In the same way, the human act of love needs the same foundation when it is considered in its specific spirituality as such; if this love is detached from its bodily and sensual foundation and its inherent structure of meaning, then it is, in a way, no longer in this world, and remains without "object" as well as "subject." And yet it is only in an integral view of the person that it can be truly understood how the consummation of human love, in the form of human marriage, can and must be expressed at the level of the body and the senses, without running the risk of "instrumentalizing" one's own or another's body.

### *A False Starting Point: The Moralization of the Natural Order*

In this perspective of an integral and therefore personal anthropology and ethics, we can understand how, and under what conditions, it is possible to speak of a *peccatum contra naturam.* In this context "nature" must be understood in a narrower sense, so that the *natura rationalis* would be excluded from consideration. Otherwise, *any* "action against reason" (*agere contra rationem*) would also be something that is *contra naturam.*

This restriction to the *natura animalis* may not make sense at first, but it is justifiable for the following reasons: to act "against reason" (*contra rationem*) is, of course, always an affront to the *lex naturalis.* The latter, as well as being an *ordo rationis,* is an "ordering" *in* the natural inclinations, which exist "by nature" (*a natura*) and as such belong to the natural law without *being* it. An offense against the *ordo rationis,* or the natural law, is an injury to what is *debitum,* an *actio indebita.* We are here considering something different from this: namely, an offense against the *proprium* of a natural inclination itself, which would be an *actio impropria,* or an act that not only carries out a natural inclination in an inappropriate way (thus injuring the *debitum,* or the *bonum rationis*), but also an act in which the natural inclination is disconnected from its "proper end and act" (*finis et actus proprius*), which thereby becomes a "denatured" act.

On the level of the natural inclinations of the *ratio naturalis,* such a denaturing is only theoretically conceivable, and in practice simply impossible. It would be a disconnection of the will from its *finis et actus proprius*, which would no longer have the "good," or even the "apparent good," for its object, but would have to will something *sub ratione mali*. This is impossible: man has no power to change his fundamental orientation toward the good.

Only in the cases where the act of an *inclinatio naturalis* arises in any way from the bodily dimension of the suppositum (as in the love between man and woman) is it possible for man to denature this act through manipulative means, and to disconnect it from its "proper end and act." Understood in this way, the *peccatum contra naturam* is possible only at this level. And precisely because of this, the distinction of a "twofold nature" (*duplex natura*) in man is meaningful in practice. But this alone is still not enough to answer the question of whether it is possible to make a moral qualification of an action *contra naturam*.

A *peccatum contra naturam*, says St. Thomas, is an act that not only goes against *ratio recta* or the *ordo rationis*, but also (and *in addition to this*) offends the *ordo naturalis* (*ordo naturae*; see *II–II*, q. 154, a. 11), which means that it offends the "natural ordering" (*ordinatio naturalis*) of each inclination to its "proper act and end" (at the level, that is, of passive participation in the eternal law). This is indeed an *ordo*, which does not come into existence by the "measuring action" (*mensuratio*) of the human reason, but rather lies before reason and exists *a natura*.[90] *Contra naturam* in this sense, then, is what contradicts the *impressio legis aeternae* in man, which is the basis of the "ordering of the reason" (*ordinatio rationis*), and thus the basis of the natural law. It has to do not with a *direct* offense against a virtue, but rather with an offense against the very foundation or presupposition or "seeds" (*semina*) of virtue, which has its natural "beginnings" (or "seeds") in the *inclinatio naturalis*.

On the basis of the precisions made up to this point, it should be clear that a *peccatum contra naturam* is not *only "contra naturam."* The *ordo naturalis* of the various urges in regard to their "proper end" (*actus proprius*), possesses in itself the character of a natural law; in this case, however, it is not a moral law of the practical reason, but rather natural law in the sense given the term by the natural sciences, such as physical, biological, and physiological regularities. A mistaken understanding of the natural law can tempt one to identify it with these laws or regularities, and this is to "moralize" the natural order as such, to identify the "*peccatum* contra naturam" with a mere "*agere* contra naturam," and thus to maintain "nature" as such to be a sufficient normative foundation for human action.

And yet it is impossible to take as one's principle that one may not act in opposition to the "laws of nature," or that whatever accords with such natural laws is by that fact alone sacrosanct, or a "natural course" of things that is God's will: the fact that something is *a natura* is not reason enough for something to be beyond the power of human control. Whoever maintains this is guilty of a crass naturalism.

This is why moral judgments about genetic experiments differ, depending on whether the experiments in question are made on human beings or animals. In both cases there is an "action against nature" (*agere contra naturam*) in respect to biological or genetic laws—the naturally founded behavior of natural processes. With animals, such manipulation as a means for a worthy end is morally justified. But it is otherwise with human beings. It is no longer merely a question of "respecting nature." Interventions into the human organism do not create moral difficulties when natural givens are changed for the better health of the whole organism. There are people with transplanted stomachs, lungs, and kidneys. All this has very little to do with what was foreseen in the "natural order." Furthermore, neither Catholic moral theology nor the magisterium has judged the use of pharmaceutical means for the regulation of fertility to be a *peccatum contra naturam*. Even the use of contraception in the case of acute danger of anticipated rape has not been so judged.

If someone argues, therefore, that "interference" in the natural order represents a moral evil, this is not maintained because of the inviolability of this order in itself, but rather because it is known that some moral evil is involved, and because of the reasons why it is evil. In other words, it is due to a recognition that certain natural things have moral significance, and that between them and the *ordo rationis* there is an intimate and indissoluble connection.

Now we cannot have immediate recourse in this instance to the will of God as the Founder of Nature, because the will of God is recognized in the created order (if we prescind from revelation) through our rational understanding of created things: "By the law of God, these things alone are prohibited, which are against reason" (*Contra Gentiles,* III, c. 125). Consequently, it must be shown in the logic of Thomistic ethics how, and to what extent, *contra naturam agere* contradicts the *reason*; since only in that case is it recognized as a "*peccatum* contra naturam" and expressly stated by Thomas to be in contradiction with the will of God.

Broad currents of contemporary moral theology have thoroughly understood some parts of this problem. Schüller has rightly emphasized that our statements about the will of God depend in each case upon our moral interpretations in regard to nature, and not vice versa.[91] But Schüller commits a fundamental error in his critique of "tradition," for he claims that a naturalistic moralization of the natural order provides the only kind of argumentation for a conclusion such as "What is against nature is prohibited." Schüller does not appear to observe that in the context of a theory of practical reason as the natural reason, it is possible to have a *differentiated* moral judgment concerning the moral significance of natural givens. His "teleological" alternative rests upon the same misconception of the natural law as his undifferentiated critique of the naturalistic tradition. The lack of differentiation goes even further in Scholz, who takes every intervention in nature, "in all areas of life," as equivalent to a "painful medical intervention."[92] By trying to move away from an undifferentiated moralization of the natural order, we arrive at an equally undifferentiated position that is no less physicalistic but tends toward spiritualism, by maintaining that manipulation of the natural in "all areas of human life" is morally permissible.[93]

### *The* 'Praesuppositio'*: An Essential Perspective*

Thomas treats of the *peccatum contra naturam* with his familiar thoroughness in the context of the vice of *luxuria,* or lust. It will be worth our while to read his justification for considering the *vitium contra naturam* to be the "greatest sin among the various kinds of lust" (*maximum peccatum inter species luxuriae*):

> In every class of things the corruption of the principle of the class is the worst, for everything else depends upon it. Now the princi-

> ples of the reason are those things that are according to nature [*secundum naturam*]. *For the reason has to presuppose what nature has determined in order to arrange anything else as it sees fit.* This appears in theoretical matters as well as in the reasoning concerned with actions. And thus, just as in speculative reasoning, that error is most serious and shameful that has to do with things of which the knowledge is naturally given to man, so in matters of action, to do that which is against the things that have been determined by nature is most grievous and shameful. Therefore, because in the vices that are against nature man transgresses that which is according to nature in the area of sexual behavior [*circa usum venereum*], in this kind of actions, this is the most serious sin. . . . With the other forms of lust, the transgression is only against that which has been determined according to right reason, but *still presupposing the natural principles.*[94]

From an integral perspective of the human person and his natural urgings, the passage just quoted will be immediately intelligible: there is little danger that it might be misunderstood through a naturalistic interpretation. The *ordo naturalis* of every natural inclination is the foundation and principle for its "proper operation and goal" (*actus et finis proprius*); it is the "presupposition" (*praesuppositum*) of the *ordo rationis*, and thereby of the natural law; and this is nothing other than moral activity as *human* activity, and in particular, every form of human love. That which is the principle and foundation of the *ordo rationis* or of the "order of virtue" (*ordo virtutis*) thereby possesses a moral qualifiability, not merely because of its "naturalness" but because of its character as a *praesuppositum* for the *ordo virtutis*, and thereby for the very *humanness* of human action.

If a voluntary action is "*contra naturam*" in this sense, it is not *immediately* "*contra rationem*," but *contra* "the nature that reason presupposes" (*natura quam ratio praesupponit*). The act of the natural reason and, with that, the entire order of moral behavior is marred at its natural foundations through such an action against nature (*agere contra naturam*)—it becomes a fundamental offense against the order of reason in its foundations. This relationship of *praesuppositio* between nature and reason is the single decisive criterion for understanding that the willing of such a clearly "ontic evil" is also a "moral evil": in other words, that it can never be *only* an "ontic evil."

Such a *praesuppositio* will be overlooked in a dualistic or spiritualistic anthropology, where all the levels of human nature that can be distinguished from the spiritual are assumed to be morally indifferent; as a consequence, they are considered to be *instruments* and not *principles* for the practical reason and the will. They appear to be a kind of "raw material" in which no order preexists that has any intrinsic connection with the *ordo moralis*: such order must instead "be created." Many moral theologians claim that every moral obligation simply consists in "avoiding as much ontic evil as possible"; in this view, no "ontic evil" can also be in itself a "moral evil." While this may offer proof of noble intentions, nevertheless one must not be deceived about the fact that such theologians misunderstand the fundamental structure of practical judgments of value and moral behavior, let alone the reality of the *lex aeterna* and man's participation in it. This is a point that should be treated more fully.

For Thomas, the specifically human acts of knowledge and of love are always based upon an "order determined by nature" (*ordo a natura determinatus*), and that means upon a definite, natural inclination with its "*proper* operation and goal" (*finis et actus* proprius), so that such acts can be accomplished and understood only within their context—at least so far as it depends on human willing. This can also be said for what pertains to the spiritual realm: for the orientation of the intellect toward the truth (such as the knowledge of God, the *desiderium naturale*) and for the orientation of the will for the good and the "Thou," which naturally make an *ordo iustitiae* possible. This in turn provides the foundation of human love and possesses a constitutive meaning especially for married love, since in the unity of the person, married love finds its fulfillment in the order of the virtue of justice.

It should be emphasized that this moral qualification of "acting against nature" (*agere contra naturam*) is not based upon a derivation of the moral order from the natural. It really goes in the opposite direction, from *an interpretation of the natural "ordo" of the natural inclinations in the light of the "ordo rationis" or virtue*; it depends on the understanding of the relationship of *praesuppositio*. Therefore the moral qualification of *agere contra naturam* turns out to be an achievement of the practical reason.

Furthermore, we are not claiming that the *ordo naturalis* that the reason presupposes *is* the natural law. We would say, rather, with Thomas, that "it *pertains to* the natural law" but is not yet itself this law, since the law arises in the *ordinatio rationalis* and in relation to the *proprium* of the natural inclinations—an *ordinatio* that simply could not exist without this *praesuppositum*. In other words, an *ordinatio* that neglects the passive participation in the eternal law (the "being measured-ness" [*mensuratum esse*] of man) would not correspond to the eternal law, and would altogether lose its character as natural law, "which is the participation of the eternal law in the rational creature." This is why we can say that such an *ordinatio* would not correspond to the will of God.

There is an *ordo naturalis* that the natural law presupposes, and without this order both the natural law and the order of reason and virtue lose their foundation. A genuine knowing and loving that is human in the truest sense of the word cannot be realized through any action thus qualified as *contra naturam*.

## Excursus: The Natural Law and Contraception

### *The Threefold* 'Praesuppositio'' *In the Act of Transmitting Human Life*

In the case of the transmission of human life, there is a threefold relationship of *praesuppositio*, that is, the *ordo rationis* or *virtutis* is based on the *ordo naturalis* in three ways.

First, the human act of procreation has a character of cooperative causality in regard to the transmission of human life. Man does not have the power to procreate as a *causa secunda*, as mentioned above (see section "Beyond Naturalism and Dualism," subsection "The Model of Married Love," in this chapter, and especially note 82). In every case there is need of the immediate intervention of God, because the human soul cannot be educed from the potentiality of the human power to procreate. The human soul far exceeds the causality of the latter. This aspect shows clearly the limitation of the human power to control human life as well as the immeasurable dignity of parenthood; nevertheless, it has not been in the foreground of the debate over *Humanae Vitae*, and will have to be mentioned here only in passing.

Second, the *ordo naturalis* is a *praesuppositum* for the "common good of the species" (*bonum commune speciei*), or the "survival of the species"; and thereby, because of a natural solidarity of man with his own kind, it forms the basis of a special type of justice.[95] This aspect of human procreation and married love is given the most emphasis by Thomas. It accounts for the unity of the person with the married "community" of the "one flesh": the unity of two wills in a supratemporal context of meaning that is greater than the individual and represents a solidarity that is specific to man. This, too, must be set to one side for the present purpose, because the question about the morality of the *type* of realization of parental responsibility (that is, through contraception or abstinence) does not arise within the context of this aspect alone.

The third relationship of *praesuppositio* is concerned with the order of human love as married love itself, which means in the dual dimension of justice (including *amor amicitiae* or fidelity and the equality of the spouses) and married chastity, a virtue closely connected with justice.

The argument of the encyclical *Humanae Vitae* is based on this third aspect. It is the fundamental context that continues to be misunderstood by many critics of the encyclical. The misunderstanding is revealed in two ways: (1) by the claim of these critics that the argumentation of the document is "biologistic" and (2) by their inability even to *cite* its most important passages.[96]

The following discussion will be concerned with this theme only with regard to the present question: Why and to what extent can someone maintain (as does *Humanae Vitae*) that contraception offends the natural law?[97] This will require determining *where* the moral problem with artificial birth control actually lies. *Humanae Vitae* and the subsequent teaching of the magisterium have stated it clearly; in the light of the foregoing analyses, we are nevertheless in a position to answer the question with the terminological precision of the Thomistic doctrine of the *lex naturalis*. We should keep in mind that we are widening and deepening the structure of argumentation for a problem that did not exist in Thomas's day.

### *The Starting Point: The Concept of "Responsible Parenthood"*

In the controversy about sexual morality, two different questions should be distinguished and kept separate. The first question relates to the significance of human sexuality in general, and to the "nature" of the human act that serves the end of human procreation, referred to in what follows as the "marital act." The question concerns the problem of the object, or the objective content of the marital act. In asking this question, we must remember that we are always thinking of a human act (*actus humanus*) and not an act of "procreative power" as such.[98]

The second question has to do not with the objective meaning of the marital act but with the act of realizing parental responsibility: May a limitation on the fertility of the marital act take place through artificial as well as natural means? This is the question that *Humanae Vitae* set out to answer and that stands in the foreground of the discussion. The understanding (or misunderstanding) of the objective meaning of the marital act, while of decisive importance, is only indirectly met with in the debate.

The intention of *Humanae Vitae* is above all to show, in the context of the second question, how parental responsibility is to be exercised in order to reach the conclusion that the way of artificial contraception is to be excluded on moral grounds. We will sketch the argument briefly, and at the same time shed some new light upon it by combining it with the results of the present study.

The human person is called to carry out the task of transmitting human life in cooperation with God's creative love, and in a rational and responsible manner, at one and the same time "interpreter" of this love and "providing for himself and others" (*providens sibi ipsi et aliis*); in other words, according to an "ordering of the reason" (*ordinatio rationis*) of the natural law. With human beings it is not a question of guidance by instincts or mere "drives," but a rational and voluntary, *responsible* parenthood. In this active participation in the divine world governance, this rational participation in God's Providence through the creation of new human beings (and although man is only a coöperator, nevertheless this creation does depend upon his willingness to cooperate), what provides the measure and rule? Not the natural inclinations as such, with their natural urgings, but the reason. The act of transmitting human life is not, therefore, an act of "procreative power," but rather a *personal act* (an *actus humanus*); an act that is essentially an act of the will that has been molded by reason—or, in the case of the voluntary joining of man and woman, an act of human love.

Responsible parenthood means, therefore, the making use of, and the compliance with, a natural striving, in the framework of an *ordinatio rationis*. Marriage itself has its source in such an *ordinatio*, and itself requires a rationally governed use of the inclination that leads to marriage. The "order of reason," according to which the transmission of human life then follows (responsible parenthood), is an "order of virtue" (*ordo virtutis*). The two virtues that correspond to this order are justice (in relation to both the *bonum commune speciei* and the spouse, through fidelity and equality) and chastity, the virtue that establishes and preserves the order and measure of human sexuality.

When one speaks of chastity, one thinks usually of abstinence, but they are not the same. Abstinence, when considered in itself, is not a virtue; it can even be a vice. On the other hand, there can be a virtuous lack of abstinence because of love; Thomas calls it *incontinentia per similitudinem,* and it occurs when "someone is completely mastered by a concupiscence that corresponds to an ordering of the reason and is therefore good" (*II–II*, q. 156, a. 2). This form of incontinence, which is peculiar to the spontaneity and genuineness of true married love, belongs, says Thomas, "to the perfection of virtue" (*II–II*, q. 156, a. 2). This kind of incontinence in no way contradicts marital chastity, which does not intend abstinence: in fact, if abstinence is without good reasons, it is *contra rationem*, and thus contrary to virtue and to love. What marital chastity requires is rational, responsibly conscious use of the natural inclination. For various reasons abstinence must be exercised in marriage, so that the virtue of chastity itself (the ordering of human love) is, as an *ordo rationis*, maintained and strengthened. But marital abstinence is always oriented toward love and (responsible) fertility, toward the responsibility to cooperate with God's creative and redemptive plan, a responsibility toward one's spouse, one's family, the human community, and oneself; in everything, the limit is ultimately set by the generosity of love.[99]

This is explained as follows in the words of *Humanae Vitae:*

> In relation to physical, economic, psychological and social conditions, responsible parenthood is exercised, either by the deliberate

> and generous decision to raise a numerous family, or by the decision, made for grave motives and with due respect for the moral law, to avoid for the time being, or even for an indeterminate period, a new birth. (10)

At the same time the encyclical teaches—and this is the contested point—that the only morally acceptable means of limiting or regulating fertility is abstinence; the "direct, temporary or permanent sterilization of the man or the woman" is judged immoral, as is any action that "either in anticipation of the conjugal act, or in its accomplishment, or in the development of its natural consequences, proposes, whether as an end or as a means, to render procreation impossible" (14).

### *The Formulation of the Problem: The Joining of the "Unitive" and "Procreative"*

Following closely upon the definition of responsible parenthood is the reference to the morally necessary maintenance of the integrity of the marital act and the natural cycles of human fertility. Most critics of the encyclical have not strayed from this point, suggesting that it is here that *Humanae Vitae*'s argument for the immorality of artificial contraception can be seen; an argument, it is claimed, that rests upon preserving the biological integrity of the act, and upon the (likewise biological) laws of cyclical fertility. But the argument does not really begin until the next section. Here lies the key statement of *Humanae Vitae*, and we will quote the passage in full:

> That teaching, often set forth by the magisterium, is founded upon the inseparable connection, willed by God and unable to be broken by man on his own initiative, between the two meanings of the conjugal act: the unitive meaning and the procreative meaning. Indeed, by its intimate structure, the conjugal act, while most closely uniting husband and wife, capacitates them for the generation of new lives, according to laws inscribed in the very being of man and of woman. By safeguarding both these essential aspects, the unitive and procreative, the conjugal act preserves in its fullness the sense of true mutual love and its ordination towards man's most high calling to parenthood. (12)

Now this formulation shows, first, that there is no question of preserving the integrity of "nature" and its biological laws, but rather the integrity of *married love* as a personal act. Moreover, it is also not concerned with the "biological–procreative" openness of the marital act, but rather with the openness of married love—that is, of the human will, or of the marital act as an *actus humanus*, as a rationally ordered act of the will, toward the "noble duty of parenthood."

*Humanae Vitae* takes as its starting point that this married love has two aspects, both equally important and inseparably connected: "loving unity" and "procreation."[100] The special character of married love in these twin aspects is destroyed by contraception. The point of controversy is not the integrity of the "natural order" but the integrity of human love, which is at once an *ordo rationis*, as well as an *ordo virtutis*.

But why is this so? The encyclical offers only a few reasons in section 13, and indicates a few of the consequences of artificial birth control in section 17, and appeals to the reasonableness of the teaching but does not provide any further justifications. Such would be the task rather of theology, which has, however, largely failed in this duty. The central statement of *Humanae Vitae* was poorly understood, and instead of entering into the actual argumentation of the document, theologians have foisted other arguments upon it that are easily criticized.[101]

The key to the argument, it appears to me, is the concept of *responsible parenthood*. The attempt has repeatedly been made to reduce it to a question of *method*: many moral theologians see natural and artificial birth control merely as two different *methods* of not having children. This misunderstanding is ultimately the result of a naturalistic treatment of human procreation.

If the limitation of the number of children is to be considered responsible parenthood, such limitation must have its origin in an act of the virtue of chastity. It would have to be a governing of the natural inclination through reason and will, and could not be realized through actions by which the virtue of chastity in regard to responsible parenthood is made *superfluous*. In other words, an act of responsible parenthood must always correspond to the structural principles of the *actus humanus*. This structure requires an indissoluble connection between responsibility and *voluntary* acceptance of this responsibility; by artificial and sterilizing interventions the structure of the marital act as a *human act* is destroyed.

It is essential to remember, first of all, that we are not concerned with proving that artificial interventions into the natural order are in themselves morally questionable. Second, it should not be maintained that the marital act that does not end in conception is morally bad: such a position must be opposed. Third, we are not debating whether there is a moral distinction between artificially contrived infertility and infertility caused by natural–biological laws. This distinction *in itself* is morally inconsequential, as can be seen in the example of a therapeutic sterilization (where the sterilization was directly caused, but not for reasons of contraception, so that it was only indirectly *willed*) or in the case of anticipated rape. Nor does it have to do with the difference between two kinds of infertility (natural and artificial); it has to do, rather, with two different relationships of the human will toward infertility—or, to be more precise, between two ways of "controlling" the result of fertility.

The alternative we are dealing with is not between "natural–biological lawfulness" on the one hand and "artificial intervention" on the other—to treat it that way would make it merely a "problem of method." The alternative is, rather, between exercising responsibility through voluntary abstinence, on the one hand, and exercising it through acts that make abstinence superfluous, on the other. To put it differently: on the one side is "the exercise of procreative responsibility through voluntary governance and mastery over the human sexual drive"; on the other side there is "the exercise of procreative responsibility through technological–artificial control of the fertility of human sexuality *instead of* such voluntary governance and mastery." The alternative is not between *natural* and *artificial* but between *voluntary* and *artificial*.[102] This is why those who defend artificial birth control maintain that human love is "impaired" by *having to abstain voluntarily*, by the need for voluntary mastery over sexuality that periodic abstinence involves.

It should be seen, first, that *making abstinence superfluous* (or *making superfluous the exercise of the procreative responsibility* that comes about through voluntary governance of a natural inclination) leads to a disruption of the order of reason (*ordo rationis*) at its root;

it should then be made clear that this entails a disruption of a specifically human (that is, *responsible*) manner of following a natural inclination (an *inclinatio naturalis* that is both fundamental to, and characteristic of, married love); finally, if all this has been established, it can be demonstrated that artificial birth control is morally wrong precisely because it offends against nature as presupposed by reason (*contra naturam, quam ordo rationis praesupponit*). It is a fundamental error (*error in principiis*) about human action *qua* human (personal action), and it truly *denatures* and morally *disorients* the activity of the practical reason itself in regard to the transmission of human life.

This is exactly what has been maintained by *Humanae Vitae* and the apostolic letter that continues its message, *Familiaris Consortio*. *Humanae Vitae* is not concerned with the observance of biological laws, although they are clearly ackowledged to be a *praesuppositum*. It is concerned, rather, with how the conjugal act can "fully and completely" preserve "true, mutual love," as well as "its orientation toward the noble duty of parenthood, to which man is called." The encyclical purposely holds itself back from a precise philosophical and theological demonstration in the strict sense. And *Familiaris Consortio* also indicates that this is a task for further scientific study. The problem is stated as follows:

> In the light of the experience of many married couples as well as of the various human sciences, theology can and must explicate and deepen the anthropological and (at the same time) ethical difference between artificial contraception and the recourse to periodic abstinence. This difference is greater than is generally understood, and is ultimately connected with *two mutually exclusive models* of the person and of human sexuality. (32)

These different models are, on the one hand, the integral treatment of the person, and on the other hand, a spiritualistic "personalism" based on naturalistic and dualistic prejudices, represented today by many moral theologians.[103]

The issue of contraception is not about the biological structure of the conjugal act, but rather about the *personal* nature of this act as an act of human love and responsibility, an act of moral virtue. The biologistic reduction of the question does not originate from the perspective of the Church's magisterium, but rather from that of its critics, who have built their arguments upon a classic sophism: the so-called *ignoratio elenchi*, or defective definition of the point of controversy.

*Sexuality and Procreative Responsibility*

The ethical discussion about contraception can profit from an integral/personal anthropology and an understanding of the *lex naturalis* and moral virtue as presented in the foregoing discussion. My thesis is the following: the virtue of chastity, and the voluntary governing of the sexual drive through abstinence that is ordered to this virtue, form the only humanly adequate basis for a responsible, rational regulation of human procreative power, and for the sensual appetites that drive that power; this is also the only basis for an integration of the *inclinatio naturalis* into the context of personal behavior, and for maintaining the personal integrity of human sexuality. This alone can lead to a steady deepening and strengthening of married love as procreatively responsible, and thus truly *human* love.

It is not only such love but also the responsible handling of the transmission of human life that results from it that provide, as human acts (*actus humani*), the *essential and indispensable* foundation for direct self-regulation through reason and will: it is the harmonizing of an *inclinatio naturalis* (right at the level of the "proper act" ordered to its natural–sensual dynamic) with the reason and the "rational striving" that love is. Here the decisive moment is the *voluntary nature* of such self-regulation; this is what stands in rivalry with a "self-regulation" that dispenses with the will, through being *artificial*.

It is necessary to grasp the real difference between a conjugal act that, even though intentionally performed during an infertile period, takes place within a context of abstinence during a fertile period, and an act that is without consequence because it was performed under conditions of artificial sterilization. The former kind of action results from rational supervision and the mastery of the will—the principles of the *actus humanus* and personal autonomy—and, furthermore, a mutual agreement of will and understanding between the two partners. In this way the fundamental uniqueness of human and married love is preserved—as well as the principles of justice, such as equality and the "love of friendship" (*amor amicitiae*)—which seeks in each case the good of the other. This is true even when the act takes place in an infertile period: the intention to do so has its source in a voluntary, personal exercise of responsibility for the transmission of human life; this responsibility must characterize *every single* marital act that is to meet the requirements of a *married* (that is, procreatively responsible) act.

Acts of self-restraint (acts of willing acceptance of this responsibility) form the context of the conjugal act, and they are *personal* acts; even when such acts take place during an infertile period, they retain their transcendence or openness to the transmission of human life, to the acceptance of a vocation to parenthood, and to the full truth of married love. This is not because there is a "biological" openness: that, indeed, is not present in *this* act, since its infertility is known. But the marital act is not an act of human procreative power *alone*; rather, it is a personal act, and that means, above all, an act of the will. The "openness" in the sense of responsible cooperation with the creative love of God (Whose "interpreters" the parents must be) is still present, because it is not a biological openness but an openness of the will and of human action. The objective qualification of the human will is not derivable from biological facts; these are not what morally "stamp" the will. *Both* personal acts of self-restraint *and* acts of marriage (carried out in the context of the former during infertile periods) are open to the transmission of human life precisely because they are both voluntary acts of *the responsible exercise of parenthood* (or of following the *inclinatio naturalis ad coniunctionem maris et feminae* within the *ordo rationis*, according to the natural law) and as such are actually carried out in the service of the human (responsible) transmission of human life—both are *objective* acts of responsible parenthood.

In the case, however, of an act of sexual intercourse that has been made to be procreatively inconsequent, the specific character of human and married love is not retained, but is attacked at its roots. For in this kind of act, the governance by reason and mastery by the will over procreative potentiality (both of which are required for a human act, and make for the personal integrity of married love) are purposely excluded, that is, rendered superfluous. The *specificum* of the human act is no longer constitutive of this kind of exercise of responsibility and becomes superfluous for the attainment of its end. The end of "responsible parenthood" is pursued in such a way that it excludes the very principle of responsibility in the means chosen to that end. Since reason and will no longer have any control over the outcome because the act is (or rather, has been) made fruitless, in relation to this particular act there is *no longer any need for procreatively responsible, rational, and will-obeying behavior.* Then the action no longer *can* be an expression of married love, unity, and fellowship in a common, responsible task, because it has become detached from the context within which the *inclinatio naturalis ad coniunctionem maris et feminae* becomes constituted, in its procreative dimension, as specifically human and married love. No longer is such an act subject to the logic of responsibility and the responsible openness to the task of parenthood, because *no responsibility is needed for an act that has no consequence.*

At this point an objection could be made. How can we speak here of excluding voluntary control by contraception, since the use of "mechanical" means of birth control (condom, diaphragm) or the practice of coitus interruptus requires, as a rule, a great deal *more* self-control and self-mastery than do periodic acts of abstinence. In such circumstances, as well as with the disciplined use of oral contraception, there is certainly a "rationally guided" willing and a "procreatively responsible" mastery over sexuality. Even surgical sterilization arises from a rational and voluntary act of procreative responsibility.

Such an objection overlooks the fact that we are not speaking merely of the "means" or "methods" of procreative responsibility; rather, we are speaking of procreative responsibility as a moral *virtue*, or as a component of the virtue of chastity. To answer the objection, it is necessary to make the analysis deeper and more precise in a few places.

First of all, it is of course true that artificial kinds of control are a form of rational and voluntary mastery over one's own acts. To the extent that one applies such measures to oneself, they imply a certain kind of "self-control." This occurs with any medicinal regimen, whether by diet, therapy, or oral dosage.

Nevertheless, using this model for understanding contraception implies treating the human sexual drive and its naturally procreative dimension as a purely biological function, as a function similar to the digestive tract or the circulatory system: in such matters there is no personally constitutive striving for personal goods, but merely physiological functions that only indirectly—to the extent that they help make up the physical integrity ("health") of the body—are bearers of personally significant goods. Physiological integrity is a human good insofar as "corporeality" is itself a constitutive *bonum humanum*; but the factors and functions that make up this integrity are not *immediately* bearers of personal goods, as are the joining of man and woman and the fruifulness of their love in view of the transmission of human life. The so-called "functions" are not subject to the dominance of the human will; their acts are not perfected through *virtues*, because they are guided to their respective ends neither through the reason nor through the will; in case they fail in some way, they are regulated by the interventions of medicinal and technical procedures—by "art," but not by moral regulation.

This also applies to the purely physiological and organic aspects of human sexuality, but not to human sexuality as a naturally procreative and unitive inclination. (Fertility is obviously not a pathological condition, unlike an irregular fertility cycle; it is consequently not the same thing to restore the regularity of the cycle with pharmaceutical means, which is to normalize a pathological condition, as to regulate the fertility of married love with what may be the same pharmaceuticals.) Human sexuality, as a natural inclination, is in no way a purely biological–physiological reality, but rather the anthropological basis of fundamentally human goods, a constitutive component of human existence qua human, as well as of the ability to exist as a human. Procreation is much more than an organic function; it is one of the most fundamental and most noble of human tasks, and not simply a necessary physiological process. It is an act which the human person undertakes in freedom and responsibility: the instinctive and sensual drives on which it is founded are subject to the guidance of the practical reason and the dominance of the will.

The human sexual instinct has a *directly* personal meaning and a personal way of being carried out, known as *moral virtue*. Together with its procreative openness, human sexuality needs an operative integration into the rational–voluntary structure of the suppositum and the *actus humanus*. But it must be emphasized that sexuality is not thereby "humanized," as though it had only a biological reality apart from such an integration.[104] On the contrary, it is respected and *confirmed* in its anthropologically foundational, already fully human meaning, and is integrated into the structure of personal actions in a manner that suits such a meaning: it is a question only of *operative*, and not *ontological*, integration (for the distinction, see the section "The Natural Law and Virtue," subsection "The Identity of the *Ordo Rationalis* with the *Ordo Virtualis*," earlier in this chapter).

We therefore arrive at our first precision: if, in the context of human sexuality, we speak about rational and voluntary governance, or self-control, we do not mean *any* kind of self-governance or control, no matter how rational and voluntary it might be, but rather that kind of rational and voluntary self-governance or control that is known as "moral virtue." Moral virtue does not consist simply in "getting hold of" the corresponding instinctual drive or its consequences; rather, moral virtue is the rational "shaping" [*durchformen*] of sensual drives at an *operative*, and not ontological level: it is the *perfecting* of them in accordance with the requirements of personal actions.

Acts of self-control, self-mastery, self-discipline *as such* are morally neither good nor bad: avaricious people and criminals, for example, can have a high degree of rational and voluntary control, of self-discipline and strength of will for carrying out disordered purposes and satisfying passions that are completely ungoverned as such. Virtue implies that form of self-control which the ordering of the reason brings about *in* the natural inclinations, which means, in relation to the pursuit of fundamental human goods. Self-control that is morally laudable is always a component of the rational–appetitive (or *operative*) perfection of natural inclinations, and not an act of negation or manipulation; similarly, that kind of self-control is not praiseworthy which has to do with actions that make possible the carrying out of a natural inclination in a manner that is destructive of the person.

Clearly, then, there are various types of rational–voluntary control or mastery over sensual urges. Contraception for the purpose of regulating the fertility of sexual acts is not an act of virtue; it is instead the manipulation of sexual acts, in order "to get hold of" their consequences by shutting them off. Coitus interruptus, of course, is not "technological" manipulation, but it *is* a manipulation, which consists in taking control of the procreative *consequences* of sexual activity while remaining irresponsible toward the sexual *drive* itself.

All contraceptive acts possess the characteristic of being a kind of control over the procreative consequences of sexual acts that is *independent of any mastery over the sexual drive itself.* The rational and voluntary governance and self-control of such acts have only to do with the procreative *consequences* of sexual activity.

Through contraceptive measures the unitive aspect of human sexuality ("loving union") on the one hand, and the exercise of procreative responsibility on the other hand, are disconnected: control over the fruitfulness is assured *independently* of the operative dynamic of human sexuality as an *inclinatio naturalis ad coniunctionem maris et feminae.* The loving/unitive aspect of married love and the acts of control over the procreative consequences of that love are made to run on two different tracks: the acts through which procreative responsibility (that is, the mastery over the procreative consequences of sexual acts) is exercised are completely independent of the act of "loving union" (or sexual activity as an act of married love); they are not integrated into the dynamic of the sexual drive, and thus in their structure are no longer acts of married and bodily love, but rather acts ("measures") of technical control over this love. Human sexuality and bodiliness, or the love between man and woman in its loving/unitive *consummatio,* is in this case not the *subject* or *bearer* of procreative responsibility, but rather the mere *object* of a regulative manipulation. Sexual union and acts of accepting procreative responsibility fall apart from one another.

The disconnection achieved by contraception, this separating of *contraceptive acts* from the *acts brought about by the sexual drive itself,* whereby sexual activity becomes a procreatively inconsequential mode of behavior, is not self-control in the moral sense. It has instead to do with a kind of "overlordship" or "tyranny" (*dominium*) that profoundly contradicts the basic requirements of moral virtue. This is because moral virtue consists, as already explained, in ordering the human inclinations, urges, and so on, with their full significance, in accordance with the reason, and to do this so that they become operatively integrated into the structure of personal responsibility. This operative integration is essentially distinct from that kind of *dominium* through which whatever opposes the reason or does not stay in unison with the reason is oppressed, shut off, and "disconnected"—in a word, *manipulated.*

Such manipulation in the case of sexuality can be legitimated only if it is assumed that the unitive and procreative aspects of sexuality do not belong together *insepararably* and that they do not form, in this *inseparable union,* a human good. The denial of this inseparable union, or the denial of the *essentially* procreative dimension of the sexual drive as an original and genuine human good, would imply that the procreative transcendence or openness of the loving union of husband and wife is *not* constitutive of this love; the procreative consequences (fruitfulness) of sexual acts would then be considered a mere "subpersonal," "biological" phenomenon, a purely physical effect of the sexual organs, over which man possesses free disposal, according to his wishes, to "bring about" new life but that do not say anything about *what* the loving union of husband and wife actually is. Such an "instrumentalization" of the procreative dimension of human sexuality and married love can nevertheless be consistently grounded only in a dualistic anthropology, and will consequently promote an instrumentalization of human life in general (as does the mode of argumentation that "weighs goods" in so-called "teleological ethics"; see chapter 8).

It should once again be recalled that human sexuality and its human perfection and fulfillment in married love cannot be understood without the procreative dimension. We simply cannot redefine human beings and their acts for the sake of controlling moral problems. The procreative orientation of the sexual drive, the procreative dimension of married love, is simply one of those "basic facts" of anthropology[105] that cannot be denied without denying man himself in his full and bodily reality, a truth that belongs to those fundamental intelligible human goods, which man grasps spontaneously in his natural practical experience and which constitute his human identity—the foundation, in turn, of all human action. To repeat: only a spiritualistic personalism based on dualistic thinking can fail to recognize, as mentioned above, that man is not an "incarnate spirit," a spiritual "I," that "finds itself" in a body that it "makes use of," but on the contrary is a *bodily* existence—a *corpus* and *animal*—that is penetrated, in singular fashion, by a spiritual soul. Man is a *person* only because of this spiritual soul, but he is not a person as a spiritual "I," but rather as *whole* man, and therefore the fertility of the sexual union between man and woman is an existentially constitutive component of the human person, who, as human, is a "body–person" (My "I" is also my body; I do not "have" this body, I "am" it; the "I" experience is unthinkable without the experience that "I am my body.")

The Cartesian and post-Cartesian model of much modern thought assumes that the spiritual powers of the human *suppositum* make use of the body "for their purposes." Through his methodic doubt, Descartes engineered a reduction of the fundamental "I" consciousness and human identity to the "I think" (*cogito*); and this can be understood, in fact, as a scientific/theoretical and methodological *manipulation* of original, basically practical experience. In reality, the bodily powers of the human suppositum help to formulate fundamentally human goods, and this is to say that they are the *bearers* (or the subject) of specifically human and natural act-intentions and of the possibility of human fulfillment and human identity. As explained above (see the section "Beyond Naturalism and Dualism," subsection "Integral Anthropology or Spiritualism?"), the phenomenon of human love, the *amor coniugalis*, is not, in a "pure" and "original" state, a spiritual phenomenon, but rather is a specifically human and *personal* shaping of a naturally procreative sexual inclination *ad coniunctionem maris et feminae*, which belongs to man in common with all other forms of life that belong to the same *genus*, animal. This is why it is impossible to understand married love, or the essential meaning of the sexual union of man and wife, without taking the procreative dimension into account.

Human sexuality does not belong to the "object world" of man—to the condition of "nature" in which man "finds himself," and with which he (however responsibly) associates, which he "uses" or "makes useful." Far otherwise, *sexuality (as an aspect of human bodiliness) belongs to the personal "subjective dimension" of man (to the "I"); it is therefore an integral and constitutive component of the human being's identity as a morally acting subject.* It is part of that nature which man *is*, and which co-constitutes the subjective character of his action as specifically *human* behavior. Sexuality is meant not as "object," but rather as the bearer, and subject, of responsible action.

Once again, the procreative potentiality of human sexuality is not simply an organic/physiological function. It is instead the essential content of the unitive inclination between man and wife: it *co-constitutes* and *co-defines* human existence and potential human existence as a moral perfection, and in the peculiar form of married love. A morally and anthropologically adequate exercise of human responsibility (which says "yes" to integral man) can never eliminate this potentiality, but will integrate sexuality in its procreative dimension *operatively* into the personal structure of rational and voluntary autonomy of action. The result of this operative integration is an indispensable component of the moral virtue of chastity.[106]

The conclusion to be drawn is that there is only *one* morally adequate mode of behavior in reference to the procreative consequences of sexual activity: the governing of the sexual drive *itself.* This is mastery of the self through acts of self-restraint when conception is not warranted. In such a case, human sexuality and its unitive character are not disconnected from its procreative dimension, but rather (in contrast to taking contraceptive measures) the unitive character of human sexuality, which is a fundamental human good, is *itself* integrated into the structure of procreative responsibility: *the loving union of the spouses in the sexual act remains in itself an act of procreative responsibility.* Human sexuality is thus confirmed in an integral way: in its twofold sense of unity and procreation, and in personal wholeness.

With this we have really reached the root of the matter. As long as there is a virtuous mastery of the *sexual drive itself,* this latter is not simply the "object" of actions (really, technical manipulations) of procreative resonsibility, but rather the *subject* or *bearer* of procreative resonsibility. This is the crucial point from an ethical and anthropological perspective. Only in this way can two essential characteristics of married love be maintained: first, that married love is essentially *procreatively responsible* love (otherwise it would not be human, since procreative *responsibility* "has not been taught by nature to all animals"); second, that married love is essentially *bodily* love, that is, a kind of love in which bodily union finds its *consummatio*. If procreative responsibility is going to be an act of married love, it is necessary that it be an act of the bodily dimension of this love, because sexual union is not only a "means of expression" or a "procreative tool" of a "purely spiritual" love, but rather an essential component and *consummatio* of love. As *acts*, procreative responsibility and sexual behavior cannot be separated from one another, because through such separation the dimension of procreative responsibility would be denied and its personal integration would be destroyed.

In order for human sexuality and the sexual relations between man and woman not to become an "object" of acts of procreative resonsibility, but rather the *bearer* of such acts, responsible control of fertility must itself become part of sexual activity as loving union. One could also say that under these conditions, sexual acts between a man and a woman are the bearers and expressions of the task that they shoulder in common: the cause of transmitting human life in a responsible manner. Control of fertility thus remains within the logic of the unitive aspect of sexuality, and within a structure of responsibility it belongs to a fully human love: the kind that attains to a union of bodies. Acts of two kinds—both those of periodic abstinence, willed because of parental (procreative) responsibility, and those of sexual union carried out in the same context but during infertile periods—are both acts whose subject (or bearer) is the sexual drive itself (because sexual behavior includes not just sexual intercourse but also acts of abstaining). In both kinds of acts, the person is confirmed as the cause of the procreative consequences of sexual activity: the causal nexus between the sexual acts of loving union and those of procreation remains fully in place; through contraception, however, this causality (or parentally responsible creating power) is negated *in the sexual act itself*.[107]

It becomes particularly clear that periodic abstinence and contraception are two completely different modes of behavior in their intentions. Acts of abstinence are acts that do have the sexual drive (together with its procreative potentiality) not as *object* but as *subject*; abstinence is itself an act of marital sexual behavior or *bodily love*. At the same time, it is an act of procreative responsibility, because the subject of this act is the human person, or the married community of persons, as the cause or initiator of procreation. The spouses are directly engaged in the task of responsibly transmitting human life when they act in self-restraint, and they remain the subject (as a community of persons) of this task. In marital sexual activity during infertile periods, they carry out the specifically sexual good of loving union in a procreatively responsible manner, wherein (it should not be forgotten) the act of abstinence is itself a special expression, guarantee, and reinforcement of the same *married* love that is equally expressed, guaranteed, and reinforced *in another way* by sexual union.

Contraception, however, is *not* a sexual act or an act of bodily love, but rather a mere "procedure" that has human sexuality for its *object*. The only content that such an act really has is the exclusion or denial of the procreative consequences of sexual acts. When they do this, spouses are not confirmed as subjects or initiators of procreation, but are excluded from being such. Contraceptive sexual intercourse is likewise no longer an act of responsible bodily love, but rather a procreatively inconsequential act in which the spouses are *not* the subjects of responsible parenthood, because the causal nexus of procreation has been willingly negated in their sexual intercourse.

Married persons who exercise abstinence seek *through their sexual behavior* to *avoid* a conception that their conscience tells them is irresponsible, by abstaining from those acts that can be foreseen as causing such a conception. Married persons who employ contraception do not, strictly speaking, *avoid* a conception, but rather *prevent* it [*verhüten*], though *not* through their sexual behavior; to *prevent* a conception without having to modify one's behavior is the point of calling it "*contra*-conception," or the "*prevention* of conception" [*Empfängnis**verhütung***].

Contraception, considered from the point of view of ethics, is totally at variance with acts of periodic abstinence: by its nature, it is an antiprocreative act. *This is true exactly to the extent that it removes the character of "being the bearer of procreative responsibility and causality" from the unitive aspect of sexual intercourse.*[108] The antiprocreative intentionality of contraception is grounded in the denial of the procreatively responsible structure of sexual acts. It equally denies the special character of sexual acts, the acts of two persons united in one flesh, who in their personal/bodily unity mutually and unreservedly give themselves to the task of transmitting human life.[109]

The objection encountered at the beginning can now be answered more fully. Procreative responsibility does not require *just any* form of rational and voluntary management of sexuality (or of its procreative consequences), but rather one that allows the single sexual acts themselves to become the *bearers* of procreative responsibility. This is a basic anthropological and ethical requirement of sexual love that represents a genuine (human) good in its procreative dimension. It is also required for human virtue.

Let's take the example of a married couple who have the full intention of respecting the good of the transmission of human life, but for very grave and legitimate reasons have come to the conclusion that another pregnancy would be irresponsible. In case they choose to contracept, then the "denial" they are making is not, to be sure, a fundamental negation of the procreative significance of married love *at the level of their intentions* (we are assuming that the couple would have been prepared, in the absence of the grave and legitimate reasons, to accept further children); the "denial" in question is, rather, directed at the procreative meaning of sexual intercourse at the level of the *means they have chosen* to the end of responsible parenthood. The choice of this means (or "method") of contraception is a conscious decision against the procreative responsibility of sexual acts—or, more exactly, *it is the voluntary decision to detach sexual intercourse from the maintenance of procreative responsibility.* In a few words: it is to make sexual acts procreatively inconsequential.

What is morally determinative of such a choice is *not* the intervention into natural/physiological structures, but the "intervention" into the personal structure of procreatively responsible sexual activity as an *actus humanus.* It is a decision against the fundamental requirement of moral virtue: to realize sexual acts (or married love in its bodily–sexual dimension) as acts of procreative responsibility. And thereby, even in an "isolated" instance, the inseparable unity of loving union and procreation is denied.

Now it may be illuminating to note that such a voluntary "discoupling" of procreative responsibility from sexual activity does not take place in the case of either pathological or age-conditioned sterility. In such cases the will is disposed in a completely different manner toward the infertility. Of course, this, too, can be "misused" in an irresponsible way, but an unwilled infertility of sexual acts does not originate from a will to disconnect sexual activity from its procreative dimension. The morally significant issue is not the infertility, as a definite "condition" or as an "outcome" of contraceptive procedures, but the *choice* to bring about such a condition or outcome.

We come now to a broader consideration, which should complete the foregoing arguments. What is decisive for judging human actions is not simply "the state of things" or "what happens," but rather what is *willed* or *chosen*. Contraception is chosen as a means and is therefore willed. To choose something as a means implies (to the extent that a real choice is in question) choosing *against* possible alternatives. The choice of contraceptive measures always implies a voluntary decision against the demands involved in the practice of periodic abstinence. Contraception as a choosing act of the will implies that the causal nexus between sexual acts and their possible procreative consequences, as well as abstinence as a responsible way to master or control this nexus, are considered evils. "Evil" in this context means a mode of action that is to be avoided, since every willing choice is subject to the first principle of the practical reason: "Good is to be pursued, evil to be avoided." The choice for contraception, in its ethical substance, is therefore not simply the "application" of a certain "method," but rather the *choice of a certain behavior* that stipulates and introduces this "application," and that voluntarily rejects the demands of human virtue, namely, the virtue of chastity. It is a decision especially *against self-restraint*, because there is no reason why people would choose sterilizing operations, ingestion of birth-control pills, the use of condoms or IUDs, or coitus interruptus unless they considered *having to exercise periodic self-restraint* as an evil to be avoided.

One could object at this point that the decision to use contraception by no means necessarily involves a decision *against* self-restraint, but could be chosen solely for the reason that such procedures are the only *reliable* or *certain* means of avoiding pregnancy. But such a description of contraceptive procedures is simply false, or at least incomplete, so that if someone bases a decision on this reasoning, he or she does so on a false assumption. This assumption consists in treating (periodic) abstinence and contraception as two technically different methods. But this is to overlook the heart of the matter. Contraception and periodic abstinence are not simply "two different methods of not having babies," but two *morally opposed modes of behavior.* The assumption gives the issue of "technical efficiency" (the question of "security") priority over the issue of moral significance and permissibility: it makes the answer to the latter, moral question dependent on the former, technical one. If someone decides on this basis, he betrays a corresponding lack of moral wisdom, inconsiderateness, or immaturity—which in various cases is more or less blameworthy—but this does nothing to alter the fact that such a decision is an *objectively* false one on moral grounds, and is equivalent, in terms of its moral object, to a decision against the demands of moral virtue (or against the requirement that the sexual act be procreatively responsible). Furthermore, the "certainty" or "reliability" of a means toward the attainment of a desired end is never a criterion, in any area of human conduct, for the moral permissibility of that means. On the other hand, if someone speaks in this connection of the "risk" of an "unwanted child," it is forgotten that this manner of speaking is altogether problematic: in a case where the married couple feels morally obliged to avoid a pregnancy, and therefore exercises periodic abstinence, for the couple to speak in this way would imply that they *don't* feel responsible for a conception that might occur despite their intention to avoid pregnancy. But such an assumption would be suited only to a contraceptive intention. The so-called "unwanted child" should in reality not be considered a "risk" (that is, as an evil), but rather as the procreative consequence of an act that has in itself a procreative dimension. It is an act that is treated by married couples who practice periodic abstinence as a good, and they consider it this way precisely to the extent that they conduct themselves according to the logic of periodic abstinence, that is, to the extent that they feel responsible for the procreative consequences of their sexual actions. The so-called "unwanted child" is a "risk," or presents a problem of frustrated intention, only under the assumption of a contraceptive attitude. If this assumption is absent, then the so-called "unwanted child" is experienced as a consequence of married love and is thus an *accepted* child.

A further objection would point to "hindrances" or difficulties of a psychological nature that would follow from the practice of abstinence. In various ways these arguments both evade the fundamental moral and anthropological dimension of the difference between periodic abstinence and contraception, and ignore the ethical and anthropological goods that are peculiar to periodic abstinence. For abstaining during certain periods as a way of exercising responsible parenthood, like any virtuous behavior, is often difficult, and involves the making of sacrifices. It should not be considered a purely "negative" act of omission, but rather as a profoundly meaningful act of married, bodily love, as well as an expression of love's growth and its fertile soil. This kind of self-restraint is always a loving affirmation of the other person, of their commonly embraced unity-in-love, and of their commonly shared burdens. These aspects of the practice of periodic abstinence, which are overlooked in such arguments, really provide the *foundation* for mastering the problems that are brought forward to prove its impracticability. On the other hand, to maintain the undesirability of all contraceptive practices *without exception* is not to cleave to "abstract" principles, but only to articulate an insight into something that is indispensable and respects the "truth about man," or the ethical and anthropological foundations for behavior that alone deserve to be called *right* and *good;* no matter how great the difficulties may be, a solution that does not respect the ethical and anthropological foundations of married love cannot be a good solution.

The idea behind the foregoing considerations has been to show that the choice of using contraception is a false one, for reasons of parental responsiblity that are justified in themselves. For the purpose of theoretical moral analysis, such a case is to be distinguished from another: the practice of contraception for a morally unjustified intention to avoid a pregnancy, that is, to take married love completely away from its orientation toward the transmission of human life—for example, to limit the number of children, or not have any children, for reasons of personal comfort, egoism, or the preference of other goods. In this case it is no longer a question of exercising parental responsibility: we are confronted here with a *thoroughly* contraceptive attitude, which comes into existence when a married couple (from the very beginning or at some later time) decide to close themselves off from handing on human life through their own love, and thus willingly give up on the task of being—through their own love—co-workers with God and interpreters of His creative love.

Such an attitude (at least in contemporary, affluent Western society) is what usually underlies the choice of contraceptive procedures. Consequently the immorality of contraception does not consist first and foremost in the choice of an improper means of exercising procreative responsibility, but rather in the willing refusal of procreative responsibility *as such*. The will is not concerned with the level of means, but rather with the final intention, and thus rejects the fundamental good of transmitting human life, and chooses against the integral, procreative meaning of married love, a meaning so fundamental for human behavior. This voluntary refusal of the task of transmitting human life, as a fundamental practical good that constitutes the horizon of meaning of human life in general, and of the love between husband and wife in particular, is a much more fundamental disorientation of the practical reason, since it turns this away from a natural principle of its own ordinative function—indeed, it even negates this principle, falsifying human sexuality and married love at the level of those ends that are given with the very nature of man.

This intention, of course, can even make use of periodic abstinence, which then, as a potentially morally adequate mode of behavior, becomes disfigured and morally perverted through the antiprocreative intention. Acts of self-restraint in this intentional context are then anti-procreative acts and are not different, at least as regards their intention, from acts of contraception, or from sexual acts that have voluntarily been made infertile. This is the case of a morally reprehensible abstinence, and not an act of the virtue of chastity. (To be sure, because of the peculiar character of abstinence, in which the sexual drive itself remains the subject and bearer—in this case of an antiprocreative intention—a smaller measure of morally depraved sexuality is present than with the use of contraceptive procedures, so that a change of fundamental attitude is at least made possible in experience. On the other hand, when a fundamentally antiprocreative attitude is combined with a denial of the procreative responsibility of sexual actions through the practice of contraception, a mentality is in the making according to which abortion is considered to be a legitimate means of "birth control," and homo- or heterosexual practices of onanism become viewed as "normal" and not as perverse sexual behavior.)

The denaturing of sexuality by contraceptive methods has its own peculiar dynamic. It nevertheless varies from case to case and has a whole palette of implications that cannot be determined in an *a priori* manner: the disintegration of sensuality; the destruction of conjugal friendship, equality, and mutuality; an increasing lack of mutual respect as persons; a tendency, brought about by the "objectifying" of sexuality and bodiliness through contraception, to treat sexuality, one's own and one's partner's body, as a mere "object" or means—all these are aspects of the disintegration of married love as the personal communion of creatures who are bodily in essence. A more detailed analysis cannot be taken up here.[110] In any case, these are many facets of a single, underlying fact: that married love loses its special quality of being *procreatively responsible love* (a love, that is, the sexual acts of which are procreatively responsible) through contraceptive procedures. And even apart from the possible consequences or implications, the immorality of contraception consists in the voluntary withdrawal of sexual activity from this procreative responsibility, thereby *falsifying* it and allowing it to become an "objectively contradictory gesture"[111]—such a gesture has nothing more to do with an act of responsible parenthood, and therefore can no longer be called the expression and *consummatio* of a truly human love, or an unconditional gift of the whole person.

The issue of contraception is not simply a problem of method; nor, on the other hand, can direct sterilization simply be called an "ontic evil" or a "premoral evil."[112] It is, rather, a matter of a fundamental "denaturing" and disintegration of the human act, which corresponds to the *peccatum contra naturam* in the classical sense. A moral evil can never be justified as a means toward an end, no matter how good that end may be: this is especially so when the dignity of the human person, the dignity of the transmission of human life, and the human capacity to love are all at risk.

Especially to be emphasized is the radical difference between, on the one side, technical mastery of the nature that surrounds man and, on the other side, what is required for the moral mastery of the powers that belong to the human person by nature. To lose track of this difference is one of the greatest dangers to contemporary man. *Humanae Vitae* pointed this out, and so has John Paul II, as follows:

> The problem lies in keeping a balance betweeen what can be called "mastery . . . of the powers of nature" (*HV,* 2) and "self-mastery" (*HV,* 21), which is indispensable for the human person. The man of today tends to transfer methods appropriate to the first area to the second. "Finally, we must consider the astonishing progress of man in his mastery over the powers of nature, and their rational utilization. Man seeks to extend such mastery over his entire life, to his body, his psychical powers, his social life, and even the laws that govern the transmission of human life." (*HV,* 2)
>
> This extension of the area of the means of "control over the powers of nature" threatens the human person, to whom the means of "self-mastery" is proper and remains so. This self-mastery corresponds to the fundamental constitution of the person: it is a "natural" means. The application of "artificial means," on the other hand, disrupts the constitutive dimension of the person, destroys his own subjectivity and makes him subject to manipulation (*The Redemption of the Body and the Sacramentality of Marriage*, p. xx)

Here is where the "naturalness" of periodic abstinence is to be found, and not in its respecting of biological natural laws. Here also is to be found the "nature of the marital act": in its personal dimension of free, voluntary, and loving self-giving of two persons, in service to the transmission of human life.

Even if there is global need for a decreasing birthrate, which in view of the emerging demographic catastrophes of the developed world is becoming ever more questionable, this would still be no argument for such a manipulative regulation of human fertility. Whoever argues in this way does not trust man to solve such a problem through his moral powers. He would deny man the capacity to overcome a human problem with the *human* means that correspond to his personal dignity. Right here is to be seen the task and responsibility of moral theologians: to awaken trust in such ability and to make known the moral necessity of its exercise "in season and out of season."

*Summing Up: The "Unnaturalness" of Contraception*

It should be clearer now why artificial birth control, or the exercise of parental responsibility through the sterilization of sexual acts, as *peccatum contra naturam*, offends against the natural law. A *peccatum contra naturam* does not consist simply in an intervention into the natural order, or in its "impairment," but rather in a *morally* unjustifiable intervention, or an intervention into a morally significant natural *ordo*; this is exactly what occurs, since the *ordo naturalis* is a *praesuppositum* for the *ordo rationis*, and thereby for the order of human virtue—and in this case, for the order of the procreative responsibility of sexual acts as an aspect of the virtue of chastity. It has to do not with an offense against any specific *praeceptum* of the natural law—to hold that would lead to a naturalistic misinterpretation of the natural law—it has, rather, to do with an offense against that *foundation* of the natural law on the basis of which (it being an *ordo rationis*) the natural law is enabled to unfold, not only in its fundamental orientation through the *ratio naturalis* but also in its preceptive demands to regulate human conduct. The offense is much more fundamental than a mere "acting against reason" (*agere contra rationem*) or "against a law" (*contra legem*). It involves, in fact, a self-caused disabling of an action *secundum rationem* or *secundum legem*: instead of an "offense" against a law, it is the *removal* of an entire area of human conduct *from* regulation by moral law (and that means the *ordinatio rationis*, and the voluntariness and responsibility formed by the reason).

And so we come to the conclusion that in the question of contraception, an *ignoratio elenchi*, or *mutatio elenchi*, or an "ignorance" or "change" of the point in dispute has frequently distorted the perspective on the problem. On the one hand, by concentrating on the question, What is the difference between naturally caused and artificially caused infertility? one then tries to deduce a moral distinction between the "natural" and the "artificial" (that is, what "harms" nature); on the other hand, when this kind of deduction has been disputed, the problem has been reduced to a purely technical question about the relative efficiency of the method chosen, and then the so-called "natural method" is only another method of contraception. I have been trying to show that the question is completely different: namely, that it concerns the difference between (on the one hand) governance and regulation of the procreative dimension of the *naturalis inclinatio* and its acts through reason and the will, and with this, the maintenance of the personal integrity of that inclination as wholly human (that is, responsible) love, and (on the other hand) the removal of the procreative dimension of the *naturalis inclinatio* from this order of virtue (or the *lex naturalis*) through a technical intervention that leads to a structural disintegration of the personal integrity of married love. The criterion for the moral qualification of natural "givens" is the order of virtue (*ordo virtutis*), which rests inseparably upon this "givenness," and not their "naturalness" per se. What is decisive is not the physiological integrity or the "wholeness" of the power to procreate, but rather the *personal integrity* of sexual *acts* as acts of human love and married responsibility. Ethics is concerned with *human actions*, and not natural givens. This makes clear the fundamental difference between the *contraception* of procreative consequences of sexual acts and the responsible *avoidance* of a conception through abstinence. Even the "artificiality" of contraception reveals itself finally as a more or less necessary supplement to the *real* morally problematic "act of contracepting."

Once the interconnection of these matters has been recognized, it is possible to look back over the course of the argument and conclude that the natural givens at the basis of this unity, including the cyclical nature of human fertility, represent a "God-given" order. We recognize the will of God because of our recognition of the natural moral law that, underlying human action, is a law of the practical reason. It is precisely through recognizing the connection between the natural order and the rational order as a *praesuppositio* that we can also recognize—in retrospect—that the natural order, in this concrete case, is a component of the *lex aeterna*, a component of that passive *impressio* of the eternal law in man: the foundation (and component) of the natural law as the law of the practical reason. It is likewise the order of virtue and moral perfection, in which the *bonum humanum* itself consists.

Once the natural basis of virtue has been recognized as such, it can also be seen as the *bonum humanum*, and consequently as the divine law, as the *lex aeterna*, and the will of God. According to the well-known words of St. Thomas, the divine law ordains nothing other than what corresponds to reason, and "God is offended by us only through what we do against our own well-being" (*quod contra nostrum bonum agimus; Contra Gentiles,* II, c. 122). And this is synonymous with that other statement, that the divine law prescribes that "all human actions be subject to reason" (*ut omnia quae sunt hominis rationi subdantur;* ibid., c. 121). Every law is thus oriented toward virtue, and "virtue consists in this, that the inner affections (*interiores affectiones*), as well as the use of material goods, be ordered by reason" (*ratione regulentur;* ibid.). Or, in an even more pregnant expression: *Praecepta legis sunt de actibus virtutum* (the precepts of law are concerned with the acts of the virtues)—and all the precepts of the law are ordered to the love of God and neighbor.

When we recall that the *lex naturalis* is essentially a participation in the eternal law, in the eternal *ordo rationis* of divine providence, and that man, through this partaking in the eternal law, becomes himself a fellow worker and fellow executor of divine providence; then in the case of married love he becomes the interpreter, and in a certain sense the bearer, of the divine creative love. We can further consider the personal acts of man as such, insofar as they are based on an "ordination of the reason" (*ordinatio rationis*) and the voluntariness of "personal autonomy," with mastery over his own acts and the corresponding responsibility. Such acts are also *part* of the divine world governance, and *part* of the execution of divine providence precisely *through* and *on the basis of* this personal autonomy of the human being. A manner of regulating conception and controlling the fruitfulness of human love that excludes *at its root* and makes superfluous the need for such rational and voluntary mastery over one's own acts, by removing human sexuality from the need of such regulation by the reason and such mastery by the will, clearly no longer has the character of a participation in divine providence, or of a formal participation of the eternal law in the human creature.[113] And even if this is possible by "technology," there is still no justification for exercising one's moral responsibility in a certain field of behavior by simply *removing* this field from the need to be governed (by will and reason, and by virtue); this is to trade away the human vocation to be the master of one's own actions for the sake of technological means. The wrongness of contraception (or the impossibility of its justification) does not follow from the inviolability of biological laws, but rather from the inviolability of human dignity, which consists in living *secundum rationem*, and through voluntary and rational mastery over one's own actions. Man is never justified in solving moral problems by refusing to be human, and this is so even if the exercise of human dignity requires sacrifice, discipline (*askesis*), and self-denial. In true love, such things are always a source of joy, fulfillment, and inner peace.[114]

## Concluding Remarks

### *The* "Lex Naturalis"*: The Law of the Practical Reason*

The result of the argument thus far is, first, the understanding that the natural law (or *lex naturalis*) is essentially an "ordering of the reason in regard to virtue" (*ordinatio rationis ad virtutem*). It is not a "law of being" in the same way that the conept of law is understood in the natural sciences, but rather is a law in the original sense of the word: a "command" (*praeceptum*) of the practical reason. This law is based on a multiplicity of natural inclinations, integrated in the context of the *suppositum*, that do not yet have in themselves the character of a law, since they are still undetermined in their *ordinatio* to what is right (*debitum*), and cannot make possible the formulation of a *praeceptum*. These natural inclinations are a participation in the eternal law that is given by nature and spontaneously experienced. In their original indetermination in regard to what is "right" (*debitum*), and as an integral component of the *suppositum*, to which even the natural reason (*ratio naturalis*) belongs, as the "natural inclination toward the right act and end" (*inclinatio naturalis ad debitum actum et finem*), they are oriented by nature to a "rational ordering" (*ordinatio rationis*) by the natural reason. This means that they are subject to a law, and that law is the natural law.

This natural law likewise arises from a natural tendency: that of the natural reason toward the "suitable" or "right" (*debitum*), which, comparable to a light—the participation in the light of the divine reason (*ratio divina*)—amounts to an inclination to the "practical truth," to the "morally true," which is the truly good or "right" (*debitum*). The truth of the natural reason is a natural truth, and for this reason is always constituted in a fundamental *adaequatio* with the "proper ends" (*fines proprii*) of the natural inclinations,[115] but it must likewise, and furthermore, determine in them the *debitum* of virtue. This determination (an *ordinatio rationis*) is the natural law.

It has also been shown how the reason—even the scientifically observing reason—reflects upon its own act and by a "complete return" (*reditio completa*) comprehends the integration of the natural inclinations in the context of the *suppositum*. This leads to an anthropological and, finally, metaphysical insight into the structure of the human person—an insight that, in its own right, has constitutive meaning for the elaboration of a philosophical ethics.

The natural law as an *ordinatio rationis* is accordingly a natural law in man, because it arises from principles that belong to human nature (*principia indita*). According to a definition of the concept "nature" that also applies to this situation, it can be called "natural," for "nature is nothing other than the principle of a certain art [*ratio cuiusdam artis*]—namely of the divine art—implanted in things [*indita rebus*], by which things move to a determined end" (*In II Phys.*, lect. 14).

This "principle of divine art" (*ratio divinae artis*) in man is the participation in the eternal law, on the basis of a divine act of creation. "Nature" here means all the natural inclinations, but in a special sense it is the *ratio naturalis*, through which man himself, indeed *because* of participation, is raised, in a certain way, to the level of the "Divine Artist." He is not just the object or the instrument of divine providence, he is "provident for himself and others" (*sibi ipsi et aliis providens*).

"Nature" is understood, in this way, to be a *cause of order* (*causa ordinationis*) that has been established within things (see *In VIII Phys.*, lect. 3). The natural inclinations are just such principles of order—are nature itself, in fact—but not *law*. In man there is another *causa ordinationis* in addition to this, which does possess the character of a law: those acts of the practical reason that, emerging from the *ratio naturalis*, direct the acts of the natural inclinations to their "right end," the *bonum rationis*, or the morally good.

It is indispensable here to keep in mind the *analogy* of the concept of nature (see *In V Met.*, lect. 5) in order to avoid confusion. Obviously, "nature" is the entire substance as well as the *forma substantialis*, and the composite of form and matter, the "essence" as the existing basis for all activity (*operatio;* ibid.). If the natural law is identified with "essence" or the "order of nature," or if one attempts to derive it from the concept of a *natura metaphysica,* the analogy of the concept will vanish, and we find ourselves on the level of a rationalist–essentialist ontology,[116] which really loses the character of the natural law as an order of reason—or, in the words of Leo XIII—as a *praescriptio rationis.*

Further precisions should now be made regarding the distinction (which has already been criticized) between an "objective natural law" as the "order of nature," on the one side, and the "subjective knowledge" of it [*Erkenntnisgrund*], on the other side: the reason, that is, as the "organ" that would "know" such a natural order. With this model, the relationship between the "natural law" and its "objective givenness" is put on its head. It is really the other way around: what is there "to begin with" [*das Ursprüngliche*] is the very constituting of the natural law through the practical reason, and only secondarily, in reflection, is the order of reason (*ordo rationis*) recognized as an "objective" natural law, as constituted through the preceptive act of the *ratio naturalis;* through the *reditio* (see chapter 1, note 47) it is likewise recognized as the "ought" that arises from human nature itself. On the basis of this reflection (the conscious "experience" of the practical reason) can then be built a habitual knowing of this law, which in the judgment of conscience finds particular applications to action. The two "fields" (of the objective natural law [*ordo rationis*] and of the subject that objectifies this natural law) do not stand "over against" one another, as "nature" and "reason," but are really "coterminous," covering the same area. When the human reason recognizes the natural law as "objective" law, it does so in reflection upon its own ordering act. In the natural law, man does not find an order of nature that stands "over against" him, to which he must "adjust" himself or that he must accept as given and "bring into execution"; rather, he recognizes *himself* in the natural law, and thereby, independently of any recognition of "theonomy," recognizes as well the *obligatory character* of this order, which is precisely that of his own practical reason.

And now, if I may be allowed a brief historical reminiscence: it appears astounding that Josef Fuchs scarcely used or even analyzed the concept of the *lex naturalis* in the principal work of his "early phase" dedicated to this very theme.[117] He concerned himself, of course, with the nature of man, with the scope, contents, and knowability of the natural law and natural right, but nowhere can be found a more specific definition of what the "natural law" really is. In his criticism of Fuchs, Karl Rahner was equally astonishing in his neglect of this decisive point; for him, too, the only problem is how human nature can be understood as the basis for natural right. An opportunity was missed. It was the chance to recognize that the question about natural right (the *naturaliter iustum*) must be answered from the point of view of the natural law, and not from "human nature"; or, to put it somewhat differently, the answer to the problem should not be sought simply "in human nature" but, rather, in this nature, *and* from the perspective of its *operative unfolding* in accordance with the order of the *lex naturalis*.

If today Josef Fuchs criticizes a "traditional Catholic natural rights doctrine," he appears to be attacking his own earlier position more than the "tradition" as such, which is in fact much richer and more differentiated than one could gather from his formulations.[118]

It is often the Thomistic distinction between *natura* and *ratio* that has contributed to such imprecise conceptions of the natural law. In a correct understanding of this distinction, however, the natural law (*lex naturalis* or *lex naturae*) is really on the side of the *ratio* and not *natura*, and yet this *ratio* is itself *natura* (without any compromising of the aforesaid distinction) because it has a natural operation. "Nature," on the other hand, is to be distinguished from "reason" insofar as it has the character of a *praesuppositum* of the order of reason: it is the "beginning" of the "order of virtue" (*inchoatio ordinis virtutis*). And this *ordo rationis* (or *virtutis*) forms the subject matter or "field" of the natural law, which in its turn (it should once more be recalled) is not "natural" because it comes into being *a natura*, or because it can be identified with physical regularities, but rather because it reflects a *natural ordering* (*ordi-*

*natio*) of the reason, which extends its "ordering" to the *proprium* of the natural inclinations and makes possible a behavior that is in accord with nature: with *human* nature, which Thomas untiringly describes as "acting in accordance with reason" (*agere secundum rationem*).

## *The "Lex Naturalis": The Law of Virtue*

The relationship of the natural law to the order of moral virtue reveals the true depth and breadth of this law of the practical reason. The relationship also reveals how the natural law can be destroyed in man: such damage is not done at its "base," as the light (*lumen*) of the *ratio naturalis*, but in its practical/cognitive unfolding and effectiveness.[119] This means that it is damaged by everything that is opposed to virtue.[120]

It remains for a later chapter to show how the concept of "theonomous autonomy," as used by contemporary moral theologians, is based on anthropomorphic conceptions. Meanwhile, in the present context of moral virtue, it is possible to speak, in the Aristotelian tradition, of a rightly understood autonomy of man. For in the natural reason (as a participation in the *lex aeterna*) man does possess an autonomy—not a "theonomous" but a "participated" autonomy, or "participated theonomy"—since the eternal law and the natural law are not two different laws. Man is capable of steering himself toward the good through his knowledge of it and desire for it, and through the *dominium* that he has over his own acts (his "personal autonomy"). Man is an entity that does not just "function," but "conducts himself." Neverthless, the natural reason is only the principle or foundation that facilitates such autonomy in the full sense of the word. In its full meaning, the "autonomous" is simply the "virtuous," the Aristotelian *spoudaios* (or serious one) who is himself the measure and mean;[121] and this is doubtless because what seems to the *spoudaios* to be good, really is so. The virtuous person is the existential and operative incarnation of the natural law, and only in the context of moral virtue is there "moral objectivity" as an irrevocable *truth of subjectivity*. It is well known that Thomas says of virtuous people that they are a "law unto themselves" (*ipsi sibi sunt lex*; *Ad Rom.*, II, lect. 3). In this autonomy and freedom (or self-determination toward the good) that belong to the virtuous consists "the highest degree of human dignity, because such a person is not led by others but by himself to what is good" (ibid.) Measure and rule in human affairs is thus moral virtue, which remains in the *ordo rationis* (see *In X Ethic.*, lect. 8; *In IX Ethic.*, lect. 4), and is itself a work of the natural reason, as is the reasoning that arises from it, as the virtue of prudence.

Now it is upon this stable ground of the *ordinatio rationis* of the natural law, and thus always in the context of moral virtue, that that unmistakable manifold of individual possibilities for realizing the human good is founded. The natural law is not a bundle of impersonal "norms" or "commands" that man must face, and that would exert pressure on his conduct through ready-made schemata of behavior, so that no "room" is left for the individual's realization of the good, or so that such "room" would be constantly endangered, making necessary a defense of human "freedom" in the face of the "law." From the outset of the modern period, a model such as this has dominated certain major developments in moral theology, but the model misleads precisely because the good can be realized *only* in an individual, singular, and concrete fashion. There is no action in accord with the natural law that would bear the universal character of its determinations; a determination must always be individualized for a moral act—an *actus humanus*—to occur. Right here arises a contrast between natural law and the "existential ethics," proposed some time ago by Karl Rahner,[122] that even today, in new terminological dress, still dominates the thought world of many contemporary moral theologians.

If I am not mistaken, Rahner posed the first questions in an unfortunate way, and improperly posed questions generally lead to plausible answers that are nevertheless incorrect. Rahner asked, "Is what corresponds to the universal norms simply identical with what ought to be done here and now?"[123] Since Rahner understood as a matter of course that the "norm" is a deduction from the specific nature of man, it was in the universal *species* that he would have to search for a moral "principle of individuation" as well as an "individual nature" of each human being. Consequently, the metaphysical principle for the constitution of angels (the self-individuating *forma substantialis*) was applied to man.[124]

Since Rahner did not trace moral norms to their true source—to their foundation, that is, in the *lex naturalis*, related, as an *ordo rationis*, to the order of moral virtue—the real moral "principle of individuation" appears to have escaped him: *human action itself*, which, as virtuous or as opposed to virtue, is morally individuated in the immensely wide variety of contingencies in human life. This is not an ontological but an *operative* individuation. It is not really a problem of norms at all, but rather a problem of the "goods" that are the subject-matter of the practical reason, and ultimately, it is a matter of what could be called "freedom to become virtuous" and "freedom in virtue."

Underlying the Rahnerian perspective is the mistake of confusing cause with effect, and what is grounded with what grounds. In the end, Rahner identifies "moral norms" with "moral value." But the norm is really *grounded* on a moral value, as it has actually been "realized" in a virtuous act. Such realization is also an "appropriation," since moral conduct is an "immanent action" (*actio immanens*) whose effect remains in the person acting. This is a "living reality" to be shaped, which becomes transparent in an ethics of virtue and not in a norm ethics, no matter how "personalistic" or "individualistic" such an ethics might be.[125]

The "norm" or law as "commandment" is, rather, as it was shown at the beginning, only a normative statement, formulated in reflection, of conduct that has been rationally ordered—of the *ordo virtutis*. Through the conscience, such a normative formulation can be reapplied to action. The natural law is by no means to be identified with the conscience, nor is it a "norm" in this sense: rather, it is the "light of the natural reason, in which is the image of God" (*lumen rationis naturalis, in qua est imago Dei; Ad Rom.*, II, lect. 3). The *lex naturalis* is not a universal norm under which particular cases must be subsumed; originally and in its essence it is not a law that I "apply," but is always the preceptive ordering (*ordinatio*) of *my* practical reason. To overlook this would be to interpret moral philosophy as the systematic of reflective "moral systems" instead of as that which underlies all such systems.

When the natural law is not understood to be a general "norm" under which concrete behavior is simply to be subsumed as a "particular case," then it can finally be understood as a *foundation* or *basis*, upon which alone human conduct can be carried out in its specifically *human* character. As a foundation it neither narrows nor endangers freedom and personality, but is their very basis: it is the starting point and bearer of an indeterminate multiplicity of possible shapings and intensifications of value on the part of the individual, in the order of concrete behavior. The intentions of the acting person contain practical truth to the extent that they are based on the foundation of the natural law and to the extent that the natural law is effective in them.

Such action is not carried out, therefore, as a mere complex of subsumptions, as is often represented by a "legalistic" moral theological tradition, or by those who attempt to overcome such a tradition on its own ground. It is instead a phenomenon with an *openness* implicit in the natural law, without being concretely defined by it: open, that is, not only to all conceivable human values but also to an uplifting into the realm of the divine life, through grace and participation in the divine nature. Through this further specification, human action can realize—can appropriate to itself—the sanctity of God; this sanctity, prefigured in Christ through His assumption of human nature, has likewise become effectively available to human participation through His meritorious work of salvation and its mediation by the Church, for "in Christ is the sacrament, that is, both sign and instrument, for the most intimate union with God, as well as for the unity of mankind."[126]

## Notes

1. It can be seen from this perspective how the conflict between "teleology" and "deontology" presents a false alternative, and is associated with a deficient understanding of the complex structure of the practical reason. The "teleological" act of the practical reason is the primary, originally preceptive, practical judgment that operates within the logic of *finis* and *ea quae sunt ad finem* (the end or goal, and that which leads to, or is directed toward, the end or goal). We can call the latter (only provisionally to avoid misunderstanding) the *means*. The *intentio* and *electio* of the will correspond to this teleological structure of human acts. The virtue of practical rational activity that leads to *electio* is prudence. The "deontological" aspect, on the other hand, corresponds to a reflec-

tive derivation from the first aspect; the corresponding "deontic" formulation of the good is not characterized by an end/means schema, but rather by the relationship between the universal and the concrete particular. As a reflective formulation of the good, it is a formulation as well of general norms that can be applied to individual cases. This in fact is what happens in a judgment of conscience, which is again practical insofar as it represents an *applicatio*. Of course, the teleological structure of prudence and *electio* is not thereby nullified. On the other hand, it seems to me to be misguided to speak of a "prudent conscience," which would correspond to a deontic understanding of the practical reason; this is mistaken because the practical reason is primarily and fundamentally teleological: the act of the conscience can be a reflective judgment on this teleological act, but it would not be an act of this teleological reason itself. It is not the judgment of conscience that belongs to it, but rather the judgment of prudence, a *praeceptum prudentiae*. This deontological misinterpretation of the practical reason as "prudent conscience" would lead as well to a misinterpretation of the conscience itself, since this would involve the conscience in the teleological structure of the practical reason and its affective conditioning, and would make unintelligible its function of providing a reflective examination in the light of universal norms, from a point of view *above* such conditioning. The very existence of such norms, or at least their significance, would thereby come into question. The call for a "prudent conscience" leads to just such consequences in F. Furger, *Gewissen und Klugheit in der katholischen Moraltheologie der letzten Jahrzehnte* (Lucerne and Stuttgart, 1965); the basic problem with this study lies in its aim: to take a deontologically conceived norm morality and to supplement (really, "weaken") this with a doctrine of prudence. What Furger fails to realize is that the practical reason is not fundamentally or primarily characterized by a deontological aspect or an act of the conscience; instead, conscience must enter in as a supplement to a morality of prudence. Accordingly, it would make more sense to speak of "prudence with a conscience"—a prudence, that is, that gives ear to the conscience and recognizes it as an unassailable source of information, as an "examiner" for an *ignorantia electionis* that is always liable to occur: in other words, as a safeguard against a false practical judgment, conditioned by affective influences, at the teleological level of the means/end relation. The present considerations can also be useful for understanding that there are two different forms of the so-called practical syllogism: one that corresponds to the original, teleological schema of *finis/ea quae sunt ad finem*; and one, the deontological form, that is not carried out by prudence as such, but rather on the reflective level of the deontically judging conscience by the logic of *subsumption* of the concrete (whether this be a judgment or an already accomplished act) under the universal. Both forms of the practical syllogism can be found in Aristotle—though without the explicit distinction between prudence and conscience. See D. J. Allan, "The Practical Syllogism," in *Autour d'Aristote: Festschrift für A. Mansion* (Louvain, 1955), pp. 325–340.

2. See *De Veritate* q. 17, a. 1: "Nomen enim conscientiae significat applicationem scientiae ad aliquem actum particularem." (The term "conscience" signifies the application of knowledge to some particular act.) A genuine act of the conscience consists, then, in an "*applicatio*" of knowledge that can be revealed or mediated through a freely acknowledged authority.

3. In his commentary on Thomas, Cajetan pointed this out elegantly: the acts of the practical reason (he is discussing synderesis and prudence) are in themselves (*in actu exercito*) preceptive acts; and yet in each case we would discuss them *in actu signato* (that is, in reflection), and this betrays their nature. He calls the final practical judgment a "*conclusio praeceptiva*, non in actu signato, id est, *ergo hoc est mihi nunc praecipiendum, eligendum, prosequendum*; sed in actu exercito, id est, *ergo actualiter sum in exercitio iudicii, praecepti, electionis, prosecutionis*." (not in a signified act, such as "therefore I must command, choose, pursue this"; but in an actual act, such as "therefore I am actually in the act of judging, commanding, choosing, pursuing.") Finally, Cajetan clarifies the difficulty in our speaking about the acts of the practical reason: "This is what deceives many [*multos decipit*] in this matter: because these propositions, belonging to the *synderesis* as much as they do to prudence, are discussed in reflection [*in actu signato*]; and yet their nature and power is seen in the actual act [*in actu exercito*]." *In I–II,* q. 58, a. 5, *Comm. VIII,* ed. Leonina.

4. See, for example, the confusion of conscience and prudence in Furger, *Gewissen und Klugheit.* Just as questionable is the concept of the "doubling" of the judgment of the conscience, which is in any case a reflection of the same mistake. A certain "synthesis" of misinterpretations of the act of the conscience, the object of the action, and the structure of the *actus humanus* can be found in J. Fuchs, "*Operatio* und *operatum* in dictamine conscientiae," in *Thomistica Morum Principia,* vol. 2 (Rome, 1961), pp. 71–79. For more detailed treatment of this theme and on Fuchs's concept, see below, Part II, chapter 9 on "Physicalism and the Naturalistic Fallacy in the 'Weighing of Goods.' "

5. One could probably distinguish a natural law *in fieri* (as prescriptive subject matter of the reason) from a natural law *in facto esse* (descriptive subject matter of the reflective reason). The truth of the matter is

that the human being is scarcely aware of the existence of the natural law *as* law *in fieri* (that is to say, of one's own part in the constitution of the natural law in his own behavior). One becomes aware of this ordering of rational action only when one reflects upon moral knowledge that has already been acquired. See the text of *Gaudium et Spes,* 16: "In the depth of his conscience man discovers a law that he has not given to himself. . . by conscience is revealed in a wonderful way that law which is fulfilled by the love of God and neighbor." See chapter 1, note 18.

6. On this see *De Veritate,* q. 22, a.4; *Contra Gentiles,* III, c. 111. The word play *non agunt sed magis aguntur* cannot be reproduced in German or English.

7. ". . . lex quaedam regula est et mensura actuum, secundum quam inducitur aliquis ad agendum, vel ab agendo retrahitur; dicitur enim lex a 'ligando' quia obligat ad agendum" (*I–II,* q. 90, a. 1).

8. ". . . quaedam rationis ordinatio ad bonum commune, ab eo qui curam communitatis habet, promulgata" (*I–II,* q. 90, a. 4). The *lex naturalis* is also related to the *bonum commune* (a. 2).

9. In q. 94, a. 2, the terms *imperium* and *praeceptum* are used interchangeably as synonyms.

10. This will be treated more fully in chapter 9.

11. The analytic distinction between the preceptive and reflective levels does not in any way imply that *in concreto* they are merely "juxtaposed" or even "successive." Reflection is spontaneous: like the conscience, it constantly accompanies the preceptive process in all its phases.

12. And this is also a *propositio universalis* (see q. 90, a. 1).

13. The same could not be said for the *distinction* between *ratio* and *natura;* but this is no full *disjunction,* since there is a natural act in the *ratio* itself.

14. Late antique gnosis and Manichaeanism provide historical examples of spiritualistic dualism; there was not only an "ascetic" or body-hating variant, there was also a "libertine" or "anything goes" school; see H. Jonas, *The Gnostic Religion* (2nd ed., Boston, 1963), especially the chapter "Gnostic Morality," pp. 270ff.). The study of historical precedents is of no small interest today, even if the justifications have changed. To quote one of Jonas' examples of a gnostic teaching, taken from Irenaeus: "for by his [Christ's] grace men were saved, not by righteous deeds. For works are not in their nature good [or bad], but by external dispensation." (p. 108). "The angels that created the world established "just actions" to lead men by such precepts into servitude." (p. 273). "Here we have, beyond the mere indifference of the 'subjectivist' argument and beyond the merely permissive privilege of freedom, a positive metaphysical interest in repudiating allegiance to all objective norms and thus a motive for their outright violation" (p. 273).

15. Of course, the ethics of Aristotle as well as those of St. Thomas are "teleological." Teleology and deontology, as stated before, really do not constitute mutually exclusive alternatives. This is because teleology is a process of norm *establishment*, whereas deontology is a process that exposes norms that are already established or (in certain contexts) not in need of any justification, or norms that are in principle incapable of being discursively established because they depend on revelation and can be understood only by the light of faith. Only in this latter case is "deontological" exposition a justification as well. See R. Spaemann, "Über die Unmöglichkeit einer universalteleologischen Ethik," *Philosophisches Jahrbuch* 88 (1981):70–89.

16. This view is represented *par excellence* by O. Lottin, "la Valeur des formules de saint Thomas d'Aquin concernant la loi naturelle" in *Mélanges Joseph Maréchal*, vol. 2 (Brussells, 1950), p. 368: "Il faut raisonner de même au sujet du rapprochement établi par saint Thomas entre la loi naturelle et la loi éternelle. Ce rapprochement est inutile, parce que lui, non plus, n'éclaire pas le concept même de loi naturelle." (One must draw the same conclusion with regard to the connection established by Thomas between the natural law and the eternal law. This connection is useless, because it does not explain anything about the concept of the natural law.) See, however, J. Finnis, *Natural Law and Natural Rights* (Oxford, 1980), pp. 398–403.

17. More extensive treatments of this question are found in chapters 5 and 6.

18. In this light, the point of departure of J. Messner's doctrine of natural law appears extremely questionable. He would like to assimilate the ethical concept of 'natural law' to the concept of natural law that is used in the natural sciences. "Just as the concept of the good should fit with the general meaning given to it by people, so, it seems to me, should the concept of 'natural law' fit in with the most common scientific terminology; the impression should not be given at the outset that "natural law" means something completely different in the human realm. . . . General scientific usage understands natural law to mean the constant, indwelling manner of operation or relation which things or living things possess by their own nature. The *most general concept of the natural law* in the human realm does not have to be anything else: it is the indwelling manner of operation of the human reason, for the control of actions in accordance with it" (*Das Naturrecht,* 6th ed. [Innsbruck and Vienna, 1966], p. 55). A large number of the stimulating and still worthwhile contributions of Messner are nevertheless, in part, very complicated and occasionally self-contradictory attempts to overcome the difficulties that resulted from this unfortunate starting point.

19. St. Thomas never calls nature a "rule" (*regula*), nor even a "remote rule" (*regula remota*) of human action or will. A rule is always reason: "The rule of the human reason is double. One is our own and like us in kind [*propinqua et homogenea*], namely the human reason, while the other is the first rule [*prima regula*], namely the eternal law, which is, as it were, the reason of God [*ratio Dei*]"(*I–II,* q. 71, a. 6); "There is a double measure of human actions: one, nearby and like us in kind [*propinqua et homogenea*], namely the reason [*ratio*]; the other, however, is the highest and transcendent [*suprema et excedens*], namely, God" (*II–II,* q. 17, a. 1). Here the relation between the two rules is one of first and second cause, which are not concurrent (or in competition with one another) but stand each at a different level; the first is constitutive of the second and at the same time contained in it: ". . . in all ordered causes, the effect depends more upon the first cause than upon the second, because the second cause does not act except in virtue of the first. That the human reason is a rule of human will [*regula voluntatis humanae*] by which rule its goodness [*bonitas*] is measured, comes from the eternal law, which is the mind of God [*ratio divina*; *I–II*, q. 19, a. 4].

20. For the concept of *inclinatio naturalis* and its history, I depend on the excellent study by D. Composta, *Natura e ragione. Studio sulle inclinazioni naturali in rapporto al diritto naturale* (Zurich, 1971).

21. "For the law of God is the natural inclination fixed in each creature [*cuilibet creaturae infixa*] for the purpose of each creature's doing what is suitable for it in accordance with its nature [*id quod convenit ei secundum naturam*]; and therefore, just as all things are held by the divine will, [*desiderio divino*], so are they held by His laws . . . and because of this it is said of the divine wisdom [see *Sapientia*, 8], that it gently sets all in order [*suaviter omnia disponit*]" (*In X de Div. Nom.*, lect. 1); "Now the inclination of each thing is in each thing according to the mode of the thing [*per modum eius*]. And so the natural inclination is in a natural thing in a natural way [*naturaliter in re naturali*]; and the inclination that is the sensitive appetite is in a sentient creature in a sensitive way [*sensibiliter in sentient*)]; and in the same way, an intelligent inclination, which is the act of the will, exists in an intellectual creature in an intelligible way [*intelligibiliter in intelligente*] as in its principal and proper subject." (*I,* q. 87, a. 4).

22. At this point it is important to distinguish the *actus proprius* (what is naturally suited) from the *actus debitus* (the morally good). The passage from the *Commentary on the Sentences* cited in the previous note makes the same distinction with another terminology: the *actus proprius* on the one hand, and the *actus conveniens* (or *competens fini*) on the other: "operationes *propriae* prodeunt *convenientes* fini"; the naturally specific acts must be oriented toward an end.

23. See *I–II,* q. 19, a. 2. For a more thorough analysis of the concepts of *ratio naturalis* and *imago*, see chapters 5 and 6.

24. This is illustrated also by the fact that in the *Summa Contra Gentiles*, the treatise on law is integrated with the treatise on providence. A parallel to this is found as well in *De Veritate*, q. 5 ("*De Providentia*").

25. Thus F. Böckle maintained that a second, passive participation of the eternal law came out of a misinterpretation of late scholasticism; see "Natur als Norm in der Moraltheologie," in F. Heinrich (ed.), *Naturgesetz und christliche Ethik* (Munich, 1970), p. 83. See, however, *I–II*, q. 93, a. 6: "Something is subject to the eternal law in a twofold manner [*duplex modus*] . . . in one way, to the extent that the eternal law is participated in through the mode of cognition [*per modum cognitionis*]; in another way, through the mode of action and passion [*per modum actionis et passionis*] to the extent that the eternal law is participated in through the mode of the first mover [*per modum principii motivi*]. And it is in this second way that irrational creatures are subject to the eternal law, as has been said. But because the rational creature has something proper to himself by being rational, *along with what he has in common with all creatures* [*commune omnibus creaturis*], *he is therefore subject to the eternal law according to both modes.*" This was stated earlier at *I–II*, q. 91, a. 2. More on the same topic will be found in chapters 5 and 6.

26. "Nè si dimentichi che per l'Aquinate il pensiero non ha funzione puramente succedanea nell' *inclinatio*, come abbiamo già notato: più che verificare la ragione costituisce l'ordine naturale" (It should not be forgotten that for Aquinas, thought does not have a purely surrogate function for the *inclinatio*, as we have already noted; more than merely verifying the natural order, the reason actually constitutes it.) Composta, *Natura e ragione*, 97.

27. "Thus under God as legislator various creatures have natural inclinations, in such a way that what is a law for one, is for another against the law [*quod uni est quodammodo lex, alteri sit contra legem*]. . . . Therefore the law for man, which he receives by the divine ordination in accordance with his own condition, is that he act according to reason [*ut secundum rationem operetur*]" *I–II,* q. 91, a. 6.

28. See K. Wojtyla, "The Problem of the Will in the Analysis of the Ethical Act," in *Person and Community: Selected Essays,* translated by Theresa Sandok, OSM (New York, 1993), pp. 3–22.

29. Even so, they are more than mere "ontological relations, which are in themselves morally indifferent, and have the quality of value only when purposes make demands, as the existential purposes of human behavior or society," as J. Messner expresses it (*Das Naturrecht*, p. 50). It would not be correct to speak of a moral *indifference* of natural inclina-

tions, but only of a moral *indetermination*. That which does not yet have the character of law, and yet forms the naturally given basis for it, can be called neither "indifferent" nor "premoral"; it already possesses in itself a *proportio ad rationem*, which has not yet been determined in relation to a *debitum*, in the order of moral actions. Strictly speaking, Messner here represents a position that can scarcely be distinguished from "teleological ethics" or "consequentialism."

30. A very confusing formula has been used in this connection by Böckle, "Natur als Normin Moraltheologie," p. 81: "The natural inclinations, so to speak, 'mark out the territory' where man must walk in his self-determination." In dependence on Arntz (see the section "The Moral Object, and How It Is Constituted," in this chapter), Böckle conceives the natural inclinations as a kind of "unformed" matter, which also emerge from a region (described in Rahner's terminology as "subpersonal" or "subhuman") that is somehow completely different from the reason; he overlooks the *ratio naturalis*, which is itself a natural inclination, as well as the personal aspect of the integration of all these inclinations in the *suppositum*, which will be discussed later.

31. This can also be said of the *horos* and the *horizein* of the *logos* of Aristotelian ethics. See the fitting remark of R. A. Gauthier (in R. A. Gauthier and J. Y. Jolif, *L'Ethique à Nichomaque,* and ed. [Löwen and Paris, 1970], vol. 2, p. 147f.): "Lorsque le verbe *horizein*, au passif et au moyen, est suivi d'un datif, le mot au datif ne désigne pas la faculté (le juge, le législateur) qui préscrit, mais la norme par rapport à laquelle la détermination est faite. . . . Notre text veut donc dire, non pas que le juste milieu est déterminé par un *logos*, mais qu'il est déterminé par rapport à un *logos*, qui est sa norme, *horos*." (When used with the dative, the middle or passive of *horizein* the dative does not designate the prescribing agent (the judge, the legislator) but rather the norm by which the determination is made. . . . The text means not that the just mean is determined by a *logos*, but that it is determined with respect to a *logos*, which is its norm, its *horos*.) See also J. de Finance, "Autonomie et théonomie," in M. Zalba, ed., *L'agire morale,* vol. 5 of *Tommaso d'Aquino nel suo settimo centenario* (Naples, 1974), p. 244. ". . . celle-ci (la raison) ne joue pas seulement un rôle *déclaratif*. . . . Au contraire, la raison est le présupposé de l'ordre moral. . . . L'ordre posé par la raison pratique n'a de sens et de consistance que par rapport à elle et c'est en cela que son rôle est ici constituant. Elle entre dans la formalité de son objet." (The reason does not play only a declarative role. . . . On the contrary, the reason is presupposed by the moral order. . . . The order presented by the practical reason has no integrity apart from it, and it is in the reason that its role is constituted. The reason enters into the formality of its object.)

32. A. Auer, "Die Autonomie des Sittlichen nach Thomas von Aquin," in K. Demmer und B. Schüller, eds., *Christlich glauben und handeln* (Düsseldorf, 1977), p. 37.

33. See also J. Maritain, *Neuf Leçons sur les notions premières de la philosophie morale,* (Paris, 1951), p. 48: "Nous sommes là en présence de la fonction explicatrice, justificatrice, manifestatrice de la verité, qui appartient à la philosophie morale. La philosophie morale est une connaissance de second regard. . . . Le philosophe découvre la loi dans l'expérience morale de l'humanité, il la dégage, il ne la fait pas; il n'est pas un législateur. . . . Il n'announce pas la loi, il réfléchit sur elle et l'explique." (Here we are in the presence of the explicating, justifying, and manifesting function of the truth, which pertains to moral philosophy. Moral philosophy is a knowledge of *the second look*. . . . The philosopher discovers the law in the moral experience of humanity, he disengages it, he does not make it; he is not a legislator. . . . He does not proclaim the law, he reflects upon it and explains it.) The second and third "lessons" are excellent expositions of the concept of the practical reason. This work is available in English translation by C. N. Borgerhoff, *An Introduction to the Basic Problems of Moral Philosophy* (Petersham, Mass., 1990): 52. The quoted passage is found on p. 52 of Borgerhoff's translation.

34. What can provisionally be called the "practical syllogism" is again only a reflective formulation of the act of the practical reason. The *conclusio* of the "syllogistic" act of the discursive practical reason, embedded in the intentionality of the act of striving/willing, is of course not a "statement," but rather a choice of action (*electio*), which is *immediately* followed by action (*ex electione immediate sequitur opus, In II Sent.,* d. 40, q. 1, a. 2, ad 1). The conclusion is therefore an action, as Aristotle maintains in the *De Motu Animalium*: *to symperasma . . . praxis estin* (7, 701a, 19).

35. *I–II*, q. 91, a. 3, ad 2um: ". . . ratio humana secundum se non est regula rerum: sed principia naturaliter ei indita [the principles naturally planted in it] sunt quaedam regulae generales et mensurae omnium eorum quae sunt per homines agenda, quorum ratio naturalis est mensura, licet non sit mensura eorum quae sunt a natura."

36. This clarifies, for example, the differentiated argumentation about the "naturalness" of marriage; see *In IV Sent.*, d. 26, q. 1, a. 1, sol. and ad 1um.

37. *See I-II,* q. 94, a.4, ad 4um: "Just as the reason is dominant [*dominatur*] in man and commands [*imperat*] the other powers, so it is fitting that all the natural inclinations that pertain to the other powers be ordered in accordance with the reason [*secundum rationem*]. Whence it is universally [*communiter*] held as right that all human inclinations be directed in acccordance with reason."

38. This holds for "the things pertaining to the end" (*ea quae sunt ad finem*), the so-called "means," as well as for the end itself; in the former case, it involves the practical intellect insofar as it is *consiliativus et ratiocinativus* (the virtue of which is prudence); the latter involves the natural reason itself, which is concerned with the *rectitudo* of the willing/striving: "In his autem quae sunt ad finem, rectitudo rationis consistit in conformitate ad appetitum finis debiti [practical truth]. Sed tamen et ipse appetitus finis debiti praesupponit rectam apprehensionem de fine, quae est per rationem" (In these things that are means to an end, the rightness of the reason consists in the conformity to the seeking for a good end. But even the seeking of a good end presupposes the right apprehension of the end, which is through reason.) (*I–II,* q. 19, a. 1, ad 2um).

39. The *actus exterior* is not simply identical with the *actus externus*, or an actually "external" behavior like speaking, talking, striking, walking, and so on It refers instead to an *actus exterior* of the will, that is, the *actus imperatus*, the act that the will brings about by way of an *imperium* over another power, in contrast to an *actus elicitus*, which the will "brings out" of itself; the *actus exterior* in this sense is treated at *I–II,* q. 20. (More detail on this can be found in chapter 9, section "Physicalism and the Naturalistic Fallacy in the 'Weighing of Goods' ").

40. G. Grisez has especially emphasized this in "The First Principle of Practical Reason," in A. Kenny, ed., *Aquinas: A Collection of Critical Essays* (London, 1969), pp. 359ff.; see *In IV Sent.*, d. 33, q. 1, a. 1.

41. On this see also *De Veritate* q. 22, a. 4.

42. This is exactly how Thomas defines the *voluntarium* in *I–II,* q. 6, a. 2.

43. A. Scola has shown this with particular clarity in his excellent study, *La fondazione della legge naturale nello* Scriptum super Sententiis *di san Tommaso d'Aquino* (Freiburg, Switzerland, 1982).

44. "Proprium liberi arbitrii est electio" (*I,* q. 83, a. 3). See *De Malo*, q. 6, a. 1. ". . . just as in natural things there is a form, which is the principle of its action [*principium actionis*] and an inclination going with the form [*inclinatio consequens formam*], which is called the natural appetite [*naturalis appetitus*], from which action follows; *but the difference lies in this*: the form of the natural thing is a form that is individuated by the matter; and so the inclination that goes with it has a single determination [*est determinata ad unum*], but the comprended form [*forma intellecta*] is a universal under which many things can be comprehended; wherefore since actions are singulars, in which there is nothing that attains the power of a universal, the inclination of the will remains undetermined toward many [*indeterminata se habens ad multa*]."

45. This would apply both to the intentional and to the elective as-

pect of moral virtue, which is, according to Thomas (who follows Aristotle), a *habitus electivus* [*hexis prohairetikê*]. To this action belongs the determination of the "virtuous mean" (*medium virtutis*), which is a "rational mean" (*medium rationis*); moral virtue is ordered to this *medium* naturally, in virtue of an *inclinatio naturalis ad virtutem*; there is still need of prudence to make this operatively concrete (see *II–II,* q. 47, a. 7, ad 3um). In the corpus of this article we read: ". . . this very thing, the being-conformed-to right reason [*conformari rationi rectae*], is the proper end of any moral virtue [*finis proprius cuiuslibet moralis virtutis*] . . . and this end has been furnished to man in accordance with natural reason: for natural reason dictates to each person that he act in accordance with reason [*ut secundum rationem operetur*]. But just how, and by what means a person is to reach the rational mean in action [*in operando attingat medium rationis*] pertains to the work of prudence."

46. This is because of the fundamental orientation of the "will as nature" (*voluntas ut natura*): ". . . naturalis inclinatio voluntatis est ad bonum virtutis." *De Malo*, q. 1, a. 4.

47. See *I–II*, q. 56, a. 4:. ". . . irascibilis et concupiscibilis dupliciter considerari possunt. Uno modo secundum se, inquantum sunt partes appetitus sensitivi. Et hoc modo [that is, in the abstract-ontological manner of treatment, at the level of the *genus naturae*] non competit eis, quod sint subiectum virtutis. Alio modo possunt considerari inquantum participant rationem, *per hoc quod natae sunt rationi obedire*. Et sic irascibilis vel concupiscibilis potest esse subiectum virtutis humanae: sic enim est principium humani actus, inquantum participat rationem." (The irascible and the concupiscible can be considered in two ways. In one way, they are considered in themselves and to the extent that they are parts of the sensitive appetite, and in this way it does not pertain to them to be the subject of virtue. But they can also be considered in another way: to the extent that they participate in reason, *because they have been born to obey reason*. And thus the irascible and the concupiscible can be the subject of human virtue: for something is a principle of human action, insofar as it participates in the reason.) The second point of view is based on their integration into the suppositum, which will be treated at a later stage.

48. The importance of this aspect has been well emphasized by G. Grisez in his article "Dualism and the New Morality," in M. Zalba, ed., *L'agire morale*, vol. 5 of *Tommaso d'Aquino nel suo settimo centenario* (Naples, 1974), pp. 323–330. The idea of man as a "spirit in the world" or as an "incarnate spirit" (which appears to underlie the anthropology of Karl Rahner) I find extrememly problematic, since it is fundamentally dualistic. See also G. Grisez, "A New Formulation of a Natural-Law

Argument Against Contraception," *The Thomist,* 30 (1966): 349: "Man is not an incarnate spirit; he is a rational animal. The dualism implied in the definition of man as an incarnate spirit threatens to become a totalitarianism which will distort the true shape of man's nature and thus destroy the only solid foundation for a realistic personalism. And Christian personalism must be realistic, as has been declared repeatedly in the past against Gnostics, Manichees, Cathars, and Jansenists."

49. In truly dualistic positions, according to which man is thought to have a "right to control" over his nature (in the sense of autonomously "giving moral meaning" to it), there is a failure to distinguish between the "nature" that surrounds man and the "nature" that constitutes the human *suppositum,* or what man himself *is*; an example of this is found in L. Oeing-Hanhoff, "Der Mensch: Natur oder Geschichte?" in F. Heinrich, ed., *Naturgesetz und christliche Ethik. Zur wissenschaftlichen Diskussion nach Humanae Vitae* (Munich, 1970) p. 41, where, with reference to Hegel, the author states: "The task of morality is really just as with external nature, which is to be shaped according to the needs of man—so also in the realm of man's own nature, morality means spiritualizing, moralizing, and humanizing natural drives and ends."

50. See the fitting remarks of Maritain, *Neuf Leçons,* p. 58: "Tout d'abord les tendances et les inclinations naturelles ne fournissent pas à la philosophie de bons instruments d'argumentation. Elles apportent une matière expérimentale précieuse, mais les raisonnements et démonstrations de la philosophie morale doivent procéder par la détermination conceptuelle, l'élucidation scientifique de ce qui est conforme ou non à la raison et aux fins de la nature humaine; la philosophie a à faire la théorie des inclinations naturelles, à expliquer leur existence et leur rôle, non à les invoquer comme preuve. Mais d'autre part, ces mêmes tendences ou inclinations naturelles sont la voie normale, la voie naturelle, et la *seule voie,* de la connaissance naturelle—non pas philosophique, mais préphilosophique—des valeurs morales." (On the one hand, the natural tendencies and inclinations do not furnish philosophy with good instruments of argumentation. They provide precious experimental materials, but the reasonings and demonstrations of moral philosophy should proceed by way of conceptual determination, or the elucidation of that which is conformable or not to reason and to the ends of human nature; philosophy has to make a theory of the natural inclinations in order to explain their existence and their role, but not to invoke them as proof. On the other hand, these same natural tendencies or inclinations are the normal way, the natural way, the *only way,* for there to be a natural knowledge—not philosophical but prephilosophical in nature—of moral values.) The passage is found on p. 63 of Borgerhoff's translation, *An Introduction to the Basic Problems of Moral Philosophy.*

51. See, *e.g.* *I–II,* q. 59, a. 4: "Moral virtue perfects the appetitive part of the soul by ordering it toward the good of the reason [*ordinando ipsam in bonum rationis*]. Now the good of the reason is that which has been governed or ordered in accordance with reason [*secundum rationem moderatum seu ordinatum*]. *Unde circa omne id quod contingit ratione ordinari et moderari, contingit esse virtutem moralem.*" (Therefore there happens to be a moral virtue concerned with everything that happens to be ordered or governed by reason.) This also provides the criterion for determining which natural inclinations, tendencies, or drives are morally significant, and which, on the other hand, are indifferent to the moral ordering of actions.

52. This *ordo virtutis* also corresponds to an *ordinatio "ad finem communem totius humanae vitae*" (*I–II,* q. 21, a. 2, ad 2um).

53. The doctrine of prudence as the *forma virtutis* belongs to this same context.

54. See *I–II*, q. 94, a. 3: Sed si loquamur de actibus virtuosis secundum seipsos, prout scilicet in propriis speciebus considerantur, sic non omnes actus virtuosi sunt de lege naturae. Multa enim secundum virtutem fiunt, ad quae natura non primo inclinat; sed per rationis inquisitionem ea homines adinvenerunt, quasi utilia ad vivendum. (But if we should speak about virtuous acts in themselves, that is to say, insofar as they are considered in their proper kinds, not all virtuous acts are of the natural law; for many things take place in accordance with virtue to which nature does not at first incline us; but people have found them out in addition [*adinvenerunt*], through the inquiry of reason, as being useful for living.)

55. See *I–II*, q. 56, a. 6: Justice pertains to three areas: to the good of the *species* (*bonum commune speciei*); to the good of other persons, and thereby the *bonum commune* of the human community; and to God, the *bonum commune totius universi*. This last aspect of justice is in fact the virtue of religion. By nature, however, the will seeks its own good more than that of others. If this becomes a habit (vice), then it is pride, egoism, envy, and so on, or "injustice" in general. Justice, by contrast, comes into play in willing the good for others, and *aequalitas ad alterum* in external actions. Thus friendship is part of the virtue of justice, since friendship consists in seeking and loving the good of another as one's own.

56. *De Verit.*, q. 11, a. 1. Next to the *inchoatio*, which the human being possesses specifically, or qua human being, there is also another one of an individual kind, caused by individual characteristics, which corresponds to the Aristotelian *aretê physikê.*

57. See *I–II*, q. 18, a. 8: Thomas is able to conceive of the indifference of an action *in specie* by maintaining that "as such" or "in itself" it

has no relation to the *ordo rationis*, such as *"picking up a speck from the floor"* or *"going to the field"* and so on. It is an entirely different matter, however, to consider acts that possess in themselves a *proportio ad rationem* as if they were independent from such relationship (e.g., the natural inclination of a man and a woman to be joined); this would involve the use of biological, psychological, and physiological methods that exclude any type of ethical judgment. The judgment that an act *is indifferent* is already a moral judgment.

58. Thomas also speaks of a *consideratio absoluta*, that is, "abstracted" from the context of moral judgment. *In IV Sent.*, d. 16, q. 3, a. 1, qla. 2, ad 2: "Some acts by definition [*ex suo genere*] are evil or good . . . however, whatever it is that causes the act to be of such a kind, although it be due to its substance in respect to its morality [*ex genere moris*], nevertheless it does not pertain to its substance [*est extra substantiam eius*] insofar as the substance of the act is absolutely considered [*secundum quod consideratur. . . . absolute*]; wherefore some acts are the same in respect to their nature [*in specie naturae*] that differ in respect to their morality [*in specie moris*], such as fornication and the marital act." Both acts, considered absolutely as sexual acts, are identical in their *genus naturae* and in the various biological, physiological, psychological, and even affective aspects that correspond to this; nevertheless, the human sexual act is no "indifferent act" (*actus indifferens*) if it is considered *in specie moris*. A confusion of "abstract" or "absolute" consideration and the view that holds such acts to be "indifferent" as such appears clearly, for example, in R. A. McCormick, "Neuere Überlegungen zur Unveränderlichkeit sittlicher Normen," in W. Kerber, ed., *Sittliche Normen. Zum Problem ihrer allgemeinen und unwandelbaren Geltung* (Düsseldorf, 1982), p. 53; L. Janssens, "Ontic Evil and Moral Evil," *Louvain Studies*, 4 (1972): 115–156. This confusion is also found in the writings of Arntz, Böckle, Schüller, and many others.

59. Unfortunately this point is often overlooked. An example is provided in Janssens, "Ontic Evil and Moral Evil," p. 121, n. 34, and pp. 135 f.; the bodily dimension of the human being is here conceived as simply a "material part of the material world," and as *human* only to the extent that this "material part of the material world" participates in the subjectivity of the human individual. Accordingly the body is understood as a "means to action," a means of subjectivity, whereby the latter is able to act in the outside world. The "human" thus becomes reduced to subjectivity: it is no longer a *personal* view of man, but a *personalistic-spiritualistic* one. The consequences are very visible in Janssens, among other ways in his characterization of "external action" (*actus exterior*) as "external *event*" (p. 120), which has no moral meaning in itself, but only insofar as it participates in the "subjectivity" of man as a "means."

60. Some time ago S. Pinckaers pointed out this danger emphatically: see *Le Renouveau de la morale* (Tournai, 1964), pp. 131ff. The general intention of Pinckaers has proven to be very opportune, even if his solution was not fully thought out in some of its aspects. See also the somewhat exaggerated criticism and refinements by T. G. Belmans, *Le Sens objectif de l'agir humain* (Vatican City, 1980), pp. 280–289. A reified and naturalistic conception of the moral object also was current among many earlier moral theologians, and persists today—this is certainly one reason why many of them were unable to understand *Humanae Vitae.*

61. *I–II,* q. 18, a. 2, ad 2um. One of Arntz's central misunderstandings should be pointed out here. This author appears to understand the material character of the natural inclinations as being analogous to the *materia ex qua.* Consequently, he can find no access to the teaching of Thomas that these natural tendencies *already belong* to the natural law. As soon as they are understood to be "indifferent matter" (as Arntz and Böckle, who follow him closely on this point, both do), they cannot be taken as a constitutive component of the natural law. They cannot be conceived as *bona humana,* as they are by Thomas. See J.Th.C. Arntz, "Die Entwicklung des naturrechtlichen Denkens innerhalb des Thomismus," in F. Böckle, ed., *Das Naturrecht im Disput* (Düsseldorf, 1966), pp. 87–120. In Arntz's view, to hold to a normative significance of the natural inclinations would lead to a "doubling" of the natural law (p. 55). Just like M. Wittmann earlier, he is unable to bring the two aspects together, and concludes too one-sidedly: "The natural inclinations offer themselves to man only as the material, in which *he himself* must create rational order" (p. 100). With this Arntz overlooks (chiefly) the cognitive meaning and normativity that the natural inclinations provide to the act of the natural (practical) reason.

62. *In II Sent.,* d. 36, q. un., a. 5, ad 4um. In the ad 5um it is made equivalent to the object, which is called the *finis proximus.* See also *I–II,* q. 72, a. 3, ad 2um; *De Malo* q. 2, a. 4, ad 9: "The proximate end of an action [*finis proximus actus*] is the same as the object, and it receives its *species* from this." And *I–II,* q. 73, a. 3, ad 1um: "Although the object is the matter concerning which [*materia circa quam*] an act is carried out [*terminatur*], nevertheless it has the character of an end [*rationem finis*] insofar as the intention of the agent is brought into it [*fertur in ipsum*], as said above. Now the form of a moral act depends upon the end [*dependet ex fine*], as is clear from what has been said before." Here the "intention" means simply the inner act of the will, which, insofar as it is an act of an acting subject, can be called an "intention" (*intentio*). This is a clear example of how rarely one comes upon a distinction between the "subjective" and "objective" elements of morality. The objective is always

also subjective; the subjective is "good" only to the extent that it is also objectively "good," that is, in accordance with reason.

63. This applies to the object of the *electio* as such, as well as to any object, that forms itself with the subject matter of an *intentio,* out of an *electio* in regard to an *intentio finis*; then the subject of the *electio* (the concrete action) is related materially to the object of the intention as its *ratio finis,* but then there is only a single object, because means and end are willed together in a single act of the will; one chooses for the sake of a goal. See *I–II,* q. 12, a. 4, ad 2um; *In II Sent.*, d. 38, q.1, a. 4, ad 1: "finis et id quod est ad finem, inquantum sunt huiusmodi consideratum, non sunt diversa obiecta, sed unum obiectum in quo finis sicut formale est, quasi ratio quaedam volendi; sed id quod est ad finem, est sicut materiale, sicut etiam lumen et color sunt unum obiectum." (the end and what pertains to the end are, insofar as they are considered this way, not diverse objects, but one object in which the end is as it were formal, as a certain manner of willing; but that which pertains to the end is as it were material, just as light and color are one object).

64. Or also as bodies to color; see *De Caritate*, a. 4: "Sed in obiecto consideratur aliquid ut formale et aliquid ut materiale. Formale autem in obiecto est id secundum quod obiectum refertur ad potentiam vel habitum; materiale autem id in quo fundatur: ut si loquamur de obiecto potentiae visivae, obiectum eius formale est color, vel aliquid huiusmodi; in quantum enim aliquid coloratum est, in tantum visibile est; sed materiale in obiecto est corpus cui accidit color." (But in the object something is considered as formal and something as material. The formal in an object is that according to which the object is referred to a potency or habitus; the material is that in which it is founded: so that if we should speak about the object of the power of sight, its formal object is color, or something like that; for insofar as something is colored, it is visible; but the material of an object is a body to which color is added.) The example that is used (*mutatis mutandis*) makes very clear what Thomas intends to say: the color (that is, the *ratio visibilitatis*) as well as the bodies indicate in each case the *whole* object, but from different standpoints. The eye apprehends in both instances "only" colors or "only" bodies; it apprehends bodies also *through* the color; and furthermore, there are no colors without bodies to which they belong. If, therefore, we distinguish the *materia* from the formal aspect (the *ordo ad finem* or the *ordo rationis*), it is no longer "visible" in its moral specificity as *materia circa quam*; on the other hand, without *materia* it can provide no *ordo ad finem* nor any *ordinatio rationis*.

65. This error is found especially in Janssens, "Ontic Evil and Moral Evil." *Louvain Studies,* 4 (1972) pp. 115–156.

66. "Bonitas autem vel malitia quam habet actus exterior secundum se, propter debitam materiam et debitas circumstantias, non derivatur a voluntate, sed magis a ratione." (The goodness or badness that an exterior action has in itself, in view of its proper matter and proper circumstances, is not derived from the will but from the reason.) (*I–II,* q. 20, a. 1).

67. "Actus exterior est obiectum voluntatis, inquantum proponitur voluntati a ratione ut quoddam bonum apprehensum et ordinatum per rationem; et sic est prius quam bonum actus voluntatis. Inquantum vero consistit in executione operis, est effectus voluntatis, et sequitur voluntatem." (*I–II,* q. 20, a. 1, ad 1um).

68. Here is perhaps the decisive misinterpretation of Janssens: he insinuates that the will can be orientated toward "ontic" goods qua ontic, and that it is possible to will ontic evils qua ontic, and to raise these to the status of the "goal of the intention" (*finis intentionis*). Only in this case, he says, is there moral evil. Such an objectification of ontic goods by the will, to the exclusion of the reason and its *ordinatio* of moral qualification and specification, is nevertheless impossible and contradicts the nature of the human will as an intellectual or rational striving power (*appetitus in ratione* or *appetitus intellectualis*). Janssens' argument, in other words, is naturalistic. We will return to this question in chapter 9.

69. Janssens simply identifies the act of the will with the *actus interiori*, the *actus exterior* (which is also an act of the will, to be sure, but a "commanded act" [*actus imperatus*]) he nevertheless conceives as an "*exterior event.*" This is why the act of the will and an intention are finally the same thing for Janssens. Only when this "exterior event" is an ontic evil and at the same time the object of an intention, is there any question of a morally evil act. The function of the practical reason appears to be omitted completely, and the argumentation is naturalistic.

70. See, for example, *In IV Sent.* d. 16, q. 3, a. 1, qla 2, ad 3.

71. *I–II,* q. 18, a. 8. It should also be observed that the same mistake is found in an influential article by P. Knauer: "Das rechtverstandene Prinzip der Doppelwirkung als Grundnorm jeder Gewissensentscheidung," in *Theologie und Glaube,* 57 (1967): 107–133. This article appeared the same year in an English translation in *Natural Law Forum* 12 (1967): 132–162, with the title, "The Hermeneutic Function of the Principle of Double Effect," and was printed again in C. E. Curran and R. A. McCormick, *Readings in Moral Theology,* vol. 1 (New York, 1979), pp. 1–39; see p. 2: "The most exact [definition of the 'morally good'] is the third definition, according to which the morally good is the 'simply good'. *By 'good' is here meant nothing other than the physical goodness of any reality whatsoever,* that goodness by which something becomes desirable

in any sense, according to the axiom *bonum et ens convertuntur.* What is 'simply' good, and therefore morally good, is such a value, if it is willed in such a way that the physical evil possibly associated with it remains objectively beyond the intention of the person willing. *Then the good alone, that is, 'the simply good', determines the intention* [my italics]." This means that the will is determined by the 'physical goodness of any reality whatsoever'! For Knauer, the practical reason has no influence upon the (in)forming of the practical good ('the morally good'); its task is limited, instead, to providing suitable reasons for the comparison of different 'physical goods.'

72. An act is thus "secundum se [objectively] malus . . . according as the action is in discord with the rectitude of the reason. A certain natural inclination toward its own end has been built into every nature [*unicuique . . . naturae indita est*]; thus there is a certain natural rectitude in the reason, through which it is inclined toward an end: therefore that which leads it away [*abducit*] from its end, is in discord with reason [*discordans a ratione*]" *In II Sent.*, d. 42, q. 2, a. 5.

73. At this point it would also be possible to discuss the constitution of prudence through the *fines virtutum*, and the double (intentional and elective) aspect of moral virtue, as well as the relationship between synderesis and prudence. See *II–II*, q. 47, a. 6.

74. Thus Thomas can say that *perversitas rationis repugnat naturae rationis* (*In II Ethic.*, lect. 2) and that *corrupta ratio non est ratio.* (*In II Sent.*, d. 24, q. 3, a. 3, ad 3um).

75. On this see Karol Wojtyla, *The Acting Person,* trans. Andrzej Potocki (Dordrecht and Boston, 1979), ch. 5.

76. See *I–II*, q. 91, a. 6, ad 3um; q. 94, a. 3, ad 1um.

77. This formulation of the Roman jurist Ulpian which had become fixed in tradition and is cited by Thomas in *I–II,* q. 94, a. 2 as well as in his *Commentary on the Sentences*, has its origin in the juridical tradition of natural law. Thomas accepted it with its limited application, and made very well-defined room for it in the context of his own teaching on the natural law. It expresses the fact that man is a species of the genus "animal." If someone does not like the formula of Ulpian, there is very little one can do about it. Charles E. Curran's rather unsophisticated thesis that the influence of Ulpian upon the Thomistic concept of the natural law leads to an inconsistent wavering between "naturalism" and "rationality," cannot be accepted. Unfortunately, Curran limits himself for the most part to the Ulpian citations by Thomas, and a more precise analysis of Ulpian's meaning and influence is lacking; see C. E. Curran, *Themes in Fundamental Moral Theology* (Notre Dame and London, 1977), p. 35ff. A more differentiated view is found in M. B. Crowe, *The Changing Profile of the Natural Law* (The Hague, 1977), p. 46ff, 141ff.

78. Marriage, because of the rational nature of man, is also a *communitas* that attains its specific nature by itself, through the foundation upon which it rests. This is why the "social" aspect of marriage has been called a *finis secundarius*; not because it is only supplementary, but rather because it is founded upon the *finis primarius*, and without this would not be possible. The "third" end of marriage as well, its sacramental character, would likewise not exist without the other two. And yet in the context of Christian life it is the decisive and most important one and includes the other two goals. The "order of rank" as first, second, or third signifies only the constitutive context, but does not imply a judgment of value about the relative importance of each end. The relationship is analogous to that between the *actus primus* (substance) and the *actus secundus* (the *operatio*); the former is foundational: without it there would be no *actus secundus*; the latter, on the other hand, is higher in the order of perfection (*operatio est ultima perfectio rei*), since it includes the foundational within itself, presupposes it, and completes it. The doctrine of the "first and second ends of marriage" is to be understood in the same way.

79. See *I.* q. 98, a. 1: "Est autem considerandum, quod alio modo intentio naturae fertur ad corruptibiles et incorruptibiles creaturas. . . . Quia igitur in rebus corruptibilibus nihil est perpetuum et semper manens nisi species, bonum speciei est de principali intentione naturae, ad cuius conservationem naturalis generatio ordinatur. Substantiae vero incorruptibiles manent semper non solum secundum speciem, sed etiam secundum individua: *et ideo ipsa individua sunt de principali intentione naturae.*" (It must be considered, that the intention of nature is directed in a different way for corruptible and for incorruptible creatures. . . . Since there is nothing perpetual and everlasting in corruptible things except for the species, the good of the species is nature's principal intention, for natural generation is ordained to the preservation of the species. Now incorruptible substances always remain, not only in virtue of their species, but even in virtue of themselves as individuals: *and thus individuals are nature's principal intention.*")

80. See John Paul II, encyclical letter *Familiaris Consortio*, nr. 28.

81. See Second Vatican Council, pastoral constitution *Gaudium et Spes*, nr. 52: "Parents should regard as their proper mission the task of transmitting human life and educating those to whom it has been transmitted. They should realize that they are thereby cooperators with the love of God the Creator, and are, so to speak, the interpreters of that love." See also John Paul II, speech before the Seminario di Studio, "La procreazione responsabile," *La osservatore romano*, Oct. 18, 1984, p. 3: "At the origin of each person stands a creative act of God; no man begins to exist by chance: each one is an aim of the creative love of God.

Because of this fundamental truth of faith and reason, the ability to procreate that has been inscribed in human sexuality is, in its deepest sense, a cooperation with the creative power of God. This truth is also the reason why husband and wife are not lords and masters over this procreative power, and yet are called to take part, in and through it, in the creative decision of God." See also J. Seifert, "Der Unterschied zwischen natürlicher Empfängnisregelung und künstlicher Empfängnisverhütung," in E. Wenisch, ed., *Elternschaft und Menschwürde* (Vallendar-Schönstatt, 1984), pp. 191–242.

82. It is very important to emphasize this in the face of many problems, for example, the correct assessment of the moral dimension of suicide. As far as the right of man to have control over human life is concerned, one cannot argue on the otherwise appropriate principle of the *causa secunda*, because as a *causa secunda* alone man does not have the power to hand on human life; he can do this only in cooperation with an immediately creative divine causality, so that he is comparable to a *causa instrumentalis*; the life of each human person is, in a very special and unique way, both "gift" and "loan," which man controls not as something he owns but as something for which he has (temporary) responsibility. Unfortunately, Bruno Schüller's criticism of traditional arguments for the prohibition of killing passes over this decisive aspect and reduces the metaphysical relationship of man's creatureliness to God's "exclusive right of dominance" (which exists in any case for all creatures; see Schüller, *Die Begründung sittlicher Urteile*, 2nd ed. (Düsseldorf, 1980), pp. 238–251). The accusation of "anthropomorphism" that Josef Fuchs has directed toward so-called "creationism" (immediate creation of the soul by God), appears to me to be based on a misconception about divine causality (see Fuchs, "Das Gottesbild und die Moral innerweltlichen Handelns," in *Stimmen der Zeit* 202 [1984] pp. 363–382). According to Fuchs, by this ("creationist") argument, God coöperates with the parents through His intervention. By creating the soul, God retains for Himself an inner-worldly prerogative. The parents would only be causes of the "biological substratum," and God the cause of the person. But God works in the world only through second causes; therefore the parents must also be causes of the whole person, that is, of the soul just as they are of the body. Now this position—that according to "creationism" the parents would only be causes of the "organic substratum," or that God is only a "cooperative" cause within the categorial world—is nevertheless mistaken. The parents are rather causes of the ensoulment, and of the personhood, but in an instrumental manner. This means that God does not work "next" to the parents within the categorial world, but instead in the moment of conception raises the parents from the

level of second causality to the level of creative causality: the parents work cooperatively with God, and not vice versa. This is not an anthropomorphic explanation; rather it appears that Fuchs has understood the "creationist" argument in an anthropomorphic manner, and then criticizes it on that basis.

83. Thomas grounds the "naturalness" of marriage above all in the context of the virtue of justice: in regard to the *finis primarius* (of procreation), extramarital conception is an injustice to the child (*In IV Sent.*, d. 26, q. 1, a. 1); in regard to the *finis secundarius* (of unity), Thomas is concerned most of all with the equality and dignity of the woman, which is secured only within the indissolubility of marriage: "Si ergo vir deserere posset mulierem, non esset aequa societas viri ad mulierem, sed servitus quaedam ex parte mulieris. (*Contra Gentiles, III,* c. 123). Long before, St. Ambrose had written in his *Hexameron*, V, 7–19 (*CSEL* XXXII): "You are not a master, but a husband; you have not gained a maidservant, but a wife." In regard to "unity" of marriage, Thomas bases his argument on the unique quality of human love: "The love one has for the other will be more faithful when they are aware of being invisibly joined" (*Contra Gentiles,* III, c. 123). See M. Rhonheimer, *Familie und Selbstverwirklichung* (Cologne, 1977); "Die Entdeckung der Familie," in Fontes, Hassenstein, Lobkowitz, and M. Rhomheimer, *Familie—Feinbild und Leitbild* (Köln, 1977), pp. 11–44; "Sozialphilosophie und Familie. Gedanken zur humanen Grundfunktion der Familie," in B. Schnyder, ed., *Familie—Herausuforderung der Zukunft* (Freiburg, Switzerland, 1982) pp. 113–140.

84. This position was represented by J. Fuchs in a very influential article, "Biologie und Ehemoral," *Gregorianum* 2 (1962) pp. 225–253. It concerns the problem of determining the *finis operis* (the object) of marital consummation as a pure "determination of fact," which must be treated from the perspective of the "inner meaning and purposiveness [*inneren Sinn und Zielhaftigkeit*] of the *capability* itself and of the act that is peculiar to it, namely the *copula*. . . . When it is clarified in this way what are the meaning and purpose of *sexual activity* (in itself) as an actualization of sexual capability, then it can be determined, what modes of sexual activity correspond to this meaning and purpose" (p. 237). Fuchs then comes to the astounding conclusion that, according to the "traditional doctrine" (which he still wants to defend), the "full nature" and "essential meaning" of human sexuality consist in "*the meaningful context [Sinnzusammenhang]* of gamete production and maturation, sexual intercourse, the joining of male and female gametes, and so on" (p. 238). Now this is more than a purely biological treatment, as Fuchs rightly emphasizes, but it nevertheless remains at the level of the *genus naturae*:

for how could one distinguish, *on this basis*, the difference between an *actus matrimonialis* and an *actus fornicatorius*, which are two different acts from the point of view of morality?

85. Thomas understands the relation of *commixtio carnalis* to married love as comparable to the relation of the *operatio* as a "second act" or *ultima perfectio* to the "first act" (*actus primus*); see *In IV Sent.*, d. 26, q. 2, a. 4 (*Suppl.*, q. 42, a. 4).

86. This does not mean, however, that the marital union is itself a "rational" occurrence. In it, man becomes "all flesh" (*totum caro*) and "his mind is constrained because of intense delight" (*detinetur mens propter delectationem intensam*; see *In IV Sent.*, d. 26, q. 1, a. 3; (*Suppl.* q. 41, a. 3). But nothing in this contradicts moral virtue: "The superfluity of passion that corrupts virtue does not only impede the rational act [*impedit rationis actum*], but also takes away the order of reason [*tollit rationis ordinem*]. And the intensity of pleasure in the matrimonial act does not do this, because even if man is not at that moment being set in order by reason, nevertheless he has been so ordered beforehand [*a ratione praeordinatus*], (ad 6). See also *In IV Sent.* d. 31, q. 2, a. 1, ad 3 (*Suppl.* q. 49, a. 4, ad 3): The pleasure [*delectatio*] that there is in the act of matrimony, although it is very intense in regard to quantity, does not exceed the limits set to it beforehand [*limites sibi . . . praefixos*] by the reason, even though reason is not able to order [*ordinare*] those limits during the pleasure itself [*in ipsa delectatione*]."

87. Pius XII, "Address of Oct. 29, 1951," *Acta Apostolicae Sedis*, 43 (1951):850. The words "expression of mutual self-giving" are not to be understood in the (dualistic) sense of an "expressive act," but rather in the sense of a *perfectio*, or *consummatio* of love through its act.

88. And also a "theology of the body"; see also John Paul II, *Mann und Frau schuf er: Grundfragen menschlicher Sexualität* (Munich, 1981); and *Communio Personarum*, vol. 2, ed. N. Martin and R. Martin (Valendar, 1984).

89. This means that the "material field" cannot obtain any anthropological value and significance at all unless *through* this actual expression of love. That would mean that its "act," and not its "existence," is constitutive for ontological integration in the suppositum. The act would have an ontological/constitutive function. Thereby, however, the bodily dimension of love becomes a mere means. See the deceptive formulation of A. Auer, "Die Autonomie des sittlichen nach Thomas von Aquin," p. 31, which Auer himself, however, considers to be anti-spiritualistic: "The human passions as well have a positive characteristic: they are natural goods, which have been given to man as dynamic powers, and they can and should be put into the service of the development of the utmost human capabilities, through man's free disposition."

90. Thomas distinguishes between *a natura* and *secundum naturam* at *I–II,* q. 71, a. 2, ad 2:. "The Philosopher is speaking here about the things that are against nature, and in such a way that what is 'against nature' [*esse contra naturam*] is opposed to that which is 'by nature' [*esse a natura*], but not in such a way that what is against nature is opposed to that which is 'according to nature' [*esse secundum naturam*], the way in which virtues are said to be *secundum naturam,* insofar as they incline toward that which agrees with nature [*ad id quod naturae convenit*]." Thus what is *secundum naturam* (but not *a natura*) is an *ordo rationis,* such as moral virtue, whereas a natural inclination is *a natura.*

91. See B. Schüller, *Die Begründung sittlicher Urteile,* p. 224.

92. See F. Scholz, "Objekt und Umstände, Wesenwirkungen und Nebeneffekte. Zur Möglichkeit und Unmöglichkeit indirekten Handelns," in K. Demmer and B. Schüller, eds., *Christlich glauben und handeln* (Düsseldorf, 1977), p. 259.

93. See the rather disturbing statements of H. Rotter, "Tendenzen in der heutigen Moraltheologie," in *Stimmen der Zeit,* 4 (1970): 264: "It is becoming ever more manifest today, that the laws of subpersonal nature are not the criterion for the rectitude of human behavior. Subhuman nature has expressly inhuman traces. It must be cultivated by man, that is, manipulated." The author refers to the laws of natural selection in the animal kingdom (weakness, disease, beasts of prey); and then to those in the human realm: wars and high rates of mortality. "They were not just evil, they also prevented greater catastrophes, such as the ruin of inherited wealth, overpopulation, and hunger. These factors of order are also very important laws of nature: in the service of the preservation of the species. And yet they are inhuman, because they sacrifice human individuals to the well-being of the human species. There cannot be any obligation to respect such laws. Man must try rather to ward them off through medicine, birth control, and political activity. The dignity of man thus requires culture, in the sense of a humanization of nature. That is possible only through 'unnatural' interventions in natural processes." Here again can be found the dualistic identification of a "subhuman" nature *in* man, with a nonhuman nature that surrounds him.

94. *II–II,* q. 154, a. 12: "In quolibet genere pessima est principii corruptio, ex quo alia dependent. Principia autem rationis sunt ea quae sunt secundum naturam: nam ratio, praesuppositis his quae sunt a natura determinata, disponit alia secundum quod convenit. Et hoc apparet tam in speculativis quam in operativis. Et ideo, sicut in speculativis error circa ea quorum cognitio homini est naturaliter indita, est gravissimus et turpissimus; ita in agendis agere contra ea quae sunt secundum naturam determinata, est gravissimum et turpissimum. Quia ergo in vitiis quae

sunt contra naturam transgreditur homo id quod est secundum naturam determinatum circa usum venereum, inde est quod in hac materia hoc peccatum est gravissimum. . . . Per alias autem luxuriae species praeteritur solum id quod est secundum rationem rectam determinatum; *ex praesuppositione tamen naturalium principiorum.*"

95. See the excellent expositions by G. DeBroglie, "La Doctrine de saint Thomas sur le fondement communautaire de la chasteté" in M. Zalba, ed., *L'Agire Morale*, vol. 5 of *Tommaso d'Aquino nel suo settimo centenario* (Naples, 1974), pp. 297–307.

96. To give one of countless examples: L. Oeing-Hanhoff, "Der Mensch: Natur oder Geschichte?" p. 17, completely distorts the argumentation of *Humanae Vitae* through incomplete citations taken out of context: "The point of the general principles formulated in the encyclical's conclusion is that man attains to truly happy, fulfilled, and moral life only insofar as he obeys the laws that God has inscribed in his nature. Such laws as 'biological' laws are primarily intended—for example, the natural infertility that precedes ovulation, which takes place according to biological laws. It is through the 'rhythm' method, and only through it, that these biological laws, inscribed in the nature of the woman, are actually followed. And that is how this method of birth control is morally justified." The problem here is not the encyclical but the interpreter, who does not imagine that there are "laws inscribed in nature" that are not biological laws, but rather *moral* laws—and these are the concern of *Humanae Vitae.*

97. By "contraception" (*Empfängnisverhütung*) is meant all technological or other practices (such as coitus interruptus); in connection with *Humanae Vitae* the field is limited to artificial methods of temporary or permanent sterilization by pharmaceutical products, mechanical devices, or surgical operations. The issue of abortifacients and abortion enters into the context of the encyclical only to the extent that they function as "a means of birth control." The so-called "natural" method is not "contraception" but *avoidance* of conception. The term "birth-control" is too undifferentiated in this context. What is being "controlled" is not birth but conception.

98. See the treatment in the section "Integral Anthropology or Spiritualism?" in this chapter, and chapter 9. In order to avoid confusion, it appears to me very important to separate the two questions about the procreative meaning of married love (the connection between married love and procreation) on the one hand, and about the act of realizing parental responsibility on the other. Contraception for the purpose of *eliminating* the procreative dimension of human sexuality is not discussed here. Rather, the single question is about the morality of the acts of

*realizing* parental responsibility, that is, the regulation of fertility, with the premise that the procreative meaning of human sexuality will remain fundamentally intact. This is because those Catholic moral theologians who support the moral legitimacy of contraception start, as a rule, from the idea that contraception seeks the same goal as natural family planning: their claim is that it does not arise from a negative attitude about the procreative meaning of married love, but is only "another" method of responsible regulation of the procreative consequence of sexuality, a consequence that in itself is not a matter of dispute. But in any case, it is clear that this equation does not quite work out, since contraception, practiced from this perspective, leads in the end to an antiprocreative attitude; and while this is a *consequence* of contraception (which must be taken into account for a full understanding of the ethical and anthropological danger of contraception), it is still not the principal reason why it is an evil.

99. See *Gaudium et Spes,* (50): "Among those couples who fulfill their God-given task in this way, those merit special mention who with a gallant heart, and with wise and common deliberation, undertake to bring up suitably even a relatively large family."

100. To recapitulate (see the section "Integral Anthropology or Spiritualism?" in this chapter): this does not mean that the marital act possesses two inseparably united "objects," procreation and expression of love. Rather, one has to recall that the act itself has its source in the *naturalis inclinatio ad coniunctionem maris et feminae.* This *is* married love—integrated in the *suppositum* and in its completely human meaning—whose object we now seek to discover. The love between man and woman is already presupposed with the question about the object, and we only need to ask what it is that specifies this love. The specifying object is the act of transmitting human life. And this is because the transmission of human life must have its origin in love, in order for it to be worthy of human life. (I have presented these ideas more fully in "Sozialphilosophie und Familie," pp. 129ff.) Love is not given short shrift: it is not object, but more foundational. It is that love whose object we seek when we ask about the object of the marital act. And this is exactly why procreation and loving union are inseparably joined. The argument also works for in vitro fertilization: just as the love between husband and wife cannot be detached from the duty of procreation, so the transmission of human life cannot be separated from the love between husband and wife.

101. The acknowledgment of this situation is increasingly widespread today and can be abundantly documented. See for example E. Wenisch, ed., *Elternschaft und Menschenwürde. Zur Problematik der Empfängnisregelung* (Valendar, 1984).

102. The voluntary (that is, the "personal") is at the same time the "natural" in a moral sense. This is why periodic abstinence is also called a "natural" method. In a moral context when such language as "natural" or the "nature of the action" is used, the personal dimension of the *actus humanus* is generally intended.

103. For example, one may cite J. Fuchs, "Der Absolutheitscharakter sittlicher Handlungsnormen," in H. Wolter, ed., *Testimonium Veritati* (Frankfurt, 1971), p. 221: "One can set person and nature in contrast with one another, so that 'nature' means the subpersonal, pregiven, of man and his world. 'Person,' on the other hand, is what forms and possesses the 'I' within this pregiven 'nature.' For a critique of this spiritualistic "personalism," see W. Kluxen, "Menschlicher Natur und Ethos," *Münchener Theologischer Zeitschrift,* 23 (1972): 1–17, especially p. 16: "One can speak of "personalism" in this sense when every natural and functional content has shed its moral relevance, and the essence of the moral is seen only in the "personal" moment. Contents count only to the extent that they are immediately contents of the reason. Pure 'personalism' is when only reason, the person, or freedom itself provides such content." Of course, in this case we cannot speak of a reason that can be conceived as "nature" when no natural act of any importance can be ascribed to it: it is the purely-constructive, "creative rationality," which is so characteristic of "teleological ethics."

104. This was the argument used in the "working paper" of the "majority" of the Papal Commission for Birth Control, which spoke *in favor* of contraception. For an exposition of the dualistic reasoning of this document see G. Grisez, "Dualism and the New Morality." One also should not forget that the moral theologians (such as Fuchs and Janssens), who were supposed to have rejected *Humanae Vitae* for its "biologism," had previously treated contraception as a problem of the "inviolability" of physiological processes, and not as one of voluntary, human acts. A symptom of this was that the "pill," as an oral contraceptive that left physiological structures "intact," was considered (with no moral justification) as a *new* problem, because others (just as incorrectly) treated contraception as the problem of an "unnatural" intervention into a "naturally" given structure. As a consequence, no small number of theologians missed the (totally different) main point of *Humanae Vitae*, since they read into it their *own* thoroughly "biologistic" perspective. See also the brief but concentrated analysis of J. Finnis, "*Humanae Vitae:* Its Background and Aftermath," in *International Review of Natural Family Planning*, 4 (1980): 141–153.

105. On the transmission of human life as a "basic fact" (*Basistatsache*), see my "Sozialphilosophie und Familie," pp. 121ff; see also the analyses

of the sexual drive in K. Wojtyla, *Love and Responsibility*, trans. H. T. Willetts (NewYork, 1981), pp. 45 ff.

106. Virginity, "for the sake of the kingdom of heaven," or apostolic celibacy, does not consist in the refusal or denial of one's own sexuality as a human good, but rather in the free *gift* of this good, a "rational obedience" (*obsequium rationale*). This sacrifice is itself a specific act of the virtue of chastity, a special form of the *dominium* over one's own sexuality that is motivated by love and *presupposes its confirmation as a human good* (self-castration for the sake of remaining a virgin is morally perverted more for this reason than because of the "self-mutilation": such a practice has nothing to do with virginal chastity or virtue, since it is a denial of sexuality). Virginity is a special mode of self-giving of the whole human person to God. Precisely because it does not consist in the *denial* of one's own bodiliness, but rather because (in a different way from married self-giving) it represents a "yes" in its giving to God (and only something positively good can be considered an object of loving giving); virginity is therefore, first, in itself a higher form of the integration of human bodiliness into the structure of love, and second, it implies *no* belittling of the *marital* gift of one's own body.

107. On this see also J. Bajda, "Verantwortete Elternschaft und Antikonzeption. Eine moraltheologische Analyse," in E. Wenisch, ed., *Elternschaft und Menschenwürde* (Valendar, 1984), esp. p. 255: "While natural family planning [*Empfängnisregelung*] in its entire essence brings to expression what is morally correct in parental behavior, contraception denies and removes exactly what is at the basis of this morally right, that is, responsible behavior: it excludes the person as creatively causal subject of parenthood. Contraception negates an essential moment of parenthood: the free and responsible disposition of oneself as a potential source of fruitfulness."

108. The argument against contraception put forward by G. Grisez and J. Finnis is based on the idea that the *will* to exclude the possibility of conception is *itself* a sign of the immorality of contraception, since in the contraceptive act the will goes directly against the fundamentally human good of procreation; see G. Grisez, "A New Formulation of a Natural-Law Argument against Contraception," *The Thomist*, 30 (1966): 343–361. Grisez has subsequently modified, in part, the ethical analyses of this article, e.g., G. Grisez, J. Boyle, J. Finnis, and W. E. May, "Every Marital Act Ought to be Open to New Life: Toward a Clearer Understanding," *The Thomist*, 52 (1988): 365–426. See also J. Finnis, "*Humanae Vitae*: Its Background and Aftermath" and, by the same author, "Natural Law and Unnatural Acts," in *The Heythrop Journal*, 11 (1970): 365–387. The same argument can be found in R. Lawler, J. M. Boyle,

W. E. May, *Catholic Sexual Ethics* (Huntington, Indiana, 1985), pp. 151–170. Unlike Grisez and Finnis, I am convinced that, *assuming the married persons' intention to avoid a pregnancy has been formed in a morally legitimate manner,* such argumentation is not immediately evident or conclusive; for some critical remarks see my later article, "Contraception, Sexual Behavior and Natural Law. Philosophical Foundation of the Norm of *Humanae Vitae,*" *The Linacre Quarterly,* 56, no. 2 (1989): 20–57.

109. On this see *Gaudium et Spes,* 51: "In regard to the balance between married love and the responsible transmission of human life, the moral quality of behavior does not depend only on the good intention or valuation of the motives, *but also on objective criteria, which result from the nature of the human person and his acts,* acts that preserve the full meaning of mutual self-giving as well as a truly human generation in real love. This is not possible without a sincere will to exercise the virtue of married chastity." See also John Paul II, *Theology of the Body: Human Love and the Divine Plan* (Boston: Daughters of St. Paul, 1995).

110. *Humanae Vitae,* 17, also speaks of such "consequences." A more exact analysis would have to show whether each case is a *possible* consequence, or a *necessary implication* of contraception. I tend to the position that the disintegration of sensuality and a corresponding "corrosion" of marital/personal love through the "heteronomy" of sensual/egocentric pleasure seeking is at least *necessarily* implied structurally in the practice of contraception; this is so, to the extent that contraception is consciously *chosen* as an alternative to abstinence. I likewise tend to think that there is a causal connection between growing divorce rates (as a consequence of disrupted marriages) and the practice of contraception.

111. See John Paul II, *Familiaris Consortio,* 32.

112. According to R. A. McCormick, for example, this "evil" consists in "damaging the integrity of the sexual organs": one must avoid this evil as we "avoid war." However, for similar reasons, in the contemporary world, war is not always avoidable. Therefore, since there is a "just war" theory, so a theory of "just sterilization" can, he maintains, be defended. "Neuere Überlegungen zur Unveränderlichkeit sittlicher Normen," pp. 53, 57.

113. Even less can such a marriage correspond to its Christian meaning as a sacrament and as an image of the relationship between Christ and His Church. The entire natural *ordo rationis* is in its own right a *praesuppositum* for the *ordo caritatis.* See also *Gaudium et Spes,* 48: "Authentic married love is caught up into divine love and is governed and enriched by the saving activity of the Church, so that this love may lead the spouses to God with powerful effect and may aid and strengthen them in the sublime office of being a father or mother . . . thus the Christian

family, which springs from marriage as a reflection of the loving covenant uniting Christ with the Church (see Eph. 5:2), and as a participation in that covenant, will manifest to all men Christ's living presence in the world, and the genuine nature of the Church. This the family will do by the mutual love of the spouses, by their generous fruitfulness, their solidarity and faithfulness, and by the loving way in which all members of the family assist one another."

114. See *Gaudium et Spes*, 49: "The constant fulfillment of the duties of this Christian vocation demands notable virtue. For this reason, strengthened by grace for holiness of life, the couple will painstakingly cultivate and pray for steadiness of love, large-heartedness and the spirit of sacrifice."

115. And this is an *adequatio* as well with the "proper end" (*finis proprius*) of its own natural act: the "good of the reason" (*bonum rationis*), which is itself the measure (*mensura*) of human action.

116. For the history of "essentialism" and a critique of it, see E. Gilson, *L'Être et l'essence*, 2nd ed. (Paris, 1972); C. Fabro, *Participation et causalité selon s. Thomas d'Aquin* (Louvain and Paris, 1961), esp. pp. 280–315.

117. *Lex Naturae. Zur Theologie des Naturrechts* (Düsseldorf, 1955).

118. See, e.g., Fuchs, "Der Absolutheitscharakter sittlicher Handlungsnormen," p. 220: "Since neither Scripture nor the Church provides a system of universal moral norms, so very much the less would one expect to obtain it from a moral natural law (or natural morality, natural order of morals, order of creation, natural right). This expectation lies at the basis of a very distinct conception of the natural law: the natural law as a collection of commands that are founded in the given and unchangeable nature of man as such, and that can be deduced therefrom." Since this is exactly the conception of the natural law that Fuchs had previously supported, it is a case of "Fuchs contra Fuchs."

119. More detailed treatment of the epistemological structure of this cognitive evolution of the natural law can be found in chapter 6.

120. This is a *destitutio* of the *ordo rationis* in man. Thomas understands it in a theological perspective that has regard for the metaphysical and salvation-historical integration of human nature in the order of grace (or super-nature). For Thomas, such destitution is a penal consequence of original sin, by which man is made liable to the danger of a "heteronomy of the senses," the *fomes peccati* (kindling of sin; see *I–II,* q. 91, a. 6). Nature left to itself (*natura sibi relicta, natura lapsa*) has now become subject to a condition wherein the *lex naturalis*, or the ordering power of the practical reason, is disrupted, and this is done through everything that is opposed to the *ordo virtutis* (every sin for Thomas is an act opposed

to some definite virtue). Therefore Thomas conceives the revelation of the basic commands of the natural law in the Decalogue and elsewhere as divine assistance, so that the natural law could regain its *whole* clarity for *everyone*: "Because the law of nature [*lex naturae*] was destroyed by the law of concupiscence [*lex concupiscentiae*], it was fitting that man be brought back to the works of virtue [*opera virtutis*], and drawn away from the vices [*vitia*]: for which the law of Scripture [*lex scripturae*] was necessary" (*In duo praecepta . . .* , Prol.). This corruption is never complete: it never reaches the first, most general principles of the natural law (see *I–II*, q. 94, a. 6). This topic will be treated again in chapter 7, section "Reason: The Rule of Morality," subsection "Philosophical Ethics and Anthropology . . ."

121. See Aristotle, *Nicomachean Ethics* III, ch. 6, 1113a, 30–34: "The virtuous man judges everything rightly, and the truth in all things is apparent to him. There are noble and pleasant things that are peculiar to every disposition [*hexis/habitus*], and the 'serious one' perhaps differs the most by seeing the truth in everything, as if he were a measure [*kanon*] or rule [*metron*] of them."

122. On the question of a formal "existential ethics," see Rahner's *Schriften zur Theologie*, vol. 2 (Einsiedeln, 1956), pp. 227–246; in English, *Theological Investigations*, vol. 2, *Man in the Church*, trans. Karl Kruger (Baltimore, 1961); also available in excerpted form in Gerald A. McCool, *A Rahner Reader* (New York, 1975), pp. 245–254. An illuminating critique can by found in W. A. Wallace, "Existential Ethics: A Thomistic Appraisal," *The Thomist*, 27 (1963): 493–515. See also D. J. Door, "K. Rahner's Formal Existential Ethics," *The Irish Theological Quarterly* 36 (1969): 211–229, and J. Stallmach, "Das Problem sittlicher Eigengesetzlichkeit des Individuums in der philosophischen Ethik," *Theologie und Philosophie* 42 (1967): 22–50.

123. Rahner, p. 233 in *Schriften zur Theologie,* vol. 2, and p. 250 in McCool's *Reader.*

124. "If (and insofar as) man, as a spiritual person, participates by his acts in the permanence-in-itself [*Insichselberständigkeit*] of the pure form, which does not resolve itself in its ordination to matter as the principle of repeatability, then he must also participate in that spiritual individuality of the spiritual which has a positive individuality, an individuality which is not merely the sameness of the repeated universal and not merely a case of the law" (p. 237 in *Schriften zur Theologie,* vol. 2; passage quoted is from Kruger's translation, p. 251 in McCool's *Reader*).

125. See the adoption of the Rahnerian point of departure in J. Fuchs, "Der Absolutheitscharakter . . . ," p. 239f.: "Once again, the real moral

task of man is not to fulfill norms—so that, to take the extreme position, the reality of living is only the material for the realization of moral values, in the sense of fulfilling norms." On the contrary, one must "creatively" shape this "living reality."

126. See Second Vatican Council, Dogmatic Constitution *Lumen Gentium*, 1.

# Part II

# Personal Autonomy, Natural Law, and Moral Objectivity: In-depth Studies

# PRELIMINARY NOTE

At the outset of this study it was maintained that recent models for the justification of moral norms were founded upon the mistaken tendencies of certain school traditions of neo-scholasticism. In particular, the so-called "teleological" model of moral justification and that of "autonomous morality" have gained plausibility and legitimacy only in front of the peculiar backdrop of a few traditional misunderstandings about the nature and justification of moral norms. In the foregoing argument, this was shown to apply to the term "natural law" and to the physicalistic–naturalistic understanding of the moral object.

What follows is intended not only to bolster this thesis but also to deepen the concept of the natural law as the law of the practical reason; in the course of it, I hope the concept will become more clearly illuminated in certain essential aspects. We will first turn our attention to the doctrine of "autonomous morality" as systematically elaborated by Alfons Auer and Franz Böckle. An exposé of the internal uncertainties of this ethical model, and the failure of its claim to be a legitimate interpretation of Thomas (in chapters 3 and 4), will lead to an in-depth analysis of the metaphysical, anthropological, and epistemological structure of the *lex naturalis* (in chapters 5 and 6). This will bring us closer to answering the relevant questions, and it will be particularly interesting to see how far the solutions were anticipated by Thomas.

On this foundation will then be erected more detailed presentations of the concept of moral action and of the normative function of the reason as the *standard* of moral action (chapter 7); this will lead in turn to a more extensive critique of so-called "teleological ethics" (chapters 8 and 9), and finally to a fuller treatment of the natural law and the objectivity of moral behavior (chapters 10, 11, and 12), which will complete what was begun in part I.

# 3

# The Model of "Autonomous Morality"

We have seen how the concept of moral autonomy is closely associated with the concept of the natural law, on the one hand, and with the need to form a self-standing method and theory for philosophical ethics, on the other. "Autonomous morality" implies a concern, fully supported in the present study, for rational insight into general human and moral claims that can stand independently of the insight of faith and theological argument. Now the elaboration of just such an "autonomous" rationality of morals happens to have been one of the principal achievements of Thomistic ethics. It should be restored to its rightful inheritance, in place of an ethics that misuses (or uses in too hasty and inconclusive a manner) a theological justification of norms. In fact, the "ethical thesis" of Alfons Auer makes good sense, in response to a predominating "ethics of faith." In the words of A. Laun, this thesis states that "there are areas of reality which are morally obliging, and man is in a position to recognize these by the power of his reason."[1]

And yet the model of "autonomous morality" that in recent years has become so widespread in Catholic moral theology cannot be reconciled with the true nature of the moral–practical reason. The deficiencies of this new approach appear, on closer inspection, to be the consequences of premises inherited uncritically from the traditional "ethics of being" (*Seinsethik*); it is on such that Auer expressly relies, and he wishes to bring them up to date and develop them. But it seems to me that the philosophical and theological consequences that follow logically from this project are untenable. Nor is it possible to find support in Thomas Aquinas for a doctrine of "theonomous autonomy," of which "autonomous morality" would be the natural development. The following discussion will show why.

In the present context only a few of the many questions that arise can be isolated and discussed, but it should be enough to show that the autonomy model is uncertain and in need of substantial correction. I will confine myself largely to the presentation of Alfons Auer,[2] who has played a leading role in regard to these questions.

## The Concept of Moral Autonomy

Auer postulates a threefold autonomy of morality: autonomy with respect to the natural law, autonomy with respect to metaphysics, and autonomy with respect to faith; the third includes autonomy toward revelation and the magisterium of the Church. (The relationships of the human reason to the natural order and to metaphysics have also been treated in chapter 1; we can leave to one side, at present, the question of the relationship of autonomy to faith.)

But what does "autonomy" mean? This is a worthwhile question. It is understood to be "self-legislation," "self-governance," "self-legislation by reason" (*Selbstgesetzlichkeit der Vernunft:* "Die Autonomie des Sittlichen," p. 52). In saying this, Auer is aware of the danger of reducing the order of reason to the order of nature, and tries to avoid it. The natural law is not simply "a law of nature," but rather a law that the reason formulates in a natural way. And yet the reason that is thus postulated intervenes "creatively" and "formatively" in the natural inclinations, the "material" of "elementary needs" that, although not freely malleable, are nevertheless there to be formed, so that moral obligations can be created (ibid.; see also *Autonome Moral,* pp. 127ff.).

The question that first occurs is whether this autonomy is to be understood in a dualistic or personalist sense, a difference which has been mentioned above (esp. ch.2, section "Beyond Naturalism and Dualism," subsection "Integral Anthropology or Spiritualism"). Auer shows his dependence on naturalistic interpretations by identifying the concept of the natural order with that of the "order of things," in the tradition of Wittmann and others. And yet, whereas for Wittmann the rational order was in fact *equivalent* to the natural order, for "autonomous morality," reason is *com-*

*pletely* divided from nature. Auer explains correctly that Thomas differed from the Stoics in noting "that the reason is not merely a mouthpiece of the order which lies in the nature of things, that the order of reason precedes the order of things" (*Autonome Moral*, p. 129).

Now such a formulation is in fact dualistic because it posits a dualism of the natural and rational orders. The "natural order" is the order or the world of things: in other words, "the natural order denotes the sum total of the physiological–biological, psychological, and sociological structures and mechanisms with which human existence is bound up" ("Die Autonomie des Sittlichen," p. 31). Auer wants to emphasize that such structures do not translate immediately into moral obligations. Now while Thomas (as was shown) sees these natural inclinations as human goods in themselves, which must also be integrated into the totality of the human suppositum (which requires that they be ordered by the practical reason), Auer remains within the dualistic schema. In order to avoid naturalism, he merely turns the schema on its head. The natural inclinations that can be distinguished from the reason itself do not directly and immediately formulate the moral "ought," but become instead the material for the shaping intervention of the reason, which uses them as instruments. In this way—far otherwise than with Thomas—human goods (*bona humana*) are distinguished from those of the natural order, from the "natural goods" contained by the order of things, "which as energizing powers are given to man, and through his *free disposal* can be made *serviceable* for the maximum unfolding of human capabilities" (ibid.; italics are mine).

Auer rightly criticizes a derivation of the moral "ought" from natural tendencies, and this appears to him to be the only plausible alternative, given the dualism resulting from the traditional reduction of the practical reason to an organ that "reads off" the natural order. The disposing power of the reason itself is what formulates the *bonum humanum*; it does not act without any relation whatsoever to the natural tendencies, as has been noted, but it does so in an "autonomous" fashion. This means that the reason itself "develops" that in which the *bonum humanum* (or "human happiness") consists, in order to accomplish it in the actual planning (subject to historical variation) of the natural, "material" level of human existence. "The "good of man" (*bonum hominis*) is founded on freedom, since man as "the cause of himself" (*causa sui*), and the "principle of his own actions" (*principium suorum propriorum actuum*), has "power over his own actions" (*potestas suorum operum*). The human good is realized through the existential achievement of reason [*Daseinsvollzug*], through "living according to reason" (*secundum rationem vivere*).[3]

Auer calls the practical reason the "organ for the discovery of human possibilities and thereby, moral obligations" ("Die Autonomie des Sittlichen," p. 37). The question that arises is, what is the practical reason? Is it *pure freedom* or does it possess in its own right a natural inclination toward the order of the good? This question has even not been raised, let alone answered, but it is the decisive question. In a later supplement to his doctrine of "autonomous morality," Auer actually characterized the answer as a scientific desideratum: "The concept of reason that is being used (or silently presupposed) in the debate must be further clarified . . . above all, we still lack an explicit comparison with the philosophically possible conceptions of reason" (*Autonome Moral, Nachtrag,* p. 237).

It can now be shown that such "unclarity" of the concept of the practical reason really belongs to the concept of autonomy developed by Auer. The autonomous reason of autonomous morality oscillates between being a "reading organ" of material structures of the material world and an absolutely free "creative reason"; it appears as an extremely vague human faculty, conceived in contradictory terms.

## The Autonomy of Reason: Self-Assertion Through Independence

More precisely, the concept of autonomy involves self-mastery of the reason, in opposition to a possible "heteronomy" (or "legislation by *another*") coming from outside. Such opposition between autonomy and heteronomy is one of Kant's legacies, and will be shown to be the chief obstacle to a legitimate understanding of autonomy.

Auer writes as follows: "The concept of autonomy expresses

the idea that man is a law unto himself; that moral norms are not imposed upon man from outside with obligatory measures, but rather are developed by himself through the power of his reason" ("Hat die autonome Moral," p. 11). This autonomy, his argument goes, arises from two sources: on the one hand, with respect to the formulation of the moral "ought" through faith, and on the other hand (and this is what primarily concerns us here), with respect to the "claims of reality," or the given structures of the external world of things.

This last definition of autonomy is nevertheless only as plausible as the starting point of the argument: it attempts a kind of "system-immanent" escape from the consequences of deriving the moral "ought" from the world of things, such derivation being the product of a definite "ethics of being" (*Seinsethik*)—Auer, in fact, is here above all the student of Joseph Pieper, whom he extols as the principal representative of Thomistic ethics (*Autonome Moral*, p. 16).

Auer begins with the following précis of his ethics of being: "The true being of reality, the inner truth of things becomes the norm and measure of behavior" (ibid.); being and the morally good are convertible, since "what exists emerges as what ought to exist" (ibid., p. 18); the "moral is the *yes* to reality" (ibid., p. 19). In this way, finally, autonomous morality (which is distinct from that which comes from faith and precedes it) is an "ethos of objectivity, which takes an insight into reality and articulates it under the aspect of obligation" (ibid., p. 160).

In this conception of ethics, which has been most clearly formulated by Pieper, the function of the practical reason is in any case reduced to that of simply grasping and carrying out the objective regularities that are immanent in the world of things. To quote Pieper: "The natural law demands of rational creatures first of all the affirmation, the imperative carrying out, and the preservation of the natural order of the world. Second and essentially, it demands that man must place himself under the obligation of the sentence, 'Become what you are,' a statement in which the inherent direction of all reality is expressed."[4]

In this view, the practical reason *as practical* does not possess any constitutive function of its own in the formulation of the moral "ought." It simply translates the recognized reality (permeated as it is with multiple potentialities) into moral claims, and can thus be reduced to what is known by the theoretical reason; to this extent, then, it is determined heteronomously.[5] The logical development of this argument necessarily leads, as we have seen, to a naturalistic grounding of moral norms, especially in the area of marital ethics.[6]

Now Auer intends to free the reason from its heteronomy on the basis of this ethics of being *without clarifying the nature of the practical reason.* While acknowledging the original rationality of the world of things, he nevertheless wants to preserve the self-determinacy of the reason, sticking firmly to the idea that man stands over against an undetermined, shapeless world as its "shaper" (*Gestalter*).[7] The concrete structures of reality are thus a pregiven field, immanently ordered at the "natural" level but open to moral ordering by man—a field upon which the autonomous reason traces out its existential designs that constantly change with history. Man has been inserted into "contexts of order" as well as natural laws. "These basic determinations of personal human existence are unchangeably stable, but they can and must be concretized in ever new existential designs" (*Daseinsentwürfe*: p. 34). Autonomous morality as a "world ethos" is consequently an "ethos of concreteness, which articulates insights into reality under the aspect of their binding force" (ibid., p. 160). The "normative articulation of the rationality of the real" (ibid., p. 36), or the task of formulating "the aspect of obligatoriness" (*Verbindlichkeit*) of the order of things, belongs to the reason.

## Autonomous Morality and the Practical Reason

Autonomous reason, therefore, stands *over against* the order of reality, but is not itself inserted in this reality. Above all, it is independent of any natural orientation toward the human good. The human good, Auer holds, must always be established anew by science as the "moral binding force" of the known order of reality; this will come about through the "human and social sciences and the insights of philosophical anthropology, in a synthesis with the necessities and demands of a good human existence, and as translated into the language of moral obligation; to discover its truth, ethics must have recourse to an ongoing and sincere cooperation with the empirical sciences and with philosophical interpretations of human existence" ("Hat die Autonome Moral . . . ," p. 13).

Auer is speaking here of "the scientifically moral knowledge" of philosophical ethics. But if we inquire as to the *practical–moral* knowledge of "everyman," of the individual human being—and that means, the immediate moral insight that is accessible to the human person for each single action (*my* practical reason)—it becomes obvious that this aspect of practical knowledge is *not* up for discussion in the system of "autonomous morality." The question of the practical reason is passed over in silence. Autonomous morality is morality in the cloak of a scientific ethical theory: in place of a moral normativity derived from metaphysical insights, it posits one derived from the human sciences and philosophical anthropology.

But since "autonomous morality" is designed to overcome the constraints that follow from an insufficiently differentiated analysis of the relationship between metaphysics and ethics, or between the natural order and the moral "ought," it overcomes these constraints by emancipating the "ought" from "being" *altogether,* so that being is placed "beneath the ethical threshold." In this way the human *ratio* is completely disconnected from its measuring function. No longer an organ that merely "reads off" norms from the order of nature; it has become instead an organ that "evolves" norms. But this means that it is no more a "measure" or "standard" than it was in a naturalistic ethics.[8]

To correct this mistaken naturalism, we must look in another direction, following the lead of St. Thomas. This requires a clear understanding that the natural reason of man (*ratio naturalis*) *itself belongs to this order of being*, or the natural order. When it is *practical* reason, though it rests in a certain way on natural foundations, it nevertheless transcends the order of the naturally given, and exercises a regulative, standard-giving function within this order, thus constituting the *lex naturalis*. Herein lies what is peculiar to man: he possesses a natural, created "light" of knowing in his existential reality—an "imprint of the divine light" (*impressio divini luminis*)—that is open to the morally good (to the *bona humana*) as an "intellectual light" (*lumen intellectuale*) naturally inclined toward the intelligible good in the practical dimension. This light of knowing is founded in the order of his being—it is "natural" knowing—but at the same time it provides a norm for this order of being when it comes to actions, and to that extent it widens the concept of human existence by perfecting it with the *esse morale*, the moral level of being.

A naturalistic ethics of being neglects the specific role of the practical reason, as does "autonomous morality"; it is forgotten that ethics is above all a theory of the practical reason, a theory of *man* in the dimension of actions, and not a theory of the moral "binding force" of the concrete structure of things, nor a theory of scientific modes for the establishment of norms. In the context of "autonomous morality," reasoning that is relevant to ethics appears to be treated mainly as scientific reasoning, so that its special subject matter is lost from view: the capability, naturally founded in human nature itself, for a self-standing (and indeed, in this sense, "autonomous") insight into the morally good and the "self-legislation" (*auto-nomía*) that is based upon this. "Autonomous morality" lacks the recognition in man as such of a basic competence for immediate insight into the moral demands of reality, and maintains instead the need for some complex and "scientific" method.

Whenever Auer speaks of the practical–moral insight of the individual, he invariably falls back on the formula that he started with, that of a "yes to reality." He writes, to give one example, as follows: "The moral moment of man's inwardness and behavior increases to the extent that he seeks the apprehended good for its own sake, insofar as the end of the doer (*finis operantis*) coincides with the end of the thing done (*finis operis*), i.e., the purpose of the acting human being coincides with the intrinsic value that is immanent to the action" (*Autonome Moral*, p. 25). What is this "apprehended good"? Or the "intrinsic value [*Eigenwert*] immanent to the action"? Auer speaks of the evolution of human dignity, of inner and outer well-being, the creative development of the person, and so on. In conclusion he refers to the conscience "in which man becomes conscious of the binding power [*Verbindlichkeit*] of the truth. Conscience does not stand for itself, but finds its measure in the 'truth of real things' (J. Pieper), the potentiality for existence that each thing has."[9]

The truth to which the conscience orients itself must be displayed by the reason; however, this reason is no practical reason that could empower an immediate insight into the human good or determine the action of the individual person; so much at least is clear from Auer's description of the "rationality of the moral," upon which he grounds its autonomy:

> The animal is led by his instincts to do what is necessary for existence. Man can only recognize the meaning of his existence, and the manner of action that is required for his fulfillment, when he consciously thinks about himself. But to do this it is essential that he clarify the social and historical contexts in which he has been placed. The rationality of the moral unveils itself less in abstract speculation than in reflection upon the historical experiences of humanity. History reveals the paths that lead to a meaningful and fruitful human existence or to the opposite." (*Autonome Moral,* p. 29)

Even a "synopsis" of the human sciences and philosophical anthropology is not enough: the historical experiences of humanity must also be considered before the human good can be determined. The autonomous reason and its corresponding morality apparently cannot be expected of the acting subject as such. "Autonomous morality" turns out to be a very questionable, scientifically theoretical model rather than a true foundation for a moral autonomy or self-legislative capacity of the acting human being.

## What Is "Proper to Ethics"?

Once the perspective of the practical reason and a real foundation of moral behavior are abandoned, autonomous morality finds itself in a strange land—that of the "world ethos" (*Weltethos*)—a morality to be deduced from a summation of scientifically produced and socially transmitted ways of behavior carried out "in the midst of the things of this world." By "world ethos" is meant "the entirety of obligations that result from the order of things in the lives of individual human beings. We are concerned here, it has been shown, with an ethos of concreteness, with an immanent ethos that is evolved autonomously and in a secular manner, in accordance with the intelligible horizon of any given historical period. It belongs to the 'truth of the world,' and thus remains within the original competence of the human spirit" (*Autonome Moral*, p. 185).

When it comes to determining such a "world ethos" in association with autonomous morality, in every case Auer reduces moral action to the category of "factual problems" in the various areas of life (see *Autonome Moral*, pp. 161–163). At the same time one can clearly see a tendency to allow what is "proper to ethics," or the ethical *proprium,* to appear as the Christian *proprium*, at the level of revelation and as an ethics of salvation. The result appears, on the one hand, as a "world ethos" of "autonomous, objective law" that is substituted for the specifically *moral* dimension of human action, and, on the other hand, as a "salvation ethics" fully taken up with moral demands, an ethics that imports theological justifications, motivations, and exhortations into such an ethos of objectivity, while having to contribute nothing to the "facts" of the situation.

The decisive point that should be emphasized here is that "autonomous morality" as an ethos of objectivity simply lacks the *ethical perspective.* Autonomous it is indeed, but it is not morality; and in so far as it does become morality (through the incorporation of "salvation ethics"), it ceases to be autonomous. There is an inner contradiction in the concept of autonomous morality as presented by Auer and others. The idea articulated in the concept of autonomy is "that man is a law unto himself, that moral norms are not imposed on man from outside in the sense of heteronomous, obligating measures, but rather are evolved by himself through the power of his reason" ("Hat die autonome Moral . . . ," p. 11). But this idea cannot live up to the claims made for it, for the following reasons:

1. A concept of the *practical reason* is missing—the recognition, that is, of a faculty of the individual, on the basis of which he can direct his own actions to the human good.

2. A concept of the *human reason* is missing, which could itself be criterion and standard for the human good; as a consequence, there is no criterion for the "moral," which has instead been dissolved into the various results of the human sciences, philosophy, or the experiences and possibilities of the history of humanity.

Moral ideals are confined to formulas like "the dignity of man" or "self-development" or "fellow feeling."

3. While autonomous morality speaks of norms, morality, and such, it nevertheless lacks an adequate concept of "moral behavior"; the moral is no longer a quality of the human act that perfects the acting person himself as an "immanent action" (*actio immanens*), something whose consequences do not primarily affect the objective surroundings of the acting person, but rather remain in the actor himself. Instead, morality is conceived as a characteristic of modes of behavior that are socially, culturally, and historically transmitted and modified, and are always becoming newly articulated in changing norms.

4. The concepts of "moral behavior" and "moral norm" are thus, on the plane of the "world ethos," drawn into the orbit of sociological and not ethical definition. Such concepts do not reflect an indwelling orientation of human behavior toward being perfected through virtue, to which the self-governance of man is ordered and in which it finds its fulfillment. Instead, norms become social regulations for human action: they are "indispensable, but have a propensity for the ethical minimum. The Christian context, however, impels us unhesitatingly toward a highly ethical understanding of morality" ("Hat die autonome Moral . . . ," p. 28; see also *Autonome Moral, Nachtrag,* p. 237).

5. Consequently, what is "proper to ethics" or the ethical *proprium*—the orientation of human behavior toward its specific perfection in virtue—is identified with the "Christian *proprium*"; the world ethos thus loses its own *moral* coherence. It is not an ethos of the *moral* self-legislation of man; rather, it is an "ethos" of the independence of "world behavior" from the specific and objective demands of morality.[10] As such, it is capable of establishing "norms of behavior," but it grounds them in their "factual determination" (*Sachgemäßheit*), and not in their morality (*Sittlichkeit*). "Factual determination" thereby becomes dissociated from what is really meant by "moral responsibility."

6. This is why autonomous morality does not adopt a concept of autonomy that would imply a moral self-legislation immanent in the human person. It offers instead a concept of autonomy as *independence.* Autonomous morality thus goes beyond its original goal. For the legitimate intention of an "autonomous morality"

would seem to consist in demonstrating the immanent rationality of a natural human morality, and the independence of its justifiability vis-à-vis Christian faith, as well as the scientific and methodological integrity of ethics alongside metaphysics. In carrying out their intention, however, the sponsors of autonomous morality have inadvertently developed an ethics of independence and sovereignty, ascribed to a reason free of any material law whatsoever; such a reason loses track of the properly ethical and becomes increasingly *an organ for the technical mastery of facts.* At the same time, and paradoxically, autonomous morality actually falls short of its claim to provide a justification for an immanent human self-governance in moral questions.

This aberrant development can best be explained in front of a peculiar background: a hasty search for a new model of ethical argumentation in the wake of the dispute over the encyclical *Humanae Vitae,* and the moral–theological misunderstanding and lack of patience that led to a contestation of the encyclical. An adequate reception and understanding of the ethical content of this document is only now beginning to make some progress,[12] revealing the tragic misunderstandings of the critics at that time, who reduced the question of contraception to a problem of "method," and thereby missed the ethical *proprium* in all its fullness.

There is a justifiable desire to develop an immanent, self-legislative, human morality that does not depend on Christian revelation and theology for its rationality, but this need has not always been satisfactorily addressed by traditional moral theology. The concept of the natural law (the *lex naturalis*) as found in St. Thomas Aquinas can provide a solution.

## Notes

1. See A. Laun, *Das Gewissen. Oberste Norm sittlichen Handelns* (Innsbruck, 1984), p. 24.

2. For this I depend on *Autonome Moral und christlicher Glaube,* 2nd ed. (Düsseldorf, 1984); "Die Autonomie des Sittlichen nach Thomas von Aquin" in K. Demmer and B. Schüller, eds., *Christlich glauben und handeln. Fragen einer fundamentalen Moraltheologie in der Diskussion* (Düsseld-

orf, 1977), pp. 31–54; "Hat die autonome Moral eine Chance in der Kirche?" in G. Virt, ed., *Moral begründen—Moral verkünden* (Innsbruck and Vienna, 1985), pp. 9–30.

3. "Die Autonomie des Sittlichen," p. 52. See also "Hat die autonome Moral . . . ," p. 22: "Since, for Thomas, the *bonum hominis* is founded on freedom and is realized through the existential achievement of reason (*secundum rationem agere*), the concept of autonomy as self-legislation is precisely realized."

4. Joseph Pieper, *Living the Truth,* trans. Lothar Krauth and Stella Lange (San Francisco, 1989), pp. 161–162.

5. This holds, of course, only in relation to *universal* and generally valid norms of morality; the peculiar function of the practical reason is in fact fully recognized by Pieper—if not always correctly—at the level of prudence.

6. This occurs, as we have seen, for methodological reasons. In other words, in itself, the connection between "nature" (as the "order of being") and the "moral order" is rightly postulated by the ethics of being; the problem lies rather in mistaking the proper methodological relationship between philosophical ethics and metaphysics, on the one hand, and the cognate relationship between the speculative and practical reason, on the other.

7. See, *Autonome Moral*, p. 23: "The world is not complete to begin with, but has been established with an amorphous beginning. The primordial form of the world is full of dynamisms and intentionalities, which operate within it as a tendency toward development [*Entfaltung*]. Through all history there is a tension between the actual form of reality, still unfulfilled and perhaps very disordered, and the form that is better and ultimately complete." This doctrine is problematic for theology, since it appears to reduce salvation to evolution.

8. Consequently Franz Böckle is forced to reduce "rational measurability" to formal "noncontradictoriness of the reason"; the reason would then provide no kind of *content*, or material consequence, for the constitution of behavioral norms.

9. *Autonome Moral,* p. 26; see also p. 36 "Because the rationality of the world is not yet a pure actuality, but is rather a potency that is always pressing toward realization, it is oriented toward a cooperation with human rationality. . . . The way to humanity passes through objectivity [*Sachlichkeit*]; in order to develop itself, human rationality is oriented toward the development [*Entfaltung*] of the world's rationality."

10. The concept of the "objectivity" of moral behavior was defined in chapter 2, section "The Moral Object, and How It Is Constituted," subsection "On the Concept of Objectivity . . . ," as "integrated in the

natural intentionality of the *ratio naturalis* and ordered, measured, and regulated through it." "Objective" also means "integrated in the context of the whole person, of the suppositum, and thereby in the purposive structure of human existence."

11. Auer writes: "What Catholic theological ethics adopted, rather, was a general concept of autonomy which was 'in the air,' so to speak, and seemed to be capable of integration into a Christian viewpoint. Its reception was a process that proved so persistent in terms of past and present developments in the Church, that it seemed to happen all on its own. It was not even discussed whether clarity could or should be attained about its precise historical connection." A new model of argumentation, in other words, had simply "emerged" in response to *Humanae Vitae*. ("Hat die autonome Moral . . . ," p. 12).

12. See especially the Bibliographical Supplement and the writings of Janet Smith in particular.

# 4

# The Concept of Autonomy

## Three Different Concepts of Autonomy

The first problem with the model of autonomy is its failure to take into account the variety and complexity of meanings that the concept has acquired, as well as the multilayered historical development[1] that has lent certain shadings to these meanings. The result is conceptual confusion and a heaping together of quite distinct kinds of autonomy. In my view, at least three different kinds must be distinguished.

### *Personal Autonomy*

A first concept of autonomy has to do with human actions that are self-determining, conscious, and carried out with a decision of the will and rational insight into the good. In this view, autonomy means mastery (*dominium*) over one's own deeds, and freedom to will and to decide. This characteristic of human actions, as expressed in the classical concept of the *actus humanus*, is an expression of the personality of the human being. It will be referred to *personal autonomy.*[2]

Thomas understood such personal autonomy as follows (see *I–II*, q. 1, a. 2): all action moves toward a goal, and this takes place in two different ways: on the one hand, when man moves himself, and on the other hand, when man is steered toward a goal by another, as the arrow by the bowman. "Those who possess reason move themselves toward the goal, because they have mastery [*dominium*] over their acts through their power of free choice [*liberum arbitrium*], which is a faculty of willing and reason. Those who do not possess reason move toward their end by a natural inclination, as if they were moved by another and not by themselves." This is so because irrational creatures are not capable of understanding the *ratio finis*, the "finality" of their ends; this is also why they are incapable of ordering any act to its end—they can only be ordered to an end. For this reason, says Thomas, the entire irrational creation is related to God as an instrument to its principal agent. It only belongs to the rational creature to seek after goals "as if leading or guiding oneself to an end" (*quasi se agens vel ducens ad finem*); the irrational creature, however, does this "as if led or guided by another" (*quasi ab alio acta vel ducta*).[3]

This mastery over oneself and one's own acts is a *dominium* and a *potestas* based upon reason and free will, and can be called personal autonomy. Indeed, precisely in this passage Thomas speaks of *freedom*.[4] From this personal autonomy of human behavior arises the dimension of morality in actions: the phenomenon of the *ought*. A creature that is "led" in a certain way, and thus has no mastery over his own acts by an insight into an order to an end, does not need an "ought." In the realm of pure nature, there is no "ought," as Kant correctly recognized: there are only necessary regularities. This "ought," a phenomenon that Kant so strongly emphasized, and rightly, is a consequence of personal autonomy, the mastery and power over one's own action bound up with reason. One "ought" only when one does not "have to," which is to say, when the action is not subject to an operative determination. Along with personal autonomy is also given the "personal autonomy of the ought," which means the insight, entrusted to the human being, into what is to be done, or into the good, in accordance with which actions are to be directed. In this personal sense, the ought is essentially autonomous. Kant saw all this correctly; the question is how this autonomy is explained or justified.

For Aristotle, the personal autonomy of human action was correctly grasped in the concept of *prohairesis* and with an insight into its dependence on the virtue of prudence (*phronesis*). Aristotle raises the question whether it is enough for ethical, virtuous action simply to do what is "right," which would mean merely carrying out materially correct deeds of justice, temperance, or courage. Second, he asks whether we really need *our own* insight into the good in order to act virtuously. Why wouldn't it be enough to do, in general, what someone does, for instance, who wants to be healthy? Simply "carry out the doctor's orders"? We certainly don't have to study medicine ourselves to be healthy (see *Nichomachean Ethics,* VI, ch. 3).

Aristotle explains that to do what is "just" is not simply that: it could also be done because "the law dictates" or because it is "the easiest way out," or for some other opportunistic reason. The "just man" is not simply one who does just actions, but rather one who does them because he recognizes the just as good, and he does this on the basis of his own insight, for the sake of the good—for the sake of virtue; in other words, one must not only do what is just, but he must do it *as* the just man does it, that is, he must *be* just.[5] This is exactly why it is not the same with prudence (the practical insight into the good that is to be done, or the concrete "ought") as it is with medicine: to become healthy is not a moral process; on the other hand, one acts virtuously if he acts on the basis of his own insight into the good. Unless someone possess prudence himself, his action will not be worthy of his personal autonomy.[6]

### *Functional Autonomy*

We now come to a second meaning of autonomy: human moral action can be characterized by the fact that it follows its own "logic" or law, since it cannot be reduced to scientific, sociological, or other categories. It possesses an integrity that is specific to it, with its own immanent rationality and consistency. I call this aspect *functional autonomy.*[7]

All created realities possess functional autonomy or self-governance, which is not identical with what has just been called personal autonomy. Even natural processes or purely animal actions operate with an immanent self-governance. Thus even the personal autonomy of the human being can itself be understood as *a kind of functional autonomy,* since ultimately this—as mastery over actions, on the basis of rational insight and free will—is in fact an immanent self-governance of human actions. The question about functional autonomy is more fundamental in the order of logic: it is the question whether a given realm is determined by its own immanent law, order, or "logic," or whether it merely follows a law that is not immanent. Such a concept of an immanent self-governance or order cannot be more closly defined until a later stage; in man, personal autonomy appears to be an essential characteristic of his functional autonomy.

If personal autonomy is treated under this aspect of being a component of functional autonomy, it retains the character of *law.* This corresponds exactly to the definition of law elaborated above, as an *ordinatio rationis*: law carries out an ordering of actions toward a definite goal, and this is precisely what is realized in the personal autonomy of human action, by reason of its immanent self-legislation.[8] In the case of animal "action," this functional autonomy does not consist in an *ordinatio rationis*, but rather in a passively received "ordering by the divine reason" (*ordinatum esse a ratione divina*). Functional autonomy and personal autonomy are not coterminous concepts. The former describes immanent self-governance as such; the second describes a certain privileged kind of immanent self-governance. It must be emphasized, however, that personal autonomy, to the extent that it is functional autonomy, is not subject to the *dominium* or the *potestas* of the person; and the same must be said of the ends toward which autonomous action orders itself through insight into the good and a grasp of the structure of finality. If this were not the case, personal autonomy would not be a functional autonomy at all—that is, it would not be an immanent self-governance—but only functional "independence," or freedom *from* any immanent self-governance. But because it *is* functional autonomy, personal autonomy is a *conditioned* (created) autonomy, and rests upon that structure of determining conditions we call "nature."

Once it is recognized that personal autonomy belongs essentially to the functional autonomy of man, it should likewise be clear that the personal autonomy of the "ought" can be treated as a functional autonomy of the "ought." What this means is as follows: the "ought"—the claim of the good—itself possesses an immanent self-governance, and as such is fundamentally independent of actual personal realization (otherwise it could never appear as an "ought"); this is what is meant when someone says that the good is founded in the reality of being, or that it follows from the "nature" of man and its purposive structure, that it brings an "objective" claim. This functional autonomy of the "ought" shows itself to be an autonomous teleological structure in respect to personal insight and effective willing; a structure that provides a foundation and orientation for all personal autonomy and for the "deontic" autonomy of the "ought" that goes with it (i.e., the nonreducibility of the "I should do *x* . . ." to extrapersonal instances). It is only this functional autonomy of the "ought"—in a way, an autonomy with a certain content—that grounds its fundamental rationality and intellective power; it furthermore provides a basis for the possibility that what is good and "what ought to be" is not simply *what I desire or think to be good*, but that there can be, within personal autonomy, a misguided and bad willing, or false and erroneous insights. It thus becomes possible to ascribe an objectively known rationality to the "ought," and to preserve its cognitive integrity—a fundamental goal, in fact, of the doctrine of "autonomous morality."

Within the concept of "functional autonomy," a further variety of autonomy can be included: *methodological* autonomy, or the cognitive integrity or self-governance of distinct sciences; in more general terms, this is a variety of *ways of knowing* ("cognitive" or "methodological autonomy"). In this way one can correctly maintain that the natural and rational knowledge of God is autonomous in relation to revealed knowledge—that it is a coherent and true knowledge, if incomplete. To this extent, there is an autonomy of philosophical knowledge vis-à-vis theological knowledge, as well as a cognitive or methodological autonomy between different branches of the same science, and among various disciplines of philosophical knowledge. In part I of this study we spoke of the cognitive autonomy of practical knowledge over against theoretical knowledge, and of the methodological autonomy of ethics over against metaphysics. As explained above, one must carefully distinguish such *functional* autonomy from "independence"; otherwise, one runs the risk of confusing it with yet a third and different kind of autonomy.

### *Constitutive Autonomy*

This third kind of autonomy, also called competence autonomy, taken from the political and legal field, is, historically speaking, the original and fundamental concept: the first two have been formed by a real, if incomplete, analogy with it. It signifies *relative* or *absolute indetermination* of an area or of an action in relation to another area that is superordinated or preestablished. A concept of autonomy as absolute independence appears in isolated instances in the ancient Greek world, where it signified the same thing as political freedom from foreign dominion. And yet the Greeks also conceived *autonomia* in a relative sense, as a *special competence*, conditioned by an external framework, in relation to certain aspects of the social order, such as the internal legislation of city-states or financial rank. It was a *conditional self-determination* (see the article cited in note 1). While the concept of autonomy was little known during the Middle Ages, it was newly taken up in modern jurisprudence, and retains there a more or less clearly circumscribed character: autonomy is a freedom, limited in certain respects by the power of the state but really preserved within these limits. To describe it in a positive way, it is an area, preserved by a framework of juridical order, in which is protected a positive special competence (not yet determined by any superior instance) to set binding norms for the area. A classic example of autonomy is the legal transaction of commercial business on the basis of civil law.

Autonomy in the juristic sense is not simply the marking out of "free spaces," but rather the recognition of the competence to realize an appointed area of the law, and to do this within a normative framework, but "by one's own rules." It has to do with conditioned and guaranteed special competence (not independence) for the lawful governance of a definite area. We can call it "competence autonomy." It can be distinguished from pure independence or self-determination, which is not fixed within a limiting framework but sets itself against any conditionality, something associated with "sovereignty" or "emancipation."[9] In both cases—competence autonomy, on the one hand, and pure independence or self-determination ("emancipation" or "sovereign autonomy"), on the other—the constitution of norms within the autonomous area is provided for, and in what follows will be referred to as "constitutive autonomy."

This last-mentioned concept of constitutive autonomy provides a basis for the concept of functional autonomy. This is because an area that is governed in conditioned or absolute independence possesses a "self-governability" (*Eigengesetzlichkeit*); this would be a certain inner coherence that could not be unequivocally derived from (or reduced to) other, "parallel" areas or the conditioning framework. Autonomously governed regions *develop* their self-governance. By analogy, any realm can be called "autonomous" that simply *possesses* such self-governability, even when this does not rest on the basis of a constitutive autonomy. For example: the pastoral constitution *Gaudium et Spes* speaks of the "autonomy of earthly affairs": "For by the very circumstance of their having been created, all things are endowed with their own stability, truth, goodness, proper law and order (*propriis legibus ac ordine instruuntur; "Eigengesetzlichkeit"*). Man must respect these as he isolates them by the appropriate methods of the individual sciences or arts" (36). This autonomy, as affirmed by the phrase "by . . . their having been created" (*ex ipsa . . . creationis condicione*) is nevertheless only a functional, and not a constitutive autonomy, because these areas have not developed their own law and order through a competence that has been "conceded" to them: they have not constituted it for themselves.

This distinction is important when the "Text from Mecheln" is considered—a text rejected by the Second Vatican Council but promoted by Alfons Auer. It reads as follows: "The world has its own consistency and is guided by its own principles and laws; the Church gladly and sincerely acknowledges *that they do not fall under her competence*, but are nevertheless ordained by God, the founder of nature." Here the concept of functional autonomy has clearly been laid aside in favor of the concept of a constitutive autonomy (note the word translated as "competence": *Zuständigkeit*). However, *competence cannot be derived from the "self-governance" of functional autonomy*; this can occur only when such self-governance has been formed from a (prior) self-competence. But that is not the case here. The question of *competence* has not even been broached, let alone answered, in a matter of functional autonomy.

This very significant distinction between functional and constitutive autonomy has been treated in an exceptionally fine manner by T. Styczeń, with special attention to the structure of the "morally obliging" or "the good."[10] He distinguishes between two questions: (1) "Does the basis upon which the morally obliging/good is built present itself *in* the subject?" and (2) "Does the basis that constitutes the morally good *depend on* the subject itself ?"

(ibid., p. 79). It is possible to say "yes" to the first and "no" to the second.[11] This is exactly the structure that corresponds to the special nature of personal autonomy: as a moral subject, man discovers normativity through his moral experience in a (functionally) autonomous manner; the truth of this normativity (as the *lex naturalis*) is at the same time *not* (constitutively) dependent on the human subject. Styczeń brings this out as follows:

> Consequently, the subject, as a conscious and freely-acting "I," can discover its own self as something ontologically preexistent and axiologically proposed, which the subject cannot at all noetically dispense with. Thus, from a noetic perspective, the self of the (self-conscious) subject is not at all dependent upon the subject, although this self is its *own* self. But it also follows that the acting subject must be noetically dependent upon the truth of his own judgments about whether the actions he is to carry out freely agree with his own ontic–axiological self. The self can see this truth or can miss it, but it cannot creatively arrange it, which would amount to determining it. The creative power of the subject is directed only to the *discovery* of reality. Nevertheless, because only the subject ascertains (can ascertain) this agreement or at least believes it can ascertain it, the subject posits moral judgments, which then necessarily count as *his own*. In this function, the subject cannot be replaced. To this extent it can be said that the subject itself posits moral judgments, which then oblige it to a definite (moral) action. Understood in this way, the identification of autonomy with self-governance or legislation [*Eigengesetzlichkeit, Selbstgesetzlichkeit*] is entirely justified. However, one can be deceived about this view, and take it to mean something else: that the truth-value or validity of this imperative—and, consequently, its obliging character—depends merely upon the ontological-axiological self of the subject (as its basis and criterion of truth) and not on this positing by the subject. This is how the supposed opposition between "autonomism" and "heteronomism" can be seen as mistaken.
>
> In presenting ethical theory, it would be advisable to place equal emphasis on two things: (1) that the subject has only his own imperatives to obey—that is, they are posited by himself, and (2) that the "own self" of the subject (which also forms the standard of its worth), noetically considered, is really found *outside* the subject (as the object of its knowing). Much confusion would thereby be avoided.
>
> With this approach, the autonomy of the moral subject acquires

full expression and is completely guaranteed. Here, the subject itself remains an entity that is completely free, *because* it is rational. It has to obey only that which it has known and recognized in its own judgment as obliging: "It obliges me, *because I posit it so*," whereby the "morally obliging" becomes a deeply *immanent category* for the moral subject. At the same time, however, the person who acts, sees that he is morally obliged by his normative judgment only for so much as he sees to be true, whereby once again the morally obliging/good makes itself known to the subject as a *transcendent category*: "It obliges me, *because it is true*." And this is the *only* way the subject can always keep his right to rationality. It is the right to ask "why" of the "ought." This right justifies neither the heteronomism nor the autonomism of Kant or Sartre. Without such a right, an "I" would no longer be an "I," and its autonomy would be an illusion. (Ibid., pp. 79–81.)

On the basis of this understanding of moral autonomy, the (functional) autonomy of moral experience can be understood as the development of a theonomy by which the "self" of the subject is informed. It would not be a "theonomous autonomy" but rather an "autonomous theonomy," if I may be pardoned for seeming to play with words. But the words are not as important as the point I am trying to make: it is a theonomy that the human subject possesses *as its own* self-lawfulness, a "participated theonomy," as will be shown later. Human autonomy is thus revealed as *created*ness, thereby becoming a medium for understanding the theonomy of its self-governance.[12] The knowledge of the morally good/obliging shows itself (as Styczeń rightly observes) as a noetically indispensable truth, which, despite its functionally autonomous positing, does not depend, *constitutively considered,* on the autonomy of the subject—that is, in its constitution qua truth. For this reason, the subject cannot claim to have the "competence" of this truth.

This is exactly the structure described in the Thomist concept of the natural law as a participation of the eternal law, as shown by the studies in part I. The doctrine is distorted by the concept of "theonomous autonomy," which would , as Styczén remarked, dissolve into a moral positivism: there is a noetic truth content of the morally good/obliging that is indispensable to the subject; if this is broken, the good or "ought" cannot be founded in its (practical) truth, but merely through a factitious positing by a (constitutively autonomous) norm-giving subject: the indispensable "truth of the good" must then yield to "self-competence."

*Forms of Heteronomy*

These three forms of autonomy entail three kinds of heteronomy.

"Personal autonomy" is opposed to a heteronomy that distorts or destroys the personal determination of an action: ignorance, compulsion, violence, fear (traditionally called *hostes voluntarii*, "enemies of free choice"); personal autonomy is subjected to heteronomy when an action is demanded or coerced from a person without inner consent.[13] As already mentioned, obedience is not heteronomy, but rather a virtue, and this is true even when immediate insight into the reasonableness of what has "just now been commanded" is absent, it being presupposed that recognition of an authority that can oblige is itself the result of a personal act.[14] Coerced "obedience," on the other hand, is by definition no obedience, but rather compulsion or the use of violence (on the part of the culprit) or mere compliance or subjection (on the part of the victim).

Functional autonomy is opposed to the heteronomy that consists in dependencies or influences that collide with the self-governance of the particular area in question; such, for example, is the interference of the "law of sin" (*lex fomitis*) with the natural law. It is that "other law" St. Paul mentions, which stands in contradiction with the "law of the spirit."

Constitutive autonomy, finally, as emancipation or sovereignty autonomy (independence), can yield to heteronomy through any kind of foreign determination or dependence. Here, and only here, "heteronomy" means "dependence," and in this sense, obedience would also be heteronomy. As competence autonomy, it yields to a heteronomy through the incursions of decision makers who are unsuitable because they are *in*-competent (in individual cases it can be questioned whether the specific area in which such limited competence is granted does not itself somehow contain an incompetence).

If we now take another look at Alfons Auer's formulation—his definition, that is, of moral autonomy—it will become clear how the various concepts of autonomy and heteronomy have been jumbled together. "The concept of autonomy articulates the notions

1) that man is himself his own law,
2) that moral norms are not imposed on man from outside in the sense of heteronomous obligations,
3) but are instead evolved by himself, through the power of his reason."[15]

"Man is a law unto himself" appears to refer to *functional* autonomy, because otherwise (2) would be meaningless, for "obligations imposed from outside" do not in fact contradict personal autonomy. The principles of personal autonomy are not essentially impaired by such obligations. "Heteronomous imposition of obligations," however, could also mean "force" or "coercion," in which case (1) would have to signify *personal* autonomy. What, then, does it mean to say that "man is . . . his own law"? The statement remains unclear, but the confusion reaches a peak with (3): "[norms] evolved by himself, through the power of his reason." This is precisely *constitutive* autonomy, for man is a law unto himself insofar as he has self-governance on the basis of the norms he develops for himself. In this area, heteronomy (imposition of obligations from outside) would mean the interference of an incompetent (unsuitable) decision maker or a foreign determination. Now if this formulation is used to explain (1), as actually happens in the foregoing definition, the meaning of the statement "man is . . . his own law" remains completely ambiguous. It can no longer be functional autonomy, but can only be constitutive autonomy—"independence," in fact. This, then, is the logic that governs Auer's autonomous morality, even if it was not so intended at the outset: a personal (and functional) autonomy, reasonably proposed to begin with, becomes subjected to the criteria that determine constitutive autonomy. In other words, Auer is able to grasp the personal and functional autonomy of the practical reason (i.e., ethics) only with the assistance of the concept of constitutive autonomy. The reason for this is that Auer (as also, for example, Böckle) on the one hand grounds personal autonomy and the autonomy of the "ought" in the manner of Kant, and on the other hand conceives the relationship between human autonomy and its cause—its theonomous origin, and its createdness—in an *anthropomorphic manner.*

## Using the Concept of Autonomy: Some Limitations

It is not clear which concept of autonomy Auer actually intends when he speaks of the autonomy of the moral vis-à-vis the natural order, metaphysics, and faith. The problem comes to the fore especially when he says, "The concept of autonomy is properly realized when the principle and measure of the moral are not sought in the natural order, nor in the metaphysical essence of man, nor in a revelation that removes man's self-governance, but rather *in the reason*" ("Die Autonomie des Sittlichen," p. 52). What does it mean, we might ask, for the moral autonomy of man to consist in such self-lawgiving of the (practical) reason?

### *The "Autonomy of the Moral Order from the Natural Order"*

If the "autonomy of the moral from the natural order" is taken to mean personal autonomy (as an aspect and form of a certain kind of functional autonomy, "self-lawgiving"), then "the autonomy of the moral order from the natural" requires that the moral behavior of man in respect to the natural order (i.e., in Auer's words, the "whole sum of physiological–biological, psychological, and sociological structures and processes in which man is bound" [ibid., p. 31]) has its own logic, consistency, and lawfulness: that of a (personal) *dominium*, a *potestas* over one's own inclinations, on the basis of reason and will; the possibility to order oneself and one's actions to a goal, to comprehend goals as such, the insight into values, the freedom to affirm the good and become obliged by it. Moral action in personal autonomy means that it possesses a functional coherence (*Eigenständigkeit*) in relation to other forms of natural lawfulness.

But if we read Auer's explanation, it nevertheless becomes apparent that although he at first intends something like this by the "autonomy of the moral from the natural," in his justification he abandons the concept of functional autonomy. He ends by defending, not a functional autonomy of the moral vis-à-vis natural realms (where the phenomenon of the moral does not occur anyway), but rather an autonomy of reason vis-à-vis the nature *that man is*. Reason, of course, has a determining, regulating, standard-giving function over the "natural order." And at this point the question takes a critical turn.

For is the autonomy of reason itself *functional* in kind? This would mean that reason possesses, in respect to the natural order in which human existence is bound, a lawgiving power of its own. Reason and nature are thereby dissociated: man would unite in himself—in his being—two levels, belonging to two functionally distinct regions; we would be engaged in a radically dualistic anthropology.

Or is it meant that the reason—and the moral order that belongs to it—forms a *constitutive* autonomy in relation to the order of nature? If this implied "competence autonomy," it would lead rather to the absurd and certainly unforeseen consequence that the natural order, as the "ordering framework" that sets conditions, leaves to the reason a limited area of self-regulation and self-competence; then the reason would be subordinated to nature, since areas of competence autonomy are always subordinated areas. But that is not what Auer intends. If it were a matter of "independence" (that is, "emancipation" or "sovereignty autonomy"), it would mean that the practical reason is independent from the natural order in its valid claims; it would evolve its own law, which it must then fully execute (*durchsetzen*) in the face of the "encroachments" and "invasions" of the natural tendencies. There can actually be found terms in Auer's writings such as "nonsubjugation" (*Nicht-Unterwerfung*) to natural purposes, the "full accomplishment" (*Durchsetzung*) of the claim of reason, and so forth.

In the final analysis, what Auer really means by the autonomy of the moral from the natural order remains ambiguous: the concept of autonomy is used too imprecisely and without adequate reflection. In addition, it can frankly be said that Auer's concept has a constant tendency to slide into a constitutive autonomy in the sense of "independence."

As has already been shown, the autonomy of the moral can be conceived as a functional, and then further as a personal, autonomy, but not as an autonomy *over against the order of nature*; for the very concept of "functional autonomy" requires that within the moral realm there be likewise an autonomous realm of the natural order, in the functional sense. Auer errs at the very beginning by identifying the natural order with those realms which are *distinct from* the reason; this has the effect of sealing off any entry to a concept of the natural reason (*ratio naturalis*).

It is quite right to speak of an autonomy of the moral over against *other*, nonhuman realms of the natural order, but it is quite wrong to maintain an autonomy of the reason over against nature *in* man. *The concept of autonomy is useless for understanding the relation between nature and reason.* The reason's regulating and standard-giving function over the natural inclinations is not a matter of autonomy. The explanation lies in the fact that the reason and all natural human inclinations are integral aspects of the individual human suppositum: together, they form a personal unity. The autonomy model is unsuitable for an analysis of the relationships between these inner aspects of the human person, because it cannot come to terms with the unity of the person. Within a substantial unity, like that of the human suppositum, there cannot exist a relationship of autonomy. As already shown, the result would be a dualistic or spiritualistic view of man.

### *The "Autonomy of the Moral from Metaphysics"*

It seems clear at the outset that the "autonomy of the moral order from metaphysics" means a functional autonomy. The question that arises is whether such autonomy requires that the moral realm—the order of "good actions," of virtue—have its own self-governance in relation to the reality that is the subject matter of the science of metaphysics. Does it mean that human *being* and human *action* belong to two functionally autonomous realms? Even to ask these questions is to answer them: of course not. Or does the autonomy of the moral order vis-à-vis metaphysics mean that the (imperative) judgments of the practical reason are not derivable from, or reducible to, metaphysical–speculative statements? This is actually what Auer maintains, and we have seen in part I how and why this is so. The practical reason does in fact possess a functional autonomy in respect to the theoretical reason. And from this emerges a third possibility: a corresponding cognitive or methodological autonomy of philosophical ethics in relation to metaphysics. Again it must be emphasized that this is a matter of functional and not constitutive autonomy; it means neither a metaphysically conditioned and delimited (methodological) "self-competence" nor "independence."

New problems arise, however, because once again Auer has formulated the problem imprecisely. There are in fact three relationships concerned in the issue. First, the relation between the realm of being, studied by metaphysics, and the order of good actions, or virtue; second, the relation between "practical reason" and "speculative reason"; and third, the relation between ethics and metaphysics. For the first relationship, the concept of autonomy is useless, since it is analogous to the relationship between nature and reason, and here, too, we are concerned with personally integral aspects of the suppositum. For the second and third relationships, there is only functional (i.e., in this instance, *cognitive* or *methodological*) autonomy.

Auer speaks of an "autonomy of the *moral* over against metaphysics." What is meant here by the word "moral" (*das Sittliche*)? If the practical reason with its specifically *cognitive* autonomy, or philosophical ethics with its specifically *methodological* autonomy is intended, I can agree with him completely. But exactly as in his treatment of autonomy in respect to the natural order, Auer substitutes another concept of autonomy in the course of justifying his thesis.

At first, he writes as follows: "We must speak of the autonomy of the moral in relation to metaphysics, since the moral knowledge of actions cannot simply be won from the *natura metaphysica* of man or of the human act through deduction, extension, or application" (ibid., p. 37). To this we can agree, in the sense indicated above. It has already been shown that a practical experience lies at the basis of every metaphysical insight of man; that, in fact, there can be no metaphysical anthropology without reflection on practical experiences. But Auer tells us something quite different in the explication of his thesis: "Moral determination can therefore not be acquired from the knowledge of being, because man must not realize a *metaphysical idea,* but rather *himself.* And this is why the practical reason does not direct itself to the *general* to be determined metaphysically, but rather to the reality of concrete human life" (ibid., italics are mine).

Here, to be sure, it is stated that the metaphysics of being has for its subject matter a certain realm, in relation to which the realm of actions is autonomous. In the one case we have a realm of "metaphysical ideas" and the "general," in the other case we have "man himself" and the "reality of concrete human life." But this also implies that the man who morally realizes "himself" is not the same reality that metaphysics understands when it treats man. Auer is not speaking of a *cognitive* autonomy of the "reality of concrete life" over against the "general" and the "ideas" to be understood by metaphysics. When metaphysics reflectively studies the actions of the practical reason, it would then be impossible to interpret this autonomous area of morality in a metaphysical or anthropological manner, since the moral remains caught, for Auer, in the concrete reality of life and, as such, cannot be comprehended by a cognition that has only the general and the idea for its object. The morally good remains concrete, ever to be newly fashioned in each concrete living reality. Universal metaphysical statements about the practical good that in any way fix the concrete shaping of living reality are not possible. Metaphysics, therefore, merely justifies (in general terms) the fact that the practical good has been left to the autonomy of the practical reason of man.

In this way the autonomy of the practical reason becomes *constitutive* autonomy. It establishes a field of practical normativity in self-competence or independence, in which only the practical reason possesses competence for the determination of norms.[16] We have arrived at the same point as before: for the sake of the autonomy of the reason, the inner, personal connection between what man is and the order of his moral realization has been broken, and along with that, the connection between ethics and anthropology. Morality, human action, and finally ethics itself are relegated to an "empty" anthropological space. *Ethics could begin only where anthropology leaves off.* The reflective, metaphysical/anthropological analysis of human conduct would be able to establish only *that* the constitution of the moral begins precisely there, where anthropological conditioning leaves off, and that, accordingly, "to be human" means to be left to realize this humanness in the freedom (the autonomy) of a "creative" reason. But this same reason will not be allowed to say anything about the constitution of the moral in its concrete determination, because this realm already has a constitutive autonomy, for which metaphysics, anthropology, and so on are not competent.

*Some Conclusions*

Without at this stage going more deeply into the problem of the "autonomy of the moral from faith,"[17] we can ask why Auer and others have come up with such imprecise and doubtful answers to the problem they have quite justifiably posed. One reason lies in a too undifferentiated use of the concept "autonomy," which encourages the use of the autonomy model in inappropriate places (such as the relation between "reason" and "nature" or between "being" and "actions"). And yet there appear to be deeper causes as well. First, there is an ideological–political factor. This has to do with showing and trying to prove in an overly hasty manner that the magisterium of the Church was wrong to reject contraception. Certainly, and in close connection with the pressures to prove this, a deeper cause has been at work: the neglect or, really, the methodical "bracketing" and exclusion from discussion of an analysis of human actions in the manner of a classical treatise on the *actus humanus* and philosophical anthropology. Finally—and paradoxically—the whole field of the *personal autonomy* of man has been avoided; the autonomy that really belongs to man was simply not brought under investigation, and this can be said for "autonomous morality" as well as for "the teleological justification of norms" that we will soon be discussing. The concept of personal autonomy is fully accessible only to a metaphysical analysis, and on its basis the fundamental immorality of contraception can be effectively established; with "autonomous morality," on the other hand, the matter can only be treated awkwardly, since this approach prefers to understand the person as pure subjectivity. Böckle maintains, for example, that what matters is the "subjective being of man," as well as the "natural inclination of the reason for norm-positing activity,"[18] and the transcendental determination of human freedom. It now needs to be shown that the guiding spirit of "autonomous morality" has been Kantian philosophy, and this is to be seen not so much in the use of the term "transcendental," as in an alleged autonomy of the practical reason and a (presupposed) opposition between anthropology and ethics.

## Kant's Concept of Autonomy and "Autonomous Morality"

It is not my contention that "autonomous morality" is a mere undiluted reception of Kant, nor even that the representatives of autonomous morality have taken on Kant's intentions and the underlying problematic of his philosophy in its innermost essence and fullest depth. The profound and, frankly, tragic achievement of Kant's thought—so influential in its historically conditioned and methodological misconceptions—could have had only an indirect influence on "autonomous morality," by way of a "transcendental" exegesis of Thomism that was never designed to do full justice to Kant's own concerns.

### *Kant's Discovery of the Autonomy of the "Ought"*

Kant attempted to pose the ethical question on an entirely new basis. He had been formed in an aprioristic–rationalistic school of thought that had recently been "purified" by a shock treatment of English empiricism, and was struggling to survive in an environment of utilitarian and hedonistic eudaemonism; unfortunately, the school was further characterized by a practically complete ignorance of the classical texts of the philosophical tradition. Kant posed his questions about ethics after he had already extolled the transcendental autonomy of the (theoretical) reason in relation to nature and experience, in order to limit the possibilities of knowledge.

For Kant, all reasoning and all philosophy are essentially autonomous. Autonomy means for him that the (functional) structural law of reason is simply independence from all that is natural or from all subjective motivations that lie in front of the pure "ought." The "ought" becomes heteronomous and "alienated" for Kant whenever it has any dependence on the empirical or on any inclination or purposively teleological (or "hypothetical") motivation. Every attempt to integrate an "autonomous morality" into the motivation structure of Christian revelation was resolutely rejected by Kant as heteronomy; on the contrary, he tried to do the reverse: to reformulate faith at the level of ethics, as a "rational religion."

Kant conceived the moral "ought" as a primordial phenomenon that could be explained only by the pure self-lawgiving of the practical reason, which formulates the categorical imperative as a purely *formal* duty. Kant's autonomism is essentially a transcendent formalism of the reason. He says nothing at all about the establishment of material norms, a problem that is scarcely even touched in his writings. His practical philosophy is a theory of the conditions that make the moral "ought" possible.

Thus for Kant this "ought" must stay free of all anthropological determination. Anthropology belongs to the empirical, and therefore is heteronomous with respect to the practical reason.[19] Here is where the problem lies: the Kantian anthropology has an essentially *negative* tone. It does not provide any positive content, not even such as provided by the concept of personal autonomy. Instead, it only speaks of freedom *from* heteronomy, and of freedom *from* everything that does not originate in the reason as such. In this way the Kantian idea of a transcendent rationality becomes an entire anthropology in itself—an anthropology of a dualistic or spiritualistic character.

As self-governance of the reason, autonomy becomes *constitutive* autonomy. It constitutes the moral as moral; its content is the "ought," independent of every material, let alone anthropological, determination.

Moral autonomy for Kant is thus justified in and through a transcendental formalism of the practical reason. He calls this formalism the "moral law" and formulates it in the various versions of the categorical imperative. For Kant, only in this way can the autonomy of the moral will be guaranteed: through the freedom of the practical reason and of the (scarcely distinguishable) moral will from every "foreign influence" that would falsify it through goal-oriented (utilitarian) or natural (inclination-conditioned) influences or—and for Kant this was the most profoundly heteronomous—through a regard for reward or punishment.

Kant displays an extraordinary sense for the necessary autonomy of the "ought": something is to be done not because it "pays" or "rewards," but simply because it *ought to be done*—and that means, because it is good. This (personal) autonomy of the "ought," its formal irreducibility to something external to the will, the fact that the experience of the "ought" and subjection to its claims, can only be understood as a movement that springs from within the person and his will—this is the fundamental ethical teaching of Kant. Only in such a law does he think that autonomy can be saved, an autonomy distinguished by the transcendent formalism of the categorical imperative.

### *The Experience of the "Ought" and the Knowledge of the Good*

But just what is this "ought"? Can we separate it, as Kant does, from the "good" in practical experience or in reflection? In the formulation St. Thomas uses—that of "the first principle of the practical reason"—the "ought" is bound up with the immediate practical experience of the good ("good is *to be* pursued, evil is *to be* avoided"; *bonum prosequendum, malum vitandum est*). Is there ever an experience of the "ought" without this experience? Without, that is, the practical knowing of the good? When there is an experience of the purely formal "I ought to . . . ," doesn't such an experience always emerge as "I ought to do this" or "This is good"? In part I, we observed that the experience of the "ought" as such, as any duty or norm, appears only *in reflection on the experience of the practical reason*. The "ought" and duty are conditioned by an immediate *practical* insight into the good. Personal autonomy (despite what Kant thinks on the matter) is not realized only when someone does something because he "ought," and for no other reason—through "pure duty." Kant takes something conditioned to be something irreducible or original. Personal autonomy is present, rather, when someone does something because he has recognized it as good—and thus that it "ought" to be done. Thomas expresses this realization of personal autonomy as follows: "He is free who is a cause of himself (*qui est causa sui*): the slave is subject to the disposing power of his master (*est *causa domini*); but he who acts on his own (*ex seipso*), acts freely; on the other hand, he who acts being moved by another (*ex alio motus*) does not act freely. The person who avoids evil not because it is evil but because God has commanded it, is not free, but he who avoids the evil because it is evil, is free" (*Ad II Cor.*, c. III, lect. 3, n. 112).

As soon as the concept of the "good" is brought into the picture—something that Kant studiously avoided, unfortunately at the price of methodological soundness—new questions emerge, such as the question about how practical insight into the good comes about, or about the conditions for knowing the true good in distinction from what only seems good (the Aristotelian *phainomenon agathon*). The good can no longer be reconstructed through a transcendent formalism of Kantian stamp, nor through a doctrine of values or ideas in the tradition of Plato. One has only to reread the Aristotelian arguments about the inadequacy of such formalism for philosophical ethics in order to become convinced that in his ethical program, Kant in a certain respect fell back to a pre-Aristotelian position.

## *The Common Deficit: An Anthropology of Moral Action*

This "archaism" of Kant is remarkable for a separation of the *founding of moral good* from the *analysis of human actions*. The Aristotelian "revolution" consisted in understanding ethics as a doctrine of *good actions* (*eupraxía*): not as an investigation into the good as object of knowledge, but rather as the object and content of *actions*; his ethics is thus to a great extent a theory of moral *action*, or of human action, insofar as it is human; ultimately it is a theory of virtue. Ethics as a doctrine of action that is based on an analysis of the structure and peculiarities of the *actus humanus* and its structure of personal autonomy reaches its summit in St. Thomas. Later nominalistic (or "legalistic") trends, followed by empirical, utilitarian, and hedonistic distortions of the doctrine of action, all had their affect on Kant. Barred from direct entry into the classical inheritance, he separated ethics not only from a doctrine of action but also from anthropology, a science that cannot do without a theory of human and moral action.

The attempt to establish ethics independently of an anthropology of human (moral) action and the resulting failure to establish a doctrine of virtue founded on an actions theory, is the characteristic legacy of Kant, which has shaped (and today continues to shape) many attempts to establish a theory of ethics. The attempt to explain the "ought" as a transcendental formalism is only one possible variant. Even the values philosophy of Max Scheler, with all its very productive and pertinent phenomenological analysis, is still marked by the lack of a concept of the good as an axiological dimension of human action *as* action. All forms of utilitarianism are essentially constituted through the *exclusion* of this problem. If they took the step of identifying the useful with the good, and thus preserved a relation between usefulness and truth,[20] there would be no need to speak of utilitarianism. A theory of operative truth or the good action is also missing from analytical ethics, which results from a method confined to the linguistic/communicative phenomena of the "ought."[21] The so-called "teleological ethics" (to be discussed later in this study) has been completely shaped by the exclusion of an analysis of human actions; it exhausts itself in a theory of "right ways of acting" and a corresponding method of establishing norms, and owes its plausibility, finally, to a presupposition that the "good" is ultimately nothing other than a formalism derived from a transcendent analysis of the "ought." Further discussion of the concept of "autonomous morality" will make clearer how much this model remains under the influence of the Kantian revolution, and how it thereby leaves aside, if unknowingly, a more than two-thousand year tradition of ethics as a doctrine of good actions and virtue.[22]

The Kantian autonomy of the reason must in principle banish from itself every "dependence"; accordingly, it must also conceive theonomy as a heteronomy. It can accept the reality of God only as a postulate of the practical reason, as a regulative idea, but not as a normative cause. This is the point where Catholic moral theologians intervene, maintaining that autonomy and theonomy must be united. But the attempt to establish a theonomy of the reason in a Kantian sense, which would have to be autonomous in respect to natural inclination and any anthropological determinateness, leads to "theonomous autonomy"; a conception that on closer analysis appears as a questionable anthropomorphism: just as for the relationships reason/nature and action/being, the concept of autonomy is useless for understanding the dependence of man and his practical reason on God and His creative reason.

## "Theonomous Autonomy": An Anthropomorphism

The first problem in regard to the concept of "theonomous autonomy" lies in the characterization of the relationship between human actions and morality, on the one hand, and the divine establishment of norms, on the other. As the term "autonomy" is generally used today, it implies that while human actions and morality are subject to a divine norm-giving and are founded upon it, nevertheless the moral action of man operates within an autonomous "free space," in which human reason exercises its "creative" function.

But this is not a functional (or personal) autonomy of man. Rather, it is an autonomy of man for the constitution of moral normativity. It is implied that the realm of moral action represents a theonomous "free space" established at creation for the shaping of the morally good. The practical reason has been constituted, through its creation, as a "creative reason" in relation to moral obligations, and in this sense it is autonomous.

### *Theonomous Autonomy of the "World Ethos"*

Whereas such autonomy of "creative" reason has usually been seen as an autonomy founded on the *lex aeterna* or the *lex naturalis* (which thus reduces it to the highest, most general, and purely formal aspects), with Alfons Auer the theme has been formulated as an "autonomy of the moral in regard to faith"; this is apparently because he believes that the created dependence of man upon God is a theme of revelation alone, and thus can be apparent only to a believer (*Autonome Moral,* p. 172). This position, that "theonomy," "God," and "creation" are as such only themes of faith and theology (as the "science of the faith," *scientia fidei*), is untenable, not least because of the whole philosophical tradition: God, creation, dependence of the world upon a first cause, and so on are also *philosophical* themes and the subject matter of rational human discourse. There is a natural, philosophical theology;[23] the question about God, and about theonomy, belongs to metaphysics as well as to ethics and to the "normal" realm of human action, independently of revelation and faith.[24] Indeed, the concept of moral action itself and moral experience are open to questions about God. Furthermore, "religion"—the virtue of religion—is part of a human and natural cardinal virtue: the virtue of justice.

Consequently, one may not maintain that questions about God and the theonomous establishment of the moral are questions that arise only through faith, and then go on to "exclude" from this any createdness of functionally autonomous earthly realities. It appears to me to be especially mistaken to divide the moral realm into two, with an autonomous "world ethos" on the one side, and a "salvation ethos" on the other, so that the question of theonomy would arise only in the latter. The question of theonomy—the relation of earthly reality, man, and his actions to God—belongs just as much to the "world ethos."[25]

The question about the theonomous justification of an autonomous morality always presents itself to Auer as a question about the relationship between autonomous, human morality and Christian faith, and as such it is no longer a theme for philosophical reflection. The starting point for this is first the concept of functional autonomy: "The laws that can be observed in the various fields of the world—we call this their autonomy—are communicated through the Logos, but are instituted by God to be self-operative" (*Autonome Moral,* p. 172). But the justification for this departs from functional autonomy: God lets "man do as he pleases in freedom and does nothing to reduce him to the status of a marionette. . . . The transcendental causality of the Creator and the total dependence of the world on His creative power do not endanger in the least the autonomy of the world, but rather make it possible. God is not the rival of man, and will not drive him from the governing position he has in the world; on the contrary, he wants him to have the most control possible. Obviously, all of this is intelligible only to the believer and could not be demonstrated to a nonbeliever" (ibid.).

It readily becomes clear how the concept of autonomy turns into a constitutive autonomy. First of all, Auer unfortunately does not distinguish between the (functional) autonomy of earthly regularities and the (personal) autonomy of human action, so that it is not known whether he is speaking of the self-governance of the world or of human action; Moreover, the concept of a human, theonomously founded autonomy is set up in contrast to a notion, presented as obviously mistaken, of a rivalry between man and God: human autonomy is then the divinely established dominance of man in the world. But the concept of autonomy here indicated is no less anthropomorphic than the concept used as "foil." Human autonomy as "self-competence," "partnership," or "independence" is nonsense from the point of view of a creationist metaphysics. It projects the legal relationship that obtains between human beings onto the relationship of creature/Creator, and comes perilously close to the Deist idea of God as the great Watchmaker.

### *"Autonomy" and "Participation": Some Clarifications*

The model of autonomy that Auer uses says both too much and too little. Too much, because man cannot have this kind of independence in relation to God. The notion that the causality of the Creator would constitute only the ordered "frame" within which the "competence" space of an "autonomous world" is found, is metaphysically untenable. The causal dependence of the creature upon the Creator is total, both in being and in actions. Through the peculiar nature of divine creative causality, there is an actually operative immanence of God in everything that is created and acts.

On the other side, Auer's anthropomorphic view of human autonomy says far too little: the actually existing personal autonomy of man is much more than a guaranteed "free space" or "autonomous" position of dominance, and this is so precisely *because* of man's radical dependence upon God. The personal autonomy of man has been created *ad imaginem Dei*; to anticipate later arguments somewhat, it is not a "competence" granted by God, but *participation in God's own "competence,"* again not in the sense of "competence autonomy," but rather through a "partaking" (participation) in God's own perfection.[26] The justification of man's personal autonomy cannot be illustrated by anthropomorphic models such as the "granting of competence" or the "transference of power." Man is not a "partner" of God, but rather His creature and image.

The relation of the creation to the Creator that is expressed by the concept of participation cannot be expressed by the category of autonomy, which is taken from human, intracreational experience. In a certain sense, "autonomy" and "participation" signify mutually exclusive situations: participation means something "seen from above," a communication of one's perfection to another in such a way that the communicated perfection becomes the possession of the receiver; participation constitutes an immanence of the "giver" in the "receiver." Participation establishes functional autonomy as participated perfection, but not as constitutive autonomy. The latter is only a "comprehending" (*umgreifende*) or "carrying" (*tragende*) framework of order, inside which any communication or participation would be left "blanked out"; it means the preservation of a participation-free "space" within which there is no immanence of the "giver," only independence to make something "new."

The relationship of (constitutive) autonomy indicates an interhuman relationship; that of participation indicates the way creature and Creator behave toward one another. Autonomy constitutes an area of freedom by humans and among humans, conditioned by ownership or legal relations; participation constitutes a created freedom brought about by the Creator, a freedom that would sink into nothingness without the immanence of God made possible by such participation—without, that is, the *imago* character of human freedom.

This may sound all too abstract, and we will return to it in the context of an analysis of the *imago* character of the natural law. Nevertheless, we have attempted to establish that the concept of autonomy, when conceived in an anthropomorphic fashion, is useless for the relation between creature and Creator.

The same anthropomorphism appears in somewhat different form in the attempts of Böckle and his student K.-W. Merks to construct a theonomously grounded autonomy of human morality by way of an interpretation of the eternal and natural laws.

### *Theonomous Autonomy of the "Creative Reason"*

Franz Böckle[27] also proceeds from the concept of creation. "According to this understanding of theology as a creative process,

God and man are not in competition with each other in the same sphere of activity. God's creative activity transcendentally embraces the whole categorial evolution of the world" (*Fundamental Moral Theology,* p. 54). Böckle rightly emphasizes that on the basis of this createdness, the Creator "founds the world and man on their being themselves and on their own activity. It is on this foundation that man is able fully to affirm his existence as an autonomous, moral rational being" (ibid.).

This speaks, in general, of the functional autonomy of the world established by creation and, in particular, of the personal autonomy of man. But what does this creation-founded autonomy involve? Böckle operates with the terms "transcendental causality of God" and "categorial" or moral (self-)development of man. God's creation "transcendentally" comprehends the categorial autonomy of the world. Now it would not exactly be obvious what Böckle meant by this, had he not made clear that he is adapting ideas like those of Auer.

At least one thing is obvious at the outset: Böckle is *not* speaking of participation, for participation would make impossible any autonomy of the categorial vis-à-vis the transcendent. He means, rather, a (participated) immanence of the transcendent in the categorial structure of created reality. The latter is a participation, with its own being, of the reality that grounds it, and this takes place through a communicated immanence of the *founding* reality in the *founded* reality (*communicatio perfectionis*).

The difficulty of understanding Böckle's position lies in the fact that he constantly confuses the concepts of functional (or personal) autonomy and constitutive autonomy. Such sentences as the following are unobjectionable if used in the sense of personal autonomy: "The man who is in accordance with maxims of action that he has given to himself is autonomous man" (ibid., p. 58), and the autonomous reason is "the *ratio* as legislative structure."[28] But Böckle does not stop at this. He understands man's participation "in divine reason" (which comes about "because he was made in the image of God") to be a "*creative activity* of human reason" (ibid., p. 61). Now, what is *not* meant by this is that man partakes of the ordering (*ordinatio*) of the divine mind itself, so that this divine *ordinatio* communicates itself to man, is immanent in him, and (in personal autonomy) is fulfilled by him. What *is* meant is that through his divine image, man himself is granted his own norm-giving competence through his "natural inclination, experienced in practical reason, to create norms with regard to his ultimate fulfillment (ibid., p. 62).

To be sure, Böckle is concerned to free his conception of any trace of anthropomorphism. He points out that God works as *causa prima*, and the creation as *causa secunda*: both are not "part-causes" of a common effect, but rather, on their own levels, in their own orders, they are total causes of total effects.[29] Now, if Böckle were consistent in his metaphysical reasoning, such an immanence of the first cause in the operations of the second would lead to very different results: it would lead, in the first place, to a treatment of the lawgiving activity of the practical reason not as *creative*, but as determined by the peculiarities of creaturely knowing; in the second place, it would preclude a spiritualistic understanding of man, and would refuse to delimit the presence of the eternal law (and the immanence of the first cause) *to the reason alone,* but would extend it to the other levels of the natural inclinations—taking into account, in other words, the *whole man.* Metaphysically this aspect is of fundamental importance. If man really acts as a second cause, then the operative immanence of the first cause is to be extended to the entirety of the created reality, which would mean the *whole man*; if one interprets the natural law in the categories of second causality, then, according to proper metaphysical reasoning, the nonrational inclinations would also belong to the natural law,[30] and the natural law in man would not be restricted to the "natural inclination to create norms" (ibid.).

The concluding formula that Böckle uses to describe the moral autonomy of the reason does not correspond to the (metaphysically defined) relationship between a first and a second cause: "The obligatory claim [i.e. the claim of the "ought"] is to be understood as a total dependence (the creatural state) in the independence of self-determination (the personal state). On the one hand, freedom implies total dependence, insofar as man is offered the possibility of deciding in favor of freedom as a gift (creation as grace). On the other hand, however, it is also total independence, insofar as man finds himself confronted with a choice with regard to the only possibility of freedom" (ibid., p. 63).

What Böckle expresses here is apparently the following: man is totally dependent on God *insofar* as he receives from Him the "possibility of deciding in favor of freedom [*Freiheitsentscheidung*] as a gift [from God]." At the same time, however, man is totally independent from God *insofar* as he exercises this freedom in the norm-giving activity of the reason. There is then no participative immanence of the divine reason and its *ordinatio*, no immanence of the *lex aeterna* in the act of the human *ratio*. The norm-giving activity of man is not completely the work of God (as would be the case with the first cause), but rather, as Böckle maintains, "totally independent." But this is to say, then, that the moral autonomy of man consists in an "independence" or "self-competence" established by God through creation, and simply "ratified" by God Himself for the sake of man's autonomy. This further implies that there is nothing naturally good for man apart from completely surrendering his action to the norm-giving and creative activity of his reason. The theonomous grounding of such autonomy means only that man possesses a God-given power, and a God-given duty as well, to shape his life in independence, on the basis of the norm-giving activity of the reason. Böckle calls this "created freedom": "In the light of faith in God's creation, the unconditioned obligatory claim is simply the dependence of a personally free self, over which a total claim is made, in this freedom, to be in control of itself, also in freedom" (ibid., p. 57).

Here any notion of participation completely disappears, and is replaced by an anthropomorphically conceived constitutive autonomy: what Böckle presents as an understanding of freedom that rests upon "faith in God's creation" really pertains to the categories used to formulate juristic relations within society. Let's imagine that as a result of a decision taken in a centralized state, a law is passed that leaves it to the competence of a certain region or community to set up a school system. Such a transfer of competence establishes for the receiver an inalienable obligation to realize that competence, and places the receiver into the dependence of an unconditional "ought," but at the same time guarantees an independence for the arrangement of concrete details within the prescribed area of competence and within the framework of the law. If the region in question did not set up the school system, it would offend against the obligation imposed upon it and could be brought to account, since it possesses no competence to establish its own autonomy. The "autonomous" region is thus required by a superordinated authority "to be in control of itself, also in freedom."

Böckle's concept of autonomy can be wholly correlated to such patterns. But it is the opposition between total dependence and total independence that really cancels out any idea of participation. For participation does not allow for an "independence" of the participating entity, but rather a "possessing on its own," an *appropriation* of something. It is a relation that in itself has nothing to do with autonomy, but *provides the basis* for autonomy in the sense of functional autonomy.

In the work of Böckle's student K.-W. Merks, the anthropomorphic distortion of the idea of participation becomes somewhat more prominent. So, for example, in the following formulation: "God's foreknowledge and governance of the world do not require His *immediate* intervention in every event, but rather provide a kind of all-embracing ordering [*umgreifend Ordnungsgebende*] in such a way that it is comprehensively effective (as freely giving a created causal power) without losing its universality; thus everything, down to the smallest detail, is governed by it, but in the way of *ratio*, which differs from *executio*: *ratio* is realized not only through the constitution of realities that have effectiveness, but also through reason's own activity—and herein is its greatness revealed."[31] Merks then characterizes God in relation to the moral order established by man as a "framework-providing good" (*rahmengebendes bonum*; *Theologische Grundlegung,* p. 194), so that in the end, Merks follows his teacher Böckle in reducing the presence or immanence of the *lex aeterna* in the human reason to "the foundation of the obligating character, independently of the immediate communication of obliging content, and as such, the foundation for the practical communication of the obligating character through the *ratio*" (ibid., p. 210). Finally, a theonomously founded autonomy, as with Böckle, means that man is obligated by God to follow his own reason "in freedom."

## Autonomy or Participation?

But these criticisms still do not solve the problem. The difficulties that Auer, Böckle, Merks, and others are grappling with rest upon a real problem contained in the Thomist concept of the natural law as participation of the eternal law. The eternal law, as Thomas always emphasizes, is as such not immediately accessible to man: it is always known by mediation, whether this be through (supernatural) revelation, on the one hand (which can for the moment be set to one side), or, on the other hand, through (natural) revelation by way of the human reason. Through the natural law man carries the eternal law in himself; it is his own possession, and he knows it exactly to the extent that the natural law unfolds itself in the acts of his practical reason.

Now one may well ask, What does it add to the picture, to know that the natural law is a participation of the eternal law? How does this help me know what I should do? Isn't it rather the case that we can only have recourse to our reason? Knowing that the moral good is grounded in the eternal law, we recognize it only through our own (i.e., personal–autonomous) reason anyway. Isn't it right, then, for Merks to treat the standpoint of the eternal law as practically irrelevant? For, he says, "The *lex aeterna* rules everything in any case. Whether something is 'right' in a moral sense cannot be judged by direct recourse to a *lex aeterna*, insofar as this is not a 'disclosing' [*erschließende*] but a "disclosed" [*erschlossene*] value, the ethical relevance of which we can determine only insofar as it has already been explicitly set forth and preclarified from some other source, namely, in some ethical position" (*Theologische Grundlegung*, p. 216).

An important distinction is neglected in this formulation. It is correct, of course, that the eternal law regulates *everything*, down to the last detail. The *ordinatio* of the divine reason is not directed only toward the "universal," but also toward the "particular." But if we are to speak of the *lex naturalis* as a participation of the eternal law, it would concern only the universal content of this *ordinatio*; the particular would be governed by another kind of human "providence": through the *ordinatio* of prudence. But precisely because this distinction between universal and particular *ordinatio* is found in the (participated) structure of human reason, it must be prefigured in the *lex aeterna*. The statement "The eternal law rules everything in any case" suppresses the fact that we can recognize that, even as a "disclosed value," it does not rule everything *in the same way*; namely, it rules one way *in universali* and another way *in particulari*.

When the question is posed as Merks has posed it, one can only come to the following conclusion: knowing that the natural law (and the practical, personal–autonomous moral knowledge of man) is founded in the eternal law in the end brings no further insights and only casts man back upon himself. The *lex aeterna* and the participative character of the *lex naturalis* would then have significance only as a metaphysical and reductive explanation[32] that says only that man's "being-left-to-himself" is theonomous—or ultimately ordained by God.

Moreover, the question of whether a recourse to the eternal law really contributes anything to the determination of norms of moral behavior is a misleading question insofar as it presupposes that the *lex naturalis*—and the practical good for which it sets a norm—is itself another law (or another realm of law) than that of the *lex aeterna*. But this is not the case. In reply to a certain objection (the content does not matter for our argument) that presupposed just such a difference, Thomas replies, "That objection would hold, if the natural law were something different (*aliquid diversum*) from the eternal law. But it is nothing if not a certain participation of it" (*I–II*, q. 91, a. 2, ad 1um). The natural law is not different from the eternal law; rather, it is the eternal law itself *as participated by man*. This implies that the eternal law is not unknown to us; that we recognize it, insofar as concerns us, in the natural law.

Once again, we are confronted with the concept of participation. If the natural law is really *the same thing* as the eternal law, which has become the possession of the creature by way of participation, this would also mean that it shows the same characteristics as all created realities constituted through participation: it reveals an order preordained and founded in God (in this case, in the *lex aeterna*), but grounded in a capability that belongs to, and is immanent in, the person (i.e., it is functionally autonomous). The participative character of the *lex naturalis* says much more, therefore, than the fact that it is founded in God. It says that *in the natural law an "ordinatio" of human actions toward their goal, existing from eternity in the divine wisdom, comes here to expression and realization.*

In such terms, the notion that the natural law leaves free an area of specifically human "creative" normativity is more than questionable, and lacks metaphysical justification. For if the natural law is participation of the eternal law and, accordingly, if there is an identity by way of participation (an immanence of the *lex aeterna* in the *lex naturalis*), then the natural law cannot be limited to a "natural inclination, experienced in practical reason, to create norms for his ultimate fulfillment," as Böckle has taken it. If it were only that, the eternal law (at least in relation to man) would be only an inclination or a "potential rationality" (of the divine reason) for norm-giving acts, the actualization of which would be left to the creature in his autonomy; it could not then be an *ordinatio* of the divine reason that is actual, universal, and perfect, and in existence from eternity, which is what Thomas expressly maintains. Böckle's concept implies that the eternal law is not an *ordinatio* of human actions toward their goal, but rather that this *ordinatio* has been left to the autonomy of the creature. As already shown, the image is anthropomorphic, and is untenable with respect to both metaphysics and the text of St. Thomas. It claims that in God there is a freedom that does not establish an order to the good. It would assume in the divine wisdom, whose *ratio* is indeed the *lex aeterna*, an "openness" or indetermination. Only in this way could Böckle's understanding of the natural law still be conceived as a participation of the eternal law.

Is it still possible to say that the *ordinatio* of the natural law (or the human reason) is *constitutively* autonomous in respect to the eternal law? Then one could no longer say that the natural law is a participation of the eternal law and is *the same* law. It would only be a law *made possible* by the eternal law, but still different from it: a law that would fall under the *ordinatio* of the *lex aeterna* only insofar as it developed within the "free-space" ordained and preserved by the *lex aeterna*. Again, this view, too, would be anthropomorphic and would obviously contradict the fundamental doctrine of St. Thomas, that the natural law is a participation of the eternal law.

On the basis of the participative structure of the *lex naturalis*, there is only one possibility: in the natural law stands revealed the eternal and universally valid *ordinatio*, through the wisdom of the divine reason, of human actions toward their end. Now this may not take us any closer to answering the question about setting norms in the concrete, but in fact it is still too early to ask that question. The question that arises now is a very different one: How does the *ordinatio* of the eternal law *come through* as the natural law? In other words, before we inquire about how the reason sets its "norms," we should ask how the participated immanence of the eternal law comes to its expression in man: "How does man participate in the eternal law?" This was sketched out roughly in part I. It would now seem worthwhile to study more exactly how the personal autonomy of man is founded as a participated autonomy. The key to the answer, once again, lies in the concept of the practical reason as the natural reason (*ratio naturalis*).

## Notes

1. See R. Pohlmann, "Autonomie," in J. Ritter, ed., *Historisches Wörterbuch der Philosophie,* vol. 1 (Basel, 1971), 701–719.

2. I have borrowed the term "personal autonomy" from sociology, where it is used to indicate individuality, spontaneity of choice, personal self-determination in the face of pressure for conformity and against behavior that is externally guided and caused by social coercion. See, for example, D. Lee, "Individual Autonomy and Social Structure," in *Society and Self,* ed. B. H. Stoodley (New York and London, pp. 223–231; further, D. Riesman, H. P. Dreitzel, and others). Of course, the concept of personal autonomy as used here will not be a sociological concept, but it appears to me to be the proper philosophical–ethical analogue.

3. See also *De Veritate,* q. 22, a. 4: "animalia non habent dominium suae inclinationis; unde non agunt, sed magis aguntur, secundum Damascenum. . . . Sed natura rationalis . . . habet in potestate ipsam inclinationem, ut non sit ei necessarium inclinari ad appetibile apprehensum, sed possit inclinari vel non inclinari. Et sic ipsa inclinatio non determinatur ei ab alio, sed a seipsa." (animals do not have mastery over their own inclination; therefore they do not "act" but are rather "acted," according to Damascenus. . . . But the rational nature . . . has the inclination itself in its own power, so that it is not necessary for it to be inclined to an apprehended good, but can be inclined or not inclined. And thus the inclination itself is not determined by another, but by itself.)

4. See also *Contra Gentiles,* III, cap. 112, n. 2857: "Quod dominium sui actus habet, liberum est in agendo, 'liber enim est qui sui causa est': quod autem quadam necessitate ab alio agitur ad operandum, servituti subiectum est. Omnis igitur alia creatura servituti subiecta est: sola intel-

lectualis natura libera est." (That which has mastery of its own action is free in its acting, "for he is free who is the cause of himself": however, that which is driven by some kind of necessity to do something is subjected to servitude, only the intellectual nature is free.)

5. In the language of Aristotle, it means to act not merely *kata logon* (according to reason, in the sense of an external following of reason) but also *meta logou* (with reason), which means, on the basis of one's own rational insight, molding the striving power or appetition (*prohairesis*); see *Nichomachean Ethics,* VI, 13.

6. It is not in any way implied that an act of obedience offends against personal autonomy; as a virtue, obedience arises immediately from prudence, that is, from the insight that it is good and reasonable to follow a certain authority. Only an obedience that lacks such rationality and freedom, and that is performed without reason, would be "heteronomous": it would come in conflict with the mastery over one's own action presupposed in moral behavior; it would originate, that is, not from one's own mastery but from the mastery of another. So long as I obey because I want to, and because I understand it to be good to do so, I keep my personal autonomy—in a certain sense, I increase it, because by doing so, I surpass the limits of my own horizon of insight into the good.

7. This concept has also been in use in sociology, and denotes the relative independence and self-legislation of, for instance, differentiated social subsystems.

8. A full analysis of the *ordinatio rationis* in its character as law was given in part I.

9. "Emancipation" is a Roman legal term and means "release from the father's power," the movement from minority to majority, standing on one's own, and self-determination. In politics, one may consider, for example, the winning of independence by regions previously controlled by colonial powers as "emancipation," and the resulting status as "sovereignty." In this case emancipation does not mean "freeing" (*Befreiung*), but "granting" (*Entlassung*), which is the concession of independence. The analogue to competence autonomy consists in the fact that this is also a "granting" of competence.

10. See T. Styczén, "Autonome Ethik mit einem christlichen 'Proprium' als methodologisches Problem," in D. Mieth and F. Compagnoni, ed., *Ethik im Kontext des Glaubens* (Freiburg and Vienna, 1978) pp. 75–100.

11. See ibid.: "Considered logically, it is possible that the basis that is valid for the morally obliging/good is fully identifiable ontically (ontologically, metaphysically) and axiologically with the self of the acting

subject, without the one who acts (as a conscious subject) knowingly placing his own ontic/axiological self creatively into 'existence' and 'existence-so' (*Da-sein, So-sein*), in the sense of *percipi—esse* (to be perceived—to be). The analysis of the judgment of conscience as a basic phenomenon of the moral sphere shows that this possibility really occurs."

12. Styczén (ibid., p. 82), in a daring but correct formulation, calls the self a "theophany" and characterizes a rightly understood "theonomous autonomy" as an "autonomy of the human being in God"; this is perhaps preferable to the expression "autonomous theonomy" I have just used.

13. Ignorance (insofar as it is involuntary) brings about an action without real consent; this is apparent from the fact that someone would act differently, had he not been in ignorance.

14. Faith is just such a personal act, and therefore the "obedience of faith" is spoken of, which is intelligible only on the basis of the freedom of the act of conscience. On this see A. Laun, *Das Gewissen. Oberste Norm sittlichen Handelns* (Innsbruck, 1984).

15. "Hat die autonome Moral eine Chance in der Kirche?" in G. Virt, ed., *Moral begründen—Moral verkünden* (Innsbruck and Vienna, 1985), 9–30.

16. This is reminiscent of the attractive, but metaphysically doubtful, thesis of Auer on the "potential rationality" of the world: "For modern thinking, the world is something formless, which waits for human shaping and releases its potential only through human undertakings. This is possible only because a potential rationality is already present in the world and in man who shapes it. Only because man is himself rational, is he able to discover and exalt the rationality of the world. Human rationality implies responsibility for the rationality of the world. Whoever is capable of bringing the world closer to its meaning and order becomes obliged by this very capability. Here is the true point of origin for the moral" (*Autonome Moral und christlicher Glaube,* 2nd ed. (Düsseldorf, 1984), pp. 35f). Through the absence of a distinction between the "world" that surrounds man, and the "world" that belongs as "nature" to the human suppositum, this thesis supports a dualistic anthropology. In the same way, Auer does not distinguish between "existential integration" (or "meaningfulness") of the natural and its cognitive and operative integration through moral virtue; see chapter 2, section "The Natural Law and Virtue," subsection "The Identity of the *Ordo Rationalis* with the *Ordo Virtutis.*"

17. Insofar as such autonomy implies a cognitive autonomy of moral knowing in relation to revealed obligations of natural–human morality

(e.g., the Decalogue), or of natural knowledge of the existence of God over against the revelation of such existence, what Auer says is correct and not anything new. The assertion of such autonomy is part of the customary teaching of the Catholic Church. The problem arises only with respect to (a) the question of the real possibility of certain, complete and error-free knowledge of these obligations in the state of fallen nature, and (b) the question about the relation between human–natural morality and revealed Christian morality.

18. See Franz Böckle, *Fundamentalmoral* (Munich, 1977), pp. 90–91.

19. For Kant, the empirical stands in a necessary opposition to the universal; the ground of the "ought," as moral imperative, must be universal in nature; otherwise, morality would be handed over to subjective arbitrariness as well as impurely moral motivation (interest). Only the reason can be the basis of a universal imperative. Accordingly, the ground of the moral "ought" can be sought only in the reason, which must remain autonomous, that is, autonomous from all heteronomy of the empirical or of particulars conditioned by motives. A. Laun has well clarified the ambiguous meaning of the Kantian autonomy concept as independence from the empirical on the one side and from impure, "interested" motivation on the other (*Das Gewissen,* 1984), pp. 31–37.

20. As was accomplished by the Aristotelian concept of "practical truth"; see F. Inciarte, "Theoretische und praktische Wahrheit," in M. Riedel, ed., *Rehabilitierung der praktischen Philosophie*, vol. 2, (Freiburg im Breisgau, 1974), pp. 155–170. It is precisely in the Aristotelian concept of *phronesis* that there is reference to a truth of action, an *operative truth*: this is the (moral) good, which is realized *in action* and has its *locus* there.

21. In this connection the works of Kenny, Anscombe, Finnis, and others are to be recommended, they have been very fruitful in some respects, but apparently have been neglected by the majority of Catholic moral theologians, who have adopted analytical ethics.

22. The study of K.-W. Merks, *Theologische Grundlegung der sittlichen Autonomie* (Düsseldorf, 1978), with its broadly conceived interpretation of Thomas, undoubtedly attempts to include an anthropological, actions-theory point of view. Merks does not succeed, however, in coming to terms with this aspect, and this can be seen above all in his confusion about the *Secunda Pars* as a treatise on virtue.

23. This is why Aristotle called his "first science" *theologia,* the science of God, because it is the knowledge of the first cause. It was called "metaphysics" only later and by chance. And Greek antiquity knew the pioneers of metaphysics—the pre-Socratics—as *theologoi.*

24. To what extent man is always and everywhere under the influence of the grace of God, whose salvation is extended to all mankind, is

a completely different question. Its positive answer does not in any case imply that someone who is *open* to God already has *faith*, because the reality of God as the ground of all reality belongs to the constitutive truth of the world in its natural dimension. Just because someone is not an atheist or an agnostic does not mean that he is a Christian, not even an "implicit" or an "anonymous" one.

25. This recieves clear expression in the documents of the Second Vatican Council (*Gaudium et Spes,* nr. 36); there it is stated that there is a false understanding of the autonomy of earthly realities which ignores the fact that created things depend upon God, implying that they can be used without any reference to their Creator; but the creature itself, without any acknowledgment of its dependence on God, would be "unintelligible." This means that an autonomous world-ethos that does not include the dimension of *createdness* and theonomy implies a concept of autonomy that falsifies the reality of the creature. Such a concept approaches that which the Council calls "systematic atheism" (ibid., n. 20); of course, Auer is no atheist, but his understanding of the "world ethos" with a God that becomes visible only through revelation and faith uses the same concept as that employed in "methodical atheism." He cannot be spared this reproach.

26. See the excellent expositions of J. De Finance, "Autonomie et Théonomie," in M. Zalba, ed., *L'agire Morale,* vol. 5 of *Tommaso d'Aquino nel suo settimo centenario,* (Naples, 1974 ) pp. 239–260.

27. I depend here on Böckle's presentation in *Fundamentalmoral,* pp. 80–92; quotations here are taken from the English translation by N. D. Smith: *Fundamental Moral Theology* (New York, 1980) pp. 54–63.

28. Ibid., p. 61. Laun's criticism (see *Das Gewissen,* p. 19) of the concept of the "legislative reason" is too undifferentiated, in my opinion, for as we observed in part I, the natural law really does arise from a legislative act of the practical reason; it is *aliquid a ratione constitutum,* and like every law, an *ordinatio rationis.* The problem does not lie in the concept of a lawgiving reason per se, but rather in the view that this legislative function is autonomous, and not participative.

29. See also F. Böckle, "Natürliches Gesetz als göttliches Gesetz in der Moraltheologie," in F. Böckle and E.-W. Böckenförde, ed., *Naturrecht in der Kritik* (Mainz, 1973), p. 177.

30. It has been shown in part I how, and to what extent, the natural inclinations do belong to the *lex naturalis.*

31. Merks, *Theologische Grundlegung der sittlichen Autonomie,* p. 193. In support of his view Merks cites I, q. 22, a. 3: "inferiora gubernat per superiora; non propter defectum suae virtutis, sed propter abundantiam suae bonitatis, ut dignitatem causalitatis etiam creaturis communicet."

Here Merks has clearly missed the whole point of the idea of participation. We have to do here with a *communicatio* of God's own perfection, which brings about participation in the divine causality, but not a release into one's own, independent causality. *Communicatio* is not to be thought of as a "delegation" or "lending" of efficacy or competence, but rather as granting a partaking in God's own efficacy and competence.

32. Reference is sometimes made to W. Kluxen who showed that "the standpoint of the eternal law is no longer a practical, but speculative one" (*Philosophische Ethik bei Thomas von Aquin*, 2nd ed. [Hamburg, 1980], p. 234). He only means by this that the concept of the eternal law as such does not emerge in the experience of the practical reason, but only in the speculative/reflective examination of this experience. Now this does not mean, that the standpoint of the eternal law must finally remain outside the methodological horizon of a philosophical ethics. This would be just as mistaken as to exclude metaphysical and anthropological interpretations from philosophical ethics. They really belong to it and serve to illuminate in a complete way the experience of the practical reason that is its theme (see part 1 of this study). The result of Kluxen's work is not a justification of a "methodical atheism" for philosophical ethics; rather, he justifies the integrity of practical experience and its priority to any metaphysical interpretation of that experience.

# 5

# Participated Autonomy: Toward A Metaphysics and Anthropology of the Natural Law

## The "Eternal Law" As A Philosophical Notion

Because of its peculiar subject matter and peculiar method of posing questions, philosophical ethics requires an anthropological and metaphysical clarification of its analyses. This is especially called for when it comes to the concept of the natural law: a complete account would provide an anthropology and metaphysics of the natural law, such as was only sketched out in part I. Now, after our encounter with "theonomous autonomy," we can fill in more detail.

The concept of "theonomous autonomy" and the attempt to reduce the natural law to a purely formal, materially undetermined "natural inclination of the reason to create norms" (to use Böckle's formula) both involve a single theme: that of the relationship between the human *ratio* (which formally constitutes the natural law) and the eternal law (*lex aeterna*), the *ratio* of God's providence and wisdom, by which all creatures are guided toward their final goal.

Among present-day Thomists there is a widespread tendency (at least in philosophical contexts) to explain away the doctrine of the eternal law: to justify it merely as the ultimate metaphysical restoration of human morality to its theonomic foundation and point of origin. Everything that philosophical analysis can conclude about the order of human actions is ultimately founded on the creative will of God, which in turn can be metaphysically resolved into the concept of the eternal law. According to Auer, as a metaphysical doctrine the eternal law anchors the activity of the practical reason in a "final context of justification" and a "comprehensive horizon of meaning";[1] as we have seen, this is supposed to explain the autonomy or "freedom to create norms" as God's unconditional moral claim upon man, which leaves it up to man's "creative reason" (Böckle's term) to shape the actual content of his actions. The doctrine of the eternal law would then simply point to a "context of justification"—namely, that formed by the coherence between theonomy and human autonomy. Any further analysis of the relationship between the eternal and natural laws would belong to the province of theology as the "knowledge of faith" (*scientia fidei*), and would be of no use for exploring the subject matter of philosophical ethics.

Time and again, Wolfgang Kluxen's name has been invoked to justify such minimalization of the meaning of the eternal law. If I am not mistaken, however, Kluxen's view that the eternal law involves not a practical but a *theoretical* position means only that the awareness of the eternal law emerges not from an act of the practical reason as such but from speculative (i.e., metaphysical) reflection upon such an act. The "standpoint of the eternal law," then, is necessary for an integration of philosophical ethics into a "metaphysics of action."[2]

A recognition that the natural law is a participation of the eternal law is thus immediately relevant for practical science. This is so first of all in the way shown in part I: the *ordo rationis* set up by the practical reason in human actions is already prefigured in the eternal law and does not need to "mirror" the natural order (*ordo naturae*) to acquire its intelligibility. Moreover, if the relationship of participation that obtains between the eternal law and the natural law is metaphysically considered, it can be understood to occur according to the principles that characterize the participation of all finite being in *esse per essentiam* (i.e., in God, Whose essence is to exist). It is only through an analysis of this kind that we can understand the participative structure of the natural law in general and of the human *ratio* in particular.

It should again be stressed that discourse about God, and about the dependence of the creation upon the Creator, are not themes reserved for theology alone. There is also (and always has been) such a thing as *philosophical* discourse about God. While the theologian speaks about God *sub ratione Dei* (under the aspect of God),[3] the philosopher speaks about God insofar as he considers the subject of his study to be God *as the first cause of all experienced finite being* and insofar as any existent's *dependence* on the first cause belongs to the finiteness of its constitution. When posing the question about the *causa prima,* philosophy as metaphysics does not seek only a "context of justification," but rather (using such coherence as a basis) tries to establish the very structure of finite being *as* participated being. This is because the knowledge of God as the first cause (and as particible, essential being) accompanies the knowledge of the truth of finite being, which otherwise would never be adequately comprehended in a metaphysical perspective. The same is true for ethics: when philosophical ethics is completed by its integration into a metaphysics of action, it entails a knowledge of the participative structure of the practical reason and the *lex naturalis.* If within the system of the *Summa Theologiae* the perspective of the eternal law is a "theological" one,[4] this should not be taken to imply that there is not also a *philosophy* of the eternal law; in fact, if Thomas had not worked out just such a philosophical notion and used it as a basis for his theological notion, the doctrine of the eternal law would not have been treated in the manner proper to it in the *Summa Theologiae.* Although the theological use of the term is predominant in Thomas,[5] this does not mean that the perspective is essentially or exclusively theological—that it is accessible only through revelation.

We will confine our methodological remarks to these, since the question of the relationship between philosophy and theology within the *Summa Theologiae* and other works of Thomas cannot be treated here in its fullness.

Meanwhile, it should be kept firmly in mind as we proceed that understanding the natural law as a participation of the eternal law in the rational creature is the key to understanding the concept of the natural law in Thomistic ethics. Our interpretation of the *lex naturalis* as an "ordering of the reason" (*ordinatio rationis*) and as "something constituted by the reason" (*aliquid a ratione constitutum*) will not be complete until we attend to its participation in the eternal law, and the same can be said for the doctrines of the natural inclinations and (on a more general level) the reason as standard and rule of morality.

## The Imago Character of Personal Autonomy

Human action is voluntary action. It comes about through one's own insight into the goal and into what leads to the goal; it is action that originates from one's own motivation—the motivation of the insight into the good—and is done with mastery over one's own inclinations and powers. This personal autonomy is not only the self-governance all creatures have (functional autonomy in general), but also *dominium* or *potestas* over one's own deeds. It is freedom: a mastery grounded in the reason and realized through the will as the "bearer" of that freedom.[6]

In his much-cited prologue to the *Prima Secundae,* Thomas follows a text of John Damascene to describe this personal autonomy as an *imago*, an 'image' or 'likeness' of the divine *potestas*: "As Damascene says, man is said to be made in the image of God because by 'image' is meant something intellectual and free in its judgment and having power over itself. Consequently, now that we have treated the 'exemplar' (that is, God) and the things that proceed from the divine power according to His will [in the *Prima Pars*], it is now time to take up the 'image' (that is, man), insofar as man is the principle of his own actions, having free judgment and power over his own deeds."[7] The theme of participation is present in this passage, because the *imago* is a participation in the *exemplar,* the divine "original."

In the *Summa Theologiae,* man was already treated in terms of the *imago Dei* in a much earlier passage of the *Prima Pars* (*quaestio* 93). Study of this earlier passage shows that the *imago* concept used in the prologue to the *Prima Secundae* is neither the first nor the most fundamental instance. This is an important point to note, in order to avoid false conclusions[8] when applying the concept to ethics.

The title of *quaestio* 93 of the *Prima Pars* (where man as the *imago Dei* is first treated) is significant: "Concerning the End or Purpose of the Production of the Human Being" (*De Fine Sive Termino Productionis Hominis*). The divine likeness of man provides a key not only to the personally autonomous character of human *actions*, but also (and in the first place) a key to the end and goal of human *existence*—and thereby, a key to the end and goal of the mastery and freedom that belong to this *imago*.

Thomas is emphasizing that man is not a *perfect* likeness of God; equality does not belong to the concept of *imago* as such;[9] a perfect image would in fact be God Himself—the *Verbum Divinum*.[10] Man possesses the image of God in a derived, incomplete way. Man *is* not the image of God, but *is made in* (or *made according to*: *ad imaginem*) the image of God.[11]

Now not every similarity makes for an "image"—only those which display a similarity of the same kind (*species*) or at least a similarity that follows upon a characteristic peculiar to the kind. For this reason only spiritual creatures (*creaturae intellectuales*) are like God "insofar as they are wise or have understanding" (*inquantum sapiunt vel intelligunt*; ibid., a. 2). Since, then, the divine likeness of man is defined by the *intellectualis natura* (ibid, a. 3), the question remains, What does this add to our understanding of human nature? Does this merely imply that man—like God, but at his own level—has the prerogatives (power and freedom) that go with intellectuality? It does indeed, but because the *imago* is incomplete (a "participation"), it *first* means something else.

What does "understanding" (*intelligere*) mean in regard to God? In Him it is not an act that is to be distinguished from His existence. Just as the divine intellective knowing cannot be separated from His existence, so the participated intellect of man cannot be considered separately from man's existence, or inner relationship to God. We are concerned with a participation, a partaking of the divine intellect, and therefore with a participation in the divine existence: since this participation is *ad imaginem*, it means an imaged participation in the divine being. This is why Thomas says that man, insofar he is in the divine likeness, does not simply possess intellect "in addition"; rather, he is saying that "the intelligent creature imitates God *above all* in respect to the self-knowing and loving of God Himself" (*Imitatur autem intellectualis natura maxime Deum quantum ad hoc, quod Deus seipsum intelligit et amat*; ibid., a. 4). And thus the *imago Dei* in man is considered with respect to his natural capacity to know and love God.[12] The *imago Dei* in man accordingly grounds a *natural inclination to participate in the divine goodness in an intellective way*. In connection with the *imago* we can therefore speak without any hesitation of a *naturalis inclinatio* toward knowing and loving God (*ad cognoscendum et amandum Deum*).

Without going into *Prima Pars*, *quaestio* 93, in any further detail, it can be established that the *imago Dei*—precisely because of its participative character—does not throw man upon himself, but rather *refers him to God.* If the intellectuality of God means that He knows and loves Himself, the participated intellectuality of man does *not* mean that man is related to himself in the same way as God is to Himself, but rather that he has been created for this relatedness to God, and this is to be realized in acts that possess a character of divine likeness—in other words, through an intellective knowing and loving. Here is where the *imago* is to be found, at the most profound level: for the human being is not a "copy" of divine perfection but rather, like every creature, a completely unique and special participation thereof. This is why the *imago* character of personal autonomy (and its power and freedom) is not really theonomously grounded autonomy, but rather "participated theonomy." Participation in the divine Self-relatedness does not consist in human self-relatedness but in human "God-relatedness."

The *imago* character of personal autonomy implies something twofold. First, it is a participation in the spirituality of God through the understanding (*intelligere*) and the love (*amare*) that are based upon it: two actions that in their participative structure refer man to God. Man is in the divine likeness because he is capable, like God Himself, of knowing and loving God. Now this is the basis for a second aspect: man, like every other creature, is ordered to the "common good" (*bonum commune*) of the creation, God Himself, and this is so in accord with the special character of the divine *imago* that he bears. The participation in "knowing and loving God" (*intelligere et amare*) grounds not only an ordering toward God but also the *manner* of this ordering: in freedom, through the mastery over his own acts, and through personal autonomy. This in fact is a characteristic of *knowing* and *loving* itself: a knowing and loving orientation toward God by its nature can take place only in freedom and through mastery over one's own acts, otherwise it would no longer be the spiritual knowing and loving orientation that becomes the *imago*. The empowered, personal autonomy of the human being provides *at the same time* both the goal of this freedom and the manner of its realization.

Thus the perspective taken up in the prologue of the *Prima*

*Secundae* does not involve an "anthropocentric shift." That would contradict the very concept of the *imago Dei.* It is not intended thereby that man realizes himself in a freedom that is univocal with reference to God, and that after having spoken about God and the effects of His *potestas*, it is now time to speak about man and the effects of the *potestas* that has been granted to him by God through the autonomy established at his creation. Instead, the programmatic opening of the *Prima Secundae* intends the treatment of man as the *imago Dei,* but not, this time, from the standpoint of his having come into being as a result of divine creation (the *processio ex divina potestate*). The new point of view takes in man's own power "of moving toward God" (*motus ad Deum*) that is grounded in the *imago* character. The perspective is not so much "anthropocentric" as "moral" (*moralis consideratio*). It is an analysis of the human actions through which the *imago*-bearing human being attains his goal, as stated in the prologue to *quaestio* 6.[13]

This also corresponds to the threefold division of the *Summa* announced in *Prima Pars*, q. 2, so that we can find there the key to understanding the prologue to the *Prima Secundae*. In the former passage Thomas states that it is not just a matter of understanding God, or God as the principle of all things, but also about God as the *goal* of all things—especially as the goal of the *rationalis creatura*. "First we will treat of God, and secondly of the movement [*motus*] of the rational creature toward Him." Thus the prologue of the *Prima Secundae* declares its theme to be the *motus* of man toward God, as treated through an analysis of the empowered, personally autonomous structure that belongs to this *motus* and its *imago* character.[14] It is not anthropocentrism but a methodological reorientation toward an analysis of human behavior involving a full use of philosophical—and for Thomas, that means Aristotelian—techniques of analysis. It should never be forgotten, however, that such an analysis consists in an explication of the finality structure of the *imago*: the intellective *cognoscere* and *amare Deum*; and that the *imago* grounds and contains a natural inclination toward the intellective and loving participation in the divine *bonitas*. It should likewise not be overlooked that, thanks to the participative character of the *imago* in man, the personal autonomy that is the theme of the *Secunda Pars* is always also treated as a participation of the divine perfection and *bonitas*, even if only *insofar* as this has become the imaged possession (precisely through participation) of the human being.

In view of these considerations it becomes possible to understand the metaphysical determinations of the natural law as set forth in Thomas's "Treatise on Law" (*I–II,* qq. 90ff.). It becomes clear how man is not an "autonomous" and self-empowered master in his own petty kingdom, but rather, because of his *natura intellectualis*, partakes in his personal autonomy and, in an "imaged" way, in the divine perfection. Such "partaking" can be brought through action—moral, *personal* action—to a humanly possible perfection; and it would have to be brought to *only* a humanly possible perfection, were man not also called, through grace, to a still higher participation in the divine perfection. Such a calling is outside the province of philosophical ethics, and leads to participation in God's holiness itself—in the divine nature qua divine—in a life that is at once human and divine.

## The Participation of Providence

The dependence of the creature upon God is not only a dependence in its existential constitution and a conservation in being; in addition, God orders all things to their end. The *ratio* or plan of this ordering is the divine foreseeing, or providence (*pro-videntia*).[15] To be subordinated to this ordering is itself a good, because it means that over and above partaking in existence, there is also an *operative* participation in the divine goodness (*divina bonitas*), a goodness of which creatures can then partake more fully through their activity.

It should at once be clear that the *imago* character of the personal autonomy of man is itself the basis for a very special mode of participation in this ordering-to-an-end (*ratio ordinis in finem*). And it should not be surprising to learn that Thomas understands the "image of God" in man to imply a special, human form of subordination to *providentia*. As a spiritual creature, man is not subordinated as something "cared for" (*provisus*), but rather as something that "cares for" (*providens*), which means that he takes an *active part* in providence.[16] Thomas does not say, "Man is in one respect subordinated to providence, but in another respect autonomous." Man's own personally autonomous *providere* is itself a determinate mode of subordination to divine providence. Since man possesses freedom of choice,[17] and thus guides and directs his own actions, this self-governing, insofar as it involves personal acts, is itself a *component of divine providence.*[18] Thomas does not mean that the self-direction of human actions as personal actions belongs to a province of autonomy that is "demarcated" by God, or that involves *only* human providence. Without any compromising of the truth that these actions are indeed actions of human providence, much more is being said: namely, that such acts are always also acts of *divine* providence. This statement cannot be reconciled with the autonomy idea.

The crucial problem of interpretation lies right here: Thomas does not think in anthropomorphic terms. He preserves the radical distinction between divine and human causality to the extent that such a distinction can be expressed in human language. The *causa secunda* is not thought of as some kind of autonomous "instrument of explication" for a master plan that provides only a framework; instead, God conceives the plan of His providence on the basis of His own omnipotence. He does not simply leave its *executio* to rational creatures, but lets them *take part* in the plan by communicating to them a participation in *providentia*; the divine ordering (*ordinatio divina*) extends itself to *all* actions of the creature. Human providence—the personal autonomy of man—is related to the divine providence as a particular cause to the universal cause.[19] This relationship implies that the causality of human providence is itself contained in the causality of divine providence: the particular cause is concerned with a certain part of the whole, while the universal cause is concerned not with just "another" (or even "higher") *part* but rather with the *whole*. The universal cause is thus present in every particular causality, and brings it about. The particular cause is also real causality, by reason of the ability that has been built into it, and not in an independent but in a participative way; it is founded and borne by the first cause, whose efficacy is simultaneously present in the second cause.[20]

Now at first, this appears to help us only by ruling out false anthropomorphic conceptions. I am aware of only one passage where Thomas explicitly counters an anthropomorphic position:

in his *Compendium Theologiae ad Fratrem Reginaldum*. There we can read the following: "Although the divine government of things takes place by means of second causes in regard to *execution*, the foregoing discussion should make it clear that the *plan* [*ordinatio*] of divine providence is in immediate relationship to all things. This is because God does not order what is first and last in importance in the way men do, by entrusting certain other people with the arrangement of the final details. It must be this way with human beings because of the limited scope of their knowledge" (cap. 131, no. 263). And Thomas can consequently say that "it is fitting that the ordering of providence be extended to the smallest effects" (ibid., cap. 130, no. 262). Thomas emphasizes that God knows and orders the effects even of the second causes that carry out the *ordinatio* of his providence, because "otherwise they would fall outside the scope of His providential ordering" (ibid.).

The *ordinatio* of divine providence is therefore extended even to the actions of man carried out in personal autonomy. They are contained in providence and underlie it as one component of the divine ordering of man to his end.

It is still too early to answer the question, "What should I do?" But it should at least be clear that the area of the personal autonomy of man, and the "empowered" (or "potestative") quality that results from his *imago* character, cannot be understood as a "theonomous autonomy," such that divine providence would provide only a "transcendental framework" within which man himself "creatively" shapes the order of good actions; or, in other words, as a "categorial" free space that God does not enter, leaving it up to man to determine what the content should be. In view of the participative character of the *imago*, such a position is meaningless. This "creative" autonomy, which casts man back upon himself and his own purposes, is like a "mess of pottage" accepted in exchange for the real greatness and dignity that belongs to man in virtue of being made in the image of God.

When we realize that there is a "plan" (a *ratio*) that underlies the divine government of the world, and that this *ratio gubernationis* is called the eternal law, then we can understand what it means to say that the natural law is a participation of the eternal law in the rational creature. Above all, it should be clear that the *lex naturalis* cannot simply ground a normative free space of creative–rational governance by man (a conception that is metaphysically useless and anthropomorphic); rather, the natural law in man is a participation in the ordering (*ordinatio*) of the divine reason itself, and it has two aspects: a participation *per modum cognitionis* (through knowing) and a participation *per modum principii motivi* (through a moving principle, or *natural inclination* see *I–II*, q. 93, a. 6).

## The Participation of the Eternal Law in Man

It would be well, before going further, to recall briefly the argument of chapter 4, section "Kant's Concept of Autonomy." The natural law is the participation of the eternal law in man. There is a twofold participation by man in the rule or standard of the *ordinatio rationis* of God's providence: in one way, through the fact that our being is "stamped" (*impressio*) with the various natural inclinations that all tend toward their own actions and goals (*actus et fines proprii*); in another way, through being "stamped" by the light of the natural reason (*impressio divini luminis in nobis*), on the basis of which we can decide between what is good and what is evil. The natural reason (*ratio naturalis*) is a natural inclination to a proper end (*finis debitus*); on its basis, the human reason is able to constitute the natural law *in* the other natural inclinations, insofar as it puts them in order; this is an *ordinatio* that corresponds to the eternal law. Both the *inclinatio naturalis* and the *ratio* belong to the *lex naturalis*; the *ratio* is the order-giving element, and through it the natural law is really and formally constituted. This reason is itself a "measure," but a "measured measure" (*mensura mensurata*): it naturally contains in itself a rule that it has received, not given to itself.

We must now study more closely the following questions: (1) What does it mean for a creature to "participate in the eternal law"? (2) What is this double mode of participation, that *per modum cognitionis* and that *per modum principii motivi*? And finally,. (3) What does it mean to say that the natural reason is an "impress of the divine light in us" (*impressio divini luminis in nobis*)? The first two questions can be answered immediately; the third will form the subject of chapter 6.

*Participation in the Eternal Law*

In order to introduce the concept of the eternal law, Thomas refers to the doctrine of divine providence. Once it is assumed that such a divine "foreseeing" exists, in accordance with which (as His "plan of governing," *ratio gubernationis*) God directs created things, then it can also be understood that this *ratio* has the nature of a law. Since God orders everything from the viewpoint of eternity, this "divine idea" (*divinum conceptum*) is eternal, and it reaches (as providence reaches) to the single actions of each and every created thing.

The eternal law can thus be defined as "the plan of the divine wisdom, in its aspect of directing all actions and movements" (*ratio divinae sapientiae, secundum quod est directiva omnium actionum et motionum*; *I–II,* q. 93, a. 1).

The eternal law is a "directive" plan (*ratio directiva*). According to it, all things have been created and possess an order toward their goal; in God the eternal law has the character of an *exemplar* or *idea* (ibid.), whereas in the creature the eternal law is "what is exampled" (an *exemplatum* or *ideatum* or *participatum*). Thomas emphasizes that the divine intellect is the measure of created things; that things "are" exactly in the measure to which they "imitate" the divine intellect (ibid., ad 3um)—and this "imitation" means nothing other than participation.[21] Participation in the eternal law constitutes the being and the operations of the creature. Every participation in the eternal law is both an existential and an operative participation in the dispositions of the divine wisdom.

In other words, we must not limit participation in the eternal law to the *operative point of view alone.* In God, all knowing that relates to creatures is a practical and creative and "measure-giving" knowing. If we are to understand the eternal law as the "plan of the divine wisdom moving all things to their proper end" (*ratio divinae sapientiae moventis omnia ad debitum finem*), we must not think of a kind of preexisting order that is now to be governed by a further, superimposed law. The *ordinatio* of the eternal law constitutes creatures not only in the order of their operations but also in their being: this, too, is a participation in the eternal law.

When it is said that the eternal law possesses an essentially practical and thereby creative, character, it should not be taken to mean that the participation of the eternal law in man would have this practical character exclusively. Because the creature represents in its own way "something ordered" (*ordinatum*), this "being ordered" (*ordinatum esse*) is itself something that belongs to the creature's participation of the eternal law.

Consequently the important distinction between two kinds of participation of the eternal law—between that in the subrational creature and that in man—cannot be said to consist in a "receptive/passive" participation (*ordinatum*) as opposed to a "practical/active" participation (*ordinans; ipse providens*). In fact, the difference is that man participates in the eternal law not only as *ordinatum* but *also* in a practical way, through practical knowing.

### *The Two-fold Mode of Participation in Man*

The existential constitution of the creature, then, belongs to the *ordinatio* of the eternal law. And precisely here arises the danger of an anthropomorphic understanding of the way in which the eternal law orders nature. It does not happen externally, through "prescriptions" applied to nature, as though it were a kind of "injunction" (*denuntiatio*) by which one human being applies law to another. God does this with regard to a created nature by "impressing the principles of its own operations upon the entire nature . . . for this reason all the movements and actions of the whole nature are subject to the eternal law."[22]

The "directive power" (*vis directiva*) of the eternal law thus affects the existential constitution of the creature; in man, it is not related just to the *ordinatio* of the actions that are unique to him and founded upon his *ratio*; it is also related to the natural inclinations that are fundamentally established in his being. These *inclinationes naturales ad actus proprios* belong to man's participation of the eternal law, which means that they pertain to the natural law as well. One cannot reduce this (as have Böckle and Merks) to a "natural inclination of the reason to create norms," nor even simply reduce it to the reason. That would curtail the reality of the human being in a "spiritualistic" way, and would neglect the fact that the whole complex of our natural tendencies belongs to participation of the eternal law, and to the plan of God's providence.

Now it has already been explained that these natural inclinations, when considered in themselves, do not as yet possess the character of *law.* They are a participation of the law, not "through the mode of law" (*per modum legis*) but "through the mode of the first mover" (*per modum principii motivi*).

For, as I have already shown, not everything that has the character of "law" in God (i.e., that which has a practical character) has the same practical or "legal" character in man. In other words, not everything that is an *ordinatio rationis* in God (and in the eternal law) is also an *ordinatio rationis* in its participated existence. Law is first of all, and in general (in relation to *all* creatures), "something ordered by reason" (*ordinatum a ratione*). In this sense, all creatures participate in the eternal law through the "mode of the first mover" (*per modum principii motivi*); it is only in the rational creature that the eternal law is, in addition, formally and really effective *as* law, and although this occurs participatively, it occurs "through the mode of knowledge" (*per modum cognitionis*), or in an intellective manner.

This "addition" must not be taken to mean a "parallelism" of knowledge and natural inclination. Practical *cognitio* and the human *ordinatio rationis* are not simply duplicates of what is already present in the natural inclinations themselves; this would imply the reduction of the human reason to an "organ that reads off" (*Ableseorgan*), and in this sense Böckle, Auer, Merks, et al. are correct. In relation to the natural inclinations, the human reason does possess a constitutive function in formulating the natural law (see chapter 6). What is to be noticed at present is that the participation of the eternal law in man is *also* expressed in his natural inclinations. These are much more than a "demarcated terrain" that the reason affects through its shaping and directive action; they belong in themselves to the participation of the eternal law. Through being ordered toward an *actus proprius* within man, they express in their being the order of divine providence founded in the *lex aeterna.*

The real difficulty here is to grasp the radical ontological difference between Creator and creature without losing the relation of analogy between them, secured through participation. Thomas's interpreters have not always succeeded in appreciating his achievement on this point.

The *lex aeterna* exists in God with the utter simplicity only God can have. It is identical, in fact, with His essence—that is, with His very existence. God *is* the eternal law, just as He essentially *is* His wisdom, His intellect, and His will. In God the eternal law exists *only* "through the mode of knowing" (*per modum cognitionis*); the divine knowing, insofar as it is joined with His will and becomes creative, can be called practical, and is the principle of all movement. Divine knowing, and therewith the eternal law as divine *cognitio,* is at the same time a moving principle. This is because in the divine knowledge (and in the *lex aeterna*) "knowing" (*cognitio*) and "motion" (*motio*) are not separate. The knowledge of God is immediately moving or "productive"—and thus creative.

On the other hand, not everything that exists as creation by way of participation of the divine being has this character of absolute simplicity, but rather is a *compositum* of act and potency, or of "form" and "matter" (whereby "matter" denotes potentiality in respect to a formal determination). This "division" (*diremptio*) in *esse per participationem* is expressed in man precisely in this twofold manner of participating in the eternal law. If this participation were to be realized only *per modum cognitionis,* it would mean that the human intellect would also have the power proper to the *lex aeterna.* But as it is, of course, the human intellect moves nothing in and of itself. It is not practical in itself, but is embedded in an *inclinative structure* of striving. Human reason is capable of an "order that moves something" (*ordinatio motiva*)—of a "command" (*imperium*) or "precept" (*praeceptum*), that is to say—only through a "moving principle" (*principium motivum*). Now if we follow Thomas's reasoning, there is no justification for confining such a principle to the will alone; if we did, it would imply that the other levels of human existence do not participate in the *lex aeterna.* This would force us not only into a dualistic anthropology but also into a dualistic metaphysics. The nonspiritual levels of man could no longer be referred to an "ordering by the plan of God's wisdom" (*ordinatio rationis divinae sapientiae*). Such a conception can find no place whatsoever in a Thomistic or post-Aristotelian metaphysics. It could at most find some connection with the teaching of Plato, who did not succeed in conceiving the unity of man as a *suppositum* of body and soul.

*Some Conclusions*

We have arrived at the conclusion that man participates in the "moving" character of the eternal law through the natural inclinations, but in the "cognitive" aspect through his reason. If one were to take the standpoint of the eternal law—to observe this participation "from above," as it were—one would have to say the following: the eternal law can be found in man both in his natural inclinations (*per modum principii motivi*) and in his reason (*per modum cognitionis*). To the extent that the natural inclinations belong to the eternal law (that is, "from above," and in connection with the divine *ordinatio*), they actually *are* law; to the extent that they are considered as a *participation* in the eternal law (that is, as something existing in nature, something created) they are *not* law (natural law), but rather are ( in accordance with the divine *ordinatio*) the "presupposition" (*praesuppositum*) for the law. They don't contain the "ordering to the right end" (*ordinatio ad debitum*) in themselves. In order to comprehend this *ordinatio*, one must consider the eternal law as it is in God, but we cannot see that. In the subrational creature such a defect is counterbalanced by the fact that this *ordinatio* takes place through an operative dimension; these creatures, and things in nature, *non agunt sed magis aguntur*; they are subordinated as instruments to the ordering of the eternal law.

Man, however, as the *imago* of God—in accordance with his spiritual nature—participates in the eternal law in a cognitive manner and thereby possesses the *ratio ordinationis* in himself, as personal autonomy. There is no question here of a "defect," since man does not need a determination of his natural inclinations to the "right" (*debitum*), nor must he be steered to his end through the divine *ratio* as an instrument; he does this himself by ordering the natural inclinations (the moving principle he receives) through his reason. The *ordinatio rationis* is thus a fuller participation in the eternal law and has itself the character of law: and this is the *lex naturalis*, the natural law.

In order for the ordering and lawgiving act of the practical reason (as cognitive participation of the eternal law) not to be falsified, the human reason can never "emancipate" itself from its moving principle, the *actus proprius* of the natural inclinations. The *ordinatio rationis* of the natural law is not a law that has these natural inclinations at its disposal, but is rather an ordering *in* the natural inclinations, since they are an expression of the plan of divine providence, at the level of the very structure of our being. They participate in the "directive power" (*vis directiva*) of the eternal law.

What is in man by nature (*a natura*)—the *praesupposita*—is not only participation of the eternal law, but also belongs indispensably to the natural law, even though it is not law *as such*.

This is why Thomas emphasizes that the natural inclinations also belong to the ordering of the divine governance: "since every inclination, whether natural or willed, of any entity, is nothing other than an *impressio* of the first mover . . . wherefore everything that behaves naturally or voluntarily arrives as it were spontaneously at that to which it has been divinely ordered."[23] This spontaneity is clearly to be seen in man who acts voluntarily: the *ordinatio rationis* is itself a natural inclination "to the right act and end" (*ad debitum actum et finem*; see *I–II*, q. 91, a. 2).

In the same way, the participation of the eternal law grounds the order of virtue (*ordo virtutis*) through the natural inclinations, since these inclinations are the "seeds" of the virtues. They provide an "aptitude" to virtue that is "from nature" (*a natura*; *II–II*, q. 108, a. 2). If virtue, then—as the "moral good" (*bonum morale*) in general—represents an "order of reason" (*ordo rationis*), so that virtue is constituted though the reason no less than the natural law that is itself formally oriented toward virtue, we are confronted with an *ordo* that is always realized *in* the natural inclinations, and not merely "occasioned" by them. This is why Thomas states that "to each natural inclination is ordered a special virtue,"[24] since virtues perfect us by helping us to follow *rightly* (*debito modo*) the natural inclinations, which belong to the natural law.

Man is a complex bodily entity that is fundamentally constituted in accordance with its inclinations. These inclinations, which he follows rationally—in the right ways—are what become the steady dispositions (*habitus*) of moral virtue. Natural inclination is an expression of the eternal law, and the foundation in man of the *ordinatio rationis*. It lends a fundamental *connaturality* and *spontaneity* to the natural law, to virtue, and to moral action that mirrors the divine goodness and wisdom; and these are fundamental qualities that can be increased by virtue or diminished by vice.

Participation in the eternal law constitutes an inner ordering of natural inclination, reason, virtue, and morality. This complex structure, which is directed toward its end through the ordering function of the practical reason, reveals the great dignity of human freedom. And to this freedom has been entrusted no less magnificent a privilege than that of realizing—of *partaking*—in the plan of divine providence.

Having reached this point, we can again reflect how little Thomas's true position has to do with an interpretation of the natural law as merely a "natural inclination" to "create norms," or as a law that contains only the purely formal meaning "to act rationally," without any determination of content. I trust that it is now clear how unintelligible the connection between natural law and virtue—or even virtue itself—would be, on the basis of such an interpretation. Lacking above all would be an adequate understanding of the nature of human reason itself, both in its character as *imago* and as a participation in the *ratio divina*.

But just what is this reason that constitutes the natural law? What, in general, does it mean to say that man must act according to reason, or that the moral good is the good of the reason (*bonum rationis*)? Finally, how is reason the standard and rule of morality? These are the questions we must now attempt to answer, in order to reach a fuller understanding of the natural law as the participation of the eternal law.

## Notes

1. A. Auer, "Die Autonomie des Sittlichen nach Thomas von Aquin," in K. Demmer and B. Schüller, eds., *Christlich glauben und handeln* (Düsseldorf, 1997), pp. 40, 42.

2. See Kluxen, *Philosophische Ethik bei Thomas von Aquin,* 2nd ed. (Hamburg, 1980), p. 234: "The standpoint of the eternal law, therefore, is not primary or immediate. It must be comprehended as the result of

reflection upon the foundation of what has been revealed in practical experience; it consequently cannot have the character of a cognition that would direct action. Just like a metaphysics of action, it is an interpretation, after the fact, of what has been practically experienced."

3. See also the very name *sacra doctrina* given to theology in *I*, q. 1, a. 7: the subject (*subiectum*) of theology is God: "omnia autem pertractantur in sacra doctrina sub ratione Dei vel quia sunt ipse Deus; vel quia habent ordinem ad Deum, ut ad principium et finem. Unde sequitur quod Deus vere sit subiectum huius scientiae." Philosophy treats of God, but He is not the subject; the subject of metaphysics is *ens qua ens* ("being as being"). God, Who is the first cause of being, is treated in metaphysics *sub ratione entis* (under the aspect of being), and more precisely as the "the cause of being" (*causa essendi*), "subsistent being" (*esse subsistens*), "being in its very essence" (*esse per essentiam*), and so on; God can also be treated with respect to the attributes that are predicable of Him by analogy, above all as "being" (*esse*), "living" (*vivere*), and "understanding" (*intelligere*).

4. As Kluxen maintains, *Philosophische Ethik*, p. 234.

5. This has recently been shown very well by G. Abba, *Lex et Virtus. Studi sull' evoluzione della doctrina morale di san Tomasso d'Aquino* (Rome, 1983). The *lex gratiae* and what it brings—the state of being a child of God (*Gotteskindschaft;* "divine filiation"), and holiness—are distinguished by the three theological virtues of faith, hope, and love, and are in fact a higher form of participation in the eternal law. In the *ordinatio* of the eternal law can be found that unity of the natural and supernatural orders which corresponds to the divine will: a unity that is restored to man through the participation in the eternal law brought about through the new life in Jesus Christ, which (also in accordance with the divine will) extends itself to *all* human beings.

6. See *I-II*, q. 17, a. 1, ad 2um: "Radix libertatis est voluntas sicut subiectum; sed sicut causa, est ratio. Ex hoc enim voluntas potest ad diversa ferri, quia ratio potest habere diversas conceptiones boni. Et ideo philosophi definiunt liberum arbitrium quod est 'liberum de ratione iudicium' (Boethius), quasi ratio sit causa libertatis." (The root of freedom is the will as subject, but the reason, as cause. For the will can be moved toward diverse things because the reason can have diverse conceptions of the good. For this reason philosophers have defined the free will [*liberum arbitrium*] as the 'free judgment concerning reason,' as if the reason were the cause of freedom.) In addition to this openness of the reason "to many things" (*ad multa*), as a spiritual faculty it possesses the power to reflect upon itself, and that is the ability to judge one's own activity and to have mastery over one's own judgment. See *De Veritate*,

q. 24, a. 2: "Iudicium autem est in potestate iudicantis secundum quod potest de suo iudicio iudicare; de eo enim quod est in nostra potestate, possumus iudicare. Iudicare autem de iudicio suo est solius rationis, quae super actum suum reflectitur, et cognoscit habitudines rerum de quibus iudicat, et per quas iudicat: unde totius libertatis radix est in ratione constituta." (Judgment, however, is in the power of the one who judges insofar as he can judge about his own judgment; for we are able to judge concerning that which is in our power. But it belongs to the reason alone to judge about one's own judgment, because the reason can reflect upon its own action, and it recognizes the dispositions of the things it judges about, as well as the things by which it judges; therefore the root of all freedom is constituted in the reason.)

7. "Quia, sicut Damascenus dicit, homo factus ad imaginem Dei dicitur, secundum quod per imaginem significatur intellectuale et arbitrio liberum et per se potestativum; postquam praedictum est de exemplari, scilicet de Deo, et de his quae processerunt ex divina potestate secundum eius voluntatem; restat ut consideremus de eius imagine, id est de homine, secundum quod et ipse est suorum operum principium, quasi liberum arbitrium habens et suorum operum potestatem" (*I–II*, Prologus).

8. This has happened, in my opinion, in the case of K.-W. Merks, *Theologische Grundlegung der sittlichen Autonomie* (Düsseldorf, 1978), p. 76, who likes to see a "change of position," an "anthropological turn" to a perspective of "anthropocentrism" in the prologue to the *Prima Secundae*. But Merks seems to have overlooked the participative structure of the divine likeness, which he interprets as a kind of "equality with God": "Man is the subject of the *Secunda Pars*, insofar as he, *too . . . just like God*, is himself the principle and master of his actions." Thomas expressly states that man, *too*, is master of his actions, and he understands this as characteristic of an "image," but not that man is a master *in the same way as God*. In any event, Merks does not take into account the *imago* treatise of the *Prima Pars*.

9. See *I*, q. 93, a. 1: "Aequalitas non est de ratione imaginis."

10. This is why the Sacred Scripture calls Christ "the image of the invisible God" (*Qui est imago Dei invisibilis*, col. 1.15; see also *I*, q. 35, a. 2).

11. "Manifestum est autem quod in homine invenitur aliqua Dei similitudo, quae deducitur a Deo sicut ab exemplari: non tamen est similitudo secundum aequalitatem, quia in infinitum excedit exemplar hoc tale exemplatum. Et ideo in homine dicitur esse imago Dei, non tamen perfecta, sed imperfecta. Et hoc significat Scriptura, cum dicit hominem factum *ad imaginem Dei*: praepositio enim *ad* accessum quendam signifi-

cat, qui competit rei distanti." (It is clear that there is found some similarity to God in man, a similarity that is derived from God as from an exemplar; nevertheless it is not a similarity by way of equality, because this "exemplar" infinitely exceeds this thing "exampled" [*exemplar/exemplatum*]. And therefore in man there is not a perfect or *complete* image but rather an imperfect or *incomplete* one. Scripture points this out when it states that man has been made *to the image of God* because the preposition *to* (Latin *ad*) signifies an approach to something, as is fittingly said about something that is far away.) See *I*, q. 35, a.2, ad 3um.

12. Thomas is speaking here (a. 4) of a *triplex modus* of speaking about the *imago*. The first is that "according to which man has a natural aptitude for knowing and loving of God"; the second mode has to do with the actual and habitual, but incomplete knowing and loving God through the "conformity of grace" (*conformitas gratiae*); the third has to do with the completion of this act "according to the similitude of glory" (*secundum similitudinem gloriae*). The *imago* as *conformitas* and *similitudo* develops at a level infinitely higher than the natural level by means of the supernatural participation in the divine nature through grace and (after death) through glory. Only the first mode is of interest in a philosophical context: the human, intellective nature of man as such is already ordered, through the *imago*, to the knowing and loving of God.

13. It is not by chance that the system of the *Summa Theologiae* as a theological work requires that the first five questions of the *Prima Secundae* deal with man's final end, or *beatitudo*; such a method starkly contrasts with an alleged "anthropocentric shift."

14. This has been very well brought out in G. Abba, *Lex et Virtus* (see below, especially chapter 7). Abba shows how the theological perspective that is constantly maintained in the *Secunda Pars* is firmly united to an authentic *moralis consideratio*. This is what gives the *Summa* its peculiar character—that of being a thoroughly theological work while at the same time (particularly in the *Secunda Pars*) realizing all the potential of a philosophical ethics and anthropology.

15. See *I*, q. 22, a. 1. "necesse est, quod ratio ordinis rerum in finem in mente divina praeexistat. Ratio autem ordinandorum in finem, proprie providentia est."

16. See *De Veritate*, q. 5, a.5: "Inter omnia vero alia spirituales substantiae magis primo principio appropinquant; unde et eius imagine insignitae dicuntur; et ideo a divina providentia non solum consequuntur quod sint provisa, sed etiam quod provideant." (Among the other creatures, spiritual substances more closely draw near to the first principle, and therefore they are consequently not only provided for by divine providence, but themselves provide.)

17. Ibid.: "Et haec est causa quare praedictae substantiae habent suorum actuum electionem, non autem ceterae creaturae, quae sunt provisae tantum, et non sunt providentes." (And this is the reason why the afore-mentioned substances have the choice of their own actions, and not the other creatures, which are only provided-for, and not providing.)

18. See *Contra Gentiles,* III, 113 (no. 2873): "Gubernatio igitur actuum rationalis creaturae, inquantum sunt actus personales, ad divinam providentiam pertinent." (Thus the governance of the actions of the rational creature, insofar as they are personal actions, pertains to divine providence.)

19. *I,* q. 22, a. 2, ad 4um: "Providentia hominis continetur sub providentia Dei, sicut causa particularis sub causa universali."

20. See, e.g., *In II Sent.* d. 1, q. 1, a. 4: "Solus Deus immediate omnia operatur et res singulae proprias operationes habent, per quas causae proximae rerum sunt. . . . Unde operatio Creatoris magis pertingit ad intimia rei, quam operatio causarum secundarum; et ideo hoc quod creatum est causa alii creaturae non excludit quin Deus immediate in rebus omnibus operatur, in quantum virtus sua est sicut medium coniungens virtutem cuiuslibet causae secundae cum suo effectu. Non enim virtus alicuius creaturae posset in suum effectum, nisi per virtutem Creatoris, a quo est omnis virtus et virtutis conservatio, et ordo ad effectum; quia, ut in libro de Causis dicitur, causalitas causae secundae finaliter est per causalitatem causae primae." (Only God can work immediately, and all particular things have their own operations, through which they are the proximate causes of things. . . . Therefore the work of the Creator pertains more to the intimate nature of things [*intimia rei*] than the working of second causes; therefore the fact that what is created is the cause for some other creature does not compromise the fact that God works immediately in all things, insofar as his power [*virtus sua*] is just like a medium [or middle term] connecting the power of every second cause with its own effect. For no creature's power could extend to its own effect [*posset in suum effectum*] except by the power of the Creator, from Whom comes all power and all preservation of power, and all ordering toward an effect; just as is stated in the Book of Causes, the causality of the second cause, in regard to its purpose [*finaliter*], takes place through the causality of the first cause.) *De Pot.,* 3.3, a. 7. "Sequitur quod ipse [i.e., Deus] in quolibet operante, immediate operetur, non exclusa operatione voluntatis et naturae." (It follows that God Himself works immediately in everything that works, without any compromise [*non exclusa*] to its will and operation.)

21. The concept of participation (*participatio*) derives from the Pla-

tonic μέθεξις, as the concept of imitation (*imitatio*) goes back to the Platonic μίμησις.

22. *I–II,* q. 93, a. 5: "sicut autem homo imprimit, denuntiando, quoddam interius principium actuum homini sibi subiectum, ita etiam Deus imprimit toti naturae principia propriorum actuum. . . . Et per hanc etiam rationem omnes motus et actiones totius naturae legi aeternae subduntur." Thomas is here distinguishing betweeen two modes of *impressio*: with man, it is an *impressio per modum denuntiationis*; with God, it is an *impressio per modum creationis* or *participationis*.

23. *I,* q. 103, a. 8: "omnis inclinatio alicuius rei vel naturalis vel voluntaria, nihil est aliud quam quaedam impressio a primo movente. . . . Unde omnia quae agunt vel naturaliter vel voluntarie, quasi propria sponte perveniunt in id ad quod divinitus ordinantur."

24. Ibid.: "Ad quamlibet inclinationem naturalem determinatam ordinatur aliqua specialis virtus."

6

# Natural Dynamics of the Reason: The Epistemological Structure of the Natural Law

## THE "LIGHT OF THE NATURAL REASON"

### *The Meaning of the "Light" Metaphor*

IT WOULD SEEM appropriate at this time to cite the relevant passage (*Summa Theologiae, I–II,* q. 91, a. 2) in full:

> Among the other creatures [*inter cetera*] the rational creature is subject to divine providence in a certain, more excellent way, insofar as this creature becomes itself a partaker of providence [*ipsa fit providentiae particeps*], "providing" for itself and others. And therefore the eternal *ratio* is participated in it [*participatur*], through which it possesses a natural inclination toward its right act and end [*ad debitum actum et finem*].
>
> This kind of participation of the eternal law in the rational creature is called the natural law. This is why, when the Psalmist says in the Fourth Psalm: "Make the sacrifice of justice" [*Sacrificate sacrificium iustitiae,* Ps. 4: 6], he adds the following, as if making reply to some who ask what the works of justice are: "Many ask, Who shows us good things? To which the Psalmist answers, saying, "The light of Your countenance has been signed above us, Lord," and this is as it were the light of the natural reason [*lumen rationis naturalis*]; by means of it we discern what is good and what is bad, and it is what pertains to the natural law, and is nothing other than the impress (or "stamp") of the divine light in us [*impressio divini luminis in nobis*].

The whole burden of the participation of the natural law "in the mode of knowledge" (*per modum cognitionis*) lies upon the *ratio naturalis*; it is a "light"[1] that is nothing other than an *impressio* (or "existential participation"[2]) of the divine light—that is to say, the divine being under the aspect of its intellectuality, its making-visible of the truth. The same argument is found in another famous passage, *I–II,* q. 19, a. 4, where the citation of the same Psalm passage shows it to be standard for this context: the human reason gets its character of being a rule for the well-being of human will from the eternal law, which is identical with the divine reason. This is why the Fourth Psalm says, "Who shows us what is good? The light of Your countenance, Lord, is signed upon us," and Thomas offers the following paraphrase: "The light of the reason that is in us can show us the good, and rule our will, *insofar as it is the light of Your countenance, which means that it comes from Your face* [*a vultu tuo derivatum*]."

The point of the article lies in the statement that our will, or the good and evil in our voluntary action, is actually ruled through the *lex aeterna*: the eternal law not only constitutes the human *ratio* as a rule but also really rules (*regulat*) the good and evil in our conduct, is in fact its "measure" (*mensura*); however, this is not in an immediate and "homogenous" way,[3] but rather *by way of* a participation of this divine light of knowing in man. This participated light of knowing operates as a second cause, and this is precisely why the efficacy—the *regulatio* or *mensuratio* of the will and of actions—must, above all, be ascribed to the first cause "because the second cause is able to operate only in virtue of the first cause" (*quia causa secunda non agit nisi in virtute primae causae* [ibid., in corp. art.]).

The same principle can also be applied once again to counter the objection that the eternal law is not known to us, and therefore cannot be a measure for our actions: "While the *lex aeterna* is not accessible to us insofar as it exists in the divine mind itself [*secundum quod est in mente divina*]; it is known to us [*innotescit tamen nobis*] to a certain extent either (1) through the ratio naturalis, which derives from it as its own image [*propria eius imago*], or (2) through some additional [*superadditam*] revelation" (ibid., ad 3um).

### *Some Reasons Why the Concept of the "Creative Reason" Is Unsuitable for Understanding St. Thomas*

These citations, as well as the notions of "light" and "image" that dominate their contexts, appear to exclude the possibility that

Thomas had in mind a notion of the reason as merely the natural inclination for one's own, rational, creative, norm-setting activity. On closer inspection, the cognitive participation of the natural reason in the eternal law makes it impossible to understand it as has Merks, depending on Böckle: it is not simply the "principle of rationality as such,"[4] as if the fact that man must act on rational grounds in order to act morally were totally unrelated to the actual content of one's actions. This is equivalent to maintaining that the good is rational action, that is, action that can be supported by argumentation. The rationality of action thus becomes a "creatively" constructive achievement of the reason, which carries this out in the area of its own autonomous competence. Moral norms—the difference between good and bad in willing and in action—therefore result from a process of rational justification, and mostly in the form of so-called "teleological weighing of goods," which is an example of just such a process of argumentative norm establishment.

Now that this is *not* what Thomas means, and that it is in fact irreconcilable with what he says about the connection between the eternal law and the natural reason, can be illustrated as follows: he associates the cognizance of the eternal law by the human reason with the further possibility of a *revelatio superaddita* (*I–II,* q. 19, a. 4, ad 3um). If one were to limit the participation of the eternal law in the human reason to the "principle of rationality," or to the "natural inclination of the reason to create norms," it would seem reasonable to ask what the content of such a revelation could then be. If the participation of the *lex aeterna* through the natural reason is nothing more than the formal principle of reason, then Thomas's reference to the possibility of an additional revelation of the same law will be meaningless.

In the *De Malo* (q. 2, a. 4), when treating the sources of knowledge of the eternal law, there is, besides revelation (in the *lex divina*), a consideration of instruction and the "infusion" of such knowledge: "People consider good and evil in human acts according to their agreement with the reason, as the reason is informed by divine law, or in a natural manner [*naturaliter*], through instruction or infusion." The text is important for understanding that Thomas is not simply pointing to the reason as such to be the standard of morality, but to the "informed" reason—a *ratio,* in other words, that is not just a potentiality for a rational process of justification, but rather one that bears a certain "in-*form*-ation" in itself. Such informing can come to the reason from outside, and this is the case with regard to revelation (and thus the *lex divina*) or through instruction or education. It can also come to the reason from within, which can happen either through "infusion" (a mode that in itself surpasses the principles of nature) or in a natural way, on the basis of the natural cognitive light, which the reason bears within itself by participation.

Equally incomprehensible under the presupposition of the "autonomistic" interpretation would be a text like *I–II,* q. 71, a. 6, ad 4um, where it is said that it is on the basis of the natural law (*ius naturale*) that human actions can be judged good or bad, independently of any positive legislation; and that such a law is first contained in the eternal law, and is only secondarily (i.e., participatively) present in the natural judging power (*in naturali iudicatorio*) of the human reason. If the natural reason were only a natural inclination for norm-creation without any "content," then the statement of Thomas to the effect that the natural criterion for judging human action is already present in the *lex aeterna,* and is participated in by the human reason, would be meaningless.

Apart from countless other difficulties of interpretation that would result from the autonomistic interpretation, one last text can be brought forward that will also be of interest later. This is where Thomas speaks of a "threefold" level of certainty and evidence of moral precepts (*praecepta moralia*)[5] that all arise from the efficacy of the natural reason's preceptive act. These levels range from the clearest commandments, such as the love of God and neighbor (the goal of all the others) through the Ten Commandments, to some that are understood only by the "wise," and go beyond the Decalogue. All these precepts, says Thomas, have their efficacy (*efficacia*) "from the very declarations of the natural reason" (*ex ipso dictamine naturalis rationis*).[6]

## "Ratio Naturalis"

The doctrine of the natural reason as a light of knowing, as the participation of the light of the divine *ratio aeterna,* as the *imago Dei* in the human soul, apparently needs to be taken seriously. It seems to contain more than the autonomistic interpretation of

Thomas is accustomed to see in it.[7] In fact, in this context the concept of the *ratio naturalis* is far too infrequently noted,[8] or is distorted by misunderstandings.[9] Thomas appears to presuppose the meaning of the "natural reason"—in the *Commentary on the Sentences,* it is usually *naturalis* conceptio[10]—as something self-evident. If we recall that for Thomas the human *ratio* is an *intellectus imperfectus,* that the agent intellect (*intellectus agens*) is nevertheless a lumen naturale, it will be understandable how the concept of the *ratio naturalis* is related to the intellective aspect of human rationality that Thomas emphasizes and explicates time and again in the most varied contexts. A final confirmation of the point can be found in formulations like the following: "Since man assents to some truth through the natural reason, on the basis of an intellective insight . . ." (*Cum autem homo per naturalem rationem assentit secundum intellectum alicui veritati*).[11]

We also find formulations in the *Commentary on the Sentences* like the following: "Laws that are inscribed in the reason . . ." (*In III Sent.,* d. 37, q. 1, a. 3: *quaedam enim sunt leges quae ipsi rationi sunt inditae, quae sunt prima mensura et regula omnium humanorum actuum*). In the *Summa contra Gentiles,* Thomas speaks of "a natural judging power of the reason that man possesses . . . in virtue of divine providence" (*III,* c. 129, no. 3011: *homines ex divina providentia sortiuntur naturale iudicatorium rationis ut principium propriarum operationum*). The famous article 2 of the *Prima Secundae,* q. 94, places the whole burden of the argument upon the concept of a "natural apprehension" of "human goods" that would remain forever unintelligible if they were not referred back to an intellective insight. The interpretation of this article is a kind of touchstone for any exegesis of the Thomistic doctrine of the natural law, and the key to the interpretation is the understanding of this term.

The human intellect accordingly appears to have a significance that comes to the fore with the light metaphor: it is a "light," and therefore a capacity in the human being to "make something visible" that would remain hidden without this light. A light does not produce the objects of its illumination; it only takes them "out of hiding." The Greek word for truth—ἀλήθεια, *alethia,* "un-hiddenness"—brings out this aspect of knowing: a power that does not "make," but "finds."[12]

## "Lumen Intellectuale"

Although Plato had paved the way by likening the source of all knowledge of the truth (for him, the subsisting form of the Good) to the sun, it was really Aristotle who first likened the mind (his νοῦς ποιητικός, the Thomistic *intellectus agens*) to the light. Thomas made full use of the metaphor in this context.

For a philosopher like Aristotle, the light function of the intellect was primarily a matter of experience metaphysically interpreted. The peculiar power of the human intellect did not make sense to him in any other way. At the same time, Aristotle was also conscious—probably thanks to his Platonic background—that the intellect in man must be something divine: he called it the "god in us."[13] This theme is present in both the *Nichomachean Ethics* (*NE*) and the *Eudemian Ethics*, and without any of the early dualistic overtones: intellect (νοῦς) and reason (λόγος) are "something divine in us," our "true self," our "best and noblest part" (*NE,* X, ch. 7, 1177a20; 1178a2). The intellectual vision is an activity proper to the gods, and he who cultivates the "god in himself" has special connections with the gods and can be certain of their special reward (ibid., ch. 9, 1179a, 23ff.).

It should not be surprising that these pre-Christian soundings of the *imago* character of the intellect find their full development in Thomas. In him they have received new force through his reception of the Platonic–Augustinian doctrine of illumination and through his own refinement of that tradition. What for Augustine was an actual illumination by the divine intellect, becomes for Thomas an intellective power, existentially anchored in man as *causa secunda,* but still participating in the divine intellect as *imago.* This power lacks nothing of what Augustine's doctrine would have ascribed to the power of divine illumination. The human intellect is in fact a participation of God's knowing light, so that Thomas can say with Augustine that "The soul knows everything in the eternal reasons [*in rationibus aeternis*], because it is by participation of them that we know anything. *The intellectual light itself that is in us is nothing other than a participated similitude* [i.e. the *imago*] *of the uncreated light, in which the eternal reasons* [*rationes aeternae*] *are contained.*" (*I,* q. 84, a. 6).[14] And it is not by chance that Thomas follows this with a paraphrase of the Fourth Psalm:

"Through the very seal [*Einprägung*; see *sigillatio*] of the divine light upon us are all things demonstrated" (*Per ipsam sigillationem divini luminis in nobis, omnia demonstrantur*; ibid.).

The human intellect, then, as *lumen naturale,* is not simply a capacity for thinking. Instead, it contains truth in a certain way. This is not to be understood in the sense of "innate ideas," but rather of its participation of that divine light in which all truth is contained, and according to which all things were made and have truth, which is their agreement with the divine intellect. The human intellect, in its truth-revealing light function, is understandable only on the basis of its participative character. And yet as *imago,* it possesses an unambiguous relevance of content. This is why we can also find the following formulation: the *lumen intellectus nostri* is an "impression of the first truth" (*impressio veritatis primae*), by means of which we know (*I–II,* q. 88, a. 3, ad 1um).

The most striking formulation, however, is to be found in the *Quaestiones Quodlibetales,* where Thomas is once again at odds with the Augustinian position that we know all truth in the first truth. He says that the participation of the divine intellect is a *resultatio* of divine truth in us, so that "from one first truth, many truths result in human minds." This *resultatio* shows itself in a double fashion: (1) in the *lumen intellectuale* itself (the Fourth Psalm is also cited here); and (2), "insofar as [truths] are naturally known by their first principles" (*veritates . . . quantum ad prima principia naturaliter notae*). From this alone comes truth, "because they are a likeness of that first Truth" (*similitudo illius primae veritatis*); and because of this, they have immutability and certainty. So Thomas concludes as follows: we recognize all truth in God, because we see it immediately not in Him but rather in the very *ratio* of His *imago* (*in ipsa ratione suae imaginis*)—that is, as the text goes on to explain, "[in the image] of the truth that has been modeled from [the first truth]" (*veritatis ab ea exemplatae*; ibid., X, q. 4, a. 1). Thus the reason's natural knowledge (which depends upon the *lumen intellectuale*)—is "a similarity of the divine truth, which is stamped upon our mind" (*similitudo . . . menti nostrae impressa*); once again there is reference to the Fourth Psalm (ibid., VII, q. 2, a. 2).

In his commentary on Proclus's *Elementatio Theologica* (the *Liber de Causis*), Thomas calls the *prima causa* a "light" (*lumen*), in accord with the terminology of another work also commented upon by Thomas and frequently cited in its own right: the *De Divinis Nominibus* of Pseudo-Dionysius. The causality of the light (*causalitas luminis*) drives from the soul all ignorance and error (*In IV De Divinibus Nominibus,* lect. 4, no. 327); God, the "supersubstantial Good," is "intelligible light, insofar as it is a certain ray [*radius*] and fountain of all intellectual light" (ibid., no. 331). This has a twofold effect: it illuminates the soul from the very beginning, that is to say, it provides it with a "natural knowledge" (*naturalis cognitio*); second, it gives something that surpasses nature: the "light of grace" (*lumen gratiae*) and the "light of glory" (*lumen gloriae*), according to the threefold gradation of the imago which has already been discussed (ibid.).[15] The end and the effect of the "causality of the light" consists in unifying all intellectual and rational existences in the truth.

### *The Truth Capacity of the Natural Reason*

For Thomas, the natural light of the intellect is a "power" of attaining truth. The human intellect possesses in a participative way the certainty and inerrancy of its source. This is expressed most clearly, as one would expect, in the Christian perspective of Thomas's commentary on the Gospel of John. It is interesting to observe that in that context a connection is drawn between the participation of the *lumen intellectuale* and the theme of personal autonomy.[16] The *Verbum Divinum* (the *vita perfecta*) that comes to man in Christ, is here referred to as "the light of man" (*lux hominum*). The Word can be "light" in the sense of an *object*—in this way it can be known only by human beings, and on the basis of the light of grace, since only man possesses a capacity for the vision of God. But the Word can also be the participated light of man, and in Christological contexts Thomas strictly distinguishes between a natural and a supernatural participation in the divine Word.[17] Naturally man partakes of this light through the light of the intellect that is in man himself, in the higher part of the soul. The citation of the Fourth Psalm follows as expected, according to which the light of the divine face is the "Son," the perfect *imago Dei.*[18]

A little later in the passage this participation or illumination through the Word is identified with the "light of the natural reason" (*lumen rationis naturalis*): whatever can be known by this latter comes from participation in the true light of the Word.[19] The words of the Gospel, "He was the true light [*lux vera*] that lights up every man *who comes into this world*," give Thomas the occasion to say that man, because of his intellect, in a certain way "comes into" this world and is not "from it." Even though, because of the bodiliness that equally belongs to his nature, he has completely "entered this world" and is a physical part of it, nevertheless, thanks to his spirituality, he has a principle of being that transcends the bodiliness of the visible world (*mundus visibilis*): whereas the physical world is only a "trace" (*vestigium*) of the Creator, the intellect is the Creator's *imago*. The point is that man is illuminated by the intellect that is in man, but not of this world.[20]

Consequently the intellect or *ratio naturalis* possesses the characteristics of certainty and inerrancy that every intellect has, in view of its participative nature. This light is always shining on everyone (ibid., lect. 3, no. 102), and without it there is only darkness. That some stay in the darkness (through ignorance or error) is not to be explained by an imperfection of the light (no. 103) but by an inordinate love in man (lect. 5, no. 138). And even if some minds (*mentes*) are "in the shadows" (*tenebrosae*), there is none that does not have some participation in the light. For whatever truth is known by someone, it is always known by way of participation of this light that shines in the darkness.[21]

Even though Thomas holds firmly to the position that all knowledge arises through the senses—that, indeed, nothing at all could be known without its first having been made present to the intellect by way of the senses, and that in every act of knowing there occurs a "turning toward phantasms" (*conversio ad phantasmata*)—nevertheless, he never in any way reduces the action of the intellect to a mere rational "reworking" of sense data in the manner of an empiricist or a sensualist. There is no compromising of the specific "making visible" action of intelligible truth through the light of the *intellectus agens*, "by means of which we can know the truth of changing things in an unchanging way" (see *I*, q. 84, a. 6, ad 1um). When intellective knowledge is said to be caused by sense perception, it does not mean that the latter is the *whole* cause, but rather that it is the material of the cause (ibid.). From the formal point of view, the cause is the intellect itself,[22] and that means that its relation to sense experience is not merely that of a "receiver," nor does it "contribute something" (and certainly not in a "creative" manner); it is, rather, as a "light" that "makes visible" what is *already there* but "hidden" because not yet presented to sense perception. We encountered this kind of relationship when we studied the relationship between the *ratio naturalis* and the *inclinationes naturales,* which can now be understood from another perspective. It may also be useful to recall at this point that the concept of "matter"—the *materia circa quam* as the *obiectum,* but with a view to its materiality—is to be understood as an analogue to the *materia* of the *intellectus agens*'s causality. Thomas illustrated the relation between the formal and the material determinations of the object (*De Caritate,* a. 4) by the metaphor of color in relation to bodies: the color is the *ratio visibilitatis* of the body, and yet it is not something distinct from the body, but is the whole body "insofar as it is visible" (see chapter 2, note 64).

### *The Natural Reason's Double Mode of Knowing*

There now remains the important, if not decisive, question. What kind of knowledge does this light of the natural reason (the intellect) disclose? Is it only a question of the first principles, as maintained by the autonomistic interpretation of Thomas? And would that imply further that the natural law is only a purely formal imperative to do the good? Would this in turn be based upon rational insight—a rationality, that is, without any shared content with the "naturally known" (*naturaliter cognitum*) and abandoned instead to a "freedom of rational discovery"?[23]

That Thomas had nothing of the sort in mind becomes clear from study of the *Secunda Secundae* (*II–II*), the particular treatment of morality and the virtues. Böckle maintains (in connection with Thomas's treatment of lying) that Thomas argues in a neo-Thomist, essentialistic manner—that, in other words, Thomas did not understand his own position or did not keep consistently to it. However, "from the whole body of Thomas's teaching, it is clear that the appeal to nature has to be seen in the context of the rational order" (*Fundamental Moral Theology,* p. 245). And yet such difficulties and allegedly mistaken argumentation have less to do with Thomas himself (or his apparent failure to carry out his thesis) than with his interpreters.

The question about the actual content of the natural law, or "what extension in content belongs to a dictum [*dictamen*] of the natural reason?" has been frequently dealt with.[24] In fact, Thomas's own statements on the matter do not always have the clarity we would like. The problem, as so often with Thomas, is that in the actual treatise on the law he presupposes certain things that are never given a special explanation in the course of the treatment. In this case it is the doctrine of the explication of intellective knowledge through the process of *inquisitio* or *inventio* or the *ratio naturalis*. If one misses the relevant doctrine, one also misses the important fact that the *ratio naturalis* as an *intellectus imperfectus* has a twofold mode of knowing: (1) a strictly natural one (related to the *naturaliter cognitum*) and (2) a *discursive/inventive* one. If Thomas speaks often of an *invenire*, he does not mean an "invention" of a "creative" kind, but rather a "finding" or "dis-covering" or grasping of the truth by the light of the natural reason; and this takes place both in the speculative and in the practical reason.[25] Attending to the *via inventionis* as a discursive process of the natural reason is decisive for understanding how the natural law is extended. For, as will be seen, Thomas clarifies a twofold act of the *ratio naturalis*: one that is natural, and another that is discursive/inventive. The second is an explication of the natural light itself. The unfolding of the natural law is explained the same way: it is first a *naturalis conceptio* or a *naturaliter cognitum* (this is the basis for its being the natural law of the practical reason), and yet in the so-called secondary precepts it is explicated in an inventive/discursive fashion.

## THE NATURAL REASON'S PROCESS OF "*INVENTIO*"

We have reached a thesis so central to Thomas's thought that its neglect by the autonomistic school of Thomas exegesis must appear striking and unintelligible: it is the thesis that the scope of the natural reason is simply not the same as the *naturaliter cognitum*: natural reason also includes discursive *inventio* and the intellective *iudicium de veritate,* these two also belonging to the *lex naturalis.* The brand of Thomism that has overlooked the concept of the natural law as an *ordinatio* of the natural reason has consequently neglected this point of view when it comes to the doctrine of the natural law itself. The autonomistic school, firmly rooted in this tradition, has not corrected the omissions; it has only repeated them and carried their consequences further. The resulting autonomistic interpretation of the natural law thus represents a fragile, stopgap solution more than a "fresh approach."

### *The Fundamental Unity of the* Ratio *and the* Intellectus

The inventive act of the *ratio naturalis* is an explication or "unfolding" of the truth grasped by the *intellectus imperfectus* proper to the human being. We have said that the human act as participated "natural light" (*lumen naturale*) represents a capacity to grasp truth; it is now time to show that, according to Thomas, the *discursive* act of the intellect belongs to this same capacity. It should suffice to cite only the most important texts where the matter is treated.

Thomas conceives the discursive process of the reason in general as an explication of what is implicitly contained in the "naturally known" (*naturaliter cognitum*) principles, but cannot be grasped in a natural or spontaneous way because of the weakness of the human intellect. Instead, it must be explicated by the intellect's discursive *inventio.* This discursive act, however, is no less an act of the intellect: it belongs to the same faculty,[26] which in the human being actualizes its whole potential only through the discursive process.

Rational discourse therefore starts out in each case from the *simpliciter intellecta*; these are the first principles, and upon them rests the path of *inquisitio* or (a synonym) *inventio.* The discursive process ends with a *resolutio* or a "return" (*reditio*) to the first principles, in which the result is tested by a *iudicium.*[27]

This is the decisive point: discursive reason is *terminatively* (i.e., in respect to its terminus, when it makes its judgment *in via iudicii*) also an act of intellection. Rational *inventio* comes to a conclusive judgment only through and in *intellectus,* and this judgment is again an intellective grasping of truth. *Inventio* itself is a transitional stage of knowing: it is not knowing itself, because knowing is always an act of the intellect's *apprehensio,* which is act and not potency. In this context Thomas emphasizes that the conclusions are fundamentally already contained in the principles, and are merely explicated through the rational process. Rational discourse, to be sure, is characterized by progress from a known to an unknown, and this is so because we are not able to grasp what is still unknown *in* the principles themselves, but we must recognize it through discursive explication "out" of the principles.[28] And yet, as will be shown again later, discursive reason is not itself knowledge, but a movement toward knowledge. Knowledge, into which discursive reasoning flows, is itself no longer *inventio,* but rather a judgment (*iudicium*) of the intellect, which is to say that it comes into being exactly at the moment when the conclusions are comprehended in the principles. This is when the discursive reasoning ends in a concluding intellective *apprehensio* of truth, which again is an *intellectus,* but now a more refined and explicit one.[29] In man, then, all knowledge is an intellective *apprehensio* of the conclusions in the principles; but the natural act of grasping the principles is not enough to attain this: it still needs the mediation of the discursive movement of the intellect, or *ratiocinari.*

Since every act of knowledge—even in man—ends in the unity of intellective apprehension, between the intellect of the pure intelligences (the angels) and that of human beings there is no essential distinction in character and capability;[30] the human intellect belongs to the same genus as that of the pure intelligences, but it is not so perfect:[31] the perfect intellect consists in a pure *uniformitas,* whereas the human intellect "rolls many things into one" (*multa ad unum convolvit*), whereas sense perception in a way expands out to many, without being able to bring them back to the simplicity of the principles (*In De Div. Nom.*, VII, lect. 2, no. 714).

### *The Actualization (Explication) of the* "Intellectus" *by Way of the* "Ratio"

Human *rationalitas* is in fact a derivation of divine wisdom (ibid., no. 713)—a derivation *ad imaginem Dei.* And this is so because it reaches its fulfillment or *terminus* in the "simple intellection of the truth" (*simplex intelligentia veritatis*), from which it goes out, in order to come back in a circular fashion, but deepened and more explicit.[32] Through this rationality the human intellect is able to have what it naturally should have *as intellect,* but that it just as naturally can obtain only through discursive processes, since it is the intellect, after all, of the human soul, and the human soul is the substantial form of a body. Now this discursive process is constantly exposed to the "risk" of deceptive influences through sense perception (imagination, a deceived common sense, etc.), and in the area of practical reasoning this means the risk of an *interceptio* or *ligatio* (binding) of the reason by disordered passions.[33]

Now this potential "self-containment" does not merely imply the fact that new truth is rationally discovered on the basis of principles. The principles as the object of the intellect are *already* a grasp of the *complete* truth. In fact, this is exactly what distinguishes a "perfect intellect" from an "imperfect" one: the latter would grasp—as it were, in an intuitive manner (that is, without discursive reasoning)—the whole sum of possible conclusions that are contained in the naturally known principles.[34]

This is why Thomas calls understanding (*intelligere*) in the strict sense the "natural apprehension of the first principles." Because of the weakness of the *lumen naturale* in man, this natural knowing power does not have the strength necessary to grasp the conclusions together with the principles.[35] Understanding human intellection in this way, Thomas shows that he does not conceive discursive rationality as a creative activity, but rather as *inventio* or, as he states in another passage, the *explicatio,* of what is already contained in the first principles.[36]

The relationship between "intellection" (*intelligere*) and "reasoning" (*ratiocinari*) is that between "rest" and "movement": the act of reasoning is an act of a potency insofar as it is potency. Rational *discursus* is thus a definite form of the actualization of *intelligere* that is a kind of process ending, again, through a *iudicium* and in an *intellectus.* Thomas emphasizes that the knowledge of conclusions (*scientia conclusionum*) does not passively consist in the intellectual potency: it is not simply reception but an *active* disclosure, since otherwise man could not by himself attain (that is, through *inventio*) to knowledge (*De Veritate,* q. 11, a. 1, corp.). To put it still more precisely: the natural knowledge of the principles is related to the conclusions not only as an accidental potency (*in potentia accidentali*), but also as an essential one (*in potentia essentiali*; ibid., ad 12um). There is an inner, "concrete" connection between them: the relation between an *explicatum* and an *implicatum*.

This is why the human reason needs the "motor" of discursive reason, of an *inventio*. Principles and conclusions are related to one another as *cause* to *effect*. And this is a crucial point.[37] The causation of the *intellectus imperfectus* is realized not only through the natural act of *intelligere*, but also through the "motor" of *ratiocinari*, a discursive process proceeding *out* of the principles "by way of discovery" (*per inventionem*). With its concluding "judgment" (*iudicium*) the reason grasps the conclusions in the principles by an act of refined and explicit intellectual apprehension—an act that could not have taken place without the discursive process.[38]

## "Inventio"—*An Act of the* "Ratio Naturalis"

In the process we are speaking of, there two are "knowns": a "naturally known" (*naturaliter cognitum*) grasped through an *intelligere*, and a "known through discovery" (*cognitum per inventionem*), grasped through the discursive reason.[39] Another way of bringing about this movement of causality in man is *doctrina*, or instruction. At every opportunity Thomas contrasts the "naturally known" with what is known *per inventionem vel doctrinam*, and he does so even in connection with the precepts of the natural law.[40]

While Thomas provides no systematic treatment of *inventio*, he does discuss *doctrina*: in the first article of *quaestio* 117 of the *Prima Pars* ("Whether One Man Can Teach Another") and in *quaestio* 11 of the *De Veritate* (see also *In II De Anima*, lect. 11, no. 372). Here can be found the essential information about *inventio* and, above all, Thomas's point that while it is not a *cognitio naturalis*, it is nevertheless an act of the *ratio naturalis*.

Thomas does not conceive of the activity of learning or teaching as the mere "conveyance" of a "supply" of knowledge to a passively receptive subject. Nor, on the other hand, does he conceive of it as pure "midwifery" in the Socratic–Platonic sense (a "maieutic" process, from the Greek *maieúesthai*, to assist in giving birth), whereby knowledge is only a "making conscious" of something already known in a latent fashion. Thomas views learning, rather, as the actualization of an intellect that stands in a state of active potency toward the knowledge of the conclusions (*scientia conclusionum*). In the process of learning, the causality of the first principles with regard to the conclusions is maintained by the fact that the conclusions are implicitly contained in the principles; the process of learning/teaching, then, which is also "inventive" but is occasioned by the movement (*motio*) of an external mover (the teacher), can likewise best be explained in terms of *inventio*.[41]

Thomas emphasizes that knowledge (even in the case of instruction) is caused by an inner principle. This can best be seen in someone who attains to knowledge by his "own discovery" (*inventio propria*). Thomas states that such discovery completes what the natural act of the intellective light is not able to do on its own, and this is done through the application or projection of principles to the particulars acquired through the senses by memory or experience. In this way the intellect progresses from known to unknown, through an unfolding of the wholly virtual power (or active potency) of the *lumen intellectuale*. (*I*, q. 117, a. 1; see also *In II De Anim.*, lect. 11, no. 372).

*Quaestio* 11 of the *De Veritate* explicates this as follows: there preexist in us certain "seeds" (*semina*) of knowledge (just as the *habitus* of the virtues is preformed in the "beginning" or *inchoatio* of the natural inclinations) through the primary and spontaneous knowing by the light of the agent intellect. Now this knowledge is that of the conclusions that follow by necessity from the principles, as being implicitly contained in them. From these universal principles flow (as from "seminal reasons") all particular principles, which of course also possess a certain degree of universality, since as "concrete principles" (*propria principia*) they are the object of *scientia*; through this process the human soul is brought to act concerning that which it had formerly recognized only in potency (i.e., "as if in a universal manner"; *quasi in universali*).[42]

After Thomas has demonstrated that this potentiality of the intellect is not something purely passive, but rather is *active*, he uses a very fruitful metaphor to show that there are two ways for a human being to come to know something: just as someone ailing can be healed through the operation of nature by itself, or through nature, but with the added external help of a medication, so there is a double mode of acquiring knowledge: the *inventio propria* (as the operation of nature itself in the metaphor) and *disciplina,* or learning from instruction (as with an external aid). Thomas is maintaining, then, that *inventio,* even in view of its distinction from the "naturally known" (*naturaliter cognitum*) of the first principles, is still a natural process. And he actually calls the inventive mode of acquiring knowledge an act of the *ratio naturalis*: "thus there is a twofold mode of acquiring knowledge: one way, in which the natural reason progresses by itself [*naturalis ratio per seipsam*] into a cognition of unknown things, and this is termed *inventio*; another way, when someone provides a support for the natural reason from the outside [*rationi naturali aliquis exterius adminiculatur*], and this is called learning [*disciplina*]."

And so both "one's own discovery" (*inventio propria*) and "learning" are processes of the *ratio naturalis,* and both always remain within the field of *scientia,* that is, of necessary and universal conclusions. Thomas says this repeatedly: rational discourse is an act of the *ratio naturalis* insofar as the whole potentiality of the *lumen intelligibile* attains to its unfolding, to its explication, which takes place through the application of the first principles to definite, particular materials (*De Veritate,* q. 11). This explains the entire epistemological substructure of *I–II,* q. 94, a. 2.

It also explains the phenomenon of any transfer of knowledge leading to the true possession of knowledge as founded on insight and understanding (*intellectus*), to the *habitus* of *scientia,* and that means through an explicative completion (through words, pictures, or other *signa*) of the natural reason's discursive movement.[43]

### *The Participative Inner Structure of the* "Ratio Naturalis"

We now find ourselves facing a new relationship of participation *within* the human intellect, because of its imperfection. The human intellect does not solely participate in the divine intellect as its creative cause; discursive reasoning also participates in the natural act of intellection (*intelligere*). This is how Thomas can speak of the light of the natural reason, because the intellect is a *lumen naturale* not only in its intellection (*intelligere*) but also in its reasoning (*ratiocinari*), even though the latter is a discursive process and not something "spontaneous." In fact, Thomas ultimately derives the *ratio naturalis* from the *imago* character of the intellect: the natural reason, as the intellect's discursive reasoning, is itself, as is the intellect, a participation in uncreated truth.[44] Because the natural reason participates in *intelligere,* the participation of the divine *lumen intellectuale* reaches all the way to the results of the natural reason's *inventio.* "We have certain knowledge on the basis of the light of the natural reason given to us internally by God [*ex lumine rationis divinitus interius indito*], by means of which God speaks to us"(*De Veritate,* q. 11, a. 1, ad 13um). This means, then, that the natural law, as the participation of the eternal law through the *lumen* of the natural reason (see *I–II,* q. 91, a. 2), extends not only to the first and most universal principles but also to the conclusions that the natural reason discloses from these principles and intellectively *grasps in* them.

A possible misconception must be warded off immediately: the *whole* process of the practical reason does not explicate itself with the *necessity* of conclusions contained in principles; what has been said applies only to the universal principles of behavior, that is, to those which have the character of law, and that would mean the natural law. Every legal norm is intended for a *multitudo,* and thus has a universal character. Now whereas speculative knowing is always of a universal character and thus attains to the necessary, human actions are always particular and are involved in contingencies. In their content and character, human actions are at once both "less" and "more" than the universality of the legal norm; the latter is insufficient for providing a norm for human actions *in particulari.* Human actions need something further: a particular measuring device or "ruler," consisting in "the right reason of things to be done" (*recta ratio agibilium*) or prudence, as well as a practical kind of truth—a truth involved in the particularity and contingency of human actions. And something else is required as well: a mode of *habitually appropriating* this practical truth, something that transcends the "natural habitualness" of the natural inclinations—what is known, indeed, as moral virtue. But of this we are still not ready to speak; we must first treat the universal and necessary conditions of the practical reason, or the *natural law* itself.

## The Extension of the Natural Law: Its Discursive Explication by the *Ratio Naturalis* and "Secondary Precepts"

In the light of the foregoing analysis of the gnoseological "infrastructure" underlying Thomas's treatise on law, an autonomistic interpretation of the natural law can hardly appear tenable. It should now be clear that an interpretation of this kind does not take in Thomas' thought *as a whole,* but submits his texts instead to a rather selective "filtering" process. Our present concern, consequently, is to show how the foregoing epistemological conceptions are implicit in the treatise on law.

### *"Conclusions" and "Concretizations"*

Our first task is to attend to the article of the *Summa* in which Thomas discusses the relationship between the natural law and positive/human laws. The question is whether all positive law is derived from the natural law, and Thomas wants to show that besides those laws which have their legal efficacy from the human lawmaker alone, there is another kind of law. These are laws that sanction material obligations of the natural law independently of any positive legislation, but do this through the *added* authority of a human lawmaker. An example is the prohibition of murder.

Now an important distinction is based on precisely this differentiation between "conclusions" that the *ratio naturalis* brings forth from its principles, and another mode of derivation from the natural law, the determination or "concretizing" of the universal (commune).[45] Everything derived from the natural law in the mode of a *conclusio* is itself part of the natural law; while what belongs to the mode of *determinatio* (concretization) is not the natural law, which is to say that it possesses its preceptive efficacy exclusively on the positive/human basis.[46]

In what does the *derivatio per modum conclusionis* consist? Thomas explains that it takes place in a manner analogous to the discursive process of the natural reason as analyzed above, "by which demonstrative conclusions are produced from principles in the sciences" (ibid.).

Thomas distinguishes the civil law from the so-called "law of nations" (*ius gentium*) in the same way: the latter, as a derivation through conclusions from natural right (*ius*) belongs to—is a component of—the natural law itself;[47] what the *ius gentium* contains, as a conclusion from the natural law, "is natural to man according to the natural reason [*secundum rationem naturalem*] that dictates this."[48]

When Thomas speaks of "conclusions," therefore, he is thinking of *necessary* derivations in the sense of "demonstration," and *inventio* pertains to this.[49] Of course, even the concretizing "determinations" are a *kind* of conclusions, but not the kind that comes from an inventive/rational *discursus*. Instead, they are conclusions from the immediately practical and concretely applied *discursus* of (precept-giving) *prudence*: always remaining within the context of virtue, they do not result immediately from an *inventio*, but rather from what Thomas now and then calls an *adinventio*. They are those concrete determinations "to which nature at first does not incline, but through the investigation of reason [*per rationis inquisitionem*] people have discovered them in addition [*adinvenerunt*] as useful [*quasi utilia*] for a good life" (*I–II*, q. 94, a.3).

### *Unity and Complexity of the Natural Law*

What must appear striking in all these texts is the rather paradoxical teaching of Thomas that what follows from the natural law is itself natural law. On the basis of this apparent difficulty, some interpreters of Thomas have maintained that according to Thomas, only the first, immediately evident, and most universal principles belong to the natural law; other scholars, no less reliant on the texts of Thomas, maintain that even the so-called secondary and "remote" conclusions belong to it.[50]

However, the problem is only an apparent one. It arises when it is forgotten that the natural law is an ordering of the natural reason (*ordinatio rationis naturalis*), and that it inherently possesses the same complexity and "inventive dynamics" that the reason does, as an explication of the human intellect.

It is only when one insists on conceiving the natural law primarily and fundamentally as a kind of "legality" of a natural order hidden in the very (i.e., material) existence of things as if it were a kind of "code" of laws, that one must conclude that what follows from the code cannot itself be a component of the code. A legal norm derived from the code of civil law (e.g., a contract drawn up for a private business) is, of course, not *itself* a part of the civil law, but only an application of it within an area of constitutive autonomy.

On the other hand, if one considers the natural law formally, as an *ordinatio rationis,* as an ordering act of the practical reason, a law formulated and constituted through the practical reason, and if the practical reason *in this sense* is itself understood to be a legislator, then there would be no contradiction in finding an inner dynamic of self-explication in such a law, a dynamic characterized by a structure of *inventive explication* of particular principles implicitly contained in other principles.

Consequently, if one accepts, first, that the natural law is an *ordinatio rationis,* and second, that it unfolds itself according to the structural principle of inventive explication of the *intellectus* by the process of the natural reason, it can then be understood how the natural law *primo et per se* (or *per essentiam*) consists in the highest and most universal principles of the practical reason (founded upon an "understanding of the principles," or *intellectus principiorum,* the *habitus* of which Thomas, along with Scholastic tradition, calls *synderesis*). Second, and by way of participation (*secundario et per participationem*), it consists in the "special conclusions" (*conclusiones propriae*), on the basis of *inquisitio, inventio,* or *demonstratio,* through the explicative process of the natural reason. Between the first principles and the conclusions there is a relationship of participation and causality, just as there is between the intellect and reason. There is semantic justice, therefore, in calling the conclusions from the first principles *natural law* in an (attributively) analogous sense.[51]

But this is not to say that the inventively explicated secondary principles do not in the strict sense belong to the natural law. It must be recalled that the inventive process of the natural reason ends in each case in an intellection; the highest, most universal principles of the natural law—above all, the primary principle *bonum est prosequendum, malum vitandum*—remain "ordinatively" present as a fundamental *ordinatio,* as "naturally known principles" (*principia naturaliter cognita*), in each discursive act of the natural reason. The *discursus,* it should be recalled, ends in each case in the first principles; in them, the conclusions can be grasped as an explication of what at first is only implicitly grasped as their explication. Every act of the *ratio naturalis* (and that is to say, every precept of the natural law) is such only in virtue of the ordinative power of the first principles—to be more precise, of *synderesis*. In this *habitus* of the first principles is founded the entire ordering and moving power, the very "essence," of the natural law; at the same time, these principles explicate and refine themselves (or, rather, the understanding of what is implicitly contained in them refines itself) in the knowledge of conclusions, by way of the discursive activity of the natural reason. The conclusions themselves, thanks to their *resolutio* into the first principles and their character as explication of the latter, truly belong to the natural law. Only in view of their cognitive unfolding do they belong participatively and analogously to the natural law; as "that which is unfolded" (*explicatum*) from the first principles, and as that which is confirmed *in* the first principles, they truly are the natural law.

This also makes more intelligible why Thomas takes little effort to spell out precisely and unambiguously which conclusions are secondary, and which are more remote; sometimes he divides them into *conclusiones primariae et secundariae* (e.g., *I–II,* q. 100, a. 11); often he simply refers to all *conclusions as secundaria* (e.g., *I–II,* q. 94, a. 6). In many passages Thomas is only or primarily interested in the formal aspect of the preceptive knowing process. Even the question of whether the very first principle (*bonum est prosequendum* . . .) is the sole highest principle, or whether others are as well, so that we would have to distinguish between the *communissima* and the merely *communia,* is really beside the point, in view of the fundamentally participative connection between principle and conclusion.[52] Thomas does not attempt a watertight terminology, but this should be irritating only to those who do not grasp the natural law as an *ordinatio* of the *ratio naturalis*: that it merely reflects the inner dynamics of human knowing, and all the flexibility and plasticity to be found there.

### *Primary and Secondary Principles*

So far, then, we have established the following: the natural law, fundamentally and essentially, is the ensemble of those most general principles that the practical reason recognizes by an "insight into first principles" (*intellectus principiorum*) and in an instantaneous–intuitive manner, by the light of the agent intellect; these principles, as something "naturally known" (*naturaliter cognitum*) form a so-called "natural habit of first principles," or *synderesis.*[53] This is a spontaneous and "natural" source of light, acquired without any discursive movement, but belonging to the practical reason and thus "bringing movement" and forming the "seeds" of all subsequent knowledge[54]—containing knowledge potentially and implicitly—so that Thomas can also call it the habit of the "natural principles of natural law."[55] The advantage of this formulation is that it expresses how the natural law[56] itself has a double aspect: that of a *naturaliter cognitum,* on the one hand, and that of a *cognitum per inquisitionem* on the other, both of which are acts of the natural reason.

The natural law is ultimately grounded—in its essentials and with all of its power—in the *synderesis,* or *habitus* of the first principles: an ordering and operative *habitus* that moves to action. Everything is implicitly contained in these principles, for these are the highest practical judgments of the human person, who is constituted according to a certain nature. The principles already possess a personal meaning, which is to say, a material [*inhaltliche*] implication by their ordering within the *human suppositum.* We are not concerned here, therefore, with "abstract" principles or "inevitable" structures of logical thinking; the intellect that grasps the principles is a power of the human soul, which is the form of a human body. The implications of these principles as the highest personal principles (that is, the practical principles of the human being)—are developed in their concrete anthropological meaning only through the inventive *discursus* of the natural reason.

The conclusions of this inventive process contain the "more concrete principles" (*principia magis propria*) that, as conclusions of a natural/discursive process of knowing, belong nevertheless (and although in "second rank") to the natural law. "Second rank" in this context does not mean "relatively insignificant," but only the "sequent" quality that they have in view of their cognitive explication[57]: they are discovered only as something secondary, or implicit. In the order of actions, however, as "less remote principles" (*principia propria*)[58] they are *more* significant than the first principles, due to their being "closer" to the object of action. Nor is it correct to consider them as *other* principles than the first and most universal; they contain these in themselves—or, to put it better, they *are* these same principles at a deeper stage of explication, and as such, they tell us more about what we should do. This means that they are also more significant in their legislative function, as determining our actions. And yet they are that only insofar as they are an explication of the first and most universal principles, and stand in an immediately inventive context with them;[59] only *as such* do they belong to the natural law at all. Now, in his teaching on the concrete judgment of action (*iudicium electionis*), Thomas will note that only prudence as the *recta ratio agilbilium* is the "proximate rule" (*regula proxima*) of action. It is the rule that has the action *hic et nunc* and the concrete "do-able" (*operabile*) for its object, and which is capable of ordering it toward its end;[60] at this level the constitutive relationship of prudence to the general secondary principles of the natural law and to the very first principle of *synderesis* is never lost.[61]

While the first principles of the practical reason or the natural law (such as "One should do good"; "Don't do anyone an injustice"; "Strive to find the truth"; "Worship God," and so on) still do not indicate any particular kinds of actions (*species*), nevertheless in these so-called secondary precepts can be found that "closeness" to concrete actions that makes possible the identification of such *species*. These derived, "discovered" principles are in content identical with the Decalogue (see *I–II,* q. 100, a. 3); with the goals of the moral virtues (see ibid., a. 2; *II–II,* q. 47, a. 6)[62], or, finally, with the order of justice (see *I–II,* q. 100, a. 8; *II–II,* q. 122, a. 1).

### *The Inventive Origin of the Secondary Principles*

The derivative relationship of these secondary precepts to the first principles is always understood by Thomas in terms of the inventive structure of the natural reason as explained above; usually, besides *inventio,* there is also mention of the other possibility, of instruction (*disciplina* or *doctrina*) or revelation, which are likewise forms of discursive actualization of the *ratio naturalis,* but with the support of some external assistance.

Let us consider a few texts. In the article on the *synderesis,* Thomas denies that this *habitus* leads toward good and away from evil by being, so to speak, "directly applied" to an action in a judgment of conscience. This is significant, because it shows that this natural *habitus* still does not possess any concrete principles (*principia propria*) that are "close" to actions. Rather, says Thomas, *synderesis* can be said to "drive toward the good, and murmur against the evil [*instigare ad bonum et murmurare de malo*] insofar as we proceed through the first principles to discovery, and judge what we have discovered" (*I,* q. 79, a. 12). The function of *synderesis* as the habit of first principles consists in its being a starting point for an *inventio*, the result of which invention is then judged *in* the first principles by the normal course of judgment (*in via iudicii*). The practical/ordinative function of *synderesis* thus operates by way of the inventive process of the natural reason.[63]

Thomas speaks the same language when he *ex professo* defines the area of the secondary principles. The best-known passage where he does so is in the *quaestio* about the moral commandments of the Old Covenant (*I–II,* q. 100), which is explained as being in agreement in material content with the natural law.[64]

There are, then, naturally known (first) principles from which every judgment of the practical reason takes its start (*II–II,* q. 100, a. 1).[65] Basing itself on these principles, the reason goes forth "in various ways" to reach a judgment about "various things" (*diversimode procedi potest ad iudicandum de diversis*). Thomas's way of expressing this suggests that such a judgment is always an (inventive) explication of principles, for he says that "some things in human affairs are so explicit that they can immediately, and with very little consideration (*statim, cum modica consideratione*), be approved or disapproved through those common and first principles" (ibid.). Other things, however, "require much consideration of various circumstances in order for a judgment to be reached about them, and such matters can be considered diligently by not just anyone, but only by the wise [*considerare diligenter non est cuiuslibet, sed sapientum*], just as it is the task not of anyone, but only of persons of special knowledge [*pertinet . . . ad solos philosophos*], to consider particular conclusions of the sciences" (ibid.).[66] It should be noted that in the area of morality, the "wise" (*sapientes*) are not the same as the "specialists" of the sciences (*philosophi*): they are the "morally wise," or the good, virtuous and prudent (the Aristotelian σπουδαῖοι or φρόνιμοι), since "prudence is wisdom in human affairs" (*II–II,* q. 47, a. 2).

The difference between some conclusions that are easily understood by everyone and others that can be arrived at only through longer and more careful deliberation, leads to the terminological distinction between "secondary" and "more remote" commands (*principia secundaria* and *remota*) of the natural law. Now this distinction can be somewhat confusing since in a certain sense *all* the precepts that are explications of the first principles are "secondary" commands (see, e.g., *I–II,* q. 94, a. 6, where this two-stage division is used). Among these secondary commands or conclusions can be found some that are "nearer" (*proxima*) and thus easily recognizable, and others that are "more distant" (*remota*) and consequently more difficult to understand.[67] This *gradation* in intelligibility of the natural law has consequences, in Thomas's view, for the communication of its contents. Whereas man has the knowledge (*notitiam*) of the proximate precepts "from God, through his own agency" (*per seipsum a Deo*), which means in virtue of man's natural participation in the eternal law, the more remote commands "go forth from God to the people [*proveniunt a Deo ad populum*] through the mediation and instruction of the wise" (*mediante disciplina sapientium; I–II,* q. 100, a. 3).

Now on the basis of our analysis of the process of natural reasoning, we know that for Thomas personal *inventio* (that is, the *notitia per seipsum*) and *disciplina* (or *doctrina*) represent two alternative modes of discursive actualization of the natural reason; in the "Quaestio de Magistro" of the *De Veritate* (q. 11), Thomas points out that the communication of knowledge through *disciplina* is in each case only an actualization of the *ratio naturalis,* which explains why a person can *understand* such instruction and be able to assent to it.[68] In this instance as well, the natural reason does not represent any compromise of the structure of participation in the eternal law. In certain cases there is need for cognitive mediation and the help of instruction, whether this be caused by the complexity of the material itself, by a lack of experience, by the habitual moral dispositions of the individual, by the social/cultural context, or by the weakening of judgment through certain habits and customs. The personal autonomy of the human being is not reduced by such instruction, nor does it involve any contradiction with the concept of the natural law. For just like the *inventio per seipsum,* instruction leads to a more certain knowledge of truth and an explication of the first principles—there is a difference only in the manner of cognitive origin. It cannot be overemphasized that the acquisition of knowledge through teaching is an *authentic cognitive process.*[69]

The teaching about the explication of the natural law through the *ratio naturalis* is summed up at *I–II,* q. 100, a. 11. The moral commandments of the Old Covenant have their efficacy (*efficaciam*) on the basis of the preceptive act of the natural reason itself (*ex ipso dictamine naturalis rationis*). They are the "natural law" in a threefold gradation: (1) first principles ("to love God and neighbor"); and then (2) precepts (the commandments of the Decalogue) that are proximate and "more determined" (*magis determinata*), but understandable to all, as conclusions drawn from the very first principles; and (3) the "more remote" and more difficult precepts, recognizable only by the wise.[70] In each case, the more apparent things are the principles of knowing the less apparent (*ea quae sunt manifesta sunt principia cognoscendi eorum quae non sunt manifesta*; ibid.), leaving intact the fundamental unity of the practical reason.

## *Another Look at* I–II, *q. 94, a. 2*

The much-interpreted article 2 of *questio* 94 of the *Prima Secundae* explains how this process of knowing arises and finds its fulfillment. It was pointed out earlier how important it is to understand precisely just *what* is being explained by the article: it is concerned to show that the natural law consists in not one precept but *in several.* In order to do this, Thomas explains how the very first principle of practical reasoning (*bonum est prosequendum . . .*) is differentiated because of the natural grasp of the human goods (*bona humana*) in the natural inclinations. Since Thomas wants to show only this, the article never departs from a demonstration of the spontaneous branching out of the first principle into *several* universal principles, each of which is grasped as it follows a natural inclination, in a natural and nondiscursive manner. Now to conclude from this, in the manner of the "autonomistic" school, that for Thomas only these principles belong to the natural law results from a neglect of the article's explicit intention.[71]

Recalling our analysis of the article in part I, we can now attempt to relate the immediate argument to our conclusions. The branching out of the principle "good is to be pursued . . ." into the areas of the natural inclinations takes place at the level of the *apprehensio naturalis* of the practical reason—that natural, nondiscursive, but spontaneous knowledge of the first and most universal principles, which remain firmly placed in the *habitus* of the *synderesis*. Here stands revealed, in fundamental fashion, the area of the *ordinatio rationis,* or the natural law. It is marked out by the natural inclinations: "Everything toward which man possesses a natural inclination, the reason grasps as good in a natural way, as something to pursue in actions, and what is opposite to this, as some evil to be avoided. The order of precepts of the natural law therefore follows the order of natural inclinations" (*I–II,* q. 94, a. 2).

Since first principles, whether of the practical or the speculative reason, are not "innate ideas," we can again appreciate the fundamental importance of these natural inclinations for the formation of the first principles of the practical reason. Without them there could be no practical knowledge at all. The human reason, even in its very first natural acts, is oriented toward some knowable content. The light of the natural reason, as the metaphor indicates, is a light that illuminates, and not a "source" from which certain first cognitions emerge. The practical reason attains its most general (practical) judgments on the basis of its intellective comprehension of the inclinations that naturally belong to the human being; such an *intellectio* includes the spontaneous recognition of these inclinations as *bona humana,* a recognition that by its intellective character brings about an integration of these natural inclinations into the order of reason. In this way, the natural inclinations belong to the natural law (1) insofar as they are grasped, and have their root, *in* the highest principle of the practical reason (*bonum est prosequendum*), a principle that is intellective and corresponds to the natural attraction of the will toward the good, and (2) insofar as they are ordered by the reason.[72] The natural inclinations cannot be treated only as a "material," only an "object" of an ordering act of the reason; that through which, as Böckle puts it, "the terrain is marked out, over which man must walk in order to shape himself," or through which "the basic needs are manifested, which must be the object of rational government."[73] The natural inclinations are not the "matter" of the practical reason; they are, rather, the strivings of a rational *suppositum,* that is, of a person, and they express the personal unity of the human being. *Before* they can be the object of an ordering act of the reason, they are the object of a natural apprehension (*naturalis apprehensio*) of the natural reason, of an intellective intuition, through which they are recognized and acknowledged in a practical manner as human goods; this is an act through which an area of human goods is already indicated and formulated in regard to content, and on the basis of which the first, self-evident, and most universal principles of the practical reason (or precepts of the natural law) can form themselves. The ordering, regulating act of the practical reason does not have power to "dispense" with these inclinations; there is always an ordering that precedes the recognition of the inclinations as human goods: it is not an ordering *of* the natural inclinations, it is an ordering *in* them. Thomas brings this out with his remark that the natural reason is a measure and rule, but *not* the measure of what is there "by nature" (*a natura*).[74]

We must also remember at this point that the intellect progresses by way of a "complete return" (*reditio completa*) over its own acts, as well as the acts of the affections (or sensitive inclinations), until it reaches a comprehension of its own essence and the soul's essence.[75] In this way it achieves a spontaneous and at the same time intellective integration—the *personal* integration—of the natural inclinations in the human *suppositum.* It does not simply comprehend the natural goal of the inclinations—their "proper end" (*finis proprius*)—it also comprehends this goal as a *bonum humanum.*

It should be now be abundantly clear that the constitution of the natural law is not completed with this natural comprehension of human goods as first and most universal principles. This *apprehensio* is followed by a discursive, inventive process of the natural reason, and by means of this process what is potentially contained in these principles is cognitively unfolded and made explicit. It takes place, as explained above, either through one's own discovery or with the aid of instruction or revelation (*Quaest. Quodl.*

VIII, q. 2, a. 2). In the discursive process, as in all knowing, man must depend on experience, and first of all on sense experience, which he is able to comprehend in its intelligible content with the light of the natural reason. This process of *inventio* Thomas also calls the "path of experience" (*via experimenti*);[76] it needs sense experience and deliberation, and finally—on the "path of judgment" (*in via iudicii*)—comes to an end by a *resolutio* into the first principles.

We can conclude, on the basis of a more thorough analysis of the Thomistic conception of the natural law, that the autonomistic interpretation of the same is untenable. The natural law does not mean an autonomy of the natural reason for its "own" norm-setting activity. The process of constituting the natural law by the natural reason is not a "creative" process, but rather an unfolding of the participation of the eternal law in man. This participation is twofold: it consists, on the one hand, in the natural inclinations and, on the other hand, in the light of the natural reason, through which these natural inclinations become cognitively integrated into the context of human goods. Through this unfolding, something is not "*created*" but *recognized*: the order of the eternal law, to which man as creature is subject. And yet, because this recognition follows from the image of God that resides in the human person, we are entitled to speak of a *personal autonomy*. The unfolding of the natural law—the recognition of the eternal law—takes place according to an autonomy that man has in virtue of being a *causa secunda*. The explication of the natural law reveals itself as an expression of the eternal law itself; in the constitution of the natural law through his own moral experience as guided by the natural reason, the human person as moral subject occasions the "breakthrough," in an autonomous way, of a *theonomy*. Man participates in this theonomy with his very being, and is noetically obliged to its normative truth since it is man's *own* normative truth, as established through personal autonomy. It is precisely this truth of moral experience—a personal, moral autonomy—that reveals, in the *imago* character of self-reflective consciousness, the entryway to understanding God as moral law-maker. It also shows in what sense "nature" can be called the foundation of moral normativity.

On this foundation, it is possible to determine more precisely *why* and *how* reason is the standard of morality. But a further problem lies before us: that of understanding how the universal principles of the natural law can be reconciled with the *contingency* and *particularity* of concrete action. Do the principles of the natural law form absolute, universal norms? What, in fact, *is* a moral norm? We thus arrive at some current problems associated with the establishment of a so-called "teleological" ethics. Treating them will lead us to consider more carefully the concept of moral behavior, and to inquire in what the proper subject of ethics (*das Proprium des Ethischen*) consists. It has already been pointed out that "autonomous morality" has not been able to come to terms with what is properly ethics, and the same will be said for the "teleological" view, since this latter is but a variant of the "physicalism" and "naturalistic fallacy" it was meant to overcome.

## Notes

1. A survey of the conceptual history of the light metaphor can be found in the articles "Lumen naturale" and "Licht" in J. Ritter and K. Gründer, eds., *Historisches Wörterbuch der Philosophie*, vol. 5 (Basel, 1980).

2. I emphasize *existential* (*seinsmäßige*) participation, in order to distinguish the Thomistic concept of "illumination" from the Augustinian. While the concept of participation is the same in both, for St. Augustine it is God Who in each case *actually* enlightens the human knowing power. For Thomas, the participation in the light of the divine intelligence (or "enlightening") is realized through an *impressio* in the *being* (*Sein*) of man, a power that works as a *causa secunda*, which man possesses as a *lumen intellectuale*. We are primarily concerned here, in other words, with the "agent intellect" (*intellectus agens*).

3. In the ad 1um Thomas calls the human reason the *mensura proxima*; the divine reason, the *mensura remota*. Only the former is a "measure homogeneous with what is measured (i.e., the human will; ibid., ad 2um). See also *I–II*, q. 71, a. 6: "Regula autem voluntatis humanae est duplex: una propinqua et homogenea, scilicet ipsa humana ratio; alia vero est prima regula, scilicet lex aeterna, quae est ratio Dei." (But the rule of the human will is twofold: one, nearby and of the same kind [homogeneous], namely, the human reason; the other is the first rule: namely, the eternal law, which is the divine reason). For further parallels, see L. Lehu, *La Raison—Règle de la moralité d'après Saint Thomas* (Paris, 1930), p. 5, note 2.

4. K. W. Merks, *Theologische Grundlegung der sittlichen Autonomie* (Düsseldorf, 1978), p. 304.

5. This teminology indicates the moral commandments of the Mosaic Law, in the center of which is the Decalogue, identical in its content with the natural law.

6. *I–II,* q. 100, a. 11: "Sed praecepta moralia ex ipso dictamine naturalis rationis efficaciam habent, etiam si numquam in lege statuantur. Horum autem triplex est gradus. Nam quaedam sunt certissima, et adeo manifesta, quod editione non indigent; sicut mandata de dilectione Dei et proximi, et alia huiusmodi, ut supra dictum est, quae sunt quasi fines praeceptorum: unde in eis nullus potest errare secundum iudicium rationis. Quaedam vero sunt magis determinata, quorum rationem statim quilibet, etiam popularis, potest de facili videre; et tamen quia in paucioribus circa huiusmodi contingit iudicium humanum perverti, huiusmodi editione indigent: et haec sunt praecepta decalogi. Quaedam vero sunt quorum ratio non est adeo cuilibet manifesta, sed solum sapientibus: et ista sunt praecepta moralia superaddita decalogo, tradita a Deo populo per Moysen et Aaron."

7. Merks's treatment of the theme "*intellectus* and *ratio*" (*Theologische Grundlegung . . .*, pp. 240ff.) shows a clear tendency to explain the *lumen* of the human intellect as ultimately only a pure "faculty of knowing" (p. 269), as the capability of making a rational/discursive *collatio* (comparison) from the material of sense experience. Even though Merks certainly wants to remain faithful to a fundamentally Thomistic epistemology that all knowledge has its starting point in the senses, nevertheless his interpretation takes on an empiricistic/sensualistic coloring through his lack of attention to the metaphorics of light and to the doctrine of human intellect as a participation of the divine intellect. Merks conceives the intellect as a "product" of the discursive reason, instead of seeing the reason, as Thomas did, as an *intellectus imperfectus;* (the mistake can be most clearly seen at p. 249, 2nd section). Merks misunderstands the nature of *ratiocinatio* as an act of the *intellect*—an act that is itself, as we shall see, "terminatively" an *intellegere.*

8. See A. Scola, *La fondazione della legge naturale nello Scriptum super Sententiis di san Tommaso d'Aquino* (Freiburg, Switzerland, 1982), esp. p. 179, where a happy exception can be found to the current trend of interpretations. "It is surprising, however, after an examination of the very plentiful literature on the subject, that so few commentators try to deepen (through the essential psychological/philosophical perspective) the meaning of this *ratio naturalis*, or of this 'natural inscribing' [*iscrizione naturale*] of the reason by a law that would be called 'natural' for this reason" (p. 180). Such a psychological/metaphysical analysis is lacking

even in L. Lehu, though he gave fitting attention to the *ratio naturalis* and rightly differed with the interpretation of O. Lottin, who always mistranslated *ratio naturalis* as *nature raisonnable.* Lehu was quite correct in pointing out that the participation of the *ratio regulae* (or *ratio legis*)—in other words, the formal participation of the *lex aeterna*—took place in the human *ratio*, and not in the *natura rationalis.* "The eternal law being the divine reason, the formal participation of the divine reason in man will be the reason of man, and not human nature" (*La Raison,* p. 159).

9. The *ratio naturalis* is understood by Böckle to be the *natura rationis*: and this latter implies for him "the structure of human knowing": "There are certain a priori insights from which man cannot seclude himself—insights that reveal themselves to him as necessarily self-evident. They arise by a necessity of essence [*wesensnotwendig*] from the nature of the human reason, and they are valid because *naturaliter cognitum*" (see "Natur als Norm in der Moraltheologie," in F. Heinrich, ed., *Naturgesetz und christliche Ethik* [Munich, 1970], p. 78ff). This consists, as we have already seen, in the purely formal idea that one should do good and avoid evil. There is a subtle but very influential "physicalistic" misconception on Böckle's part. He reduces the *naturaliter cognitum* of the natural reason to the structures of the "nature of the reason," and thus the "natural light" of this reason is reduced to *nature.* In order, then, to rescue the reason as the rule of free and personally autonomous actions, he must reduce the area of the *ratio naturalis* and the *lex naturalis* in general to purely formal, self-evident principles that are indifferent to any content.

10. See above all *In IV Sent.*, d. 33, q. 1, a. 1: "It is fitting that in the knowing power [*in vi cognoscitiva*] there be a natural cognition [*naturalis conceptio*], and that in the appetitive power [*in vi appetitiva*] there be a natural inclination [*naturalis inclinatio*]. In ibid., d. 26, q. 1, a. 1, the term *naturalis ratio* is used: "*naturalis ratio* dictat ut homines simul cohabitent." (The natural reason dictates that human beings live together.) Once again, an example of how the natural reason formulates not just purely formal imperatives. In this passage one sees the natural–rational justification for married and community life.

11. *II–II* q. 9, a. 1. Here, as in some other passages, *naturalis ratio* refers to the natural reason as opposed to the reason illuminated (supernaturally) by grace or faith. Although these different meanings of "natural" must sometimes be distinguished from one another, when it comes to the reason, there is a real overlap of the two aspects: the *ratio naturalis* is for this reason something natural (as distinct from supernaturally illuminated) precisely because there is an existential (*seinsmäßige*) participation of the *lumen intellectuale.* In any case—and this is decisive for the present

context—in every act of the human *ratio* there is an *intellectus*, which lends it a *natural capability* of "assenting to the truth."

12. See also the *In III de Anima,* lect. 10, no. 730: "Unde dicit quod est habitus, ut lumen, quod quodammodo facit colores existentes in potentia, esse actu colores. Et dicit 'quodammodo,' quia supra ostensum est, quod color secundum seipsum est visibilis. Hoc autem sollummodo facit lumen, ipsum esse actu colorem, inquantum facit diaphanum esse in actu, ut moveri possit a colore, ut sic color videatur. Intellectus autem agens facit ipsa intelligibilia esse in actu, quae prius erant in potentia, per hoc quod abstrahit ea a materia; sic enim sunt intelligibilia in actu, ut dictum est." (Wherefore he [Aristotle]says that it is a *habitus,* as the light, which in a certain way makes colors existing in potency be colors in act. And he says 'in a certain way,' because it has been shown above that color in itself is visible. But light does only this: it makes color actualized, insofar as it makes a being-transparent in act, so that it can be moved by color, and that in this way color might be seen. Now the agent intellect makes what is intelligible actualized, which was before only potential, and it does this by abstracting the intelligibles from matter, and thus they are intelligible in act, as has been said.)

13. As he says in his early work the *Protrepticus,* which was so Platonic in inspiration: "For man there is nothing divine or holy apart from that one thing that is worth all the trouble: namely, that which is in us of understanding and spiritual power. This alone seem imperishable of that which we possess, this alone seems divine. Thanks to our capacity to have a share in this, our life is so wonderfully equipped, despite its natural poverty and wearisomeness, that man seems like a god in comparison with other creatures. For the poets are right when they say, 'The *nous* is god in us' or 'Human life has some part of a god in itself' (B 108–110).

14. "Et sic necesse est dicere quod anima humana omnia cognoscat in rationibus aeternis, per quarum participationem omnia cognoscimus. Ipsum enim lumen intellectuale quod est in nobis, nihil est aliud quam quaedam participata similitudo luminis increati, *in quo continentur rationes aeternae.*"

15. It is interesting to notice how Thomas speaks here of the "power of illuminative virtue" (*potestas illuminativae virtutis*), on the basis of which God has "all dominion" (*omnis dominatio*). The *gubernatio* of the *lex aeterna* thus can also be conceived as an *illuminatio.*

16. *Super Johannem,* I, lect. 3, no. 99. To illustrate the "perfection and dignity of this life, because it is intellectual and rational," there follows, as always, a comparison with the animals that "move by necessity, and not freely" (*ex necessitate moventur, et non libere*). Moved by this kind of principle, they "are act-ed" (*aguntur*) rather than "act" (*agunt*). But man,

since he is the master of his own actions, moves himself freely toward everything that he wants; and thus man has a "perfect" (or "complete," *per-fectam*) life, just as any intellectual creature.

17. See ibid., no. 104: "Alio modo . . . exponitur secundum fluxum gratiae, quia irradiamur per Christum." This second "irradiation" presupposes the first, and in fact includes it in its own content. The metaphysics of light can also be extended in Christological terms to a *theology of light*, within which a continuity can be demonstrated from the natural order to the supernatural. This continuity is one that, on the one hand (with regard to the *modus participationis* and seen from the human point of view), fully respects the difference between the natural and the supernatural but, on the other hand (with regard to the *participatum*, the origin or original image, Christ), keeps both aspects indivisibly together, but without confusion (as the two natures of Christ). The distinction is also found at ibid., lect. 4, no. 129/130: "being illuminated" (*illuminare*) can occur, on the one hand, *ratione suae creationis*; on the other hand, *pro lumine gratiae.*

18. Ibid., no. 101: "Potest etaim dici lux hominum participata. Numquam enim ipsum Verbum et ipsam lucem conspicere possemus nisi per participationem eius, quae in ipso homine est, quae est superior pars animae nostrae, scilicet lux intellectiva, de qua dicitur in Ps. IV, 7: 'Signatum est super nos lumen vultus tui,' id est Filii tui, qui est facies qua manifestaris." (There can also be a participated light of men. For we can never look upon the Word itself or upon light itself without a participation of it, which is in man himself, and which is the superior part of our soul, namely the intellective light, which is mentioned in the Fourth Psalm, verse 7: *the light of Thy countenance is signed above us* . . . that is, the light of Your Son, who is the face by which You are manifested.)

19. Ibid., lect. 5, no. 129: "illuminare secundum quod accipitur pro lumine naturalis rationis . . . quia homines . . . illuminantur lumine naturalis cognitionis ex participatione huius verae lucis, a qua derivatur quicquid de lumine naturalis cognitionis participatur ab hominibus." (because human beings . . . are illuminated by the light of natural cognition by way of participation of this true light, from which is derived whatever of the light of natural cognition is participated in by them.)

20. Ibid.; "ostendit enim Evangelista quod haec illuminatio est secundum illud quod est ab extrinseco, scilicet intellectum, cum dicit 'venientem in hunc mundum' " (for the Evangelist shows that this illumination is in respect to what comes from outside, namely, the intellect, when he says, "coming in the world"). As mentioned earlier, the second causality of the corporeal creature cannot be the source of an intellect. Every human soul springs from an immediate act of divine creation.

21. Ibid., lect. 3, no. 103: "quia quidquid veritatis a quocumque cognoscitur, totum est ex participatione istius lucis, quae in tenebris lucet."

22. And this is something that is not at all clear in Merks's account. He calls the intellect the "kernel of experience and reflection" that does not bring upon itself "the instability of discourse" (*Theologische Grundlegung*, p. 254); the "connection with sense perception . . . constitutes the specifically anthropological understanding of the intellect" (p. 257). The intellect here appears to have become a *perceptively conditioned* achievement of the *ratio*. It begins with an *intellectus* of a few first principles (having only a formal significance), so that this contentless intellect can then be "filled out" with the results of its "discourse" with the senses.

23. See O. H. Pesch, *Das Gesetz* (Heidelberg, 1977), p. 53: "A natural law that would give only an 'outline of behavior' obviously leaves man in the freedom of a rational 'invention' [*Erfindung*]." L. Oeing-Hanhoff, "Der Mensch: Natur oder Geschichte?," in F. Henrich, ed., *Naturgesetz und Christlich Ethik* [Munich, 1970], p. 29, also translates the term *inventio* as *Erfindung*.

24. The standard work on this theme is still R. A. Armstrong, *Primary and Secondary Precepts in Thomistic Natural Teaching* (The Hague, 1966). This very circumspect and comprehensive study has not won the attention it deserves from many scholars of St. Thomas.

25. See *I–II*, q. 68, a. 4: "Ratio autem est speculativa et practica: et in utraque consideratur *apprehensio veritatis quae pertinent ad inventionem*; et iudicium de veritate." (But the reason is speculative and practical: in either one there is to be found an *apprehension of the truth that pertains to discovery*, and a judgment about the truth.)

26. *I*, q. 79, a. 8: While simple, natural intelligere *means simpliciter veritatem intelligibilem apprehendere* (simply apprehending the intelligible truth), *ratiocinari*, on the other hand, means *procedere de uno intellecto ad aliud, ad veritatem intelligibilem cognoscendam* (proceeding from one thing that has been understood to another, in order to know intelligible truth). Rational discourse is related to *intellectus* (here, the act of simplex *apprehensio*) as movement is related to rest (rest being at the same time starting point and end point of movement), or as "acquiring" is related to "having." Thus both belong to the same faculty.

27. Ibid.: "ratiocinatio humana, secundum viam inquisitionis vel inventionis, procedit a quibusdam simpliciter intellectis, quae sunt prima principia; et rursus, in via iudicii, resolvendo redit ad prima principia, ad quae inventa examinat."

28. See *I*, q. 14, a. 7: "quia talis est procedentis de noto ad ignotum. Unde manifestum est quod, quando cognoscitur primum, adhuc ignoratur secundum. Et sic secundum non cognoscitur in primo, sed ex

primo." (This is what happens when someone proceeds from what is known to what is unknown. Wherefore it is clear that when the first thing is known, the second thing is still unknown. And thus the second thing is not known in the first, but out of the first.).

29. Ibid.: "Terminus vero discursus est, quando secundum videtur in primo, resolutis effectibus in causas: et tunc cessat discursus." (But the end of the *discursus* takes place when the second is seen in the first, once the effects have been resolved into the causes.)

30. See *In De Div. Nom.,* VII, lect. 2, no. 713: "Homines habent intellectus quodammodo Angelis aequales, scilicet secundum proprietatem et possibilitatem animarum." (Human beings have intellects equal to the angels, that is according to what is proper to and possible for their souls.)

31. *I,* q. 79, a. 8, ad 3um: "Et ideo vis cognoscitiva angelorum non est alterius generis a vi cognoscitiva rationis, sed comparatur ad ipsam ut perfectum ad imperfectum." (And therefore the knowing power of the angels is not different in kind from that of the human reason, but stands compared with it as perfect to imperfect.) For this reason, Thomas can call the human intellect a participation in the intellect of the pure intelligences.

32. Ibid., "Inquisitio [= inventio] enim rationis ad simplicem intelligentiam veritatis terminatur, sicut incipit a simplici intelligentia veritatis quae consideratur in primis principiis; et ideo, in processu rationis est quaedam convolutio ut circulus, dum ratio, ab uno incipiens, per multa procedens, ad unum terminatur." (The investigation or "discovery" of the reason is completed at the simple understanding of truth, just as what is considered in the first principles begins from the simple understanding of the truth; in this way, there is a certain "turning around" as in a circle, while the reason begins from one thing, goes through many, and comes to a stop with one again.)

33. The theme of moral virtue belongs in this context, because it brings about the conformity of the senses with the ratio, and it does this not only in a negative way (in the sense of "not disturbing" it) but also positively, since virtue is perfected when it supports and even provides orientation for the reason in its practical discursiveness.

34. For the divine intellect, see *Summa Theologiae I,* q.14, a. 14; for the angels, which are pure intelligences, *I,* q. 58, a. 3: "Sic igitur et inferiores intellectus, scilicet hominum, per quendam motum et discursum intellectualis operationis, perfectionem in cognitione veritatis adipiscuntur; dum scilicet ex uno cognito in aliud cognitum procedunt. Si autem statim in ipsa cognitione principii noti, inspicerent quasi notas omnes conclusiones consequentes, in eis discursus locum non haberet.

Et hoc est in angelis: quia statim in illis, quae primo naturaliter cognoscunt, inspiciunt omnia quaecumque in eis cognosci possunt." (And thus also do the inferior intellects [namely, human intellects] acquire perfection in the knowledge of the truth through a kind of motion and "running about" [*discursus*] of intellectual activity, while they proceed from one thing known to another thing known. But if, in their very act of knowing the first principle, they were to see all the conclusions that follow as if they were also known, there would be no place for "discursus" in them. And this is what occurs in the angels: they immediately see, in those things which they naturally know first, all the things whatever that can be known in them").

35. Ibid. "Et ideo [angeli] dicuntur intellectuales: quia etiam apud nos, ea quae statim naturaliter apprehenduntur, intelligi dicuntur; unde intellectus dicitur habitus primorum principiorum. Animae vero humanae, quae veritatis notitiam per quendam discursum acquirunt, rationales vocantur.—Quod quidem contingit ex debilitate intellectualis luminis in eis. Si enim haberent plenitudinem intellectualis luminis, sicut angeli, statim in primo aspectu principiorum totam virtutem eorum comprehenderent, intuendo quidquid ex eis syllogizari posset." (And thus the angels are said to be intellectual: because even in them, what is naturally apprehended is said to be "understood," and thus understanding [*intellectus*] is called the habit of the first principles. But human souls are called rational, since they acquire a knowledge of the truth through a certain "*discursus.*"—And this happens because of the weakness of the intellectual light in them. For if they possessed the fullness of intellectual light, as the angels do, they would immediately understand in the first glimpse the whole power of those principles, by seeing whatever could be syllogized from them.)

36. See *De Veritate,* q. 11, a. 1, ad 12um: "Sed potentia intellectiva, cum sit collativa, ex quibusdam in alia devenit; unde non se habet aequaliter ad omnia intelligibilia consideranda; sed statim quaedam videt, ut quae sunt per se nota, in quibus impliciter continentur quaedam alia quae intelligere non potest nisi per officium rationis ea quae in principiis impliciter continentur, explicando." (But the intellective power, since it brings together, proceeds from some things to other things, so that it is not equally disposed toward considering all things that are intelligible, but it immediately sees certain things as if they are known in themselves, in which are implicitly contained certain other things that [the human intellective power] could not understand except through the functioning of the reason, by explicating the things that are implicitly contained in the principles.)

37. See *I,* q. 58, a.3, ad 2um (once again, in a comparison with the

pure intelligences): "Angeli syllogizari possunt, tamquam syllogismum cognoscentes; et in causis effectus vident, et in effectibus causas: non tamen ita [that is, in the manner of human beings] quod cognitionem veritatis ignotae acquirant syllogizando ex causis in causata, et ex causatis in causas." (Angels can syllogize, as if they knew syllogisms, and they see the effects in the causes, and the causes in the effects: nevertheless, they do not do this as human beings do, who must acquire a knowledge of an unknown truth by syllogizing from causes to things caused, and from things caused back to causes.) See ibid., *I,* q. 108, a. 7, ad 2um: "Inveniuntur autem in nobis multae intelligibiles actiones, quae sunt ordinatae secundum ordinem causae et causati; sicut cum per multa media gradatim in unam conclusionem devenimus." (Many intelligible acts are to be found in us that are ordered according to the order of cause and that which is caused, just as when through many intermediate steps we gradually arrive at a single conclusion.) A deeper understanding of the causal relationship of this kind would require a treatment of causality itself, which cannot be undertaken here. For the moment the following can be emphasized: there is an "essential connection" (*Wesenszusammenhang*) between cause and effect. The effect is already contained in the cause, and in a certain way represents an explication of what is virtually in the cause; as long as it is not merely an accidental cause, there is always an inner, formal connection between cause and effect. Now understanding (*intelligere*) is not a *causa per accidens* (see *De Veritate,* q. 11, ad 12um); it does not simply leave the *ratio* to the creative freedom of discursiveness; for the *ratio* can explicate only what is already implicit or virtually contained in the *intelligere.* This is why the causality under discussion is not simply a *successio,* a "series," in which one act of knowing follows another. Thomas clearly distinguishes the *discursus secundum causalitatem* from the *discursus secundum successionem tantum*; the former designates the connection between principles and conclusions, which is precisely what makes it possible for an *intellectus perfectus* to grasp the conclusions in the principles without any discursive process (see *I,* q.14, a. 7).

38. See also *De Veritate,* q. 15, a. 1. In this context one should also keep in mind the doctrine about the "confused" way of knowing of the *cognitio communis,* which corresponds precisely to the cognitive structure of the *praecepta communia.* "It is manifest, however, that to know something in which very many things are contained without having a special knowledge [*propria notitia*] of each of the things which are contained in it, is to know something confusedly [*sub confusione quadam*]. In this way both the universal whole [*totum universale*] can be known, in which the parts are contained in potency, as well as the integral whole [*totum integrale*]: for both of these wholes can be known in a kind of confused way

[*in quadam confusione*], without the parts being distinctly recognized. But to know distinctly what is contained in the universal whole is to have a knowledge about something that is less general [*cognitionem de re minus communi*]." In this passage the process of explication is described as a movement from a *cognitio confusa* to a *cognitio distincta.*

39. See *I,* q. 60, a. 2: "For the intellect understands the principles naturally [*naturaliter*]: and as a result of this understanding [*ex hac cognitione*] the knowledge [*scientia*] of conclusions is brought about in man: conclusions that are not known by man naturally [*naturaliter*] but by discovery or teaching [*per inventionem vel doctrinam*]."

40. And in most cases revelation enters the picture as a mode of instruction, as in the passage already quoted from *Quaestiones quodlibetales,* VIII, q. 2, a. 2: "For there are in us by nature [*naturaliter*] certain complex first principles, known to all, and out of which reason proceeds to the actual knowing [*ad cognoscendum in actu*] of the conclusions that are potentially [*potentialiter*] contained in the said first principles, and this takes place either through one's own discovery [*per inventionem propriam*], or through being taught by another [*per doctrinam alienam*], or through divine revelation [*per revelationem divinam*]." This passage brings together all the elements characteristic of rational discourse that we have so far treated.

41. The fruitful consequences that result from this for the conception of knowledge *per doctrinam* and *per revelationem* cannot be gone into in detail in the present context. The benefits are many in regard to understanding the relationship between human reason and revelation, and thus between faith and the *magisterium.* The autonomy theses of Alfons Auer would need substantial revision in the light of Thomas's teaching on these matters.

42. *De Veritate* q. 11, a. 1: "And the same thing can be said about the acquisition of knowledge: that there pre-exist in us certain seeds of knowledge [*scientiarum semina*] or first conceptions of the intellect [*primae conceptiones intellectus*] that are immediately known by the light of the agent intellect, through species abstracted from sensed particulars, whether these be complex, such as axioms [*dignitates,* i.e., *propositiones per se notae,* such as form the basis of the process of practical reasoning in *I–II,* q. 94, a. 2, the first being the principle *bonum est prosequendum* . . .], or uncomplex, such as being [*ratio entis*] or one [*ratio unius*] and suchlike [in the practical realm this would be "the good," or *ratio boni*: "the good is what all things seek," see *I–II,* q. 94, a. 2], which the intellect immediately apprehends. From these universal principles all principles follow, as if from certain seminal reasons. When therefore the mind is led out [*educitur*] from these universal cognitions [*ex istis universalibus*

*cognitionibus*] so that it actually knows [*actu cognoscat*] particulars that it first knew in potency and, as it were, in a universal way [*quasi in universali*], then someone can be said to acquire knowledge."

43. Ibid.: "And thus someone is said to teach another, insofar as one presents [*exponit*] to another through signs this discursive movement of the reason [*discursum rationis*] that is naturally carried out in oneself [*quem in se facit ratione naturali*], and thus the natural reason of the student, making use of these as some kind of instruments, attains to the knowledge of unknown things. In the same way as the doctor is said to bring about health in the sick person through nature's operation, just so is man said to cause knowledge in another by the operation of the natural reason of that other, and this is teaching." Thomas retains the functional (personal) autonomy of the student in the process of learning. Without the autonomy of the *ratio naturalis* (an autonomy that is neither constitutive nor creative), the process of learning itself would not be possible; there would only be the phenomenon of a "conditioning"of thought, as a kind of "thinking process" or cognitional behavior, or (alternatively) a matter of making the student believe that things are as they have been explained. Neither accounts for what really happens in learning.

44. See *De Veritate*, q. 11, a. 1: "The light of this reason [*huiusmodi . . . rationis lumen*], by which principles of this kind are known to us [*principia huiusmodi . . . nobis nota*; this refers not only to the first principles but also to the particular *principia propria* disclosed through invention], has been established in us by God [*est nobis a Deo inditum*] as a certain likeness of the uncreated truth shining in us [*similitudo increatae veritatis in nobis resultantis*].

45. *I–II*, q. 95, a. 2: "Sed sciendum est quod a lege naturali dupliciter potest aliquid derivari: uno modo sicut conclusiones ex principiis; alio modo, sicut determinationes quaedam aliquorum communium."

46. *I–II*, q. 95, a. 3: "Utraque igitur inveniuntur in humana lege posita. Sed ea quae sunt primi modi, continentur lege humana non tamquam sint solum lege posita, sed habent etiam aliquid vigoris ex lege naturali. Sed ea quae sunt secundi modi, ea sola lege humana vigorem habent." In regard to the second mode, this means that the preceptive power rests solely upon human *positio*; from the point of view of content, the connection with the natural law is still present, since even *determinatio* is a "mode of derivation" (*modus derivationis*); indeed, human law otherwise would not be law, but rather a kind of coercion. If the power of its *content* to oblige [*inhaltliche Kraft*] did not originate from the natural law, it would stand in conflict with the natural law (see also ibid., q. 96, a. 4).

47. See ibid., q. 95, a. 4: "For those things that are derived from the

natural law as conclusions from principles pertain to the 'law of nations' [*ius gentium*], as just purchases and sales, and other things of this kind, without which human beings would not be able to live together [*ad invicem convivere*]; and this *belongs to the natural law* [*quod est de lege naturali*], because man is naturally a social animal, as shown in the first book of the *Politics*." In his reply to the first objection, then, Thomas emphasizes that the *ius gentium* and the *lex naturalis* are not coterminous. A comparison with *II–II*, q. 57, a. 3 shows why: the *ius gentium* extends only to a part of the whole area of natural law, and furthermore, it obtains its validity not from natural knowing but from the *consensus hominum*, since it is, after all, the law *of nations* (see *I–II*, q. 95, a. 4 ad 1um: "men easily agree on conclusions of this kind" [*de facili . . . consenserunt*]).

48. *II–II*, q. 57, a. 3: Thomas once again emphasizes that this "law of nations" (*ius gentium*), as a conclusion from the *lex naturalis*, is a work of the natural reason; see ibid., ad 3um: "The natural reason dictates the things that pertain to the law of nations, such as the right to obtain justice from one's neighbor [*puta, ex propinquo habentia aequitatem*]; this is why they do not require any special legislation, but rather are instituted by the natural reason itself." And yet it is ever enclosed within a historical context through the *hominum consensus*, or the culturally and historically varying insight into the natural law. The historical evolution of the "law of nations" does not result from an evolution of the natural law, but from an evolution of the *insight* into the natural law and from an evolution of its *application*.

49. It is to R. A. Armstrong's credit (*Primary and Secondary Precepts in Thomistic Natural Law Teaching*, pp. 95, 136) that he called attention again to the significance of *demonstratio* in this context.

50. For further details see ibid.; that only the highest and most universal principles of *synderesis* belong to the natural law was maintained early in the twentieth century by V. Cathrein, who was among those who held nature, and not reason, to be the standard of morality. This does not appear to me to be accidental: there is a connection between the limitation of the natural law to the highest and most universal principles, and misunderstanding the standard-giving and normative function of the practical reason as *ratio naturalis*. On the basis of this misunderstanding one can reach the view, as did Cathrein, that "nature" is this standard, or one can go further and maintain that the practical reason is "creatively" normative. Both errors have a common root.

51. On the semantic question of participation and attributive analogy, see C. Fabro, *Participation et causalité selon S. Thomas d'Aquin* (Louvain and Paris, 1961), pp. 509ff, 634ff.

52. This can be seen clearly at *I–II*, q. 91, a. 3, where Thomas ex-

plains the development of human law as follows: "And in this way it is necessary that the human reason proceed from the precepts of the natural law as if from certain more common and indemonstrable principles to the laying down of certain more particular dispositions [*ad aliqua magis particulariter disponenda*]." On the basis of this statement, Merks (*Theologische Grundlegung . . .*, p. 244) concluded that for Thomas the natural law is reduced to the most universal and indemonstrable principles, out of which human law autonomously determines all material content without the intermediary of any "material" (*inhaltlicher*) principles also belonging to the natural law. This misinterpretation consists in overlooking that Thomas argues here (as always) in a formal (or structural) manner: the principles of the natural law are, in relation to the human lawmaker, just like general, indemonstrable principles; they have, that is (to use Aristotelian epistemological terminology), an "underlying" (*hypothetical*) character. This means that they are *presupposed in* the process of human lawmaking—they do not "receive confirmation" in and through the process, but *presuppose it* as a foundation and starting-point.

53. See *I–II*, q. 94, a. 5: "to the natural law pertain *first of all* [*primo quidem*] certain most universal principles [*praecepta communissima*], which are known to all." Q. 100, a. 3: "the first and common principles [*communia*], which require no . . . publication [*editionem*] other than that they be written in the natural reason as if known in themselves"; *II–II*, q. 47, a. 15: "The first, universal [*universalia*] principles are naturally known [*naturaliter nota*]." *I*, q. 79, a. 12: "Wherefore the principles of things to be done [*operabilium*], naturally planted in us [*indita*], do not pertain to any special faculty, but to a special natural habit, which we call *synderesis*." *III*, q. 94, a. 1, ad 2: "Synderesis is called the law of our intellect, insofar as it is a habit containing the precepts of the natural law, which are the first principles of human deeds [*prima principia humanorum operum*]"; note how synderesis can even be called a *law* because of its practical nature. The connection with an epistemological metaphysics (*Erkenntnismetaphysik*) is especially clear in the *Commentary on the Sentences:* "It is fitting that all reasoning proceed from some knowing that has a certain uniformity and rest [*uniformitatem et quietem quandam*]; and this does not happen through a *discursus* of investigation, but is offered immediately to the intellect: for just as the reason in speculative matters . . . so must the practical reason be guided by some principles known in themselves [*principiis per se notis*], such as that evil is not to be done, that the commands of God are to be obeyed, and likewise with the rest; the *habitus* of these is synderesis . . . which is somehow inborn in our mind through the very light of the agent intellect."

54. *De Veritate*, q. 16, a. 1: "Wherefore, in human nature as well,

insofar as it touches the angelic nature, there ought to be a knowledge of the truth without inquiry [*cognitionem veritatis sine inquisitione*] both in speculative and in practical matters; this knowledge ought to be the beginning [*principium*] of all subsequent knowledge both speculative and practical, since principles ought to be more certain and more stable [*stabiliora et certiora*]. And therefore this knowledge [*cognitionem*] ought to be naturally present in man [*homini naturaliter inesse*], since he recognizes it as a certain 'nursery' or 'seedbed' [*quoddam seminarium*] of all subsequent knowledge; just so in all natures there preexist certain natural seeds of the operations and effects that follow upon the natures. And this should also be habitual, so that it be ready for use whenever necessary [*in promptu . . . ea uti*]."

55. Ibid.: "Now just as there is a certain natural *habitus* of the human soul by which it knows the principles of the speculative sciences—a *habitus* we call 'understanding of the principles' [*intellectus principiorum*]; . . . there is in souls a certain natural *habitus* of the first principles of things to be done [*operabilia*], and these are the natural principles of the natural law [*naturalia principia iuris naturalis*]." It can be seen here how the theme of the *synderesis* is practically reduced to that of the *intellectus principiorum*. Since for Thomas *synderesis* is still only the *habitus* of these principles, and no longer a peculiar faculty (as it had been treated before his time, in some some very long *quaestiones*), there is only mention of it in passing after the treatment in *I*, q. 79, a. 12. What is decisive for Thomas—in accordance with the Aristotelian theory of the sciences—is the derivative connection between first principles and conclusions. This is in preparation as early as the *Commentary on the Sentences* (*In III Sent.*, d. 33, q. 2, a. 4, sol. 4): "thus in the practical reason are inborn connatural ends for man [*sunt innati fines connaturales homini*]; in regard to them there is neither an acquired nor an infused *habitus,* but a natural one, such as the *synderesis,* in the place of which the Philosopher (at VI *Ethics*) posits an *intellectus* in things done [*in operativis*]." On this point I am in agreement with M. B. Crowe, *The Changing Profile of the Natural Law* (The Hague, 1977) pp. 136ff.

56. It is not necessary *in this context* to distinguish "natural right" (*ius naturale, Naturrecht*) from "natural law" (*lex naturalis, Naturgesetz*), since we are concerned here with the derivative connection, which is the same for both *ius* and *lex*.

57. Armstrong, *Primary and Secondary Precepts . . . ,* emphasized this point well. Unfortunately he did not pay adequate attention to the cognitive process of the *ratio naturalis*.

58. Thomas uses this expression for the conclusions (e.g. in *I–II*, q. 94, a. 4 and a. 5). For the origin of this concept in the Aristotelian theory of the sciences, see *In I Post. Anal.*, lect. 18.

59. Thomas also calls them *principia propinquiora*, the principles that "stay closer to" the first principles; see Armstrong, *Primary and Secondary Principles . . .*, pp. 92ff on the use of the term *propinquus*.

60. This connection between the *ratio naturalis* as general but insufficient *regula* and prudence is very clearly brought out in the *De Virtutibus in Communi*, q. 1, a. 6. The correct placement of prudence within the process of practical reasoning and its significance as the *regula proxima* of actions has been grossly neglected by traditional handbooks of Catholic moral theology. In the context of a modern moral theological tradition, which arranges the material of morality by the antitheses law/freedom/conscience, one finds instead of a teaching on prudence, a correspondingly larger treatment of conscience as the so-called "subjective norm" of action. Aside from the fact that conscience belongs to the level of reflection, the result of this has been the misleading, but today very dominant, antithesis of "objective/universal norms," on the one hand, and "subjective/concrete norms," on the other. Moral action is then conceived of as either the mere application of universal norms to concrete instances (even though these norms are inadequate for concrete application) or as the "adjustment" of general norms to the individual case, whereby one is brought into a situation ethics. In all of this it is overlooked that the judgment of prudence is dependent upon, and formed by, the intentional rectitude of the moral virtues, the cognitive content of which is shaped by the precepts of the natural law; and that this judgment of prudence is thus a rule for actions at once objective *and* concrete.

61. See *II–II*, q. 47, a. 6, ad 3um: "Sed synderesis movet prudentiam, sicut intellectus principiorum scientiam." (But synderesis moves prudence, just as the understanding of principles moves science.)

62. In this article (*II–II*, q. 47, a. 6), which treats the ends provided by prudence, the expression *principia naturaliter nota* is used (here, differently from natural law contexts) to indicate everything presupposed by prudence; what leads to a goal and is the object of prudence is designated as a *conclusio*. This is an example of Thomas's terminological flexibility and of his interest in formal connections; his vocabulary, with regard to analogy, shows a corresponding plasticity of function. The thesis of Arntz, that the ends of the virtues (which he calls *prima principia propria*) form an "intermediate level" between the primary and secondary principles, will be discussed below.

63. And also by way of prudence, in the ordering of prudence; see *II–II*, q. 47, a. 6, ad 3um: "*Synderesis* movet prudentiam, sicut intellectus principiorum [movet] scientiam." In this way it is left to prudence to show moral virtue the way to reach those ends (*quae eis viam parat*), the

ends that the moral virtues "possess beforehand" through the natural reason (*virtutes morales . . . tendunt in finem a ratione naturali praestitutum*).

64. The moral commandments of the Old Covenant and the Decalogue are treated in this context as components of the *lex divina*, that is to say, as commandments in the context of a law that leads man to his real, supernatural end. The interpretation of Pesch (*Das Gesetz*, p. 618), is that the natural law presupposes faith (!) and that its first commandment is the supernatural love of God; and further that Thomas recognizes no distinction between the natural and supernatural orders, even though he was "not conscious of having introduced a fundamentally new conception" (p. 624). Such an interpretation makes sense only by the logic of an ideologically motivated hermeneutics that bends or suppresses certain passages. This can be seen, for example, with regard to Pesch's claim that the First Commandment presupposes faith. *I–II*, q. 100, a. 3, ad. 1um: "These two precepts are the first and common precepts of the law of nature, which are self-evident to human reason either by nature or by faith [*vel per naturam vel per fidem*]." Here again there is reference to a double possibility of natural knowledge or of revelation. Or, at *II–II* , q. 122, a. 1: "The first three commandments concern acts of religion, which is the most important part of justice [*pars potissima iustitiae*]." The virtue of religion as part of justice (it is discussed in the treatise on justice) is a human/natural virtue and not a theological one (see *II–II*, q. 81, a. 5); for this reason it is also distinguished from *caritas* and does not presuppose faith. Pesch makes the mistake of inferring a theological and supernatural *structure* of the natural law from the *context*, where it is treated as a component of the Old Testament.

65. *I–II*, q. 100, a. 1: "Just as every judgment of the speculative reason proceeds from a natural knowledge of the first principles, so every judgment of the practical reason proceeds from certain naturally known first principles." Thomas maintains here as well, with regard to the relationship between "principles" and "conclusions," a functional parallelism between speculative and practical knowing. And yet one must recall the equally fundamental distinction between the theoretical and practical reason as analyzed in part I of the present work—a distinction that is explained by the embedding of the practical reason in the *appetitive* structure of the human *suppositum*.

66. In the context, Thomas is soon to mention the "things to be believed" (*credenda*), those principles of action that disclose themselves only to believers, and for which *instructio divina* is required. Thomas thus shows that what is naturally known can also be the object of such divine instruction (that is, can be a command of the *lex divina*), which is the case with the Decalogue, understood in its historical setting as the law on the two stone tablets given by God to Moses.

67. At *I–II*, q. 100, a. 3, Thomas explains that the first principles—"inscribed in the natural reason as if self-evident" (*scripta in ratione naturali quasi per se nota*)—are *contained* in the commands of the Decalogue, as principles contained in the "near" or proximate conclusions. ("For those principles that are first and universal [*prima et communia*] are contained in the commands just as principles are contained in proximate conclusions [*sicut principia in conclusionibus proximis*]."). The precepts, however, that are recognized by the wise ("which through careful study by wise persons [*per diligentem inquisitionem sapientium*] are found to agree with reason [*rationi convenire*]") are—in an "opposite manner" (*e converso*)—contained in the commands of the Decalogue "as conclusions in the principles (*sicut conclusiones in principiis*)." These latter are secondary principles of the second class. It can be seen here that Thomas considers proximate secondary principles to be commands of the Decalogue only in the strict sense; and yet, just as the proximate conclusions belong to the natural law insofar as they are conclusions from the first principles, it is possible to consider the more remote commands as also belonging to the Decalogue, insofar as they are conclusions that have been explicated out of the proximate ones.

68. See once more the *De Veritate*, q. 11, a. 1: "In the same way, someone teaching another leads him to the knowledge of unknowns, just as someone leads oneself by discovery [*sicuti aliquis inveniendo deducit seipsum*] to the knowledge of what is unknown . . . Accordingly, someone is said to instruct another by pointing out with signs the discursus of reasoning that the teacher already carried out within by natural reason. For just as the doctor is said to bring about health in the sick person by the operation of nature [*natura operante*], so the human being is said to cause knowledge in another by the working of the natural reason in that other [*operatione rationis naturalis illius*], and this is to teach." Thomas also relates this process by analogy to mere opinion, on the one hand, and to faith, on the other. It is always the light of the natural reason that makes possible an assent to a truth, on the basis either of one's own *inventio* or of another's instruction. See also *Quaestiones Quodlibetales*, VIII, q. 2, a. 2: Both in *inventio propria* and *doctrina* or *revelatio*, there is an actualization, through *principia naturaliter cognita*, of what is potentially contained in the first principles.

69. This should always be kept in mind (although it has not been) in regard to the question of the relationship between personal autonomy, conscience, freedom, and the magisterium of the Church. The last-mentioned appeals not only to the *lumen rationis naturalis* but also to the *lumen fidei*, the reason as illuminated and supported by faith. The magisterium is above all something that *teaches*, which means that it con-

veys *knowledge and insight.* If it fails to do this in the case of a believer, the problem is lack of faith—and in certain cases, also a lack of reason. The same could be said about conscience, since the authority of the magisterium rests primarily on the conscience, which is illuminated and "motivated" by faith. This point has been excellently treated in A. Laun, *Das Gewissen. Oberste Norm des sittlichen Handelns* (Innsbruck, 1984).

70. Thomas provides at this point a number of examples of such "remote" conclusions; to them belong, for instance, the prohibition of blasphemy: the commands not to hate anyone and not to injure one's neighbor; the prohibition of adultery, and of usury and fraud in business dealings; the command to make true judgments. One can certainly observe that, according to the cultural and moral condition of a given society, certain norms of behavior become moral "standards" to the extent that there is an awareness of their need to be justified, and when the difficulty of doing so is discovered, certain "obvious" matters—often through a moral decay of civilization—are lost sight of. By no means should one conclude that such "obvious" or "self-evident" matters are merely customary "ways of thinking" or "cognitive" habits. They are, rather, the expression of something at a moral (and *also* a cognitive) level, which implies a true and knowable but also *socially lived,* and thus *transmitted,* insight into the structure of moral behavior. We are often not conscious today of the high level of morality that the divine pedagogy has given to the history of the human race in the Mosaic Law, nor of the significance for today's civilization of its confirmation and fulfillment in the law of Christ. The fact that we need new and deeper justifications for moral standards may be, on the one hand, the necessary and positive sign of scientific progress; on the other hand, as a social phenomenon, this is the sign of a deep crisis: the destruction of a lived *ethos* and the *cognitive* as well as behavioral assumptions that go with it. It therefore seems to me foolish to reproach so-called "tradition" for being deficient in its justification of normal norms. It did not need such justifications, because what was *lived* had itself a justifying function.

71. Merks places the whole weight of his interpretation (an interpretation heavily dependent on Böckle) upon this article. He poses the question "What did Thomas intend in this article?" but never mentions the title, even though that should have provided an answer. Merks wants to show that here, as with the *lex naturalis* in general, there is nothing having to do with any content, but rather with a "statement about the structural unity of the *lex naturalis*—in relation to varying contents—and with respect to its rational justification" (*Theologische Grundlegung,* p. 281). This reduction of the natural law to "rationality" is a sign of its "detachment from all content" (p. 283).

72. *I–II,* q. 94, a. 2, ad 2um: "Omnes inclinationes quarumque partium humanae naturae, puta concupiscibilis et irascibilis, secundum quod regulantur ratione, pertinent ad legem naturalem et reducuntur ad unum primum praeceptum, ut dictum est. Et secundum hoc, sunt multa praecepta legis naturae in seipsis, quae tamen communicant in una radice. (All the inclinations of whatever parts of human nature, such as the concupiscible or irascible parts, insofar as they are regulated by reason, pertain to the natural law and are reducible to the one first precept, as has been said. Accordingly, there are many precepts of the natural law as such, although they share in one common root).

73. F. Böckle, "Naturliches Gesetz als göttliches Gesetz," in Böckle and E.-W. Böckenforde, eds., *Naturrecht in der Kritik* (Mainz, 1973), p. 181.

74. See *I–II,* q. 91, a. 3, ad 2um: "Ratio humana secundum se non est regula rerum: sed principia ei naturaliter indita, sunt quaedam regulae generales et mensurae omnium eorum quae sunt per hominem agenda, quorum ratio naturalis est regula et mensura, licet non sit mensura omnium eorum quae sunt a natura." (The human reason in itself is not a rule of things, but the principles naturally implanted in it are certain general rules and measures of all the things that are done by man; the natural reason is the rule and measure of these things, although it is not the measure of all things that are there by nature.) The word *res* here does not mean only "things" in the narrower sense, as noted earlier, but rather a reality that is independent of all human knowing and striving; a natural inclination can therefore be called a *res* in Thomas's terminology. See also *I–II,* q. 64, a. 3.

75. See part 1, ch. 5.5; and above all *De Veritate,* q. 10, a. 9: "Therefore the action of our intellect first moves toward [*primo tendit in*] that which is apprehended through phantasms, and then returns to understand its own act [*redit ad actum suum cognoscendum*]; and then progresses further [*ulterius*] toward species and habits and faculties and the essence of the mind itself." In the case of the moral virtues, whose foundation is the natural inclinations, the concluding judgment (*iudicium*) is attained on the basis of a natural cognition (*naturalis cognitio*), "the ends of which [the goals of the virtues] are dictated by the natural reason" (ibid.). Thomas emphasizes the unity of the suppositum that leads to the integration of the *apprehensio* of the natural inclinations into the good for man as a whole: "Nor are those two parts (namely, the intellect and the affection) to be thought of as being situated in two different places in the soul, like sight and hearing, which are the acts of organs; thus what is in the affection [*in affectu*] is also present to the understanding soul [*animae intelligenti*]. Wherefore the soul does not only return through the

intellect only to an understanding of the act of the intellect, but also to understanding the act of the affection [*affectus*] just as through the affection it returns to an appetition and loving (*ad appetendum et diligendum*) not only of the act of the affection, but also of the act of the intellect" (ibid., ad 3um in contr.).

76. See *II–II*, q. 47, a. 15. He first speaks of the *universalis cognitio* of the *prima principia universalia*, which are "naturally known" (*naturaliter nota*). These are also the general principles of prudence. "But other, posterior universal principles [*principia universalia posteriora*], whether they be of the speculative or the practical reason, are not possessed by nature [*per naturam*], but through discovery [*per inventionem*] according to the path of experience [*secundum viam experimenti*] or through teaching."

# 7

# The Normative Function of Reason and Its Fulfillment in Moral Virtue

## Reason: The Rule of Morality

In the course of the foregoing study it has been emphasized more than once that the Thomistic doctrine of reason's normative function does not imply that the reason is merely the normative "instance" of morality, as though it were an "organ," or a "subjective" norm that "applies" measures; on the contrary, the reason (ultimately, the *intellectus* in its rationally discursive explication) is *itself* the rule, standard, or norm of morality.

The purpose of this chapter is to draw out the meaning and consequences of this doctrine in its fundamental aspects. We have here to do, it seems to me, with the very axis around which Thomistic philosophical ethics revolves, as a *normative* ethics. With this question we are located on the boundary between ethics and metaethics, because we are trying to determine just what Thomas means when he speaks of "rationality," or, to be more precise, what he means by such expressions as *secundum rationem agere, vivere secundum rationem, ordo rationis, bonum rationis, proportio ad rationem*, and so on.

### *Traditional and Tradition-Critical Misunderstandings*

Now this very group of questions has been neglected both by the autonomous school and by the so-called "teleologistic" school. These forms of justification of moral norms are in many respects based on the same foundation as the representatives of the so-called "traditional" teaching, since these latter were often insufficiently aware of the meaning of the practical reason as "ethical reason" or as "evaluative reason."

It may be astonishing to learn that the critique of traditional models of justification launched by the teleologistic (or "consequentialist") school actually assumes the same naturalistic foundation as those models, in order to work out new varieties of argumentation;[1] in any event, this was not done primarily in the interest of overcoming shortcomings in the older justifications, but rather for the purpose of bringing in new contents, and above all in relation to the question of an intrinsic morality of actions (i.e., the so-called *intrinsece malum* or *malitia ex obiecto* independent of circumstances or consequences) and the question of indirect willing. It cannot be denied that this critique, which in some points can be considered justified and beneficial, has in many cases presented the "traditional" doctrine in too undifferentiated a way, providing a caricature more than an objective analysis.

In many cases, traditional arguments are represented as *normative* justifications that were never really meant as discursively justifying arguments, such as the formulations of moral systems in "probabilistic" or "probabilioristic" form, which do not arise from a context of norm justification. These were, rather, elaborated to provide bases for practical decision-making, criteria for pastoral praxis, in order to judge whether a concrete behavior fell under one norm or another, or to determine how much ambiguity must be eliminated for the "subsumption" of morally responsible behavior under such and such a norm.[2] Another example of the criticism of argumentation for being rationally discursive, even though the arguments in question were never intended as such, is the disparagement of theological recourse to the "will of God" as an unreliable and insufficient justification.[3] In this context as well, it cannot be said that the "tradition" *in general* made use of this recourse as a substitute for the discursive justification of norms, even if a few authors can be found who did so.

This makes quite doubtful B. Schüller's contention (it is essential to his whole argument) that "classical moral theology" or the "tradition" *ignored* the basic question of normative ethics (the discursive–philosophical question about the difference between "good" and "evil") and *replaced* it with mere "exhortation" (*parainesis*).[4] Such criticism is not only the result of an inadequate methodology; one also gets the impression that the moral theologians who are critical of tradition are themselves only transmitting an abridged, "handbook" version of that tradition.[5] Moral theological handbooks are not the source of moral theology: they cannot reproduce the entire range and greatness or developmental potential of the scientific labors of a certain era or tradition; it is expected that they will be continually improved upon and replaced, primarily to provide compendia for the continuing education of pastors, for whom the unsolved or disputed problems are usually left "in brackets." Furthermore, the discursive justification of the normative foundation of ethics does not really belong to the discipline of "moral theology" as such, but rather to "philosophical ethics," whose results moral theology must presuppose and make integral to itself. It is true that the evidence for such presupposition and integration is not always as explicit as one would like, and that not all moral theologians have had the same philosophical training or possess the same degree of awareness of problems. This has also led to the presentation as self-evident of normative statements that really appear so only to the reasoning of a person with faith. In the forum of the philosophically reflective reason, such statements are not at all self-evident: they need discursive justification.

It would not be fair, then, to point to this kind of inadequacy in the area of discursive justification, often met with in the manuals, and infer the complete *absence* of such justifications in the moral theology of the past. Nor is it correct to ascribe the philosophical shortcomings or the mistaken attempts at such justification on the part of individual authors to the works of an entire epoch or to "tradition" as a whole. Mistaken or provisional hypotheses occur in every field of knowledge, and can create the conditions for progress by encouraging a deeper investigation of certain difficulties. There are many flaws and gaps in our classical moral theological handbooks; as someone said, they are like baroque churches whose originally strong and graceful lines have gradually been obscured, with the passing of centuries, by all sorts of added decoration.

In a certain respect, Bruno Schüller is quite right: in the course of recent centuries, a highly praxis-oriented moral theology has encouraged a neglect of philosophical reflection on the justification of norms while, unhappily, becoming subject to certain heterogeneous influences. Examples that come to mind in this connection are nominalism, with its tendency to a legalistic treatment of morality, the rationalistic *ius naturale* school of the early modern period, and an exaggerated casuistry that tended to bury the basic normative inquiries.[6] In the very widespread traditional compendia of moral theology, one meets again and again the startling phenomenon of normative justifications of a low quality, far below the level that would be expected, given the real philosophical bases of this moral theology. Clearly, the interest in such justifications—and even the need for having them at all—was relatively limited in view of the pastoral context for which they were designed.

But circumstances have profoundly changed in the meanwhile: amid the conditions created by the progress of science and technology, and by the new moral problems of a pluralistic civilization with mass communication, it is no longer only a problem for academic investigation; it is also a pastoral responsibility to lay bare the normative foundations of ethics and morality. This task is necessary because the things that are morally self-evident—the "lived contexts" and all the "proofs" that go with these contexts—are disappearing, so that conflict reaches increasingly into the field of the fundamental normative justification of any given moral claim. Moral theology cannot be spared this necessary task; it needs a philosphical basis for its specifically theological statements if it wants to keep those statements from being dissolved into uncertain discourse that cannot go beyond philosophy.

The controversy over contraception showed that Catholic moral theology was not adequately prepared for such a task. The incapacity to create arguments drove many of the most gifted moral theologians to the hasty conclusion that the huge chasm between the moral claims made by the Church and the available possibilities of norm justification made it necessary to give up on the claims. This phenomenon amounted to a capitulation that was all the more regrettable because certain mistaken notions—such as the naturalistic interpretation of the concept of the object of action (or *finis operis*)—were used as the foundation for a new normative ethics. But the task of contemporary philosophical ethics, in my view, is to work out the neglected normative foundations of moral theology from its sources. That a few normative justifications have proved inadequate, or that some others have not yet been elaborated, should not compel the conclusion that the (admittedly high) claims of Christian morality ought suddenly to be changed.

This is particularly true for the doctrine of the measuring function of the reason, which is crucial for the normative foundation of ethics. Unfortunately, this function has now, more than ever before, been obscured and forgotten by the contemporary critique of the "tradition." It is the normative function of the reason that does not merely consist in what is known in the English-speaking world as "reasonableness," or an "acting for the sake of reasons," a rationally grounded action.[7] The human reason, relying on an intellect, is not only an anthropological constant but also an action, in the preceptive judgment of the practical reason, and as such is the foundational norm of morality; it is that which constitutes the difference between good and evil, not in a "creative" manner but rather as a participative, cognitive completion of the "ordering" (*ordinatio*) of the natural law.

We will now attempt an exposition, in general terms, of the measuring (or standard-giving [*maßstäbliche*]) function of the reason, without going into a detailed historical analysis. It will also be possible to draw a few consequences for some basic problems of normative ethics and the justification of moral norms. I would like to limit myself to those aspects of the issue that are so fundamental that their practical significance may not be immediately evident. This would be expected only from a normative ethics meant to justify concrete actions and provide answers to current problems. Moreover, the doctrine of the measuring function of the reason as it is found in Thomas implies an image of the human being, and of the worth and meaning of human existence, that may be considered by some to be irrelevant to contemporary practice. And yet the image does possess relevance, and it does so by viewing human life in a context of meaning that has been lost in many ethical studies of the present day. Here again the remark of Aristotle is pertinent: "If a general sketch of a subject is first presented, then each person can work on it further and articulate it with details."[8]

## *The Telos Character of the Reason*

Let us begin by recalling the basic anthropological significance of the reason as the inventive explication of the intellect. We grasped this significance through reflection upon the act and experience of the practical reason, and then by the integration of this reflection into an anthropological and metaphysical interpretation (the latter aspect implying both a metaphysics of actions and a metaphysics of creation). While this required emphasizing the original independence of practical experience from metaphysics, it was also acknowledged that such experience can in the end be fully illuminated only by metaphysical and anthropological analysis.

In the human soul, and more specifically in the intellect as "natural light" (its participation as a being in the intelligibility of the divine being), there are to be found, on the basis of this participative structure and the participation of the divine *intellectualitas* as such, not only the traces (*vestigia*) of the Creator but also His very image (*imago*). The intellect as such already says something fundamental about the human being, because this intellect (or, to be more precise, this intellective soul) is at the same time the form of a body, so that it establishes through its very spirituality—its *imago* character—an order of rank or "hierarchy" within the anthropological structure of the human *suppositum*. By its nature, the intellect is oriented toward the knowing of truth, and that means it is oriented toward God, in Whom all truth is grounded. We have already observed how much Thomas sees man's fundamental God-relatedness, his orientation toward God, as lying in the *imago* character. In anthropological terms, this character is grounded in the *intellectualitas* of the human soul, for in it can be found, as has been shown, a formal participation (i.e., not merely a likeness or a trace) of the divine fullness of being in its intelligibility.

The human intellect—and along with it, the reason as explication of the intellect—in its fundamental relatedness or orientation toward truth is not just an organ of knowing. Its essential act (the grasp and vision of the truth) already has in itself the character of a *telos* for the actions and emotions of the human person. It constitutes as well the final orientation of humanity *as* community, and the *bonum commune* that corresponds to this.

We are not concerned here with theological statements or even with a specifically Christian moral theology. The recognition of this *telos* character of the reason is a philosophical recognition; in particular, it is the inheritance of Plato, and lies at the basis of

Aristotelian ethics. It was received by Thomas and integrated into the Neoplatonic metaphysics of light; in its fullness, the teaching can become the foundation for the Christian theology of participation in divine holiness that can exalt human nature itself.[9]

Aristotle defines happiness as the ultimate good of man; this must lie in virtue and must consist in activity, perfected in accordance with the most perfect "part" of man's soul (*Nichomachean Ethics* I, 5–6). This activity is the intellective vision of the highest truth. Virtue is accordingly a life according to reason, that is, a life in which all the powers and emotions of a human being are deployed to such an extent and in such a manner that the "work" of the intellect—the vision of truth—is not only not hindered, but also promoted.

While Plato with his dualistic anthropology spoke of the "death of the philosopher" as the desired liberation of the soul from the fetters of the senses that obstructed the vision of truth,[10] Aristotle, by contrast, saw the fundamental moral task of the human being as the creation of a rational ordering in the powers and faculties of the soul that were not rational in themselves.[11] This rationally "normativized" order in the soul is a *hexis* (*habitus*), or moral virtue. And Thomas makes this doctrine his own: "The good of man, insofar as he is human, consists in the reason attaining to a complete knowledge of the truth, and the subordinate appetites being ordered [*ut . . . regulentur*] in accordance with the rule [*regulam*] of reason" (*De Virtutibus in Communi*, a. 9). Thomas then goes on to ground this truth in an anthropology: what is specific for man is *rationalitas* (see ibid: *nam homo habet hoc quod sit homo per hoc quod sit rationalis*); the rationally endowed soul is the form of the human being. The doctrine of the measuring, standard-making function of the reason thus widens out to an anthropological thesis by which Thomas takes over the Aristotelian doctrine of the hierarchy of the parts of the soul[12] and the natural orientation of the nonrational powers toward the reason (see *I*, q. 81, a. 3; *I–II*, q. 56, a. 4).

### *"Telos" and "Imago," or the Requirements of Being Human*

We see, then, that the concept of "morality" must be reduced to the more fundamental concept of the "good of the human being insofar as one is human" (*bonum hominis in quantum est homo*): this arises from the question, In what does the good of man consist? The good is that toward which all things strive, and we call the fulfillment of this striving "happiness." That we all strive toward this good in our action and willing—and the very "nature of the good" (*ratio boni*) that is formulated in reflection has this striving as its foundation—provides the real starting point for our practical experience and for ethics. And because the "good" is always an "apparent good" (since everything that we strive for, we strive for because it appears good to us), it is now time to develop the distinction between what *only seems* good, and what *both seems and is* truly good. To put it another way: Under what conditions does the truly good also *appear* good, or (conversely) under what conditions is the apparent good the *true* good?

The concept of the moral, and of the moral norm, is thus reducible, for its fundamental constitution, to the concept of the good that comes to light in the elementary practical experience of striving. Or to be more concrete: it is reducible to the concept of the *bonum hominis in quantum est homo*, to the specifically human good, and to the good *for* the human being. We cannot take the question "back" any further: when establishing a science, it is not possible to go behind the elementary givens of experience or to try to justify these givens. The very point of departure for ethics as the analysis of "the truly good striving" (or "morality") is the *fact* that we all strive for the good, and more particularly for the truly good, or happiness.[13] Whoever quarrels with this, quarrels with the evidence.

The reason, then, is both *telos* (end or goal) and *regula* (rule); that is to say, it is rule and norm precisely because of the fact that it is a *telos*. The goal is what gives the measure, and *is* the measure; and through the explication of the practical reason it is applied to human action, whether in the form of *external* operations or in the form of *internal* actions of the sensitive appetites and of the will.

By showing the *telos* character of the reason, we do not simply establish an ethics that envisions knowledge of the truth as the "single goal" or "exclusive moral content" of human life. The anthropological and ethical content of the doctrine is far deeper and much more comprehensive. The human being is fundamentally a *striving* being: in the will, man possesses a natural inclination toward a good that fulfills and satisfies this striving. In the body, the human person is filled with inclinations that seek their own fulfillment and affect the soul as "emotions." Man is fundamentally a being who possesses a certain "momentum of the soul" (*pondus animae*) toward the good in all its varieties; in the intellective and sensitive inclinations, the human being has a "natural love" (*amor naturalis*) that belongs to every creature according to its kind. In the strictest sense, man is an existent that is meant for *loving*. This is a special form of love that has been created *ad imaginem Dei*; it is spiritual in nature, molded by what participation in the divine intellect requires; and it is by these requirements that the *imago* is constituted.

The demonstration of the *telos* character of the reason does not simply mean that "morality" consists in knowledge of the truth; it means, rather, that it consists in satisfying the requirements of the *imago* in one's human striving and loving: to strive on the basis of one's spirituality and in accordance with it.[14]

As the metaphor of light expresses, the intellect has a natural relatedness to truth and to reality (and that means, finally, to God as to the ground of all truth and intelligibility); this is what makes it possible for man to meet the demands of being human (the divine likeness itself) in his striving.

The natural reason, in which that formal participation of the eternal law is realized, makes possible this self-realization of one's humanity. In his actions and willing—loving—man must bring the light of reason into the open, for this alone is what illuminates the demands made upon him: the goal striven after (the knowledge and love of God) as well as the right order in his soul, or in the powers both of his soul and of bodiliness and soul. And it is only this light of the reason that can suitably order one person toward another as a "thou" constituted in the same dignity and vocation; and this is an ordering that lies at the basis of all justice and love of neighbor.[15]

Pointing out the *telos* character of the reason—or of the *imago*—also serves to clarify how the fundamental demands of morality (that is to say, of a further *bonitas* of the human being that goes beyond nature and perfects it) consist in ordering all the striving powers in man—the will, the senses—in such a way that they follow the good that is accessible to man only through the cognitive power of the natural reason. For it is only thus that man (who, unlike the nonrational creatures, is not guided by instinct) can meet the demands of personal autonomy. This is to be guided by one's own *providentia* to the goal; this is what moral behavior consists in, and it explains why the practical judgments of the natural reason are identified with the *lex naturalis*.

This ordering of the reason (*ordo rationis*) is always fundamental and primarily implies an *orientative* ordering of the will and the sensitive powers *toward* the reason, so that the latter can exercise their "mastery," or practically imperative, preceptive function, which leads toward the good. This ordering must be realized by the individual human person within his or her own striving powers, and that is the work of the moral virtues, which Aristotle once referred to as the "tool of the understanding" (*organon tou nou*; *Eudemian Ethics,* VIII, 2 (1248a40).

### *The Constitution of the "Morally Good" by the Reason*

At the basis of Thomistic anthropology and ethics lies a conviction that originates in the profoundest discoveries of Greek philosophy: in his intellective power, man possesses an unerring light that is naturally ordered toward, and open to, truth; this light, if it is not hindered in its proper action by the will or the disorder of sensitive appetites, infallibly reveals the good to man.

On the one hand, it is the will that above all can hinder the natural knowing process of the human intellect in its explication or practical effectiveness; this is because the will possesses a "command" (*imperium*): "I know, because I want to" (*intelligo enim, quia volo. De Malo*, q. 6, a. 1). This is a command over itself as well as over the reason: the will itself cannot will the willing of a good that is known by the reason. Because by nature the will is oriented only toward its own good, it needs habitual perfecting in order to become oriented toward the good that is God (*bonum divinum*) or the good of one's neighbor (*bonum proximi*), and this is the virtue of justice (see *I–II*, q. 56, a. 6). Now there is a justice of *equality* among human beings because of a fundamental sameness, just as there is a justice of *inequality* between God and man because of a fundamental difference. The virtue of *religio* is what brings to God the thankfulness, worship, and love that He justly receives as Creator, and that man can provide because of his position as creature.[16] If this habitual perfecting of the will is absent, man will follow the requirements of justice that his reason recognizes in a manner *contrary* to the natural willing of, and preference for, his own good. Sooner or later, he will acquire a habitual disorder in the will: *malitia*, malice of the will, or the vice of injustice.[17]

Expressions of injustice, or factors that induce one to injustice are, for example, avarice, envy, jealousy, pride, and arrogance, all of which, in one way or another, permit the good of another, which ought to be known as such by the reason and to be loved, to be experienced instead as *one's own evil*, and to this extent confuse and disturb the judgment of the reason. By this disordering of the human will, the light of the reason can be obscured and lose much of its ability, not without the person's own fault.

On the other hand, with certain other effects (less subtle, perhaps, because more obvious) the reason can be distorted and hindered in performing the act of knowledge through disordered sensuality or passions. This is so because the reason can never know something without the help of the sensitive powers, and these can influence the reason through disordered inclinations. Moral virtue consists not in supressing or shutting off the sensitive drives, but rather in *ordering* them in such a way that they do not impede but rather support the reason, that they in fact lead man to the good *qua* sensitive drives. In this perfection the perfection of virtue is first, according to the words of Psalm 84:2. "My heart and my flesh give praise to the Living God," where the "heart" can be understood as the will, and the "flesh" as the passions and/or senses.[18]

Acts involving the will and the sensitive appetites, insofar as they are human acts, are always subject to the command of the will. The criterion for the moral good with respect to such acts, then, is that these acts correspond to the reason, which means that they must not hinder or disturb the reason but support it, and follow what the reason presents to them as good.[19] The principle "living according to reason" (*secundum rationem vivere*) implies a whole anthropology, epistemology, and metaphysics, and cannot be understood without that background.

This is an anthropology that not only views man in his incomparable dignity as an intellective being created *ad imaginem Dei*, but also understands the consequences of that view. The personal autonomy of man is bound up with freedom, and stands or falls as freedom stands or falls. For only in freedom can reason fully exercise its function as an intellective light, and make good its claims in all the actions and emotions of the human person. Through this light of the reason—a formal participation in the eternal law—man is able, in all his actions and strivings, and ultimately in all the forms of love that he realizes, to correspond to the truth of his own personal being, and thereby to find realization *as* a human being and *in* his humanity.

### *The Measuring Function of the Reason: Three Aspects*

Once the true nature of the human intellect is recognized, as well as its place within the whole complex of the human suppositum, it can be seen how the reason, in a fundamental way, is the *measure* of moral good. On the basis of the foregoing, it can be said to do this in three ways. First, as *telos*, as end or goal (*finis*) of human life in general, which consists in the knowledge and love of truth (or really of God, who is the Truth *per essentiam*); this knowing and loving is possible only through man's intellective powers, the intellect and the will. The intellect is the "light" of the will, and the will can only strive after that which has been presented to it by the intellect. Second (and this depends on the first), the intellect or reason is a measure because the free, unhindered, and undistorted accomplishment of its action provides the criterion for ordering the other powers of the soul: it is in this ordering, by which the sensitive powers become in a way "stamped" with the "seal" of reason, that moral virtue consists.[20] Within the complex unity of the *suppositum,* then, the reason is a *telos*: it is the *telos* of the nonrational appetitive (or "striving") powers, which are able to participate in rationality through moral virtue. Third, because of its *telos* character, the reason is a measure because it is embedded in the rationally ordered appetitive powers, and is supported by them, or at least not hindered by them, in making its practical judgments—in formulating its preceptive dictates (*dictamina*)—

and these are what belong to the truth of human existence as practical truth, and order it to its end.[21]

J. de Finance has effectively conceptualized this constitutive and measure-giving function of the reason as follows: the reason does not have a merely *declarative* task; it is not limited to presenting the will with a ready-made moral order. Instead, the reason is itself a prerequisite for the constitution of the moral order; the order created by the reason is not simply the "execution" of an objective order of being but is itself thoroughly formed and fashioned through a constitutive relationship to reason itself.[22] This is the expression of an autonomy that we have called *personal autonomy*. This *constitutive* meaning of the reason, with all its ethical and anthropological breadth and normative effect, is completely lost sight of in autonomous and teleological ethics, where it is reduced to mere "reasonableness."

As already shown in part I, the practical reason presents neither a pregiven, necessary order of being nor an act of reflection upon a speculative judgment as follows: "What I have (theoretically) observed, will now be carried out." What is recognized by the practical reason in a preceptive judgment—and I emphasize that it has been *preceptively* recognized, or "prescribed" in the sense of a constituted order of reason—has itself been formed by this practical reason and has no moral consistency apart from its relation to the reason (ibid., p. 244), but would remain in its merely physical species (*genus naturae*). The same can be said about the comprehension of the acts and ends of the natural inclinations through the *ratio naturalis*: in this "grasp" (or *apprehensio*), the relation to the reason is what has already constituted them to be taken as *bona humana*. This constitution of the practical (moral) object, or of the object of the practical reason, is itself something "objective,"[23] which means that it constitutively depends upon the nature of the human reason, or on the *inclinatio ad bonum secundum naturam rationis* (*I–II*, q. 94, a. 2). That should never be forgotten when someone speaks about the "object" of an action, or what is generally referred to as the *finis operis*.

De Finance goes on to explain why human reason has this power and authority: because our autonomy is a participation of the divine reason, it is a *participated* autonomy. Consequently, it is not because the reason is human reason that what corresponds to the reason is morally good; rather, it is because man is rational—as bearing within himself a participation of the divine reason—that conformity with the reason is also a human good, and that such conformity defines the human good as such. The human good, in other words, is not merely any particular good that the reason manages to obtain through some kind of argumentative process (for example, "the proportionate assessment of values" or the "weighing of goods" [*Güterabwägung*] ); rather, the human good is the "good of the reason" (*bonum rationis*), the good that lies in the reason, corresponding to its nature and purpose, and naturally known by it (ibid., p. 246).

At this point some remarks can be made by way of anticipation. At the basis of the Thomistic "ethics of virtue" there are a "weighing of goods" and a "teleology"—beyond all other practical judgments—that constitute the very concept of the morally good and that ground an unassailable human dignity. The human good lies in the *bonum rationis*, in a life according to reason, and thus in the realization of a *personal* autonomy. No "consequences" of a person's actions can have any weight against the consequence of losing his human worth. "Teleologist" (or "proportionalist") ethicists consider Thomistic ethics "deontological"—that it insists, in other words, that there are actions that are always wrong, *regardless of their consequences*. But this is not true. On Thomistic principles one thing at least is certain: that one consequence—namely, the loss of the dignity that is proper to man and that corresponds to the *imago Dei*—would remove *any further* weighing of consequences, and thus stands revealed as the unassailable ground condition for the morality of actions. An action is "intrinsically evil" (*intrinsece mala*) precisely, then, when it has the *consequence* that the human being loses his or her undeniable and fundamental dignity by doing it. "Deontology" as defined by teleologists simply does not exist; their view (that deontology requires that some actions be qualified without any regard for their consequences) could be maintained only under certain conditions: that "consequence" is very narrowly (and unjustifiably) restricted, that vague terms like "goods" or "values" are used, and that man in his anthropological constitution utterly disappears from the field of ethical analysis.

*The "Autonomy" and "Theonomy" of Reason*

The reason, then, itself possesses an "axiological consistency" by being a participation of the divine intellect (ibid., p. 247). The whole strength of the human reason lies in the fact that it is not an "autonomous" norm or measure, but rather receives its regulating power "from outside," even though it bears this normativity *in itself*, as a participated and received normativity. It is thus a "normed norm" (*norma normata*), a derived (or participated) reason. The personal autonomy of man consists in the fact that man is a creature, that in a constitutive sense he is really *not* autonomous, because the law that grounds his personal autonomy is the eternal law itself, as participated.

And this participation, to state it again, is an existential participation in the divine light of knowing, or the eternal law. It has to do with a "reason in being" (*raison dans l'Etre*), which is capable as such of formulating the requirements of human existence, because it is itself an existential and, indeed, normative component of human existence; as Aristotle would say, it is the *dominant* part of the human *suppositum,* and thus belongs above all to that "nature," which defines what is "according to nature" for man.

The human reason, then, as a natural light of knowing, is "admitted" into the divine reason, and is molded in its intentionality by the intentionality of the divine reason, or eternal law. It has its autonomy precisely *in this way*, and not as "freed" or "independent" *from* the jurisdiction of the divine reason. When it is unhindered in its operation as reason, it expresses the deepest claims of human existence, participating effectively and formally in the nomothetic function of the divine reason: "Our autonomy is the expression in us of an *ontonomy*, known to metaphysical reflection as *theonomy*" (ibid., p. 251). And thus it is quite proper to say, without fear of committing an anthropomorphism, that "God gives us His law, not as an external lawgiver, whose measures presuppose a constituted structure of obligation in order to bind us; he gives us his law by giving us reason."[24] The human reason is therefore a "*médiation de la théonomie*" (ibid.), the *communication of theonomy;* this also clarifies why theonomy as such should not be considered merely the "grounding" for human autonomy—human autonomy, rather, *is* theonomy, and in theonomy finds its fulfillment. Other forms of the communication of theonomy, such as revelation, or teaching by the magisterium of the Church, are thus not *restrictions* on human autonomy, but rather its *empowering* and fulfillment.

If we are saying, then, that reason is the standard of morality, we are faced with a dictum full of metaphysical and anthropological implications. If the doctrine of the measuring function of the reason is detached from its metaphysical and anthropological foundation, it becomes unintelligible and a merely formal structural statement, an "empty formula" (*Leerformel*) for normative ethics.[25] The doctrine of the measuring function of the reason rests upon a metaphysics and anthropology that in any event represent the reflective, after-the-fact interpretation of the original experience of practical reason. As a metaphysical and anthropological integration of ethics, therefore, the doctrine shows the reason's normative character from the outset.[26]

### *The Need for an Operative Concretizing of the Practical Reason*

The doctrine of the normative, measuring function of the reason has not yet been completely expounded. Much the opposite: for what is really at issue is its capability of extending all the way to concrete actions. That is to say, we are now asking how the universally grasped good at the level of the precepts of the *lex naturalis* is communicated to the good *hic et nunc*, and in all the contingency of particular actions.

This is the task of the *recta ratio agibilium* (right reason of things-to-be-done), or prudence, the truth of which is a practical truth. This right reason is constituted as the agreement of what is willed in action (or of the final practical judgment that stamps this elective willing) with the rectitude of the willed end. The rectitude of the willed end is a work of the *lex naturalis*; action itself is never unambiguously determined by this end, since the matter of actions is contingent. Various possibilities of action—although not just *any* possiblities whatever—are capable of the same rectitude of end.

Now the measuring function of the reason comes to its fulfillment, and becomes immediately relevant and effective right here, where the universal practical judgment of the reason is communicated to the level of those judgments that trigger concrete actions; where, that is to say, there is a concretization of what is recognized *in universali* as good (or bad). We can point this out only in general terms, since an exposition of the doctrine of prudence would transgress the limits of this study, which is concerned with the concept of the natural law, or the universal law of the practical reason. A few questions will be treated later (in chapter 9, section "The Hidden Deontologism of Teleological Ethics"), concerning concretization through the so-called "means" (*ea quae sunt ad finem*). This will have to do with the problem of whether the validity of universal precepts of the natural law are in any way restricted by the contingency of actions, or whether the natural law retains its unrestricted validity in all cases, even under the conditions of "merely" practical truth. This is important for the question of whether, on the basis of the natural law, there are ways of acting that can be objectively—universally, and in all circumstances—characterized as morally good or bad in themselves.

### *"Obscuring" or "Distortion" of the Natural Law*

The placing of the doctrine of the natural law within the terms of the more general definition of moral action as "action done according to reason" brings clarity to the question of what Thomas means when he speaks of a "distortion" or an "obscuring" of the natural law.

In general, it can be said that the *lex naturalis* comes to have significance in the human being (and is able to develop all its preceptive, action-guiding power) to the extent to which virtues are developed—that is, to the extent that striving (or appetition) is ordered according to reason. In the case of the virtuous person, the sensitive appetites and the will participate in the order of reason (the *ordinatio rationis*) and support it, allowing the natural reason to develop its full practical–cognitive effectiveness. Conversely, vice is the habitual dis-ordering and misdirection of the appetites, causing the *lex naturalis* to become "obscured" in man.

Thomas's famous treatment of this question is in the *Prima Secundae*, question 94, article 6: the first and most universal *principia communia* in their universal validity can never be deleted from the "heart" of man, even though it is quite possible for their application to be hindered in the concrete instance through appetitive influences or a passion. The secondary principles, discovered by *inventio*, can actually be deleted from the heart, or at least their cognitive presence can be so deleted, and this can take place through false but purely intellectual convictions (cognitive fallacies), such as can occur in speculative knowledge or through bad morals, customs, or vices (*I–II*, q. 94, a. 6).

This shows that the "clouding" or "distortion" of the *lex naturalis* in man is the same thing that happens in the habitual distortion of the *ordo rationis* through vice. Both themes concern the same subject matter from a different angle; it shows once more how the topics of natural law, moral virtue, and right reason (*recta ratio*) compose a single subject matter for Thomas.

In various cultural contexts, the natural law will be effective to varying degrees. The social environment, historically evolved customs, morals, and usage all exercise an influence. To understand the natural law is to understand the phenomenon of its partial obscuring in whole cultures. The partial discrepancy of moral norms among various cultures is no argument against the existence and unity of the natural law; it is an argument for the existence of human freedom as well as its dangers. It also explains the possible and actual progress—or decadence—of the moral conscience of entire cultures.[27]

### *Philosophical Ethics and Anthropology and the Problem of "Fallen Nature" and the* Fomes Peccati

At the present juncture brief mention can be made of the concept of original sin, or the "kindling matter of sin" (*fomes peccati*). For Thomas, this law of sensuality, which belongs to humanity as a punishment for the first sin, is a consequence of the loss of the originally perfect condition. This condition was a natural one, insofar as it did not concern *gratia elevans*, but the more-than-natural condition of *integritas*; as Thomas explains, this integrity was nothing other than the gratuitously bestowed possession of virtue, the subordination of the reason to God (justice), which brought with it the subordination of the will, as well as the sensitive appetites to the reason.[28] This condition of "sound nature" (*natura integra*), of the complete possession of moral virtue, is also the condition in which the *lex naturalis* as the law of the practical reason possessed its full effectiveness and undistorted rule.

The loss of integrity destroyed this perfection, not through the disruption of nature, but through the loss of the gift of *integritas*, or nature-perfecting virtue, which man acquires "according" to nature (*der Natur gemäß, secundum naturam*), but which he does not possess "by" nature (*von Natur aus, a natura*), rather, he acquires it through action, and herein lies its character as a gift "more-than-natural" (*donum praeternaturale*) but not "supernatural." Through its loss, nature falls back on itself and to the *defectus naturae* that it has as a body–soul nature. The concept of the *fomes peccati* reflects this *natura sibi relicta* (nature left destitute);[29] in the perspective of salvation history and theology it is a "lack" or "privation," and thus a *malum poenae*, the evil of a punishment.[30] The rebellion of the will and especially of the senses against the reason is, on the one side, considered philosophically and anthropologically, quite simply a part of the *conditio humana*, since the will, as we have seen, is not by nature *habitually* oriented toward the good of neighbor or of God; and still less are the sensitive appetites in relation to the good of the reason (*bonum rationis*)—the sensitive appetites naturally seek a sensible good (*bonum sensibile*). But the will and sensitive appetites (or "strivings") are by nature set up to strive *according to reason*, and therein consists their perfection, or moral virtue.[31]

This anthropological situation, which belongs to the *conditio humana*, can be treated in a theological (and salvation-historical) perspective as the condition of a fallen nature, and this is only because "in the beginning," thanks to a gift of God that surpassed the powers of nature, "it was not so."[32] On the basis of anthropological experience, Platonic philosophy found an inner contradiction in human nature, a conflict between soul and body, and, drawing dualistic consequences, explained it with the *mythos* of the demiurge in a creationist–theological way. In the young Aristotle there are still hints of that "saying of the old ones" that the "soul had to pay a price, and we live in punishment for some huge mistakes" (*Protreptikos*, B106). Later, after abandoning the dualistic anthropology, he would only grant that "a kind of wickedness" sticks to our nature (*Nichomachean Ethics,* VII, 15;

1154b29). "Historical" explanations like the Platonic *mythos* no longer satisfy him, but a certain pessimism arises about the moral potential of the "many," and true happiness seems to be confined only to the few, to the philosophical elite and the "serious" (the σπουδαῖοι). The Stoics will solve the problem through a model of "cosmic harmony"; the modern period will attempt the same through a philosophical–historical evolutionary model, as derived from the mistaken early modern theodicy that attempted to reconcile the goodness and wisdom of the creator God with the obvious shortcomings of human nature. The Aristotelian anthropology and ethics offer the only paradigm for a realistic, and purely *philosophical,* anthropology of "fallen nature" that at the same time *leaves intact the mystery of this condition.* It describes human nature as it really is, but it cannot explain why it is so: that is, why it is a "fallen" nature. And no human science can explain that. The ancient *mythos* had the intuition that only a *historical* explanation is possible, but that particular *mythos* was not the true explanation. The true history was revealed by the One Who knew why and how He had created man, in order to set clearly before us our need of salvation.

If one speaks of the natural law within this perspective of theology and salvation history, then the present condition would be a "distortion," representing the disturbance of the original perfection that once existed in a condition of integrity and virtue, and that can now be won back only through effort and struggle.[33] To the degree that this condition of "nature left to itself" is considered "punishment," it can also be considered "law"—as the ordinance of the *ratio* of divine providence, which has dispensed a punishment to the human race.[34]

It seems to me to be crucial to point out and carefully define this philosophical–anthropological equivalent of "fallen nature," if we are concerned to integrate the doctrine of the natural law into moral theology. The connection has not been sufficiently studied: contemporary moral theology is oriented toward salvation history, and it has difficulties with the concepts "natural law" and "human nature."

For some time, many moral theologians—and also dogmatic theologians—have been working, it seems to me, "against" St. Thomas, with an artificial distinction between a "pure nature" (*natura pura*) and another, fallen nature that *in itself* is less perfect than the former; they do not appear to have noticed that the "fallen nature," considered *in itself* and as a subject of philosophical–anthropological and also ethical analysis, is nothing other than human nature as such, but that its "fallenness" represents a salvation-historical, and *not* a metaphysical or anthropological, statement.[35] The influence of the distinction can be seen in that what it implicitly denies has become explicit doctrine: namely, that the *only* analysis of human nature that is possible is a salvation-historical one. Karl Rahner prepared the way for this development with his (incorrect) view that philosophical anthropology (that is, the knowledge of human nature) was founded on a generalization of empirical data; now, empirically, the only kind of human being that exists is *in some way* situated within salvation history, so that one could never know what belongs to human nature *independently* of the influence of historically operative grace or super-nature. "Human nature" is thus a "residual" or "remainder" concept (*Restbegriff*), and what belongs to human "nature" cannot be determined. Rahner also wanted to distinguish a "pure," philosophically objectified (but de facto nonexistent) nature from an actual nature. In the tradition of Baius, he thereby turned the salvation-historical situation of humanity into a metaphysical and anthropological statement about human nature.[36]

It is not possible to go into any more detail here about the errors, and the enormous influence, of the Rahnerian position. It arose as the expression of a very widespread failure to harmonize the dogma of original sin with the doctrine of a "natural" morality that would also be valid for "fallen nature."[37]

The development introduced by Rahner led finally to the complete breakdown of an understanding of the concept of nature, as can be seen in much salvation-historically oriented moral theology.[38] It also had corresponding effects upon the concept of moral action and the question of determining what is the real business of ethics, or the "properly ethical" (*das ethische Proprium*). This, repeatedly identified with "Christian morality" as such, loses its specific character and becomes a purely *human* morality clothed in theological jargon. The apparent Christocentrism of this moral doctrine is then used as a way of speaking about man *as man*.[39]

## The Concept of Moral Action and the Proper Subject of Ethics

Part II began by showing how so-called "autonomous morality" has lost sight of what is properly the subject matter of ethics; it could recover its peculiar subject matter only through integration into a Christian and theological ethics. This pillaging from theology unfortunately brings dangers from two directions: it threatens the independence and self-consistency—the functional autonomy—of a human morality (seemingly the original desideratum of autonomous morality), as well as the radical novelty and specificity of the Christian ethos, which should transcend all human claims to morality.

### *"Morality": A Characteristic of Actions*

"Morality" is a characteristic of human *action*. That means, in the final analysis, a characteristic of the human *will*, which becomes "incarnated" in an external action, or which, if only an inner act, does not become manifest on the outside. Moral action is an *actio immanens*, an action whose effect and consequences remain in the doer and do not "produce" something, for what is produced exists independently of the action.[40] When someone kills an innocent person, the *moral* evil is not in the death of the innocent person but in the injustice of the murderer's will, in the deformation of his will. The moral evil, in other words, consists in the unjustly caused death of a human being. The real *malum morale* is thus not death but the "killing of the innocent," an *act* of injustice, a deformed action that willfully departed from the rule of reason.[41]

A morally (good) action is an action that sets up the order of reason *in action itself*: and this means ordering one's powers that are subject to the will, and ordering the will itself, toward the "good of the reason" (*bonum rationis*), or the good that corresponds to reason. And that means for the human person, in his or her action, to be ordered toward the good and to the transcendence of the good as such, to the truth and perfection of God, and finally toward the good of one's fellow human beings. What counts is not merely "doing good" but "being good" *on the basis of doing* (or of "choosing," *eligere*) the good.

It could be objected—as Bruno Schüller would surely do at this point in the argument—that such a distinction is not required. Of course we are concerned only with "being good," but in order to know how one is to be good, one must discover which acts are good. Therefore ethics can be restricted to the task of discovering *which ways of acting* are right or wrong, since it is understood that only someone who does something "by free decision" and by trying to act "rightly" and "well," acts morally.[42]

The objection is both subtle and suggestive. It permits Schüller to eliminate from ethics the perspective of virtue in the classical sense, and reduce it to an analysis of "right" and "wrong" ways of acting. In contrast, I would emphasize that a treatment of virtue belongs *constitutively* to the concept of "right action," insofar as virtue is the immanent, habitual perfection of actions.

### *"Morality," "Right Action," and "Virtue"*

The underlying error of Schüller's argument, at least with regard to content, and not its logical form, is a mistaken definition of moral virtue. This is surprising in view of Schüller's stated aim to clarify definitions.

The derivation of the concept of virtue from the concept of right action is made plausible only by way of an overly general definition of virtue as a "good operative habit" (*habitus operativus bonus*); this is not specific for moral virtue, since it also holds for the intellectual as well as infused and theological virtues.[43] Schüller then defines virtue as the habitual, free decision to do the good that corresponds to right ways of acting, for the sake of that good. Moral virtue is thus the "right way of acting" and the "free decision" as well. What is "virtuous" in virtue appears, at least superficially, to remain attached to the concept of the right way of acting.[44]

And yet, when we study more closely the concept of virtue as found in Aristotle and Thomas, it is striking to note that the case is exactly the opposite: the concept of "right action" is derived from the concept of "moral virtue." The former, in fact, is only an abstraction that keeps its significance when it is constitutively related to the concept of moral virtue. The generic definition of virtue that Schüller uses does not express the specificity of *moral* virtue. It is no wonder that the distinction between "right knowing" and "right action" also disappears, and that the problem of the normative justification of morality is reduced to the problem of the discursive justification of norms, and ultimately to a question of "right thinking."

Thomas devoted an article of the *Summa Theologiae* to the Augustinian definition of virtue: "Virtue is a good quality of mind, by which one lives rightly, which no one can misuse, which God works in us without our help" (*Virtus est bona qualitas mentis, qua recte vivitur et nullus male utitur, quam Deus in nobis sine nobis operatur,* see *I–II,* q. 55, a. 4). But, because it is not sufficiently specific,[45] it is not further used in the context of the treatise on moral virtue, and Thomas adopts the Aristotelian definitions instead. The definition *habitus operativus bonus* can do nothing more than characterize what intellectual and moral virtue have in common: the quality of being able to direct the *operatio* of a faculty to its proper perfection; thus the *habitus operativus* is distinguished from the so-called *habitus entitativus* (for example, grace), as well as from every form of *habitus malus.* But *both* intellectual and moral virtue have something further in common: *Virtus est quae bonum facit habentem et opus eius bonum reddit* (Virtue is what makes its possessor good, and renders his work good);[46] as operative habit, virtue in general is defined as the perfecting of its possessor and of the possessor's power or potency. The same can be said for the definitions of virtue as the *dispositio perfecti ad optimum* (disposition of what is perfected toward the best; see *Phys.* VIII, 3, 246a10; see also *I–II,* q. 62, a. 1, arg. 1.), or as the *ultimum potentiae* ("the finality of a power," see *De Caelo,* I, 2, 281a14–19).

When moral virtue, in turn, is distinguished from intellectual virtue, care must be taken not to forget the fundamental and general determination of the *genus* as a *habitus operativus bonus.* On the other hand, the definition of virtue must be completed with regard for the specificity of *moral* virtue as that kind of *habitus* which perfects human action or the *actus humanus.* This is how Thomas, taking up the formula of the *Nichomachean Ethics,* arrives at a complete definition of moral virtue that takes into account what is proper to ethics: "[Moral] virtue is an elective habit that consists in a mean, determined by reason in respect to ourselves, and just as the wise person would determine it" (*Virtus est habitus electivus existens in medietate, quoad nos determinata ratione, ut utique sapiens determinabit*; see *Nichomachean Ethics,* II, 6, 1106b–1107a2; *In II Ethic.*, lect. 7, no. 322). At *I–II*, q. 58, where the treatise on moral virtue begins, Thomas shows that right acting (*recte operari*) means right choosing (*recte eligere*); this understanding of moral virtue as an elective habit—a habit of "right choosing" and consequently of "right acting"—is of decisive importance.

Moral virtue is what causes the *rectitudo* of choosing, the choosing act of the will that immediately triggers action. As such, it does not form the content of an *intention,* but of an *action.*[47] This *electio* is shaped according to a mean determined by reason "with respect to the doer"; this mean is such as to correspond to prudence: it is "right reason" (*recta ratio*).

It would take us too far afield to present all the implications of this very rich definition. In the present context, the following consideration appears especially relevant: the concept of moral virtue is already related to a fully elaborated psychology of human behavior, to its elective structure. This is the truth that action takes place in a choosing appetition or striving that is molded to a certain rightness by the reason; finally, it means that we are morally "good" or "bad" according to the actions that we will in our act of choosing, on the basis of the disposition of our appetitive powers. What the concept of virtue as *moral* virtue adds—to distinguish it from "pure" right reason—is the reason-conforming disposition of the appetites, a disposition that is habitual precisely because it is a *stable* disposition stamped upon the appetites to act *according to reason*, according to the rule laid down by reason. The "essence of virtue" (*ratio virtutis*)—what makes moral virtue be virtue—is not only the habitualness, as Schüller implies (for this is common to intellectual virtue as well), nor the character of "free purposiveness" (*freie Entschlossenheit*) (for this is true of any moral action as an *actus humanus*); what is specific for moral virtue is the agreement of the appetition with the reason.[48] The concept of moral virtue is thus related essentially and constitutively toward the doctrine of the *telos* character and the measuring function of the reason, and not merely a "habitual, free purposiveness" to do right. The concept of "right action" as action that belongs to a virtue already implies (as bound up with the idea of virtue) the normative foundation of right action's *rectitudo*. This is its "being in accordance with reason," as defined in regard to the concept of moral virtue.[49]

Schüller's definition of moral virtue, however, is inadequate for an analysis of the phenomenon "morality," because it is practically empty of content. And it is only by presupposing such a definition it that he can make his position plausible—the position, that is, that virtuous action can be determined merely by the analysis of "ways of acting" for their rightness or wrongness. By confusing what grounds and what is grounded, he loses sight, as do teleologistic ethicists in general, of the normative foundation of human action, as contained in the concept of moral virtue as such. All that remains is an abstraction, erroneously conceived as the starting point for the discursive justification of norms. Normativity must then be reconstructed upon this mere corpse of moral action, divided into "goods" and "values." The instrument of reconstruction is reason as *discursive rationality*: a technique for the justification of norms that is called "weighing of goods" or the "proportionate assessment of values" [*Güterabwägung*]. The understanding of reason as a *standard* [*Maßstab*] has been lost sight of.

## *The Proper Subject Matter of Ethics*

It should be emphasized, then, that the concept of "right action," seen with reference to the concept of moral virtue from which it originally arose, must possess its anthropological foundation in the doctrine of the *telos* character of the reason.[50] This is why the distinction Schüller maintains between right/wrong, on the one hand, and good/bad, on the other, is not workable for the determination of ethical norms. A "wrong" action is an action that does not correspond to the order of virtue, and thus not to reason. If it is voluntary—that is, if it is *not* based on (nonculpable) ignorance or on coercion—it is also morally bad or "evil."[51]

The concept of moral action (or "the right way of acting"), in other words, becomes clear only through an analysis of the concept of moral virtue. Moral action always involves preserving (or establishing ) the order of the soul, as measured by the reason as *telos*. A moral act is accordingly one through which the human appetites (and external actions, to the extent that they arise from these appetites) are directed to the "good of the reason"—the good that is recognized in the process of the natural reason in a practical (i.e., preceptive manner). At the same time, moral virtue itself, again, provides the condition that this moral good (the good of the reason) really comes to realization in concrete appetition and action. This is precisely why moral perfection—the fulfillment of personal autonomy—consists in virtue, through which the natural reason and its lawgiving function reach their "breakthrough" and through which the appetitive, "striving" powers of the human being (the senses and the will) come to bear the "seal" (*sigillatio*) of the reason. As a result, these powers habitually strive for the good that corresponds to the *imago Dei* in man. The virtuous man is the one who strives for the good according to reason with his will and his sensitive powers; this is the person to whom the good appears attractive and pleasant, and who carries it out cheerfully and with ease. The virtuous person is also the one to whom the *true* good (the good in accordance with reason) also *appears* good, and thus he does the good as it were spontaneously, without a great deal of deliberation, and without having to fight against himself. He is the *prudent one* (the σπουδαῖος) of whom Aristotle speaks, the one he calls the measure and rule of the morally good;[52] the virtuous person, finally, is the one Thomas, following St. Paul, can call "a law unto himself."[53]

At first, this may sound rather abstract, and not very "close" to the realities of life. It is in the *Secunda Secundae* (*II–II*) of Thomas's *Summa Theologiae* that we find the particular treatment of morality. There, the intimacy with lived experience embodied in this conception of human action is visible in all its breadth and depth. And this will remain clear to us as long we are always conscious of (a) the nature, meaning, and origin of the human reason as the *imago Dei* and as natural light, and (b) of the reason's *telos* and measuring (or standard-making) functions.

The "connection with life" is relatively easy to grasp when it concerns the order of the reason in the sensitive appetites. Here are the virtues that order the concupiscible (desiring) and irascible (angering) powers in the individual. The issues are more complex when it comes to the virtue of justice, which has to do with relations of the individual person toward others as well as toward external goods.

The confidence and skillfulness of Thomas's presentation of certain arguments in the area of justice follow from the depth of his insight into the structure of the *imago* in man, and the fact that we are called to recognize it and love it in the "thou" as well as in ourselves. To establish or continue this relationship of *aequalitas* (or sameness) from one person to the next, in the strivings of the will and in external actions, and also in their relation to external goods, is the real "essence of justice" (*ratio iustitiae*). As the first principle of natural law, it becomes intuitively spontaneous through the experience of the other as a human being, *the same as I*: because of the lived experience of (especially) *linguistic* communication, I discover in the other the same *imago Dei*.[54]

Only the reason is able to grasp the "proportion of one to another" (*proportio unius ad alterum*) in which justice consists: *ratio ordinat in alterum* (reason orders to another), so that justice consists in the conformity of the will with this ordering of the reason (*ordinatio rationis*; see *II–II*, q. 58, a. 5c, also ad 2um, ad 3um).

Unjust behavior consequently causes the destruction of human community and communication *because* the will of the unjust person becomes divorced from the reason and thereby becomes bad. The moral evil of the death of the innocent person (as in abortion) or the moral evil of lying does not consist primarily in the death of the innocent or the "false statement" as such, but rather in the injustice or the distortion of the will of the person acting. Insofar as he departs from the order of reason in his striving and in his actions, he destroys the foundation of all interpersonal order and justice: namely, the recognition and love for the *imago* or the mastery of reason in oneself. *And this alone makes it possible for man to discover, know, and love this* imago *in others, and that means becoming able to see the* ratio iustitiae *and the* proportio ad alterum, *and to act accordingly.*

This is also why the so-called Golden Rule, "Do unto others as you would have them do unto you," and the definition of justice as "the firm will to give to each according to his due" are not merely "empty formulas" (*Leerformeln*). With the doctrine of the *telos* character of the reason and the *imago* as background, these formulas have a clear normative meaning, since they ground an immediately effective *ordo rationis* in each human being that needs to be concretized in action.

Man's openness to the *bonitas divina* (which transcends him but at the same time grounds his existence and constitutes its meaning and goal) is founded in the *imago*. The unfolding of this *imago*'s potential is at the same time the ultimate self-transcendence of man. Moral action as a life according to reason, and the "being good" that goes with this, are the condition and way to the fulfillment of human potential. The knowing and loving "turn" toward God[55] is an "orientation" that forms the stable foundation for all interpersonal justice. Justice is thus the highest virtue, because in justice the highest degree of the "good of the reason" comes to light; it is closest to reason because it has its seat in the intellective appetite, the will, and not only orders man in himself but also orders him to others—to fellow human beings and to God.[56]

This potentiality of the *imago*, finally, is also the basis for the capacity the theologians call *potentia oboedientialis*. The ability of human nature to be *capax Dei*, to be able, without self-contradiction, to join oneself to an "uplifting" by God (a capacity that is founded in the *imago* and leads to its perfection), and to be brought to a supernatural fulfillment; this is to meet God in a way within oneself through the elevation of grace, to "reach God" (*attingere Deum*), to become a participant in the intimacy of His divine nature—to correspond, in other words, with the divine call to *holiness*.[57]

Human behavior is not primarily a matter of realizing definite "ways of acting," nor even the habitual and freely chosen realization of actions. Rather, it is a matter of "*being* good," which means directing all appetition and will according to reason. Only in this way, on the basis of a determination of good action in the context of moral virtue, can an abstraction like "right ways of acting" be employed without losing the normative foundation of rectitude.

The allegation of Bruno Schüller that the "tradition" overlooked, or did not even raise, the basic question of a normative ethics—the question about the difference between good and evil—not only is untenable but contradicts itself; on closer inspection, the "tradition" in fact posed and answered this question as far back as its roots go in the Greek and Hellenistic periods, and it posed it in a much deeper and more comprehensive way than is seen, for example, in Schüller's so-called "teleologistic" school. For like "autonomous morality," this school of thinking has lost the perspective of moral virtue, and that means losing the perspective of an anthropologically based ethics of virtue, and the sense of what is "proper to ethics" (*das ethische Proprium*). Instead, it follows the tradition of a "norm ethics" in which one thinks first of "moral norms," "right ways of acting," "commandments," "duties," "law," and so forth, only to conclude that someone acts virtuously who does "by free choice" what is "right," or what his "duty" is, what is "commanded here and now." The concept of moral virtue has no self-consistency or significance in this view: it becomes a mere "epiphenomenon" or mere *name* for what is "right." But virtues are not grounded in norms. It is the other way around: norms are formulated on the basis of the single moral virtues. *Totam materiam moralem ad considerationem virtutum reducere*—"to reduce the whole matter of morality to a consideration of the virtues"—was the method of St. Thomas, working in the tradition of Aristotle. This is the real foundation and justification for a "normative ethics" that speaks not only of norms but also, finally, of the *human being*.

This loss of the "proper subject matter of ethics" is characteristic not only of "autonomous morality," as shown in chapter 3, but also of the so-called "teleological ethics," which is the model of norm justification usually chosen by the defenders of "autonomous morality." We can now embark on a closer analysis and criticism of this teleologistic model.

## Notes

1. Reference must once again be made to T. G. Belmans, *Le Sens objectif de l'agir humain* (Vatican City, 1980), who fully details the survival of physicalistic-naturalistic argumentation in today's moral theology.

2. This very restricted function of a "moral system"often appears to have been completely misunderstood. See for example B. F. Furger, *Was Ethik Begründet. Deontologie oder Teleologie—Hintergrund und Tragweite einer moraltheologischen Auseinandersetzung* (Einsiedeln, 1984), p. 19. One

should realize in any case that the hair-splitting debates over these moral systems often led in the past to a neglect of the fundamental questions about the normative justification of morality; many contemporary moral theologians were trained in this atmosphere and consequently have been influenced by an abbreviated moral-theological perspective, as well as by a lack of philosophically discursive training for the discursive justification of norms. See also R. Spaemann, "Wovon handelt die Moraltheologie?" in *Internationale katholische Zeitschrift* (1977): 289–311; Spaemann's remarks on the so-called "reflective moral systems" are fitting: "The reason for these systems was to provide handy criteria for cases when the 'objective' judgment of an action was controversial. This emerged from the common experience that one must often act before something has been thoroughly discussed. Moral philosophy is concerned with the problem of making discursive justifications of actions. Theologians were formerly called on to provide handbooks for confessors, which means that they were faced with the need to make judgments and provide counsel *hic et nunc*" (p. 298).

3. See B. Schüller, *Die Begründung sittlicher Urteile*, 2nd ed. (Düsseldorf, 2nd. ed., 1980); and his "Neuere Beiträge zum Thema, 'Begründung sittlicher Normen,' " in *Theologische Berichte*, vol. 4 (1974), pp. 109–181. Of course, Schüller is right in pointing out instances of inappropriate or pointless recourse to the "will of God" or the "wisdom of God." But I cannot agree that such misuse was the characteristic method of traditional norm justification; that is surely an oversimplification. Again, his distinction between *parainesis* (or "exhortation") and scientific theology is in principle correct, but Schüller overlooks the fact that there are theological statements that, while being no substitute for rationally discursive norm justification, are nevertheless genuine theological formulations and *not* mere *parainesis*. For example, consider the Augustinian formulation of sin as a "violation of the eternal law." This definition, it is true, does not provide any concrete determination of what would constitute such violation, and Thomas adds to it that such would have to be determined by reason or by revelation. But that by no means requires that an action, once it *has* been discursively analyzed, could *not* be qualified in the end as in fact a violation of the will or wisdom of God. The formulation is not *only parainesis*; it also sets the particular action within a new and more profound theological perspective.

4. See B. Schüller, *Die Begründung sittlicher Urteile*, p. 272: "It appears that the tradition, even though it had elaborated a very comprehensive and detailed normative ethics, never really posited or developed the basic question of normative ethics."

5. For example, the works of Schüller are practically innocent of any engagement with any studies outside of the textbook tradition, let alone with Thomas Aquinas himself. F. Böckle's criticism of the "tradition" depends only on a single author (A. Vermeersch), to whom, within a certain limited context, "decisive importance" and great influence can indeed be ascribed; see F. Böckle, "Natürliches Gesetz als göttliches Gesetz," in F. Böckle and E.-W. Böckenförde, eds., *Naturrecht in der Kritik* (Mainz, 1973), p. 188.

6. Certainly, casuistry has a very great pedagogical and heuristic value, even in other areas; thus one should carefully differentiate between the legitimate and even necessary use of casuistry in moral theology, and a *casuistic morality,* which must be avoided. The studies of S. Pinckaers are still quite apposite to these matters: "La Nature de la moralité: Morale casuistique et morale thomiste," in *S. Thomas d' Aquin, Somme Théologique, Les actes humains,* vol. 2, *Renseignements techniques* (Paris and Tournai, 1966) pp. 215–273.

7. See, for example, the trivialization of the Aristotelian doctrine of *kata logon prattein* in F. Siegler, "Reason, Happiness, and Goodness," in J. J. Walsh and H. L. Shapiro, eds., *Aristotle's Ethics: Issues and Interpretations* (Belmont, Calif., 1967), pp. 30–46. On the other hand, Anglo–American Aristotelian research has contributed much to the rediscovery of the morally constitutive meaning of *logos.*

8. Aristotle, *Nichomachean Ethics,* I, 7, 1098a 22–24. An original and very valuable study that systematically develops and formulates the doctrine of the rationally determined nature of human action (*recta ratio*) is the theory of the "first principle of morality" and its distribution into eight different "modes of responsibility," in G. Grisez, *The Way of the Lord Jesus,* vol. 1, *Christian Moral Principles* (Chicago, 1983), esp. pp. 184ff. and 205ff; see also the no less systematized theory of the "basic requirements of practical reasonableness" of J. Finnis, *Natural Law and Natural Rights* (Oxford, 1980). Both Finnis and Grisez, in my opinion, lack the necessary attention to what I call the "telos character" of the reason; they use instead the category of "integral human fulfillment." Nevertheless, the two categories can, it seems to me, be joined into one: the latter points out that human fulfillment has for its subject *all* the levels of existence in the *suppositum,* whereas the former looks instead to the charcterization of the reason as the *normative ordering principle* for this "integral human fulfillment." It appears to me that this second aspect does not receive enough attention from Grisez and Finnis.

9. A more comprehensive study of this process of reception would be in order.

10. See *Phaedo* 63e–69e. The basic ethical question that Plato poses

is "But when does the soul grasp the truth?"(65b). The answer is "Is it not, therefore, if anywhere, in the act of reasoning [ἐν τῷ λογίζεσθαι], in which the truth of things is offered to it? And the soul surely reasons then in the most perfect way, when it is not disturbed by anything, not by hearing, nor seeing, nor pain, nor pleasure, but rather when it is as much as possible drawn into itself, and has taken leave of the body, and associates with it and touches it as little as possible, and strives after what is real" (65c). Not only does Plato think dualistically, he also makes no distinction between speculative and practical knowing.

11. This is the fundamental doctrine of the *Nichomachean Ethics*. Some formulations of the *Magna Moralia* (now recognized as Aristotelian at least in content) are especially clear: "In the soul there is a lower and a higher part; the lower part is nevertheless always there for the sake of the higher, just as with the body and soul the body is there for the sake of the soul. We say that the body is in good order when it does not hinder the soul, but rather supports and encourages the soul to complete its own function. The lower is ordered to the higher, in order to cooperate with it. If the passions do not hinder the soul [νοῦς] from accomplishing its work, then the action is carried out according to right reason [ὀρθὸς λόγος] (*Magna Moralia*, II, 10, 1208a 13–21). Aristotle is no longer thinking dualistically: he is not concerned with getting free of corporeal conditions, but rather with their good ordering, their being in harmony with the rational part. This good ordering is what moral virtue achieves.

12. See for example, *Contra Gentiles*, III, 129, no. 3015: "According to the natural order, the body of the human being is for the sake of the soul, and the inferior powers of the soul are for the sake of the reason. . . . But because it is oriented toward another [*ad aliud ordinatum*], it ought to provide help [*auxilium*] to that other, and not an impediment [*impedimentum*]. Therefore it is naturally right [*naturaliter rectum*] for the human body—and even the lower powers of the soul—to be treated in such a way that the act of the reason and the good of the reason be as little impeded as possible [*minime impediatur*], and instead be helped; if it happens otherwise, there will be sin against nature [*erit naturaliter peccatum*].

13. See *Nichomachean Ethics*, I, 7, 1098a34–b4: "One should not inquire after the cause in the same manner for all things. In some matters, it is enough for the 'fact that something is so' to be plainly shown, such as when it comes to principles: 'the fact that something is so' is first and a principle. Principles themselves are known partly through induction, partly through a kind of habituation, partly in still other ways" (in every instance it has to do with forms of discursively underivable, immediate experience).

14. See chapter 1, section "Practical Reason and Philosophical Ethics," subsection "The Subject of Philosophical Ethics: The *Ordo Rationis,*" where the subject matter of ethics was defined as the "ordo rationis" within human striving and action.

15. The distinction between natural love of neighbor and Christian love of neighbor has been made intentionally; the former belongs to the field of classical human friendship (*amicitia*), as described in the *Nichomachean Ethics* of Aristotle; it is part of the cardinal virtue of justice, the foundation and bond of all human communities. Christian love of neighbor greatly exceeds the just requirements of human/natural love; it goes beyond justice to mercy and is thereby not only human love but also the reflection of divine love toward man, which is revealed in Jesus Christ, and goes far beyond what is required from a purely human point of view. The distinction is indispensable, in my opinion, especially to keep the category of "sanctity" in Christian moral doctrine free of trivialization, which unfortunately is no rare occurrence in contemporary moral theology.

16. Only supernatural justice (which rests upon grace and consists formally in the virtue of *caritas*) has the character of perfect justice, because it is founded upon a certain created *equality* or *friendship* between God and man, made possible by grace (a supernatural participation in the divine nature).

17. While the ethical–philosophical concept of *malitia* is a habitus of the will that is a vice, or a habitual inclination toward evil, the theological term *malitia*, as one of the four "wounds of nature" (*vulnera naturae*) that resulted from original sin, denotes the condition of nature as fallen or as "left to itself" (*natura sibi relicta*). This *malitia*, insofar as it is treated as a "wound of nature" resulting from original sin, is not the habitual malice of the will as a vice, but rather that original, natural (and philosophically analyzable) lack of habitual orientation of the will toward the good of neighbor and God, thanks to which man possesses a natural readiness and propensity to seek his own good. This propensity is what we may call the fundamental tendency of the human being toward pride and wrongful self-love. It can be treated as a "wound" of nature only *theologically,* which means in reference to a historically prior condition of a *natura integra*, which involved the possession, by gift, of all the virtues. The auxiliary notion of a *natura pura* is thus superfluous and confusing (see below, subsection "Philosophical Ethics and Anthropology, and the Problem of 'Fallen Nature' and the *Fomes Peccati*").

18. See *I–II*, q. 24, a. 3: "For the perfection of moral good it is essential that man be moved to the good not only according to the will [*secundum voluntatem*] but also according to the sensitive appetite [*secundum appetitum senstivum*]; according to what is stated in Psalm 83:3 . . ."

19. See, for example, the *Summa Contra Gentiles,* III, 129, no. 3015: "It is naturally right [*naturaliter rectum*] that the body be managed in this way, and even the lower powers of the soul, so that the act of the reason and its good be as little as possible hindered, and instead be helped; but if it happens otherwise, it will be naturally wrong [*naturaliter peccatum*]. Therefore, drunken parties and gluttonous feasting and inordinate sexual activities (all things that impede the acts of the reason), and because they are subjected to passions *that do not allow the free judgment of the reason*, are naturally bad [*naturaliter mala*]." A great abundance of examples could be cited from the *Secunda Secundae* as well, in which this argument is crucial.

20. See *De Virtutibus in Communi*, a. 9: "the virtue of the appetitive part [moral virtue] is nothing other than a certain disposition, or form, that has been 'sealed' and 'stamped' [*sigillata et impressa*] upon the appetitive power by the reason." Other formulations are found at *Summa Contra Gentiles,* III, 121, no. 2944: "For virtue consists in this, that both interior affections, as well as the use made of corporeal things, be governed [*regulentur*] by the reason." At *I–II*, q. 59, a. 4: "Moral virtue perfects the appetitive part of the soul by ordering it toward the good of the reason [*bonum rationis*]. For the good of the reason is that which is governed or ordered [*moderatum seu ordinatum*] according to the reason."

21. That this may at first glance seem like circular reasoning, Thomas himself was aware (See *In VI Ethic.*, lect. 6, no. 1131). But the circle is opened by the fact that the ends are given to man by nature—in other words, they present a *naturaliter cognitum* in the act of grasping the first principles. The process of forming moral virtues is in fact a complex one and not *spontaneous*; experience has shown that it requires the aid of instruction, models, advice, and, above all, loving, wise, and strong guidance. This is also why Thomas sees the propagation of human life as guaranteed only in marriage, and considers it to be among the precepts of the natural law, for marriage is the foundation for human reproduction. On this, see M. Rhonheimer, "Sozialphilosophie und Familie. Gedanken zur humanen Grundfunktion der Familie," in B. Schnyder, ed., *Familie—Herausforderung der Zukunft,* (Freiburg, Switzerland, 1982) pp. 113–140.

22. "Autonomie et théonomie," in M. Zalba, ed., *L'agire morale,* vol. 5 of *Tommaso d'Aquino nel suo settimo centenario* (Naples, 1974), esp. p. 244: "When speaking about an order constituted by the reason, we do not mean that the reason plays only a *declarative* role, nor that its function is limited to proposing to the will a moral order that is already given as such [*déjà donné comme tel*]. Its role in fact goes much farther . . . the reason is the presupposition [*le présupposé*] for a moral order."

23. Ibid., p. 245: The practical judgment "has an objective content,

that is, it is different from the act [*bonum et malum sunt in rebus*], but this content includes in itself a relation to my reason, and by it, across it, and beyond it [*par elle, à travers elle, au delà d'elle*], it has a relation to the horizon upon which it opens and to which it refers as reason," that is to say, to the universal, intelligible truth—finally, to God, as well as in a special way to the "thou," in which the *imago* of God is found, an image that reveals itself fundamentally in the experience of spoken communication, through which we have an entry into the intimacy, the *mens*, of our fellow human beings.The formulations of J. de Finance show how well Thomas respects the demands both of the practical reason as constitutive, and of the foundation of all moral objectivity in reality; but reality is not merely an order that is "objectified" for the knowing reason, since the practically knowing reason is itself reality. It is finally the whole of the reality of the human *suppositum*, which constitutes itself only as a moral magnitude through the act of the practical reason.

24. Ibid., p. 252. De Finance rightly emphasizes (p. 258) that the moral "ought" does *not* presuppose an explicit knowledge of God. On the other hand, this position also implies that every sin has an intrinsic ordering to God, is indeed an offense to God, because it means a refusal to recognize his *imago* and slights the participation in the eternal law that God established (thus there is no "philosophical sin" [*peccatum philosophicum*]). Here is the ultimate grounding for the truth of the dignity of conscience and that one should not act *against* the conscience, or *with* a doubtful, insufficiently informed, or culpably erring conscience.

25. This is clear in K.-W. Merks, *Theologische Grundlegung der sittlichen Autonomie* (Düsseldorf, 1978), esp. p. 295. Here it is no longer the *ratio* that is shown to be a standard, but rather *rationality*, that is, the mere fact of the rationally discursive foundation of norms, the material content of which, according to Merks, only human law can achieve. See also p. 297: "The *bonum secundum rationem* is, fundamentally, rationality itself . . . man strives fundamentally toward rational existence, and thus the rational governance of action is as such the fundamental 'good' to which the reason spontaneously assents, and which it spontaneously ratifies as the affirmation of itself." The interpretation of Bruno Schüller seems equally problematic; it tries to place the *recta ratio* in the area of metaethics (metaethical "cognitivism"). As applied to the area of normative ethics, the recourse to the *ratio* would be equivalent to an "empty formula" that says nothing about what is "in accordance with reason." See *Die Begründung sittlicher Urteile*, p. 161.

26. This is the chief reason why a methodology of this kind excludes the naturalistic fallacy. Now in principle, Schüller quite rightly recognizes this (*Die Begründung sittlicher Urteile*, p. 160, n. 11); I would not

express it as Schüller does—that anthropology is grounded in ethics or that moral theology is grounded in dogmatics—but rather, I would say that the anthropological and metaphysical deepening or broadening of ethics rests upon the reflective interpretation of an originally practical experience. Unlike philosophical anthropology, metaphysics (and dogmatics) are constituted independently of this practical experience.

27. See also R. A. Armstrong, *Primary and Secondary Precepts in Thomistic Natural Law Teaching* (The Hague, 1966), pp. 151–156: "It is clear from our reading of St. Thomas that he was perfectly aware of the possibility of man's rational development giving rise to an apparent change in natural law" (p. 152).

28. See *I*, q. 95, a. 3: "Such was the rectitude of the original condition [*primi status*], that the reason was subjected to God, and the inferior powers to the reason. For virtues are nothing other than certain perfections [*perfectiones quaedam*] by which the reason is ordered toward God, and the inferior powers are disposed according to the rule of reason [*secundum regulam rationis*]; and this will become clearer in the treatment of the virtues. Whence the rectitude of the original condition required that man in some way have all the virtues."

29. On the concept see *I–II*, q. 87, a. 8: "Primarily, the punishment for original sin is that human nature is left to itself [*sibi relinquitur*], destitute of the help of original justice, and from this follow all the punishments that happen to human beings *by a defect of nature* [*ex defectu naturae*].

30. In his *Commentary on the Sentences* Thomas made the most explicit differentiation between the philosophical and theological methods of treatment. See above all *In II Sent,* d. 30, q. 1, a. 1: "Man could not cleave to his final goal [the supernatural vision of God] by love, nor could reach it except by his supreme part, which is the mind and intellect, or reason [*mens et intellectus, seu ratio*], in which the *imago Dei* is inscribed [*insignita est*]; and so, in order for that part freely to reach God, the inferior powers were subjected to it, so that nothing could happen in them that would hold back the mind and obstruct it in its journey toward God [*quod mentem retineret et impediret ab itinere in Deum*]; . . . by a like reason the body was so disposed that no passion could happen in it through which the mind's contemplation could be impeded. And because all these things, as stated, were in man through an order to his end [*ex ordine ad finem*], therefore, when there occured a dis-ordination from the end by sin, all these things ceased to be in human nature, and man was left *only to those goods which come to him by natural principles* [*ex naturalibus principiis*]. . . . Accordingly, I say that these defects can be considered in two ways with respect to human nature [*possunt ad naturam humanam dupliciter considerari*]: either with respect to how it is considered in its

natural principles alone, and without a doubt these are not punishments, but only natural defects, such as to have come out of nothing [*esse ex nihilo*], and to need preservation [*indigere conservatione*], which is a natural defect that belongs to every creature and is not a punishment for anyone; or [it can be considered] as *being begun* [*prout instituta est*], and without a doubt this is a punishment, because someone can be said to be punished by being deprived of what has been gratuitously given [*quod gratis alicui conceditur*]."

31. This twofold perspective of a philosophical or theological treatment can be found in the most varied stages of development in Thomas; see, apart from the *Commentary on the Sentences* (at *In II Sent.* d. 31, q. 1, a.2, ad 3um; d. 32, q.1, a. 2; q. 2, a.1; d. 33, q.2, a.1), *De Anima,* q. 1, a. 8; *De Malo,* q. 4, a. 2, ad 4um in contr.; *Contra Gentiles,* IV, 52; *I–II,* q. 17, a. 9, ad 3um. This last passage is very fruitful for the whole treatise on original sin in the *Summa Theologiae,* because the point is made immediately after a defect has been treated as a punishment for original sin: "Sed quia per peccatum primi parentis, ut infra dicetur, natura est sibi relicta, subtracto supernaturali dono quod homini divinitus erat collatum; ideo consideranda est ratio naturalis quare motus huius modi membrorum specialiter rationi non obedit. Cuius causam assignat Aristoteles. . . . (But because, through the sin of the first parent, as will be explained below, nature was left to itself, once the supernatural gift had been taken away that had been divinely granted to man, the natural reason must be considered, and why this kind of motion of the members does not give special obedience to the reason. Aristotle explains it as follows . . .). This perspective is entirely at one with other passages where Thomas still speaks as a theologian, and very starkly contrasts the *natura integra* of salvation-historical perspective with the *natura corrupta* that exists afterwards (as at *I–II,* q. 102, a. 2, where it might appear that Thomas thinks the *natura corrupta* is instead a nature altogether "beneath the threshhold" of human nature).

32. See *I–II,* q. 92, a. 2: "Therefore there is a law of man [*hominis lex*] that he has by the divine ordinance in regard to his own condition, that he act in accordance with reason. This law was so strong in the original state that nothing could steal upon man [*subrepere*] that was beyond reason or against reason. But when man drew back [*recessit*] from God, he became liable to being carried by the impulse of sensuality [*quod feratur secundum impetum sensualitatis*]; and this happens to each person, the more someone departs from reason, so that in a certain way one becomes like to the beasts, which are borne about by the impulse of sensuality."

33. Thomas achieved a complete synthesis of the philosophical and theological methods of treatment, as seen, for example, at *In Duo Prae-*

*cepta Caritatis et in Decem Legis Praecepta Expositio*, Prol., I, no. 1129ff.: "The first law is said to be that of nature, and this is nothing other than the light of the intellect planted in us [*insitum nobis*] by God, through which we know what we are to do and what to avoid [*quid agendum et quid vitandum*]. God gave this law and this light to man in creation. . . . But even though God gave this law to man at creation (that is, the law of nature), nevertheless the devil sowed another law in addition [*superseminavit*], namely, the law of concupiscence . . . and thus it happens that the law of concupiscence frequently corrupts the law of nature and the order of reason. . . . Because the law of nature was torn down [*destructa*] by the law of concupiscence, it was necessary that man be brought back to the works of virtue, and be led away from vices, and for this a written law was necessary." Here is the reason why there was need, morally and historically, for a revelation of the precepts of the natural law. See also *In VII ad Romanos*, lect.1, no. 520: "And this law lives, as long as the natural reason is effectively thriving [*efficaciter . . . viget*] in man. But the law of nature dies [*moriatur*] in man as long as the natural reason succumbs to passions." This *efficaciter vigere* has its full force of meaning in an anthropological–ethical perspective, under the conditions of moral virtue; or in a salvation-historical perspective, in the original condition of *integritas* (or the *natura redempta* and *sanata*).

34. *I–II*, q. 91, a. 6: "But insofar as man, by divine justice, has been deprived of the original justice and strength of reason [*vigore rationis*], the very impulse of sensuality that drives him has the nature of a law, insofar as it is penal and a consequence of the divine law, which has deprived man of his proper dignity [*lege divina . . . hominem destituente propria dignitate*]."

35. Jacques Maritain spread this misconception very widely in *An Essay on Christian Philosophy*, transl. E. Flannery (New York, 1955): "Man is not in a state of pure nature [*in statu purae naturae*], he is fallen and redeemed. Consequently, ethics . . . insofar as it takes man in his concrete state, in his existential being, is not a purely philosophical discipline" (p. 39). According to Maritain, philosophically analyzed human nature is an abstraction that does not exist in reality.

36. On this see Karl Rahner, "Bemerkungen über das Naturgesetz und seine Erkennbarkeit," in *Orientierung* 19 (1955): pp. 239–243; "Über das Verhältnis des Naturgesetzes zur übernatürlichen Gnadenordnung," *Orientierung* 20 (1956): 8–11; "Über das Verhältnis von Natur und Gnade," in his *Schriften zur Theologie*, vol. 1, (Einsiedeln, 1956), pp. 323–345. For an English translation of some of these materials, see G. A. McCool, ed., *A Rahner Reader* (New York, 1975), esp. pp. 185–190. For another selection and bibliography of Rahner's writ-

ings in translation, see G. B. Kelly, ed., *Karl Rahner: Theologian of the Graced Search for Meaning* (Minneapolis, Minn., 1992). It appears to me that Rahner, like many of his students, did not understand the Thomistic concepts of "nature" and "natural law": he writes, for instance, that "people begin all too easily with the idea that whatever is 'always and everywhere' observed about man belongs *eo ipso* to that unalterable existential situation of 'human nature,' which would then form the basis for the *lex naturae*. . . . it may be asked whether the scholastic 'nature-concept' as applied to human nature, was interpreted too much after the model of the subhuman (as a consequence of ancient philosophy, which was so oriented to *physis*)." Numerous misconceptions and terminological confusions have, unfortunately, been uncritically adopted from Rahner. There is a repeated failure to see that knowledge of human nature is obtained from specific philosophical–anthropological analysis, and not from the generalization of empirical data.

37. This reproach can also be directed to Joseph Fuchs and his classic text, *Lex Naturae: Zur Theologie des Naturrechts,* trans. by Helmut Reckter, S.J., and John Dowling as *Natural Law: A Theological Investigation* (New York, 1965). The erroneous tendency of Fuchs was to work with an "abstract" concept of a *natura metaphysica* as a hypothetical *natura pura.* This became explicit in his later work, *Moral und Moraltheologie nach dem Konzil* (Freiburg im Breisgau, 1967), esp. pp. 94–98. There can be found the sudden assertion that there is no "purely" natural order of morality, or order of morality related to a *natura pura*, but only one that is *always* (i.e., not only through the actual history of salvation but also *metaphysically*) related to an *assumptio* in Christ. Like others, Fuchs reached this conclusion because he held that a "pure nature" could be thought of that was fundamentally *different* from the "fallen nature" that was being treated in itself.

38. For example, in H. Rotter, "Zwölf Thesen zur heilsgeschichtlichen Begründung der Moral," in H. Rotter, ed., *Heilsgeschichte und ethische Normen* (Freiburg, 1984), pp. 99–127.

39. The Christological *kenosis replaces* the reality of the *assumptio* of human nature in the divine nature as realized in Christ; see, for example, F. Furger, " 'Kenosis' und das Christliche einer christlichen Ethik. Eine christologische Rückfrage," in K. Demmer and B. Schüller, eds. *Christlich Glauben und Handeln* (Düsseldorf, 1977), pp. 96–111. Furger does not deny that the Incarnation, acccording to the Athanasian Creed, is not a *conversio Divinitatis in carnem* but an *assumptio humanitatis in Deum*, but he neglects it. The consequence is a reduction of the Christian to the human. The only thing specifically Christian that remains is the explicit awareness that this pure humanity was revealed in Jesus Christ.

In its most radical form, the consequences of this christologically defective tendency are seen in certain types of liberation theology.

40. See *Contra Gentiles,* III, 10, no. 1944: "Vitium morale in sola actione consideratur, non autem in aliquo effectu producto: nam virtutes morales non sunt factivae, sed activae." (Moral vice is considered in action alone, and not in any effect produced, because moral virtues are not productive but active.)

41. See *De Malo,* q. 2, a. 2: "Peccatum non est deformitas, sed actus deformis. Deformitas autem actus est per hoc quod discordat a debita regula rationis vel legis Dei." (Sin is not the deformity, but rather the deformed act. The deformity of the act consists in its being against the fitting rule of reason, or the law of God).

42. See B. Schüller, *Die Begründung sittlicher Urteile,* pp. 299ff. It is surprising how Schüller neglects his supposedly so important distinction between "morally good" and "morally right" when he defines virtue: he describes the foundation of virtue as "the phenomenon of a free decision of the human being for a morally good or bad, morally right or wrong, behavior" (p. 300). Is the free decision of virtue related to the morally *good* or the morally *right*? Schüller appears to have split the concept of moral virtue into a "morally good fundamental attitude," on the one side, and a "right manner of acting," on the other.

43. For the generic definition of human virtues that also includes the intellectual virtues, see *I–II,* q. 55, a. 2.

44. Something else that appears to go unnoticed by Schüller is the way his doctrine implicitly recalls the voluntaristic conception of Duns Scotus (which then becomes rigoristic) that only the *will* is the seat of moral virtues. According to this position, virtue perfects only the will, but not the sensitive appetites. These latter would not, then, attain to their own perfection as a participation in the rationality of the "politically ruling" part of the soul (Aristotle) but would, rather, as powers that always remain *immanently* irrational, be subject to a "despotic" mastery of the reason.

45. The last clause of Augustine's definition applies only to the infused virtues; in the *Commentary on the Sentences,* Thomas had already reduced the first part to the Aristotelian definition of virtue, which would remain his standard definition (see *In II Sent.,* d. 27, q. 1, a. 2).

46. See, for example, *I–II,* q. 20, a. 3, arg. 2, taken over from *Nichomachean Ethics,* II, 5, 1106a15–17 and 23–24; *I–II,* q. 56, a. 3. Thomas makes the further comment here that this definition really applies only to moral virtue, since it makes man good in the strict sense (*simpliciter bonum*), or morally good.

47. Only *as a consequence* does the choosing [*electio*] also shape the

intention, which *either is formed on the basis of* a *habitus* of choosing, or *is* this habit itself.

48. See *I–II*, q. 58, a. 2: "Sicut appetitus est principium humani actus secundum quod participat aliqualiter rationem, ita habitus moralis habet rationem virtutis humanae, inquantum rationi conformatur" (Just as appetition is the principle of the human act insofar as it participates in the reason in some way, so moral virtue has the nature of human virtue insofar as it is conformed to reason.)

49. In addition to the passages already cited, see *I–II,* q. 59, a. 4: "Moral virtue perfects the appetitive part of the soul by ordering [*ordinando*] it toward the good of the reason. And the good of the reason is that which is ordered or governed [*moderatum seu ordinatum*] according to reason. Therefore, concerning everything that happens to be ordered and governed [*ordinari et moderari*] by the reason, there exists a moral virtue [*contingit esse virtutem moralem*]. Now the reason does not only order the passions [*passiones*] of the sensitive appetite, it also orders the operations [*operationes*] of the intellective appetite, which is the will, and not subject to passion, as said above." Ibid., q. 60, a. 5: "The perfection of virtue depends on the reason"; q. 61, a. 2: "The formal principle of virtue, of which we are now speaking, is the good of the reason [*bonum rationis*]"; *II–II* , q. 58, a. 3 (on determining the "virtuous character" of justice): "The human act is rendered good by its attaining to the rule of reason, according to which human actions are justified." See also ibid., a. 8.

50. This relationship has significance for that most fundamental distinction between the good and the bad habit (*habitus bonus* or *malus*): see *I–II*, q. 54, a. 3: "A good *habitus* is that which disposes someone to an act that suits [*convenientem*] the nature of an agent; a bad *habitus* disposes to an act that is unsuitable. Just as acts of the virtues suit human nature, because they are in accord with reason [*eo quod sunt secundum rationem*], so acts of the vices, since they are against nature, are discordant with human nature. And thus it is clear that *habitus* are distinguished by type according to the difference between good and bad."

51. It seems good to distinguish further between only "bad" actions and, *beyond that,* "evil" actions; so long as they are voluntary, both types can be considered culpable actions and, thus, moral transgressions. Merely "bad" actions (willfully wrong because of consent) can be equated with "sin by weakness" (*peccatum ex debilitate*); evil actions (willfully wrong because of deliberate purpose), with "sin by choice" or "malice." A theft made out of weakness when an opportunity presents itself is not as bad or wrong as that of the theft of a professional burglar. The former thief behaves badly of course, and is culpable, but he does

not possess the vice of injustice; the latter is habitually bad and is really a criminal (see *II–II*, q. 59, a. 2). Schüller's distinction makes this differentiation inapplicable, and leads in the end to an intolerable moral rigorism; the only escape from such rigorism would be to claim that whoever has *not* acted out of "free determination" (and that means deliberately and with a malicious intention), *never* acts morally badly or errs culpably.

52. See *Nichomachean Ethics*, III, 6, 1113a30–34: "The virtuous person judges everything rightly, and in everything the truth is apparent to him. For each *habitus* there are special things that are fine and pleasant, and the virtuous person differs from others most of all, perhaps, in this ability to see the truth in each thing, so that he is the *canon* and measure of things." But whoever does not possess this order in the soul—in whom *logos*, or reason, does not have the mastery—"is deceived by pleasure, which appears to be a good without being so." Everything appears good to someone according to the state of the person's soul, and people want to do what appears good. Virtue is what ensures that the seeming good is also the *real* good. The virtuous one participates in the cognitive infallibility of the reason in his appetites; he judges rightly by inclination and is therefore himself the rule and measure of the good. He always does what is good, rejoices in doing so, and lives in complete harmony and peace with himself, whereas the vicious person, while doing what appears to him as good, nevertheless lives in discord with his conscience and is plagued by its "gnawing," and if he stays in this state, he will, as a rule, become *strengthened* in the habit of neglecting reason. This leads in the end to what theologians, following Scripture, have called "the sin against the Holy Spirit."

53. See *In II Rom.*, lect. 3, no. 217. This is related to the natural law as well (no. 216): "quod est lumen rationis naturalis, in qua est imago Dei."

54. In this context the special character of the virtue of truthfulness or sincerity (*veracitas*) is treated, and so is the fundamental wrongness of lying, its opposite.

55. It is fulfilled in the intellectual virtue of *sapientia*; in relation to it, *prudentia* (itself dependent on the existence of moral virtue) stands as a "ministress" (*ministra*): "introducit enim ad eam, praeparans ei viam, sicut ostiarius ad regem" (*I–II*, q. 66, a. 5, ad 1um). See also *De Card. Virt.*, q. 1, a.1: "Actio moralis est ostium, per quod ad contemplationem sapientiae intratur." (Moral action is like a door, through which there is an entrance to the contemplation of wisdom.)

56. See *I–II*, q. 66, a. 4: "In general [*simpliciter*], virtue is considered greater, according as a greater good of the reason is reflected in it [*relucet*], as has been said above; accordingly, justice is preeminent among all the

moral virtues, as it is closer to the reason [*tamquam propinquior rationi*]. And this holds true in regard to the subject as well as the object. In regard to the subject, because it is in the will [*in voluntate*] as its subject, for the will is the rational appetite, as is clear from what has been said. But in regard to its object or 'subject matter,' it is so because it is concerned with the operations, by which man is ordered not just in relation to himself but also to others."

57. Karl Rahner posed a question in this regard that is very revealing of his position ("Das Verhältnis von Natur und Gnade"): "One must inquire why a supernatural goal could be set for man that would not destroy his nature, and why God could not do this with a subhuman creature." This question, as well as the solution he offers with his "supernatural existential" that is supposed to ground all personal recourse to God, show immediately that Rahner cannot avoid identifying nature *as such* with what he calls the "subhuman." Further, his (now very widespread) erroneous and spiritualistic opposition between human "nature" and "personality" is thus revealed as mistaken in its grasp of the concept of human nature, in which the *imago*, along with reason, is *constitutively* present. Human nature, understood rightly, is the basis of the functional self-governance of man, which can be called *personal autonomy*.

# 8

# "Teleological Ethics"(I): Utilitarianism and the Deontology/Teleology Distinction

## "Utilitarianism": An Escape From The Irrational?

For a comprehensive critique of so-called "teleological" ethics, the essential points of departure arise from a normative ethics that, as an ethics of *virtue*, has for its object the *human being*, and not an abstract analysis of "goods" and "values" weighed against one another.[1]

We did not arrive at this conception of ethics by holding that man must "realize" an "essence" known theoretically by metaphysical analysis. Rather, we have attempted to show how the starting point of ethics consists in the immediate, personal experience of the practical reason—an experience that can be reflectively understood and then widened, through metaphysical analysis, into a comprehensive anthropology, which in turn provides an understanding of ethics as a doctrine of moral virtue. The axis upon which the entire ethical–philosophical enterprise turns is the practical reason, recognized thereby to have the character of a law and measure.

Now, as an alternative to a "traditional" form of normative ethics, so-called "teleological ethics" (or "proportionalism") has credibility only because its "teleologism" is built upon—and draws the ultimate consequences of—an uncriticized (and "traditional") *physicalism*. In order to show that "teleological" ethics is merely the utilitarian variant of traditional "irrationality" (physicalism) or of the "naturalistic fallacy," it will be necessary to begin with a brief explanation of utilitarianism.

In making this identification, I do not assert that teleological ethics teaches such reprehensible doctrines as "the end justifies the means" or "the good is what is useful"; Bruno Schüller has rightly opposed the idea that these popular conceptions underlie "teleological utilitarianism." Indeed, what is commonly understood as "utilitarian" does not exactly correspond to the original philosophical import of the word.

## Classical Utilitarianism

### *"Utilitarianism": A Deceptive Name*

According to John Stuart Mill, actions have the character of "utility" when they promote happiness.[2] Actions, then, are morally good or bad according as their consequences promote happiness or hinder it. It is immediately apparent—as critics of utilitarianism have always pointed out—that the problem of this formula is not with "utility" nor with "consequences," but rather with "happiness": what criterion is being used to define it? The name "utilitarianism" is itself deceptive in a way, because it distracts attention from the fundamental thesis of the doctrine. The intention of "utilitarianism" as such was to understand ethics in a manner opposed to that of an intuitional or sentimentalist ethics that held that *feeling*, as an infallible "moral sense," determines what one should do. The utilitarians, in contrast, were concerned to point out that in order for someone to know what actions were morally right, *rational consideration* was required: one must *think* about the cause-and-effect relationship between action and purpose, about the "usefulness" (utility) of an action for the attainment of its goal.

Now so far, the "useful" is really not different from what Aristotle called *tò sýmpheron* and Thomas, the *actio debita, conveniens*, or *proportionata fini*—the fitness of the means (an action) toward the attainment of an end.[3] "Utility" as a moral criterion is certainly not unique to utilitarianism.

The problem with the "utilitarian" concept of utility (although most contemporary proportionalists seem not to be aware of this) is that utilitarianism is a eudaemonistic ethics without a theory of happiness: it simply lacks a criterion for human *eudaimonia*. Historically, this lack has its origin in Benthamism, and has long affected the question of the connection between "utility" and "practical truth." The best illustration of the defect can be found in Mill himself, not because the British philosopher was unaware of the problem, but precisely because his attempts to defend the utility principle were driven by the desire to provide just such a connection between utility and truth—to ground the concept of utility as an "objective" moral principle—and to do this without betraying the basic utilitarian position of his teacher Bentham. It would seem worthwhile at this point to sketch something of the problematic of utility and practical truth in utilitarianism, in order to set in a clearer light the weakness, on the one side, of contemporary proportionalist moral justification, and the strength, on the other side, of an Aristotelian ethics.

### *J. Bentham and Social Eudaemonism*

Bentham begins his *Introduction to the Principles of Morals and Legislation* with lapidary prose: "Nature has placed mankind under the governance of two sovereign masters, *pain* and *pleasure*." These two empirically undeniable principles determine what we should do.[4] Since every human being strives toward pleasure, or happiness, and flees pain, there is only one rational position to take: to recognize our natural subordination to, or conditioning by, this law, and to pursue human well-being by means of reason and law.[5] Thus the "good" is what is necessary for happiness (pleasure), and "bad" is what is opposed to this. According to the empirical pleasure principle, the "good" is the "rational" because it is "useful" for happiness. The reason is here merely a means or instrument for the determination of what is useful for happiness. The actual criterion for the morality of an act is the relation of *utility* between that action and happiness.

Bentham is taking a "natural," empirically verified fact for his starting point: man is subject to the mastery of a natural tendency to experience pleasure (and by no means is this pleasure confined to "sensual" pleasure: it also includes the pleasure spiritual good can bring). Utilitarianism seeks to find the criterion for moral rectitude under the conditions of satisfaction/dissatisfaction. The criterion is the principle of utility: the good is what is useful for well-being (satisfaction). An action is good if its *consequence* is well-being, but, as Bentham emphasizes, not the well-being of the individual but that of the greatest possible number of people in a given society. There are, then, a total of four principles in Benthamism: the pleasure principle, the utility principle, the consequence principle, and the social principle.[6]

The question that now arises is, How can I distinguish between "what I *want* to do" (what pleases me, what is "useful") and "what I *ought* to do"? Is it possible to win through to the concept of the useful on this basis, independently of the limitations of my own subjectivity? Is whatever *appears* pleasurable the same as that which indeed promotes happiness (i.e., is it *truly* pleasurable)? Or must the problem even arise? Isn't it enough to satisfy the empirical attraction toward pleasure in order to attain happiness?

The truth of the matter is that Bentham did not pose such questions. These are questions that arise in an ethics concerned to discover what human happiness *is*, to discover wherein lies the true realization of human existence as such. Bentham was concerned with finding moral criteria for making laws in the context of society. Benthamism, and utilitarianism in general, was in its original form a *social ethics*, or an ethics of social reform for the *praxis* of legislation; it can be called "social eudaemonism."

This is precisely why the original form of utilitarianism set aside (or did not even pose) the question about the fundamental moral principle, or about the "measure" of morality. In fact, for Bentham the reason possesses only an instrumental character, but in this "instrumentality" it can never be a "standard" for the moral; it remains, as pure "rationality," a mere organ with the function of judging actions according to their consequences for happiness. When it comes to actions, only the *telos* itself could have a "measuring" role. In this case, however, the "*telos*" is such (desire, and its satisfaction) that it must necessarily fail in this task, since every pleasure, both the desire for it and the attainment of it, is a subjective perception. Every morality—even utilitarianism—seeks a principle that is independent of "*my* feeling," or at least seeks to bring "my feeling" into harmony with the truly good or useful. If this were not the case, there would be no need for an ethics, but only for laws effective enough to protect people from one another in their search for "happiness."

It is revealing that for Bentham neither the reason nor the *telos* (satisfaction of desire) is capable of exercising a measure-giving function. Pleasure is something subjective and relational: it is objective only as a natural–empirical fact, and not in its axiological character. Utility is likewise something relational: the "useful" is constituted by way of the *telos*. But now we have an equation with two unknowns and only one conceivable constant: the natural fact of the desire for pleasure. In its origin, therefore, utilitarianism is primarily naturalistic, and there is no rational support for its derivation of "I *ought* to do this" from "I *want* to do this."

But the Benthamist ethics nevertheless still aims at *objectivity*: it still claims to provide objective criteria for "good" and "bad." But it can do this only on the basis of the *social* principle: the criterion or standard for the well-being or (subjective) pleasure attainment of the greatest number, the "community." The objectivity of Benthamist ethics is thus an objectivity of the "majority," which makes for a "sociological" and "historical" objectivity; the question about happiness, or in what happiness "truly" consists, becomes superfluous. To be happy is to "feel that one is happy," and the largest possible number of people attaining to this is the criterion for utility—for the "moral rectitude" of a certain kind of behavior, or of a law.

It should seem very obvious here that this grounding of the "objectivity" of the good only circumvents the really fundamental question of ethics: the question about the connection between the utility (of an action) and truth. To put it more exactly: What grounds the *goodness* of the "useful"? Nobody would dispute that the good is always useful in an *ethical* sense—for that is the classical meaning of *utilitas*.[7] But in order for what is useful to be good (and thereby *truly* useful), the *telos* must be understood under its aspect of "good": only then will we have a concept of the "useful" that is in every case related to the "good"—a "useful," in other words, that comes to be through agreement with *right* appetition (or striving) for the *telos*—and is thus *practically* true, or true *by practical reasoning*.

Recourse to the social principle, of course, obviates having to deal with this question. To determine the morality of an action, something further is needed: all the consequences of that action for the whole of the given society must be taken into account; the person who acts needs to have a view of the "entire social context"—something he is naturally incapable of having. This can lead to the recognition that an ethics that aspires to provide standards not only for the legislator but also for the individual person must be able to provide a criterion for the morally good that is in fact independent of the "sum total of possible social consequences."

### *Mill and the Problem of the Relation Between Utility and Truth*

The problem of the relation between utility and truth became virulent in Mill's attempts to found an ethics on the basis of utilitarianism. In response to the objection that it is impossible always to act in view of the general interests of society, Mill explained that this "social principle" is only a *motive* for actions, not the standard or rule for them. Although this was to revolutionize Bentham's position, he maintained that ethics must teach us what our duties are and how we can know them.[8] In his efforts to found an ethics on the basis of the Benthamist principles, Mill explains that the motive (the utility of the greatest number) has nothing to do with the morality of an action, but only indicates something about the worthiness of the agent.[9] In fact, Mill searched for a criterion of the moral quality of human actions *independent* of the sum total of social consequences, and *independent* of the motives and intentions of the person acting. Nevertheless, it is apparent that he was not aware of what might be implied by this way of posing the problem.

Mill set himself the task of working out a criterion of truth for the concept of utility. This involved marking out the field of the "useful" in such a way as to permit the definition of an action as good independently of *other* possible consequences. This meant that he would have to set aside, at least in part, the principle of pleasure, maintained by Bentham in its purely empirical actuality. Mill started by discussing the natural feelings and inclinations of man, and indeed the very question of what human nature is.[10] He displays a whole "palette" of natural inclinations, saying that they must all be subordinated, finally, to the higher instincts or inclinations of human intelligence.[11] Using associative psychology, Mill grounds the formation of these inclinations even as far as the concept of virtue.

In the end, the concept of utility flows into the concept of virtue, which then becomes the essence of "happiness." And happiness is no abstract idea, but rather a "concrete whole" (ch. IV), the formal principle on the basis of which everything is desired; what someone desires is desired not only as a means to happiness but also as a component of it. Here is the final proof for the principle of utility: the fact that all human beings necessarily strive after a goal, and that this goal is happiness.[12] This is a matter of experience, which is based on evidence and is comprehended only by reflection, self-observation, and the observation of others.

Now what for Aristotle was the *starting point* of the search for the standard of morality—the fact that everyone seeks happiness—is for Mill the *standard itself.* The pursuit of happiness presents itself empirically as a pursuit of pleasure. Mill does not get beyond this definition, even though he tries to counter the subjectivity of such a pursuit, seeking objective criteria for its "naturalness" and suitability by way of an empirical, associative-psychological anthropology.

If Mill had understood more metaphysics, and a philosophical anthropology based upon metaphysics, he could have overcome Benthamist utilitarianism and eventually made his way to a more "Aristotelian" approach. Much of what Mill says is quite solid; much not only "sounds" Aristotelian but is actually inspired by Aristotle. Unlike Bentham (who had written "It is not necessary to consult Plato, nor Aristotle"), Mill had indeed read Aristotle, and the form of his ethics is very indebted to the ancient philosopher. But the retention of the Benthamist principles prevented correction, and Mill's ethics remained inconsistent and, in a way, "bifurcated."

What Mill particularly failed to do was to differentiate the concept of the good, as the aspect under which everything is desired, from the concept of pleasure: the good as the formal object (or goal) of all striving or appetition remains identified with "what gives pleasure"—and this means adopting the tradition of hedonism.[13] That the "good" as the object of the reason (*bonum rationis*) can empirically and psychologically be shown as also at times *not* being under the aspect of the "pleasurable," is never considered, nor is the fact that the "pleasure bringing" (*delectabile*), even though it belongs to what is good, is not necessarily an intentional object, but is often only a side effect. Mill remains trapped in the idea that the reason is only an instrument, and overlooks its character as the goal, as the *telos*. Thus even the "practical good" and moral action also have only an instrumental character. Despite his efforts, Mill could not succeed in grounding moral action as a component of happiness.

To accomplish that, it would have been necessary for utilitarianism to define the concept of the moral good on the basis of an anthropological analysis of the *telos*, and would have required distinguishing the *truly* pleasurable from what is only *apparently* so. In this way, one would arrive at an anthropologically founded concept of happiness and virtue. This would make it possible to interpret actions and their "utility" *anthropologically*, that is, in their constitutive function in relation to the end. And that, in turn, would enable an understanding of the empirical fact that the first principle is not "Pleasure is what every man desires," but rather "The good is what all things seek" (*bonum est quod omnia appetunt*). Finally, the concept of the *true* good, as distinguished from the *seeming* good, could be shown to be the specific and practical object of the reason, as the *bonum rationis*. But then utilitarianism would not be utilitarianism; indeed, it was never such on the basis of "utility" anyway, but only by the identification of the good as such with the "pleasurable."

Aristotle was well aware of the crucial importance, for ethics, of the phenomenon of pleasure (*hedonê*). He clearly recognized that good action, especially virtue, had something to do with pleasure and its opposite. The good, which always "seems" good, appears also as "the pleasant," "the enjoyable," or the "useful," about which, however, only the virtuous person judges rightly.[14] The two feelings of pleasure and pain are "thus the cardinal points of our entire theory, for it is no small matter for actions whether they are rightly or wrongly experienced as pleasurable or painful" (*Nichomachean Ethics*, II, ch. 2, 1105a5–6).

The question about the *rectitude* of the perception of pleasure remains unexamined in Bentham's and Mill's utilitarianism, leaving the doctrine trapped in a naturalistic–empiricistic phenomenalism. The same holds for the concepts of "consequence" and the "useful." What is the *truly* useful (because *truly* good)? What consequences of an action are constitutive of happiness, as opposed to other consequences? What is "moral" action or "human action," in general? A utilitarian ethics has never been able to answer these questions, nor have contemporary "proportionalism" and "teleologism," which are utilitarian for the precisely the same reasons.

The decisive characteristic of all forms of utiliarianism is the lack of a metaphysically and anthropologically grounded concept of the *bonum humanum*—itself the principle of all "utility"—as the good brought about in man himself by moral action. The "teleological" ethics practiced by many Catholic moral theologians of the present day is a utilitarian ethics, as can now be verified in detail.

## "Deontology" and "Teleology": A False Disjunction

A distinction of ethical theories into "deontological" and "telelogical" has now become familiar. A deontological ethics, it is maintained, judges the moral quality of actions *independently* of their consequences, whereas teleological ethics judges actions in the light of their consequences, and is thus also known in the English-speaking world as "consequentialism."

Probably no one will maintain a "pure form" of teleological ethics, that is, without any admixture of deontological elements. If we confine ourselves to the teleology of Catholic moral theologians, a position generally held is that the final goal of all human action cannot itself be teleologically grounded, and second, that teleological justifications can ultimately be formulated "deontologically" (as "duty").

Nevertheless, it is also held that there are "milder" and "harsher" forms of deontology, the former having some degree of regard for consequences and the latter *morally qualifying* a certain number of human actions in complete independence from their consequences. Such a position, it is maintained, was at the basis of traditional Catholic moral theology, with its absolute prohibitions of such actions as contraception, abortion, and lying.

Now this sharp separation between "teleological" and "deontological" seems to me misleading, and not only when used as a hard-and-fast disjunction (which no proportionalist will do anyway.) But it is false *even as a distinction* between two types of norm justification. "Teleology" and "deontology" do not ground two types of *justification* of normative statements, but rather two different *levels of involvement* with such statements. To put it concisely: every ethical theory, insofar as it works with discursive justifications, is necessarily "teleological," and every theory is at the same time "deontological" insofar as it frames the results of its justificational discourse in normative statements such as "this is what must be done . . ." and then, as in many cases, proceeds to find *further* reasons for the unconditionality of this "ought."

A "teleological" ethicist, then, would say, "Action *x* is good [i.e., "should be done"], or is my duty [*deontological* formulation], because . . ." (*teleological* justification). On the other hand, how could we imagine, by contrast, a so-called "deontological" ethicist who would say, "Action *x* is always, under all conditions, bad," *without* adding "because . . ."?

Those who claim that there is a deontological type of norm justification assume that the deontologist speaks only in tautologies: "*X* is always wrong, because one may not do *x*," or ". . . because *x* is forbidden," or ". . . because *x* is against the will of God," or ". . . because I have no right to do *x*," and so forth. To maintain the existence of a deontological type of norm justification is to maintain that there is a type of norm justification that states: "One may never do *x*, because *x* is always forbidden." But this would not even be a justification, only an expression in the form of a normative declaration. And at this level, even a "teleological" ethics could be considered "deontological," since a "teleologist" can form sentences as follows: "*X* is always wrong, since *x* always has bad consequences for everyone concerned."

The above sentence intends a "deontologically" absolute prohibition: if it is true that "*X* is always bad," what is meant is that "*X* brings a consequence that is always bad," or that "action *x* is defined precisely by a consequence that is immanent in it, and that is always bad." The so-called "deontologists" are distinguished from the so-called "teleologists" not by the fact that they do not consider consequences, but (1) by what they consider as "consequences" and (2) by the criteria according to which they judge them. To be more precise: a "deontologist" argues exactly like a "teleologist," except that he has a criterion for distinguishing between those consequences which are constitutive of the moral value of an action, and are thus *always* at issue, and those consequences for which such is not the case. And he possesses this criterion because his concept of actions and their consequences has an anthropological commitment. The so-called deontologist, unlike the teleologist, is able to identify those consequences which are constitutive for the moral qualification, for the "definition" or "specification" of an action. He can thus attain to an identification of the morally objective connection of consequences, or of a context that constitutes the human meaning of single actions, which he can then distinguish from nonconstitutive consequences, in the context of which such actions may be embedded without being constituted by them in their fundamentally *human* meaning.

If, then, it is maintained that the formulation "*X* is always morally bad" is specifically deontological, it is being assumed that whoever says this *means* that "doing *x*" is without consequences—since such a person is supposed to be judging actions independently of their consequences. But this is absurd. If someone says, "*X* is always bad," it is not meant that "doing *x* is without any consequences, but still bad because of other criteria," but rather that "doing *x* indeed has a consequence—one that cannot be accepted, no matter what other consequences may be foreseen." This consequence is the destruction of the constitutive conditions for the fundamentally human or moral significance of the human action in question.

## Anthropological Differentiation of "Consequences"

So-called "deontological" norm justification exists where one would least suspect it: the ethical theories characterized as "deontological" are in fact based on a differentiated, anthropologically grounded teleology, whereas so-called "teleological ethics" works with an anthropologically *undifferentiated* concept of "consequences."[15] To put it more precisely: the "deontological" theories have in themselves a criterion for the moral qualification or ranking of "consequences," whereas "teleological" theories, in the tradition of utilitarianism, are only capable of judging any consequence in the context of *all* possible consequences. For the deontologist there are consequences that morally qualify an action independently of other consequences; for the teleologist every consequence is in principle a "premoral" quantity. The deontologist brings the criterion of "moral difference" into the concept of consequence, while the teleologist argues physicalistically.[16]

This can be shown in regard to *Humanae Vitae*, which is constantly (and mistakenly) cited as a classical instance of "deontological" argumentation. Its argument is quite openly teleological, with a teleology anchored in the anthropology of married love, specifically, in the anthropological connection between "loving union" and "procreation." As explained in chapter 2, section "Beyond Naturalism and Dualism," the central argument of *Humanae Vitae* is that contraception is wrong because it has *as its consequence* the severance of this connection and the disruption of the whole meaning of married love.[17] Can any other consequences be "weighed" against the fundamental destruction of the meaning of married love? Do not the other consequences acquire the qualification of being "side effects" through this qualifying of the consequences of contraceptive actions? Such consequences are judged in completely different ways when the fundamental meaning of married love is preserved and when it is not preserved, for in the latter case, the distinction (between action-constituting or action-specifying consequences and other, less important kinds of consequences) is not being made.

The conclusion should be clear: every Aristotelian ethics is frankly teleological—that is generally granted. And yet Aristotle himself speaks of actions that are in themselves bad and always wrong (φαῦλα): "Therefore it is never possible to do these things rightly, but rather always to do wrong in doing them. For the question whether they are done rightly or wrongly does not consist in considering, for instance, whether one commits adultery with the right person, or at the right time, or in the right manner, but simply to do anything of this kind is wrong" (*Nichomachean Ethics,* II, 6, 1107a14–17; see also *Eudemian Ethics,* II, 3 1221b19ff.).

Thomas likewise argues teleologically when he maintains that marriage is indissoluble, because its dissolution would have as a consequence that the woman would no longer be the companion, but rather the slave, of the man; that lying is wrong, because it makes human communication, community life, and so on impossible. Drunkenness is morally reprehensible because man loses his dignity as a being who acts according to reason; procreation is permitted only within marriage, because anything else is an injustice against the child, and because any other mode of human procreation would have the consequence that the child would be deprived of the specifically human foundation of his development; and so on. Of all these consequences it can be said that they not only are possible, contingent consequences but also are consequences that are constitutive in a *specifically human manner* for the action in question: they reveal its objective content. To overlook the connection of certain actions with this kind of consequences is to overlook the human meaning of the action (of procreation, speech, etc.).[18] And all other possible consequences, on the other hand, must be weighed on the basis of the real human meaning of actions. Their occurrence can in effect be grounded on the basis of a constitutive, "objective" qualification of consequences that issue from actions of different types of moral behavior, such as self-denial and sacrifice. In their very character as "unpleasant" consequences, they can lead to a deepening of the constitutive meaning of human actions. So, for example, the virtue of honesty is strengthened by refusing to lie in a difficult situation, and that leads not only to the human fulfillment of the individual honest person but also to the well-being of the society. Suffering injustice can itself become a moral value: What would have happened to Western philosophy if Socrates had "weighed" the consequences of his love for truth "on the scale"? Or, to take another example, the so-called "unwanted child," in the context of genuine married love, can become the very proof of the genuineness of that love, and an opportunity for its deepening. All these matters can be "teleologically" established, provided there is firm anchorage in an anthropologically grounded *hierarchy* of consequences.

A "teleological ethics" that does not possess any means of distinguishing between (a) consequences that are constitutive of the action in a moral sense (since they specify the action in question as a human and moral action) and (b) consequences that are only contingent, circumstantial, and possible (and may burden the action or render it more difficult), must necessarily define the object of action at a natural, physicalistic level. The possible contents of actions are then only "premoral" goods, whose moral qualification can be determined only through the whole ensemble of consequences, as "weighed" in a porportionate "assessment of values" (*Güterabwägung*).

Even though the consequences that are constitutive of action are real consequences, they are usually not referred to as such, and this is what leads to the appearance of a "deontologism." In popular language that has now become academic terminology, a "consequence" implies a contingent, situationally conditioned effect of an action. The whole complex of consequences or effects that specify the objectively human or moral content of an action is normally expressed by concepts like "the nature of the act itself." Thus the "nature of speech" in this sense is understood as the ensemble of the consequences and effects that flow from the speech capability of the human spirit and from human sociability, which permit the qualification of certain speech acts as "lies"; the "nature of the marital act" is really the ensemble of consequences and effects that occur within the whole human suppositum, indicating that it is an act of married and fully human love.

So-called "teleological ethics" is a theory that in principle considers *all* consequences as only contingent, circumstantially conditioned, and therefore morally *nonconstitutive*. It proceeds from a radical freedom from moral content, or from an "indifference" toward human actions, in order to reconstitute moral content through a "weighing" of the goods brought about by the consequences.

But questions such as the following emerge: According to what criterion is this "weighing" or "assessment" to be carried out? Must it not again result in a "premoral" good? If not—if, that is, there *are* criteria of value—where do these values come from? For they cannot themselves be teleologically gounded. Finally, how can someone reconstitute a "moral value" from the assessment of a combination of "premoral" goods? The suspicion arises not only that there is a *naturalistic fallacy* hidden in this "teleological ethics" or "proportionalism," but also that there is, in order to make up for the fallacy, a disguised—and extreme—*deontologism*, or "value idealism."

## DEONTOLOGICAL FORMULATIONS, TELEOLOGICAL JUSTIFICATIONS

Schüller calls "teleological" any ethics that gives a priority to the concept of "the good" over the concept of the "ought" (ibid., p. 289). This characterization seems accurate enough: the good has the character of an end, and if the "ought" is grounded in the good, then every "ought" would be treated as the imperative demand to do that which brings about this "good'. According as the action (or nonaction) that effects the good stands in a necessary or contingent context of consequences and circumstances, an imperative will be formulated in the mode of "I ought to" ("I ought not to") or "I may, am allowed to" ("I do not have to"). These are instances of deontological *formulations* (normative statements) of practical judgments that have been *teleologically* grounded.

### *Two Levels of Involvement with Normative Statements*

A "strict" deontologism, which, in Schüller's view, Catholic moral theology was supposed to have represented, would maintain that the "goodness" of an action is based upon the "oughtness" of the action. That such an approach is inconsistent has already been shown. But we should be careful not to get lost in our use of words. In the framework of a teleological ethics, which grounds the ought upon the good, the following would hold: action *x* is good because it ought to be done, that is, it corresponds to what one should do here and now. Here and now, one should do *x*, because *x* leads to the accomplishment of a definite good, because *x* is good. In brief: to do *x* is good precisely because one should do *x*; and one should do *x* because it is good to do *x*.

Now this is not circular reasoning because the word "good" is being used in two different senses. First, it is used deontologically—for *formulation* and *exposition* (not justification) of a normative statement. It means that what is really good is what one should do. If one does not do what one should, then one acts badly, that is, one acts contrary to that which one has recognized as obliging. Or it could be said that one acts against one's conscience.

In the second instance, "good" is used for the teleological *justification* of the ought: what one should do, one should do *because* it is good, that is, because it is what brings about good. "To do good," then, has two meanings: (1) to do what one should (otherwise, one acts against conscience) and (2) to do what one should because it is good (because otherwise one would behave immorally).

This could also be formulated in another way, if it is assumed that what one "should do" because it is good in each case corresponds, in the moral sense, to the nature of man or to the will of God. Or, because one is not justified in *not* doing what one should do because it is good, since everything that one should do because it is good corresponds to the will of God.

Accordingly, if someone deontologically *formulates* (i.e., does not justify) that one should do something because it corresponds to the will of God or to nature, or because one is not justified in acting otherwise, and that such behavior is thereby morally "good," then the teleological *justification* is presupposed: one should do it, in other words, *because it corresponds to the will of God or to nature*; or one cannot be justified in doing otherwise, because it is good, *as teleologically grounded.*

Teleology and deontology are not, then, two different forms of the *justification* of norms; rather, they correspond to two different levels or aspects of the approach to normative statements. The formulation of a normative statement as an "ought" is deontological: for example, one may not do what one ought not to do, that is, what is not good. Otherwise, one would act against the conscience or against the will of God, which indeed is recognized on the basis of what is good; or, similarly, one would act against nature, or because one is not justified in doing so. The recourse to nature, to the will of God, or to the failure to be justified is only an "intensification" and putting-into-order of the deontological formulation, but not a *justification* of the ought. Such deontological formulations have a grounding function, but only in another respect. Namely (and this is domething that Schüller also correctly points out), for an admonition, that is, for justifying why one "does what one should," or that what someone has *recognized* in a judgment of the conscience as an "ought to do," one ought *actually* to do; otherwise, how could the ought have an unconditional claim, one that is independent of consequences or other circumstances? In other words, the deontological "use" of normative statements serves to justify why only *those* actions are morally "good" (in the first of the two senses) that correspond to what has been recognized as an "ought-to-do." Such deontological formulations are especially frequent in texts intended for instruction, admonition, or (in the case of the Church's magisterium) for the authoritative exposition of moral norms. And usually in the following form: let no one think that what one should do because it is good, one should not always do; one would otherwise act "against human nature" or "against the will of God" or "without justification," and such an action could never be morally good.[19]

To sum up: the argument of Schüller and these who follow him plays on the ambiguous meaning of "good": it apparently escapes notice that there are deontological formulations about moral norms that intend to show that only an action which respects the "ought" is good, because in this "ought" the claims of human nature, or of the will of God, are ultimately expressed. Nor is it further acknowledged that such deontological statements can be made without any compromising of the fact that the "ought" that they contain has itself been teleologically grounded. In other words, independently of the deontological statement, it has in fact been established why action *x* represents an "ought," or why it corresponds to "nature" or to the "will of God."

Some authors may have been content with deontological formulations, where justifications were called for. But Schüller goes much too far in assuming that the deontological formulations of the "tradition" have in general been meant as *justifications* of a "deontological" kind, and that they were meant be taken as such. In fact, a few examples will suffice to show that Schüller's view is unfounded. The examples he cites fall into three classes: (1) simple citations of deontological formulations that are merely *assumed* to be "justifications"; (2) Schüller's own (imagined) "reconstructions" of an argument; (3) statements that do in fact justify something, but *not what they are cited as justifying.*

### *The Critique of the Formula, "Prohibited Because It Is Against Nature"*

We can observe an example of the first category, where Schüller claims to see the fallacy "prohibited because it is against nature" in the position taken by Pius XII about the impermissibility of artificial insemination: "One should not forget: only the conception of a new life that is according to the will and plan of the Creator includes the realization of the intended goals to a wonderful degree of perfection. It is at the same time fitting for the bodily and spiritual nature and dignity of the spouses as well as for the normal and happy development of the child."[20]

Now according to Schüller, the (fallacious) "traditional" argument here is as follows: the physiological fact of sterility in a certain case is just as much a sign of the will of God as fertility is in most cases. The natural givens "sterility" and "fruitfulness" are expressions of the will and plan of the Creator. The given facts of nature reflect the intentions of God. So Schüller concludes, the argument is that "married persons who can have a child only through artificial insemination must understand that God intended childlessness as their destiny. And as painful as it is, they must nevertheless come to this realization: *God knows better than we do whether it is good for us to have a child or not*" (*Die Begründung sittlicher Urteile,* p. 227).

Now the question at this point is not whether artifical insemination is bad or good, but only how this is justified in the quotation. Schüller contends that the recourse to the will and plan of the Creator has the function of a (deontological) norm justification: the will of God is understood as expressed in "physiological givens," so that acting "against nature" is not permitted.

That such an interpretation is more than questionable immediately becomes clear when one considers the difference between deontological–parainetic *formulation* and teleological *justification.* The meaning of the quoted text is that there is a definite order of human procreation that corresponds to "the bodily and spiritual nature and dignity of the spouses, as well as to the normal and happy development of the child." This order is suited to the natural mode of human procreation. If someone were to replace it with an artificial technique, the fully human meaning of married love and the transmission of human life would be lost. The question is not, as Schüller assumes, "childlessness—yes or no?" but rather, "What price would one have to pay in order to overcome the problem of childlessness?" With a solution such as artificial insemination, the price would be the destruction of the fully human meaning of the transmission of life. Schüller, however, looks at the problem as only the question "What can be done to have a child in spite of the failure of physiological function?" In other words, he avoids posing the moral question, and considers the situation as a solely physiological and technical problem. The physicalistic premise is here completely on the side of Schüller, and not on the side of the magisterium.

It is only on this basis of the teleological context of human love, marital unity, and procreation that the will and plan of the Creator can be recognized. And this explains the deontological and paraiinetic formulation: only when we attend to the will and plan of the Creator's wisdom can we reach the intended goal (human procreation) in a manner that corresponds to human dignity. Behind this stands an entire anthropology of married love, and it is this, and not simply "recourse" to the Creator or to nature, that has the function of justifying the norm.

### *The Critique of the Argument About "The Frustration of Natural Purposes"*

A second example—this time, of an imaginary "reconstruction" of inconclusive arguments—has to do with acts that are considered "unnatural" because they frustrate natural purposes. Schüller asks himself, "How does the tradition arrive at the impermissibility of *every* intentional frustration of these purposes? . . . Man created neither his language nor his sexuality—both appear to have been given to him by God (by nature). According to the traditional viewpoint, man must be prohibited, even in the interest of values that may seem more important to him, from frustrating God-given purposes. Why? The only plausible answer—at least at first sight—seems to be the following: *God (or nature) knows better than man himself what will turn out better for man in the long run;*

*God (or nature) simply has the superior wisdom and understanding.*" And Schüller adds: "I am not in a position to say whether the actual argument has to be reconstructed in precisely this fashion."[21]

So, then, must it be so reconstructed? Schüller's reconstruction is in fact plausible, but again, only under the assumption of a physicalistic interpretation of the concept of "natural purpose," and that implies an equally physicalistic treatment of "speech" and "sexuality," for Schüller argues as follows: "A clock and a book also have their essence in a determination of purpose. Nevertheless, nobody thinks that every nonpurposeful use of a clock or a book is impermissible. And why not? Probably for this reason: that it has been entrusted to man to judge whether one value that has been created by him should be sacrificed to another, higher or more urgent value."

But "man did not create either his language or his sexuality: both appear to have been given him by God (or by nature)." Thus man is not justified in "using" them contrary to their purposes.

The difference between a clock or a book and human speech or sexuality consists only, according to this "reconstruction," in the fact that the former are made by man, while the latter are "given" to man. Man may not change the purposes of what he has not created himself. And so on. The reconstruction assumes that language and sexuality are physical things like a book or a clock that are "used"; since they are "given in nature," their "naturalness" is assumed to constitute their moral unchangeability. Schüller is assuming a physicalistic interpretation of the concept of "natural purpose," and the result, of course, is a physicalistic argument.

Now if Schüller seems incapable of detecting the naturalistic presuppositions of his own argument, it may be because he is working within the framework of a dualistic anthropology, as will become apparent in the following passage. There is a first, correct meaning of "according to nature" (*naturgemäß*): (1) "according to the purposeful determination of a personal being, that is, morally good (right)." A possible synonym for this is "human" (*human, menschlich*). If someone should say of true statements that they are according to nature (or natural), and of false statements that they are contrary to nature, the object of these predications is not *man*, but his *language*. "According to nature" (*naturgemäß*) in this second sense would mean "according to language" (*sprachgemäß*), and "contrary to nature," in a second sense, would mean "contrary to language" (*sprachwidrig*). The same thing would hold if the adjectives *natural* and *unnatural* were used to describe a particular realization of the sexual act or a particular use of the corporeal organs of the human body. Insofar as one cannot simply identify man, as a personal being, with his language, with the sexual act, or with one of his bodily organs, so one certainly may not assume that a particular action, because it is contrary to language or to sexuality, is for that reason "contrary to the definition of man as a personal being" or "morally wrong" (Schüller, "Neuere Beiträge zum Thema, 'Begründung sittlicher Normen,' " p. 147).

This "assumption," indeed, would only go along with a naturalistic interpretation of human sexuality and language. These would both be located—as "exterior events"—*beneath* the personal level, or merely as functions of bodily organs, and not in their human sense, in their personal integration in the human *suppositum*. Schüller's anthropology is dualistic and spiritualistic: the "true" man is then the person only as the subjectivity of the spirit; this "personality" determines the morally good or the "human." Whatever is connected to the function of a bodily organ is a natural given, beneath the threshold of the personal, "used" by man for the realization of his "personal" existence (as a book or a clock), and existing for his "free disposal."

Accordingly, what eludes Schüller's notice is, first, that if someone speaks of lying or of certain realizations of the sexual act as "unnatural," the object of these predications is *not* in fact language or sexuality in its physiological "naturalness," but rather *man*. Second, if someone calls, in this context, on the "superior wisdom of God (or nature)," it is because, in the framework of a teleologically grounded ethics and anthropology, he has already established the *human meaning* of language and sexuality. The physicalism, once again, is that of Schüller, who has "reconstructed" the traditional view from a physicalistic perspective.

### *The Critique of Recourse to the "Superior Wisdom of God"*

In Schüller's writings one can also find an example of a third variety of critique, whereby citations are supposed to provide justification for something that in their original context they were never intended to provide. There is a particular sentence from *Humanae Vitae* that has been cited over and over by a wide range of authors—a sentence that allegedly illustrates the naturalistic argumentation of this encyclical: that the natural and physiological laws or regularities of human fruitfulness are themselves the justification for the prohibition against not observing these laws or regularities. The sentence reads as follows: "God has wisely disposed natural laws and rhythms of fecundity which, of themselves, cause a separation in the succession of births" (*Humanae Vitae,* no. 11). Schüller comments as follows: "One gets the impression that this sentence functions as an answer to the following objection: since the marital act, on the one hand, is somehow the necessary expression of the love of the spouses, but, on the other hand, should always have the purpose of creating new life, then this leads, as we know by experience, to overpopulation. Can *that* be the will of the omniscient Creator? No, of course not. *God, in His wisdom, has already seen to it that overpopulation does not have to take place*" ("Neuere Beiträge zum Thema, 'Begründung sittlicher Normen,' " p. 142).

The truth of the matter is that this sentence does *not*, in fact, have the function that Schüller says it has. The sentence has only to be read in its context: the argument serves instead to show that an act, known beforehand to be unfruitful, nevertheless remains "ordered to the conception of human life." Therefore, no one should think that the marital act is morally good *only* when it actually brings forth a human life—in other words, that it is *solely* a means of procreation. Rather, it is also "ordered toward expressing and consolidating the union of the spouses" (*Humanae Vitae,* no. 11). In fact, a key teaching of *Humanae Vitae* is contained in the following quotation from the immediate context: "These acts, by which husband and wife are united in chaste intimacy, and by means of which human life is transmitted, are, as the Council recalled, 'noble and worthy' (see *Gaudium et Spes,* no. 49], and they do not cease to be lawful if, *for causes independent of the will of husband and wife,* they are foreseen to be infecund" (ibid.).

This statement is fundamental for the anthropology of married love that lies at the heart of the encyclical. The justification for what is being said in paragraph 11 appears immediately afterward in paragraph 12: "That teaching, often set forth by the magisterium, is founded upon an inseparable connection, willed by God and unable to be broken by man on his own initiative, between the two meanings of the conjugal act: the unitive meaning and the procreative meaning."[22] The sentence quoted by Schüller, then, has the function only of showing that a marital act foreseen to be unfruitful is nevertheless in accord with the full significance of marital love, because the cause of the infertility does not lie in the will of the spouses, and thus allows the full meaning of spousal joining to be unsullied, as a "human act" (an *actus humanus*) or as a voluntary, personal act.

The quoted passage, furthermore, has nothing to do with the question of "birth control" to prevent overpopulation, as assumed. This question belongs instead to the theme of "responsible parenthood," and when dealing with that question, *Humanae Vitae* did not refer to the "natural laws and regularities" of fertility, but rather to the structure of the marital act as an *actus humanus*, that is, a fully human, voluntary act. Responsible parenthood is carried out either through the generous decision to raise a numerous family or through self-denial (abstinence): in both cases it is a matter of human acts arising from the intellect and will. It has to do formally (or essentially) with acts of married love itself, and not a "technical" intervention that would make these acts inconsequential, and thus alter their human and personal significance.[23]

Sadly, the richness of *Humanae Vitae*'s argument has gone unnoticed by many moral theologians. Usually, physicalistic prejudice or the unconscious adoption of a dualistic–spiritualistic anthropology blinds them to the real value of the arguments. So-called "teleological ethics," in fact, appears, from this standpoint, to have made a virtue out of necessity, bringing a physicalistic interpretation of the object of human actions into moral theology "through the back door," as it were, to take up seemingly "permanent" residence.

## The Naturalistic (Physicalistic) Basis of Teleological Ethics (Proportionalism)

Schüller, we said, was right in saying that an ethics is *teleological* when it gives the concept of the "good" priority over the concept of the "ought." And yet precisely here is where the great weakness of the proportionalist (or "teleological") ethics lies: it knows no concept of the *morally good* that the concept of the "ought" can presuppose.

*On the Distinction Between "Morally Right" and "Morally Good"*

According to Schüller, "The *consequences of an action* means the good and evil that are effected for all concerned. Therefore the teleological (or "proportionalist" or "consequentialist") thinker is one who holds that of two alternative ways of acting, the way that is morally right brings about more net good than the other."[24] Now there are two evaluational terms here: "morally right" and "good." It is clear that the "morally right" determines what someone should do. There will be a priority of the "right" in relation to the "ought." At first, one may think the "right" is simply another name for the "morally good," but Schüller explains why this is not so.

"People are generally in agreement that the conviction and intention of the agent are what determine whether he is morally good or morally bad, whether he is acting morally or immorally. But because of this consensus it is also considered appropriate to direct one's attention to the question of how the moral *rightness* of an action must be determined. Accordingly, a teleological ethics maintains that whether an action is *right* or not is measured exclusively by its consequences."[25]

Now this is a surprising statement—but not because it says that it can be "immoral" to do something "right" with a bad intention. There is in fact agreement about this: a bad intention can make an action, no matter how "right," morally bad. If it is assumed that someone is doing something right, then only the intention remains to determine whether the actual carrying out of the action is morally good.

What is astounding about the statement is that the concept of the "morally good" is completely separated from the concept of "right action." One would rather have to say that there is a double source of the moral goodness of an action: the rightness of what someone does (the object) and the rightness of what one intends by the action (the intention). In every instance "right" is also "morally good," but the real, decisive moral goodness of an action flows from *both* kinds of "rightness."

The distinction between "right" and "good" has a curious effect. The above quotation, "the conviction and intention of the agent determine whether he acts morally or immorally," actually means not only that the intention is ultimately decisive, but also that the *entire* determination, whether one is acting morally or not, lies on the level of inner conviction.[26] This leads to the consequence that that person acts morally well who actually carries out the "ought" recognized in the "morally right"; the one who does what is right, who does as he ought. One performs a morally good action, then, exactly to the degree that one intends the "right," recognized as the "ought." It appears that the foundation of the moral goodness (not the "rightness") of an action is *deontologically* determined. It is a mere derivation of the morally good from the "ought."

In accordance with the (in itself, excellent) definition of a teleological ethics as an ethics that grounds the moral ought in the moral good, so-called "teleological ethics" would properly be so named only under the assumption that it is able to speak of a moral goodness of the morally right. It cannot do this, because in its physicalistic understanding of "right action" it has opened up an uncrossable abyss between the "right" ("in accord with reality," *sachgemäß*) and the morally good. The chasm can be crossed only by using the naturalistic fallacy.

### *The Concept of "Premoral Goods" and the Problem of Reconstructing a "Moral Claim"*

This "chasm" is immediately apparent in the following formulation: "Of two alternative courses of action, that one is morally right that brings about more good in comparison with the other." Rightness is determined through the "weighing" of goods. Now what is meant by "good" in this case? Is the rightness of an action determined through the comparison of *moral* goods or values? Schüller, Böckle, and others answer "no." The goods to which the "weighed" consequences are related are not moral goods, but nonmoral, premoral, physical goods (or evils). "A possible subject of the evaluative predicates *morally good* and *morally bad* is only a rational entity, only a person, insofar as the person freely takes up an attitude toward a moral claim through adoption or rejection; in particular, it is the act of free determination of the person, as well as the free state (conviction, attitude) and all the free actions and omissions that freely issue from this."[27]

This reveals first of all that Schüllerian ethics (to the extent that it *is* an ethics and not a "technology of actions") is *radically deontological* according to the above definition, because the *moral* good presupposes the *moral* demand, or the "ought." That person is morally good who takes a positive, free attitude toward the ought; that person is morally bad who does the opposite.

If the moral good results from the "attitude" taken by the person, how can we speak of the object of this attitude, of a "moral demand"? What is the "moral," or the "moral good" in this claim? It cannot be the "morally *right*," which is only the optimization of "pre-moral," physical goods. There appear to me to be three ways of escaping this impasse, methods that have in fact been used by teleologist or proportionalist thinkers:

*Method number 1*: "Moral demand" is attributed only to persons, and not to definite actions. Moral demand would then only be the "thou" of another person (or of oneself). Now this solution, in its "sympathetic" manner, is radically deontological, since the person of the other is taken as an immediate, moral "ought" claim that cannot be further justified teleologically. But this would contradict the Schüllerian definition of ethics as an "analysis of the rectitude of actions," since ethics, according to Schüller, has nothing to do with the morally good—a proposition that in itself can hardly be maintained. Since Schüller maintains both—that ethics has to do with the analysis of the rectitude of actions, and that a particular moral claim can be a person, then one may conclude that his theory is self-contradictory—like any physicalistic theory of moral action.

*Method number 2*: Certain criteria of value—so-called "ethical principles"—are posited for the "weighing" of goods (*Güterabwägung*): justice, love of neighbor, generosity, fairness. This is in order to reintroduce, "through the back door," as it were, the moral good that had been lost. I use the expression "through the back door" because these criteria of value cannot themselves be grounded. They must be deontologically posited.

*Method number 3*: By simple application of the "naturalistic fallacy," the "optimization" of "premoral" (physical) goods results in a moral good or "value." The objection to this is simply that *ex nihilo, nihil fit.*

In the following chapter, we will treat these methods in the following order: the third method (the "naturalistic fallacy") will come first, and then the first and second methods ("disguised deontologism"). In this way, methods number 1 and 2 will already be deprived of any refuge in the principle of the "optimization of premoral goods" (method number 3).

## NOTES

1. In the following discussion I focus on the so-called "teleologistic" or "teleological" ethics that predominates in German-speaking lands. It is largely identical with what is called "consequentialism" or "proportionalism" in English-speaking countries. See J. Finnis, *Fundamentals of Ethics* (Oxford and New York, 1983), pp. 80ff. An important treatment of teleological ethics which I was not able to refer to in this discussion is J. Seiffert, "Absolute Moral Obligations Towards Finite Goods as Foundation of Intrinsically Right and Wrong Actions. A Critique of Consequentialist Teleological Ethics: Destruction of Ethics Through Moral Theology?" in *Anthropos* 1 (1985): 57–94.

2. J. S. Mill, *Utilitarianism*, ch. II: "The creed which accepts as the foundation of morals, Utility, or the Greatest Happiness Principle, holds, that actions are right in proportion as they tend to promote happiness, wrong, as they tend to produce the reverse of happiness." The principle goes back to Bentham, who formulated it as follows: "By utility is meant the property in any object, whereby it tends to produce benefit, advantage, pleasure, good, or happiness (all this in the present case comes to the same thing) or (what comes again to the same thing) to prevent the happening of mischief, pain, evil, or unhappiness to the party whose interest is considered" (*An Introduction to the Principles of Morals and Legislation*, ch. I, 3).

3. See, e.g., *I–II*, q. 7, a. 2, ad 3um: "Bonum ordinatum ad finem dicitur utile, quod importat relationem quandam . . . et ideo, *cum bonitas actuum sit inquantum sunt utiles ad finem,* nihil prohibet eos bonos vel malos dici secundum proportionem ad aliqua quae exterius adiacent." (The good ordered to an end is called "useful" [*utile*], because it brings in a certain relation . . . and therefore, *since the goodness of actions is to the extent*

*that they are useful for an end*, nothing prevents them from being called good or bad according to the proportion they have toward things that exist outside of them.) See also Cicero, *De Officiis*, III, 30: "Nothing can be useful that is not at the same time morally good. And it is not morally good because of its utility, but because it is good, it is also useful."

4. Ch. I, 1: "It is for [pain and pleasure] alone to point out what we ought to do, as well as to determine what we shall do. On the one hand the standard of right and wrong, on the other the chain of causes and effects, are fastened to their throne. They govern us in all we do, in all we say, in all we think: every effort we can make to throw off our subjection, will serve but to demonstrate and confirm it."

5. Ibid.: "The *principle of utility* recognizes this subjection, and assumes it for the foundation of that system, the object of which is to rear the fabric of felicity by the hands of reason and law." In a note, Bentham explains that the "principle of utility" is a short-hand synonym for the "greatest happiness" or the "greatest felicity principle."

6. In this list I am following O. Hoffe, *Sittlich-politische Diskurse,* (Frankfurt, 1981), p. 55. Höffe combines all four principles into a single "principle of utility": "That action or rule of actions is good or right in the moral sense, the consequences of which are optimal for the well-being of all concerned."

7. Translator's note: This original meaning of *utile* can be seen very clearly where it is *contrasted* with pleasure (*dulce*); in the context of ancient literary criticism and rhetoric, the *utile* is the preceptive or instructional value ("ethical content"), as contrasted with the "pleasure" or "sweetness" of aesthetic, imaginative and sensual value (versification, imagery, figures, etc.). See the verses of Horace, *Ars Poetica*, 343, describing the best kind of (ethical) poetry: *omne tulit punctum qui miscuit utile dulci, lectorem delectando pariterque monendo* (He makes every point, who mixes the *useful* [the good, the right, the ethical instructional content] with the sweet [the pleasurable, formal, or aesthetic elements], equally delighting the reader [through the *dulce*] and providing moral instruction [through the *utile*]."

8. Mill, *Utilitarianism*, ch. II: "They [the critics of utilitarianism] say it is exacting too much to require that people shall always act from the inducement of promoting the general interests of society. But this is to mistake the very meaning of a standard of morals and confound the rule of action with the motive of it. It is the business of ethics to tell us what are our duties, or by what test we may know them."

9. Ibid.: "Utilitarian moralists have gone beyond almost all others in affirming that the motive has nothing to do with the morality of the action, though much with the worth of the agent."

10. See, e.g., ch. II: "It is natural to man to speak, to reason, to build cities, to cultivate the ground"; Mill calls *natural sentiment* "the desire to be in unity with our fellow creatures. . . . The social state is at once so natural, so necessary, and so habitual to man . . . etc. . . . there is at least a temporary feeling that the interests of others are their own interests . . . the good of others becomes to him a thing naturally and necessarily to be attended to. . . ." Mill speaks of *intellectual instincts* and says, "we have natural feelings of justice" (ch. V).

11. This is found in ch. V, "On the Connection Between Justice and Utility."

12. Ibid.: "If the opinion which I have now stated is psychologically true—if human nature is so constituted as to desire nothing which is not either a part of happiness or a means of happiness, we can have no other proof, and we require no other, that these are the only things desirable. If so, happiness is the sole end of human action, and the promotion of it the test by which to judge of all human conduct; from whence it necessarily follows that it must be the criterion of morality, since a part is included in the whole."

13. Ibid.: Ch. IV: "to think of an object as desirable (unless for the sake of its consequences) and to think of it as pleasant, are one and the same thing."

14. *Nichomachean Ethics*, II, ch. 2, 1104b30–1105a1: "There are three things that are the objects of choice, and three things that are avoided: the morally good [or noble; τὸ καλόν] the useful [or advantageous; τὸ σύμφερον]; and the pleasant [τὸ ἡδύ], and their opposites, the shameful, the disadvantageous, and the painful, and in regard to these the virtuous person is a good judge, and the unvirtuous a poor judge, but especially when it comes to the pleasant; for this is common to all creatures with senses [τὰ ζῷα], and is connected with everything subject to choice, so that even the good and the useful appear pleasant."

15. Not even Kantian ethics is deontological. But its teleology is a "transcendental teleology" or a "teleological formalism." For Kant, an action is morally bad when it has as a consequence that carrying it out could not become a universal law, or that a human being would become used by it as a means. Certainly, according to Kant, one should always act according to duty. But "duty" is itself grounded in a transcendental teleology. But then for Kant, the reason, and more exactly the practical (categorical) imperative, is the *telos*, which defines what "duty" is. Because this is only a transcendental formalism, reason is incapable of developing any (material) standards for action. Kant comes to make deontological formulations for just this reason, that he has a differentiated conception of consequences: for him, there are some consequences that

are morally constitutive—namely, those that concern the transcendental formalism of the reason.

16. B. Schüller, *Die Begründung sittlicher Urteile* (Düsseldorf, 1980), p. 173, expressly emphasizes this reduction of consequences to "nonmoral evil." A premature decision of fundamental importance has been made: for if, as with Schüller, all relevant consequences of an action exist in principle on the "nonmoral" level, but these are the consequences that make the difference between the "rightness" or "wrongness" of actions, then the question about whether an action is right or wrong is made in principle on the premoral level. This physicalistic approach leads to an ethics of "good sense" and to the inconsistencies that we will study in detail below.

17. *Humanae Vitae,* no. 12. The anthropological context is again teleologically clarified at no. 17: "Upright men can even better convince themselves of the solid grounds on which the teaching of the church in this field is based, *if they care to reflect upon the consequences of methods of artifical birth control.*"

18. It was exactly this aspect of the *anthropological* structure of human acts that was overlooked by Schüller in his treatment of the indissolubility of marriage (*Die Begründung sittlicher Urteile,* pp. 252ff.). Schüller actually argues on the basis that, according to canonical practice, a marriage undertaken with a mental reservation against its indissolubility is invalid. That is correct, of course, but this invalidity is itself based upon an anthropological and ethical reality: that indissolubility is one of the most essential elements of married love; thus, a marriage "with reservation" is not, for this reason (its canonical invalidity), considered not to be a marriage but, rather, is judged invalid in canon law, because it is no marriage. If this is attended to, Schüller's argument breaks down, since the very thing is being observed that he himself says is needed for a valid conclusion: "From insight into the moral character of an action, it is immediately apparent whether God commands, allows, or forbids the action" (p. 263).

19. See the "abbreviated form of speaking" discussed in chapter 1, section "Why a 'Reconstruction' of the Concept of Natural Law is Necessary."

20. Schüller, *Die Begründung sittlicher Urteile,* p. 227.

21. B. Schüller, "Neuere Beiträge zum Thema, 'Begründung sittlicher Normen,' " (in his *Theologische Berichte,* vol. 4 (1974), p. 141.

22. The fact that this connection of the two meanings correponds to the "will of God" must of course itself be justified through anthropological and ethical analysis. Such an analysis is is not to be found in *Humanae Vitae,* because it is an encyclical and not a moral theological treatise.

Too many "justifications" have been looked for in *Humanae Vitae*. An encyclical is intended to present the teaching of the Church, and as such to be a source for theological work, without itself performing that work; its authority does not consist in arguments, but rather in the apostolic authority of the magisterium. Rather than justifications, what one finds in *Humanae Vitae* are indications where, and from what perspective, such justifications must be looked for, always preserving the legitimate freedom of theological research. Unfortunately, many moral theologians were not prepared from the outset to accept the doctrine of *Humanae Vitae*, and consequently were not able to take advantage of the new perspectives that it opened.

23. See the fuller exposition above in chapter 2, section "Beyond Naturalism and Dualism."

24. Schüller, *Die Begründung Sittlicher Urteile*, p. 284.

25. Ibid., p. 283. See also pp. 133ff, where the application of the distinction between right/good (*richtig/gut*) and wrong/bad (*falsch/schlecht*) is justified. I think Schüller considers this distinction plausible because he understands the "objective" only in an opposition to the "subjective"; on this, see chapter 10.

26. It even appears that Schüller would like to separate moral goodness from "right insight," see ibid., p. 141: "The morality of a man stands entirely upon his free self-determination, not upon his better or worse insight. . . . Nobody acts morally well because he had a better insight in contrast with another who acted poorly. Of course, nobody can decide for the morally good without winding up at the same time with the better insight and the morally right. But whether one actually attains to the morally right that one began with is not as much in one's power as the free decision for the morally good." It is not difficult to see that this argument is inconclusive. First, we are told that morality does not depend on the insight into what is right; then it is maintained that morality does in fact depend on putting one's efforts into the right moral insight. Now someone has to provide criteria for the moral sufficiency of this effort, if he is going to distinguish a *culpable* lack of right insight [as in the untranslatable German expression *was ich nicht weiß macht mir nicht heiß*] from an *inculpable* one. This distinction would imply that the statement "The morality of a man . . . does not depend on his better or worse insight" is false. This is why Schüller does not introduce the distinction but only adds, by a leap of thought, that *as a whole*, man has only a limited power over attaining an insight into the morally right. In place of the difference between culpable (immoral) and inculpable ignorance, there is the notion that a lack of right insight is based on an *incapacity* for right insight, and thus is inculpable in principle, an idea that is never once justified.

27. Schüller, "Neuere Beiträge zum Thema, 'Begründung sittlicher Normen,' " p. 154.

# 9

# "Teleological Ethics" (II): Physicalism and Hidden Deontology

## Physicalism and the Naturalistic Fallacy in the "Weighing Of Goods"

### *"Values" and "Goods"*

Very little of a concrete nature can be found on this theme in Schüller's writings. Franz Böckle, who follows the basic ideas of Schüller, has been more explicit. He calls "concrete action" the "practical association with already existing goods and values" (*Fundamental Moral Theology*, p. 234). For Böckle, values are axiological givens like "justice," "faithfulness," truthfulness," and so on: it is never morally permissible to act unjustly, unfaithfully, untruthfully, and so forth. Values have an immediate moral character and should never be directly harmed (ibid., p. 240). Moral commands in regard to these values are therefore always *apodictic statements*; they are analytical judgments or tautologies. Thus the Fifth and Sixth Commandments have the function not of prohibiting definite kinds of actions but, rather, of prohibiting the injury of certain values. They say, for example, "It is unjust to kill unjustly" or "It is unfaithful to leave one's wife unjustly."[1]

According to Böckle, these values tell us nothing about what we are supposed to *do*. Objects of an action are not values but "goods." "Goods," for example, are life, health, procreation, marriage; their opposites, "evils," are death, disease, lies, and so on (and this "so on" is somewhat misleading, since rather few examples are to be found in Böckle's account). Values and goods are "already given." Values, it seems, can be determined only transcendentally. As far I know, no teleological or proportionalist ethicist grounds values teleologically. They simply appear from "out of the blue," like rays of sunlight from *value heaven*. It is possible they have been adopted from the phenomenology of values, except that there is no trace of phenomenological analysis.

The "goods," which will no longer concern us here, are treated like things, or natural givens, already "there" for action. In the case of "life," this may be plausible to some extent, but the price one pays for it is heavy: human life is reduced to its natural (physical) structure (its physical integrity) and to its sociological externalities. Now it simply will not do to call "human life" a "pregiven reality"—one that must be "respected in action" even though, as Böckle says, the very duty to "respect" cannot be derived from it—if "human life" is to be considered in its true depth, according to its own horizon of meaning and developmental potential, according, that is, to its character as *imago*, with the fundamental determination of the human being that such a character provides.

### *The Derivation of Moral Claims from Premoral Goods*

How does Böckle arrive at this concept of "goods" as realities "already given" to action? As givens, or "natural facts" that one recognizes as meaningful in a simple "ascertaining judgment"? He tells us that he means by "goods" nothing other than was intended in traditional moral theology by "object (the objective aim of action)." Thus Böckle belongs among those moral theologians who conceive the concept of the object of action in a physicalistic manner, as a pregiven, naturally given "thing." Object or "goal of action" (*finis operis*) designates those natural givens (and the purposes inscribed within them) in the "environment" of which human action takes place. This concept corresponds to a widespread tradition in the manuals, to which we will return.

Now what should surprise us here is the unquestioning ease with which Böckle asserts that a "judgment" about a "situation in which we have to consider a definite good such as human life [*daß Leben sei beachtenswert*, "that human life is worth one's esteem"] can, of course, easily be changed into a judgment about action, in other words, a moral judgment." The "easy change," unfortunately, is wrought by the naturalistic fallacy. Böckle himself says that "what is worth esteem" (*beachtenswert*) means nothing other than "what has to be respected in action" (*im Handlung zu respecktieren*)." But what does it mean to "respect in action"? If I am planning to rob a bank, I would have to "respect" the fact that the bank probably has an alarm system. One must always "respect" many things in any action. Now if we want to use "respect" (*respektieren*) for a positive judgment of value—which seems to be implied, since Böckle also speaks of "esteeming" (*achten*)—then one would have to object that such esteem (*Achtung*) is possible only because the object of "esteeming" is a moral value. But goods are premoral values. And Böckle also stresses that the obligation to "respect" does not ultimately emerge from these goods—not even from the "dignity of man"—but rather "is the result of man's own understanding of the situation and his responsibility. As a moral subject, man is transcendentally called upon to take up a position with regard to the reality involved in the situation. What is revealed in our observation of the situation and our consequent judgment [*Feststellungsurteil*], is that a certain good—for example, life itself—is unmistakably the object of moral responsibility. It is morally right to esteem that object [*beachten*] in action and morally wrong not to" (*Fundamental Moral Theory*, p. 233).

From the obscurity of the discussion at least one question should arise: How can one "easily" transform the "judgment about the situation" into a *moral* judgment, when the obligation to respect these goods does not ultimately come from these goods? And how is it "morally right" to "esteem" them? They are not supposed to be *moral* goods!

In fact, two fallacies are at work. First, from the experience of a premoral good it somehow emerges that it is "worth esteeming," that it is to be "respected in action"; and second, it is then concluded that a premoral good, respected in action, is "morally right." The predication "moral" is arrived at in two steps from a premoral good. But at the same time, "what must be respected" and the "morally right" presuppose the morally good, which can be ascribed only to values. How can this incongruity be removed? Through the "optimization" of premoral goods, or the "negative optimization" of premoral evils. By this means, a moral value is in each case realized and someone "acts morally."

There is no other way to solve the dilemma, since value judgments are always analytic and tautological: there is no other criterion for the ordering of values (such as "justice") in relation to concrete actions, except for the "weighing" or optimizing of premoral goods.

But it is impossible to establish *which* premoral goods are to be respected (or *how, when* and *how much* to respect them) on the basis of a purely analytical standard that lacks any relation to concrete actions: "one should always act rightly." Rather, what is maintained is that values ("justice," etc.) *emerge* from the "weighing" optimization of premoral goods. Böckle's position leads to the consequence that values are merely the *designations* of various "optimizings" of goods; they are "empty formulas" but have the function of providing a moral predicate (or morally qualifying "names") to a calculus of premoral goods. Nothing could show more clearly that we are dealing here with a version of the "naturalistic fallacy."

The problem can be formulated in the question What is the standard for the optimizing "weighing" of goods, or for the optimizing of the consequences of actions? By what criteria does the "weighing" itself take place? Although Böckle provides no explicit solution, there appear in fact to be two principal roads taken by the teleologists: (1) recourse to deontologically formulated "ethical principles" and (2) recourse to a so-called "love ethics," which then often leads to the understanding of concrete actions as "expressive acts" or "signs" of Christian conviction or Christian faith. Both ways lead in the end to a *hidden deontologism* and must finally go back to the formula (introduced by Böckle) of moral values as equivalent to "optimized" premoral goods. One may then go on to argue in the typical utilitarian fashion. This is also found in Schüller, who supports what is basically a "love ethics."

## The Hidden Deontologism of Teleological Ethics (Ethics of Principles and Ethics of Love)

The foregoing argument has maintained that so-called teleological ethics rests upon a distinction between two fundamentally different levels: first, there is the level of the "morally good" (or moral values), to which also belong good intention, conviction, and so on; the other level, which "lies in front of" the former, is that of "premoral goods," concrete actions, "right" actions, and so on. That person is morally "right" in his action who brings about the optimum of (premoral) "good," after a consideration of the consequences of his action for all concerned. That person is morally "good" in his action who acts on the basis of a decision for the moral good, meaning that he acts with sincere intention and conviction.

### *The Hiatus Between "Goods" and "Values," or Between "Right" and "Good"*

This approach, as we have seen, requires a gap between the "morally right" and the "morally good." It is not completely clear how the concept of "right action" attains to the predication of "moral." It is apparent at least that this predication "moral" (as in "morally good") can result only from the optimization of "weighed goods" or from the optimization of consequences. And here once again is the "naturalistic fallacy": for the consequences of "premoral" goods would only be "premoral" consequences! How can their optimization set up a claim of moral significance? Is it because the very process of the "weighing of goods," or the optimization itself, constitutes "morality"?

If that is the case, then one must establish the grounds of this "morality-causing" power of the weighing process. How does the "weighing of goods" provide a fundamental moral value? This would explain how moral action—as rational action—can be an action that is based upon the weighing or balancing of premoral goods. Since it is impossible to establish this, at least in a teleological manner, the reasoning is inescapably circular.

One rather large part of the problem is that no one has clarified the concept of "morality." There is instead a reliance on mere intuition. Apparently it is possible to count on a general consensus about the meaning of "morality" or "morally good" and so forth. This consensus in turn rests on the idea that that person acts morally "rightly" who promotes, realizes (and so on) his own human existence and that of others. While this could be an adequate idea of morality, but it would nevertheless still mean that man realizes or promotes his and others' human existence *through* the "weighing of goods." And we are still caught in the same circle.

There seems to be only one way out: one has to offer moral criteria for the weighing process. In order to close the gap between (pre-) moral goods and (moral) values, one must make the "weighing" on the basis of value criteria. Something like this has in fact been maintained by Schüller, in response to "inaccurate" criticism of teleological ethics, since such criticism "appears to imply that a teleologist wants to determine which action brings about more good, without offering any standards like justice or fairness" (*Die Begründung sittlicher Urteile*, p. 285). Now it is clear that these criteria or "standards" cannot themselves be the result of a "weighing" process, or we would fall into an infinite regress. As directive "goals" of any weighing process, they will have to be deontologically formulated. This is in fact readily admitted by teleologists, since it is the only way they can avoid an *obvious* naturalistic fallacy.[2]

### *The Problem of Reconstructing a Hierarchy of Actions and Moral Values*

We have now reached the decisive point of our analysis, or the old familiar question of philosophical ethics: What is justice? What is love? or beneficience or friendship? or courage, moderation, chastity, etc? In other words, what is the moral good? The teleologists claim that it has to do with standards of value, in reference to which the weighing of goods, or the judgment of the consequences of actions, must be carried out. Here they adopt a Platonic position, which says that every action treated *in itself* is meaningless—it has a meaning only insofar as it intends a good. Ethics treats of the good, and is essentially a "metaphysics of value"—or, perhaps more concretely—a metaphysics of the good.

Aristotle rejected this definition of ethics: the metaphysics of the good is irrelevant for ethics. This is not because a metaphysics of the good is irrelevant, but because ethics does not investigate the good as such, but rather the "bringing about" or the "effecting" of the good (in Aristotelian terms, the *sýmpheron,* or "useful"). Ethics is not concerned with "justice" but rather with the "just man" or the "just action." Indeed, justice is a characteristic of human *actions*, and not a "good" or "value" that would exist *prior to* any actions or exist independently of them. Ethics has to do with the "practically good," that is, with that good which man realizes *in* his action and *through* it. The practical (moral) good that is sought is not an idea on the basis of which man could judge which actions are "good . . . as if the good were an ideal model, with whose help we could judge what is better for ourselves, and once we know it, could attain to it." This is already contradicted by the reality of human craftsmanship (an image Aristotle uses), since it wouldn't do any good for an artisan or craftsman who wants to reach a certain goal to look at the "idea" of the good. "It would be strange (and how would it help?) for a weaver or carpenter in their trades to know *the good in itself*; or how would a miltary general or medical doctor be better at their occupations by having seen the idea of the good? The doctor does not have 'health in itself' in view, but rather 'the health of the person' or rather 'the health of *this* person.' For doctors heal individual cases." (*Nichomachean Ethics,* I, 4, 1097a 8–15).

Aristotle means that the practical good is a characteristic of actions; moral values result from the analysis of actions that are in accord with human being: from an analysis—grounded in an anthropology—of those actions which correspond to virtue and bring it into existence. Moral virtue is the moral good that has been effected in the human being as an "elective habit" (*héxis prohairetikê*).

Any ethics that holds to the Aristotelian tradition treats moral values as a characteristic of human *actions*. Values are not intuited ideas or "social" or "socially transmitted" standards of action. They can be objectified as ideals by abstraction; they can be socially transmitted and adapted as ideals, but the origin of values is not there—it is to be found, rather, in human action as *such*. Accordingly, the recognition of values is possible only in the framework of a philosophical anthropology.

So-called teleological ethics is a Platonic kind of ethics. This makes very clear where to locate the distinction between the so-called "strictly deontological" and the so-called "teleological ethics." It consists in the fact that so-called deontological ethics treats moral values as qualities of actions; thus, within an ethics of virtue, an analysis of types of action can be assumed that is *at the same time* an analysis of moral values. It also can attribute moral values to concrete actions; and since (as everyone grants) one should not act immorally, but certain actions can be described as "wrong," so there are certain actions that are always evil. And this is not compromised at all by the fact that the qualification of such actions has been teleologically arrived at, so long as it is a teleology that maintains a fundamental connection between act analysis and value analysis—that is, that grounds the latter in the former, on the basis of an anthropology. This connection is achieved in the doctrine of the reason as *telos* and standard of human actions, as outlined in chapter 7.

So-called teleological ethics is neither "more teleological" nor "less deontological" than so-called "deontological ethics." In fact, "teleological ethics" is, in a certain sense (at the level of the justification of moral values), *exclusively* deontological; it argues teleologically only on the level of the analysis of actions (the "rightness of actions"), which however, is no analysis of human morality, but instead an analysis of the consequences of human action on the level of premoral goods. Through the separation, or rupture, of action analysis from value analysis, the concept of human action falls back to the level of premoral, physicalistic determination (the area of premoral goods). The morality of actions must then be reconstructed in reverse through standards of value that are applied to the "weighing of goods." These standards must then be established in an exclusively deontological manner.

This will shortly be explained. But it should also be shown that this "reconstruction" of the concept of moral action—through a "weighing of goods" calibrated by deontologically established standards—is impossible. There are only three possiblities left for a teleological ethicist who wants to show that a concrete action is morally called for, or morally right: (1) he must use the naturalistic fallacy; (2) he must argue in utilitarian fashion; or (3) he must posit the moral good only in the "good intention"—in a "conviction" that is good *independently* of what one actually does, as long as one has come to the decision responsibly, that is, through the "weighing of goods." Actions thus have value only as expression or signification of the moral intention, and this is a solution that is found (above all) among those who combine a so-called teleological ethics with a Christian ethics of faith, hope, and love or a so-called *ethos of imitation*. In any event one can maintain, as something that holds for all these variants, that there are no human actions capable of being described as intrinsically evil (*intrinsece mala*); this means that of no action can it be said that it is always in and of itself evil. If not *every* action is in principle good or indifferent, nevertheless every act is in principle morally possible and defensible, under the condition that someone believes, loves, hopes, and has subjected the "goods" to be touched in action to a "weighing" process.

A reconstruction of the concept of moral action on the basis of a deontologically grounded, teleological "weighing of goods" that is to be both a measure and a criterion of measures, cannot work. The point can also be stated as follows: there is no immediate derivability from the physicalistic treatment of actions (in their *genus naturae*) to their moral treatment (in their *genus moris*). Moral values and "premoral" goods are two mutually irreducible quantities. In the words of Thomas, "Moral ends are accidental to a natural thing, and conversely, the character of a natural end is accidental to what is moral" (*I–II*, q. 1, a. 3, ad 3um).[3] If someone wants to predicate "moral" of an action, one must draw upon a theory that allows understanding the axiological, moral value content of actions *qua human (personal) actions*. Like St. Thomas Aquinas in the Aristotelian tradition, one must have a moral concept of the object of action (*obiectum morale*), as opposed to the merely natural or "physical" object relations of human action. The present thesis, in other words, is that the reconstruction of a concept of moral action in the framework of so-called "teleological ethics" cannot succeed, because this ethics is based on a physicalistic theory of the object of human actions.

### *"Love" as a Fundamental Principle*

The justification of our thesis rests upon the fact that the mutual correspondence of values and actions is not possible under the condition just mentioned, that of a *separation* of action analysis from value analysis. Consequently the correlation of the value "justice" to "action *x*" would not be possible, so that one could not say that "action *x* is a just action" or "action *x* is an act of justice."

This impossibility can again be shown with reference to the expositions of Schüller, who attempts to solve the problem as follows: teleological ethics possesses three "distinguishing marks" that mutually "explain and supplement" one another. The fundamental measure for all moral goods is the commandment to love (in the sense of Romans 13: 8–10), the "call to love, as both good willing and good acting." It is always related to a *person* and is the foundation and root of all other conceivable principles (values), such as justice, fairness, sincerity, loyalty, thankfulness, and self-fulfillment.[4] Thus the fundamental distinguishing mark of teleological ethics (at least in this systematic perspective) is that "the love of man has its obligatory standard in the goodness or value of that to which it stands in relation." Of course, since we have seen that moral goodness for Schüller can only be the characteristic of a person, so the binding standard is always a person; but it is not the *human person* as such that is intended here (in the sense of "human nature"), but rather the actual and situationally bound "thou" to which an action is related.

This fundamental standard "not only tells us how the morally right is to be understood, namely as acts that promote love. It also tells us that moral good consists in love as an inner conviction." Apparently, this principle cannot say anything definite about the correlation between moral values and actions: it merely states, first, that moral goods consist in the intention (the love for a person) and, second, that love must express itself in actions. The fundamental principle "love" *basically* fosters the correlation of moral values (such as love) and actions, without being able to say *which* actions are a realization of love. It likewise fosters a correlation between "inner conviction" and "deed," without establishing in what sense such a correlation is itself determinative of the "inner conviction," that is, whether a conviction *x* can in fact be fundamentally expressed or realized by *any action whatever.*

### *"Particular Principles"*

This makes it necessary to have additional principles. The second distinguishing sign of teleological ethics is the following: "Love (in the sense of Romans 13: 8–10) is the ultimate ground of determination for the moral rectitude of all actions; all other ethical principles must be considered as particular forms of this love." The basic principle of love thus becomes differentiated into a series of what Schüller calls "particular principles," such as "justice," "fairness," "fidelity," and so on.

Here at least one serious problem appears. When Schüller writes that all particular principles (we could also say "the single virtues") are only differentiations or concretizations of "love," he seems at first to be saying something quite traditional. And he clearly thinks so too, when he says, "It is inconceivable how a Catholic theologian could justify distancing himself from his tradition on this point." As witness, he introduces a fine "traditional" formulation of the idea by R. Carpentier (1953): "The task of teaching moral theology consists, above all, 'in the formulation (concretized and specified in a thousand ways) of charity, the mother and root of the virtues [*mère et racine des vertus*].' "

But Schüller's idea is not at all "traditional," for the simple reason that the tradition (correctly) did not treat the virtue of love (*caritas*)—which is at issue here and in Romans 13—in philosophical ethics, but rather as a *theological virtue* in the framework of moral theology. And since moral theology treats of human nature as raised to the life of grace, it *presupposes* the teaching of moral action and of moral virtue (prudence, justice, moderation, courage). The "tradition" never used the theological exposition of the virtue of charity to establish the "natural" morality of human action. In *Romans* 13: 8–10 the virtue of *caritas* is not introduced to ground the moral commandments, but rather to fulfill them and sum them up. Assuming the justification of morality in the sense of a virtue ethics, the "tradition" treats the theological virtue of love as the *forma virtutum*, and as "mother" and "root" of the virtues. This is meant in reference to the success of their production and to the completeness of their operation,[5] *and not in reference to their axiological constitution or specification*. Charity, rather, *presupposes* the integrity and the self-consistency of an act of moral virtue (formally molded, directed, and axiologically specified by prudence),[6] which is something that is related to "love" (or *caritas*) as matter is to form or as the body is to the soul. For Thomas, and for the tradition along with him, it is completely clear "that moral actions do not become specified through their final goal [that is, neither through the person of God or through charity], but rather through their proximate goals [*fines proximi*]; there are many of these and they are related to various actions [*plures diversorum sunt*], just as natural goals are many and various" (*In II Sent.*, d. 38, q. 1, a. 1, ad 3um). The human good (*bonum humanum*) is not formulated through the ultimate end or even through the virtue of charity that orders man to that end, but rather through the right use of reason (*recta ratio*).[7] Here we see the proper understanding of the goals that naturally belong to man, and whose demands he both *recognizes* by natural reason as the "natural law" and *brings into action*, in dependence upon those goals in the judgment of prudence, a judgment that for its own part depends on the possession of moral virtue.[8]

And so Schüller is doing something "new" after all, by using a theological position to solve a philosophical problem. The quotation from Carpentier only means that the virtues that concern moral theologians are *specified* forms of love: that is, they already possess a moral species independently of *caritas*, which is not constituted by this (divine) love, but rather becomes thoroughly penetrated by it. "Specified forms of love" means a certain concrete incarnation of Christian love in the various human virtues, which are themselves thereby raised to a supernatural level and, while remaining *human* virtues, become an integral component of Christian morality. The supernatural virtue of charity, which is formally divine and has the divine Person as subject, becomes incarnate in man in an existentially human way: it is the form or the "soul" of an action that, as it imitates the divine love, is nevertheless always still a *human* act. Grace presupposes nature, and elevates and perfects it; it does not *redefine* nature, nor make it necessary that what a human being is or what a morally good or *humanly* just action is, be defined on the basis of grace.[9]

Schüller's contention that the "particular principles," or the moral values to be correlated to the various human virtues, are merely branches or various forms of Pauline *caritas* is neither "traditional" nor a solution to the problem of correlating actions and values. The "particular principles" cannot do anything more than the basic principle "love." They define an inner conviction without ordering this conviction to any definite actions. They require an act without saying what (further) actions correspond to it. "The second characteristic mark [of teleological ethics] assumes the particular manifestations of the morally right as givens, and points out their common foundation in love. Through this proof, teleological ethics opposes the notion that ethical principles like justice and fidelity can make a claim to validity completely in their own right." But how are these "manifestations" *given*? Through an intuition of values? Through social convention? Through an analysis of actions? How, in general, can one determine the "moral rectitude" these principles categorically comprise, in a manner specific for actions?

### *The Principle of the Optimization of Premoral Goods*

Consequently there is need for a third "characteristic" of teleological ethics, upon which the whole matter rests, for good or for ill. This third characteristic is as follows: "the moral rectitude of all actions is determined exclusively by their consequences for the welfare or misery of all concerned." It appears that the "weighing of goods" is now being introduced as a criterion for determining which action can realize which specific moral value. For this, it would be necessary for the "particular principles" to be the measure for the process. But can they do this? No, because the weighing of goods, which has been introduced to determine the morally right, is already being used to determine what "justice," "fidelity," and so on mean, in a way specific for actions. Since Schüller already wanted to determine moral action "from above" (i.e., starting with love), he must now, for good or for ill, elevate the "optimization" of premoral goods (carried out by the "weighing of goods") into a measure for "justice," "fidelity," and so on. But this is not what is intended by Romans 13: 8–10. Love, as the "fulfillment of the law," *pre*supposes which actions are good, and which actions *therefore* tend toward love and find their fulfillment or consummation there. "Love" does not constitute the commandment; rather, the commandment shows wherein love toward God and neighbor consists—that is, in what fundamental types of actions.

At first glance, the circularity of the argument may not be apparent, since in the enumeration of "characteristics" the last one ("weighing of goods")—and really, the one most in need of justification—comes first, so that it seems to be justified by the other two ("particular principles" and love), which then would provide the standard for every "weighing." In reality, love is the fundamental principle, the particular principles are derived from it, and the whole burden of correlating values and actions in the end comes to rest upon the "weighing of goods."

This is why, once again, we have a "weighing" without a standard. Schüller's mistake becomes visible when he calls the "welfare and suffering [*Wohl und Wehe*] of all concerned" the criterion of judging consequences. Had he said "The moral rectitude of actions is determined exclusively by their right or wrong consequences, their consequences for fidelity, and so on," he would have been correct, but he would also have had to admit that his argument was circular and tautological. This is because the burden of proving what is right or wrong is laid precisely upon the "weighing of goods." The expression *welfare and suffering of all concerned* is apparently a remedy for the situation. Such "weal or woe" [*Wohl oder Wehe*] now become the necessary and ultimate criterion for every "weighing." But since a correlation between values and actions is not possible, no more can this criterion be correlated to the "particular principles." The standard of "welfare and suffering" *can* be defined only on the level of the premoral goods.[10]

Now that is what is probably being said in a statement like the following: "Someone is thinking teleologically who is convinced that of two alternative choices of action, that one is morally right that effects comparatively more net good than the alternative." Now since only the optimizing of premoral goods can be considered "good" in this instance, this optimization can itself be assumed only on the basis of an (equally premoral) judgment about the priority of certain goods, since any criterion of the correlation of such optimization with moral values is precisely what is lacking. Even so, Schüller maintains that the correlation between moral values (particular principles, love) and actions must result from this optimization. But that is simply the naturalistic fallacy.

At this point, however, Schüller finds himself in a terminological crisis. The concept "welfare and misery" (*Wohl und Wehe*) appears to indicate this, as well as the characterization of (negative) consequences as "devastating" (*verheerend*) or "catastrophic" (*katastrophal*).[11] But terms like these cannot achieve the correlation of actions (or consequences of actions) with moral values any more than the concept of human "welfare" can. Accordingly, Schüller must operate with a vocabulary that appeals to the emotions rather than the reason.

The questionable nature of the argument is readily apparent in an example he uses: a sheriff of a small town in the southern United States is judging a case involving the sexual assault of a white woman. A black man, whom the sheriff knows to be innocent, is suspected by the whole town. If the sheriff were to condemn this man to execution, he would prevent the outbreak of civil unrest that would cost the lives of many innocent people. Should he then judge the innocent man guilty, for the welfare of the whole town? Schüller holds that it is not at first evident how the sheriff should decide. "It must be considered carefully whether the killing of one innocent person for the rescue of other innocent persons is wrong because it is murder, when not doing it is a decision that permits the killing of other innocent persons." Nevertheless, *in this case*, "the sheriff should not in fact allow the one innocent man to be executed, in order to save the lives of many innocent people." And this is for the following reason: if he were allowed to condemn the innocent man, the institution of criminal justice would have to be equipped with the following exception clause: "the judge should condemn a man known to be innocent as "guilty," if he thereby can keep worse evil from others; nevertheless, the judge must have moral certainty that apart from him, everyone is (wrongly) convinced that the man is guilty. Now, since it is more than doubtful that the institution of criminal justice would be able to fulfill its function for the welfare of society if it were equipped with this exception clause, then the exception must be rejected as being contrary to the welfare of the community and as unjustified."[12]

This is a typically utilitarian justification. It shows that the teleological weighing of goods, as Schüller understands it, is not capable of achieving the correlation of actions and moral values, but only determines moral values (in a utilitarian manner) at the level of premoral goods. The "welfare of those concerned" is here only the "welfare of society." Conditions could be such that if a crime is committed and innocent persons are condemned, the public institutions could still function. Would it not then be a moral commandment to create the social conditions in which, "for the welfare of all concerned," such exception clauses would be possible *without* endangering the smooth functioning of society?[13]

But there is a still more serious problem: according to the inner logic of Schüller's argument, the life of the innocent does not deserve unconditional "esteem" in itself. The concern for the human person is here no longer an inviolable value. It has, rather, become a means for reaching "higher" values. By the utilitarian argument here applied, the value that absolutely merits attention is not the individual human person, but rather the "institution of criminal justice," or "public order," or indeed "society" or *collective* humanity. A false understanding of "the common good" is implied, set dangerously against "individual well-being." Concern for the life of the individual becomes merely a *means* of preserving the "institution of criminal justice" or public order. Consequently, I take Schüller's justification to be *inhuman* in structure: that he must have recourse to it by the logic of his approach shows, at the very least, that the approach is inconsistent. Without a doubt, Schüller intends his ethics to be humane. But how can an ethics be consistently human in its intention when it permits a justification that instrumentalizes an unconditional concern for the person?

### *Escapes, Emergency Solutions*

In order to avoid such possibilities, a teleological ethics can only argue deontologically. Moral values and their correlation with certain definite actions (or the prohibition of certain other actions) must simply be posited or maintained as self-evident. One may appeal, as does F. Furger, to historical experience, which is supposed to show that torture, betrayal, blasphemy, and unchastity in no way *actually* correspond to the dignity of man; that is, "such prohibitions have as norm the condition of an unconditional obligation that does not recognize any exceptions. For ethical *praxis* such behavior is absolutely excluded, as quantities that can never be included in a 'weighing of goods,' because, according to experience, the consequences (especially the long-term ones) of such an action are definitely worse than the good that such actions have achieved" (*Was Ethik begründet*, p. 46). But is that a criterion of value? What happens if someone does not know about these "long-term consequences"? Is it then only up to the state to set moral norms? Would right conduct then require a competence (such as an insight into social conditions and historically long-term consequences) that an individual could never possess? What would oblige me to take such historical considerations into account at all? Agreed that "betrayal," "torture," "blasphemy," and "unchastity" are moral values (or, rather, *unvalues*)—statements about them are analytical or tautological; the diffculty is in knowing if *this* action is connected to *this* value.

What Furger calls "secondary deontology" appears, rather, as "hidden" deontology, brought in to make up for the fact that the method "weighing of goods" lacks all relevance to the ordering of actions with moral values.

This hidden deontology becomes still clearer when Furger speaks of the necessity of a deontological establishment of the *telos*. At the basis of every "weighing of goods" lies the free positing of a *telos* as the final goal of all action. This positing cannot itself be teleologically grounded; it arises, rather, from an act of faith, carried out through a "freedom option." "Formally, it makes no difference in principle whether this positing of value in relation to a *telos* is based on 'philosophical' (or 'secular') or religious belief" (ibid., p. 53). In a teleological ethics, values cannot be disclosed through an analysis of human actions. They must instead be established by an act of faith, and this is what Furger calls *deontological teleology*: "All further ethical judgments must then result teleologically from this *telos*, from the reference to the *telos* of the various conditions, values, goods, and duties that can govern the particular decision in a concrete situation" (ibid.). But this "reference" to the *telos* is just what cannot be obtained. It is impossible to achieve, with rational discourse, a reference of actions to this *telos*, because the "transcendental" level of values (or of the *telos*) is incommensurable with the "categorial" level of actions, as has been shown. One would need a theory of the correlation of transcendental values (the *telos*) with categorial "goods" subject to actions. Such a correlation would be possible only if these "goods" would not be premorally determined, but rather comprehended in their practical value character. There would also be needed an anthropological analysis of human action and its axiological structure, an analysis that is exactly what is lacking in so-called teleological ethics.

The confusion here of the objective value character that is immanent in human action with the so-called premoral goods (physicalism) is notorious. For example, Böckle is of the opinion that in principle every action is open to a "weighing of goods." "This applies to all contingent goods, including the good of procreation. We cannot say, in other words, that it can never contradict a greater good and therefore that it is obligatory for everyone in an absolute way (that is, the absolute way implied in the encyclical with regard to the norm of regulation of contraception)" (*Fundamental Moral Theology*, p. 238). Böckle is completely unaware that the question of contraception has to do not with the "good of procreation" but rather with the *act* of procreation as human, personal action in the context of married love—that is, with this married love itself and its meaning. The "object" of this act is not simply the "good of procreation"—that would be a purely physicalistic way of treating it. The "objective" meaning of this act is defined by the significance of married love in its anthropological dimension, and in the dimension of cooperation with a divine act of creation, which relates both to eternity and to the human soul that bears the *imago*. When responsible parenthood is realized, the "good of procreation" must sometimes be put behind other goods, and no one would dispute that. *Humanae Vitae* is concerned to instruct *how* that can happen, without destruction of the significance of married love.

Through the integration of this physicalistic interpretation of human action into a "salvation-historical" Christian ethics, moral action becomes indefinable as human action in its axiological content. Human action in its "concrete empirical form" does not have an unequivocal moral sense: it forms only the "outer surface of morality." Only the realization of faith, hope, and love, "which in any case expresses itself symbolically in concrete external actions," is truly moral.[14] Human action becomes merely expressive action, a sign or a symbol, which, brought into service through the "weighing of goods," becomes the "bearer" of a Christian conviction. In this way, philosophical ethics is finally rendered irrelevant. Only by an "inner preparedness and a corresponding attitude of faith" is one enabled to see into the deeper moral meaning of concrete actions. "Where these conditions are not present, there can perhaps be an agreement in theory about the factual or social intentionality of a norm, but not about the deeper moral significance" (ibid., p. 145). How is this different from saying the following: nonbelievers can only be utilitarians—only believers can go further and understand the real, *moral* meaning of their action! Once again, the determination of what is "proper to ethics" would fall victim to a "theological absolutism," with the double result of depriving philosophical ethics—or human morality—of its autonomy, while depriving Christian morality, too, of its proper subject.

## Concluding Remarks: How Teleological Ethics Misses the Value-Objective Character of Human Action

So-called teleological ethics, or proportionalism, is based upon physicalism. It breaks down the whole moral field into "goods" that are in competition with each another. It completely lacks a theory about which goods in such a conflict are "absolute" or inviolable, and must *unconditionally* be taken into account in order to preserve the *human* and *personal* meaning of actions. In teleological ethics such meaning is never grounded with ethical philosophical methods. The function of "grounding" is taken over by a theology of what is proper to Christian morality. Theological positions are introduced in an illegitimate fashion to solve philosophical problems.

But ethics is nevertheless its own philosophical discipline, independent of theology and faith. Its object is the acting *human being*, possessing both inner dignity and operative realization; what counts is not the realization of "goods" but the achievement of the goodness of the human being—the justice, courage, moderation, trustworthiness, and so on of the human person. The point is not to realize "goods," but rather to become fully human.

So-called "teleological ethics" does not fully recognize this priority of the human being because its ethical methods, analyses, and statements lack the necessary anchoring in an anthropology. It is from such a foundation that a correlation of human actions and moral values is to be obtained: and it is only under the condition of such an anthropologically founded correlation that a concept of human action as *moral action* and not as "natural event" comes to the fore; and this happens when ethics is understood as a doctrine of moral virtues.

The concept of moral action *includes* the mutual interdependence and complementary inter-penetration of "right action" and "good will" (intention, conviction). This is an expression of the fact that moral action is an "immanent action" (*actio immanens*), a "doing" that is specified by the fact that its effect remains in the "doer." Actions also are always externalizations of an inner conviction, but they are not only "bearers" of values (to use Scheler's term); but rather, they have moral value themselves, and thereby have an effect upon inner conviction. The intention is molded by human actions while having formative power for preserving the genuinely moral meaning of those actions. There is a mutual, constitutive relationship between the inner act of the will and external actions.[15]

From this perspective we can see how human action affects human goodness. Morality is concerned with the "interior," with the heart of man. This interior, this good will, intention, or conviction, is primarily, fundamentally, and objectively affected by what we *do*. The Bible calls this the basic characteristic of moral action; from the heart come not *values* but very distinct *actions*: "From the heart come evil thoughts: murders, adulteries, fornications, thefts, false testimonies, blasphemies. These are what make a man unclean" (Matt 15:19–20). It is also Matthew who provides, in the sixth beatitude, the deepest—indeed, the truly *teleological*—perspective on moral action so understood: "Blessed are the pure in heart, for they shall see God" (Matt. 5:8).[16]

The connection between action and "intention" can be understood only when it is kept in mind that every moral action is formally an act of the will, in which *that which is done* is as matter to form (the will); it is a matter that is a suitable object of the human will, which again only the reason can achieve. It is not "things" that destroy the intention and make unclean the heart, but rather *actions*, which compromise the light of reason.[17]

Human action is essentially elective, or in Aristotelian terms, *prohairetic* (from *προαίρεσις*, "choice, preference"). Every action is essentially a willing, and the objects of actions are always the objects of a willing, whether this be on the level of concrete choices of actions or on the level of the intention that helps form these choices (*intentio*), which itself is always related to the objects of action, but such as can be reached only by way of other actions (*ea quae sunt ad finem,* the so-called "means"). The intention is not the "subjective" conviction that extends out to the objective element of the action, but rather itself always possesses an objective, reason-formed character; as an act of will, the intention is a component of my interior, of my subjectivity, just as much as the concrete choice of action: the inner conviction is formed both by what I do and by what I ulteriorly intend with this "doing." Both at the same time acquire an objective meaning: what I do and what I intend possess an objective content, which is both *stated* and *formed* by the reason in a practical (preceptive) judgment. The supposed "juxtaposition" or "superposition" of "good intention" and "right action" in teleological ethics is mistaken in view of a theory of actions. It misses the peculiar character of moral action: that indivisible blend of action and intention, of reason and will, of objective and subjective meaning.[18]

It is also impossible to treat the actions that take place only interiorly as moral actions, and finish by including the "conviction of the heart" in an ethical analysis.[19] How could one form a "teleological" judgment as follows: the consequence of the murder of an innocent (even the will to perform such a murder) is "uncleanness of the heart," the badness of the inner conviction? A "teleologist" could only limit himself to the external, and finally *interpersonal,* consequences of the action, and would have to leave out of account the *inner-personal* ones.[20] I know of no teleologist's "calculus" that has included "good intention" or "purity of heart" in the *weighing of goods.* From the perspective of this ethical theory such an internal state would be meaningless, since the theory contends that the "rectitude" of actions arrived at by the *weighing* process is constituted prior to, and in complete independence of, all intention, since the intention is a moral good but the goods to be *weighed* are premoral.

On the other hand, from the perspective of another kind of ethics, which has the capacity to determine and analyze the value-objective character of human action, even deontological *formulations* can be presupposed for the conditions of action that must be preserved independently of all conditions or consequences, so that the value and significance of action as *human action* can be preserved. Such deontological formulations are always based on an anthropologically founded teleological justification, even if this does not always have to be fully explicated in certain circumstances (as in pronouncements by the magisterium). Such justifications form the special contribution of philosophical ethics.

This is how ethics can speak of the "objective" meaning of human action, whereby "objective" does not refer to the purposiveness of actions at the natural level (the *genus naturae*), but rather the human–personal, and thus moral, content of definite actions. This objective content (the so-called "moral object") corresponds in each case to a specific moral virtue.

In so-called teleological ethics, there is no room for this kind of analysis of the objective structure (or value structure) of human action as specifically *human* action. Actions are specified at the level of premoral goods, while values are analyzed independently of this, on a "transcendental" level that is itself grounded in a hidden deontologism. This makes it impossible to correlate concrete actions with moral values. And when at last an attempt is made to reconstruct the meaning of an action through the weighing of goods, the process amounts precisely to the naturalistic fallacy. By this gap between moral values and actions, man is endowed with a practically unlimited power over his existence.

Completely omitted from all of this is the natural reason, made *ad imaginem Dei*, and its measuring function. And yet this is really nothing other than the reason, which, in its setting within the human suppositum (in its *personal* meaning, that is to say), constitutes human action in its moral species (*genus moris*). As the practical reason, its acts form a *natural law*—the law of the practical reason—that molds human action in a normative way and constitutes it as moral action.

Of course, in addition to this (i.e., the human significance of human actions) there are many other points of view from which to consider the determination of a morally right action, such as the consideration of circumstances or consequences; but that is not in question at present, and is something that has always been acknowledged. What is *not* acknowledged by proportionalism, however, is that the specifically human meaning of an action, its moral significance, does not in fact depend on the situational context, nor even on consequences, except insofar as those consequences include those which are constitutive, from an anthropological perspective, of human action *as human*.

Hence it is fitting to associate proportionalism and teleological ethics with *utilitarianism*. This ethical theory is utilitarian because it maintains that every action is fundamentally good, or that no action can be *fundamentally* bad. This is exactly what is meant by utilitarianism: that in principle, every action must be formulated in a "calculus of utility" to determine its moral value, and thus can be totally reformulated in each situation; its moral value is fundamentally at the disposal of the agent.

But this will be denied by someone who maintains that there are actions that *always* and *in themselves* are evil: that there are actions that *always* impair human "utility." Such actions have consequences that could not be "at our disposal" without also having "at our disposal" the very meaning of human action *as such*.

An ethics that takes into account the existence of "moral objectivity" must also inquire how such actions may be identified. How can it be said of an action that it is *objectively* unjust? What, indeed, *is* moral objectivity, or the "moral object" of an action? This question will now be treated, as a conclusion of the foregoing investigations.

## Notes

1. *Fundamental Moral Theology*, p. 234. In this way Böckle does not at all pose the very interesting question of how infidelity is unjust, or how the relationship between justice and infidelity is constituted. I don't believe he *can* ground it, in fact: for he would probably have to say that the judgment "to leave one's wife unjustly is unfaithful" can be reduced to the judgment "to unjustly abandon one's wife is unjust," so that one simply calls "injustice" in this context "infidelity." But then all the commandments of the Decalogue could be reduced to the one command "Thou shalt not act unjustly." And then these commandments would no longer have the function of "reminding the people of the most important goods and values," but only of reminding us that in various contexts we are only *speaking* of the single value "justice."

2. See, for example, F. Furger, *Was Ethik begründet* (Einsiedeln, 1984) p. 49ff. As a teleologist he shows how every teleological weighing of goods must rest upon the *telos* of a deontological valuation, which provides the criterion for teleological justifications. See also O. Höffe, "Die Frage nach dem Moralprinzip," in his *Sittlich-politische Diskurse* (Frankfurt, 1981), p. 65: "Ethics is deontological in the grounding of the highest moral axioms, and teleological in its application of the axioms to definite areas of life and concrete situations."

3. See also T. G. Belmans, *Le Sens Objectif de l'agir humain* (Vatican City, 1980), p. 84ff.

4. Schüller, *Die Begründung sittlicher Urteile*, 2nd ed. (Düsseldorf, 1980), pp. 285ff. This list follows the so-called prima facie duties, or "presumptive duties" in the "milder" form of deontological ethics in the English-speaking world. Schüller is probably correct in thinking that such a "milder" deontology like this one, which does not generally oblige to definite actions but only gives a presumptive and provisional validity to such duties, is in practice not to be distinguished from a teleological ethics. In fact, this "Anglo–Saxon" form of deontology is intelligible only within a utilitarian perspective: it attempts, under the conditions of the utility principle, to establish definite models of action as at least presumptive duties, although they are in principle "elastic" and capable of being superseded.

5. This is so that the acts of the virtues can also reach their ultimate, supernatural goal—namely God—something possible only through the virtue of love (because in actuality, by God's plan of salvation, man possesses *only* a supernatural end, and therefore is effectively ordered *only* to God—that is, as a servant—through *caritas*). Those acts which are ordered to their final end, and are thus "of service," nevertheless do not determine the axiological qualification of actions on the natural–human level; see *In II Sent.* d. 28, q.1, a.1: "Opus meritorium non determinat genus actus, sed efficaciam." (A meritorious deed does not determine the kind of action, but rather its efficacy.)

6. See *De Caritate*, q. 1, a. 3, ad 9um: "A proprio fine et a proprio objecto quaelibet virtus habet formam specialem, per quam est haec virtus; sed a caritate habet quandam formam communem, secundum quam est meritoria vitae aeternae." (Any virtue acquires its special form from its intention and from its object, through which it is *this* virtue, but from charity it gets a certain universal form, by which it becomes meritorious for eternal life.)

7. See also *De Virtutibus Cardinalibus*, q. 1, a. 2: above the natural inclinations (representing the *semina virtutum* to the extent that they are not yet molded by reason), there are two further levels of virtue, which

must be clearly distinguished: "The second grade of virtues is of those which meet with right reason, but still do not reach God Himself through charity. These are perfect in a way [*aliqualiter sunt perfectae*] with respect to [*per comparationem ad*] the human good, but they are not absolutely perfect [*simpliciter perfectae*], because they do not reach the first rule [*primam regulam*], which is the the last end [*ultimus finis*]. . . . The third level is that of perfected virtues, which are joined to charity [*simul cum caritate*]; these virtues make an act of a man absolutely good [*simpliciter bonum*], as reaching the last end."

8. Ibid.: "Ad ipsam autem rectam rationem in quolibet genere requiritur quod aliquis habeat aestimationem et iudicium de principiis, ex quibus ratio illa procedit. . . . Principia autem agibilium sunt fines; ex his enim sumitur ratio agendorum." (For right reason in any matter it is required that someone have an estimation and judgment about the principles from which that reasoning proceeds. . . . The principles of things to be done are their ends, for from these is taken the reasoning of things to be done.) These *fines* are the "proximate" *fines*, that is, the goals of the virtues, which are constitutive of the objects of those actions which belong to each of the virtues.

9. The present issue would have to be treated much more fully in a theological work, because the position of Schüller and many contemporary moral theologians depends on abandoning the distinction between nature and grace, and between the natural and the supernatural. The resulting jumble of philosophy, theology, philosophical analysis, biblical citations, and "theologoumena" is an obstacle to the philosopher, and seems to me to serve the interests neither of philosophy nor of theology. Two different tendencies appear to come to the same result: an ethics derived directly from faith, and an "autonomous" morality debilitated by the loss of what is proper to ethics. Both agree in this basic respect, and have similar effects on the justification of moral norms on the human level.

10. In another context, Schüller clarifies what he means by this "weal or woe": (in "Die Bedeutung des natürlichen Sittengesetzes für den Christen," in G. Teichtweier and W. Dreier, eds., *Herausforderung und Kritik der Moraltheologie* [Würzburg, 1971], p. 125). First, in the "single unconditional necessity," namely, "to be loved by God in Christ and thereby to gain salvation." Second, in "one's own moral goodness" (but wherein this consists, ethics must say, since it cannot itself be a standard, but some measure must be provided for it). Third, he mentions "health and illness, wealth and poverty, honor and dishonor." It is clear that "salvation" and "one's own goodness" are never themselves subject to a "weighing" process. But what, then, do these "standards" say for human

conduct? Nothing, as such. And then *everything else* "that otherwise makes for the welfare or suffering of the human being . . . can immediately be judged as *indifferent*." Thus the criterion of *Wohl oder Wehe* is shown to be a morally "empty formula."

11. See *Die Begründung sittlicher Urteile*, p. 283: "because both types of conclusion 'morally wrong, because against nature' and 'morally wrong, because unjustified,' lead to the judgment of certain actions without regard to how many devastating [*verheerende*] consequences their omission might lead to." "A definite action (such as a lie) is supposed to be morally reprehensible, no matter what catastrophic consequences *not doing it* may lead to."

12. See Schüller, ibid., p. 291. The argument of J. de Lugo, introduced in the same context, concerning the validity without exception of the secrecy of the confessional, is no proof that such typically utilitarian arguments for the grounding of moral norms was known to the tradition. For this argument does not serve to ground the validity of the secrecy of the confessional as a natural or professional secret. Rather, it establishes why such secrecy may never be violated, which does not unconditionally apply to a professional secret. The argument, in other words, does not intend to establish the *exception* to a command that in itself is valid without exception; it does the reverse: it seeks to justify the *intensifying* of a norm (that in itself allows exceptions) to the point where it allows *no* exception. This means that it establishes why, in the case of the secrecy of the confessional, the purpose of professional secrecy can be secured only through an *exceptionless* validity. In other words, it is precisely the opposite kind of phenomenon as in Schüller's example.

13. This example is also discussed by J. Finnis, *Fundamentals of Ethics* (Oxford and New York, 1983), pp. 95ff. Finnis points out further problems with Schüller's argument.

14. See H. Rotter, *Christliches Handeln. Seine Begründung und Eigenart* (Graz, 1977), p. 143.

15. Thomas explains this especially at *I–II*, q. 19–20, and at *De Malo*, q. 2.

16. In this context, the reduction of all practical goods to premoral goods is the crucial mistake in principle. All goods then become "contingent" and are treated as morally "relative." And here is where Böckle locates the "main argument" for the "teleological justification" of moral norms. "The main argument consists in showing that the goods and values presented to our action are ultimately *conditioned, created*, and therefore *limited* values. Moral judgment can then succeed only through regard for this conditionality, as well as through the weighing of occasionally competing goods. To be sure, man is unconditionally obligated

by the absolute ground of the ethical, but as a contingent being in a contingent world, he can realize that absolutely required *bonum* only in and through the *bona* that show themselves as contingent goods or values or even relative values, and as such never as the a priori greatest good, which could never compete with a higher one. With a view toward the *bona*, the only question possible is about the preferable good, and that means that every concrete, categorical decision *must* ultimately (in order to avoid absolutizing what is contingent) rest on a choice made on the basis of the priorities of goods and values." (*Fundamentalmoral,* p. 307 [translated by G. Malsbary; see p. 236 of *Fundamental Moral Theology* for translation by N. D. Smith]).

In this quotation the whole problem of teleological ethics, with its weakness and inconsistency, can be seen clearly. It is inconsistent because suddenly goods *and* values (the latter are not supposed to be premoral for teleologists) are associated together upon the same contingent and relative level. The weakness of the argument consists in the fact that in *every* moral action, the moral goodness of the person is in question, and that this goodness always depends upon *what* one does. Practical goods, which are chosen and pursued in a moral action, are not simply "things" with which one negotiates and calculates. The morality of an action, in which the whole person is involved, is nevertheless always an *absolute* and *unconditional* good, even if the person is a nonabsolute, created existence. This is so because it is precisely in moral goodness that man establishes his relationship with God, the unconditional and absolute ground of every moral demand. In relation to the goodness involved in concrete action, there can never be an occasional "higher" or "competing" good. To someone who has adopted the idea that our actions have to do only with premoral goods, this argument will hardly appear plausible, because such a person has lost sight of what is "proper to ethics" to begin with.

17. See *I–II,* q. 86, a. 1, ad 1um: "Anima non inquinatur ex rebus inferioribus virtute earum, quasi agentibus eis in animam: sed magis e converso *anima sua actione se inquinat, inordinate eis inhaerendo, contra lumen rationis et divinae legis.*" (The soul is not made unclean by things inferior to it in power, as though they acted against the soul: rather, the soul by its own action makes itself unclean, by inordinately clinging to them, against the light of reason and of the divine law.)

18. Note added by the author to English edition: When mention is made here of "intending" or "intention," it is meant in the strict sense—that is, in the sense of Thomas's *intentio* as opposed to *electio.* In subsequent works I have often pointed out that the object of action always includes within itself a basic intentionality formed by the reason. In the present work, however, the emphasis is upon the connection between

object and practical reason. For the intentional structure of the object of action, see my later writings " 'Intrinsically Evil Acts' and the Moral Viewpoint: Clarifying a Central Teaching of *Veritatis Splendor*," *The Thomist* 58, 1 (1994): 1–39; "Intentional Actions and the Meaning of Object: A Reply to Richard McCormick," *The Thomist* 59, 2(1995): 279–311; and in more detail in *La prospettiva della morale. Fondamenti dell' etica philosophica* (Rome, 1994). See also a similar approach to the matter by J. M. Finnis, "Object and Intention in Moral Judgments According to Aquinas," *The Thomist* 55 (1991): 1–27.

19. See also Matt. 5:27–28: "You have heard that it was said, 'You shall not commit adultery,' but *I say to you*, that everyone who looks at a woman lustfully has already committed adultery with her in his heart." Such an "adultery of the heart" is, of course, *without consequence*, so that one would have to consider the consequence in the heart of man. And this is not just any consequence, but adultery. But in the framework of an ethics that puts everything in terms of the "rectitude of actions" on the basis of a weighing of goods, the so-called inner act cannot be conceived as moral action.

20. This is clearly to be seen in Böckle, *Fundamental Moral Theology*, p. 308, n. 7: "It should be stressed that it is only in the interpersonal sphere that moral norms can be justified on the basis of the predictable consequences of man's actions." Böckle completely overlooks that every *interpersonal* action (in regard to the virtue of justice) possesses an *innerpersonal* dimension, and this is finally of the highest significance for the *interpersonal* realm as well. We are concerned here not only with external goods but also, as always, with human actions and acts of the will that extend to the good of another.

# 10

# The Objectivity of Human Action: The Object of Action and the Practical Reason

THE EXTENSIVE CRITIQUE of teleological ethics (or "proportionalism") should reveal the need for a fuller and deeper analysis of the "objective meaning of human action" as presented in a preliminary fashion in chapter 2, section "The Moral Object, and How It Is Constituted." What do we mean when we speak, with Thomas, about the "object" of an action giving the action the moral quality of "good" or "bad," or correlating the action to this "vice" or to that "virtue?" And what connection is there between this objectivity of human action and the natural law?

In many traditional handbooks, the theme of the morally specifying and qualifying object of actions is inadequately, or in some isolated instances incorrectly, treated, at least when compared with Thomas's treatment. Consequently certain preconceptions survive among contemporary moral theologians when, on the basis of such interpretations, they do not understand why not only "moral actions" or "values," but even *actions* as such, can be morally qualified independently of the concrete intentions of the agent.

The very precise, if dryly technical, term *object* can easily make us forget that it signifies the *moral finality* that pertains to single actions (and that at the same time constitutes the moral content or meaning of such actions).[1] Over and over again it is the concept of the object—or the *finis operis*—that is being misunderstood "naturalistically." The connection, furthermore, between this "objective meaning" of human action and the natural law as the law of the practical reason is not brought to light with sufficient clarity. In the following chapters, the interconnections of these various themes will be shown by way of a concluding synthesis of the foregoing studies—a mere sketch of a vast subject.

## The Conceptual Relationship Between "Object of Action" and "Actus Humanus"

What is in question now is the objective content of a "doing"; however, this is not any "doing," but only that which St. Thomas calls the *actus humanus*. "Human actions"—a synonym for "moral actions" (see *I–II,* q. 1, a. 3: *nam idem sunt actus morales et actus humani*)—are acts over which a human being possesses a mastery (*dominium*), or acts considered insofar as one possesses such *dominium* over them. They are actions, in other words, that man carries out in personal autonomy, in freedom, and with rational consideration: through the will and intellect, man is master of his own actions (see *I–II,* q. 1, a. 1).

Accordingly, there are activities that the human being carries out that cannot *as such* be called human (or "moral") actions: for example, pure acts of cognition (as such) or productive acts (technical or artistic). "Human actions" always belong to the area of a moral virtue, or of a vice, which is opposed to virtue. Making a shoe or constructing a building, carrying out an act of knowing or painting a picture can all *as such* be correlated to no specific (moral) virtue. If we can say that the "object" of shoemaking is the shoe, or that the "object" of house construction is the house, the "object" of scientific knowing is, for example, the brain of a white laboratory rat, or the "object" of the painting, a particular landscape, we are not speaking of "objects" as the content of *moral actions*. Even if we were to consider these objects as the *goals* of the corresponding activities (the goal of shoe-making is the shoe, that of construction is the house, that of scientific research is the knowledge of the functioning of the rat's brain, that of painting is the image of the landscape), even then we would not be concerned with the goals of moral actions, but rather with the goals of other types of actions that are characterized both naturally and (on the part of the agent) artificially, *as producing certain effects*, which effects can then be pursued as goals.

All this may sound somewhat banal, but in fact this distinction is not infrequently overlooked: many moral theologians try to understand the concept of the object of moral actions by the model of such *productive* actions.

Now this is not to imply that these kinds of actions (human

making, knowing, or artistry) cannot *also* be "moral actions"; indeed, it must even be said that they are always *de facto* moral. The shoemaker, the house builder, the biological researcher, the landscape artist, all do what they do because they are pursuing a definite *practical* good: houses are not built for the sake of houses but so that people can live in them; human beings need houses for reasons of shelter, survival, and sociability. The architect qua architect in his action pursues first and foremost the "building of a house," but as *a human being* he pursues a human good that is more than the purely technical construction of a "building"; and he acts on the basis of his own deliberate decision. The researcher with his action *at least* wants to know the truth, even if his activity would serve no other purpose. The "knowledge of the truth," even of the brain functions of a white rat, is a human good, and an action based on this good is accomplished by a human person who orders his action voluntarily and according to reason, since otherwise he could have no interest in white rats. Thus his action is a "human action," and morally qualifiable.[2]

In this way we reach a second concept of the "object" of action: even if the architect builds "houses" (the *material* aspect of his doing), what he does is *formally* and in the moral sense essentially an act that goes beyond the mere fact of "constructing houses" (an act of justice, one might say, insofar as the houses are meant for people to live in them). The architect pursues a human good, and as a rule does so for others. If he were not to do so, he would perhaps not be a bad architect, but his doing would be objectively different in the moral sense. This would be the case, for example, if instead of working with a view to the general well-being of human life, work, and culture, and making something humanly "useful," he were to use his ability to deceive other people by his skill and make unjust profit for himself.[3]

It is important to emphasize here that the question of the *intention* has still not been broached.[4] This would be the case if, in addition to what has been said, the further possibilities were taken into account that the architect is carrying out his activity in order to earn a living, in order to win a prize, in order to become famous and admired, and so on. Such intentions, which go beyond the objective meaning of the action, as a rule are prior to it and extremely significant—indeed, they are crucial in the final analysis. Nevertheless, the object we are speaking of here is the goal that is pursued in the action as such, or "objectively," and that first lends the action its character and specificity as a "human" or "moral" action, its moral distinctiveness.[5]

The examples we have mentioned all involve actions that are in fact not the most typical or elementary "moral actions," since they do not originate from the area proper to moral action. But analogies from the nonmoral areas, if correctly applied, can be very helpful in making clear the specific conditions that belong to these areas. With some actions this can be very difficult. Acts like "eating" (self-nourishment), "having a child," "speaking" (apart from the rhetorical art of persuasion), "killing a human being," and so on all have the peculiarity, that they *originally* belong to the realm of moral action, that is, they can be treated *only* as moral actions, as *actus humani* and objects of "doing" (as opposed to "knowing" or "making"). It makes sense to distinguish an architect qua architect from an architect qua human being, but it would make no sense to distinguish someone who *as such* nourishes himself from someone who nourishes himself *as a human being*, and the same holds for the other examples. Naturally, we can study the process of nourishment or metabolism in the abstract, in its physiological characteristics, and the same could be said for the act or process of procreating a human life, for the physiological function of human speaking, or for the technology of abortion. But these actions are not carried out on that level alone. They do not (like the productive actions of building a house or shoemaking, or like the act of researching the brain structure of a white rat) belong first to another sphere, to which the character of moral actions must be *further* attributed; they are neither "products of skill or artistry " nor "acts of knowledge." If we treat them in their natural (e.g., physiological) determinacy—as the act of procreation produces a life through the combining of gametes, and so on—we presume an abstraction, and we could not say that these acts as such belong to another sphere of human action, which then "additionally" has a moral dimension. It would be meaningless, therefore, to treat a "procreator of human life" *as such* in distinction from someone who does the same qua human being.

To put it another way: an architect who is a good or competent architect is still a good architect even if we exclude all consideration of the moral components of his action as human action. But it is not possible to imagine the act of procreating while excluding its quality as an *actus humanus*: we would consider as a "bad" or ("incompetent") procreator or "transmitter" of human life precisely someone who does not consider, or who wrongly considers, the moral dimension of his or her action.

In the domain of human actions, in most cases the sphere of "productive" (or artistic or technical) actions is mixed with that of genuine moral action. The most diverse sorts of productions, technical abilities, and means enter into the area of human action. This makes it somewhat difficult for us today to recognize *two areas* of human actions in particular as actions of a genuinely moral nature, and to distinguish them from merely productive actions, or from technical skills or abilities, and so on: these are the realms of human *language* and human *sexuality*. This is especially manifest in the contemporary reduction of the object of moral actions to "premoral goods."[6]

When, in the following discussion, the concept of the object of human (moral) actions is used, it must be made clear just what is meant by this "object": it means neither the object of a productive enterprise (technique, artistry, making), such as a "building," nor the object of a knowing activity (e.g., scientific research), such as "the structure and function of a white rat's brain," nor the object of natural, physiological acts or processes, such as the functioning of the digestive system or the action of the "generative power." The object we are speaking of here, as already explained, is the goal or practical good that is pursued in doing and that, at the same time, gives the act its character as a "human" or "moral" act at the very outset.

The definition of the concept of the *actus humanus* appears in Thomas in an article bearing the title "Whether It Is Proper to Man to Act for the Sake of an End?" (*Utrum Homini Conveniat Agere Propter Finem? I–II,* q. 1, a. 1). The answer to the question depends on the definition of the *human act* as that kind of activity "that proceeds from a deliberate will." Whatever springs from the will is pursued for the sake of a goal or end, since the object of the will is a goal or end. Thus it is the goal or end that the will seeks that lends human action its *objective* character, giving it moral qualification and specification.[7]

The definition of the object of action as a "goal" or "end" (*finis*) of the will is fundamental for Thomas. The conventional neo-scholastic terminology that distinguished sharply between "objects" and "ends," or the *finis operis* and the *finis operantis*, has led to the neglect of this truth, even though the terminology is still useful in practice, and was not foreign to Thomas himself. In using it, one must be careful not to overlook the fact that the "object" is always a goal or end for the will, and that the goal of the intention is *also* an "object."[8] It makes no sense, that is, to set the "objective" in opposition to the "subjective": such an opposition usually implies physicalism. In the interplay of action and intention there is an object of the first order and an object of the second order. What is "subjective" is often only the *correlation* or *ordering* of concrete actions and intentions. To use Aristotle's example, if someone steals for the sake of committing adultery, he both *does* and *intends* something objectively bad. The intention is only to that degree subjective (and a *finis operantis*), since the orientation of theft to adultery in no way belongs to the objective meaning of the theft;[9] the intentional ordering is something that belongs to the acting subject, but this does not impair the fact that the morality of such an intention must be judged according to objective standards.

At this point, there is something that must be firmly grasped: the concept of the object of the action in a moral sense depends upon the concept of "human action." Accordingly, the object of a moral action is not the object of some kind of *power*, or of human making, but rather is exclusively the object of the will, and that means a goal and good pursued by the will. Of course, objective elements of other powers and productions can be integrated into these objects of the will, as usually happens. As material components of the moral object, they will form the so-called *materia circa quam*, and they already *are* this *materia* as components of the moral object; but in order to be able to appear to the will as a good (or object), they must be molded and ordered by the practical reason (see the earlier treatment of the *materia circa quam* in chapter 2, section "The Moral Object, and How It Is Constituted").

An example is in order. The "good of procreation," which according to F. Böckle is the object of the human act of conception, is as such *not* the moral object of this act; the "good of procreation" is, rather, the good (or object, or *finis naturalis*) of the human procreative or generative *power*, that is, of its natural–biological purposiveness. But if we treat the object of the human act of procreation as a "moral object," that is, as an *actus humanus* (which it really is), and not merely as an "act of the generative power" (*actus potentiae generativae*), then the object is not simply the "good of procreation," for while that would materially determine the action, the action is by no means exhausted in that. The object of the human act of procreation (as an *actus humanus*, or a personal act) is the *human good* of the transmission of human life.

The *natural* intentionality of the procreative power is not "concerned" with the fact that the (natural) object of the (purely physically considered) act of procreation is a *human* existence; for this good is capable of being intended only by the human being, insofar as the human being acts *as such*. And he can grasp this good in all its dimensions, insofar as he clearly understands what a human being is and wherein consist the dignity and meaningfulness of human life: that man possesses an immortal soul directly created by God; that human procreation is a cooperation with a divine act of creation; and that the transmission of human life signifies the transmission of the image of God, the building up of the human community and—from a Christian perspective—of the Church as the mystical Body of Christ and the People of God. These objective contents are not included in the "good of procreation" as the *finis naturalis* of the generative power. They are constituted in the fact that this generative act is an act of a human being, which in the framework of the human suppositum (even without consideration of the supernatural order of grace) possesses a more comprehensive meaning than the purely natural, and if it is carried out, it is an *actus humanus*. *These objectively moral contents are objectifiable to man only as* a *humanly acting* being, and thereby become the object of his action ("*human* procreation").

In this way, two aspects are taken into account: the material content of the object, and its integration into the moral context of the *actus humanus*. In the former aspect, the act of conception is *materialiter* the act of the procreative power. But it is this always in the context of a human suppositum, and is thus more than a mere biological event. It is a specifically human act and not merely a "biological one"; it is a *personal* act.[10]

This point can be clarified by a formulation of St. Thomas: *finis usus genitalium membrorum est generatio et educatio prolis*. (The end of the use of the genital organs is the generation and education of children; *De Malo*, q. 15, a. 1). It may appear at first that Thomas is thinking here of a *finis naturalis* of the act of the human organs of conception; but this is not the case, and to take it so would require a physicalistic interpretation. Thomas is not speaking here of the *finis* of the human procreative act in its physiological and biological dimension, but rather of the *finis* of the *usus genitalium membrorum* (the end of using the genital organs); the *usus* refers to the last, immediately practical level of the unfolding of the *actus humanus*: it is the effective action that results from the deliberative process and is subject to the command of the reason and will. "To *use* [or exercise or apply; *uti*] is properly and primarily an act of the will, where the will is as it were the first mover [*tamquam primi moventis*], while the reason provides the direction [*rationis . . . tamquam dirigentis*], and the other powers follow along [*aliarum potentiarum . . . tamquam exequentium*]; but to use [apply or exercise; *uti*] is properly an act of the will" (*I–II*, q. 16, a. 1).

This teaching does not speak, then, of a (physiological) *finis naturalis* of the organs of generation, but rather of a human, voluntary act, which is only *materialiter* an act of the organs. Formally, it is an act of "reasoned will" (*voluntas deliberata*), and thus in substance an *actus humanus*. The *generatio et educatio prolis* is taken as the goal (*finis operis*)—and we could also say: as the *object*—of an act of *this kind*.

The formulation itself points this out. How could the natural–physiological goal of the procreative power be understood to consist in the "education" or "raising" of children?[11] The passage shows the constantly *moral* perspective of St. Thomas. He is talking about human, moral actions, and not natural-physiological processes.

## The Objects of Actions as Objects of Reason and Will

Apart from those human acts which are carried out by the will alone (such as an internal act of loving God, or wishes), the human act displays a "composite" structure: as an act moved and "commanded" by the will, it is composed of an *inner* act of the will (*actus interior* or *elicitus*) and an *external* act (*actus exterior* or *imperatus*). The overwhelming majority of human acts are carried out (through an *usus*) by means of another power of the soul and by one or another bodily organ. The will governs or "rules" these acts of the other powers of organs by its command (*imperium*). The inner act of will and the outer *actus imperatus* are related to one another as form and matter, and form a single act.[12]

Human acts are thus always personal acts: that is, they are not carried out by a power or an organ, but by a knowing and willing human being, and with the means of other powers. It is man who procreates man, and not the "human procreative power." The unity between the inner and outer act, between the *imperium* and the *actus imperatus,* is ultimately an expression of this personal structure of human acts: in human action there is a personal integration of all the levels of human existence.

The distinction between an "inner" and "outer" act does not entail that the "outer" act be externally manifest or visible, but rather that it be that very act of a power of the soul *insofar* as it is subject to the *imperium* of the will. So, for example, in a willing act of sensual desiring, the "outer" act is the act of the sensitive "concupiscible power" (*vis concupiscibilis*), to the extent that it is subjected to the power of the will, even if this act does not reveal itself outwardly and the person "does" nothing; the "inner" act of the will, which has the outer act as an object or goal, and "wants" this desiring.[13]

The so-called "exterior act" is likewise an act of the will, and yet not an act that the will "brings from itself" (*actus elicitus*), but rather an act that the will achieves through the means of other powers and bodily organs. It would consequently make sense to distinguish further between the *actus exterior* and the *actus externus*: the latter would be the externally visible "outer doing," as opposed to a purely inner wishing, feeling, and so on. If, with this distinction in mind, Thomas calls the *actus exterior* the object, he does not mean the object of the "outer doing," but rather the object of the will, insofar as the will, through its command (*imperium*), reaches out to the act of a power other than itself.

The object of moral actions is always the object of the will. To the extent that an *actus humanus* is achieved (as is normally the case) through the command of an act of another power, the object of this human action is not the object of the act of the other power but rather the act itself, *insofar as it is subject to the command of the will*—and that means insofar as it is ordered by the reason as the *bonum rationis*.

This command (*imperium*) that the will exercises over the other powers and their acts is essentially the act of the "ordering reason" or an *ordinatio rationis*.[14] This is set into motion by the will and is embedded in the will's appetitive (or seeking, striving) dynamic.[15] The *imperium*, therefore, is precisely equivalent to the *preceptive structure of the practical reason*, as presented in part I.

We can therefore treat one and the same object of an action from two different points of view: first, in abstraction from its "being willed," as an *actus exterior* ordered through the *imperium* by the *ratio*, that is, as the object of the (practical) reason; and second, we can consider it as the object of that inner act of the will that lies at the basis of the *imperium*. Objects of actions are always objects of the practical reason *and* the will, and only to that extent are they the objects of an actus humanus, or so-called *moral objects*.

## Actions as Objects of the Practical Reason

We can begin by turning to the moral qualification and specification of the "exterior act." Thomas says that its object is that *circa quod est actio exterior* (*I–II*, q. 18, a. 6), or that the object that gives the exterior act its moral species ("good" or "bad," "right" or "wrong") is the *materia circa quam* (*I–II*, q. 18, a. 2, ad 2um).

Now if we think that the exterior act is not the act of the will but rather the act of another power, this object of the exterior act could seem simply to be the object of the power in question, one of the *fines naturales* of the various powers, or even the "things" that we seek for, use, distribute, take or steal.

But this is not supported by Thomas's texts. For he clearly points out how, in human action, the acts of the single powers specify the action not in its natural aspect (*genus naturae*) but rather in its moral aspect (*genus moris*). The classical example of this is once again the procreative act: in its natural determinacy as an act of the *potentia generativa* it does not specify human action in a moral way and is not at all a moral object; only insofar as this act is objectified by the reason and, consequently, *ordered* by the reason, is it an object of action in the moral sense. On the level of its determination by the reason, then, there is a difference, in a moral respect, between the procreative act of a married couple and the *naturally* identical act of nonmarried persons (e.g., in an adulterous relationship). Considered in their *genus naturae*, the marital act and an act of adultery are identical; as objects of an *actus humanus*, however—and that means as moral objects of actions considered as being ordered by the reason—we find ourselves faced with two morally and *objectively* different—radically different—actions (see *I–II,* q. 18, a. 5, ad 3um; see also *De Malo,* q. 2, a. 4). In the same way, there is an objective (moral) difference (and a *natural* identity) between "killing an innocent person with a pistol" and "carrying out a legitimate death sentence with a pistol," or between lying as such and lying in a harmless parlor game.

The morally objective qualification of actions thus is not simply derived from the "nature of the act," if one means by that the natural determination of the act. Thomas constantly emphasizes that by the "object" he means in each case the *genus moris*, or the *esse morale* of the act. This moral determination of an object is constituted through the relation between an act and the reason: "The human act, which is called the moral act, obtains its specification from an object related to the principle of human acts, which is the reason.[16] As stated earlier, Thomas calls the species of moral action formed by the object "forms as conceived by the reason" (*formae prout sunt a ratione conceptae*), and thus distinguishes them from the "natural forms" (*formae naturales*), through which natural things (*res naturales*) are specified and through which acts can be treated at the merely natural level of the *genus naturae* (*I–II,* q. 18, a. 10).

At this stage in our presentation, a rather significant nuance should be noted in Thomas's formulations: the object, which morally specifies actions, is not simply the "object" of such actions (as the *finis naturalis* of single actions, or the "use of things," such as "to take money" or "to fire a shot"), but rather the "fitting object" (*angemessene Objekt*): "The first morality of an act is found in the *fitness of the object*" (*Prima moralitas actus attenditur ex obiecto convenienti*). For an example, Thomas distinguishes "using one's own" (*uti re sua*) from "taking what belongs to another" (*accipere aliena*: *I–II*, q. 18, a. 2). The relationship of possession does not consist in the things—no more than a marital relationship can be distinguished from an extramarital relationship ("sleeping with one's own spouse" as opposed to "sleeping with another's spouse"; see *De Malo*, q. 2. a. 4) by the "nature of the procreative act." The "fitness" (*convenientia*) that is *included* in the concept of the moral object, and that first constitutes it in its *genus moris*, has its origin in an *ordinatio rationis*.

By this, Thomas shows that the specification of actions through the object does not simply mean "if the object is good, the action is good." Money, "things" in general, and acts such as the procreative act are always "goods" in their natural state—and this means on the "premoral," "ontic" level of the *genus naturae*—so long as the money is not counterfeit (whereby it would still keep the "goodness" of a skillfully made counterfeit, or at least of the worth of the material) and so long as the procreative act is physiologically normal ("sterility" in this sense would be a physical evil).

But *not* in this sense are the moral objects of actions, or the actions that pursue these objects, "goods": they are only so, Thomas says, through a *debita proportio ad hanc vel illam actionem*,[17] or insofar as they are a "fitting object" (*obiectum conveniens*).

A third formulation to the same effect can be taken from the *De Malo*. After the point has been made that human acts become specified through the object in its relation to the reason, Thomas makes this precision: a good action is one that is related to a "fitting" or "proper" matter (*actus cadens supra debitam materiam*), for example, "giving a hungry person something to eat"; a bad action is one that is related to an "improper matter" (*materia indebita*), as for example "to take something that belongs to someone else." We have here a *materia circa quam* that in one case is "right" (*debita*), and in another case is "wrong" (*indebita*). Now this "matter concerning which," as we have emphasized before, is not simply the material aspect of the action in its *genus naturae* (which would be "matter out of which"; *materia ex qua*), but is already a *materia debita*. In a certain way, "it possesses, insofar as it gives the *species*, the characteristic of a form" (*I–II,* q. 18, a. 2, ad 2um); this *materia circa quam* is therefore the same as the (moral) object of action.[18]

The concept of the object and that of the *materia circa quam* include the element of *convenientia* (or *debita proportio,* or *debitum,* fittingness, reasonableness, etc.) by means of a *comparatio ad rationem.* Once again, it is seen how the objects of action are "forms as they are conceived by the reason" (*formae prout sunt a ratione conceptae*). This perspective is confirmed in the *quaestio* where Thomas speaks expressly about the "good and evil" (*bonitas et malitia*) of the *actus exterior:* this moral qualification originates neither from the will nor from the matter nor from the circumstances as such (i.e., independently of their relation to the reason). On the contrary, the "goodness [*bonitas*] or evil [*malitia*] that the exterior act has in itself [*secundum se*], on account of the rightness or fittingness of the matter or circumstances [*debitam materiam, debitas circumstantias*] is not derived from the will, but rather from the reason [*sed magis a ratione*]" (*I–II,* q. 20, a. 1, ad 2um).

And finally we have our conclusion: the moral object, or the morally objective content of human actions, is constituted through understanding the *convenientia,* the *debita proportio,* the *debita materia,* or simply the *debitum* of definite exterior actions. In other words, the grasping of the objects of actions or of the objective moral content or meaning of an action is a task of the (practical) reason. This *debitum* lies neither in "things" nor in the "nature of the act" as objectified in the *genus naturae.* Rather, it is these that must be ordered by the reason, and fundamentally so in acts that we have already thoroughly analyzed: we are concerned here again with the (preceptive) acts of the *lex naturalis,* since these arise from the *ratio naturalis* and, as a participation of the eternal law, from a *naturalis inclinatio* "to the right act and end" (*ad debitum actum et finem; I–II,* q. 91, a. 2).

This doctrine of the rational constitution of the moral objects of actions, in leading us to the reason, leads us as well to the concept of the natural law. The concept of the *debitum* is included in that of the moral object. Exterior actions will be "objectified" in the moral sense, and the "objective meaning" will be brought out, exactly to the extent that the *debitum* is grasped and *constituted* in them through an ordering (*ordinatio*) of the reason—and this does not work in reverse, as the naturalistic fallacy would maintain. The concept of the object *presupposes* that of the *debitum* or the *ordinatio rationis*. The rule and measure of the objective meaning of our actions is the reason, and with it, the natural law of the practical reason, however its contents are conveyed, since "good and evil in human actions is considered with regard for how the act accords with reason [*concordat rationi*] as informed by divine law, by nature, or by instruction" (*De Malo,* q. 2, a. 4).

This can now be illustrated by the example of human procreation: the "moral object" or, preferably, the "objective moral content" of the human act of procreation does not simply consist in the "conception of a living thing,"[19] but rather in the "transmission of human life." What a human being is, is not contained in the act of conception considered in its *genus naturae*, nor may that act as such (in its natural potentiality) ever bring about a human being. This is because the act of conception is really capable only of producing a body that is informed by a soul that does not originate from that act. But even if we recognize this, we still have not determined the "moral object" of the act. This is constituted, rather, through a grasp of the value of human life, of its meaningfulness and orientation, and of the connection of the transmission of human life with married love. It has to do with the practical knowledge of a *bonum humanum,* as grasped and preceptively formulated in one of the highest principles of the *lex naturalis*.

We can be still more precise: the moral object (or the objectively meaningful content) of the act of human conception as an *actus humanus* is the loving unity (*commixtio carnalis*; the "mixture of the flesh") between man and woman, which in itself nevertheless already contains the meaningful content of the transmission of human life, since the bodily unity of husband and wife is the *consummatio* or fulfillment of married love, which for its part originates from a corresponding *naturalis inclinatio*, as integrated into the *ordinatio rationis* (see chapter 2, section "Beyond Naturalism and Dualism," subsection "Integral Anthropology or Spiritualism?"). In this objectively meaningful content will also be found a "right commensuration of matter and circumstances" (*commensuratio debita materiae et circumstantiarum*): the relationship between the transmission of human life and married love (which requires separate justification[20]), as well as the openness of the human procreative act to the conception of new life. Married love is a personal act—essentially, an act of the will—that reaches out to the good of the transmission of human life. Its openness toward the transmission of human life is not a "biological–physiological" openness of the *potentia generativa*, but rather the openness of married love toward the transmission of human life.

The object (or *finis operis*) of the marital act cannot simply be grounded by the act of the *potentia generativa*; rather, it needs the formal consideration of what married love *is*.[21] Only in the personal dimension of the *actus humanus* can the objectively-meaningful content of the act be seen—as well as what it means to be open to the transmission of human life.[22]

Formulations like "object of the marital act," the "object of lying," and "object of theft" conceal a dangerous ambiguity. If we take the case of theft, the object of which is neither simply some "thing" nor "something belonging to someone else" (*res aliena*), but rather the *substractio rei alienae* (the *taking away* of something): the *res aliena* in itself can only be the object of an act of envy or of shared joy. Only in relationship to an act of "taking away" does this *res aliena* become "wrong matter" (*materia indebita*).

And so we arrive at the seeming paradox that the object of theft is really *theft*. If I should say, "The object of theft is the *taking away* of what belongs to another, " then I am not saying what the action "theft" is here *concerned with*; I am saying what theft *is*, that is, I am defining it. If one does not attend to this, one must immediately go "one step lower," to the level of the *genus naturae*, or "things." This is possibly the route taken by so many moral philosophers and theologians who looked for the object of the marital act in the "object" of the generative power as such, and thus fell prey to the naturalistic fallacy. In a certain sense, then, it would be preferable to speak of the "objective contents" or "meaning of the exterior act" instead of the "*object* of the exterior act," since the "object" is the exterior act itself, as ordered by the reason: the action's *materia circa quam*, or "proper matter" (materia debita).[23]

The seeming paradox of an action that is the "object of itself" is removed when we consider that our treatment thus far has depended on an abstraction. Hitherto we have treated the object of action as an object integrated into an *actus humanus,* but still "isolated" within its relationship to the reason and not yet an object of the will. The "exterior act" that gains its specification through the object is an *actus imperatus,* a "commanded act"; as an *actus humanus* it is essentially a *willed* act, and only as such does it enter the sphere of the practical, of the reason as practical reason—or is even accomplished at all. The object of such an *actus humanus,* which originates from a "deliberate will" (*voluntas deliberata*), is now precisely the *actus exterior,* which we have hitherto been considering as abstracted from the will.[24] *If we speak of the object of human actions, we will henceforth mean the object of an act of the will.* Only from this standpoint can we attain a full insight into the meaning of the concept "the object of the action."

## Actions as Objects of the Will

To conceive of actions as objects of acts of the will does not mean adding a new and different aspect to our investigation, but only entering into the perspective of a complete vision of human action. We should not forget the subject matter of ethical–philosophical inquiry: the order, which the reason establishes in the acts of the will, or the ordering of willing acts; or man, insofar as he voluntarily acts for the sake of a goal, the good (*In I Ethic.*, lect. 1; see chapter 1, section "Practical Reason and Philosophical Ethics," subsection "The Subject of Philosophical Ethics"). We attend to this perspective of voluntariness as soon as we know we are inquiring about "human acts" as "acts of persons," and not as acts of powers or organs. The personal–integrative factor is thus the will and its *imperium*, which in any event is morally significant only to the extent that it depends upon the *ordinatio* of the practical reason.

*Quaestio* 19 of the *Prima Secundae* is devoted to this topic: it treats the moral qualification of the inner act of the will (*De Bonitate et Malitia Actus Interioris Voluntatis*). Thomas begins by making it clear that the distinction between the *genus naturae* and the *genus moris* arises when the will is involved: the will is the one power whose object possesses per se a moral dimension, because the object of the will is the moral good, and if something is willed, it is always willed according to its *esse morale*.[25] Insofar as the will extends to the "good" (object or end) of other powers, it wills this not on the natural level that corresponds to those powers, but as (moral) will. The will does not seek premoral goods; or, to be more precise, premoral (ontic) goods, insofar as they are objects of the will, are already within the moral dimension.

But why? At first, the naturalistic argumentation of the teleologists may seem more plausible, since it maintains that the moral quality of an action is actually based upon the "value" that someone "wills." This willing would always have the character of an intention (or "conviction"). The will that directs itself to (premoral) goods, and to the goal or end of each power in question, nevertheless would at first not contain any more moral content than this ontic good contains in itself qua ontic, premoral good. The morality of the will could then, in this view, not depend on such purely premoral objects; rather, it is the intentional "value willing" that lends moral significance to each instance of striving for a premoral good. This means that teleological ethics denies that the "good" or "end" (*finis*) of other powers (such as the procreative power, speech ability, etc.) is already being willed under the aspect of the *esse morale* that comes to them insofar as they are objects of the will. According to the doctrine, they would remain premoral goods, and the moral quality of their being observed or not observed would hinge *only* and *originally* upon the inner act of the will, as a "value intention."

It should be clearer now how such a position is bound up with a radical naturalism or physicalism on the one side, and with a value idealism on the part of the intention, on the other side, so that the personal structure of the *actus humanus* is split into two spheres—a dualism of the will as opposed to the other powers and their "natural ends," the premoral goods. It is interesting to note that Thomas himself made explicit reference to such a view. He answers an objection (*I–II*, q. 19, a. 1, obj. 3) that maintains it is impossible for the will to be *morally* specified by the object, because such objects, which possess only the *bonitas naturae* (that is, considered as "premoral" goods), could not lend moral goodness to the will. It would then have to follow that the inner act of will creates its moral quality out of itself.

The answer to the objection explains why the will can be morally qualified by "objects," that is, why the objects of other powers, insofar as they become objects of the will, have already entered into the dimension of the *esse morale,* the *genus moris*, and morality. The reason is not far to seek, but is significant and confirms the foregoing analyses: "The good is represented as an object to the will through the reason; and insofar as it falls under the order of reason, it pertains to the area of morality (*genus moris*), and causes moral good in the act of the will. This is because reason is the principle of human and moral acts" (ibid., ad 3um)."

This is then confirmed in the third article, so that while the first article (just quoted) asked whether the goodness of the will depended on the object, the later article brings out the dependence of the will on the reason, and we learn that it is one and the same dependence, since "the goodness of the will depends on the reason in the same way as it depends on the object" (a. 3). And the reason for this is that (as explained earlier) the objects of the other powers are really not adequate objects for the will. The will cannot strive toward the "good" of another power *as such* (a sensible or imaginable good), since these goods have an adequate *porportio* only to the seeking power that corresponds to them (i.e., the "sensitive appetite," *appetitus sensibilis*). The universal nature of the good (the *ratio boni*), toward which the will reaches, is not yet present to the various particular goods of the other powers. It is only by the comprehension and *ordinatio* of such goods through the practical reason that they become objects of the will, and this is because they are already, as determined by reason, *within* the dimension of morality as *bona intellecta.*[26] Only a "practical good," as objectified by the reason, is capable of moving the will, and not a "premoral" good.

There are, then, two statements that are identical in meaning: "The moral qualification of the will depends on the object" and "The moral qualification of the will depends on the reason." Thomas explains as follows: the "goodness" (*ratio boni*) of this object is constituted through its relationship to the will; the "truth" or "practical truth" (*ratio veri*), is constituted through the reason.[27] Thomas uses a brief but profound formulation: *Appetitus voluntatis non potest esse de bono, nisi prius a ratione apprehendatur* (The striving of the will cannot be a striving for the good, unless it [the good] has first been apprehended by the reason; ibid.).

Here can be found the clearest answer to the "naturalism" and irrationality of teleological ethics, a theory that ignores the constitution of the object of the will through the practical reason, and consequently must take all "goods" to which the will reaches as "premoral" goods, in order to reconstitute the moral dimension through a value idealism of "pure intentions of the will" or "basic attitudes."[28]

Only the reason can move the will "from the side of the object" (*ex parte obiecti*), and this in turn is so only because these objects—the objects of human, personal acts—are a *conceptio rationis*. In the constitution of the object, the reason possesses an actual, morally measuring function through its participation in the eternal law, as Thomas explains in the article to follow. The moral goodness of the will thus depends, by way of the practical reason, upon the eternal law, as this has already been presented. The ordering power of the practical reason, as participation of the eternal law, is nothing other than the *lex naturalis*. This is also, finally, what determines the objective meaning of human action in a fundamental and universal (i.e., specifically human) way.

This object presented to the will by the reason—a *materia debita*—is nothing other than the *actus exterior*, the so-called exterior action. Previously, we encountered a seemingly paradoxical conclusion that the "object" of an *actus exterior* is this *actus exterior* itself. But the paradox arises only from the abstractive point of view. If I ask, "What is the object of theft?" I am *really* asking, "What is the object of the inner act of the will?" (whether *intentio* or *electio*), or "What does this *actus humanus*, that is, this considered act of the will, have for an object?" Now the object is precisely the exterior action, "the taking of someone else's possession." It has to do with an action already specified through the reason in the dimension of morality, with regard to the *debitum*. In this case, one would have to say of the act that "it is not accompanied by the right circumstances" (*non est vestitus debitis circumstantiis*) or that it is "deprived of the right mode, species, and order" (*privatus debito modo, specie, et ordine*; *De Malo*, q. 2, a. 4).

When, in other words, we treat an action "abstractly" or "in itself," we treat it only in its relation to the reason. When we ask, then, about the "object" in this connection, we are not asking about the "natural goal" (*finis naturalis*), nor about the powers of the soul engaged in this exterior act, nor even about the natural characteristics of the "things" that are at the basis of the act in question; rather, we are asking about the *modus*, or the "fitting order" (*ordo debitus*), and this of course with reference to the *ordinatio* of the practical reason. To use a different formulation, we are asking about the *specifically human and personal*, not the "natural," meaning of this act. The expression "object of the exterior act" can be deceptive, and it has deceived many. If, like Thomas, we understand from the outset that the "object" is a *conceptio rationis*, then the "object of the exterior act" (or its *materia circa quam*) means the same as the human–personal meaning of the exterior act, or the "rightness" (*ratio debiti*) of the exterior act, constituted with relation to the order of reason. In every instance, we mean the moral dimension of this action. It would perhaps be better to speak of the "objective *meaning*" (moral value content) of the exterior act rather than of the "object of the exterior act."[29]

But if we consider human action in its whole extent as *voluntary* action, as a doing that arises from an intentional and elective *imperium* of the inner act of willing, then when we speak of the "object" of such an action, the *actus exterior* means this object, just as it is "presented" to the will by the reason. As Thomas explains (*De Malo*, q. 2, a. 4; *I–II*, q. 20, a. 1), while the exterior act possesses the same moral quality in the "order of execution" as the act of the will that underlies this *executio*, the *bonitas* of the inner act of the will comes from the reason, in the order of moral specification or *apprehensio*. The object of the will is thus the *actus exterior,* "according as it is in the ordering and apprehension of the reason."[30] If we speak of a human action, we mean fundamentally and essentially the exterior act "insofar as it has been presented to the will, by the reason, as a certain good [*quoddam bonum*] comprehended and ordered [*apprehensum et ordinatum*] through the reason" (ibid., ad 1um). The object also means the exterior act as *goal of the will,*[31] since what one wants is the *goal* or *end* (*finis*) of the will, completely independently of any further intention: the object itself possesses a *ratio finis* when considered with respect to its objectification through the inner act of the will.[32]

## INTENTION, "*FINIS OPERIS,*" "*FINIS OPERANTIS*"

The investigation can—and really must—be taken further, to the more complex structure of the interplay between the objective moral value content of the exterior act, and the *finis* or "goal" of an intention that goes beyond that object. But since that investigation would bring nothing new to the concept of the object as such, we can leave it aside at present. To resume, then: an "aiming toward an end" (*intentio finis*), which is related as "form" to the "matter" of the object (the exterior act), does not encounter a morally neutral or "premoral" quantity in that object, but rather an action that is already morally specified. Every intention not only possesses its own objective content but also informs something else, and not in a "supplementary" way but formally, or "essentially": a concrete human action that already bears in itself an objective moral content. Thomas is emphatic in saying that an act that is provided with a further, intended "goal" can as a whole be bad, even though that intention is good, if the *actus volitus*, that is, the exterior act as object of the *voluntas eligens*, is bad (see *I–II*, q. 2, a. 2). There are exterior acts (objects of actions) that are in themselves unsuited to be the "matter" for even the best intentions, because they contain an *indebitum* by being contrary to the order of reason. To use a metaphor: if someone wants to survive by eating stones, his intention may be flawless. But stones simply cannot be used for nourishment.

His *Commentary on the Sentences* contains Thomas's clearest presentation by far of the connection between the will as the intended goal and the will as directed to the immediate object of action (*In II Sent.*, d. 38, q. 1; d. 40). In this passage, his teaching on the immediate object of action and the intended goal is applied to the Aristotelian analysis of the intentional and elective act of the will: the "object" as immediate goal of the action is the subject of the *voluntas eligens*; the goal of the intention, on the other hand, is the subject of the *voluntas intendens*; both acts nevertheless form *one single* complex act of willing in a concrete action, in which something is intended "by way of" (or by *means* of) another action. And in order for the will to be good, Thomas reasons, the *electio* must simply have to be good, because this is what unleashes the action, and because what is intended is *intentionally* present in it.[33] The goodness (*bonitas*) of the intention is not enough by itself to make the will good.[34]

Both the intended goal (the object of the *voluntas intendens*) and the object of *electio* (the *actus volitus*), to the extent that one is willed for the sake of the other, are no longer two different objects, but rather, in one single act of the will, they are one single object in which the intentional and elective objects relate to each other as form and matter.[35] This shows once again how flexibly, and in how *rationally determinate a manner,* the "objectivity" of human action is constituted. Since an ordering act of the reason lies at the basis of the intention as well, the question about the possible correlation of actions and intentions is reduced to the question about the constitution of the object of this complex act of the will. And this means, provided the intention is morally good, that the question is whether the action through which this goal is intended is a *materia debita* or *conveniens.*

This gives a new demonstration of the truth that the immediate object of the action or the *finis operis* cannot be treated as a mere *finis naturalis,* nor as a simple "given" or "thing." Nor is it an *operatum* (thing done) that takes place independently of the ordering practical reason.[36] On the contrary, the "object" or the *finis operis* is an *actus volitus,* that is, the object of an inner act of the will, "objectified" for the will through the ordering power of the practical reason, which morally specifies this will as morally good or morally bad.

The word *opus* in the expression *finis operis* cannot be taken to mean an action without reference to its relation to the *bonum humanum* or to the person. This *opus* is not simply a "given," which man "encounters," "takes up," and "carries out" to its "natural end" (*finis naturalis*). In the human act of procreation there is not simply an "application" of the generative power according to its natural end. The *opus* in the expression *finis operis* (object) is an *actus humanus,* and its purposiveness is not simply a naturally present "natural purpose," but rather this natural purpose as integrated in the whole of the suppositum. That means it is governed by the practical reason to its goal, which is not only "natural" but also "human–personal." The goal, which is not simply "there," nor simply "read off" from nature, is defined and constituted, once again, not without relation to the reason, and thereby not without relation to the knowing human person. Thomas defines the expression *finis operis* as follows: "*finis operis est hoc ad quod opus ordinatum est ab agente, et hoc dicitur ratio operis*" (The *finis operis* is the goal to which the deed is ordered by the doer, and this is called the nature of the deed"; *In II Sent.*, d. 2, a. 2, a. 1). And precisely this "nature of the deed" (*ratio operis*) is what is considered in the "abstract" treatment of actions. In the concept of the *finis operis*, as also in that of the object, an "ordering by an agent" (*ordinatio ab agente*) is included, and this is of course nothing other than an "ordering of the reason" (*ordinatio rationis*).

Since the object is always the object of an *actus humanus*, or of a personal act, it in each case expresses the meaning content of such personal acts and possesses an inner axiological coherence founded on a relation to the practical reason that constitutes this coherence. Because the objective meaning of the exterior act represents both an *ordinatum a ratione* and a *volitum*, it is not "morally neutral," and not every action will be suitable, no matter how good the intention may be. And thus Thomas adds dryly: "If someone wills an evil in order to pursue something good, then this good is not the goal of the will, but only a goal that the agent has proposed to himself in a disordinate way."[37] The goal of willing, and with that, the moral content of the corresponding act, is the morally bad object of action, which is simply incapable of being formed by an intention that is good in itself, as the *finis operantis* (the "end conceived by the doer").[38]

The obvious conclusion from this is that the terminology of *finis operis* and *finis operantis* should be used with caution. Indeed, it must be said that the *finis operis* is always a *finis operantis*. If Thomas remarks that occasionally they differ from one another, it means that there are cases in which the agent is acting with an intention that is different from the *finis* of the immediate act (or object). This occurs when someone pursues a further and final purpose above and beyond the meaningful content of a concrete action, or when the intention is contradictory to the meaning of the action.

Thomas rarely uses the distinction. It occurs for the most part in the context of "building": one can build a house, but the goal that the builder is pursuing in doing so may be something other than "building a house" (such as "making monetary profit," see *II–II*, q. 141, a. 6, ad 1um). The example is meaningful in its place, but it has the disadvantage of presenting a special exception, namely, that of the moral qualification of an *artistic/productive* action, which does not primarily belong to the area of moral action. The *finis operis* is here the goal of technical production, and the house is the characteristic "product" of this action.

But if these examples are taken as paradigmatic for moral action, one would easily incur the danger of treating "objects of actions" or the *finis operis* as "things" (houses, buildings) that can then be given a distinct moral determination by the acting subject. To do so, however, would mean losing the perspective of moral behavior, of the *actus humanus* or the personal act.

Such misunderstandings are found not only in critics of the tradition but also, to a certain extent, in its defenders. K. Hörmann provides an example (unfortunately followed by F. Scholz): for Hörmann, the concepts *finis operis* and *finis naturalis* are simply identical. It has to do, he states, with the "natural effect" of an action, which for Thomas too is supposed to be "the characterization of a natural end [*finis naturalis*] or goal of action [*finis operis*], namely, the goal to which the thing or the action by its nature, and independently of human willing, is directed [*in quem tendit naturaliter*]; house construction has by nature the end of the house."[39] And now this goal must be distinguished "from the goal that the doer pursues" (*finis operantis*). Like J. Fuchs, he calls the object an *operatum*, or an "objective action."

But this is wrong simply because the concept of human action cannot be treated independently of "human willing," that is, independently of its relationship to the *actus humanus*. If an action *is* treated independently in this way, then it would be considered only at the level of its *genus naturae*. The object of action can be the object of a personal, human act only by being carried out by an *agent*, so that it is in a certain sense also a *finis operantis*. In this way it becomes objectified for the will by the practical reason, and is no longer an "objective happening" or a "natural effect." Only in retrospect and with reference to this total view can an object also be considered abstractly in its moral content. Finally, Hörmann is neglecting something very important: even in the case of an "abstract" investigation of the exterior act as object, and independently of the inner act of the will, this object must nevertheless *always* be treated as an object of the *apprehensio* and *ordinatio* of the practical reason, and *not* as a natural event. Once again, what we are seeing is the ordering function of the practical reason in the constitution of the object.

At any rate, this is how Hörmann arrives at his ethically meaningless position (here he seems to be following the approach of J. Fuchs) that one "could follow Thomas" in "agreeing that the sexual intercourse of spouses, of whom at least one has no gametes, could not, in its concrete actuality, have the conception of a child as its *finis operis*."[40] Now, to put it simply, this is not a statement about the marital act as an *actus humanus*, but rather is a statement about the (natural) act of the *potentia generativa*. This latter, in cases of temporary or permanent sterility, cannot actually have conception as a *finis operis*, taken in the sense of a "natural effect." And of course, no more could one say of a marital act, considered *only* as a "use" of this power, that it is oriented toward the transmission of human life, or that it *objectively* signifies an act of responsible parenthood.

Considered as an *actus humanus*, however, the marital act, even if known to be biologically unfruitful, very much retains its objective meaning as an act of married love ordered toward the transmission of human life. The *finis operis* is not affected *in its moral content* as an act of the will or an act of human love, since this content transcends the current physiological disposition of the generative power. It is only when the act is *willingly* made unfruitful that there are consequences for the *finis operis* of the marital act: namely, because in that case the spouses no longer will, in their marital act, an act of love that is ordered to the transmission of human life. The objective difference does not lie in the fact of sterility as such, but rather in the willed nature of this sterility—that is, in the alteration of the object of the act of married love. To put it more clearly: it is not a question of the *finis* of the generative power, but rather of the *finis* of married love. As already shown in chapter 2, section "Excursus: The Natural Law and Contraception," the problem of the sterilization of this power does not consist in the sterilization as such, but rather in the making unfruitful (*Unfruchtbarmachung*) of married love, which is thus changed in meaning; it likewise has as a consequence the alteration of the objective meaning (of the *finis operis*) of a marital act carried out under such conditions.

For exactly the same reason, there is an objective, moral difference between naturally caused and willingly caused sterility, although both may come to the same thing with respect to the generative power. And this objective difference is not there because the "natural" is being "moralized," but rather because the natural, insofar as it is not willed, does not touch the objective meaning of this action. Marital acts carried out in this condition of natural (unwilled) sterility are still per se "open" to the transmission of human life, because this finality has not been excluded.[41] This shows once again that the marital act must not be understood simply from the point of view of the function of the generative power (as Böckle has it, the "good of procreation"), but from the point of view of the full, personal meaning of married love.

We must reject the identification of the *finis operis* with the *finis naturalis*.[42] With St. Thomas, we can call the *finis operis* or "the object" a *finis naturalis* only if we have abandoned the ethical point of view for the naturalistic. For we are concerned with the "natural," in the sense of what is "natural to man," as constituted by the reason and above all by the *ratio naturalis*. In this way, one could speak, in the ethical sense, of the "nature of an act." A text from St. Thomas can clarify: "What is natural to something is what is suited to its form [*quod convenit suae formae*], through which it is constituted in such a nature. . . . But the form through which man is man is the *ratio* and *intellectus*. Therefore it naturally tends toward whatever is suited to man's reason and intellect. The good of any virtue [*cuiuslibet virtutis*] is suitable for man according to the reason: because such goodness [*bonitas*] comes from a certain commensurability [*commensuratio*] of the act to the circumstances and to the end, *a commensurability that reason brings about" (In II Sent.,* d. 39, q. 2, a. 1). In order for the object and the *finis operis* to be constituted, it needs this "*commensuratio* of the act to circumstances and to the end, brought about by the reason"; it needs an "ordering, standard-giving configuration, made by the reason, of the act in relation to the circumstances and end." Without this, the act remains in its *esse naturae* and is never capable of revealing its moral content. It would mean studying the "corpse" of a human action, and not the real, "living," human–personal action that has "life" through the intentional and elective command of the will, as founded on the ordering function of the practical reason.

## "Objectivity," or the Moral Dimension of Human Actions

"Object" and "objective meaning" do not refer, then, to some material or natural "reality" that is independent of action, nor even to an "objective event" that would then be formed by a "subjective" will, even if this will "wills" a natural event to take place. In general, it has nothing to do with something *opposed to subjectivity.* The opposition between "subjective" and "objective," in fact, is counterfeit coin in the realm of morality. The "objectively moral" is what has been objectified for the will of the acting subject through the practical knowing of the reason, and carried out as personal action, as an *actus humanus.* "Objectively good" means, as we formulated it earlier, an action's *being integrated* into the natural intentionality of the *ratio naturalis* and being ordered, measured and regulated thereby; or its integration into the context of the whole person, of the suppositum, and thus into the finality structure of the human being. In order for "subjective" moral intentions to be "good intentions," they must be *objectively* good, that is, they must be according to reason. And the object of an action is not constituted without relation to the action of the agent, or to that agent's will and reason. Even though it can also be objectified "abstractly" as "a kind of action" or "manner of acting," this is *never* independent of its constitutive relationship to the practical reason. For the abstract objectification of an action and its *finis operis* (or object) is never the objectification of a purely "external fact," but rather a consideration of the action "according as it is ordered and apprehended by the reason" (*secundum quod est in ordinatione et apprehensione rationis, I–II,* q. 20, a. 1). Anything else would mean investigating only the "corpse" of the action, something that is no more a moral action than the dead body of a man is a sound organism.

The "objectivity" of human action is not set in contrast to the "subjective." Concepts truly opposed to the *morally* objective are, for example, the *naturally* objective (*genus naturae*), and the "not rationally ordered," that is, that which is not objectified for the will through the reason. The "subjective"—insofar as it can be understood in contrast to "objective"—is mere "appearance" (the Aristotelian *phainomenon agathon*) or the "apparent good" (as opposed to the *really* good), or mere "opinion" (*doxa*), which has not ascertained the "objectivity" of truth. But if the "subjective" is simply identified with the *moral* or *personal,* then the objectivity to which it is opposed cannot be a *moral* objectivity, but rather an objectivity of "things," of the natural or social environment of man. Now to confuse this second concept of "objectivity" with that of *moral* objectivity, and then set it in opposition to moral "subjectivity," not only is the influential error of many "tradition-oriented" moral theologians, but is especially to be found in Karl Rahner,[43] as well as his students Schüller,[44] Rotter,[45] and Böckle (primarily with regard to the concept of the object of action,[46] but also with regard to the relation between the "subjective" and "objective," or the object intention[47]); the error is no less obvious in F. Scholz,[48] J. Fuchs,[49] and many others.

The reason is objective exactly as much as it is subjective, that is, as it is *my* reason on the basis of which *I* understand and decide what is good or bad. *Objectivity in the moral sense is finally nothing other than the truth of subjectivity,* a truth that results from the *ordinatio* of the practical reason and that shows itself, in a fundamental and universal way, as the *lex naturalis.* The distinction between *subjective* and *objective morality* has meaning only in this sense—the reason and the conscience under certain circumstances can err without culpability. But even this kind of subjectivity has in a certain (*per accidens*) sense the character of objectivity: namely, the undeniable fact that man, if he would stay man, must act according to the dictates of his reason.

## NOTES

1. In its essential lines, the following exposition agrees with S. Pinckaers, "Le rôle de la fin dans l'action morale selon saint Thomas," in his *Le Renouveau de la morale* (Tournai, 1964), pp. 114–143. Even so, Pinckaers did not adequately emphasize the reason in his analyses. And

that is the advantage of the analyses of T. G. Belmans, *Le sens objectif de l'agir humain* (Vatican City, 1980), who, in my opinion, criticizes Pinckaers's position subtly but not always with due care.

2. This must be expounded in more detailed fashion with the starting point of *I–II*, q. 56, a. 3. In this passage the following observations are made on the distinction between moral virtue, on the one hand, and *ars* or *scientia*, on the other: "And because virtue is what makes its possessor good, and renders his work good, habits [*habitus*] of this kind [i.e., moral virtues] are called 'virtues' pure and simple [*simpliciter*], *because they render the deed good in its actualization* [*reddunt bonum opus in actu*] and make the possessor good in general [*simpliciter*]. But the first kind of habits [*habitus*], [namely, *scientia* and *ars*] are not called 'virtues' pure and simple [*simpliciter*], *because they do not render the work good except in some certain faculty* [*non reddunt bonum opus nisi in quadam facultate*], nor do they make the possessor good in general [*simpliciter*]. For someone is not said to be good in a general sense [*simpliciter*] by being knowledgeable or by being an artist [i.e., "skilled," *artifex*], but he is said to be good only in a certain respect [*secundum quid*], as, for example, a good grammarian or a good carpenter." Since moral virtue is an elective habit (*habitus electivus*), and as such is the perfection of the *actus humanus*, its special character does not consist in some "ability," but rather in the fulfillment of a certain *striving or effort*, and ultimately the "good use" (*bonus usus*) of an ability (*aliquis habitus non solum facit facultatem agendi, sed etiam facit, quod aliquis recte facultate utatur*).

3. Thomas's distinction between moral and "artistic" activity derives from Aristotle, and is explained as follows. An artist (or artisan, "skilled" person) who *purposely* makes a mistake is no bad artist for doing so—indeed he shows his mastery of his craft by being able to do so; but if he commits mistakes accidentally, then he is known as an incompetent artist. In the moral realm it is the opposite: the one who purposely does wrong is bad; the one who does wrong accidentally is not considered bad. Since we can judge the artist either qua artist or qua human being, in every artistic action a double sin is possible: "in one way, through a deviation from the particular end [*fine particulari*] intended by the artisan, and this sin [*peccatum*] will be proper to the art, as when an artist intending to make a good work of art makes a bad one. In another way, through deviation from the common goal (*fine communi humane vitae*) of human life: and in this way he will be said to sin, if he intends to do a bad deed, and brings it about that someone is deceived. *But this sin is not proper to the artist* qua *artist* [*artifex*]; in the second case he sins qua human being [*homo*]" (*I–II*, q. 21, a. 2, ad 2um). The "particular goal" of the *ars* and the "common goal of human life" ground two different spheres

of action and "objectivity" that can neither be *reduced to* nor be *derived from* one another.

4. We are not speaking of so-called "indifferent actions," because these are actions that are neither artistic acts nor acts of knowing. They actually belong to the realm of "doing" (*agere*), but when considered in themselves (*ex objecto*) they have not yet been morally specified; for instance, the action "to pick up a stick from the ground" does not have a morally objective meaning as either an *agere* or a *facere*; it is related neutrally or indifferently in relation to possible intentions, which alone specify it. But one cannot say the same of the act of the architect: it already possesses, as a *facere*, the immanent meaning of a work of art (or "making," production). As Thomas points out, it is already, and always, oriented toward a *bonum*, even if it is still not being considered as a *moral* good, which enters only with the *bonus usus*, or the integration of artistic action in an *actus humanus*; see *I–II*, q. 57, a. 3, ad 1um: "Wherefore, just as knowledge [*scientia*] is always oriented toward [*se habet semper ad*] the good, as has been said, just so is art [*ars*]; and accordingly art is said to be a virtue. But in this respect it falls short of the full essence of virtue [*perfecta ratione virtutis*] because it does not make the *use itself good* [*non facit ipsum bonum usum*], since something further is required for that; still, the *good use* [*bonus usus*] could not take place without the art." As *agere*, artistic or scientific ("knowing") activity is thus neither neutral nor indifferent to objective moral content.

5. On the concept of the "moral distinctiveness" (*moralischen Differenz*], see W. Kluxen, "Menschliche Natur und Ethos," in *Münchener theologische Zeitschrift* 23 (1972): 1–7.

6. See the purely technical conception of sexuality in J. Fuchs: "Morally *right* action is conceptually apparent as the realization of *premoral* goods/values [for man]. Which attitude toward sexuality, the mass-media, nuclear power, etc. serves the well-being of man, when considered in an inner-worldly and interpersonal manner?" ('*Intrinsece malum*': Überlegungen zu einem umstrittenen Begriff," in W. Kerber, ed., *Sittliche Normen* (Düsseldorf, 1982), p. 84. Can we really speak of human sexuality in the same breath as the mass media and nuclear power?

7. See *I–II,* q. 1, a. 3: "Actus dicuntur humani, inquantum procedunt a voluntate deliberata. Obiectum autem voluntatis est bonum et finis. Et ideo manifestum est quod principium humanorum actuum, inquantum sunt humani, est finis . . . actus morales proprie speciem sortiuntur ex fine: nam idem sunt actus morales et actus humani."

8. See S. Pinckaers, "Le Rôle de la fin dans l'action morale selon saint Thomas," pp. 131ff.; his critique of Billuart is still quite valid: ibid., p. 128ff.

9. Thomas distinguishes an ordering of actions per se from one that is *per accidens: to "fight"* is per se oriented toward "victory," whereas "stealing" is only *per accidens* oriented toward the "giving of alms." In the latter relationship, an "intentional organization" of actions is carried out, freely accomplished by an agent, and extends beyond the objective meaning of the immediate action (and in this sense the intentional organization is "subjective"; see *I–II*, q. 18, a. 7).

10. See the quotation from Pius XII (chapter 2, note 87): "The marital act within its natural context is a personal action."

11. See also *In IV Sent.*, d. 33, q. 1, a. 3; q. 1a, 1: "Finis autem quem natura ex concubitu intendit, est proles procreanda et educanda." By *natura* here is not intended simply the "nature of the act of conception," but rather "human nature," or the nature of the act of conception, insofar as it is a human act. This should also be clear in the following formula (ibid., q. 2, a. 1): "Matrimonium ex intentione naturae ordinatur ad educationem prolis." This is because matrimony, whose nature is here in question, is already a consequence of a human act and not a natural happening. It belongs to the region of the "natural," "to which nature inclines, but which is completed with the mediation of free choice [*mediante libero arbitrio*], just as acts of the virtues are said to be natural; in this sense even matrimony is natural, because the natural reason inclines to it in two ways: first, in regard to its principal end, which is the good of the offspring [*bonum prolis*], for nature intends not the generation of offspring but also its transmission and its furtherance [*traductionem et promotionem*] to the complete human state, insofar as one is a human being, which is the mutual obedience [*mutuum obsequium*] given by the spouses to one another in affairs of the household. For just as the natural reason dictates that human beings live with one another [*cohabitent*], because one person is not sufficient unto himself in all the things that pertain to living . . . wherefore, nature moves toward [*movet ut . . .*] a certain association of the man and the woman, which is matrimony" (*In IV Sent.*, d. 26, q. 1, a. 1).

12. See *I–II*, q. 17, a. 4: "Imperium et actus imperatus sunt unus actus humanus, sicut quoddam totum est unum, sed est secundum partes multa." (The command and the commanded act are one human act, just as a whole is one, while being "many" in view of its parts.)

13. See the example given in *De Malo*, q. 2, a. 2, ad 6um: the hand of the murderer sins only insofar as the death-bringing movement originates from the will of the murderer. If I were to fire a gun while holding it in another person's hand, that other person's hand would not be committing sin, since it is purely a tool. Human procreative power is no tool, but rather a part of the suppositum, and as such its act is always a

human act. Not even the partner is a "tool" for the other, since both have "one flesh" through the bond of matrimony; their common marital act has a single personal meaning, for which the *uniting of two wills* is of crucial importance.

14. *I–II,* q. 17, a. 1: Imperare autem est quidem essentialiter actus rationis: imperans enim ordinat eum cui imperat, ad aliquid agendum." (To command is essentially the act of the reason, for the person who commands "orders" [*ordinat*] the one he commands to the *doing* of something [*ad aliquid agendum*].)

15. See ibid.: Inde relinquitur quod imperare sit actus rationis, praesupposito actu voluntatis, in cuius virtute ratio movet per imperium ad exercitium actus." (And thus it must be concluded that to command is an act of the reason, with a presupposition of the act of the will, in virtue of which the reason moves or impels—through a command—to the exercise of the act.)

16. *I–II,* q. 18, a. 8; see also ibid., ad 2um: "Every object or end has some goodness or badness [*bonitatem vel malitiam*], at least in the natural sense; but it does not always bring in some goodness or badness in the moral sense, which is considered through comparison with the reason." Ibid., a. 5: "In human actions, good and evil are said to be through comparison with the reason [*per comparationem ad rationem*]; ibid., ad 1um: "And in the same way, good, insofar as it is according to reason, and bad, insofar as it goes beyond reason, are what diversify the moral species." See also *De Malo*, q. 2, a. 4, and ibid., ad 5um: "The moral act, as said, gets its species from its object, in accordance with a rational consideration [*secundum quod comparatur ad rationem*]." In the language of many handbooks (in the tradition of Billuart), this *proportio ad rationem* becomes a *proportio ad normam moralitatis*, which in itself is not incorrect, since the reason is indeed this *norma* (measure, standard). But Pinckaers (*Le Renouveau de la morale*, p. 129) was right: "For Billuart, the object of the moral act is the physical object, simply clothed with a relationship to a rule of morality, transported into the realm of the moral by its relationship to the law, to its precepts and prohibitions." In this way, the relationship to the *norma moralitatis* becomes something "external," something "imposed" upon the object already constituted on the premoral level. It is overlooked how this *norma moralitatis* is fundamentally the reason, which constitutes the object as a moral object, and that the relationship to law, commandment, and so on (further expressions of "moral norms") represents a *derived* or *reflective* relationship. The penetrating statement of Thomas that "law" and "commandment" have their origin in an *ordinatio rationis,* and thus do not represent limitations *externally imposed on the reason from the outside*, is practically forgotten. This is

quite probably the relevant background for understanding certain contemporary moral theological attitudes that favor a "new formulation" of Christian ethics.

17. *De Malo*, q. 2, a. 4, ad 1um: "Licet res exteriores sint in seipsis bonae, tamen non semper habent *debitam proportionem* ad hanc vel illam actionem. Et ideo, inquantum considerantur ut obiecta talium actionum, non habent rationem boni." (Although exterior things are good in themselves, nevertheless they do not always have the *right proportion* to this or that action, and therefore, insofar as they are considered objects of such actions, they do not have the character of goodness.)

18. *De Malo*, q. 2, a. 4: "Materia enim actus, dicitur obiectum eius"; see also *I–II,* q. 72, a. 3, ad 2um: "Obiecta, secundum quod comparantur ad actus exteriores, habent rationem materiae circa quam; sed secundum quod comparantur ad actum interiorem voluntatis, habent rationem finium." (Objects, according as they are compared with exterior acts, have the nature of *matter concerning which*; according as they are compared with the interior act of the will, have the nature of *ends*.) We will return to this extremely important qualification. It may be helpful to recall the remarks made in chapter 2, section "The Moral Object, and How It Is Constituted," subsection "The Object of Action": the *materia circa quam* is not to be thought of as analogous to the *materia ex qua* as a "coprinciple" in the hylomorphic structure of being. Matter and form in human actions are related to one another as are "body" and "color": the matter is the *whole object* in its rational determination, but seen from the material point of view. Body and soul, as hylomorphic coprinciples, do not separately characterize the whole person, but only partial aspects. A man "is" neither body nor soul, but a composite of both.

19. This expression presupposes that we have to do here with a so-called "univocal causality," in the sense that a "human being conceives a human being," that the living thing conceived by a human being has the same species as the conceiver, that it is likewise a human being. But that has meaning only on the level of the *genus naturae*: the physiological process of human conception is oriented, physiologically speaking, toward the conception of a living thing that corresponds to the one conceiving, or is identical in regard to species. In other words, the human act of conception conceives a human being because the one conceiving is a human being, but not because the act of conception intends the conception of a human being. This it could not do, because what a human being is as a whole (including the direct and exclusive creation by God of the soul) goes far beyond the physiological potentiality of the act.

20. See M. Rhonheimer, "Sozialphilosophie und Familie," in B.

Schnyder, ed., *Familie—Herausforderung der Zukunft* (Freiburg, Switzerland, 1982), pp. 113–140.

21. In this connection one can see the weakness of J. Fuchs's very influential article, "Biologie und Ehemoral," *Gregorianum* 2 (1962): 225–253: though it is intended to confirm "traditional sexual morality," there is a clear tendency to determine the *finis operis* on the level of the *genus naturae* (esp. at p. 236ff.), while the act of human procreation as an act of married love is considered a "secondary" *finis operis.*

22. *See Humanae Vitae*, no. 11: "Necessarium esse, ut quilibet matrimonii usus ad vitam humanam procreandam *per se destinatus* permaneat." (It is necessary that every exercise of the marital act stay intrinsically destined [or ordered, or open] to the procreation of human life.)

23. It is essential to stress that "objects" in the moral sense are *human actions* and neither "things" nor *fines naturales* of single powers. For example, in the handbook of Mausbach and Ermecke (*Katholische Moraltheologie*, vol. 1, *Die allgemeine Moral,* 9th ed. [Münster, 1959], pp. 242ff.) , this is excluded, because of the apparent paradox just mentioned, with a questionable reference to Thomas and a perhaps more justified reference to the Thomistic school: "Many theologians understand by the object the action itself, and in its very core and essence (as opposed to the circumstances), and so with theft as such, in a sacrilegious church robbery. But in this point alone our question is different. We are trying to establish morality by going back to its basic components [*principia, elementa*]. *And thus the action itself is eliminated, for it cannot be its own object* . . . following the precedent of St. Thomas and his school, we understand the object as the real subject matter [*Gegenstand*] toward which the action is oriented in its essence, and therefore in the example of theft, the thing that has been removed from another's possession." How questionable this interpretation is, can be seen as follows: If Thomas calls theft the *ablatio occulta rei alienae* (the hidden removal of something belonging to someone else)—and here *ablatio occulta* means the same thing as *substractio*—he also calls the action of "removal" the "object." If the object were the *res aliena ablata* (the thing belonging to another that has been taken away), it would no longer be possible to distinguish the object of "theft" from the repossession of this "thing taken away" by the police for the purpose of restoring it to the rightful owner. If the police "repossess" the *res aliena ablata*, they commit no theft, but only the "repossession of a stolen thing"; theft is removal, the "hidden removal of something belonging to someone else" (*occulta ablatio rei alienae*).

24. Thomas is fully conscious of doing this: see *De Malo*, q. 2, a. 3: "Actus exterior dupliciter considerari potest: uno modo secundum quod est in apprehensione secundum suam rationem; alio modo secundum

quod est in operis executione." (The exterior act can be considered in two ways: in one way, according as it is apprehended with respect to its own reasoning; in another way, according as it is carried out in deed.)

25. Ibid., a. 1: "Bonum et malum sunt per se differentiae actus voluntatis. Nam bonum et malum per se ad voluntatem pertinent; sicut verum et falsum ad rationem, cuius actus per se distinguitur differentia veri et falsi . . . unde voluntas bona et mala sunt actus differentes secundum speciem." (Good and bad are per se differences of the act of the will. For good and evil pertain *in themselves* to the will, just as the true and false pertain to the reason, the act of which is distinguished by the difference between the true and the false . . . therefore a good will and a bad will differ in species.) And this is why with the will, in contrast to the other powers of the soul, the *ratio obiecti* and the *ratio finis* are one and the same, because "the *finis* is the object of the will, but not of the other powers" (ibid., a. 2). See also *In II Sent.*, d. 40, q. 1, a. 1: "Therefore the very acts of the will, which in themselves and immediately [*per se et immediate*] pertain to the will, are as such [*per se*] in the *genus moris*; wherefore interior acts of the will are absolutely [*simpliciter*] divided into good and bad, just as into essential differences; but the acts commanded by the will, since they are brought forth [*eliciti*] through other powers, pertain to the *genus moris* only *per accidens*, according, that is to say, as they are commanded by the will. And thus those acts are not distinguished according to *species* into good or evil, but *per accidens*, according as they pertain to the *genus moris*." This doctrine of St. Thomas, that "good" and "evil" are "essential differences" (*differentiae essentiales*), was new and original in comparison with the traditional standpoint (represented by Peter of Tarantasia, Albertus Magnus, and Bonaventure).

26. Ibid.: "The goodness of the will depends properly on the object. But the object of the will is proposed to it through the reason. For the intellective good [*bonum intellectum*] is an object of the will that is proportionate to it [*proportionatum ei*]; but sensible good, or imaginable good, is so proportioned not to the will but to the sensitive appetite. This is because the will can direct itself toward the universal good [*in bonum universale*], which is what the reason apprehends; but the sensitive appetite is directed only to particular good [*bonum particulare*], which is what the sensitive appetite apprehends." The "conception of a human existence" is an object of the generative power only as a *bonum particulare*, or as a physical good. *As such*, it does concern "premoral" good. But this nevertheless becomes objectified for the will, in its totally human, personal dimension, through the mediation of the reason. That this *ordinatio rationis* is an act of the *lex naturalis* has been already explained in part I.

27. Ibid., ad 1um: "bonum sub ratione boni, id est appetibilis, per prius pertinet ad voluntatem quam ad rationem. Sed tamen per prius pertinet ad rationem sub ratione veri, quam ad voluntatem sub ratione appetibilis." (The good in itself, that is, the seekable, pertains to the will before it pertains to the reason. But even so, it pertains to the reason under the aspect of the truth before it pertains to the will under the aspect of the seekable.) The "aspect of the truth" (*ratio veri*) is thus materially (*materialiter*) the prerequisite for the "aspect of the good" (*ratio boni*), even though the latter as such (*formaliter*) is constituted through the will. That the will *actually* wills the good, and not just a "seeming" good, is the achievement of the practical reason.

28. See also chapter 2, section "The Moral Object, and How It Is Constituted," subsection "The Object as the Goal of the Will." The most explicit form of this error is found in L. Janssens.

29. This is the (in my view, very well founded) suggestion of T. G. Belmans, *Le Sens objectif de l'agir humain*. *Obiectum actus* would mean *le sens objectif de l'agir effectué* (p. 16). The term "object" or "moral value," far from belonging to the order of things, represents nothing other than the properly human sense of deliberate action (p. 110). In very clear terms the author brings out the moral dimension of practical reason (*raison éthique*) in the constitution of the object. In Pinckaers, on the other hand ("Le Rôle de la fin dans l'action morale, selon saint Thomas") this aspect is too little considered; Pinckaers is concerned above all with emphasizing the peculiarity of human action as voluntary action, and with criticizing a reified understanding of the object. In Pinckaers, despite the soundness of his interpretation as a whole, there are nevertheless some confusions about the concepts of *finis operis*, *obiectum*, and *materia circa quam*; there is a mistake particularly, it appears to me, in his dissociation of the concepts "object" and *finis operis*. Pinckaers refers the object in general to the level of the *genus naturae*. See also the criticism by Belmans (p. 282), which is oversimple in some points.

30. *I–II*, ibid.; see *In II Sent.*, d. 40, q. 1, a. 3: "actus exterior comparatur ad voluntatem sicut obiectum."

31. *De Malo*, q. 2, a. 3: "actus exterior comparatur ad actum voluntatis ut obiectum quod habet rationem finis."

32. This also holds for the *materia circa quam*; see *In II Sent.*, d. 36, q. 1, a. 5, ad 4um: "Est duplex materia: ex qua, vel in qua, et materia circa quam; et primo modo materia dicta non incidit in idem cum fine; sed secundo modo est idem cum fine: quia obiectum finis actus est." (There is matter in two senses: from which [or in which] and matter concerning which; in the first sense, it does not coincide with the end or goal; in the second, it is the same as the end.) In *I–II*, q. 72, a. 3, ad 2um, the

double point of view of the object as "matter" and as "goal" is explained still more clearly: "Obiecta, secundum quod comparantur ad actus exteriores, habent rationem materiae circa quam; sed secundum quod comparantur ad actum interiorem voluntatis, habent rationem finium; et ex hoc habent quod dant speciem actui." (Objects, according as they are compared with exterior acts, have the nature of matter concerning which, but according as they are compared with the interior act of the will, thay have the nature of ends, and from this they have the ability to give specification to the act.) This shows how flexible Thomas's terminology is: he thinks, to express it in a contemporary fashion, both "structurally" and "functionally."

33. *In II Sent.*, d. 40, q. 1, a. 2: "Cum igitur electio sit quasi consilii conclusio, ut in *III Ethic.*, c. 6 dicitur, oportet quod ad bonitatem voluntatis eligentis concurrat bonitas finis et bonitas eius quod ad finem ordinatur; et si hoc sit, proculdubio actus exterior bonus erit; si autem alterum desit, erit voluntas mala et actus malus." (Since therefore choosing is a conclusion of taking counsel, as said in *III Ethics*, c. 6, it is fitting that the goodness of the end [and the goodness of what is ordered to the end] should agree with the goodness of the choosing will; and if this is the case, without doubt the exterior act will be good, but if this is lacking, there will be a bad will and a bad action.)

34. Ibid., "Non autem bonitas voluntatis intendentis sufficit ad bonitatem actus: quia actus potest esse de se malus, qui nullo modo bene fieri potest. Si autem consideratur voluntas secundum quod est eligens, sic universaliter verum est quod a bonitate voluntatis dicitur actus bonus, et a malitia malus." (But the goodness of the *intending* will does not alone suffice to make the goodness of the action: this is because an action can be evil in itself, and cannot in any way be rightly done. But if the will is considered as *choosing*, then it is universally true that a good act is so named from the goodness of the will, and the bad act from the badness of the will.)

35. *In II Sent.*, d. 38, q. 1, a. 4, ad 1um: "Finis et id quod est ad finem, in quantum huiusmodi consideratum, non sunt diversa obiecta, sed unum obiectum in quo finis sicut formale est, quasi ratio quaedam volendi; sed id quod est ad finem, est sicut materiale, sicut etiam lumen et color sunt unum obiectum." (The end and that which is *ad finem*, so far as it is considered such, are not different objects, but one object in which the *finis* is like something formal, as a certain reason of willing; but that which is *ad finem* is like the matter, just as light and color are one object.)

36. This notion has been popularized by J. Fuchs, see " 'Operatio' et 'operatum' in dictamine conscientiae," in *Thomistica Morum Principia*,

vol. 2, (Rome, 1961), pp. 71–79. The object of action, treated as the fundamental "source" of the morality of an action, is merely an "impersonal," "material," and "static" *operatum,* and not an *actus moralis* at all; it is, in other words, a purely premoral quantity. See also Fuchs's "Der Absolutheitscharakter sittlicher Handlungsnormen," in H. Wolter, ed., *Testimonium veritati,* (Frankfurt, 1971), p. 232, where it is stated even more clearly that "a moral judgement of the action cannot be presupposed in anticipation of the intention of the doer, since this would not be a judgement about a *human* action." The radical physicalism of Fuchs is based on the fact that he overlooks how the objects of actions are the objects of acts of the will and, as such, are subject to an *ordinatio* and *apprehensio rationis,* which remain constitutive even when actions are considered abstractly, in independence from the will. They do not collapse to a mere *operatum,* to their *genus naturae.* Fuchs, however, wants to limit the ordering and evaluating function of the *ratio* to the "whole view" of the context of "action, circumstances, and purpose (intention)"—a combination, he says, of three "premoral elements."

37. *In II Sent.,* d. 38, q. 1, a. 5, ad 1um: "Quando aliquis vult malum propter bonum, illud bonum non est finis actus voluntatis, secundum se considerati, sed est finis a volente inordinate praestitutus." The reason for this is that the object of a good intention is not capable of specifying the elective will, if this will is already bad *ex obiecto* by its willing of a bad action. And this is so because the *actus exterior* already possesses an objective content that is determinative for the will. To use a classic example: the will "to give alms" cannot be justified if it is already a bad will through the *actus volitus* of "stealing money" (i.e., as a means for giving alms). The moral judgement does not result from a "calculus" of premoral goods, but rather has its foundation in *what someone wills.*

38. The goal, insofar as it really is capable of specifying the act, is always a goal in relation to which the exterior act stands in (moral) proportion (a *materia debita* or *conveniens*). Otherwise, it is not really (effectively, objectively, and *specifiably*) the "goal of this exterior act," but only a goal "disordinately provided by the doer" (*inordinate ab agente praestitutus*). See also ibid., sol.: "*finis autem dicitur ad quem actus proportionatus est* [the goal is said to be that to which the action is proportioned], et ita etiam si finis est bonus, et actus bonus; quia actus malus non est proportionatus ad finem bonum [because a bad action is not proportioned to a good end]. Unde dicit Philosophus in IV Ethic., de his qui per malos actus bonos fines consequi intendunt, quod 'quaerunt sortiri finem inconvenienti medio'; sicut etiam non quaelibet materia est disposita ad quamlibet effectum, nec quodlibet medium ad quamlibet conclusionem; ita nec quilibet actus ad quemlibet finem." (Wherefore the

Philosopher says in the fourth book of the *Ethics* concerning those who intend to pursue good ends through evil actions, that "they seek to have the end by an unfitting means." Just as not any matter is disposed to any effect, nor any middle term to any conclusion, so not any act is suitable for any end.)

39. K. Hörmann, "Die Prägung des sittlichen Wollens durch das Objekt nach Thomas von Aquin," in F. Böckle and F. Groner, eds., *Moral zwischen Anspruch und Verantwortung* (Düsseldorf, 1964), pp. 242, 243.

40. Ibid., p. 244: The text continues as follows: "A married couple aware of this could not in any meaningful way make conception their *finis operis*. For such sexual activity, one could maintain conception as the *finis operis* only by ignoring the actual situation: what someone does is carried out in such a way that it would lead to conception with gametes available from both parents; in other words, the abstract object, seen without the proximate circumstances, remains oriented toward conception, but not the concrete object, as considered with all the circumstances."

41. Even an originally unwilled sterility can, of course, be "misused." Everything depends on the will that lies at the basis of love.

42. See the excellent article of C. Caffarra, "Die Unmoral der Empfängnisverhütung," in E. Wenisch, ed., *Elternschaft und Menschenwürde* (Vallendar-Schönstatt, 1984), pp. 261–273. The author puts his finger exactly on the problem of the naturalism of a seemingly "antinaturalistic" position. "It exchanges the concept *objectively bad* for the concept of *naturally bad*, and the concept of the *finis operis* of an act for that of its *finis naturalis*. The concept 'objectively bad' is really a *moral* qualification, insofar as it says that the inner finality of an act is such that it may not be carried out by a will that makes a choice in accord with reason. The concept 'naturally bad,' on the other hand, says that an act is incapable of accomplishing a natural capacity of the person (*finis naturalis*); this excludes any reference to the will as governed by reason."

43. See K. Rahner, "Das 'Gebot' der Liebe unter den anderen Geboten," in his *Schriften zur Theologie*, vol. 5 (Einsiedeln, 1962), p. 513; English trans. by K. H. Kruger as, *Theological Investigations*, vol. 5, *Later Writings* (Baltimore, 1966) p. 456: "The basic meaning of the Christian ethos is not that we must respect objective material norms which God has imposed on reality. For all these material norms become real norms only once they become the expression of the very structure of the person. All other structures of things are placed *below* man. He may alter them, he may twist them as far as he possibly can, he is their master and not their servant. The only ultimate structure of the person that expresses it perfectly is the person's basic capacity for love, and this capacity

is boundless." Note the opposition of "objective" and "person," and the identification of the "objective" with "things" or the "factual," "subhuman," or "not yet morally significant."

44. See B. Schüller, "Die Bedeutung des natürlichen Sittengesetzes für den Christen," in G. Teichtweier and W. Dreier, eds., *Herausforderung und Kritik der Moraltheologie* (Würzburg, 1971), pp. 123–124: "We began by asking in what sense the nature of man is the measure for good and evil; we were investigating the nature of man as moral subject, as a person who behaves freely . . . it is crucial that . . . we have introduced the concept of nature to characterize the *object*, toward which I freely relate as subject, in order to determine what kind of 'love-worthiness' [*Liebens-Würdigkeit*] this object consists in, and in what consists its well-being, which is to be fostered. . . . We have apparently taken our investigation in the wrong direction, but we need not feel regret, since in any event we had to become sure whether and in what degree our behavior takes its moral character from the object to which we are relating ourselves. But now let us direct our attention to man as moral subject."

45. See H. Rotter, "Subjektivität und Objektivität des sittlichen Anspruchs," in K. Demmer and B. Schüller, eds., *Christlich Glauben und Handeln* (Düsseldorf, 1977), pp. 196, 203: "The ability of man to go out to the world in an inner distance and to grasp things as objects simultaneously conditions his ability for subjectivity. . . . The concept *objective* is used in a very different sense. Here it is understood in opposition to those subjective dimensions of the human act that are characterized by feeling and freedom. Objective factors in the moral claim are those givens that are presupposed independently of a personal attitude." It is understandable why so many moral theologians want to free themselves from so distorted a concept of "objectivity." Observe how the object is that which has nothing to do with the really human and personal, and stands "apart" or "prior" to man. It is opposed to *freedom*. In reality, what is "objective" are the specifically human meaning and contents of action, as constituted by the practical reason in the context of the person. The rationally objective is not *opposed* to freedom, nor does it represent a *narrowing* of it or a *threat* to it, but rather provides its foundation; as Thomas says, it is the *radix libertatis*.

46. See F. Böckle, *Grundbegriffe der Moral*, 8th ed. (Aschaffenburg, 1977), pp. 40–41; English trans. by W. Jerman as *Fundamental Concepts of Moral Theology* (New York, 1968), pp. 38–39: "By *object* we mean the objective value to which an act by its very nature is ordered. . . . Thus a thing that does not belong to me (*res aliena*) is not, in the order of justice, an object that lends itself to my attempts to possess it; on the other hand, a thing that has been lost (*res derelicta*, e.g. a piece of wood in a forest)

neither obliges me to get it nor forbids me to look for it. . . . If we consider the human act exclusively from the point of view of the *subject* (the person who performs the act), it is a striving or an acquiescence; only from its object does it become a striving *for something* or an acquiescence *in something*. . . . To prevent any misunderstanding, it should be expressly noted that the object of an act is always a being—and thus also a good—to which the freely willed act is ordered." Böckle is here repeating a point of view common to many traditional handbooks. It is not the *res aliena* that objectively specifies an act of the will, but rather the exterior act that directs itself to the *res aliena*; the object is not the *res* that belongs to someone else but the *taking* of the *res*.

47. See ibid., p. 43 (p. 41 in Jerman's translation): "To distinguish the purpose or end of an act that pertains to the nature of the act itself (*finis operis*), the [doer's] intention is here called the "reason for acting" (*finis operantis*). Because the purpose of an *act* (*finis operis*—the end of a particular act) coincides with the object of the act, it is called the *objective* purpose; and the purpose of *acting* (*finis operantis*—the purpose of the one acting), because it lies entirely within the subject (the person acting), is called the *subjective* purpose." Here, too, the concept of the objective (*finis operis*) is treated as a "given" constituted independently of the will of the agent as molded by his reason, and not as a goal of the will, *apprehensum et ordinatum a ratione*, whereby the *ordinatio rationis* is really that of the acting person's.

48. See F. Scholz, "Objekt und Umstände, Wesenswirkungen und Nebeneffekte," in K. Demmer and B. Schüller, eds. *Christlich Glauben und Handeln* (Düsseldorf, 1977), pp. 243–260. Scholz correctly understands the "object" as a "doing" (*Tun*) (p. 243), but it becomes evident that he places this "doing" on the level of the *genus naturae*, without any constitutive mediation by the reason in relation to the will. The result is once again a dualism between the "objectively impersonal" and the "subjectively personal." The "matter concerning which" (*materia circa quam*) that according to Thomas is a "fitting matter" (*materia debita*) becomes merely a de facto "ordering of external factors" (p. 251). Thus "the *materia circa quam* that gives shape to the object is external to begin with and is internalized only by the will" (ibid.). Scholz rightly fights against a "physicalistic manner of treating the object," but he seems not to have avoided doing so. He refers, for example, to an illustration incorrectly applied by K. Hörmann from *I–II*, q. 7, a. 3, ad 3um, where "pouring water upon someone" is said to be the "object" and "washing"(*ablutio*) the "natural consequence"; what Thomas means, however, is that "washing" is the object of the exterior act "pouring water on someone"; that is, *cleaning someone* is the objective meaning of this action: the "pouring" as such would be the deed *in genere naturae*.

49. This occurs above all in reference to the supposedly Thomistic distinction between the *operatum* (the "objective–material" element) and the *operatio* (the personal carrying out of the action). Fuchs finds support in a single passage where Thomas uses this terminology, in the Commentary on the *Ethics* (*In I Ethic.*, lect. 1, nos. 12–23). By *operatum* Thomas intends the *product* (standing independently of the doer) of an *operatio transiens*, which he calls a "making" (*factio*), "just as when an artist/artisan [*artifex*] makes [*facit*] a house or bed," whereas the "action" (*actio*), on the other hand (as an *operatio immanens* like "seeing," "knowing," "willing"), does not have an *operatum*: its goal is not an external product, but rather the action itself. Fuchs constructs his analysis of moral action after the schema of "productive action," with consideration of the "management" and "production" of materials—which is what in fact is denoted by the term *operatum*. See J. Fuchs, 'Operatio' et 'operatum' in dictamine conscientiae," in *Thomistica Morum Principia,* vol. 2 (Rome, 1961), pp. 71–79.

# 11

# The Objectivity of Human Action: Detailed Treatment of Some Classic Problems

## Lying and the Virtue of Truthfulness

The problem of the moral qualification of lying has become one of the favorite themes of contemporary moral theology. One approach has been to point out the issue as a classic instance of "physicalistic" norm justification on the part of the tradition. The moral evil of lying was supposedly founded on the "nature of language," that is, on the natural function of words as a sign of mental contents, so that the moral evil or "unnaturality" of lying was derived from this "nature": "Since words [*voces* ] are naturally signs of intellections [*intellectuum*], it is unnatural [*innaturale*] and not fitting [*indebitum*] that someone signify with a word something that he does not have in mind [*id quod non habet in mente*]" (*II–II,* q. 110, a. 3).

Another approach has been taken by L. Janssens, who tried to show that Thomas did not in fact argue physicalistically, but that for Thomas a lie is not simply a material-physical *falsiloquium*—that would be only an "ontic evil" (or "exterior event"); only an *intention to deceive someone* on the part of the one who makes the false statement (*intentio fallendi*) could make this "ontic evil" into a "moral" one. In other words, Janssens reduces the problem of lying to the *intentio fallendi* that arises in the willing of an ontic evil.

In my view, not only is it incorrect to say that Thomas derived the evil of lying from the natural signifying function of speech, but it also is not true that he limited the nature of lying (the *ratio mendacii*) to the "intent to deceive" (*intentio fallendi*). The former position is based on a faulty analysis of the lie as an *actus humanus* that contradicts the "manifestation of the truth" (*manifestatio veritatis*), which amounts to a mistaken understanding of its objective–moral content. The position of Janssens, on the other hand, is based simply on the omission of a few words in the text of St. Thomas's *Summa Theologiae* cited in its support. Since the theme cannot be handled exhaustively, a few remarks will suffice at present.

The *quaestio* about lying belongs to the treatise on the virtue of veracity or truthfulness (*veracitas*; *II–II,* q. 109–113). This virtue perfects the human being with regard to the fact that language, and also external actions, manifest something "internal" and are thus *communication*. Man enters into communication with his fellow man not with thoughts or intentions but with the bodily dimension of his being: with his language and with his (external) actions. To confine our attention to speech: the bodily dimension of human communication clarifies the natural connection of human communication with language, as well as the inner intelligibility of language, which is not only an event in nature but also an act of *human* sociability. Without it there could be no human community, trust, or friendship. The virtue of truthfulness thus belongs to the virtue of *justice* (see *II–II,* q. 109, aa. 2 and 3).

The peculiar act of this virtue is the *manifestatio veritatis*. And the objective content (the "object") of this act could be called "interpersonal communication" or "the manifestation of the truth" (or *dicere verum*), because "even saying the truth is itself a good act" (*quia hoc ipsum quod est dicere verum est bonus actus,* q. 109, a. 1). And this *manifestatio* is precisely a *debitum morale* to the extent that it is constitutive for the virtue of truthfulness—to the extent that it brings about the order of *communication*. This order consists in two things: first, and above all, in the order of human *willing* of the good of human community life; and second, in a *trusting* human community life, upon which all communication is based.

But the "manifestation of the truth" (*manifestatio veritatis*) is an act of the will, and as an *actus humanus* it is a "commanded act" (*actus imperatus*) of the will.[1] As a willing, personal *actus humanus,* an *apprehensio et ordinatio rationis* accordingly underlies the human act of communication with language. As shown before, the act of the will is never simply and "directly" oriented toward the act of a power in its *genus naturae*, or toward an "ontic good." Likewise, the act of the will that presently concerns us does not orient itself toward the natural sign relationship between "word" (*vox*) and "thought" (*intellectus*). This is why Thomas expressly says: "This expression [*manifestatio*] or statement [*enuntiatio*] is an *act of the reason*, which correlates sign and thing signified; every 'representation' (*repraesentatio*) consists, in fact, in a certain correlation (*collatio*) that is the specific task of the reason"(*II–II*, q. 110, a. 1). Thomas illustrates this by contrasting the "language" of animals: here the *manifestatio* is not based on an act of the will (*non tamen manifestationem intendunt*), but rather is brought about by a natural instinct, through a *naturally determined* correlation of sign and signified. Man, however, grasps and establishes the relationship between *signum* and *signatum* through an ordering act of the reason. Human "speaking" is not a natural event, but rather an act of the reason. "Insofar as this *manifestatio* or *enuntiatio* is a moral act, it must be willed, and must depend on the *intentio voluntatis* (ibid.).[2]

Consequently, the *manifestatio veritatis* is to "bring together sign and thing signified" (*conferre signum et signatum*); this *collatio* is an act of the reason, and this act specifies the will. To the same degree as "true speech" grounds an *ordo rationis*, a false statement is essentially or objectively an act that is contrary to reason, an act that destroys the rational ordering of communication, and thus lying objectively and formally consists in the "will to make a false assertion" (*voluntas falsi enuntiandi*).

The problem, then, is in understanding the meaning of the following statement: "Lying [*mendacium*] is an act that has to do with a wrong matter [*indebita materia*]: since words [*voces*] are naturally the signs of intellections, it is unnatural and wrong [*indebitum*] that someone signify with a word [*voce*] what he does not have in the mind" (ibid., a. 3).

This statement does not establish the objective evil of lying, as is so often claimed. The title of the article is the question *Utrum Omne Mendacium Sit Peccatum*, "Whether *Every* Lie Is a Sin." The article is intended to show that lying is an evil *ex genere*, that the *voluntas falsum enuntiandi* is *always* a moral evil.

It is not the objective badness of lying that is being established here (i.e., the *ratio mendacii* or the *species mendacii*)—that was the business of the first article of the *quaestio*. It is only the "always" of the objective evil that is being established here, in the third article. And the justification is evident: words by nature, on account of the corporeal constitution of the human being, are signs of mental contents. In no case is it conceivable that someone could make use of a false *collatio signi et signati* and at the same time claim that in this instance the linguistic sign did *not* intend some mental content (an *intellectus*). The natural relationship between *vox* and *intellectus* (established in the body–spirit constitution of the human being) is a *praesuppositum* for the *ordo rationis* of human communication; therefore the voluntarily false *collatio signi ad signatum* that the reason achieves is *always* an act which is opposed to the nature of human communication and the virtue of truthfulness, and thus is a lie and a moral evil.[3]

We need only to consider the structure of Thomas's argument to see not only that it avoids physicalism, but that it avoids spiritualism as well, by respecting the natural and corporeal contingency of human communication.

Speech, in other words, is not merely an "ontic," freely disposable "means" that in itself can be used toward any purpose. Speech, or language, is itself a constitutive *medium* of communication, and as such is a human good (*bonum humanum*). From this perspective it is also possible to recognize that even the "forced lie" (in which the *intentio fallendi* is not present) attacks communication, and thus directly attacks as well the relationships of justice among human beings. This takes place fundamentally with regard to weakening the habitual ordering of the liar's will toward the "good of another" (*bonum alterius*), the good of one's fellow human being. The profound difference can also be seen between a lie and a clever "hiding of the truth by some dissimulation" (*occultatio veritatis sub aliqua dissimulatione*; ibid., ad 4um), or the so-called "mental reservation" (*reservatio mentalis*). There is not always a duty to "manifest the truth": sometimes, in fact, one is obliged to omit it. But the "reservation" consists in not disturbing interpersonal communication or the orientation of the will toward the *bonum alterius* (justice), despite the *occultatio veritatis*, and therefore it is not lying. Of course, many "techniques" of mental reservation have been used for "easing the conscience" that in reality are only refined forms of lying.

We can take a closer look now at Janssen's exegesis of Thomas.

The following text is cited in support of his position that for Thomas, only the *intentio fallendi*, or the deliberate purpose of deceiving another, is constitutive for the *ratio mendacii*:

> Now the intention of the disordered will can be led to two things [*potest ad duo ferri*]: one is the stating of something false [*ut falsum enuntietur*]; the other is the proper effect of the false enunciation, that somebody be deceived [*ut . . . aliquis fallatur*]. If the following three are present together, namely (a) that what is stated is false, (b) that there is a will to state something false [*voluntas falsum enuntiandi*], and (c) an intention to deceive [*intentio fallendi*], then the falsity is material [*materialiter*], because something false has been said, formal [*formaliter*], because of the will to state something false, and effective [*effective*], because of the will to impress the falsehood [*propter voluntatem falsitatem imprimendi*]. But the nature of lying [*ratio mendacii*] is taken from *formal falsity (b* –from the fact, that is, that someone has to will to state something false. (*II–II,* q. 110, a. 1)

Thomas is speaking here of three stages: the material *falsiloquium,* or the *enuntiatio falsi,* is as such not a lie, since it can be coerced. Only what is *ex intentione voluntatis* is a moral act, and thus a lie. But this *intentio inordinata voluntatis* can be directed in *two ways* (incidentally, the phrase *potest ad duo ferri* is replaced by an ellipsis in Janssen's exposition): either to the *falsiloquium* itself (the *voluntas falsum enuntiandi*) or to the "impression of falsity" (*impressionem falsitatis*) upon another person, which is actual deception (*effective*). This is the *intentio fallendi*, an actual intention. And what, according to Thomas, makes for a lie? The formal falsity, the *voluntas falsum enuntiandi*; the *intentio fallendi* is only the full achievement of the lie (*quaedam perfectio eius*), but does not constitute the very nature of the lie (the *ratio mendacii*). Janssens, however, identifies the formal reason simply with the *intentio fallendi*, which seems plausible because Thomas's distinction is replaced by Janssens with his ellipsis![4]

But Thomas's solution is comprehensible only when it is kept in mind that the inner act of the will is not only *intention* (as Janssens insinuates[5]) but also the *electio*, or that *voluntas* which relates to the object of the action (*dicere verum, falsum*); this object is not merely an "ontic" *falsiloquium*, but also a false "correlation by the reason" (*collatio rationis*), a disorder in the act of the practical reason (*malum rationis*), and thus a moral evil. The "correlation of sign with thing signified" (*collatio signi ad signati*) in an act of truthfulness is an act of human communication, and thus an act of the *practical* reason, or an *actus humanus*.

What Janssens wants to emphasize, and he is correct in doing so, is the fact that every lie *objectively* includes a "will to deceive." And in fact Thomas himself says that the *ratio mendacii* is grounded in formal falsity (*sumitur a formali falsitate*), through the *voluntas* of saying something false, and not in the mere *falsiloquium* itself, in its material aspect. It appears to me that this is not simply the same thing as the difference between "formal" and "material" sin; otherwise the statement would be trivial, and the reader would wonder why it was specially mentioned here, when it is something that applies to *all human* acts.

What Thomas wants to emphasize, rather, is that the *ratio mendacii*, the morally-objective content of a lie, does not consist in misjudging an external good. Thomas would certainly not say, for example, that the *ratio adulterii* consisted in the *voluntas adulterii committendi*: adultery is formulated objectively in its "matter concerning which" (*materia circa quam*), that is, through the "matter" of "having intercourse with the spouse of another" (i.e., not one's own spouse). If someone seduces a married woman without knowing that the woman is married, he *objectively* commits adultery, even if, because of the ignorance on the part of the man, he does not commit *formal* adultery. But if someone makes a false statement (a *falsiloquium*) with the intention of speaking the truth, then this is not *objectively* a lie, since a lie is constituted in the *voluntas* to say something false.

I believe that Thomas's solution to the problem is in harmony with the Augustinian definition of the lie, which may be clearer in a way: *mendacium est quippe falsi significatio cum voluntate fallendi*[6] (lying is the signifying of something false, with the will to deceive). The Augustinian *voluntas fallendi* is exactly identical with the Thomistic *voluntas falsi enuntiandi*: in order for a *falsiloquium* to be a lie, there must be the will to deceive as well. And this applies to every kind of lying. Even a "forced" or playful lie is *intended* to deceive, since otherwise it would make no sense—the deception is willed, but only at the level of a "means." What remains distinct from this is a lie that is spoken with the *intentio fallendi*, the "intention to deceive," that is, not in order merely to get the "better" of someone or to play a joke on someone, but *with the intention to deceive.* And this distinction is important: for when I lie in order to maintain a—perhaps legitimate—advantage in a "game situation," I cannot have recourse to claiming, "But I didn't *mean* to deceive him." Even if, on the level of intention, the intent to deceive is not present, nevertheless, I *did will*—at the level of the "means"—to deceive the other, in order to reach my goal. But if the "choosing will" (*voluntas eligens*) is bad, then the entire will is bad, no matter how splendid the intention may appear.

## "Indirect Action," "*Voluntarium Indirectum*" and a Few Remarks on the Misuse of Casuistry in Moral Theology

Many contemporary moral theologians hold the view that the classical doctrine of "indirect action" (or *voluntarium indirectum*) is untenable and must be replaced by another principle: that one is permitted to carry out directly a (physical) evil (e.g., perform an abortion, make a false statement with the intent to deceive, kill noncombatants in war) so long as there are serious enough reasons for doing so.[7] The tradition maintained that, for example, the death of an innocent, if caused only "indirectly," can never be *intended* as a goal or *chosen* as a means, but at the most can be *tolerated* as a secondary consequence.

Moral theologians who would like to replace the doctrine of indirect action with the dictum "also *directly*, but only for sufficiently grave reasons," are adopting an ethics that makes man morally responsible, in principle, for *all* the foreseeable consequences of his actions.[8] They also hold it as conceivable, and within the bounds of discussion, to justify morally the imposition of a death penalty upon a defendent *known to be innocent* by the judge, if thereby the lives of *many* could be saved (the so-called Caiaphas principle, referred to in chapter 9, section "The Hidden Deontologism of Teleological Ethics," subsection "The Principle of the Optimization of Premoral Goods," with the example of the American sheriff).

G. E. M. Anscombe brought up an excellent example to show

the absurdities to which such "consequentialism" can lead.[9] Someone, known as Mr. X, is responsible for the upbringing of a child. It would clearly be wrong for Mr. X to neglect his duty or deprive the child of some assistance, and it would make no difference were he to do so for reasons of personal advantage or for some very noble cause. But now let us say that Mr. X is suddenly confronted with the choice between committing some misdeed, on the one hand, and being condemned to a very long prison sentence for not committing it, on the other. If he goes to jail, he can no longer fulfill his duty to care for the child. According to the "consequentialist" (or "teleological" or "proportionalist") position, there would be no difference between the two alternatives with respect to the responsibility for the consequence "interruption of child care": in the first case, Mr. X would do this for some definite purpose; in the second case, the consequence is foreseen as an unavoidable result of the noncommission of an evil deed.

This is enough of the example for our purposes, although Anscombe does develop it further.[10] The tradition would call the interruption of the child's care a "direct" action (whether as end or means). And since it concerns an evil act (going against one's duty to be just), which is here intended as a goal or as a means, the action is impermissible. The object of the action belongs here to the moral species of "injustice." In the second case, the action is "indirect": what is done is good ("not committing the crime"); the end or goal is likewise good ("striving for justice"); the evil consequence is not immediately intended, but mediated as a side-effect of the fully accomplished action (a voluntary *avoidance* of something is also an action), and there is also a serious reason ("avoiding the doing of misdeeds").

From the teleologistic standpoint, on the other hand, one would argue as follows: if the foreseeable consequences of doing *x* (only prematurely called a *crime* or *misdeed* by "deontologists") are *less evil than* the interruption of support for the child, then I am obliged to do this deed—and doing *x* would no longer be a "misdeed" after all. If I didn't do it, I would be morally responsible for the situation of the child that will result from the deed's omission. In this way it is possible to justify abortion, active euthanasia, lying, the condemnation of persons known to be innocent, the bombardment of civilians, and so on (this is how President Truman justified the bombing of Hiroshima). This is how many contemporary moral theologians argue, even though they (usually) manage to produce a reason why someone should *not* do such things after all (see the example of the American sheriff, chapter 9). But at the basis of such questioning of absolute prohibitions lies, it seems to me, a grave disruption of what is called "morality."[11]

What is "indirect action"? If I have someone murdered by a hired killer, or if I set someone's house afire and let him die, have I murdered him directly or indirectly? Seen from a strictly technical viewpoint: "indirectly." But as far as the intention is concerned (that is, to consider it from the moral point of view): "directly."[12] Can I say, then, that the death of the person is only an indirect consequence (a secondary consequence, a side effect) of the action of "hiring a professional killer" or of "setting a house afire"? In the technical sense, yes. In the moral sense (considered as an intentional act), no. This means that from the ethical perspective a (technically) "indirect" action is not unconditionally the same as what is called an "indirect action" in ethics. We speak of "indirect action" (in the moral sense) only when the consequence is not *willed*, that is, if it falls outside the intentional structure of the action and is not objectified for it (again, in the moral sense). For objects of action (here, "to kill a man") are always objects of the will.

This may appear trivial at first. But we can narrow the scope of the question: Is it possible for a consequence, "technically" necessary and foreseeable with respect to the natural context of causality, to be—*from the moral perspective* (i.e., when treated as an intentional act)—a mere side effect (*voluntarium indirectum*) for which no responsibility is borne by the agent? This question has a fundamental significance, since what is technically caused does not (on the level of "natural effects") coincide with what has been morally caused. If we were to treat objects of actions principally on the level of the *genus naturae*, and thus concentrate on the technical or natural cause–effect relationship, we would have to say that a directly caused consequence is always the object of a (morally) caused action. To take the example used earlier, the condemnation to a prison term is a direct, unavoidable, necessary and foreseeable consequence of the noncommission of a certain crime, and the inability to exercise the duty of child care is a direct consequence of being in prison. If it is assumed that this context is exactly as necessary and foreseeable as the death of a man, once I set his house afire, then the sad plight of the child has been as directly caused as the death of the man whose house I have set aflame. But this is absurd. The foreseeable causal necessity of a consequence does not determine the amount of responsibility one should take for it. In other words, there can be a (morally) indirect action even in the case of a foreseen causal necessity.

The same holds for the "legitimate defense": if the death of the attacker is only a consequence of the action of "self-defense," then this will not be contradicted by an autopsy that shows that the action of self-defense (e.g., the firing of a shot that went straight into the heart of the attacker) was the *direct* cause of the attacker's death, and that, medically considered, it was certainly no mere "side effect" of the shot. To use another example, a doctor gives a drug for pain relief to a patient who is terminally ill, and an autopsy shows afterward that it was the drug and not the disease that actually killed the patient. Has the doctor directly killed the patient in the moral sense? No, since his action was intentionally (and morally objectively) that of "reducing pain," and not "shortening life"; in view of the patient and the diagnosis, the lethal effect of the drug is reduced to a nonintended (not willed) side effect, even though the death, from the medical–technical perspective, was *not* a side effect, but rather the direct result of the dispensed pain-reliever.

When we speak in the moral perspective of indirect action, we are speaking of indirect *willingness* (*voluntarium indirectum*), since the question is ultimately "What is the objective meaning of this action?" And the object of an action is always conceived as the object of the will, informed by the judgment of the practical reason. Not simply what merely *happens* when someone does something (on the level of the *genus naturae*), but what someone *wants to do* on the basis of a rationally formed intentionality—which is what specifies an action.[13]

"Willing," then, can be taken in two senses: either as willing a goal or end, or as willing the means to a certain end. What results as a consequence (even as a foreseen consequence) from an action chosen or from an action chosen as a means, but that is itself neither end nor means, is not willed but merely permitted insofar as a sufficiently grave reason justifies permitting such a thing to happen. A consequence of this kind is a *voluntarium indirectum* not because it is willed "by the way" or "in passing," but because only the *cause* is willed (the concrete action), from which this consequence nevertheless emerges as a foreseen effect.[14]

Some years ago, F. Scholz attempted to show that most of the actions that were formerly justified by moral theologians as indirect actions were in reality not indirect at all, that the so-called "unwilled side effect" was really just a means camouflaged as a side effect.[15] But Scholz's analyses are based on a physicalistic understanding of the object of action, so that ultimately, actions are being treated not as intentional acts, but rather as "event-like" complexes of effects disconnected from the agents.[16] Scholz thus supports the position that (to use his terminology) so-called "essential consequences" (*Wesensfolgen*), or consequences that result with natural necessity from an action and can *therefore* be foreseen, simply *have to* be willed as means, since they inevitably enter into an action and are thus a *conditio sine qua non* for the action. The death of a certain number of civilians is unavoidable in the bombardment of a military target, even though it is not the goal of the bombing. It is therefore really a means to the end of destroying the military target. The killing of the civilians is thus a necessary consequence of the military action and a sine qua non for its accomplishment ("Objekt und Umstände . . . ," pp. 256–257). In the same way, Scholz maintains, there is no moral difference between the killing of a fetus in the womb as a consequence of rupturing the amniotic sac and the killing of the fetus as a consequence of removing a cancerous uterus (*Umwege und Auswege* . . . , p. 95). In both instances, the fetus is deprived of its essential life-support system: its death is in both cases an "essential consequence" of the action, and thus directly caused.

From the perspective of moral theory, however, this argument appears absurd. The object of action is being treated on the purely natural level of physiological cause-and-effect relationships. But an analysis of the intentional structure of the action shows that in the first example, the "breaking of the amniotic sac" is not the object of a choice for its own sake: it is only a means for bringing about the death of the fetus ("indirect" action in the technical sense). If someone did not want to do this, there would be no reason for breaking the amniotic sac. The action of "letting out the waters" obtains its intentional significance *only through* the consequence "death of the fetus." This is an action, then, that exists at the level of the example of "burning a house, in order to let the inhabitant be killed." In the second example, on the other hand, the extirpation of the uterus is not at all a means of killing the fetus, but a means of freeing the mother from cancer: in contrast to the other example, the intentional significance of the willed action is here constituted in the action "extirpation of the organ that is endangering the mother's life," and not in the consequent death of the fetus. The abortion here is not the goal of the action.

Now one may object with Scholz that it is still only a means to an end, for without the death of the fetus, the gravid uterus could not be removed. Its death is a *conditio sine qua non* for the success of the operation. But this objection does not hold. While every necessary means is a *conditio sine qua non* for reaching an end, not every *conditio sine qua non* is a means. If it were, then the wages earned by policemen would be considered "dirty money," since the crimes committed by criminals are the *conditio sine qua non* for the exercise of the policeman's profession! What must be proved is not that certain consequences are a *conditio sine qua non,* but rather that within the intentional structure of the action, a *conditio sine qua non* has the character of a means. That abortion is *not* the means in our example of the cancerous uterus is seen in the fact that the death of the fetus is not actually *chosen*, so that the *preference* of uterus removal (i.e., the undertaking of that action) does not stand in an intentional context to the death of the fetus. Considered from the point of view of the intention, I do not need the killing in order to save the mother. I cause the death, but not because I want to do so but because it follows from what I want to do. What I want to do here is completely independent from the consequence "death of the fetus"; and further, it is doubtless a good will both at the level of the means and at the level of the end. If we follow Scholz's reasoning, however, we would have to consider (in the previous example) the "withdrawal of support for the child" as the *means* (as *conditio sine qua non*) for the just act, "not committing a crime." This would again be absurd, because in moral questions it is always a matter of the human *will*, not the structure of physiological or other nonwilled cause–effect connections.

This may at first sound all too "subjectivist," giving the impression that everything is fine so long as the will has been suitably "directed." Thanks to a presupposition of Cartesian origin that intentions of the will are "directable" (*lenkbar*) in some way, since the seventeenth century the most unimaginable things have been understood as morally possible, and still are.[17] The most absurd kinds of mental reservation have been justified by this method, and Scholz refers to a few for the purpose of demonstrating the invalidity of the doctrine of indirect action. Another example is justifying the dropping of the atomic bomb on Hiroshima (or the firebombing of German cities), because what was *willed* was the end of the war, and not the death of civilians. But this cannot hold. *Certain things cannot be done without willing them also.* To put it more clearly, perhaps, whatever one does *directly*, one also *wills* to do. An analysis of the intentional structure of the action "total bombing" can show how this is so: What intentional meaning *in itself* could there be in the death of the civil population, and its effect of threat and warning of *another* such event, as a *means* for ending the war? The intended goal of "ending the war" can only lead to the action of "total bombing" *because* thereby masses of civilians are to be killed. One could not maintain that not this was willed, but only the end of the war: the killing of the civilian population was a chosen *means* to an end, and the recourse to the principle of the "directed" intention (*Lenkbarkeit*) is only a disguise for the principle of "the end justifies the means."

The example of the removal of the uterus is different. In this case, without any "direction" of the intention, it can be established that it was not the death of the fetus that was willed, but only the healing of the mother. The removal of the uterus would make sense independently of the fact that there is a human life contained in it; in case there were no child, it would be chosen rightly and without hesitation. Only when viewed physiologically, and not intentionally, can the death of the fetus be a *conditio sine qua non* for the healing of the mother. In the case of the bombing of Hiroshima, as it was impossible for "the killing of civilians" not to *be willed* for the purpose of ending the war (this is an intentional *conditio sine qua non*, a means), so it is clearly *possible* to will to remove a cancerous uterus even if it does not contain a living fetus (or, in other words, not to will its death). This consequence is therefore *praeter intentionem* (not because the will is "directed" away from it, but because it is not directed *toward* it in the first place). Now it may be the case that someone "*also* wills" the death of the unborn, so that there is relief at its death ("it's better this way . . . "). It is in the will—in the human heart—that it is determined whether someone is good or bad. And whether one is good or bad is what is proper to ethics. It is not the consequences one brings about but *what one wills*—and *does* in accordance with that will—that makes for moral goodness. One can naturally "will" certain consequences, and this willing then informs the doing, but "willing" consequences and effecting them are still two different things.

The importance of taking into account the intentional structure of an action is seen in the reverse situation: let us suppose that the cancer has not progressed far, so that it will be possible to delay the operation, without risk to the mother and child, until after the birth of the child. In this case, there would be no sufficiently serious reason to tolerate the consequence of the unborn child's death. But if someone decided to perform the operation at this moment (knowing that it was not necessary), the death of the child could no longer be "beyond intention" (*praeter intentionem*), even though it would have been caused in the same way as before with regard to its medical or physiological nature. One would, rather, have to consider that the death of the fetus is here not merely tolerated, but "*also* willed." One may even be content to "kill two birds with one stone." This was formerly used as a method of justifying removal of the uterus without sufficient medical reason. The consequence of sterilization, the direct willing of which was not permissible, could be labeled a mere "side effect," and thus justified, it was believed, as "indirect" action. But in the absence of a serious reason, the so-called side effect is in reality the (hidden) goal of the action, without the medical–physiological, or "natural," context being different from that of a morally justified sterilization. This difference will be apparent, however, only when actions are considered as intentional acts and not, as Scholz would prefer, in terms of merely natural causality.

Scholz is thus guilty of a grave methodological error, and not only because his treatment of indirect action is done in a typically "physicalistic" manner, with attention paid only to the natural causality, but also because he "puts in brackets" the condition, "*sufficiently serious reasons must be present before one can tolerate evil consequences*" (*Wege, Umwege, und Auswege* . . . , pp. 79, 84), and believes that it is possible to analyze indirect action without regard for this condition. He overlooks the fact that the morally indirect is always an *intentionally* indirect (*praeter intentionem*), and not a naturally–essentially indirect. Scholz argues with a physicalistic concept of the object of the action, and must assume (along with other consequentialists) that the only consequences for which one is *not* responsible are *un*foreseeable consequences. The conclusion is that since one must in any event bear responsibility in the same way for everything, one cannot avoid doing evil, and must be permitted to do it *even directly* if the reasons are sufficiently serious[18]—one must choose evil *as a means*. It is astonishing to see the old (legalistic) doctrine of the "direction" of the intention emerge in Scholz's remark that the lack in the agent of an "intent to harm" (*animus nocendi*) is decisive for the moral permissibility of direct "physical" evil ("Objekt und Umstände . . . ," p. 259).

We can sum up the matter in the following terms: what is decisive for the existence of a *voluntarium indirectum* is, first of all, not the fact that the bad effect is indirect *technically or physically*; what matters is that such bad side effects be also only indirectly *willed*, that they take place *praeter intentionem*. Something is "not willed" in not being willed as a means or as an end. And a sufficiently serious reason must *always* be presupposed.

The "indirectly willed" (*voluntarium indirectum*) is something that someone simply *does not want* (it is *praeter intentionem*), even though it may enter as a side effect into certain actions that one is morally obliged to undertake in certain circumstances. In order to determine what a side effect is in the moral (i.e., intentional) sense—an effect, that is, that does not shape the *objective* content of an action, and in *this* sense does not follow immediately from the action—the following formula would apply: a (foreseen) effect is a *side effect* (or does not immediately follow from an action's accomplishment) if, *first,* its being willed is *not intentionally necessary* for the accomplishment of the action, and if, *second,* a reason exists for its tolerance that is sufficiently serious in view of the intended goal. In regard to the first condition, some observations are in order. Whether or not something is intentionally necessary for the accomplishment of an action naturally depends on *what one does.* The question is not answered at the level of the intended goal (in the sense of the *finis operantis*), but rather at the level of the object of the action (the *finis operis*); but this cannot be determined, as Scholz maintains, at the level of natural "existential contexts." The first condition ensures that the evil effect is not chosen as a means, whereas the second ensures that the evil effect is not intended as a "hidden" goal. And so we can say of a not-willed (in the general sense of being "not-intended") side effect that the person does not want it, and only insofar as one does not want it (i.e., only insofar as it enters *praeter intentionem*), does it *not affect* the objective meaning of the corresponding human act. Since it is often difficult to judge this, all the handbooks provide traditional "rules of thumb" to facilitate the determination. Such rules are an aid for someone who *must* make a speedy judgment *whether or not* an indirect action is at issue. But for a genuinely theoretical ethical analysis of indirect action, these rules of thumb must first be understood in terms of the action theory on which they were originally based.[19]

Once we have understood such "rules of thumb" in terms of their theoretical background, some of the current arguments against the doctrine of indirect action will no longer seem so persuasive. It begins to become clear that not every action with a double effect entails the structure of the *indirectum* (it is not necessary that one of the two effects be a *side* effect), so that many of the examples used for the analysis and criticism of the *indirectum* are not really appropriate: they may be good examples of the *praeter intentionem,* but not of indirect action. Take, for instance, the example (introduced by Cajetan and thoroughly explored by Scholz) that has become a typical textbook case: a rider on horseback who is fleeing for his life across a narrow bridge and finds his way blocked by a child. The ethical question is whether or not the evil effect enters *praeter intentionem.* Now this is something, it seems to me, that can be decided neither by a moral-theological handbook nor by a critic of the handbook, but rather by the rider himself—and by God, the searcher of hearts.

For in order to judge such cases, one must keep in mind first of all that we are not concerned here with a "solvable problem," in the sense of a classical *casus conscientiae*. On the side of the agent, the question is not "May I, or may I not, ride over this child?" for as soon as the horseback rider posed this question, he would come to the conclusion "Yes, in order to save myself, I may ride over the child, because I intend to escape, and not to kill the child." This would mean (as Scholz rightly notes) that he would be choosing the killing of the child as a *means* for his own survival. But if we follow Thomas, this is not morally permissible.[20]

The decisive characteristic of the structure of action that is *praeter intentionem* (as in certain cases of self-defense) seems to me to be the fact that it never even comes to the question "May I or may I not?," and thus never to the choosing of a means (such as "to ride over the child"); rather, the rider simply wants to escape over the bridge. The child that he sees, and whom he tries by reflex to avoid, still remains outside the intentional structure of his action. He kills the child without ever having the chance to pose to himself the question "May I do this?" But now there is another question: Is the rider to be held responsible for the death of the child? Is it not rather—intentionally considered—an *effectus per accidens*?[21] Is he morally responsible for it? Should he be convicted of murder? And the answer would have to be "no," for this consequence was *praeter intentionem*, in no way willed. We must realize that here we are not judging a case that will be relevant for the justification of moral norms; we cannot use the example for the analysis of moral "decision-making," *because no decision is being made*. It is not an example that stimulates the question "Did the rider act rightly?" The only really meaningful question is "Is the rider responsible for the death of the child?"

Let us assume, now, that the rider did have time to stop and consider "May I kill the child in order to save myself?" The affirmative answer to this question would point to the choice of "killing the child" as a means. But in fact it is highly unlikely that the rider would even pose that question (he would do so only in such circumstances in a moral theological handbook), or that he would even choose a means at all. What he intends is to escape from his pursuers, and he would simply be trying to get over the bridge without hurting the child. He may not succeed in doing this, but it is still not a case of decision-making in casuistic terms: the death of the child comes about *praeter intentionem.* Now *whether or not* it really is, in the last analysis only God and the rider himself know. It would be better if moral theologians found themselves in situations like this before they made judgments about them. In any case, a casuistic argumentation pursued "at any price" is suited only to the reality of its own method, and falsifies the intentional structure of the action being investigated.

I am inclined to believe that such examples (like that of legitimate self-defense) are highly *unsuitable* for analyzing the structure of indirect action. When such examples are used as "cases" for the general application of norms in decision-making, a fundamentally false perspective is at work: that of the casuistic understanding of morality, which sees all moral questions as principally instances of the "application of " (or "exception from") legal norms, and forces them into the alternative of "permissible" or "impermissible." Even critics of the doctrine of indirect action like Scholz remain deeply influenced by this tradition, so that they cannot be spared the reproach of having a false perspective and a lack of sympathy for concrete, lived situations. Reality has to be faced and understood before a human situation can be judged.[22]

A further issue can be raised with regard to the question of the misuse of "borderline cases": these are hypothetical constructs that leave out the multifaceted conditions and alternatives of concrete life in order to show that certain norms or commands are not exceptionless: situations are "discovered" in which following the norm or command would lead to absurd consequences. The case of the execution of the innocent person is an example of where *not* doing so would have the consequence that many other people lose their lives. The discussion of such borderline cases (with Scholz and Schüller it becomes a methodological principle) is not so much a helpful tool of analysis as a dialectical artifice not really useful at all for analysis and yielding only (apparent) consequences through the help of a fallacy. The usual pattern is as follows: a case is found where obedience to a certain moral prohibition leads to very difficult or "inhuman" (for Schüller, "catastrophic," "devastating") consequences. Therefore, one concludes, the prohibition is not without exception. And finally, in principle *not every* norm may be valid in any concrete situation: one can measure its concrete validity *hic et nunc* only through the particular actions involved (through a "weighing of goods" or "teleological" assessment).

This style of argument is based on a *petitio principii*, or circular reasoning. What is to be proved is already assumed as proved. What is to be proved here is that "all actions can be judged morally only on the basis of their consequences, or *teleologically*, and not on the basis of absolute criteria, independently of the concrete case." What is rejected is the proposition "Doing *x* is morally bad in all circumstances." And yet this very proposition is tacitly assumed when someone says the following: "In the given situation (illustrated by the borderline case), obeying the absolute norm leads to seriously evil consequences; *consequently* this norm does not apply here." But *consequently* it is this that is in need of proof, that is, it would have to be proved *why* the "seriously evil" consequences that may result from following a certain moral norm can say anything at all about this norm not being valid in this case, and (it comes to the same thing) *why* the avoidance of the seriously evil consequences through *not* obeying a moral norm is *more humane* than following the norm with the readiness to face serious consequences. And this is exactly what is *not* proven here, since the conclusion "A prohibition cannot have exceptionless validity (i.e., compliance with it cannot be humane) if serious consequences result from it" is already *presupposed* as a premise. Or consider the following question: "If it is known in advance that a mother will not survive the birth of a child, is it not simply *better, more humane,* and thus *morally right* to purchase the birth of the child with the sacrifice of her own life, than to abort the unborn child, in order to avoid the serious consequence (for the family as well) of her own death?" Such a question is rejected as not even worthy of mention by many contemporary moral theologians, thanks to the *petitio principii* we are discussing. But questions like this cannot be merely swept away. For they implicitly bear that fundamental moral question of Socrates, "What is worse, to *suffer* evil or to *do* it?" And this is the question whose correct answer determines the existence of humanity or inhumanity in this world.

Extreme cases and borderline cases say almost nothing about the universal validity of a norm. They only show that in certain circumstances, heroic sacrifices are demanded of the human person in order to preserve purity of heart. For Christians, there is only *one* morally supportable answer—that of the Sermon on the Mount: "Happy are those who are pure of heart, for they shall see God" (Matt. 5:8), and "Seek first the kingdom of God and His righteousness, and everything else [such as earthly needs] will be given to you as well" (Matt. 6:33). If such statements were made irrelevant to moral theology by the "weighing of goods" and the dissolution of every unconditional *non licet*, "the very point of Christian life would be lost, through losing the possibility of taking that life seriously."[23]

Borderline cases also show how little justification there is in judging a man who may actually be involved in one. The (pagan) anxiety about the serious consequences (by earthly standards) of morally upright action has crippled many, and the overcoming of this fear has given the Church many martyrs. What is in question is the moral significance of the *not-intended consequence* known as martyrdom. How far, on the other hand, denial is to be counted as morally culpable—that only God knows, Who alone governs all things. We human beings do not always have to be ready to pass judgment. For those who fail in such situations, those who with more or less culpability have done evil, and feel sorry for doing so, God—and the Church—have a quite different answer: *mercy and forgiveness*. The "exception rules" of many moral theologians, on the other hand, make for an irresponsible game with the human conscience.

There are situations in life that simply do not permit an unambiguous solution. Contemporary moral theologians habitually bring up such cases and treat them in a distorted casuistical manner, in order to disprove absolute prohibitions. The best-known example (although practically irrelevant de facto) is that of the medical doctor who claims that during an operation on a tumor in a gravid uterus, he was faced with the alternative of letting the mother bleed to death, or aborting the baby to stop the bleeding and so preserve the uterus. He takes the latter action, even though a moral theologian had told him it was morally impermissible. The same theologian informed the physician that it *would* have been permissible if he had surgically removed the baby *and* the uterus, since that would be an instance of indirect killing. The implication? The doctrine of indirect action leads to absurd consequences.[24]

There is only one thing to say about this: beware of misusing casuistiry! It is more than questionable to draw consequences for a normative ethics on the basis of an isolated occurrence. In this case, the conclusion is based on a manipulation of the argument that may not at first be apparent: the indirect killing of a fetus (as the consequence of a morally justified removal of the uterus) can be morally justified, as shown above. *But this does not provide alternatives of action relevant to the present example,* because as a meaningful instance of indirect action, it belongs to a completely different context of action and presents a quite different intentional structure. If the counseling moral theologian had advised the doctor to act in accordance with this (other) case, he would have been giving the wrong advice.

For the apparent choice of alternatives in the earlier example was based on the concern *not* being the preservation of the uterus; since the uterus was already cancerous and irretrievable, it had to be removed in order to save the life of the mother. In this example, however, the "removal of the uterus," is not being sought for, but rather its *preservation* (which was also the reason for the operation to remove the tumor in the first place). This is precisely why, in this particular intentional context, the alternative, "stopping the bleeding by removing the uterus" is rejected as foreign to the intentional structure. It contradicts the original goal of the operation. Removal of the whole uterus is not a *meaningful* (i.e., rationally coherent) alternative. To suggest that the doctrine of indirect action is supposed to *make* it meaningful is a manipulative argument.

The intentional conditions for a meaningful removal of the uterus and the permitted (because indirect) killing of the unborn child are *not* present in the case. It is simply not possible to offer an intentional (or morally consistent) alternative of action. One must take care not to "simplify" the casuistic discussion of the case by abstracting the action structure "removal of the fetus for the purpose of stopping the bleeding" from the entire context of the original action structure "removal of the tumor in order to heal the mother." This would only distort the intentional structure of the situation. For these reasons, the case appears to me to be beyond casuistic discussion. It is impossible to arrrive at a normative judgment about what the doctor *should have done* in this situation. The only thing that one can judge here (and not in a casuistic manner) is the concrete action of the doctor in *this* situation—without trying, of course, to subsume the case under a general rule, not even a "weighing of goods." It is a question of *responsibility* and not of "*permission.*" Consequently, I would incline to the judgment that the killing of the fetus here is *praeter intentionem*: the will of the agent is not related to the object of the action "killing the fetus" as a *choosing* will. It is completely different from a situation where one deliberately arrives at a decision to abort the unborn child directly, "in order to save the life of the mother." But if experience has shown that this situation was in fact foreseeable and *avoidable,* and if the same thing should happen to the same doctor again, I would characterize the action as negligence (and thus a *voluntarium in causa*).

In any case, it is only "sensationalism" to reason on the basis of such an example that there are cases in which one may directly kill an innocent person in order to avoid a greater evil. The example doesn't work, simply because the doctor was *not* permitted to do what he did. There are situations that elude any casuistry and any subsumption under a general norm that would allow us to say that one "may" or "may not" do such and such. The tradition was conscious of this when it was maintained that the doctor acted "in good faith" (*bona fide*), since he made a rational decision in a crisis that did not admit of a rational decision. He could not be reproached, on the one hand, and yet on the other hand, the norm that one may *never* choose the killing of an innocent as a means to some end remains undisturbed. But to derive consequences for normative ethics from such situations means (1) giving up on valid argumentation, (2) committing the fallacy of making a norm out of an exception, and (3) misusing casuistry, and implying that a casuistically unambiguous normative solution is possible for *every* situation. Casuistry, let it be recalled, is an *aid* for the making of normative judgments—not *a standard.*

The method of arriving at exceptions to norms from the use of borderline cases appears to me to be logically inconsistent as well. For one cannot (on the one hand) maintain that "borderline cases show that a supposedly absolute norm admits of exceptions" and (on the other) maintain *at the same time* that "the possibility of such exceptions shows that all actions must be judged on the basis of their consequences." If the second proposition is valid, one cannot even speak of "exceptions," since exceptions imply a universal norm, and according to the same proposition, universal norms are not even supposed to exist. The latter proposition *negates* the former, which is it own presupposition. A syllogism whose conclusion refutes its own premises is rightly regarded as inconsistent. The result of the "reasoning" is self-contradictory. Borderline cases in the area of "indirect action" do not point to (normative) exceptions, but only to the fact that in certain cases one must plead for "mercy" without being driven to change the "law."

The question about the *voluntarium indirectum*, then, is ultimately the question of how far man bears the responsibility for his own actions, how far consequences affect the morally *objective* content of his actions. The concept of "responsibility" is closely connected with that of *willingness*. And while teleological ethicists are inclined to make man responsible for *all* the consequences of his actions, this claim comes at the price of treating all chooseable contents of actions as, in principle, only *premoral* goods. But this destroys not only the concept of the indirectly willed but also, it seems to me, the concept of moral responsibility itself, and its morally objective and personal meaning. For if, "for serious reasons," I may will *anything* in principle (even something normally considered evil, but by exception willed as a means to a worthy end), then the object of my willing no longer has any moral meaning. Only the "serious reasons" can have moral meaning. But what is the criterion for moral responsibility? (It was shown in chapters 8 and 9, how something like this cannot be consistently provided in "teleological ethics," but can at best be postulated only "deontologically.")

Now the traditional solution appears at once *more consistent, more realistic*, and *more humane*. It is more humane not because it is more "pleasant," but because it respects man as a being who has significance in his own essence, and who is not condemned to have constantly to "construct" from proportionate "reasons" what this being is or should be. It is more realistic because such *total responsibility* leads either to total irresponsibility or to the normative dictatorship of experts, politicians, and laws. Now in theological terms, this could make sense in a theory of "theological absolutism," according to which *anything goes* in principle, because there exists only "a single inwardly evil action, that of turning from God" (Scholz, *Wege, Umwege, und Auswege* . . . , p. 153), the equivalent of giving up on morality and ethics altogether for the sake of the love of God. But such a position forgets that Scripture instructs us otherwise: that man's love for God is to be judged on the basis of his *actions*—that not everyone who merely says "Lord! Lord!" will enter the kingdom of heaven.

## The Concept of the "*Intrinsece Malum*" and the Ethical Context

According to a very widespread usage, the ethical term "intrinsically evil action" (*actio intrinsece mala*) denotes an action that is morally bad in its own objective structure, and *not* because it has been positively prohibited by legislative fiat (*mala quia prohibita*), *nor* because of circumstances or consequences. There are actions, therefore, that are *never* permissible, independently of whether they have been positively prohibited and independently of *any* situations or consequences.[25]

This is how Scholz describes the doctrine (*Wege, Umwege, und Auswege* . . . , pp. 16–17):

> It has to do with actions that can be described only in physical terms and that must nevertheless be rejected *morally* without exception, such as (direct) contraception, artificial insemination, direct intervention on an incipient life (even after exhausting all other possibilities) in order to save the mother, and so on. Such actions, according to this leading doctrine, are characterized by an "absolute, inner wickedness," so that they *never*, no matter what the motive and no matter how extreme the situation, are permissible.[26]

On the basis of our presentation of moral objectivity, it should be immediately apparent that this description of *intrinsece malum* is based on a physicalistic theory of the object of action. For to say "doing *x* is evil *in itself*" means that "to do *x* is *objectively* (i.e., on the basis of the object of action) evil." In order to describe "what is being done," an action that lies under the verdict of being *intrinsically evil* must be described with respect to its *object*. If an action is described "in physical terms," that means that the *object* of the action has been determined at the physical–ontic level, or at the level of the *genus naturae*. But at this level it cannot be subject to a *moral* qualification ("doing *x* is evil in itself"). To maintain that the doctrine of intrinsically evil actions is inconclusive because no moral judgments can be made at the physical-ontic level, is simply begging the question (*petitio principii*), since it is assumed that the action which is being so judged is being described "in physical terms." But no moral judgment at all can be made about actions described in that way. The conclusion only repeats one of the premises.[27]

The judgment "doing *x* is in itself (*intrinsece*) evil" is nevertheless a moral judgment. If an action is going to be described correctly as *intrinsece malum*, this qualification must relate to the level of the *genus moris*. This involves taking into account what we might call the *ethical context* of the action. The ethical context is the context into which a certain action is integrated through the ordering act of the practical reason: it is the context of the *suppositum*, of the person, or the context of moral virtues, all of which transcend the level of the mere *fines naturales*. In order for the judgment "doing *x* is in itself (objectively) morally bad" to be valid, the description of "doing *x*" must take into account the ethical context as well as the physical elements.

Thus it is quite possible for the same action that has been described "in physical terms" to be judged *differently* in view of the ethical context. This is a very well-known doctrine, and it is astounding that it has been so easily forgotten in the treatment of the *intrinsece malum*. The classical example is the difference between a marital act and an act of adultery: they are distinguished in their moral species insofar as they possess a relation to the reason (*secundum quod comparatur ad rationem*). The marital act is praiseworthy; the adulterous act is the opposite. But insofar as they are compared in regard to the use of the reproductive organs (*secundum quod comparantur ad potentiam generativam*), they do not differ at all in their species. The species at the level of the *finis naturalis* is identical, but it is not the *moral* species and does not allow the judgment of (morally) "good" or "evil" (see *I–II,* q. 18, a. 5, ad 3um.).

It would be logically inconsistent to maintain this well-known distinction between the *genus moris* and the *genus naturae*, and at the *same time* maintain, for instance, that "contraception, as understood in physical terms (i.e., as an intervention into the functioning of the generative powers), is always evil in itself." The judgment "contraception is evil in itself" cannot be made good as an ethically relevant judgment at this level, but only at the level where the use of the generative power is understood as being integrated into an ethical context, that is, at the level at which the *genus moris* of this act is constituted. This level is the level of chosen human actions, the field of the practical reason that constitutes the natural law, the level of *moral* objectivity.

This should clarify why it is not enough to describe the morally qualifiable human action "contraception" in "physical terms"—to describe it as a "surgical, pharmaceutical or mechanical intervention that causes sexual intercourse between a man and a woman to be without conception." This is just as meaningless as to maintain that sexual intercourse between a man and a woman is in itself (that is, as considered independently of any ethical context) morally "good" or "evil," or that it is even *a human action* at all. Rather, the questions should first be "Are the man and woman married?," and "Are they married *to one other*?" "Is it a voluntary action or is it rape?" "Is it marital, or pre- or extramarital, or coerced sexual intercourse?" Only at this level of the *genus moris* is any ethical judgment possible.

"Contraception" must be described within the ethical context for an *ethical* judgment. This differs from a purely *medical* judgment: for if the question is whether a contraceptive is "effective" or "harmful," "reliable" or otherwise, it is completely immaterial whether the contraceptive has been used for canceling the fruitfulness of marital acts or for a precaution in case of an anticipated rape.

The encyclical *Humanae Vitae* holds that "every action [is excluded] . . . that, either in anticipation of the conjugal act, or in its accomplishment, or in the development of its natural consequences, proposes, whether as an end or as a means, to render procreation impossible" (14). This statement is framed within the ethical context of a certain type of *human actions*: the free, consciously chosen sexual union of a man and a woman. It is not a statement about the "inviolability of the physical integrity of the generative power," but a statement about the sexual union of man and woman as an *actus humanus* (and thus *Humanae Vitae* is concerned with the sexual acts of *married persons*). It is not a question of a "natural prohibition" (to use Scholz's expression), where "nature" refers to the "physiological structure of the generative power and its integrity." If the expression "natural prohibition" were used, then "nature" would have to mean the "nature of the sexual relations between man and woman" (i.e., *natural* in the sense of the natural law as expressed through an *ordinatio rationis*; see chapter 2, section "Excursus: The Natural Law and Contraception").

For example, an affirmative answer to the question of whether a woman may be permitted to use a contraceptive in anticipation of rape does not constitute an "exception" to this norm.[28] A woman neither intends nor chooses sexual intercourse with the rapist. She thus bears no procreative responsibility for the act. The rape cannot be described as a human act of "sexual intercourse" on the part of the woman, but rather as the suffering of an act of physical aggression, or the misuse of her sexual organs through the act of the aggressor. The ingestion, for example, of an oral contracpetive has for its purpose the hindering of a possible conception; this contraceptive act is not related to the ethical context "hindering the procreative consequences of sexual union between X and Y," but rather to the context "hindering the procreative consequences of sexual aggression of X upon Y"; the contraceptive act of the woman X has no relation to the *human act* of sexual union. To characterize the permissibility of contraception in this instance as an "exception" to a general prohibition would be possible only if the act of contraception (or sexual union) were being described independently of the ethical context, that is, at the level of the *genus naturae*. At this level, nothing "happens" in a rape that is different from any other act of sexual intercourse. But the act cannot be described in that way, as we have already shown.

*The expression* "intrinsece malum" *is always to be understood in relation to an ethical context.* The qualification "intrinsically evil" only and exclusively concerns the *morally objective* content of an action. This is precisely what "teleological" ethicists have overlooked in their critique of the category, and that is because, having lost sight of the concept of *moral* objectivity as the object of the practical reason, they are compelled by physicalistic prejudice to consider such a distinction as impossible.

The case of the moral qualification of lying is similar, although the matter is somewhat more complicated. The elements that constitute the ethical context within which a false saying becomes a lie are complex. A lie injures the virtue of truthfulness, which is oriented toward the good of human communication (see the section "Lying and the Virtue of Truthfulness" earlier in this chapter). Certain borderline cases that have been discussed by some theologians appear to relate to situations that *totally lack* such a communicative context.

We can consider, for instance, the case of the prisoner of war interrogated about the strategy of his own troops. Of course, it could not be said that a "context of human communication" between the two army camps is *totally* lacking: it is there at least potentially, and in fact we would have to acknowledge that its eventual *restoration* would be a principal goal of all the war efforts, and the very condition of a peace treaty. But it could not be said, on the other hand, that the interrogation of a prisoner of war really exists within a "context of human communication." Far the opposite: the interrogation of the prisoner is just as much an "act of war" as the surprise attack that could be made on his own troops as a result of his giving the correct information to the enemy. If someone were to call a false statement by the prisoner *morally* bad, that is, a "lie," then every deceptive action in war could also be so judged. And assuming that the "killing of a man" in a just war is morally permissible, such a consequence would be absurd. The ethical context is here completely different from that in which a lie is defined as being "always" and "in itself" bad.

Now, to maintain in this way the relativity of the *intrinsece malum* with regard to its ethical context is completely different from the attempt of "teleological ethics" to characterize actions as "good" or "bad" solely on the basis of their consequences. The ethical context of actions in itself is not modified "in the concrete situation" by foreseeable consequences. The ethical context of an action is, rather, a part of the *morally objective* dimension of human action, objectifed by the practical reason; this context can delimit the area of an *intrinsece malum.* A teleological "weighing of goods," on the other hand, if the "concrete case" and the "foreseeable consequences" required, would subordinate the good of social communication (or the virtue of truthfulness) to some *other good* considered more important—in other words, it would justify telling a lie for a "good purpose." But the doctrine of an *intrinsece malum* as related to an ethical context, while never considering a lie permissible, would in fact allow a false statement that in no way injures the good of communication or the virtue of truthfulness.[29] Such "noncommunicative" situations are extremely rare, and can usually be described in exact terms. There will always be "gray areas," of course—but that changes nothing about the difficulties inherent in lying: no more so, indeed, than, when you are walking in foggy weather, you see something, and a doubt arises: "Is that a cat or a dog?" The problem in such a case is not any doubt about the true nature of a cat or dog, but rather about *whether or not* that animal there is (in fact) a cat or a dog.

We can conclude this excursus with a discussion of the problem of murder. It has been questioned whether or not the commandment "Thou shalt not kill" is exceptionless. If it means "Thou shalt not *unjustly* kill," or "Thou shalt not kill *any innocent person,*" then the command is without exception. But this would only delay the problem for a while, for questions remain, such as "When does one kill *unjustly?*" or "Who is *an innocent person*?"

Because of this difficulty, some have come to the conclusion that the fundamental permissibility of the death penalty, of killing in a just war, and killing in legitimate self-defense are "exceptions" to the general prohibition of killing. The very existence of such exceptions, they reason, shows that "to kill a human being" cannot be considered as an *actio intrinsece mala,* that the prohibition of killing is valid only "in most cases" (*ut in pluribus*), and not universally.

These and similar references to "exceptions," however, are based on making the moral assessment of the action "killing a human being" subject to a description of actions on the plane of the *genus naturae* (in other words, to a description in physical terms). Now it seems quite possible to describe the "killing of an innocent person" (murder, unjustifiable killing) as distinct from "killing as such" in view of the ethical context, that is, on the level of the *genus moris*. The action of "killing someone" can at first, of course, be identified in a purely physiological or technical description. As long as we know, for instance, what happens when a person is shot, we can describe "killing a human being" as "shooting a human being." But if we wanted to conclude that "killing an innocent person" means nothing other than "unjustly shooting someone," we would find ourselves in a logical impasse. In such a case a sentence like "It is morally bad to shoot an innocent person" would be a pure tautology, identical with the statement "It is morally bad to shoot a person unjustly." But this difficulty is only the consequence of describing the action "killing someone" independently of any moral context.

Let us say we describe the action "killing a man" as "taking another person's life into one's hands in an act of personal competence (i.e., as a *private person*)," where "taking life into one's hands" means the same thing as "ending life by killing." The problem lies not in *grounding* the badness of such an act, but rather in adequately *describing* the action "murder." If I describe murder as I have above, then I can say, "This act is *always* and *in itself* bad. There is no exception. "Killing a man in legitimate self-defense" does not arise here as a possible "exception," because such a killing is permissible only when it happens *praeter intentionem*, that is, when the killing is not *willed* (intended as a means); what happens *praeter intentionem* has *no moral species whatsoever*, and thus cannot be an "exception" (see the section " 'Indirect Action,' '*Voluntarium Indirectum*,' and a Few Remarks on the Misuse of Casuistry in Moral Theology," earlier in this chapter).

The death penalty and "killing in a just war," as morally qualifiable actions, exist within a different ethical context and must be described in accordance with that context. The traditional justifications of capital punishment and killing in a just war[30] are based on the idea that the lives in question are not at the disposal of private persons, but rather of representatives of the public interests, to whom a responsibility for common good has been entrusted, especially for the restoration of justice when it has been harmed.[31] It is also implied that the competence that legitimizes this power (no matter what its concrete organizational or personal configuration) comes from God (see Romans 13:1ff.) and not from men. Here again, it is not a matter of *justifying* whether or not capital punishment and killing in a just war are permissible, but rather of showing that these actions have a different objectively moral structure because of their different ethical context. Consequently, they must be differently described.[32] The permissibility of such actions would not then be "exceptions" to the prohibition of killing, because they are actions that would never be subject to this prohibition in virtue of their *genus moris*. This does not mean they *are* permissible. It means that their moral qualification is different from that of a case of killing under "private competence."

In this connection, then, it can be said that "It is *always* morally wrong to kill an innocent person."[33] How can we describe the action "killing an innocent person"? We do this by indicating *who* an innocent person is. For example, we can call "innocent" anyone who is the object of an act of killing carried out by a representative of the legitimate public authority when that representative acts in a manner contrary to the principles that constitute public authority and its exercise. As a result, any form of "judicial murder" is rejected. This means that a person is "innocent" who is convicted of a crime even though the judge does not know whether he has in fact committed it (or even though he knows in fact that he *has not* committed it). Such a person is innocent because a public action of this kind would be contrary to the principles that constitute the legitimacy of the public administration of justice (one naturally must be in a position to describe those principles, which may not be an easy task). To the extent that a judge acts for purely *personal* reasons, such an action would belong to the ethical context of simple murder.

This brings us once again to the importance of attending to the ethical context in our description of an action, in our description of a *human act* (*actus humanus*) as governed by the practical reason and will—a morally qualifiable action. "Execution of someone sentenced to capital punishment" and "killing in a just war" do not appear as exceptions, but rather as (physical) actions of killing that belong to *another ethical context*. Killing in legitimate self-defense, on the other hand, due to its *praeter intentionem* structure, is a morally nonspecified and nonspecifiable action—neither good nor bad—but rather a consequence for which one is not responsible.[34] The commandment of the Decalogue, "Thou shalt not kill," is best understood as being addressed to private individuals and not to public authorities qua public authorities. In this way it can be taken as exceptionless, even for those persons in public authority who are subject to the temptation to misuse their office for "private" purposes, and thus become murderers.

To recapitulate: actions that must be described differently because they are in a different ethical context appear as "exceptions" only when it is believed that human actions are to be described "in physical terms," that is, at the level of the *genus naturae.* The contemporary critique of the *intrinsece malum* has its origin in a *petitio principii.* For if someone maintains that the moral judgment of actions must be made in "physical terms" only, and not in view of their morally objective content, that person is saying nothing other than "The content of an action that is *the object of the practical reason* is never moral but always premoral." This view negates (without support) what is assumed for good reasons by someone who holds that human actions possess a specific, objectively moral dimension for the practical reason. An ethical theory that is founded on such a negation and that thus denies the existence of actions that in themselves are *always* bad, can rightly be called "physicalistic."

## NOTES

1. See *II–II,* q. 109, a. 3, ad 2um: "Veritas secundum quod est cognita, pertinet ad intellectum. Sed homo per propriam voluntatem, per quam utitur et habitibus et membris, profert exteriora signa ad veritatem manifestandam. Et secundum hoc, manifestatio veritatis est actus voluntatis." (Truth, insofar as it is *known,* pertains to the intellect. But man brings forth external significations for the manifestation of truth *through his own will,* through which he exercises habits and bodily members. In this sense, the manifestation of the truth is an act of the will.)

2. *Intentio* here does not mean the "intention," but only the *willing* in general, as will be clear from what follows.

3. For the concept of the *praesuppositum,* see chapter 2, section "Beyond Naturalism and Dualism," subsection "The '*Praesuppositio,*': An

Essential Perspective"; for lying as *intrinsece malum,* see below, section "The Concept of the Intrinsece Malum."

4. See L. Janssens, "Ontic Evil and Moral Evil," *Louvain Studies* 4 (1972), pp. 115–156.

5. See ibid., "To be a lie, this material element must be embraced by the *formal* element, viz., the end of the inner act of the will, the *intention* to utter something that is not true (*intentio voluntatis inordinatae . . . ut falsum enuntietur*)."

6. Augustine, *Contra Mendacium,* 12, 26 (PL 40, 537). T. G. Belmans sees an opposition betweeen the definitions of Augustine and Thomas, but it is probable that Belmans overlooked the meaning of *voluntas* for Thomas in the constitution of the *ratio mendacii.*

7. First and most influential in supporting this position was P. Knauer: "Das rechtverstandene Prinzip von der Doppelwirkung als Grundnorm jeder Gewissensentscheidung," in *Theologie und Glaube* 57 (1967): 107–133; the English translation can most conveniently be found in C. E. Curran and R. A. McCormick, eds., *Readings in Moral Theology, No. 1: Moral Norms and Catholic Tradition* (New York, 1979) pp. 1–39. The article first appeared in English as "The Hermeneutic Function of the Principle of Double Effect," *Natural Law Forum* 12 (1967): 132–162.

8. See B. Schüller, *Die Begründung sittlicher Urteile,* 2nd ed. (Düsseldorf, 1980), p. 290: "The third characteristic of teleological ethics calls into question this restriction of human responsibility. For since it maintains that the moral rectitude of an action is determined exclusively by its consequences, it makes one responsible for all the foreseeable consequences of one's action." This position, whose most influential proponent was the English utilitarian philosopher Henry Sidgwick (1838–1900), was shown as early as 1903 to be untenable in this form by G. E. Moore (*Principia Ethica,* [rep. Cambridge, 1984], p. 149; see chapter 13, note 5, of the present work). See also G. E. M. Anscombe, "Modern Moral Philosophy," in *The Collected Papers of G. E. M. Anscombe,* vol. 3 (Oxford, 1981), esp. pp. 34–36.

9. Anscombe, "Modern Moral Philosophy," p. 35.

10. The equation of "means" and "unavoidable consequence" then leads Mr. X to consider the following: If I am equally responsible for the consequences in either case, then it is fundamentally indifferent what I *do.* I only have to pay attention to the consequences that follow from my action (or nonaction). Accordingly. Mr X will feel justified, if he has the opportunity, in doing an even worse crime, since he is no longer obliged to consider whether the act is good or bad. If bad consequences that he did not foresee result from this, he will say, "I am not responsible

for that, because I couldn't foresee those consequences." After all, an action is good or bad according to the *foreseen* consequences (see Moore, *Principia Ethica*, pp. 149–150). This means, then, that it is not the consequences as such that determine the moral quality of my actions, but only the consequences that *I* foresee, which are perhaps different from consequences foreseen by Y or Z. So, then, the *actual* consequences are no longer relevant after all, but only the *anticipated* ones. In this way no one is responsible for the consequences of his actions, so long as he can give reasons for not foreseeing them. But in response to this, we must say, with Anscombe, that this is absurd. On the contrary, every person is responsible for the evil consequences of his misdeeds, and gets no credit for their (occasionally) good consequences; and *nobody* is morally responsible for the (occasionally) bad effects of one's good actions. Rather, everyone gets credit for the good consequences.

11. See G. E. M. Anscombe, "Modern Moral Philosophy," p. 40: "But if someone really thinks, *in advance,* that it is open to question whether such an action as procuring the judicial execution of the innocent should be quite excluded from consideration—I do not want to argue with him; he shows a corrupt mind."

12. "Intentional" means that actions are not natural events, but rather acts of the will, guided by the reason. In a human act there is always a concretized *intentio voluntatis.* This is first of all the *intentio finis*, the intention in the real sense, and secondly the *electio eorum quae sunt ad finem,* the "means," which are chosen for the sake of the end; the choice of means (*electio*) is nothing other than an operative concretization of the *intentio.* The concrete, accomplished action is thus from the ethical point of view, an operatively concretized *intentio voluntatis.* In order for moral actions to be analyzed and judged, they must not be considered merely "physical" processes, but rather intentional acts.

13. See also Thomas: "Morales autem actus recipiunt speciem secundum id quod intenditur, non autem ab eo quod est praeter intentionem" (*II–II,* q. 64, a. 7). Here, *intendere* is used in the most general sense for "willing"; in this sense the *intentio finis* and the *electio* of the means are equally an *intendere.* Useful comments on this can be found in J. M. Boyle, " '*Praeter intentionem*' in Aquinas," *The Thomist* 42, 4 (1978): 649–665.

14. As Scholz rightly points out with reference to Garrigou-Lagrange's commentary on the *Prima Secundae* (1951) in his article "Objekt und Umstände, Wesenwirkungen und Nebeneffekte," in K. Demmer u. B. Schüller, eds., *Christlich glauben und handeln* (Düsseldorf, 1977), pp. 243–260, one clearly cannot identify indirect action with the *voluntarium in causa* (p. 253). A typical case of *voluntarium in causa* would be

someone who causes the death of a person through culpable negligence (speeding, drunken driving, a doctor's carelessness in surgery, etc.). In this case, one *is* responsible for the consequences; and in distinction from the *voluntarium indirectum*, this is because *although* one *did not* foresee the consequences, one *should* and *could* have foreseen them. In other words, it is a special case of direct action. In indirect action, one would have to say, "The evil effect is not willed *in causa*, but is instead *not*-willed." The *voluntarium indirectum* is precisely what brings it about that an evil consequence (brought about by the willing of its cause) is *not even willed in the willing of its cause,* and thus one does not bear responsibility for it.

15. F. Scholz, *Wege, Umwege, und Auswege der Moraltheologie* (Munich, 1976); see also Schulz's "Objekt und Umstände. . . ."

16. See above all "Objekt und Umstände . . . ," pp. 247ff. Scholz analyzes the concept of the object of action on the level of the *finis naturalis* of an act, or of a potency, without considering in the slightest way that objects of actions are always objects of the will, and thereby of the practical reason. The *finis operis* is finally reduced to the "effects of the inner essential possibilities, that is, the potencies of the essence" (p. 249). His concept of the "side effect" is likewise determined on this physicalistic foundation.

17. See also G. E. M. Anscombe, "War and Murder," in *The Collected Papers of G. E. M. Anscombe,* vol. 3 (Oxford, 1981) pp. 51–61; also in W. Stein, ed., *Nuclear Weapons: A Catholic Response* (London, 1961), pp. 43–62—see p. 58 for the Cartesian "directability" of intention. Various attempts at such justifications through the "direction" of intention have brought censure from the magisterium.

18. See the cynical "compromise" theory of sin proposed by C. E. Curran, *Themes in Fundamental Moral Theology* (Notre Dame, Ind., and London, 1977) pp. 31–32: "Recently, I have proposed the need for a theory of compromise in moral theology precisely because of the existence of sin in the world. The surd brought about by human sinfulness is so oppressive that occasionally we cannot overcome it immediately. The presence of sin may force a person to do something one would not do if there were no sin present. Thus in sin-filled situations (notice all the examples of such situations in the current literature) the Christian may be forced to adopt a line of action, which one would abhor if sin were not present." Can a Catholic moral theologian forget that salvation means not only "forgiveness of sins" but also the *presence* and *effectiveness* of grace that heals, helps, and *overcomes* sin?

19. This has been shown by J. M. Boyle, "Toward Understanding the Principle of Double Effect," *Ethics* 90 (1980): 527–538. Only the two conditions named above are specific for indirect action, as Boyle

shows. The bad consequence may not follow from the action immediately (in the intentional sense), as the good effect does, so that for the sake of it the action is really accomplished (it cannot be a means, in other words); and there must be a sufficiently serious reason (since the evil may not be willed as an end, and, in view of the fact that a morally permissible action must be either good or indifferent, this holds for *every* action). Now there is a moral theological tradition according to which the good and bad effects may both be immediately and simultaneously derived from the action. I hold this view to be completely untenable, since it rests on a failure to understand what the object of action is. On its basis, someone could justify any killing as a means to an end with an argument like the following: "If I kill an innocent person, and a physical good immediately results (the only thing I am intending), then the death of the person is *praeter intentionem*. In reality, the immediate consequence, the death of the person, belongs to the object of the action, because it has the character of a means: here the killing of the innocent person is *intentionally* necessary in order to attain the goal, and is thus directly willed. For an effect follows *immediately* from an action when its being willed is intentionally necessary for the accomplishment of the action: (in other words) if I cannot do *x* in an intentionally meaningful way without *y* (the evil effect) following from it (as, for example, it was impossible to "drop an atomic bomb on Hiroshima for the purpose of forcing a surrender" *without* having the result of the death of masses of civilians).

20. See *II–II*, q. 64, a. 7, where Thomas handles the question of killing an aggressor in legitimate self-defense: "Illicitum est quod homo intendat occidere hominem ut seipsum defendat." Here *intendere* clearly means choosing to kill the aggressor as a means of self-defense. Even though he wants to affirm at any price its "Thomistic" nature, Scholz's interpretation of this passage is inconceivable, since it is *clearly* in contradiction with the text (*Wege, Umwege, und Auswege . . .* , pp. 115–117). Scholz maintains, first, that *intendere* always and exclusively means the "*intentio finis*." This is supposedly why Thomas says that it is impermissible to choose the death of the aggressor only as an *end* (this, according to Scholz, is what Thomas means by *praeter intentionem*); on the other hand, one may choose to kill him as a *means* (since *eligere* is not *intendere*). Apart from the fact that this restriction of the terminology is *in no way* justified by the text of Thomas, Scholz's interpretation is directly contradicted by the sentence quoted at the beginning of this note, which Scholz does not mention: "Illicitum est quod homo *intendat* occidere hominem *ut* seipsum defendat." (It is not permissible for someone to *intend* to kill someone as a *means to the end* of self-defense.) Thomas indeed uses the word *intendere* here to indicate choosing a means!

21. Seeking support from Thomas, Scholz tries to limit the category of the accidental (*per accidens*) to the unforeseeable consequences. Because of the physicalistic perspective, however, he is unable to see that Thomas also acknowledges a *per accidens* in the intentional sense, which is coextensive with the concept *praeter intentionem*, in regard to the specification of the object (see for example *I–II*, q. 72, a. 1).

22. Thomas's manner of handling the legitimate defense has been commented upon many times. It seems to me that a meaningful interpretation can be possible only when it is understood that Thomas is not understanding a real decision-making situation (with an end–means structure). The person who defends himself is simply trying to save himself in a spontaneous reaction (the object of the action) *without* intending the death of the attacker as a means thereto. What really indicates this is the condition for a legitimate use of force: the amount of force used must be proportioned (*proportionata*) to the end: "Si aliquis ad defendendum propriam vitam utatur maiori violentia quam oporteat, erit illicitum" (see *II–II*, q. 64, a. 7).

23. R. Spaemann, "Wovon handelt die Moraltheologie?" *Internationale Katholische Zeitschrift* 6 (1977): 308ff. Moral theology may not forget that such serious cases, which are connected to the condition of original sin, reveal a positive moral meaning completely and clearly only under the conditions of Christian faith and its promises. Man's need of salvation is shown in the fact that the human reason *alone* in such serious cases cannot make understandable just what the will of God is.

24. The example was first used by B. Häring, *Das Gesetzt Christi*, 8th ed., vol. 3 (Freiburg, 1967), p. 126. Even though this is something that practically *never* happens, it is constantly brought forward as *the* example for the absurdity of a "deontological" ethics that holds to the doctrine of indirect action. See B. Schüller, "Direct Killing/Indirect Killing," in C. E. Curran and R. A. McCormick, eds., *Readings in Moral Theology*, No. 1 (New York, 1979), pp. 153ff.; Scholz, *Wege, Umwege und Auswege*, pp. 47–49; F. Furger, *Was Ethik begründet* (Einsiedeln, 1984), p. 19. It is, of course, highly questionable whether so far-reaching a thesis can be based on one such "case."

25. Aristotle speaks in the *Nichomachean Ethics* (II, c. 6, 1107a9–27) of such actions that can never be done rightly in "moderation" and that, independently of circumstances, "are evil in themselves" (*tà autà phaûla*), such as murder, theft, and adultery.

26. See also (in a somewhat more subtle style) J. Fuchs, " '*Intrinsece malum*': Überlegungen zu einem umstrittenen Begriff," in W. Kerber, ed., *Sittliche Normen. Zum Problem ihrer allgemeinen und unwandelbaren Geltung* (Düsseldorf, 1982), pp. 74–91.

27. It is to the credit of J. Fuchs ("Der Absolutheitscharakter sittlicher Handlungsnormen," in H. Wolter, ed., *Testimonium Veritati* [Frankurt, 1971], pp. 211–240 ) that he first argues in a more exacting manner: "Morality in its proper sense (without exaggeration or use of analogy) can be used only for a *human action*, and that means for an action that arises from the free consideration and decision of a human person." One can fully agree with this statement, but not with the one that immediately follows: "There is no action of this kind without the intention of the agent." As said several times before, Fuchs treats the goods that are the objects of the elective will as only premoral goods. Accordingly, an action is constituted as human only through the intention. But this view is based on the physicalistic prejudice that we have been studying, which assumes that the objects of actions presented to the practical reason (independently of any "intention") are only physical goods or evils, that they possess no moral dimension at all.

28. This was Scholz's view (*Wege, Umwege, und Auswege*, pp.44–45) about the case of the nuns in the Congo mission, much discussed in the early 1960s. The moral theologians Hürth, Palazzini, and Lambruschini declared in an affidavit that the use of contraceptives by the nuns who anticipated being raped by guerrilla soldiers was morally permissible. When Scholz held that the principle "Contraception is always intrinsically evil" was here subject to an exception, his conclusion was based simply on the (false) presupposition that the action "contracepting" was being judged independently of an ethical context, that is, at the level of the *genus naturae*.

29. See the discussion of Thomas's treatment of the lie (in the present chapter, section "Lying and the Virtue of Truthfulness"). It must be noted that Scholz speaks of a "secondary never" (*Wege, Umwege, und Auswege* . . . , pp. 156–157). At a deeper level, one could come to the conclusion that an action is *always* intolerable for the attainment of a certain goal. Scholz uses this example: "You may not have an abortion in order to avoid an interruption in your professional education." This is always valid, because there can *never* be a suitable proportion between "abortion" and "not interrupting one's professional education." Whether that is *always* apparent to the agent, is another question. The problem with the principle of the "secondary never" can be seen in Scholz's justification of the impermissibility of the extermination of the Jews under the Third Reich. "The proportion between means and end is intolerably skewed." Scholz does not realize the problem with his own statement. Even if he meant to say, "The proportion is in such a case *always* intolerably skewed," the justification still depends on the assumption that the protection of human life needs justification:

whether, that is, the destruction of human life can *sometimes* be a "proportionate means" for the attainment of an end—a type of moral justification that is both morally repellent and dangerous.

30. According to Prümmer's manual, for example (*Manuale Theologiae Moralis,* vol. 2, 130), the following points belong to the "just war" doctrine. First, the war must be an act of the legitimate public authority. Second, it must be justified with respect to the preservation of the common good: in general, only defensive wars are morally permissible; offensive measures are considered just only when they restore a state of justice that had been seriously harmed. Wars for territorial expansion, forced religious conversion, or the acquisition of personal glory are excluded. Third, there must be purity of intention (*recta intentio*): the goal of a state engaged in a war must be the fastest possible restoration of peaceful community life between the nations involved. Under the conditions of contemporary military technology, the possibilities for a just war must certainly be reduced; see G. E. M. Anscombe, "War and Murder."

31. See J. Finnis, *Fundamentals of Ethics* (Oxford and New York, 1983), pp. 127ff.; see also *II–II*, q. 64, a.2 and 3.

32. In *I–II*, q. 1, a. 3, ad 3um, using the distinction between the *genus naturae* and the *genus moris*, Thomas argues that the *conservatio justitiae* grounds a special species of acts of killing; the "restoration of justice" is the responsibility exclusively of public power, and not of private persons (as in *II–II*, q. 64, a. 3), and Thomas calls it the *finis proximus*, or the moral object, of such an act.

33. In a more extended sense, even killing under "private competence" could be called "killing an innocent person." This simplifies the language used, since it makes a positive statement as follows: "Killing a person is permitted *only* on the basis of a just exercise of the public power." The disadvantage of speaking this way, however, is the confusion about the fact that a "just killing" and a "killing by a private person" belong to very distinct ethical contexts. Killing through the just exercise of public power appears as an "exception" to the prohibition of private killing, without in fact being so.

34. However, it does not make sense to describe "killing in a (just) war" in accordance with the structure of the *voluntarium indirectum*, as "indirect killing" or as "killing in a legitimate defense." This view can be supported only by showing that the direct killing of combat troops by combat troops is morally justified: it is not a matter here of the actions of private persons, but rather of persons who are acting in obedience to the public authority. The immorality of large-scale bombardments of cities and using the nuclear bomb, on the other hand, depends on the immorality of acts of war directed against (noncombatant) civilians, who cannot be described as aggressors.

# 12

# The Objectivity of Human Action: The Object of Action and the Natural Law

## The Central Concept of the Debitum

One result of the foregoing analysis of the concept "object of the action" consists in knowing that the "objective" content of a concrete human action cannot be formulated in terms of the action performed by the particular human power subject to the command of the will, but only in terms of the practical reason that orders the act. For it is only through the *apprehensio et ordinatio rationis* that the act can be objectified as an *actus exterior*, as a good for the will: in its moral species, that is, or *esse morale*. As such, it is the "material concerning which" (*materia circa quam*—as treated materially, but still *in apprehensione et ordinatione rationis*) or, as treated formally, the end of the will.

The will is dependent on the reason in order to be specified through the *actus exterior*; the accomplished exterior act (*in ordine executionis*) obtains its moral significance through the command of the will: that is, by being "willed" (by being a *volitum*), it becomes an object of the elective or intentional act of the will.

From this perspective, the decisive point is the "fitting"or debitum (*ratio debiti*, the moral value, "ought character," or order of reason, *ordo rationis*) and its *constitutive priority* over the meaningful content of those actions that, at the level of the *genus naturae*, do not immediately arise from the will as actions of other powers or areas of the human suppositum. Only the will is directed per se to the morally good, to the "good of the reason" (*bonum rationis*). The act of the will, in its very *genus naturae*, is oriented toward the *esse morale*, and this is so because the object corresponding to its nature is itself constituted though the reason.

Now this *ratio debiti*, which makes it possible for a *materia circa quam* to become an *obiectum conveniens* (proper object) for a certain action, is thus not derived from an entity *theoretically* presented to the reason (i.e., an ontic good, or an act in its *genus naturae*). Instead, it presupposes a *practical* and thereby value-recognizing, value-judging, and (to a certain degree) value-constituting relationship of the reason to the matter. The "suitability of matter and the circumstances" (*commensuratio materiae et circumstantiarum*) to an object of action is a task of the practical reason, a task that reveals a "standard-giving" function and through which the matter of the action is configured under the aspect of the *ratio debiti*. This morally evaluative function of the practical reason, as shown in the foregoing discussions, comes fully into play in the *constitution of the object of action*. Accordingly, such objects are in each case an expression of action in the context of the human suppositum—the expression of a personal act and of the personal autonomy of man.

This also reveals that the constitution of the object of action and the constitution of the *lex naturalis* have an identical structure. In part I, the object of a moral action was shown to arise from an "ordering of the reason" (*ordinatio rationis*) *in* the matter of the action (which only in this ordering of the reason is a *materia circa quam*, the form and end of the will), precisely as the *lex naturalis* is an "ordering of the reason" *in* the natural inclinations.

The function of the *lex naturalis* as the law of the practical reason is based on the fact that as a participation in the *ratio aeterna*, it represents an *inclinatio naturalis* to the "right act and end [*debitum actum et finem*] . . . by which we discern what is good or bad" (see *I–II*, q. 91, a.3; and chapter 2, section "The Natural Law as Participation in the Eternal Law," subsection "Man's Double Participation in the Eternal Law"). In the language of the *Commentary on the Sentences*, it is a *naturalis conceptio* and a *naturalis inclinatio* "by which an operation suited [*conveniens*] to the kind or species of action is rendered fitting [*reddatur conveniens*] to the end."[1] Thus the practical reason does not simply objectify things, or the actions proper to the various human powers, in order to put them, as such, into the mode of the "ought." Rather, the practical reason orders them according to the criterion of the *debitum* as specifically presented to it. The reason brings its own claim, which is in fact the claim of human "existence" (as person and as the wholeness of the suppositum), *into the configuration of the object.*

The natural law, therefore, turns out to be the ordinative or preceptive foundation for the constitution of objects of action. But even so it is only the foundation, since the range of possible objects of human action (or of possible *intentiones* and *electiones*) extends far more widely than the range of the precepts of the natural law. The latter orders human action essentially in the area of the natural inclinations: it constitutes the *ratio virtutis* (see *I–II*, q. 94, a. 3). The order of the natural law is the order of virtue. In the constitution of the objective meaning of human action, the natural law has a *foundational* function. This is what guides human action in performance toward its foundationally objective meaning, making the action *human* and thus in accordance with moral virtue. All the same, the natural law does not formulate the objective meaning of every concrete action. That is the function of prudence. But every objectively moral or even prudential action must be referred to the natural law as to its foundation, on which it depends and in which, in a certain manner, it is "integrated." Another way of understanding this is to say that the precepts of the natural law receive a suitable "concretization" or "individuation" in the precepts of prudence.

This connection between the natural law and prudence (related to concrete action *hic et nunc*) is to be observed above all with respect to those actions in which the fundamental humanity of action is in question. Perhaps the most frequently discussed example of this is the marital act of transmitting human life. The concrete good (*in concreto* or *utile*; *cf.* the Aristotelian *súmpheron*, which prudence must establish) may not dispense from consideration the foundations of human action—those which guarantee the action to be human in a fundamental sense.

It is not enough for some action to be done "for some reason" or "freely": it must also be a *personal* action, and that means an action that preserves the meaning of single acts and tendencies in the context of the human suppositum. What this meaning is, becomes clear through reflection on the act of the practical reason, and through the anthropological and metaphysical explication and illumination such reflection brings. The moral claims of human existence or nature are thereby revealed, so that human existence or nature is already standing within a practical context: this does not mean simply as the object of a theoretically observing reason, but rather as a metaphysically and anthropologically illuminated personal experience of the practical reason. *This is a being and nature whose concept and meaning already imply and have present the ordering and evaluating effectiveness of the practical reason as the "natural reason" (ratio naturalis).* It has been called a "structured, ordered unity of reason, person, functionality, and naturalness."[2] This unity is constituted as such by the reason, which itself becomes objectified in reflection *as nature.*

Now our reasoning could be circular at this point if we were not to take into account the intellectual power and truth capability of the human reason (as a participation in the divine light of knowing). This ability of the human intellect not only to recognize the truth but also (as practical intellect) to bring it about in human willing and action, and thus orient the human person to the truth, authenticity, and fullness of human existence, has a consequence. It means that man can recognize himself as man, and thus be able to live in harmony with himself, only in a life that satisfies the claims of the reason. Now such a "life according to reason" does not at all mean a "rationalistic" life, or a "calculating" life, but rather a life that corresponds to the demands of human spirituality, to its *imago*—an existence that is ultimately a life of love, a love that goes beyond itself, moving out toward fellow human beings and toward God. Now, the reality that man, with this ability to love, is in fact estranged from himself and his goal, and is thus in need of a saving power in order *fully* to realize his humanity, is not the business of philosophy. But no more is it the business of the theologian to find models for reducing the demands of a morality in the context of salvation (a Christian morality) to "merely human" demands. This would make man himself unintelligible to himself: the "alienation" and paradoxes of his existence, as seen in the context of what is human, would then become tolerable only by setting aside the very demands of human existence and retreating behind the "merely human."[3]

This can also be seen in the attempts of many moral theologians to prove that there can be no actions that are always evil in themselves, or that are always immoral. This question was articulated above in connection with the concept of the natural law. Now, with reference to Thomas's statement that "the same rectitude is not found in all" (*non est eadem rectitudo apud omnes*), and the consequence that the precepts of the natural law are effective only "for the most part" (*ut in pluribus*), it has been inferred by some that even for Thomas the concept of the natural law could not be reconciled with the existence of intrinsically evil actions (*operationes intrinsece malae*). The commands of the natural law, also as expressed in the Ten Commandments, point to the goals of the virtues; these are to be understood, according to this interpretation, only as "approximations" or "ideals" that can be variously realized in various historical and personal circumstances. And with that, as a supporter of this view has said, "the ideal of a strict universality of ethical judgments is abandoned."[4]

Again, this problem will have to be analyzed in order to demonstrate that we are confronted once more with a questionable exegesis of Thomas. This concluding study should throw further light on the character of the natural law and the objectivity of human action as constituted through the practical reason.

## THE PROBLEM OF THE CONTINGENCY OF THE MATTER OF ACTIONS

### "Non Est Eadem Rectitudo apud Omnes"

In the fourth article of *I–II*, q. 94, Thomas poses the question "Whether there is one natural law for all" (*Utrum lex naturae sit una apud omnes*)—whether or not the natural law is one and the same for all human beings. Of course, Thomas will answer this question affirmatively, and in the corpus of the article two phenomena are analyzed that appear to show the contrary. First, the fact that it is simply irrational in certain circumstances to hold to some precepts of the natural law as if they were at the level of "nearer principles" or "secondary precepts" (*principia propria, praecepta secundaria*): for example, the command of justice "to return what has been loaned" (*deposita sunt reddenda*). Such commands oblige only "for the most part" (*ut in pluribus*) and seem to demand some variability in the natural law. What holds in one situation under certain circumstances will not hold for all situations. Second, Thomas speaks of a nonidentical *rectitudo* of the natural law based on a defective or faulty knowledge (*notitia depravata*) of it caused by passions, bad habits, or natural dispositions. "Thus formerly, theft, although it is expressly contrary to the natural law, was not considered wrong among the Germans, as Julius Caesar relates in *De Bello Gallico* (vi., ch. 23)."

We are concerned at present with the first problem. When it comes to the concrete conclusions (*conclusiones propriae*) of the practical reason, there is not an identical truth or "rectitude" for all: what someone has obtained through trust or loan or deposit must be returned. While this is certainly a requirement of justice, is it also required of me, in justice, to return a shotgun that has been lent me by a friend if he asks for it back at a time when I know his wife has betrayed him and when he clearly wants to shoot her in a fit of anger and confusion? Does the command "return what has been loaned" have validity here? It appears that the law as formulated here has only a general validity, and that following it in this concrete instance would be both irrational and unjust.

Of course, there are many moral theologians who take refuge in the view that after all, no moral law is without exception: that there are in fact no actions of which one could say that they are intrinsically bad. "It all depends on the situation. . . ."

And they are not exactly wrong to hold this view. To a certain extent, they are protesting against a theory of morality that would lay down everything with certitude and precision: a theory that would force human action into a structure of preformulated, exactly defined models, a system of "dos and don'ts." In fact, life is much richer than the formulations of morality textbooks. The virtue of prudence does not consist simply in the application of "norms," but rather enters into each concrete situation in order to realize *there* the truth claims and moral demands of human action—the underlying intention of the "command." In the context of the Old Testament, when someone performs an act of kindness on the Sabbath by healing the sick or pulling an ox out of a well, that person does not violate the law of the sabbath but really fulfills its underlying intention, even though he may go against it "literally" or superficially.

But then does this in fact mean that in principle all actions are good or bad "according to the situation"? That there is no way for any actions to be qualified as morally bad in all circumstances? Does this mean that the secondary commands of the natural law (e.g., "Thou shalt not kill," "Thou shalt not commit adultery," "Thou shalt not bear false witness against thy neighbor," etc.) are valid only *ut in pluribus*, "in most cases," according as circumstances permit? Does it mean (as Arntz tries to argue) that only the "ideals of the virtues" (i.e., "You should act justly, moderately, etc.") have an exceptionless validity? And that one may never attach predicates of value (right or wrong) to any actions as such (such as "stealing is wrong")? Can one consequently conclude that voluntary sterilization, active euthanasia, abortion, and lying are *usually* morally reprehensible, but not *always* so in principle, depending on the circumstances? In the light of the maxim "There is not the same rectitude for all" (*Non est eadem rectitudo apud omnes*), the morally right or good cannot always be the same for all.

This deserves a closer look. Our first question is whether this view is really to be found in Thomas, and the second question is whether this position is not in fact based upon a profound misunderstanding of the constitution of the objective meaning of human action.

The most important points made in article 2 of *quaestio* 94 of the *Prima Secundae* are the following. Like the speculative reason, the practical reason moves from the universal to the particular (*ex communibus ad propria*). Unlike the theoretical reason, however, the practical reason is related to human actions, and that means to contingencies, to a matter that is not always necessarily the same but can "also be otherwise" (in Aristotle's phrase, *endechómenon kaì allôs échein*). The more one approaches the particulars, the more deficiency (*defectus*) is to be found.[5] The material of actions changes, or is no longer identical with the material on the basis of which a general principle was formulated. In the example given, it appears that in the concrete circumstances the principle that "things loaned are to be returned" (*deposita sunt reddenda*) is no longer suited to the situation at hand. Thus, "according to rectitude" (*secundum rectitudinem*), the natural law is only the same as the "common principles" (*communia principia*); in relation to some particular principles (*secundum quaedam propria*), which are related like conclusions to the universal principles, there exists merely a "rectitude for the most part" (*rectitudo ut in pluribus*); in a few instances (*in paucioribus*) they can fail to hold good (*potest deficere*) because of a few impediments (*propter aliqua particularia impedimenta*).[6]

The text makes it clear that Thomas understands that this phenomenon occurs only with a *few* "propria": it cannot be applied without further ado to *all* "*principia propiora.*" But leaving this matter to one side, there is a second problem of even more urgent interest: Does Thomas conceive of a *defectus* of this kind as an "exception" to a commandment? Does he mean to say that in certain circumstances a command is not "valid" or does not "bind"? Or is it rather that the formulation of the command is not adequate for certain situations? Are there actions, in other words, that change their objective meaning in certain circumstances so that they are no longer covered by the command—so that the command can no longer express what needs to be done in this particular case?

Thomas takes the latter view, and this needs to be shown. The maxim that "rectitude is not the same for all" (*non est eadem rectitudo apud omnes*) in no way means that the *principia propria* of the natural law are *not* valid without exception. Rather, it means that because of the contingency of the matter of actions, situations arise that are exempted from the command in question. This occurs because even though the exterior action appears to be identical with other actions, through some circumstance it has changed in its *esse morale*—that is, *objectively.*

Before we complete this analysis, we should pause to observe more carefully the problem Thomas was facing in the article under consideration (*I–II*, q. 94, a. 4). It should seem surprising at first that Thomas speaks of a defect in regard to *rectitude* (*defectus quantum ad rectitudinem*), and not of a defect in regard to the validity or binding force of a certain moral commandment. What is meant by this "rectitude" or "truth"? Clearly it is not "rectitude" or "truth" of the commandment, since the formula says, "There is not the same truth [*veritas*] or rectitude [*rectitudo*] for all [*apud omnes*] in regard to the proper principles." It means that it is a matter either of a faulty knowledge of the natural law or—our present question—a matter of a certain command of the natural law no longer being applicable. The natural law contains within itself the *ordo virtutis,* in this case the "order of justice." But there can be cases in which, because of an impediment (*aliquod particulare impedimentum*), the mode of establishing this order in accordance with the natural law is not practicable, and the application of the command *in this case* would go against the intention of the command (justice). The reason for this (seeming) "exception," then, does not lie in the command, as if it would no longer "be valid" here, because it is too "general" or "abstract" to apply to this particular case. The reason is the reverse: it is a "defect" of the matter of action, an "impediment" that brings it about that the order of justice can no longer be preserved in the way that suits *this* command of the natural law.

The "defect" or "change" of *rectitudo* thus appears to originate not from the command but from the "matter" to which the command is supposed to relate. You could say that the present situation (of the husband who wants his rifle back in order to take revenge on his wife) is no longer the "right matter" (*materia debita*) for being governed by the commandment "return what has been borrowed." A "return of something loaned" at this time would not in fact be an act of justice but an act of assisting in murder.

We reach the conclusion, then, that whereas the "common precepts" (*praecepta communia*) are usable in all instances (e.g., "one should preserve the order of justice"), this does not in fact hold true for the "nearer precepts" (*propria praecepta*), which represent concretizations of the universal law for application to definite human actions. It does not hold for them because of what happens "in a few cases" (*in paucioribus*): the morally determinative conditions that are presupposed in the concrete formulation of the law *have changed.*

These are conditions that pertain to a person involved in the action. The principle that "things borrowed are to be returned" (*deposita sunt reddenda*) presupposes that the person who lends something to another is the rightful owner of the thing. The relationship between the owner and the thing loaned (in the order of justice) constitutes the moral obligation for the return (the *redditio*) of the thing borrowed. If something should change in the justice of the claim to ownership, the obligatory character of the *redditio depositi* would also change. And this is exactly what has happened in the example: the original *rectitudo* of the relationship "owner—thing owned" has changed. The claim to ownership of the rifle, with which the man intends to shoot his wife, no longer corresponds to the order of justice. There is a particular "impediment" to the use of the principle *deposita sunt reddenda* in this situation. The corresponding action would constitute a "wrong matter" and would *objectively* be a just action no longer.

Now there happens to be a very explicit parallel passage to *I–II,* q. 94, a. 4 that makes it quite clear that this in fact is what St. Thomas is saying. The passage is in the *Secunda Secundae* (*II–II,* q. 57, a. 2, ad 1um): "That which is natural to something that has an unchangeable nature ought always and everywhere to be of the same type [*semper et ubique tale*]. But the nature of man is changeable [*mutabilis*]. Thus what is natural to man can sometimes not be present [*potest aliquando deficere*]. For example, man has a natural equality, so that when something is borrowed, it should be returned to the lender; and if it were the case that human nature never erred [*semper esset recta*], or was always oriented to what is right, the precept would always have to be obeyed. But since it is the case that sometimes the will of man is depraved, a situation can arise in which a thing lent should *not* be returned [*depositum non est reddendum*], lest a man with a perverted will exercise that will—if, for example, a man who is beside himself with anger or who is an enemy of the state asks that his weapon be returned to him."

"The nature of man is changeable" (*natura hominis mutabilis est*) does not mean that human nature itself changes through the course of history,[7] but rather that human nature does not have the kind of immobility that God has in an absolute fashion and that the purely spiritual creatures have in virtue of their choices (*electiones*), made once for all time.[8] Because of his nature, it is characteristic of man to possess a changeable will. And consequently in our example the fundamental *rectitudo* of the will of the gun's owner has changed. This fundamental *rectitudo* is presupposed by the command "things borrowed are to be returned" (*deposita sunt reddenda*), because this obligation applies only to a justified relationship of owner to thing owned, and does not apply to the relationship now in question, which is opposed to the order of justice through a "depraved will" (*depravatio voluntatis*). The "change of the matter" (*mutatio materiae*) is what makes it possible for an act that is in obedience to the command *deposita sunt reddenda* to be *not an act of justice at all* in this instance. Objectively speaking, it would be unjust to give back the thing borrowed, and to precisely the same extent would it be *just* to take a weapon away from the enemy of the state who was refusing to surrender his weapon.

In this customary example, it should not be forgotten that for Thomas, private property is essentially related to the community. The goods of this world have been created for the use of all, but by the natural law there is a personal "power of procuring and dispensing" (*potestas procurandi et dispensandi*), according to which man may possess property.[9] In relation to the *usus* of things, however, man must never consider himself as their owner, but must always use them for the utility of the community.[10] The principle *deposita sunt reddenda* presupposes the rightful use of things as ordered to the well-being of the community. The very nature of justice (*ratio iustitiae*) includes the "right use" of things. Thus certain moral commands that rest upon *legitimate ownership* become inapplicable through *illegitimate use* of such ownership (or through an emergency situation that demands a community use of goods), and cannot determine *this* kind of situation. But this is not because the commandment admits exceptions. It is because the situation in question no longer pertains to this commandment.

A *mutatio materiae* means, then, a change of the "matter concerning which" (*materia circa quam*), a change that is visible to the practical reason alone and that concerns the "nature of the right" (*ratio debiti*) of the matter of action. The reason for the change (in our present example) lies exclusively in the *depravatio voluntatis*, the "depraved will" of the lender of the thing. It consists in the fact that his request for the thing no longer corresponds *objectively* to what a just claim to recover property entails—it corresponds, rather, to an action of preparing to murder someone. Precisely for this reason, the return (*redditio*) of the loaned item would in turn, *objectively speaking* (in regard, that is, to its object or "matter concerning which"), not be an act of justice but rather an accessory act to a murder. This means that the *practical truth* or *rectitude* of the action of "returning borrowed property" (*reddere depositum*) has changed *in this instance*. The change has occurred because the object of the action has changed, and not because an exception has been found to the command *deposita sunt reddenda.*

This example appears as an exception only when the "object" of the action is identified with its purely "external" aspects. This would imply thinking only of the original relation of property owning, that the thing borrowed is "someone else's" thing (*res aliena*) for the borrower. In that kind of "abstract" consideration of the problem, only the "corpse" of the action comes into view, and any further consideration is excluded—such as understanding that the *object* of a recovery of property and the corresponding obligation to give it back is not simply a "thing" that belongs to "me" or "someone else" (*res propria/aliena*), but the "just possession of a thing" (*iusta possessio rei*) or its legitimate use (*usus rectus*). That a change has in fact occurred in this *objective* sense will be apparent only when it is not forgotten that the objective meaning of an action can be understood only in the context of its objectification through the will, on the basis of an ordering of the reason.

The very widespread notion that the "nearer principles" (*principia propria*) of the natural law are abstract formulations that allow exceptions in concrete instances is based on false assumptions. Such a view overlooks especially how every object of action already stands, thanks to the practical reason, in a relationship to the *ordo virtutis* (here, the order of justice). Therefore, it is not the commands of the natural law that are inadequate or that "admit exceptions"; rather, there are concrete situations or cases where actions change their objective meaning and can no longer fall under the same command—or can no longer be governed by that command.

Now an objection can be made that this is an oversubtle distinction, irrelevant in practice: it makes no difference whether you say that "the commandment admits of exceptions" or that "the situation has changed and the commandment is still valid but doesn't apply to this situation." But it does make a difference. The latter alternative is very different from saying that there are cases (due to circumstances or the intention of the agent) where it is permissible not to give back something borrowed to the person who rightfully asks for it back, for the sake of a so-called "higher good." In such a case one could not argue that the owner is not "rightfully" asking for the thing. The argument could only be that the good of just possession must yield to another good, judged to be of "higher" value in the concrete situation because of serious circumstances. And this is exactly the structure of argument of "teleological" ethics, for which some writers have claimed the authority of St. Thomas.

Consider the following case. A good friend lends me a substantial sum of money to start a business. He stipulates that I pay back the principal within five years, and that I can postpone such repayment only if he has no pressing need for money at that time, and that this is a very real possibility I must consider. There is no written contract. I start my business, and five years later, with luck and skill, I have done well enough to hire a hundred employees whom I can pay, thanks to my friend's capital. My friend has a business with only ten employees. We are both married; I have four children, he has none. Now at this point a serious economic crisis occurs. My friend desperately needs the capital he had lent me: without it, he will not be able to pay his ten workers or meet his other obligations. His firm is on the edge of bankruptcy, and he asks for his money back.

If I pay him back, my business will go bankrupt, since it is still dependent on the borrowed capital. I may think along these lines: "If I pay him back, a hundred jobs will be lost, and I won't be able to support my family. If I don't pay him back . . . his business provides jobs for only ten, and he has no children to support. I can associate him with me as a partner and absorb his ten workers, which is something he could not do for me and my hundred workers. *Ergo,* I am not obliged to pay back the borrowed capital. After all, the consequences will be catastrophic if I do—certainly a hundred jobs and a family with four children outweigh ten jobs. . . ."

It remains an open question to what extent my friend is morally obliged to do everything he can to save the hundred jobs in my company, but *I* cannot oblige him to that. What is certain is that this example is essentially different from the earlier one. The claim of my friend is a real one. There has not been any "change of matter" (*mutatio materiae*). If I don't pay him back, I could say that the rule "one should pay back what is borrowed" (*deposita sunt reddenda*) is not valid without exception. There are situations in which the circumstances, the possible consequences, the goodness of the intention, and so on (I do, after all, want to save a hundred jobs and support my family) all contribute to making a person's just claim . . . something of less value. In fact, his "right" is really only something "abstract," a "premoral good." His insisting on his right is just as *immoral* as my determination to realize a greater good through my action is *moral.* What I propose is simply reasonable, and any other course of action would be irrational. And so on.

I could probably convince others (using tears, perhaps) that my friend is truly inhuman, and that I am not obliged to pay him back—that this command of the natural law is really too abstract, that it doesn't take adequate account of life in the concrete. With a "clear conscience" I could end up committing a great injustice: I let my friend's business go bankrupt—the friend who so generously lent me capital. In doing so I completely forgot that I was behaving immorally in creating a hundred jobs despite my awareness of the very real possibility of having to return the capital. In order to avoid the consequences of my irresponsible action, I have recourse to "humanity" and "catastrophic consequences."

This should make clear how great the difference is between saying, on the one hand, that a certain commandment of justice is not applicable in concrete cases because the situation has removed itself from the commandment through a "change of matter" (*mutatio materiae*) and, on the other hand, saying that a certain command admits of exceptions in certain circumstances when "higher values" are at stake. The commandment "return things that are borrowed" (*deposita sunt reddenda*) is quite applicable to our second example. It shows its real meaning in cases like that. Its unconditional validity is *presupposed* by my friend in the very moment of lending me the capital. How could I claim that this "situation" calls for an exception?

Practical irrelevance of a commandment by reason of the contingency of the matter of action (*mutatio materiae*), on the one hand, and "exceptions" to a precept of the law, on the other hand, are fundamentally different things. An "exception" is when someone is dispensed from fulfilling a certain commandment: "When, for example, for the purpose of defending a state, it is decreed that certain persons in various villages be assigned as guards, but for some higher purpose certain persons can be dispensed from this duty" (*II–II*, q. 100, a. 8). Since this is only a concrete determination of the "mode" (*modus*) of realizing the intention of the lawgiver, the dispensation or exception here does no damage to the realization of that intention. But to look for a dispensation from the precept *deposita sunt reddenda*, to allow exceptions, would mean dispensing someone from acting rightly, from being virtuous, from acting according to reason, as a human being should. When it comes to the natural law, then, there exist in principle neither exceptions nor dispensations.

### *Exceptions, Dispensations,* Epieíkeia

A few precisions are necessary. The standard example of *deposita sunt reddenda* can be found in various contexts of Thomas's works, and we are in a position now to understand better the differing meanings it can have. So far, we have studied texts of the *Prima Secundae* (q. 94, a. 4) and the *Secunda Secundae* (q. 51, a. 4), where this command was understood as a command of the natural law. But there are other contexts where not the natural law but the *positive law* is under discussion: *I–II,* q. 100, a. 8 discusses the positive *divine* law (the Decalogue), and *II–II,* q. 120, a. 1 speaks of positive *human* law.

The Decalogue is a positive, and thus linguistically fixed, presentation of the natural law and contains the "ordering toward the common and ultimate good, which is God" (the first tablet, see *I–II*, q. 100, a. 8), as well as the "order of justice to be observed among men" (the second tablet; ibid.). The command *deposita sunt reddenda* is not a part of the ten laws of the Decalogue, but is implied or contained in it. The second tablet determines "that nothing be wrong to anyone [*nulli . . . indebitum*] and that the right [*debitum*] be done to everyone." Insofar as the Ten Commandments express this, they are "absolutely indispensable" (*omnino indispensibilia*; ibid.).

A first objection to the argument attempts to show that dispensation from the Decalogue can be allowed, thanks to the *mutabilitas* of human nature. Thomas's answer is in keeping with the phenomenon already analyzed: "There is not to be found the same justice in all people" (*non est eadem rectitudo apud omnes*).[11]

A further aspect can be discovered in the answer to the third objection. Among other things, Thomas introduces this example: if someone takes something from someone (or does not return something) that belongs to him in the first place, this is not theft, so long as the taking corresponds to what is right (*debitum*). This is in complete harmony with the principle *non est eadem rectitudo apud omnes*. But Thomas introduces further cases that go beyond this principle: it is possible for certain actions to change their objective character in virtue of a higher authority (such as a divine command). Abraham (Gen. 22) would not then have been a murderer if he had in fact sacrificed his son Isaac. This was an *occasio debita per mandatum Dei*, since God is the Creator of life and, unlike man, He can determine when this life can be granted or taken away. In the same way, Hosea (Hosea 1:2) did not commit adultery, since he did what he did on the basis of the divine behest, and God is the One Who instituted marriage in the first place (*I–II*, q. 100, a. 8).

Thomas is not saying that these are dispensations or exceptions from the natural law. They consist, rather, in a "change of matter" (*mutatio materiae*), and this happens not because of their contingency but because of an *ordinatio* of the divine Lawgiver.

For many moral theologians, this position of Thomas seems arbitrary or nominalistic. It would necessarily have this appearance to someone who judges human action as an "external action event," completely severed from an ordering of the reason. But the object of an action is constituted through an orientation of behavior toward the personal meaning of action. In a concrete situation this will be the case when an action does not correspond to the "natural order" through Him Who established that order—that is, it is not done on the basis of "nature" but rather by a commandment of God (*per mandatum Dei*)—but is nevertheless ordered to its right end (*finis debitus*). This implies that it is unthinkable that God can redefine what "divorce" or "theft" or "murder" is, but that an action that according to the natural, God-created order would be a divorce, or a theft, or a murder, can become ordered to a *finis debitus* within a higher *ordinatio* of the divine providence, which is "beyond the order of nature" (*praeter ordinem naturae*) but nevertheless enters into the natural order of second causes. This would be an extraordinary event (like a miracle[12]), something reserved exclusively to God's direct intervention. Thus this is *not an issue for moral philosophy*, and no further conclusions can be drawn in its regard from the present perspective. Thomas omits justifying or explaining the "case of Abraham" and similar cases with the normal categories of a normative ethics.[13] We could never have understood or justified the significance (or even the fact) of such a "command of God" (*mandatum Dei*) in the cases of Abraham and Hosea, if there had not been explicit revelation concerning them. We would be confronted by a riddle, and would have to blame both Abraham and Hosea for unintelligible and unjustifiable behavior.

This is why Thomas emphasizes that such "changeability" (*mutabilitas*) in things ordained by God (such as marriage) is possible only through divine authority. Human authority can do something analogous only in those orders of reality that come into being through human lawgiving. For example, within the framework of an economic system established by human ordinance, while the taking over of capital for the purpose of the common good is prohibited, nevetheless, by legislative authority, which intends the good of the community, it can be arranged that for certain persons or situations the prohibition is waived. The same action, then, would be right for one person and wrong for another.

The whole thrust of the argument of this article points out that there is no exception from the commands of the natural law or the Decalogue. Only a *mutatio materiae* is possible. This can take place through a change of will (*depravatio*) of a person involved in the particular action structure ("there is not the same rectitude for all"), or through the authority of the one who constituted the meaning of the actions involved. In the areas of the "naturally just" (*naturaliter iustum*) this is God alone; in matters subject to human legislative authority, it is that same human authority.

Now there is a third context where the example *deposita sunt reddenda* is treated, this time in an explicit fashion (*II–II,* q. 120, a. 1): the passage has to do with ἐπιείκεια or "equity," and Thomas describes this virtue as follows: "Since human acts, for which laws are established, occur 'in individual contingencies' [*in singularibus contingentibus*] that are capable of an infinite variation, it is not possible to lay down a rule that would never be waived; lawgivers are concerned instead with what happens 'for the most part' [*ut in pluribus*], and pass their laws accordingly. Following the law in some cases would injure the common good, which the law was intended to promote. And so, just as the law determines that things borrowed must be returned, which is something that 'for the most part' [*ut in pluribus*] is just, nevertheless it can happen that this can be injurious, for example, when an unbalanced person gives up his sword but asks for it back during a spell of madness, or if someone asks for a weapon to attack his own country. In these and similar cases it would be wrong to obey the positive law. It is better to ignore the letter of the law and to do what justice and the common good require. This is what was called ἐπιείκεια [by the Greeks], and what we [i.e., Latins] call *aequitas* [English, "equity"; German, *Billigkeit*]. It is clear, then, that this is a virtue" (ibid.).

Here a brief commentary should suffice. What Thomas is saying here is *not* that the command "things borrowed are to be returned" (*deposita sunt reddenda* ) is based simply upon the "creation" of positive human legislation, and that it can thus be subject to dispensation. *Epieikeia* is not any "dispensation," since the one who does not obey the letter of the law is not the lawgiver but the person to whom the law is addressed. Second, this argument cannot be imported into the natural law, in the sense that someone could say that occasionally one must act against the "letter" of the natural law, in order to carry out one's intention.

What the argument assumes, rather, is that the command *deposita sunt reddenda* is a law of *natural justice*. It is considered from the point of view of formulation within positive human law. There is no absolute disjunction between the area of the natural law and that of the positive human law: most commands of the natural law are also sanctioned in some way or another by human and positive law.

The case considered shows that in relation to the *ordo iustitiae* as established by the natural law, there can be a *mutatio materiae*. In regard to the practical reason, what this means is that the action has changed its objective meaning and belongs to a moral species no longer grasped by this commandment of the natural law. This also holds, in principle, for the positive/historical formulation of that law. The difference is that the positive human law, because of its rigid linguistic fixation upon the external aspect of human action (it presumes to regulate nothing further), cannot take into account or foresee such a change of matter. In this case human law is inadequate because its formulation is inadequate, because it cannot reach this particular case with its formulation. But the natural law is in essence *not* a written law, but rather an *ordinatio rationis* previous to all linguistic formulation. Accordingly, the natural law does not really have this defect; it only *appears* to have it, insofar as it has been linguistically formulated. The imperfection of human law, however, which in certain cases is inadequate in its formulation, can be overcome only by acting contrary to the "letter" (or linguistic formulation) of the law—for the purpose of fulfilling its intention. And this is the virtue of *equity.*

We must carefully distinguish, then, between the working out of a *mutatio materiae* with respect to the natural law and its working out with respect to the positive law. In the case of the natural law, the "change" causes the objective meaning of the action to change, and in such a way that the new kind of action "withdraws" from being regulated by the same commandment of the law. In a case of human law, however, which results from the same *mutatio materiae*, this change does *not* bring it about that the new kind of action withdraws itself from the applicable law as regards its "letter"; it withdraws itself from the intention, which has an inadequate expression in the letter and thus is not applicable to all cases. This is why we must act against the "letter of the law" in such cases.

The tendency of contemporary moral theologians to use the model of equity (or ἐπιείκεια) for a *mutatio materiae* in relation to the natural law is based on a fundamental misunderstanding. The natural law is improperly treated according to the model of human/positive law, where, looking to the letter of laws and norms, one ascertains that not every case is covered, and then arrives at the conclusion that the natural law is not always valid because it, too, admits exceptions. But the natural law does not originally consist in (linguistically) formulated commands and norms. It is an "ordering of the reason" (*ordinatio rationis*), an ordering act of the practical reason. This ordering applies to all possible "cases," and thus there is no "equity" in its regard.

Here again it may appear that we are only disputing about terminology. But this is not the case. If I believe that the natural law (*essentially* an ordering of the reason) is subject to equity, I am claiming that there are cases in which the *ordinatio* of justice, "things loaned are to be returned," is inadequate, and that the demand of justice must then yield to a "higher good." Recurring to our example, then, the intention of the command would be respected if I abandoned the demands of justice "in itself" or "in the abstract" for a higher good—that is, if I did not pay back the borrowed capital. After all, it would seem more just (and justice, after all, was the intention of the command) to put only ten workers out of work instead of a hundred, and to ensure the safety of my family. This is a situation the command of the natural law simply could not have foreseen!

But the principle "things loaned are to be returned" is only an ideal approximation to justice. It expresses the "nature of justice" (*ratio justitiae*) in a manner specific to certain actions, and cannot be made invalid because of circumstances or consequences.

We have two positions that are fundamentally the same: (1) "the natural law admits of exceptions because of circumstances or consequences" and (2) "equity is applicable to the natural law." The natural law's formulation of absolute prohibitions would then be deficient for individual cases—and that would in principle hold true for all possible actions. The question, ultimately, is this: "Is a *mutatio materiae* conceivable for all areas of action, or only for some?"

The question is a decisive one, since the argument for a natural law that admits of exceptions provides a basis for considering abortion, euthanasia, and artifical contraception as immoral "only for the most part" (*ut in pluribus*). It is an argument claiming that in principle there are no intrinsically evil actions, that there are no actions that are always and under all conditions immoral.

But the question is difficult to answer. To apply Thomas's argument to contraception for example, there must exist situations in which the objective meaning of the marital act is changed. Because the meaning of this act is constituted in the context of the human *suppositum* (of human nature) and in the context of the meaning and finality of human life in general, such a *mutatio materiae* would require a change of human nature itself. And this would not be the "variability of nature" (*mutabilitas naturae*) of which Thomas speaks—a vacillation or *depravatio* in the "choosing power" (*vis electiva*) of the human will—but a total alteration of the ontological structure of the human person.

The human nature, or person, is not a contingent structure that defines itself anew in every situtation. A *mutatio materiae* is possible only for actions whose meaning is constituted in the context of a *contingent* structure of actions, such as the relationship of someone who borrows a rifle to the owner of the rifle—or, to put it in general terms, in the area of the *usus* of external goods, an area related essentially to the common well-being and ordered by the virtue of justice.

The indiscriminate use of the principle "rectitude is not the same for all" cannot be justified, nor can the consequence that *some* "nearer principles" (*principia propria*) are relevant only "in general" (*ut in pluribus*) be applied to *all* areas of human action. If this doctrine has been derived from Thomas, it reveals a very superficial exegesis of the relevant texts. Since J. Th. C. Arntz has attactively presented just such an interpretation, it would seem worthwhile to look a little more closely at his argument.

### *The Universal Validity of the Secondary Principles of the Natural Law*

Our starting point will be article 8 of the *Prima Secundae, quaestio* 100, a passage discussed above. Arntz argues as follows. The commands of the Decalogue—and by that he means the "secondary principles" (or "nearer" [*propria*] principles)—are not exceptionless *as such,* but only to the extent that they bring the "nature of justice" [*ratio iustitiae*] to expression.[14] Arntz quotes a. 8, ad 3um for support: "And thus the precepts of the Decalogue are unchangeable [*immutabilia*] to the extent that they contain the nature of justice [*rationem iustitiae*]. But to the extent that some determination is being made through an application to particular actions [*per applicationem ad singulares actus*], such as that this or that action is or is not murder, theft, or adultery—that is changeable [*mutabile*]." From this Arntz concludes that the "command" is only a possible expression of the "nature of justice"; it can occur that the same order of justice might require someone to act *against* the letter of the command, and that would constitute an exception. It must first be shown that "the command is inadequate to the idea of the virtue," and then that "the very comprehensiveness of the idea is really the reason why the command never fully corresponds to it, and why the command is applicable or has validity only in the majority of cases" ("Prima principia propria," p. 10).

Furthermore, the command is also "inadequate to concrete reality in which we must follow the command" (ibid.). Arntz refers here to the Thomistic teaching that "circumstances can enter into the definition of the object," and this is something that can be explained from the epistemological standpoint by "the inner indeterminacy of the abstract concept." "The abstract concept," he explains (meaning the "object" of an action or command), "is always a mere approximation [*Annäherung*] to reality, so that the ethical judgment in which this concept plays a role has only an approximate [*approximativen*] character. This is why a concrete ethical judgment does not have an exceptionless validity, nor—to say it in Thomas's own words—*can* it ever have one: *non est eadem rectitudo apud omnes*" (ibid., p. 11).

Arntz then proceeds to pit prudence against conscience: the latter lacks the required flexibility to attend to concrete circumstances (ibid.). He proposes a teleological ethics, and would give the role of the "first nearer principles" (*prima principia propria*) not to the secondary commands of the natural law, but rather to the "ends of the virtues" (*fines virtutum*) that would then represent an "intermediate level" [*Zwischenschicht*] between the very first principles and the second ones (ibid., p. 4). Prudence is able "creatively [*schöpferisch*] to form the goal of the virtue in accord with the situation, or (in other words) to find the most rational solution to the problem capable of taking into account all the circumstances. If the law has become an ultimate, neither the law nor its application can be put in question. . . . The 'end of virtue' [*finis virtutis*] gives scope for profound cultural changes as well as for unique situations. . . . The same ideal can be formed in several ways, a different configuration does not mean a betrayal of the ideal. . . . The most important thing is knowledge of the concrete, not mere observation of the universal. . . . Neither the idea nor the philosopher is the norm for action, but rather prudence. This means giving up on the ideal of a strict universality of ethical judgments" (ibid., pp. 13–15).

Arntz concedes that, according to this interpretation, Thomas proposes "a model that can scarcely be reconciled with his own model of the evidence" (ibid., p. 12). Whatever we may make of that, at least the following can be said about Arntz's argument.

1. It appears that Arntz's concept of the natural law is much too dependent on the model of positive human law, so that he projects the inability to cover all particular cases (typical for this kind of law) onto the natural law itself; further, his abstract presentation of the object of action has a naturalistic point of departure; third, he represents the value idealism of teleological ethics criticized earlier in this study, a view that neglects the value dimension of *actions*.

2. A closer study is needed of the passage (*I–II*, q. 100, a. 8, ad 3um) that forms the basis of Arntz's argument. It is true that Thomas states that the commands of the Decalogue (or the secondary precepts of the natural law) are indispensably and without exception valid *insofar as* they contain the "essence of justice" (*ratio iustitiae*). In saying this he does *not* mean that they contain this *ratio iustitiae* in a merely abstract and approximative form, in formulations not applicable to all individual, cultural, or historical situations. What Thomas asserts, rather, is that the order of justice at all times requires precisely what is formulated in this command: that theft is not only "in most cases" (*ut in pluribus*) an offense, or only a "possible" offense, against the order of justice, but rather that stealing *is* wrong and that the commandment "Thou shalt not steal" for this very reason has an exceptionless validity *because* and *insofar as* it formulates the *ratio iustitiae* for specific actions.[15]

3. There is a qualification, however, that may raise a doubt here: "as to any determination by application to individual actions—for instance, that this or that action be murder, theft, or adultery , or not—in this point they admit of change" (*quantum ad aliquam determinationem per applicationem ad singulares actus, ut scilicet hoc vel illud sit homicidium, furtum, vel adulterium, aut non, hoc quidem mutabile est; I–II,* q. 100, a. 8, ad 3um). Now this does not mean that it is *impossible* to make predications of moral value about any action independently of concrete circumstances, or that it is impossible for anyone to say *of any action* in advance that it would be a matter of "theft" or "murder" or "adultery," and thus would constitute an offense against justice. Thomas is not supporting the principle of indifference toward the moral value of actions. Rather, as the text proceeds to show, his statement has

to do with the cases of Abraham and Hosea. The *mutabilitas* of which Thomas speaks in the context is brought about by the "ordering" (*ordinatio*) of the lawgiver; and since he writes expressly about matters that have been ordained by God (and here the natural law is relevant) only God has the power to make such a change. The human lawgiver, on the other hand, can make such changes or exceptions only in matters that belong to human legislation.

This should already make it obvious that Thomas's argument intends something quite other than what Arntz wants to derive from it.[16] In regard to the order of *natural* justice, human beings have no business determining whether this or that action is going to be murder, theft, or adultery or not. This kind of mutability can come only from a "command by divine authority" (*mandatum ex divina auctoritate*).[17] The text provides no support whatever for Arntz's argument.

4. The "ends of the virtues" (*fines virtutum*) are, as "first, nearer principles" (*prima principia propriora*), supposed by Arntz to represent an "intermediate stage" between the "common principles" (*principia communia*—such as "Do no one an injustice") and the "secondary principles" (*principia secundaria*). But this does not in fact correspond to Thomas's teaching. A qualification needs to be made that Arntz unfortunately leaves out of the picture: even though the commands of the Decalogue are "proper conclusions" from the "common principles," and are thus also "secondary precepts" of the natural law; "conclusions from the first principles" are nevertheless not strictly identical with "commands of the Decalogue." The commands of the Decalogue are a possible system of formulation of the "common principles," under the point of view of the "essence of justice" (*ratio iustitiae*). The goals or "ends" of the virtues are implicitly contained "naturally" (*naturaliter*), like "seeds" (*semina*), in the common principles.[18] This is why the whole virtue of justice is potentially contained in the twofold command "Love the Lord thy God . . . and love thy neighbor as thyself." This is also how it can be said that the end of all the virtues is contained in the common principles (under which, as universals, *all actions* can be subsumed): the goal to which all the virtues are ordered is the love of God and neighbor. In this sense, the goal of justice as a "common principle" is treated

as the goal of justice as *virtus generalis* or *principalis*.[19] As conclusions, single forms or "varieties" of justice can be recognized as a "less common" and "nearer" (*magis proprium*), such as "distributive" and "commutative" justice (types or species of justice), as well as virtues "associated" with justice (*partes potentiales*), such as religion, sincerity, generosity, and friendship.

Now the goals of all these virtues are *communia* (even if some already are derived from a conclusion) insofar as they relate in each case to a different action. But they can already be action-specific, for instance, the commandment to "Love one's neighbor as oneself." This would involve, then (as Arntz is correct to point out), one of the "first nearer" (*propria*) principles. But in the precepts of the Decalogue, nevertheless, it is not these goals or principles, but rather *acts*, that are of concern (see *I–II*, q. 100, a. 2). To this extent Arntz is quite right. The command does not say, "You should love the life of your neighbor as you love your own," or "You should take care of the possession of your neighbor as you would your own," but rather, "Thou shalt not kill," "Thou shalt not steal," and so on. As a result of his identifying "conclusions within the natural law" with the "commands of the Decalogue," Arntz overlooks the fact that the *prima principia propria*, or goals of the virtues as special virtues, already arise from an inventive conclusion from the very highest command: "Thou shalt love thy neighbor as thyself" or "Do not do to anyone what you would not want someone to do to you."

The "first nearer principles," then, are already principles that are specific for action (they couldn't otherwise be rightly said to be *nearer*). This means, too, that they are conclusions and "secondary principles"—they stand on the same level as the commands of the natural law. Only the mode of formulation differs. Thomas says that the commands of the Decalogue are the *prima principia legis* (the first principles of the law) to which, as is very evident, the natural reason immediately assents (*quibus statim ratio naturalis assentit sicut manifestissimis*). In these commands shines the "nature of the right" (*ratio debiti*), or the order of justice, in the clearest possible way (*manifestissime*; see *II–II*, q. 122, a. 1). This is even clearer at *I–II*, q. 100, a. 8: there are some commands that convey the intention of the lawgiver and are thus without exception, and there are others that are instituted to realize that intention, and thus permit exceptions when a particular case arises where following the letter of the command would actually go against the lawgiver's intention.

Arntz thinks that the commands of the Decalogue belong to the second class, but Thomas thinks otherwise: "The precepts of the Decalogue contain the very intention [*ipsam intentionem*] of the lawgiver, that is, God"—and this means the "preservation of the common good [*conservatio boni communis*] or the very order of justice and virtue" [*ipsum ordinem iustitiae et virtutis*]—"so that no one be wronged, and everyone would receive his due [*ut scilicet nulli fiat indebitum, et cuilibet reddatur debitum*]. This is how the precepts of the Decalogue are to be understood, and why they are completely indispensable" (*omnino indispensabilia*).[20]

Arntz's interpretation thus runs quite contrary to the text. The misunderstanding seems to arise from a too narrow concentration on the Ten Commandments and an attempt to determine what a conclusion from the common principles would be, solely on their basis. It is the identification of *conclusio* (that is, a "secondary principle") with "commandment" that creates the problem. The system of the Ten Commandments is not at all the same thing as the "system" of the inventive process of the natural reason. The former are a *representation*, for the purpose of instruction, of the *results* of this process. They explicate the goals of the virtues (the "first nearer principles," *prima propriora principia*) under the aspect of their "most evident nature" (*ratio manifestissima*) by prohibiting the acts that contradict the goals of the virtues. The pedagogical wisdom of the Decalogue consists in its naming of the acts that contradict virtue. With its negative formulation, it cannot speak of virtues, but of vices. And this is how its commands (indeed, its prohibitions) convey the "intention of the lawgiver"—the ends of the virtues.

But the conception of "first proper principles" (*prima principia propria*) as an "intermediate stage" [*Zwischenschicht*] between the first and universal principles, on the one hand, and the second and derived principles, on the other, can furthermore be shown to be a consequence of "value idealism." Value idealism cannot understand how moral values are the characteristics (objects) of *actions* and not of *cognitions* or "intuitions of value." The secondary principles of the natural law (of which the Decalogue presents only a determinate, pedagogically motivated formulation) are not "possible" applications of abstract "value-principles." Rather, general principles (for example, the *ratio iustitiae*) are the universal formulation of those moral values that define concrete actions as being specific modes of human action. We must recall in this connection the inventive origin of the secondary principles: in epistemological terms, they are (implicitly) contained from the start in the universal principles, but are explicated in the discursive act of the *ratio naturalis*. But one can never arrive at a knowledge of these universal principles (which implicitly contain the secondary principles) unless they are grasped *in* those secondary principles through concrete human action and the *ratio debiti*. Arntz's position assumes that the universal principles (or the grasp of the *ratio iustitiae*, or of moral value in general) come into existence *independently of* and *prior to* the grasp of the value character of concrete *actions*. But such a view is an idealism: in Arntz's formulation, universally valid norms of action are only "abstract" and "approximative" ideals. Just as in "teleological ethics," there is a great chasm between moral values and human actions.

5. Arntz's argument, then, is deficient in its foundation. But there is another special problem: the illegitimate confusion of two phenomena that must be distinguished: (1) the *mutatio materiae* that comes about through a change in the structure of the action complex, and thus in the objective meaning of an action (this is what prevents an action from being subsumed under a certain "proper conclusion"—*non est eadem rectitudo apud omnes*), and (2) the *mutatio materiae* that is caused by the *ordinatio* of the lawgiver, a change that in certain circumstances can have the character of a dispensation or exception.

But to follow Arntz in analyzing the former with the categories of the latter is to treat the change in the structure of the action complex (or the change in the objective meaning of the action) as if it were an "exception." And this can be plausible only if we treat the natural law itself in the categories of human law. This would mean treating it as a law that conceives and grasps actions and regulates them only in their external appearance, applying the same law to actions that *seem* to be the same but in reality are different. In certain concrete situations the intention of the lawgiver, and justice, could be neglected.

Granted, *in practice* it may be relatively unimportant to know whether we speak of an "exception" or not when there is a change of the matter of action or of the object. In other words, I could say, "The commandment 'things borrowed must be returned' (*deposita sunt reddenda*) does not apply to this situation (in the sense of an exception)," or I could say, "This action is not covered by the commandment *deposita sunt reddenda* because in this case the 'return' (the *redditio*) is not 'right' (*debitum*)." Now in a moral philosophical analysis, whereby we seek to attain a deeper insight into the structure of moral action, we must go beyond the resources of everyday speech to show that this distinction is indeed quite important.

If we neglect the distinction, we can adopt the viewpoint that the "proper conclusions" (*conclusiones propriae*) of the natural law are not valid in all circumstances. If we preserve the distinction, we will have an understanding that, due to the contingency of the matter of actions, the particular principles of the natural law do not cover all the situations or actions that *may appear alike* from the outside. In our example, the commandment "return what has been borrowed" cannot cover every instance of an owner "asking for something back"—it does not apply to all these situations. And this is because, at times, "asking for something back" or "returning something borrowed" may *objectively* be something else. In one case it could be a rightful claim—in another case it could be preparation for murder.

The apparent inadequacy of certain principles of the natural law is due to their (reflective) linguistic formulation. But these principles are originally and *essentially* an "ordering of the reason" (*ordinatio rationis*), and thus a preceptive act of the practical reason. Armstrong makes an excellent argument that the principle *deposita sunt reddenda* does not have any exceptions, but that it is formulated in a way that cannot contain all the conditions for its universal validity.[21] The principle assumes and even implies that the "return" of what is borrowed is right (*debitum*); but this does *not* mean that there are circumstances where "right" (*ratio debiti*) is not called for, or must "yield" to a "higher good" on the basis of a "weighing of goods" or because of "serious reasons." Rather, the formulation does not take account of the fact that, because of the contingency of the matter of actions, there are situations when the "return of something borrowed" is simply not "suitable" or "right" (*debitum*). The problem is not whether there is exceptionless validity; the problem is with the formulation, because the formulation of the *principia propria* is oriented toward typical cases (*ut in pluribus*) and often leaves aside the explicit conditions that would express the absolute validity of the principle.[22] The reflective linguistic formulation of such principles can leave the impression that there is something analogous in the natural law to the *epieíkeia* of human law. The difference is that the human law is valid only *by way of* its linguistic formulation, and is valid only *to that extent.* The natural law, however, is valid by way of the ordering act of the practical reason and can become more differentiated as its linguistic formulations try to express it ever more adequately on the basis of reflection.[23]

Now, apart from this important difference between the natural law and human positive law, a second point needs clarification. Let us say that someone insists on judging the objective content of the action (the object of the action) only on the basis of the "external" appearance of the action—and that would mean on the basis of the *actus exterior* in abstraction from its objectification through the practical reason and as the object of an inner act of the will—only the "corpse" of the action, as it were. This fundamental difference between an "exception to a command" and "change of the object due to the contingency of the matter of actions" would be lost on the person in question. If Arntz treats the binding force of the secondary commands of the natural law (along with the *ratio virtutis*) as an "approximative abstraction," he can do this only because he has a very "abstract" notion of the constitution of the object of action. The object, he says, contains "only the *abstract concept* of an action," but this concept contains an *openness* needing to be defined more precisely through circumstances before it can approximate reality. There is something both correct and incorrect in this formulation.

It is correct that the circumstances can change an action in its objective meaning: a circumstance can become a "principal condition of the object" (see *I–II,* q. 18, a. 10). This is precisely what happened in our example: the change in the intention of the owner has become a new condition of the original complex *owner–thing borrowed–borrower,* a condition that causes a new determination of the objective meaning of his request for the borrowed item. This means that it is no longer *merely* a "circumstance" but is in fact a "principal condition of the object."

But Arntz is incorrect in thinking that the object as considered in itself is a still more abstract concept, something more removed from reality, and thus a "premoral" quantity. The command to "return what is borrowed" is a specification of the general *ratio iustitiae* ("give back what is owed" [*reddere debitum*] or "give to each one his due" [*ius suum unicuique tribuere*]). The original object, then, was not "returning what does not belong to one" (*reddere rem alienam*), but rather "returning what it is *right* to return" or "*the right returning* of what does not belong to oneself" (*debita redditio rei alienae*). And that is not an abstract, value-neutral description of an action. Arntz assumes that "object" is the object of an action as treated in its *genus naturae*, its "natural species." The example he chooses—"killing"—shows this. "Killing" is an action considered at the level of the *genus naturae*. The (moral) object of action would be "killing an innocent" (or "murder"), or "carrying out capital punishment," and so on.

This is to confuse two possible approaches to "circumstances" that Thomas is always careful to distinguish: one can treat an action in its "natural species" (*genus naturae*), and consider only the "essence of what is done from the outside" (*substantia facti exterius*, *In IV Sent.*, d. 16, q. 3, a. 1, sol. 2); from this perspective, what really belongs to the (moral) object will appear as mere circumstance. What in reality must be attributed to the object of an action, to its *substantia . . . inquantum est ex genere moris* (i.e., its very essence as considered from the moral perspective), becomes a mere circumstance "according to a consideration of the substance of the act in an absolute sense" (*secundum quod consideratur ipsa substantia actus absolute*; d. 16, q. 3, a. 1, ad 2um). Now this "absolute" consideration—"released" [*cf.* the meaning of the verb *ab-solvere*] or "abstracted" from the context of the *genus moris*—is the view of actions and their objects that Arntz has used as a basis for his concept of the object of action. In this, however, he is only following an unfortunate tradition of the handbooks of moral theology.[24]

Arntz is proceeding from a naturalistic and reified concept of the object of the action. He explains: "To understand the indefinite nature of these concepts, we must attend to the fact that Thomas is a moderate realist. This means that *universalia sunt in rebus*. It says nothing about *how* they are in things. The image comes to mind that the essence of the thing, what something is called, is tightly 'locked up inside' the thing like a nut in a shell. Further determinations are added as pure accidents to this inner kernel. The same is true for human actions: they are specific by the object, and the circumstances are related to it as accidents to the substance."

But this interpretation is far too oversimplified, so Arntz attempts to improve it by citing the Thomistic doctrine that circumstances can emerge as the "principal condition of the object" (*principalis conditio obiecti*), that the object is thus "flexible" and "open" to new determinations that enable it to be closer to reality.

The error here is in the starting point, which falsifies the concept of the object. Thomas never assumes that the "object" that is changed by certain "circumstances" (and in the present example they are no longer merely circumstances)—that this object is the object in its natural species (*genus naturae*), or that all objects, when abstracted from their circumstances, are indifferent, value-neutral, and "open" to any circumstantial conditioning. Nor does Thomas think that the object "lies inside things"; rather, the object is human *action,* in its fundamentally human–moral content, "ordered" (or "measured") by the practical reason in an *ordinatio* of the *ratio naturalis* and thereby objectified for the will. This shows clearly how Arntz's conception rests upon a naturalistic view of the object of action.

We arrive at the conclusion, then, that according to St. Thomas even the secondary principles of the natural law have an exceptionless validity, and that the contingency of the matter of actions does not create "exceptions" or cultural and historical changes. The *occasional* (*ut in paucioribus*) inability of single "nearer principles" is not caused by "exceptions" to them but by the contingency of the matter of actions that brings it about that the objective meaning of an action can change. This also means that those actions whose objective meanings are defined not within the context of a contingent action structure but within the context of the human *suppositum* do not permit such a phenomenon to occur. Whereas a certain circumstance can objectively change the moral nature of the action "returning what was borrowed"—which "circumstance" is then no longer merely a circumstance—there is no circumstance imaginable that can change the moral–personal nature of the marital act, since human nature itself would have to change. Such a change, in fact, could not even be postulated through assuming a constant historical evolution of this nature.

### *The Historicity of the Natural Law*

On the basis of the foregoing, then, something further can be seen: the extent to which the "realizations" of justice, as regulated by the natural law or *natural right* (at the basis of all positive legislation), are subject to historical and cultural-civilizational change. If we define "natural right" as the "rights" regulated by the natural law, we can understand that "natural right" represents a kind of realization of the natural law or "application" of natural law to the human social order.[25]

Of course, "historical and cultural variability of natural right" is to be distinguished from "historical and cultural variability of the way natural right is *understood*." Now this may seem an obvious or trivial point, but in fact it is often missed.[26] We are not discussing now the fact that over the course of the centuries, the conceptions of what "natural right" is have changed, nor that there have been changes in the style and manner of natural rights arguments used to justify certain kinds of actions. Thomas was also well aware of the existence of such development. Because of the complexity of the matter, or cultural conditions, or progress and regress in the understanding of the natural law, the *ways of conceiving* the natural law certainly do change.[27]

We are not disputing change in the understanding of the natural law, but change of the natural law itself. The question is, Is it possible that a certain demand of justice is valid by a natural rights justification today that will not be so tomorrow? Or vice versa? Can something like this be valid in one cultural–civilizational context but not in another? When we consider the contingency of the matter of actions, it should be clear how and why something like this is possible. But this is not because the natural law itself changes, but because the configuration of the matter of actions is contingent in the sense that certain concrete demands (or laws) can be justified by natural right at one period, but not at another. This is so because certain legal measures are necessary only under certain circumstances in order to bring about conformity with the precepts of the natural law that are permanently valid.

In this way, we can understand why certain human rights and laws can emerge, in view of a particular social context, that would not have emerged at an earlier time or in another place. For example, no one will dispute that the state has a naturally justified right to run a school system. But the state did not always have such an obligation: it results from the existence and structure of the modern understanding of education. Another example that has become classic is the prohibition of usury. In the Middle Ages, capital and usury had a completely different economic significance than they do today, so that giving credit at interest was a completely different kind of action then than it is today.

This should make clear how false would be an understanding of natural right that presented a timeless system, independently valid of all historical conditions, with natural law commands that would be valid "always" and "everywhere." This would mean claiming that only *one* form of government, one economy, and one taxation system truly correspond to the natural law. On the other hand, an example of the connection of the supratemporal and permanent moral requirements of natural right with a changing realization of them at particular times is provided by the social teaching of the Church. Indeed, the development of the Church's teaching in this matter can best be understood in this light. To be sure, there are advances in the understanding of the structure and requirements of political and economic justice. But circumstances also change. The Church has been teaching since Leo XIII that the state has the duty to intervene in the economic sphere in order to protect the worker. But this demand came about only as a result of the economic and social changes of the nineteenth century, the context in which the encyclical *Rerum Novarum* applied unchanging principles of the natural law.

Thomas concerns himself with these connections in a few passages. In the *De Malo,* he distinguishes a formal aspect from a material aspect in regard to the justice of positive human laws. The formal justice of these laws is founded in their agreement with the "principles of justice that are found in the natural reason"; these principles are immutable (and contain, in virtue of the extension of the *ratio naturalis,* both primary and secondary precepts). On the other hand, a material justice must be considered: "From this perspective, the same thing is not right and good everywhere and for all people, but must be settled by laws. This results from the mutability in human nature (*propter mutabilitatem naturae humanae*) and from the diverse conditions of human beings and things, according to the diversity (*diversitatem*) of places and times" (*De Malo,* q. 2, a. 4, ad 13um).

Thomas establishes the necessity for human laws here on the basis of the contingency of the matter of actions. It is a contingency that exists both in place (according to culture or civilization) and in history. But it is also based on the "changeableness" of human nature, which means that man in his nature changes in regard to *willing,* as has been shown. A law against drug trafficking will not be needed where drugs are not used or do not affect behavior in a way dangerous to the common good, but this can change because of human habits—the *rectitudo* of the will can indeed change, and then the common good requires suitable laws.

In the *Summa Theologiae* as well (*I–II,* q. 94, a. 5), Thomas puts the question directly of whether or not the natural law is changeable. Now this change can be understood in two ways: first, there is change by addition, and this is of course possible, "since many things are added [*superaddita sunt*] to the natural law that are useful for human life [*ad humanam vitam utilia*], whether by the divine law or by human laws"; second, there can be change by way of subtraction [*per modum subtractionis*], which works by the structure of the validity of the precepts of the natural law "for most cases" (*ut in pluribus*), and Thomas refers to his earlier exposition of the matter (in article 4 of the same question).

What is particularly of interest here is that Thomas views the addition by positive human law that establishes what is "useful [*utilia*] for human life" as a change of the *natural law itself.* And how is this to be understood? It means that natural law (or natural right) always appears as "incarnated" in each particular historical and cultural context. An example of this is that it accords with the natural law that there be punishment for crime. But no human legal code restricts itself to this requirement: particular punishments are stated for particular crimes. But this positive human law is a derivation "through the mode of determination" (*per modum determinationis*) of the natural law, and the precept "evildoers must be punished" (itself a secondary command of the natural law) is "incarnate" in that particular law. Its validity stays alive by means of the natural law, and only *to this extent* does the concrete positive law belong to it (or is a derivation *from it* "by way of determination"). Historical and cultural conditions lie at the basis of its concreteness. A state that would not respect this concretization offends against the natural law. A law that sets out certain penalties for certain crimes corresponds to the natural law, and at the same time can change in its concrete manifestation. It is exactly in this sense that the natural law can "change."

Such concretizations are conceivable that would appear to be the only ones possible in a given civilizational–historical context. They show the only way to create validity for a definite command of the natural law. In this case, you could say in the strict sense, "This law, here and now, is a command of natural right," without forgetting that the circumstances, and thereby the human–positive determinations, can change. *To that extent,* the natural law changes, always understood as the natural right that is culturally and historically "incarnate." The error of natural law doctrines (especially those under the influence of modern rationalism) consists precisely in failing to distinguish this "incarnate" natural right from the principles that are always valid.

## Natural Law, Virtue, and Prudence

We have seen how the complexity of many situations often makes it very difficult to know what one should do. The governance of concrete action through the natural law of the practical reason becomes more ambiguous and more indefinite the closer one gets to the level of the concrete *operabile.* In many cases, several courses of action are, or at least appear to be, morally justified. A simplistic orientation toward universally formulated norms of action fails or proves insufficient, not because these norms of action are inadequate but because we often find it difficult to determine *the objective content of the action in question.* This is due to the material contingency of actions in certain circumstances—above all in the area of justice. When it comes to the making of laws, it is particularly difficult to see which measures would be adequate to the objective moral demands.

It belongs to prudence (especially legislative prudence)—and to the moral virtues always attached to prudence—to judge concrete situations rightly for their objective meaning,[28] which is to order human actions to their goal—to the good—according to the order of reason. The act of prudence is nevertheless fundamental and not originally regulated by "norms." And this means too, that prudence is not in conflict with the "conscience," nor does it have to "modify" it. Prudence depends, rather, on the intentional act of the moral virtues, and that means the universal *ordinatio* of the natural reason and its habit (*habitus*) of the first principles, which tradition (for one reason or another) has called *synderesis.*

The fundamental rule of the practical reason as the *recta ratio agibilium* (right reason of actions) is a natural rule that lies in front of the reason and constitutes its normative power, a rule that arises from the practical reason itself on the level of the *ratio naturalis.* This rule is the natural law, and not "moral norms" that represent only an "after the fact" formulation on the reflective level. The various forms of contemporary moral theology we have treated in this work must be reproached for having failed to overcome a perspective that is already centuries old: the view that wrongly assumes that moral "norms" and the reflective formulations of the natural law are the fundamental phenomena. All the new theological approaches criticized in the foregoing discussion depend on arguments that operate on the level of a norm ethics. From that perspective, the starting point of moral discourse must be the phenomena of "commandment" and "law" as reflectively formulated norms of action; these norms are then *opposed* by such things as "conscience" and "freedom," by the uniqueness of the situation, or by the intention of the subject.

This abstract point of departure unavoidably creates a "tension" that would otherwise not be there "between the necessarily required and generally formulated norms and the concrete demands of the individual."[29] The business of the moral theologian then becomes a search for arguments that make such "tension" tolerable.[30] In certain traditions of legalistic moral theology that operated in this fashion, the "tension" was removed in the favor of the norm, and the forms of argument that came into play for the clarification of exceptions could easily appear as "ways out" or "emergency solutions." The plausibility of these arguments was more intuitively than discursively based, but always fulfilled their practical purpose. The disadvantage was that the "legalistic" moral theologian ran the risk of becoming a mere "expert in law."

To the present day, little or nothing seems to have changed—except that now the decision is generally made in favor of "individüal freedom." The moral theologian is still an expert in law who tells us when, how, and why certain norms do *not* apply, and that someone may act otherwise. Freedom appears to have been rediscovered, as the power of moving around in the spaces of "well established" exceptions.

This puts the relationship between what grounds and what is grounded on its head. Human freedom is much more than this, and the demands of being human are much greater—so much so, indeed, that at times they seem to exceed our powers. This would certainly be the case if we only had the kind of autonomy that puts a person completely on his own. But man has not only been created by God, he is also, by the operation of grace, the child of God. The Christian moral theologian must never forget this, and must maintain that "Christian morality" has nothing specifically new and different to say to man. Among other things, it can tell him that he cannot come to terms with the demands of being human without the grace, or divine assistance, that becomes ours through and in Christ, and as communicated by His Church. Salvation is not salvation from the moral demands of being human, or from the "moral law"; it is salvation from the human *inability* to correspond completely with these demands—and that means, salvation from the inability to live in accordance with real human dignity.

## Notes

1. *In IV Sent.*, d. 33, q. 1, a. 1; one should keep in mind that Thomas distinguishes this *operatio conveniens* from the mere *operatio propria* of the single powers (*genus naturae*). The *proprium* is also the *debitum* only for the reason and the will—that is, the (practical) truth and the moral good. The "proper operations" of animals are ordered to the *debitum* through their "natural judgment" (*naturalis aestimatio*, or instinct). In human beings, this function is carried out by the *lex naturalis*.

2. See W. Kluxen, "Menschliche Natur und Ethos," in *Münchener theologische Zeitschrift* 23 (1972): 1–17, esp. 17.

3. An example of this is the general tendency to replace the concept of the "indirect voluntary" by "direct, but for proportionate reasons." According to F. Scholz, the latter expression "fits more effectively the bitter reality of life, and gives a literal interpretation of it . . . the basically broken human situation with all its tragedy is more fully illuminated. Man comes inevitably to the awareness that he cannot have, keep, or preserve all goods at the same time, but that he can even be called, in the service of higher goods, to injure lesser premoral values without any intent to harm (*animus nocendi*). This is familiar to us in painful medical operations, and applies to all areas of life. Paradise appears to be permanently lost." ("Objekt und Umstände," in K. Demmer and B. Schüller, eds., *Christlich glauben und handeln* [Düsseldorf, 1977], pp. 258–259). This theological pessimism, designed for the creation of a "more human" morality, seems to me rather unpersuasive, and its consequences are immense. If moral action in all areas of life is equated with a "painful medical operation," then anything can be justified. What is proper to ethics is lost from sight, for moral action has to do not with "operations" on premoral goods but ultimately with the very humanity of man. On the question of the "indirect voluntary," see above, *Excursus II,* ch. 7.1.8.

4. J. Th. C. Arntz, "Prima principia propria," in W. P. Eckert, ed. *Thomas von Aquino. Interpretation und Rezeption* (Mainz, 1974), p. 15. See also F. Scholz, *Wege, Umwege, und Auswege der Moraltheologie* (Munich, 1976); W. Ernst, "Universalität sittlicher Normen—heutige Tendenzen," in W. Kerber, ed., *Sittliche Normen: Zum Problem ihrer allgemeinen und unwandelbaren Geltung* (Düsseldorf, 1982), pp. 58–73; F. Scholz, "Durch ethische Grenzsituationen aufgeworfene Normprobleme," in *Theologisch-praktische Quartalschrift* 123 (1975): 341–355 (the exposition that follows in the text will suggest a critique of this article in particular).

5. *I–II,* q. 94, a. 2: "Quanto magis ad propria descenditur, tanto

magis invenitur defectus"; and "Quanto enim plures conditiones particulares apponuntur, tanto pluribus modis poterit deficere."

6. See also, *I–II,* q. 94, a. 5: "Potest tamen immutari in aliquo particulari, et in paucioribus, propter aliquas speciales causas impedientes observantiam talium praeceptorum."

7. This was the interpretation in J. Fuchs, *Theologia Moralis Generalis* (Rome, 1960), p. 77; L. Oeing-Hanhoff, "Thomas von Aquin und die Situation des Thomismus heute," *Philosophisches Jahrbuch* 70 (1962): 17–33; C. Fay, "Human Evolution: A Challenge to Thomistic Ethics," *International Philosophical Quarterly* 2 (1960): 50–80; see also M. B. Crowe, *The Changing Profile of the Natural Law* (The Hague, 1977) pp. 280–283. The clear impossibility of this interpretation of Thomas's text can no longer be held, at least not since its thoroughgoing refutation by R. A. Armstrong, *Primary and Secondary Precepts in Thomistic Natural Law Teaching* (The Hague, 1966), pp. 173–179.

8. See *I,* q. 9, a. 2 : "Sic igitur in omni creatura est potentia ad mutationem: vel secundum esse substantiale, sicut corpora corruptibilia [this means that they are contingent, that they can be or not be]; vel secundum esse locale tantum, sicut corpora caelestia; vel secundum ordinem ad finem et applicationem virtutis ad diversa, sicut in angelis. Et universaliter omnes creaturae sunt mutabiles secundum potentiam Creantis, in cuius potestate est esse et non esse earum." *I,* q. 9, a. 2, ad 3um: "angeli boni, supra immutabilitatem essendi, quae competit eis secundum naturam, habent immutabilitatem electionis ex divina virtute: tamen remanet eis mutabilitas secundum locum." The concept of *mutabilitas* means in this context the same thing as *mobilitas*; see *I–II,* q. 64, a. 2: "Unde et voluntas hominis adhaeret alicui mobiliter, quasi potens etiam ab eo discedere et contrario adhaerere; voluntas autem angeli adhaeret fixe et immobiliter . . . liberum arbitrium hominis flexibile est ad oppositum." *In IV Sent.* d. 26, q.1, ad 3um: "natura humana non est immobilis sicut divina." See also *I,* q. 19, a. 7; *III,* q. 57, a. 1, ad 1um.

9. See *II–II*, q. 56, a. 2; see also *I–II,* q. 56, a. 1: This *potestas* arises from a *naturale dominium exteriorum rerum* founded in the rational and voluntary structure of human action. Thomas emphasizes that this "natural dominion" belongs to man "according to reason," in which consists the *imago Dei*.

10. This can be seen as well in the permissibility of stealing for the reason of hunger in an *evidens et urgens necessitas*. Thomas emphasizes that "this does not properly have the essence of theft [*rationem furti*] or of rapine (*II–II,* q. 56, a. 7); the act in question is only apparently theft. In reality it corresponds to the just *usus* of material goods, which are ordered to the well-being of the community.

11. *II–II,* q. 56, a. 7, ad 1um: "Philosophus non loquitur de iusto naturali quod continet ipsum ordinem iustitiae: hoc enim nunquam deficit, *justitiam esse servandam.* Sed loquitur quantum ad determinatos modos observationis iustitiae, qui in aliquibus fallunt." The action of "returning what has been borrowed" (*reddere depositum*) is therefore a mode of realizing justice that with certain persons (and under certain circumstances) ceases to be such; that is, it is no longer an act of justice.

12. See *I–II,* q. 94, a. 5, ad 2um: "Nec solum in rebus humanis quidquid a Deo mandatur, hoc ipso est debitum; sed etiam in rebus naturalibus *quidquid a Deo fit, est quodammodo naturale.*" (Not only in human affairs is whatever God commands right in itself; but also in things of nature *whatever God commands is in a certain way natural.*) See also *I,* q. 105, a. 6, ad 1um: "Cum igitur naturae ordo sit a Deo rebus inditus, si quid praeter hunc ordinem faciat, non est contra naturam." (Since the order of nature is imposed on things by God, if He does anything that goes beyond this order, it is not against nature.) This is to say that God transcends the order of second causes created by Him, but still preserves order as related to the "first cause," and thus to the *ordo iustitiae*; see also *I,* q. 105, a. 6, ad 2um: "the order of justice is according to a relation to the first cause, which is the rule of all justice. And thus nothing God can do is outside of this order [*praeter hunc ordinem*]." But man is himself *not* able to dispense himself from the order of second causes: "the natural reason is rule and measure, although it is not the measure of things which are by nature" (*I–II,* q. 91, a. 3, ad 2um). If man could do so, he would no longer be able to keep to "the order in relation to the first cause" (the *finis ultimus*), because he would not have the orientation that the natural reason provides him, which is itself ordered to the *naturaliter cognitum* as to its principle and fundamental orientation.

13. In the *I–II,* q. 94, a. 5, ad 2um, this becomes still clearer: death, the passage states, is a punishment ordained by God for original sin. "And thus death can be inflicted upon any human being, innocent or not, according to the command of God, without any injustice. Adultery is *concubitus* with another man's wife, a woman who has been given to that other man by the law handed down from God. But if someone should lie with any woman because of a command of God, it is neither adultery nor fornication." The same goes for theft, "which is the taking of something belonging to someone else. Whoever takes something by the commandment of God, Who is the Lord of all, does not in fact take something without the will of God, which is what stealing is." This is also how Thomas explains the dispensation of the Old Testament patriarchs from the commandment to be monogamous: "the law of having a single wife is not humanly, but divinely established, nor is it handed

down anywhere by word or in writing, but is stamped upon the heart: just so for the other things that pertain in some way to the law of nature; there is dispensation from these only through an *internal inspiration*, by God alone" (*In IV Sent.*, d. 33, q.1, a. 2).

14. Arntz, "Prima principia propria," esp. p. 9.

15. To repeat: since the *usus* of all private ownership is oriented toward the common good, the case of "stealing to ward off starvation" does not constitute an exception to the commandment, "Thou shall not steal." The act is objectively not an act of stealing.

16. And Arntz goes even further: a command of the Decalogue is "left to human law and justice systems for its application," is "left to the jurisdiction of human society," and even to "the wise jurisdiction and decision of the private person" ("Prima principia propria," p. 9).

17. What *can* occur is that, due to the complexity of a certain situation, it may be difficult to *judge* whether an act of adultery, theft, or murder is in question. For the analysis of this case of the "intrinsic complexity of certain particular situations," see Armstrong, *Primary and Secondary Precepts in Thomistic Natural Law Teaching,* pp. 156–161. Armstrong concludes as follows: "For implicit throughout his teaching on natural law is the idea that no matter how complex an issue may be, no matter how many different and oftentimes contradictory solutions may be suggested as being the right course of action, it nonetheless remains true that there is one correct solution; there is one action, out of all actions, whether suggested or otherwise, which is the right action to do" (p. 159).

18. See *II–II*, q. 47, a. 6: "in ratione practica praeexistunt quaedam ut principia naturaliter nota, et huiusmodi sunt fines virtutum moralium, quia finis se habet in operabilibus sicut principium in speculativis." (Certain naturally known principles preexist in the practical reason, and this is what the ends of the moral virtues are, because an end in 'things done' [*operabilia*] is like a principle in 'things known' [*speculativa*].)

19. In other words, according to the "common rational formula" (*secundum communem rationem formalem*) and not as a particular virtue (*virtus specialis*); see *I–II,* q. 61, a. 3.

20. Ibid. This article, furthermore, has no mention of "exceptions" and addresses the question in terms of "dispensability." God Himself could not dispense from these commands without contradicting His own wisdom.

21. See Armstrong, *Primary and Secondary Precepts in Thomistic Natural Law Teaching,* p. 168: "It is clear from the teaching of St. Thomas that the question is not one of variability, but rather one of reformulation, particularly in the case of the remote conclusions. As we stated earlier,

the reason there appears to be variability present, is that the formulations of some particular precepts neglect the conditions that ought to be included if the principle is to be binding in all instances."

22. "It is clear from St. Thomas's teaching that he was aware that the formulation of a secondary natural law precept may omit the conditions that require to be expressed if the law is to be absolute" (ibid., p. 167).

23. We should recall that Thomas refers to the precepts of the *lex naturalis* as "universal propositions of the practical reason" (*propositiones universales rationis practicae*), that is, as practical *judgments* and not as "normative statements" (chapter 2, section "The Natural Law as a Work of the Reason"). The commands of the natural law are, *as* the *lex naturalis*, just as essentially judgments of the practical reason as the commands of positive law are, *as* positively *formulated* normative statements. These latter, apart from having a different basis for their justification, have validity and bind only *insofar* as they are formulated and promulgated *in language*. But the natural law is promulgated with the human reason itself and has validity and binding power on the basis of the practical *judgments* of this same human reason.

24. This can often be seen in the inability to distinguish objectively *indifferent* acts from acts considered in their *genus naturae*. For example, Merkelbach uses "giving money" (*dare pecuniam*) as an illustration of an *actio indifferens* (*Summa Theologiae Moralis,* 2nd ed., vol. 1 [Paris, 1935], p. 142). But this is not an indifferent action; it is an action like "giving alms" or "paying a reward," but treated in respect to its *genus naturae*. "Giving money" as such does not exist, because "giving money" *as such* is already and *always* a *proportio ad rationem,* and thus has the moral species of "good" or "evil." An action is morally indifferent only when such a *proportio* is not found in it, but only in the circumstances or the intention. The standard examples Thomas uses are "scratching one's beard," or "going for a walk," and so on. The difference between this kind of action and "giving money" should be obvious.

25. We need some terminological clarification at this point. In the strict sense, natural right is ordered to the virtue of justice; it is then an expression of the part of the natural law that is related to the virtue of justice. In a further, less specific sense, one speaks of "naturally right" as equivalent to "being in accord with the natural law." Thus one can speak in general of an ethics based on natural rights even in contexts where the virtue of justice is not concerned. But in the present context I am understanding "natural right" in the former, narrower sense.

26. As J. Finnis has pointed out so clearly in *Natural Law and Natural Rights* (Oxford, 1980) p. 25.

27. See Armstrong, *Primary and Secondary Precepts in Thomistic Natural Law Teaching,* ch. 6.

28. This concrete moral evaluation is the task of the so-called *ratio particularis* or *vis cogitativa*. See for example, *In VI Ethic.*, lect. 1, no. 1123; lect. 9, no. 1255. For a historical and systematic analysis of its meaning in the context of the Thomistic theory of knowledge, I would recommend C. Fabro, *Percezione e pensiero*, 2nd ed. (Brescia, 1962), especially vol. 1, ch. 4, pp. 193ff.

29. See W. Ernst, "Universalität sittlicher Normen," p. 61.

30. It is astonishing to see how seriously such theologians underrate the classical doctrine of moral virtue. See the following interpretation by Ernst, "Universalität sittlicher Normen": "In order to make this gap tolerable, and do justice to the decision of conscience in the concrete situation, the traditional moral theology has developed those well-known doctrines that are meant to provide "help" or a "way out" of the difficulty, such as the doctrines of prudence and of conscience, from the sources of morality, the principle of double effect, the doctrine of the virtues and of *epieíkeia*, of probablism and the problem of the lesser evil." One must ask how it would be possible to interpret the doctrine of prudence and the moral virtues as "a help and a way out," in order to make "tolerable" the gap between norm and subject. The point of view has been turned on its head. Isn't it rather that the doctrines of virtue and prudence form the starting point for understanding what a moral norm is? Shouldn't we begin by speaking about the human person, and only afterward about norms and commands? Otherwise, when one finally does begin to speak about man, man must be "defended" from the norms and commands, instead of moral norms being understood as really an expression of the demands of being human, of a life lived according to virtue.

# 13

# Some Philosophical Conclusions—and an Orientation for Moral Theology

We can conclude now by reviewing some of the most important results of the foregoing studies, and by taking a glance at some of the consequences for moral theology.

## I

The natural law, in its fundamental structure, is an expression of personal autonomy. This autonomy encompasses a whole series of fundamental elements, the organic unity of which ultimately rests upon the fact that the human person is a living thing that has has been created *ad imaginem Dei*—a free and spiritually ensouled entity of the corporeal world, which, participating in the eternal law and oriented toward God by knowing and willing, transcends the "visible" world of bodies. The natural law is not an ordinary "natural phenomenon," since it does not have a "natural" structure so much as a "personal" one, in accordance with the personal nature of human existence. "Being a person" is itself (in the unity of the *suppositum*, cognitively and operatively mediated by the natural reason) a special, and superior, form of "being natural," that owes its superiority to the reason; and reason, as the "natural reason" (*ratio naturalis*), plays a special role in the constitution of the person through its standard-giving function. To refer justification of moral normativity to "nature," or to argue "by the natural law," always involves an appeal to this *conditioned nature* that belongs to the rational–personal structure of the natural law; an appeal, that is, to a "natural order" that is revealed in reflection upon moral experience as just such an "order of reason" (*ordo rationis*), although the experience in question is spontaneous, partly intuitive, prescientific, and conditioned by personal dispositions or moral virtues.

The natural law is thus to be identified neither with the "natural order" in a purely metaphysical sense nor with the (rational) nature of the human person. The natural law is rather the law of the practical reason, that is to say, an ordering (*ordinatio*) of the practical reason as the natural reason, which orients actions in accordance with the natural inclinations toward the goal that is proper to the human being as a person. Now, this does *not* mean that the natural law can be called the "law of the practical reason" only to the extent that it gives precepts, as if the practical reason were only the "voice" that obeys the natural order objectified for it with regard to any particular content. The practical reason does not simply constitute the "preceptive" side (the *ratio praecepti*), does not merely transform natural tendencies or action structures into moral commands; rather, the human reason has an axiological self-consistency even in its practical mode, and thus constitutes the moral "ought" (the "order to an end"; *ordo ad finem*), and it does this, again, with regard to particular contents. However, it does *not* do this in a "creative" fashion: practical knowing is still *knowing,* and as such constitutes the moral ought in an ordering act without constituting *the truth* of this "ought" in "creative" (or "self-competent") fashion. To put it more precisely, while it is true that the practical reason constitutes this truth *cognitively,* this occurs in a *participative* manner, and not in a way that permits "manipulation" of that truth. This is because the ordering of the practical reason that is known as the natural law is a "participation of the eternal law in the rational creature."

In the natural law, then, the eternal law is explicated in the context of the autonomy of subjective moral experience. The natural law is not the "imitative" reflex of a "natural order," but rather a practically cognitive, cooperative completion of the ordering of the eternal law. The natural law in this sense has an ordering function in relation to every order that is "only nature" insofar as it can be distinguished from "reason."

The Stoic model of the natural law was founded on the identity of *physis* and *logos*, with the reason as immanent, and *therefore* normative; and the logos that governs the natural order of the cosmos is identified with the "eternal law." This leads to a circular conception of identifying what is "according to reason" (*secundum rationem*) with what is "according to nature" (*secundum naturam*), and vice versa. For Thomas, on the contrary, the moral standard-providing reason is not the *logos* (or structural principle) of a natural order, but rather an ordering power that has power over what is *only* natural, an ordering that brings into manifestation the *logos* of a *transcendent* eternal law existing in the mind of the Creator. Human reason is not a "microcosmos" that mirrors the cosmic order in miniature; rather, it is the place where the *imago Dei* is found, whose truth and ordering power it at once shares in and effects. The practical reason is accordingly a cognitive principle as the *natural* reason, which is transcendent over all the rest of nature; at the same time, as a created reason, and originating from a spiritual soul that is the form of a body, it is also *nature*. And Thomas has stated this most clearly, as we have seen, in his Commentary on the Gospel of John: "Man, according to his intellectual nature . . . *which is "from outside"* [*ab extrinseco*] . . . comes from God through being created" (see chapter 6, section "The 'Light of the Natural Reason,' " subsection "The Truth Capacity of the Natural Reason"). The reason thus has a *telos* character in relation to all nature that is other than reason; its practical activity cannot be reduced to "reformulating" natural inclinations into moral commands. To be sure, the reason is constitutionally oriented toward these inclinations in order to acquire knowledge and in order to establish precepts that are true for the praxis of human behavior, since the human being *is* both body *and* soul, and since duality does not mean dualism! All the same, in relation to the inclinations, the reason has its own axiological consistency and an ordering function. The order that is built by the practical reason within the natural inclinations is the order of virtue, in which the integrity of the person is revealed in all its operative abundance.

Consequently, moral norms, which in this way possess their validity in the natural law, are norms that bring personal existence to expression in the most fundamental, comprehensive, and developed way, and thus never constrict or suppress human spontaneity or authenticity. On the contrary, they really make possible "being human" in the first place, because they do nothing other than bring to expression what is *fundamentally* true about the human being for *all* human actions. This is the truth that makes the difference about human action, what makes it *human* action; it is a difference that is not "given" with the necessity of nature (because human beings are free), but must be realized in actions. The real alternative to a legalistic or naturalistic conception of moral justification is a personal understanding of the natural law, and not an escape into "historical consciousness."

## II

This personal understanding of nature as the foundation of morality makes clear how a "law of the practical reason" unfolds as a natural law that comes into being through the autonomy of the practical experience of the moral subject, or the *person*. At the same time, nothing other than the eternal law of the Creator is explicated in this natural law of the practical reason—and not only as "transcendentally founding" or as merely "providing a framework," because the eternal law is *identical* with the natural law as autonomously explicated by man. Indeed, the natural law is nothing other than the "participation of the eternal law in the rational creature," and this participation, thanks to the personal existence of the human being, is a complete, or *cognitive and active* participation.

Human autonomy is therefore "autonomous theonomy" or "the autonomy of man in God," or a participative theonomy that has been translated into autonomy. God's moral lawgiving is not that of an "overlord" or "master" who *imposes* a law on the creature through "interventions" or by "retaining privileges to Himself," which is the inadequate (and anthropomorphic) model increasingly used of late to characterize the (supposed) "anthropomorphism" of traditional moral doctrine.[1] From the point of view of this study, God is neither "overlord" or "master," on the one hand, nor mere "partner" or "employer," on the other; He is *creator*, and that means that God has given man a law by *creating* him with a definite nature and its inclinations, especially the natural reason. Any subsequent divine lawgiving (positive and revealed) would then have for its basis the eternal law as first conveyed at creation; otherwise, such legislation would be seen as a "divine ordinance" founded exclusively on an act of divine fiat—and it could not be called a *moral law.*

III

The human being participates in the eternal law with his entire being. The human person is body and soul, which in an undivided unity define human goods and the parameters of meaningful human existence. *Anima mea non est ego* (St. Thomas, *Comm. ad I Cor.*, 15, lect. 2, no. 924) is the truth that must be held up against those who spiritualistically limit the human person and its "I": "My soul is not I," or "I am not my soul"; man *has* a soul, but he *is* both body and soul. That means "I am not only my soul, I am also my body," or, rather, "I am a soul-endowed body." Bodiliness is constitutive for the understanding of the human person, for the human "I" or self-consciousness. The body must not be considered "subhuman" (Rahner), since that would lead to the equation *human being* = *person* = *soul,* which leads straight to an anthropological dualism that has been combated since the very beginnings of the Christian teaching on creation.

This can also help us understand why the constitutive conditions of human bodiliness have a personal significance that is there from the beginning (and not only through "expressive action," which would *endow* them with meaning). We have seen how this dimension of human existence is to be understood in a nonphysicalistic way, and how it becomes normative. In particular, it was pointed out how the sum total of natural inclinations, even those which arise from the bodily nature of the human being, are always *ontologically* integrated in the *one* human suppositum, as created. The ordering function of the natural law, and ultimately of moral virtue, does not bring an *ontological,* but rather a *practically cognitive* and *operative,* integration into being in the suppositum, and this brings about the practical truth of human action.

To repeat once more, and to remove all possible ambiguity, the bodily nature of man is not a "neutral" area, something that is in itself "less than human" or "subpersonal," even if recognized as being "morally more significant." On the contrary, our bodily nature *formulates* fundamental human goods (or goals) that are specific to the potentialities of being human, and are constitutive for *personal* action. The nature of our body is therefore such as to give rise, in the bodily joining of man and woman, to the elevation of flesh to a "creative transition" (Styczén). If this is not intelligible, neither is the "word becoming flesh" (*Verbum caro factum est*), which is the fact that the divine Word, in order to unite human nature with God, became not merely a human *soul* or *spirit*, but also human in body.

## IV

Understanding the personal structure of the natural law also clears the way for understanding human action as moral action, and for understanding its objectivity, which is finally nothing other than the fundamentally human and personal meaning of behavior, as it emerges from the objectification achieved in the practical reason. The distinction between "good" and "bad" action becomes clear in this context, a distinction that is identical to the difference between "right" and "wrong" actions, since moral value pertains immediately to *actions*, and not just intentions or "fundamental options."

This personal understanding of human action is thus directly opposed to a legalistic and formalistic understanding of ethics, because it defines the morally "right" (and likewise the very concept of the moral law) from the morally "good," and not the other way round; this moral "good"—understood in the context of a *virtue ethics* and not a *norm ethics*—means the good as the expression of the constitutive requirements of the person. Of course, these goods of the person, ultimately summed up in the good of personal integrity, are only contingent goods from a metaphysical perspective, since they are created goods. Nevertheless, from a *moral* perspective they are *absolute* goods: *persona est affirmanda propter se ipsam* (The person must be affirmed for its own sake), and this is the relevant and fundamental principle for an ethical personalism. If the "dignity of man," metaphysically considered (that is, as considered in non- or premoral terms), is a contingent, nonabsolute (because *created*) good, a good that is limited (there is more than one human being, after all), both constituted by God and ordered toward Him, nevertheless, in the sphere of human action, the *practical* good is "*esteem for* the dignity of man," which (in the moral sense) is an absolute and noncontingent good. In the same way must be distinguished the "death of an innocent person" from the "killing of an innocent person," or murder. So-called teleological ethics has completely overlooked this all-important distinction between what is *metaphysically* absolute and what is *morally* absolute.[2] And we also noted the cause of this oversight: teleological ethics is still bound up with a naturalistic (or "physicalistic") conception of the object of action.

## V

Upon this foundation, it becomes clear what we mean by the "proper subject matter of ethics" or the "properly ethical." Morality does not consist in the achievement of any good consequences or effects whatsoever in the human sociohistorical environment; rather, it is concerned that the *acting person* be good. As Plato said, it has to do with the "good of the soul," and, as Aristotle said, not in doing what is right so much as *being* right in doing the right. Precisely for this reason there are two different kinds of effects or consequences, which, in the calculus of teleological ethics, are indifferently "weighed off" against one another: *suffering* wrong and *doing* wrong. The latter is a moral evil; the former is not.

The most likely reason for the failure of teleological ethics (and the method of "weighing of goods") to grasp what is proper to ethics, is the use of a technical, or technological, model of action instead of a practically cognitive one: there is neglect, in other words, of the difference between praxis and poiesis, between "doing" and "making." A discourse that is dedicated to "optimizing" (premoral) goods and "minimizing" (premoral) evils will usually stay beneath the threshold of the moral. The method appeals at a superficial level, and has plausibility because of its technical calculations. The situation is comparable to that of a surgeon who tries to cause his patient the least possible pain in a certain operation, presuming that the *moral* question of the permissibility of the operation has already been settled, and is no longer an issue. However, the suffering that unavoidably follows a certain operation tells nothing about the *moral* permissibility of the operation in question: an immoral operation will be no less immoral by being less painful, but this could not be proven through the model of teleological "weighing of goods." To derive moral obligation from the technical model, teleological ethics must take refuge in a new version of the "naturalistic fallacy."

Further, teleological ethics is constantly controlled by an "often unconscious legalism"[3] that seeks unambiguous solutions for all ethical problems, particularly in the area of "borderline" and difficult cases. This is connected with a dependence on models of juristic decision-making, where competing rights must be weighed and a decision *has to be made* for one side or the other. Apart from the fact that such juristic models overtax the powers of the individual,[4] it appears to be forgotten that ethical discourse is not concerned with the question of the preservation or infringement of *rights*, or of something that is interchangeable between the parties; not, that is, with the question of whether *A* suffered any injury of his rights from *B*, but rather *whether B acted rightly or wrongly*. Teleological ethics likewise overlooks the basic structures of the practical reason, since in the concrete situation there will not be absolutely *one* solution. That such a solution does exist, and that for it alone there can be moral responsibility is presupposed by a method that holds that the acting person bears direct responsibility for all forseeable consequences, and that the morally correct action in each situation is that by which the smallest amount of evil and the greatest amount of good are effected. But if these amounts cannot be determined in every situation, which seems more than likely, the "proportionalist" model implies that an insight into what is morally right and obligatory is not really possible after all; an ethics thus based solely on the "weighing of goods" stands revealed as an irrational ethics.[5]

This inherent irrationality ultimately results from the fact that human beings are not obliged to bear, or even be capable of bearing, the responsibility for all consequences, at least without emptying the meaning of moral responsibility altogether. A right understanding of this issue presupposes a theory of moral action that is founded on a thorough analysis of voluntariness.[6] There are consequences, that is to say, that cannot be the intentional object of practical decisions; they are thus not *chosen*, and that means they are not *willed* as either means or ends—they are "indirectly willed" or "tolerated." If this kind of consequence is placed at the same level as the (directly) chosen or willed kind (as in teleological or "proportionalist" ethics), the concept of moral responsibility will disappear from view. For the concept of responsibility is reducible to the concept of the choosing will, and this relationship is lost when *all* consequences are put at the same rank. If, in a practical judgment, chosen consequences are put at the same level with other consequences that are not chosen, but only tolerated as unavoidable side effects, then the choosing will and the tolerating will are identified, and the category of choice itself (*prohairesis*, *electio*) begins to disappear. For instance, by this reasoning someone could maintain that an executive of a firm who undertakes fraudulent measures for his personal enrichment while deliberately driving the company to bankruptcy is no more responsible for ruining his firm than another man who refuses to do something fraudulent to rescue his business even though the "damage" (if he carried out the fraud) would be "minimal" and it is the only way to rescue the firm and the jobs involved.

By considering as equivalent a merely "tolerating" will (as with the second) and a "choosing" will (as with the first), responsibility is reduced to the capacity to "cause" certain things. In this technical and no longer moral conception of responsibility, it makes no difference whether the causation takes place "directly" or "indirectly." In the same way, one could no longer distinguish between the direct killing of the fetus in the mother's womb and a necessary operation that has the death of the fetus as an anticipated side effect. The latter is a consequence that the physician would "cause" (in the technical sense), but for which he would bear no responsibility under the condition that his will only *tolerates* it, and does not *choose* it, either as means or as end. If teleological ethics has a certain attraction, it is most likely due to this simplifying confusion of moral responsibility with purely "technical" causation of effects or consequences.

The reduction of the psychological structure of human action to the logic of technical action, then, lies behind the assumption (of the teleological ethicists) that the tolerating will is only a form of the choosing will; yet a still deeper confusion lies behind this one: the misunderstanding of human responsibility and "fore-thought" as such. In the proportionalists' "weighing of goods," human responsibility is overburdened. It is assumed that the person not only is capable but is even *obliged* to be the master of *all* the consequences of his actions, and to harmonize them all into an "optimum." To begin with, this is a position that simply cannot be reconciled with Christian revelation, which maintains that only divine intervention at the end of time will fully reform this temporal world, and that the individual cannot be responsible for the situation of the world in its totality. The "consequentialist" and "proportionalist" position makes the single human person responsible for the "whole," and thus confuses divine and human foresight. This has the effect of negating the theological significance of humanly tragic "borderline cases" as situations in need of divine redemption. An oversimple concept of responsibility throws upon the individual the whole burden of responsibility for unambiguous solutions to such difficult situations. At first, the vision of such a burden, or of such a "competency," may enhance the sense of freedom, but this will come true only by an inconsistent life. For in order to act at all, the infinite chain of "foreseeable consequences" must be "cut" at some point or other by a "decision" made on the basis of some criterion that will not be subject to the "weighing" process. What results is a subjectivism which cannot be rationally justified: a method which violates the very principles of a "weighing of goods" and invites any available form of moral justification.

The ultimate cost of using this method, however, is the surrender of the distinction between moral action (and that means acts of the practically choosing will, which mold the goodness of the will) and technical "optimization" of premoral goods or evils; this is to give up on the difference between the judgment "It is always wrong directly to kill an innocent person," and the judgment "It is better (whether "right" or otherwise) to cause the death of an innocent person than to cause the death of hundreds of innocent persons through not doing so." The latter judgment—also known as the Caiaphas principle—"It is better for one man to die than for the whole nation to be destroyed" (John 11:50)—makes no sense in a genuinely ethical context, where an action that is "less wrong" is still "wrong." and is recognized as morally impermissible. The point of Caiaphas's logic is precisely the placing of the question on the level of "premoral" goods, since the "death of a man" is being weighed against the "destruction of the nation," which keeps the whole consideration short of the moral realm. If Caiaphas had said, "It is better to *kill an innocent man* than to let the whole nation be destroyed," his suggestion might have stirred up some moral questioning. As it was, he succeeded in cloaking the morally problematic issue by weighing the "death" of *one* against the (possible) "death" of *many.* But the "death" of an innocent is surely different from the "killing" of an innocent!

When a truly moral decision is made, the acting person knows that he does not bear responsibility for consequences that he could hinder only through wrong action. If he insists on taking this responsibility, he must finally deny that there exist types of actions that can be described as "wrong," absolutely and universally, and must maintain instead that such a qualification can come only from the end, or from the intention, or from the whole context of the concrete situation. When proportionalist thinkers say they have no dispute with the truth of the statement "One may never do evil as a means to good" (Romans 3:8), they have really emptied the statement of any content, for according to their theory, the only evil actions are those which *have not* been done for a good end. No human being would be *capable* of making a moral judgment with the method of the teleological "weighing of goods," which could allow him or her to do what this statement forbids (with the exception, conceded by a few, of a temptation to sin). But the fact that people nevertheless do make such judgments and can act on them is proved not only by moral "common sense" but also by the history of humanity. It appears, then, that fundamental ethical principles become meaningless in the context of the teleological or proportionalist model of "weighing goods," because this model has lost sight of what is proper to moral judgments and moral action. It is a method that has not come to terms with the phenomena of morally practical judgment.[7]

## VI

The "properly ethical" or "ethical *proprium*" delimits only those consequences of an action as constitutive of its moral value that constitute the action in its *specifically human meaning*. This perspective has a liberating effect on human praxis that actually strengthens a true, rational responsibility. Only those normative areas are seen as morally indispensable that constitute the specifically *human* meaning of human action, and to act contrarily in such areas can thus be described as *intrinsece malum*. At the same time, there opens up, upon this human–personal basis, a whole spectrum of possible, still undefined moral actions that do not have to be subjected to the (finally, *rigorous*) necessity of being subjected to a determination, in each case, of the "optimal good." Such an ethics, which recognizes absolute moral norms while being uncompromising in what constitutes human action as truly *human*, is in fact flexible, even "creative" in the area of the immense variety of possible realizations of responsible human actions that are founded in human nature.

## VII

A metaphysically adequate understanding of this foundation of the specifically human possibilities of action and its character of being the "natural order" of human actions as grounded in the *lex naturalis*, has more than once required reference to the concept of the *eternal law* as a key concept. Originally of Augustinian inspiration, the doctrine was worked out with a more consistent anthropology by St. Thomas, where the natural law is understood as the participation of the eternal law. This opens up an abundance of moral theological perspectives and analytical possibilities, an abundance very far from being exhausted. The participation of the eternal law in man is not limited to the *lex naturalis*. By divine providence, and from the very beginning, man has been called to a life that is part of an ordering to a far higher goal: by the "law of grace" (*lex gratiae*), which has become "law of Christ" (*lex Christi* or *lex evangelica*) through Christ's incarnation and the redemption He has brought, human life is ordered to the holiness of God.

Now the participation of this *ordinatio* of the eternal law through grace and the theological virtues of faith, hope, and love is not a "foreign body" added to human nature, or a "second floor" of man's existence. It belongs, rather, to the original, human meaning of our existence, not by reason of the "nature" of man, but rather by the divine will for salvation and the *single* ordering (*ordinatio*) of the divine law. In the human person this constitutes an indivisible (but unconfused and distinguishable) unity of the natural and the supernatural.

This unity was destroyed by the first sin, by the resulting fall of man, and by the condition of original sin. Through this fall to what is *merely* natural and *merely* human, a deep chasm appeared within the "ordering" (*ordinatio*) of the eternal law and the participation in it of the human being. The contradiction (between God's will to save and the condition of humanity) as a *moral situation* (*peccatum naturae*) bears the character of guilt because of the estrangement of the human will from its true goal. Only the atoning intervention of the mercy of God can remove this guilt. This saving intervention was crystallized in a new law, which by becoming incarnate in Jesus Christ (the divine wisdom become man) is the "law of Christ," which heals human nature from the wounds of the fall and leads it to its true destiny.

The *ordinatio* of the *lex naturalis* keeps its integrity within the *lex gratiae*. "What is of the law of nature is fully decreed there [i.e., in the law of grace]" (*ea quae sunt de lege naturae, plenarie ibi traduntur*). The natural law is the presupposition for the law of grace and is elevated and completed in it "since many things are decreed there that are beyond nature" (*cum multa tradantur ibi supra naturam*; *I–II*, q. 94, a. 4, ad 1).

This elevation and fulfillment of human nature in the order of divine holiness is revealed in Christ. "The distinction between the supernatural order of salvation and the temporal ordering of human life must be seen within the one plan of God, to unite all things in Christ."[8] In the participation in the life of Christ by the power of the Holy Spirit—the personal love between the Father and the Son—occurs the full participation in the *ordinatio* of the eternal law, a participation, that is, that is in accordance with the divine plan of salvation. This is the specific perspective of moral theology: it must be fundamentally *Christological*. It must treat of Christ as the *Way, Truth,* and *Life* of the human person. But moral theology can do this only when it understands man as a *natura elevata*, just as it can understand Christ only by holding fast to the unity in the divine Person of *two* natures, the divine and the human, that has been *assumed* by the divine nature "unmixed, unchanged, without division or separation" (Council of Chalcedon). Since "the human" has been taken up in its integrity in Christ, the magisterium of the Church has the duty not only to teach Christ and the Life in Christ, but also "the human," and that means *to teach the natural law*. And because Christ cannot be reduced to His human nature, the peculiar concern of Christian moral theology must be the themes of filial adoption by God, sanctification, and identification with Christ; and this implies a morality of sharing in the prophetic, priestly, and kingly mission of the Redeemer of man.[9]

## VIII

In order to provide an adequate answer to the much agitated question about what is proper to Christian moral doctrine, a certain distinction should be *abandoned*, that is adequate neither to a true theology of the eternal law nor to the Christological perspective that runs like a scarlet thread through the documents of the Second Vatican Council. This is the distinction between a "worldly ethics" [*Weltethos*] and a "salvation ethics" [*Heilsethos*], as well as the parallel distinction between "worldly (categorial) action" and "transcendental" intentions, motives, or fundamental options. (I do not mean by this the necessary distinction between the temporal *order* and the *order* of salvation, but rather the dualism maintained in the distinction between a worldly ethos and a salvation ethos). Instead, it must be affirmed that the Christian salvation ethos is also an ethos for the world, and that a worldly ethos becomes transformed and elevated for Christians into a salvation ethos. In Christian living, both the temporal order and the order of salvation must be understood as distinct, yet united in a single ethos, one that is at once a "worldy ethics" and a "salvation ethics," both supernatural faith *and* action in the world.

If, on the other hand, someone restricts the "Christian" aspect of Christian morality to *transcendental, faith-determined intentions* or *fundamental options*, at least two things are overlooked. First, that through the incarnation of the divine Word in Jesus Christ, everything human—and that means all worldly action—acquires a new salvific meaning and a new moral normativity that it could never possess on its own without the *assumptio* of human nature. For example, the Christian love for enemies, which exceeds human justice, represents in the Christian context a *commandment* of a higher justice, and the same goes for the whole content of the Sermon on the Mount, especially the Beatitudes, which are summed up in the command "Be perfect, as your Father in heaven is perfect," or in the apostolic command "As my Father sent me, so send I you." A second truth overlooked (as already emphasized) is the fact that in many cases, the moral requirements of being human overburden or simply go far beyond the moral capacity of man in his fallen condition. The gap that thus appears between what one *ought* to do and what one *can* do is a serious threat to the autonomy of moral insight. *For in itself, no moral "ought" can be grasped that reaches further than the moral "can."* That means that in the long run, *and at best,* it will be recognized as an "unattainable" ideal, and will never be acknowledged as a truly obliging norm of action.

For such a contradiction as this, there is only one authentic and responsible theological answer, deriving from revelation but apparently too frightening for many contemporary theologians: only a life that is in accordance with Christian morality, the fulfillment of which lies in the mystery of the Church and is founded on the grace of the Holy Spirit, can give the human being the means and the hope of corresponding fully to the demands of being human. A moral theology that refuses to be faithful to this (redemptive) claim of the Christian message is, it seems, no longer a truly Christian morality. One has only to consider the subject of divorce to realize how the limited moral capability of the person who no longer takes seriously the efficacy of redeeming grace has become the norm of a "purely human morality," or secular humanism. A moral doctrine of this kind falls short of being truly human.

## IX

In their option for "autonomous morality," many theologians are motivated by serious pastoral reasons, particularly the concern for a method of proclaiming the Christian message of salvation in an effective way to people who are frequently quite secularized or even atheistic.[10] In these terms, the most accessible path might seem to lie in showing that norms of behavior that pertain to the world are common to the Christian and non-Christian alike. Only the *motivations* differ: the motivations that provide the ultimate meaning of action and the perspective of hope are the only element specific to Christian life.

Now this assessment would be correct if it were not for the chasm that exists between the "ought" and the "can." For the (unbelieving) humanist, it is not clear in the least that demands that can be met only through the help of the grace of God belong to the morally normative dimension of human nature. Depending on the moral standard of the surrounding society and his personal disposition, the unbelieving humanist will tend to set the threshold of a minimum human morality somewhat lower than does the believing Christian. This is because the latter will have, through faith alone, a somewhat larger grasp of what is morally *possible*, and, finally, of what is morally *obliging*, since he knows that man is called to "be able" to do more than he actually "can." If the Christian wants to maintain that Christians and non-Christians have the same standard of morality at the human level, the question still remains, Whose standard will yield to whose? The fact of the matter is that on the basis of the practical principles of an "autonomous morality," the Christian will have to yield, since in any historical and cultural situation he will take the recognized moral standard as the standard of human morality. And yet precisely then, the truly "human" will be missed.

In reality, the believing Christian is *not* on the same level as the (unbelieving) humanist when it comes to the actual capacity to grasp the human moral standard. To begin with, the Christian can appreciate all genuine human values that can be found outside the Christian context as human values, and thus as Christian values. This can lead to a refined sense for an authentic pluralism in temporal affairs and respect for the freedom of conscience. But the Christian must go further. In all humility he must show that the way to meet the demands of being human is the "wisdom of the Cross," which will appear as foolishness to the (unbelieving) humanist. Although the Christian, as only "one among many" striving for the noble goals of human existence, knows that he is united with all men of goodwill, and is "at home" in all fields of society, nevertheless, in the midst of a secularized world not distinguished for its faith, he is at the same time often "the other" and a sign of contradiction. He stands for a *human morality* that is *specifically Christian.*

And it is precisely here that the real dignity of faith, the proof and the attractiveness of the Christian message of salvation, has been located from the earliest times. It has not been a matter of presenting newer or higher "motivations" for meeting the moral demands that are more or less obvious to everybody, and more or less attainable by everybody, but rather in showing the way to bridge the chasm (which tortures every man of goodwill) between the rational and autonomous moral insight into what one *ought* to do, on the one side, and, on the other side (at a lower level), the moral *ability* to do it. Or, to put it somewhat differently, when someone has reduced his grasp of the *ought* or of "doing what is good" to his *own* ability and will, the Christian is called to invite that person to what is called *conversion*, to seek reconciliation with God the Father.

Now this does not mean that the moral demands of being human are mostly apparent only to the believer, or that there is not an inner, autonomous rationality that belongs to everyone. What it means is that, first of all, thanks to the gap between "ought" and "can," not everyone will even *have* such an insight; indeed, sometimes whole societies will lose sight of it, even though in principle it is always available because of its inherent rationality. This is why faith, founded on revelation, is the corrective needed in practice: a light that will not be "extinguished" by any historical or social pressures that illuminate the true requirements of being human. Second, it must be remembered that human moral teaching is not concerned only with external actions but, like any morality, must reach within, to the will of the human person. Here again, what is "asked of" and what is "possible for" the Christian will go far beyond the "merely human." Third, it means that "being human," simply as a way of acting in the world, has a *new meaning* by its being assumed in Christ, a meaning that is related to God's own holiness, something that cannot be restricted to "motivations," "intentions," or "fundamental options." Holiness consists in action, in a doing that acquires its full meaning only in the mystery of Christ (and in the mystery of the Church), but that is also a way of acting in the world, a "worldy ethos." Where else must a person act in this life, if not in the "world"?

The distinctions between a "salvation ethos" and a "world ethos,," and the related distinction between a specifically Christian "intentionality" (at the transcendental level) and a principally human "worldly behavior" not specified by the Christian message, both appear to fall far short of one of the primary themes of the Second Vatican Council: the teaching that the salvation Christ is to bring should not simply be reduced to "the rescue of the soul"; that after this worldly existence one will reach salvation by leaving the world behind, and in unity with God. The latest Ecumenical Council has reminded us that salvation is comprehensive, that it has to do with the condition of the world and with overcoming the sin of the world; Christian behavior is therefore *redeemed* and *redemptive* action in the world that must change this world "in order to renew everything in heaven and earth in Christ" (Eph. 1:10). The Kingdom of God is not *of this world*, to be sure, and its growth must be sharply distinguished from worldy progress (see *Gaudium et Spes*, 39), but it is not only to be erected "beyond" this world: the "other world" is not meant as a category that reduces the worldly character of human existence (an existence that will be definitively assured only in the Resurrection), but rather lessens the "bound of death" of the individual, and points to the life after death. The Kingdom of God, we must say, includes the world and earthly progress—to the extent that it comes from love and is oriented toward love—and is of great significance for the growth of that kingdom (ibid.). Nevertheless, it will appear in its fullness only at the end of time, through a divine act of re-creation when "the shape of this world will pass away," and will prepare the way "for a new earth, where justice will abide," where love will remain, "and all that creation that God made on man's account will be unchained from the bondage of vanity" (ibid.).

An action that neither arises from the consciousness of the fallen state of the creation nor lives in the eschatological hope of the Resurrection and the New Creation is an action that is specifically other, a "worldly" but non-Christian action. This would point to a different situation of man, a different interpretation of his possibilities and hopes, and thus different norms of behavior. Since such action would lack both the "eschatological presumption" and the Christian hope that rises above the usual human horizon, the only meaningful actions would be those which have some measure of human success. This kind of behavior, which remains adrift between the anticipations of a fallen but redeemed creation, on the one hand, and an eschatological hope, on the other, will be understood in human terms as meaningless and inconsequential, as "inhuman" and without any binding moral force. Once again, a non-Christian ethos will reduce what is morally binding to the "humanly possible," and have only a partial grasp of the true possibilities of human action. To insist that the "worldly" norms of behavior of non-Christians are substantially identical with those of Christians is a position that requires abandoning the connection of the Christian message with any restoration of the fallen creation. (To impute to non-Christians an "anonymous" Christianity—to attest to an "unconscious" or "implicit" hope that they supposedly have—is to refuse to take seriously their *not being Christian* and ultimately, their freedom of conscience).

Theologians who put in brackets the relation between salvation and the world implied in the concept of a comprehensive salvation grow accustomed as well to avoid speaking of original sin, just as they tend to reduce the specifically Christian moral content to a matter of mere *intentions* that relate to an "other world." They forget, that is to say, that what is specifically Christian must come into realization in the world, because salvation is finally salvation of man *and his world*. Restoration of all things in Christ is not only a restoration on the horizon of hope for a future destiny, it is also a *present-day, worldly* responsibility of Christian love. The reality of human love, of its open possibilities and challenges, needs a Christian interpretation in the light of revelation. This in turn can lead to formulations of norms of action that could never be understood outside the context of the reality of love.

## X

The question of whether the Christian thereby shuts himself up in a "faith ghetto" (J. Fuchs), is finally not a question of theory but one of practice. If, in regard to his grasp of human moral capacity, the Christian is "not of this world," then in what regards his life, action, witness, and solidarity with *all* other human beings, he must be "of this world." "I do not ask that you take them out of the world, rather that you guard them from the evil one" (John 17:15). This means that essentially the Christian is called to live the Christian salvation ethos *as* a worldly ethos: to translate his faith into action in the world. This does not mean a call toward "secularization" (at least as usually interpreted), but rather toward a *secular existence* lived in faith. Such an existence is likewise a new, *specifically Christian, worldly ethos* of sharing in the priestly, prophetic, and kingly offices of Christ. It is an ethos that shapes new (categorial) ways of worldly action, in which the Christian promotes justice and understands himself to be building a "Civilization of Love" (Paul VI) as the "light" and "salt" of the world. This practical demand for a *Christian secularity* that brings faith in the Redeemer into all fields of society cannot be replaced by a demand to reduce concrete Christian norms of action to norms of the "merely" human. That would be a tragic misunderstanding. As long as one does not fall prey to this, the path is cleared to a truly supernatural, Christian, and Christ-centered morality of the Sermon on the Mount and the Beatitudes . . . and this is when the Philosopher must yield to the Theologian.

## NOTES

1. See especially J. Fuchs, "Das Gottesbild und die Moral innerweltlichen Handelns," *Stimmen der Zeit* 202 (1984): 363–382.

2. See J. Seifert, "Absolute Moral Obligations towards Finite Goods as Foundation of Intrinsically Right and Wrong Actions," *Anthropos* 1 (1985): 57–94.

3. J. Finnis, *Fundamentals of Ethics* (Oxford and New York, 1980), pp. 93ff.

4. This has been established by R. Spaemann, "Über die Unmöglichkeit einer universalteleologischen Ethik," *Philosophisches Jahrbuch* 88 (1981): 70–89.

5. This was established by G. E. Moore in opposition to a one-sided consequentialism. In considering various alternatives, our knowledge of the causality of consequences is too incomplete to permit an unambiguous judgment: "Accordingly it follows that we never have any reason to suppose that an action is our duty: we can never be sure that any action will produce the greatest value possible" (*Principia Ethica* [Cambridge, 1903], p. 149).

6. On this see J. M. Boyle, Jr., "Toward Understanding the Principle of Double Effect," *Ethics,* 90 (1980): 527–538.

7. For a thorough critique of this aspect of teleological ethics, as seen above all in the work of J. Fuchs, see G. Grisez, "Moral Absolutes. A Critique of the View of Josef Fuchs, S.J.," *Anthropos* 2 (1985): 155–201, esp. 156–163.

8. Congregation for the Doctrine of the Faith, *Instruction on Christian Freedom and Liberation* (March 22, 1986), p. 80.

9. *See* Second Vatican Council, dogmatic constitution on the Church *Lumen Gentium*, esp. chs. 2, 4, and 5; and the decree *Apostolicam actuositatem*, esp. chs. 1 and 2.

10. See A. Auer, "Hat die autonome Moral eine Chance in der Kirche?," in G. Virt, ed., *Moral begründen—Moral verkünden* (Innsbruck and Vienna, 1985), pp. 9–30, esp. p. 11: "The theological significance of the autonomy concept consists in disclosing the truth of salvation in a new way to contemporary man." See also J. Fuchs, "Autonome Moral und Glaubensethik," in D. Mieth and F. Compagnoni, eds., *Ethik im Kontext des Glaubens* (Freiburg, 1978), pp. 46–74, esp. p. 68: "Is it a meaningful possibility for us Christians to have an objectively ethically correct behavior amid our secularizing and secularized, humanistic and atheistic fellow men? Or do we necessarily live in a 'Faith ghetto'?"

# AUTHOR'S POSTSCRIPT (1995) TO THE ENGLISH EDITION

## A Few Remarks on the Origin of *Natural Law and Practical Reason*

In the Foreword to the original German-language edition of this book (*Natur als Grundlage der Moral*, 1987), I noted that "Since *better* is the enemy of *good*, not only must many gaps of material be anticipated, but also imperfections in a style of presentation, which will eventually prove to have been only preliminary, and in need of improvement." Indeed, my labors on *Natural Law and Practical Reason* have now turned out to be only a beginning.

To be exact, a whole new beginning! It was occasioned by two principal factors. First was my interest in the Thomistic reception of Aristotelian ethics. In this work (begun in 1981 but only recently published[1]) I discovered that my understanding of the "Thomistic" doctrine concerning the relationship between "nature" and "morality" (or the natural moral law) could not be reconciled with Aristotle's action theory or his doctrine of virtue. It seemed that I would have to decide between Aristotle and Thomas, until I realized that I had been imposing a viewpoint upon Thomas that was not at all his own. This is the assumption that practical judgments are ultimately grounded in theoretical judgments about the "order of nature"—that is, in a "knowing" of what I took to be the natural law. For Thomas, however—as it became increasingly clear to me—practical judgments are not derivations from theoretical judgments. Instead, the natural law itself, no otherwise than law in general (*ratio legis*), is a set of *propositions of the practical reason* (see *I–II*, q. 90, a. 1, ad 2um). This meant that a theory of the natural law was at the same time a theory of practical reason. This proved to be the key to Aristotle's action theory. It also meant that ethics has its starting point *not in metaphysics* but in reflection upon subjective experience of the person who acts, or the *practical reason.*

The second factor coincided with this fortunate "crisis" in my understanding of Thomas: an increasing involvement with the "autonomistic" school of Thomas interpretation. By this I mean the attempts of A. Auer, J. T. C. Arntz, F. Böckle, O. H. Pesch, K. W. Merks, and others to show that the "real" Thomas was the originator of what was then being called "autonomous morality": morality as the free creation of a rational being, completely free of any naturally given norms, and needing to be rediscovered in changing historical and cultural contexts. I understood the intention that lay behind the attempt, and it partly coincided with my own interests (see the Introduction). Especially challenging for me was a remark Franz Böckle once made in my direction (we were both giving talks at the Freiburg "Symposium on the Family" in 1981): what he was saying had already been said by Thomas, and the contrary doctrine had its source in misinterpretations of modern neo-scholastics.

I didn't have much in the way of reply at the time, but started to work on the problem. A catalyst for the process was the well-known attempt of the time to establish, in some way, the teaching of *Humanae Vitae* in human "nature," which was also the problem that lay behind the rise of "autonomous morality." The reproach of "biologism" directed by the critics of the encyclical did not seem to me to be off the mark—*as criticism not of the encyclical but of certain attempts to provide it with an argumentative justification.*[2] This led to a conviction that the current understanding of what makes an action "according to nature" was inadequate, as was the method of justifying such "correspondence."

At this point I came across an article by Germain Grisez, "The First Principle of Practical Reason."[3] Grisez was a foe of the "new morality" and a defender of *Humanae Vitae*, but at the same time was sharply critical of Neo-Thomism. Even though today my position is by no means identical with that of Grisez, I have him (as well as John Finnis[4]) to thank for a decisive impulse toward a new—and I think, better—reading of Thomas. This orientation was further reinforced by Wolfgang Kluxen's *Philosophische Ethik bei Thomas von Aquin* (a favorite source, by the way, of German-speaking representatives of "autonomous morality"). At first I had been skeptical about the book because of my earlier prejudices, but eventually both Kluxen and other scholars convinced me of the methodological autonomy of ethics vis-à-vis metaphysics.[5] I had also become certain that holding this position did not require me to adopt the position of "autonomous morality."

And that is finally how my point of view, as developed in *Natural Law and Practical Reason*, came to be formed.[6] I was in agreement with the representatives of "autonomous morality" in rejecting certain neo-Thomistic tendencies (especially those connected with Cathrein, Elter, Rommen, Manser, Mausbach, Ermecke, Prümmer, and the early Fuchs). Nevertheless, the Thomas interpretation of the "autonomist" school did not hold up under close inspection: it was clearly too ideologically "interested," and could make sense to me only in front of the "background" of an inherited dualistic antithesis of "nature" and "reason"; there was also a persistence of certain "physicalistic" thought patterns. The autonomistic school had unconsciously retained one of the greatest shortcomings of neo-Thomism: a physicalistic concept of action.

Nothing of the kind could be found in Thomas, who holds an intentional view of action. My perspective on the matter was sharpened by a few works of the analytical school (Kenny, Anscombe), and fuller treatments of the theme can now be found in my works that have appeared since: *Praktische Vernunft und Vernünftigkeit der Praxis* (1994) and *La prospettiva della morale* (1994). In any event, *Natural Law and Practical Reason* found itself in a no-man's land between two hostile fronts: traditional neo-Thomism, on the one side, and the "autonomous" interpretation of Thomas, on the other. A brief review of some of the more important reactions to my book since 1987 will show this clearly.

## The Reception: A Thematic Survey

The Foreword of the first edition includes a catalog of shocking statements made by Catholic moral theologians. These were statements that I considered the sorry fruit of the moral theological tendency I would be subjecting to criticism in my book, and

I placed the list at the very beginning of the study in order to alert readers to the seriousness of the issue. But this rather polemical start did not prove entirely successful.

The Foreword, in fact, was judged by many to be an act of aggression, and the moral theological establishment seemed to be puzzled about who had ever said such monstrosities! As I said in the Foreword, none of the statements were invented, and if someone read my book, he could have found an illustration of every one of the statements; I even made up a separate list for private circulation.[7] I received written queries from some moral theologians who were skeptical about the authorship of certain statements; after giving the reference, I was told "it was not meant in that way," or that I had improperly taken the statement out of its context.[8] I have decided to omit the Foreword in this edition, together with its disturbing catalog of quotations.

And yet all the stir about the "ominous Foreword" (which apparently spread quite widely) seemed to have been a kind of "distraction" maneuver. For the representatives of "autonomous morality," the book was perhaps more than anything else a challenge to their beloved alternative between "traditional neo-Thomism" and "autonomous morality," which the book tried to show was not so complete a disjunction after all. Because he considered this point especially "dangerous," Franz Furger[9] may have reduced his mention of the book to a footnote, with a brief aside to the reader that it needed no further attention, since it was merely another warmed-over version of the "neo-scholastic, deontological natural law doctrine of rationalism" that incorrectly sought support in Thomas Aquinas and stood in opposition to the movement of the Second Vatican Council. There were also a few remarks that apparently served to cast doubt on the honesty of my intentions.[10]

But other voices were also to be heard, such as that of J. Römelt,[11] who, although critical of my position, nevertheless attested that the book successfully showed that Franz Böckle, for example, had no justification in calling on Thomas Aquinas for support of his position. As Römelt said, one didn't need to go back to Thomas or call on him for support in order to defend the idea of "a free, creative subject." So this was one victory—at least with regard to Böckle's interpretation of Thomas.

By the professional Thomists, on the other hand, I was accused of grossly misinterpreting St. Thomas, and this came from the most diverse camps: not only traditional Thomists but also prominent Thomas scholars who interpret him more along the lines of modern subjectivist philosophy. But the book also received praise from the "Thomistic" side, for quite different reasons. And there was yet another debate that had less to do with my criticism of the "autonomy" concept than with "teleological ethics." In the following sections I will briefly review the reactions, according to theme.

*The Relation Between Practical Reason and Human Nature*

The first question concerns my basic thesis that the natural law is in its essence "practical reason" and cannot simply be identified with the "natural order." The morally good is thus not simply to be derived from "nature," whereas whatever of nature is morally relevant should always be thought of as being ordered by the practical reason.[12]

An important opposing voice in this connection was that of Leo Elders;[13] he saw me as a Kantian and a follower of Maréchal (I have never read Maréchal). Elders tried to break a lance with me in defense of the genuine Thomas: according to him, for Thomas "nature," and not "reason," is the foundation of morality.

My view that the natural law is a "participation de l'intellect humain à la sagesse avec laquelle Dieu gouverne le monde" is incomprehensible to Elders.[14] How could I have arrived at such an idea? Even though he thus refers to chapter 1, section "Statements about Natural Law . . . ," subsection "A 'Forgotten Text of Leo XIII . . .", he does not mention that in that very passage I was expressly repeating the teaching of Leo XIII on the matter (the encyclical *Libertas Praestantissimum*), and that I was expressing regret that this encyclical and its perspective had been largely forgotten by neo-Thomism. Elders may now have to revise his criticism in the light of the encyclical *Veritatis Splendor.*[15]

In any event, Elders continues, instead of doing what Thomas did—that is, ground morality on nature (as the title of the book would lead us to expect)—I had driven a new wedge between practical reason and human nature. But it is barely possible to refute Elders's criticism, since he has incorrectly reported my position and does not appear to have glimpsed the fundamental problem. This is the epistemological and methodological problem about how knowledge of the moral good (*bonum morale*) naturally arises in man: a knowledge that really belongs to the person (and *to that extent* is autonomous).[16] This also applies to the (very brief) remarks of J. Endres,[17] who at least considers my view possible.

A reaction similar to that of Elders comes from A. F. Utz,[18] who attacks above all my presentation of the relationship between metaphysics and ethics, between the "being"/"nature" of man and practical judgments; he finally arrives at the position that I have radically misunderstood Thomas's concept of the natural law.

I have good reason to fear that Utz also has completely missed the point that my critique of "essentialism" is concerned with a *methodological* problem. I do not in the least deny or call in question the connection between the "being of man" and the "moral good." In anticipation of such misunderstanding, I had expressly called attention to the point several times in the course of the argument. If Utz, in his disagreement with me, points to the fact that for Thomas, moral requirements follow unambiguously from "human nature," and not simply from the reason, he seems to have overlooked the fact that the question I was trying to answer was how a normatively relevant concept of "human nature" comes into being at all. Now, since the reason is itself a *component* of this human nature so constantly attested to, then the "nature" that is human can be grasped as *morally normative* only through the reason and its ordering function.[19]

As it turns out, Utz maintains precisely what I thought I had argued against in my book, namely, the position that "For Thomas, the natural law is a law in the sense of the natural sciences, that is, a law of being."[20] This statement is historically untenable. In Thomas's day, there was no "law" in the sense used in the modern natural sciences, with the meaning of "physical regularity." For anyone who lived before the modern era, the expressions *lex naturalis* and *lex naturae* could refer only to the phenomenon of *legislation* or *lawgiving* (*Gesetzgebung*), implying either an act of the reason (*ordinatio rationis*), as in Thomas, or an act of the commanding will, as in the voluntaristic tradition.

But even leaving that aside, it is sufficiently clear from studying the text that Utz does not come close to Thomas's point of view. Thomas's own words for law—*ordinatio rationis, propositio universalis rationis practicae, aliquid a ratione constitutum, opus rationis*, and *dictamen rationis*—all contradict the view that Thomas understood the natural law as a "regularity of nature" (like the "law of gravity"). And even if he *had* understood it so, the important question would still remain unanswered, namely, how such "laws" could be normatively binding, and which ones bind—or, rather, why does the "law of gravitation" not formulate anything of a morally binding nature whatsoever?[21] The reaction of this prominent neo-Thomist is a valuable confirmation that it is quite possible *not even to see* the problem that provided my point of departure.[22]

Utz entitled his review "In What Direction Does the Conscience Orient Itself?" "Wonach richtet sich das Gewissen?"). What he means is that the conscience orients itself toward the "laws of human nature," the "being of man," man's *physis*. Without wanting to dispute this in the least, my question was, rather, How does this "law of nature" or "being of man" come to *practical* application?[23] Utz may be surprised to read, in the encyclical *Veritatis Splendor* (59), that the conscience derives its truth from the "natural law," where natural law is described (with the words of St. Thomas and Leo XIII) as the "human reason itself, which commands us to do good and counsels us not to sin" (44), so that the practically preceptive knowledge of good and evil is exactly what is referred to as the "natural law." Thus the encyclical concludes that "The truth about moral good, as that truth is declared in the law of reason, is practically and concretely recognized by the judgment of conscience" (61). The conscience, therefore, is oriented toward the "natural law," that is, toward the knowledge of moral principles that belongs to human nature.

Of course, it was cause for rejoicing that this methodological refinement, as well as the rediscovery of the identity of the themes "natural law" and "practical reason," did win support from influential authorities in Thomistic philosophy. This was the case especially with regard to the relationship between *inclinatio naturalis* and the reason.[24] A. Léonard, in particular, has grasped and fully appreciated the complex problematic of the *lex naturalis* as the work of the practical reason.[25]

My perspective on the "practical reason," and the *lex naturalis* doctrine as a theory of the practical reason have been recognized by Thomists such as T. G. Belmans[26] and above all, G. Abbà,[27] to both of whom I am much indebted. The latter especially appreciated the Thomistic distinction between the *proprium* and the *debitum* that I found to be so important with regard to the natural inclinations, as well as the crucial differentiation of the immediately "preceptive" level from the reflectively "descriptive" level of rational acts.[28]

G. Abbà is also associated with a movement to rehabilitate classical virtue ethics. One of the purposes of my book was to establish the constitutive connection that exists between practical reason as natural law and the order of moral virtue. While this aspect was immediately noticed in the English-speaking world,[29] it appears to have been almost completely overlooked in the German-speaking world.[30] The same point also appears to be overlooked when it is objected that there can be a conflict and collision between natural inclinations, so that there must be a "weighing" after all—and this is precisely the task of a teleological theory of norms.[31] The theme of "moral virtue" will be treated again below.

### *The Relation Between Reason and Nature, the Problem of the "Natural Inclinations" and the "Human Good"*

Another reproach came from a totally opposite direction. Despite all my efforts, it was held that I had misunderstood Thomas, so that reason still wound up being "subordinated" to nature. This criticism was especially represented by Georg Wieland,[32] not only an outstanding scholar of medieval ethics but also one of the most prominent students of Wolfgang Kluxen. It appears particularly fitting to listen to what he said, especially when his voice harmonized with authors of similar leanings (e.g., W. Korff, L. Honnefelder, and J. Römelt[33]).

Wieland formulated his critique in a paper read before the International Union of German-speaking Moral Theologians and Social Ethicists.[34] Wieland's principal objection was that although

I knew that reason and freedom held supremacy in man over all natural determination through the natural inclinations, I nevertheless fell short of drawing the consequences of this insight. This consequence should have been a concept of the natural moral law, according to which this law would be largely reduced to the structure of practical reasonableness, but in such a way that no concrete moral norms, or indeed any norms of a universal and historically invariable kind, could be "derived" from it.[35]

In particular, Wieland faulted me for incorrectly judging the relationship between "natural inclinations" and "practical reason," which meant that I allowed the naturality of the *inclinatio naturalis* to become the rule for the reason, instead of recognizing that in truth it is the reverse: that the reason is there "to begin with," and not nature. Referring to Kluxen, Wieland writes as follows: "For in order for nature to be at all significant for the context of human action, man must be in a position to conduct himself in relation to nature, and that means that man must be thought of as rational and free at the outset. Thomas formulates the basic principle of all morality in the first principle of the practical reason, which must be presumed whenever someone is in a relation to nature at a practical level."[36]

Along with L. Honnefelder (likewise a student of Kluxen), Wieland maintains the position that the "structure of practical reasonableness in general"[37] is to be understood as normative with regard to nature. But this would imply that "morally good" ultimately means "reasonable." The norm "act morally" would be equivalent to the norm "act rationally." I do not maintain that this is absolutely an "empty formula" (*Leerformel*)—it can mean, for example, "always act on the basis of a responsible weighing of goods," or it can mean much more—and yet with Wieland the formulation "reasonableness" (*Vernünftigkeit*) seems to be reduced to a *formal* thought structure that appears completely undetermined with regard to content, and certainly without any determination through natural givens.

In the book I tried to make it clear that Thomas did not hold such a view. I believe that Wieland's (very differentiated) critique applies more to the traditional position than to my own. I do not maintain, in fact, that practical reason is normatively governed "to begin with" by the "natural tendency"; I maintain that the standard is ultimately the practical reason, but that the practical reason is nature, too. I understand that the reason, including the practical reason, can be thought of in all its actions as not independent from a determination through natural givens. This does not require, as Wieland appears to think, a dependence of the practical reason upon theoretical judgments (he thinks I have "flattened out" the difference between practical and theoretical judgments). Wieland's criticism presupposes the view (a physicalistic view, in fact, very questionable from the standpoint of action theory) that it is even possible in principle to conceive of voluntarily following the dynamic of a natural inclination *independently* of any judgments by the practical reason. This seems to me to posit a dualism between "reason," on the one side, and "natural inclination," on the other, which is what gives rise in the first place to the question, Which has the priority, "reason (freedom)" or "nature"?

Nevertheless, a human being who behaves "rationally and freely from the outset," and *only then* puts himself into relationship with the nature *that he himself is*, in order to dispose of this nature in a normative fashion and thereby fulfill the demands of moral responsibility, is inconceivable, at least insofar as we understand man to be a personal, existential unity of body and spiritual soul. "Natural inclination," that is to say, is *realiter* (that is, under the condition that we find ourselves in the realm of free action) always a *voluntarily followed* inclination, and that means it must be conceived *through reason* and must be seen within the horizon of reason as a "good," intelligible striving. This means that "natural inclination" is already something more than "mere nature," and yet, without the natural given, there could be neither an act of the will nor an act of the reason. *Reason would be grasping a void* like a light that has nothing to illuminate, and illuminates nothing until it is lost in infinite space.[38]

I mean to say that human "practical reason" and its principles are constituted in the voluntary carrying out of the natural inclination, and that this process, insofar as it requires an act of the will, is already cognitively integrated by the reason as a *bonum humanum*. Of course, this is what occurs in a fundamental way in the first principle of the practical reason (*bonum faciendum est . . .*), but to think that this act contains in itself the "structure of practical reasonableness in general," on the basis of which it then "makes a judgment upon" the natural inclination, would be mistaken. This judgment is not carried out *as such* in any given action: instead, the first principle of practical reason branches out into intelligible strivings that are nevertheless distinct in content; these strivings at the same time correspond to the first and most fundamental principles of the practical reason, giving the reason practical effect within a multiplicity of action fields.[39] This is why the concept of a structure of reason that "precedes" nature cannot be maintained. The human practical reason only exists *in* nature, is always bound up with nature, and is conditioned by nature. It is not "reason" that knows, but rather the *body–soul* unity, *as constituted in the person*, that knows *by means of* the reason. Wieland's interpretation, it seems to me, is still far too close to the dualism of reason and nature. It puts the two factors "side by side," and conceives of them as "added to" one another, instead of understanding them, as Thomas shows again and again, to be in a relationship of act and potency, or as a unity of form and matter.[40]

According to Wieland, this would mean "understanding the relationship of nature and reason in an essentially *reciprocal* fashion" ("Secundum naturam vivère," p. 25). I do not know if "reciprocity" is the proper expression for the relationship of matter to form. One could easily fall into a quarrel over terminology at this point. At any rate, I will return later to the real significance of this critique of "reciprocity."

I follow the explicit statement of St. Thomas[41] in holding that the *inclinatio naturalis* has a standard-giving function in relation to the ratio naturalis. This has the simple epistemological meaning that every act of knowing is somehow determined by a *res naturalis*, by some object that comes "from outside." Wieland appears to take the opposing position, that there are certain "principles originally present to the human reason" that are independent of determination through any natural inclination (ibid., p. 22, n. 33). But where do these "originally given" principles come from? The only thing given to the reason is the (in any case) formal structure of reasonableness (since everyone knows there are no "innate ideas" for Thomas). Why, then, this talk about a plurality of "given principles"?[42]

The question that had to be answered here was "How does it happen that survival, life, nourishment, and sexuality (i.e., the bond between man and woman) are human goods? Does the practical reason get these things "out of itself"? Or is it not, rather, the consequence of the fact that this practical reason is the reason of a bodily and sexually constituted human person? To repeat Wieland's statement, "For in order for nature to be at all significant for the context of human action, man must be in a position to conduct himself in relation to nature, and that means that man must be thought of as rational and free at the outset."

This sentence can be taken to have at least two different meanings. It can be understood first in a trivial sense, not significant for our present concern, that without reason and freedom, "nature" could not become meaningful for action, for there would be no "behavior" at all and man would not be the kind of being whose "doing" has anything to do with "morality," he would be merely a natural existent, and human action would be only a natural phenomenon. In a second sense, which is not at all trivial, the statement is not entirely without ambiguity, and this is something that becomes obvious when we posit some concrete example of "nature": the sentence, for example, would then say, "For in order for life (or "nutrition" or "sexuality," etc.) to be at all significant for the context of human action, man must be in a position to conduct himself in relation to it (i.e., life, sexuality, etc.), and that means that man must be thought of as rational and free at the outset." I think that the reality is the reverse: "In order for man to be rational and free in relation to life (nutrition, sexuality, etc.), these must be thought of at the outset as significant for human behavior . . . ." But this significance, as a natural given, does not arise from "naturalness" as such, but rather from the fact that such realities belong to the substantial unity of the "human person."

The question Wieland asks is "Whether the natural inclinations are already *bona humana* through their 'belonging' to the human being, or do they not become goods only through the ordering and integrating activity of the reason?" Now the very way this is formulated appears to present us with a false alternative. My answer would be, "Of course the natural tendencies (or, to be more precise, the ends to which they are oriented) are already *bona humana* by the fact of their belonging to the human being. But they become practical goods only in the context of action, and that means as objects of willing, which in turn means as objects of rational judgments." In other words, within the dimension of the practical, the natural inclinations cannot emerge onto the horizon of subjective experience except as objects of the *reason*. And they do this in each case as *intelligibilia*, as goods grasped as such by the reason, and judged on the horizon of rationality.[43]

When it comes to how "nature" is reflected in action, or "what I should or should not do" (the *debitum*) with respect to "life," "nutrition," or "sexuality," in each case this—so my argument goes—does not result from natural givenness. For this, human reason is the measure. This is why I wrote the sentences that Wieland takes to be a fundamental misinterpretation of Thomas (the emphasis was not in the original quotation): "the natural inclinations in themselves are only an 'indirect' rule or standard, or in other words they form the basis of the standard; *they still do not have the power to govern actions*. They are rather a standard and rule for the natural reason, *which in its turn is the rule and standard for actions, through its 'causing of order* [ordinatio] *in the natural inclinations'* " (chapter 2, section "The Constitution of Natural Law Through the *Ratio Naturalis*," subsection, "The Spontaneous Comprehension of Fundamental Human Values"; p. 79 in the German orig. ed.).

The underlying question that remains relevant for the whole issue is "How are we to think of the relationship between the *actus* or the 'proper end' (*finis proprius*) of the natural inclinations (their natural orientation) and the *debitum*, that which 'ought' to be done, the 'right' thing, the only way it can be objectified for the practical reason?" This question, as emphasized in the present work, is not answered by *I–II*, q. 94, a. 2, as I explain in the subsequent subsection ("The Integration of Fundamental Human Values into the Structure of Human Action"). Wieland appears to have seized upon the wrong passage for his criticism.

But to return to his critique that I (incorrectly) understand the relationship between reason and nature as "reciprocity," or as a mutual relationship of conditioning and dependence: instead of this, Wieland supports the idea that the "structure of rationality in general," as revealed in the first principle of the practical reason (*bonum faciendum est . . .*), is the practical a priori of every attitude taken toward the natural strivings. These strivings are not at the free disposal of man, but are still "the necessary condition for the rightness of the normative region."[44]

At the basis of this idea lies the presumption that "nature" (as the "natural") is merely "restrictive condition and limit," but not the "origin of ethical normativity."[45] This purely "negative role" of the natural, as seen in Wieland's thinking, means that nature "marks out," so to speak, the territory of the normative; it determines where, or in which areas, ethical normativity is required, without saying anything about the content of such norms.

My position, on the contrary, says that it is not possible to maintain a purely negative norm-giving role of the reason as a "limit," without understanding this "negative norm" as at the same time establishing norms that are positive in content. That would be just as impossible as to maintain that the "negative norm" *Thou shalt not kill* says something about death (i.e., that it "marks out" the boundaries of a normative field) without at the same time saying something about life, or about the relationship between human persons, or, in other words, about what is within the boundaries of the normative area.

To be sure, if "natural" (and thus "preethical") negative normativity were simply the ensemble of those givens that are not at the disposal of human power, this would be plausible to some degree. In any case, one would have to say that "nature" would in this case "set the boundaries" for very little, and, in fact, for increasingly less with the progress of technology and medicine. The "rightness of the normative region" would then be repositioned at every stage of progress. Then the "natural" would no longer be a "limiting norm" (*Grenznorm*), but simply the index of the actual state of technological capability.[46]

Therefore, if nature is going to be an actual limit, even a negative one, it can reveal this limiting character only in the framework of an ethical normativity, about what "nature" means as an ethically relevant limit. There is need, in other words, for an understanding about which "natural" structures not merely are beyond our control and "given," but that *ought to be* (since, given continual technological progress, any given structure could at any moment become subject to our control).

If nature is going to become understood as a limiting concept in the sense of an ethically relevant metanorm, then it must be something more than the "naturally given," to the extent that it provides the "necessary condition for the rectitude of the normative area." It is this only on the horizon of the reason, which here works as a measure, but only insofar as it meets with as "given" what it regulates.[47] "Reciprocity" is scarcely avoidable, although the term does not seem quite right. For the very point of my interpretation was to make clear that here we are dealing neither with "reason" nor with "nature," but with human persons, in whom nature and reason form a unity, where reason is itself "nature," and where the natural becomes visible as "human nature" only on the horizon of the reason.

On the other hand, the conception of a reason that stands over against the natural, in order to impose norms upon it in free but rational self-determination, seems very questionable. And in *Natural Law and Practical Reason* I presented a number of arguments on this matter, both in itself and with regard to the interpretation of Thomas.[48] In any event, Wieland and I are in agreement (in opposition to naturalism) that in actuality the reason does not simply grasp the natural and merely reproduce it in its own logic or simply confirm it in the mode of the "ought," to use Kluxen's formulation, in order to make it immediately subject to the moral difference between good and evil.[49] The objectification, through the reason, of every originally nonspiritual natural inclination gives that inclination, as a *practical good*, a new "form" at the level of spiritually formed personality. Thus human sexuality is essentially more than the naturally given "sexual drive"; human sexuality on the level of practical good that has been objectified by the reason and pursued by the will—that is, human sexuality in its truth—is nothing other than "married love," that is, a free, mutual self-giving of indissoluble permanence between two persons of opposite sex, in the totality of their body-soul existence: a love that serves the transmission of human life, whereby this transmission, again, is not merely a "natural function," but rather the very meaning of love as personal fulfillment. This is what I call the "truth of sexuality," and sexual acts that stand outside this context are in contradiction to it—that is, they are "immoral" in the objective sense—not because they are "unnatural," but rather because they contradict the (practical) *truth* of the natural, as it appears on the horizon of apprehension and regulation by the reason.

It should be clear that for such a complex structure, the term "reciprocity of nature and reason" would be inadequate, since there can never be a question of treating the relation between nature and reason (reciprocal or otherwise) as a relation between two "factors" that remain distinct from one another. There simply is no nature that stands over against a free, rational, "I"—no more than there is a free, rational "I" that has a body for it to stand over against. My body is what I am, and I am my body. To conceive of this bodily–spiritual unity of the "I" in categorial terms has ever been one of the most difficult tasks of philosophical reflection. As long as we speak of the nature *that we ourselves are,* it seems inappropriate to say that nature becomes "meaningful for the context of actions" only when the human person is thought of as "already at the outset rational and free." This is true, but trivial insofar as there can be action only through reason and freedom. But there is less truth about being "meaningful," since this reason—as practical—would simply grasp a void without the nature that we ourselves are. Without nature, the reason would have no meaning, even as reason.

### *The Problem of "Autonomous Morality" and "Teleological Ethics"*

This response to Wieland's very important criticism can be of service in bringing to the fore certain deeper dimensions of the problem, as well as its significance for anthropology. Although the question has first to do with the interpretation of Thomas, it has a decisive importance for contemporary philosophy as well.

However, when it comes to the question of "autonomous morality" and "teleological ethics (or "proportionalism"), we are only at the margin of Thomas exegesis, with the possible exception of the theme "object of the action." I would like to make a few matters clear in this regard, since I have recently treated the topic more fully in my book *La prospettiva della morale.*

Klaus Demmer took me to task[50] for constructing an argument that was intelligent, perhaps, but finally a *magnus passus extra viam*—a kind of overreaction, a false alarm, "overinterpretation" caused by a faulty understanding of the contemporary problems of moral theology and the true intentions of "autonomous morality"; the latter does not deny the necessity of objective moral norms, but only tries to ground this "objectivity" in a more comprehensive way.[51]

The representatives of an autonomous ethics point out over and over—often with irritation—that tradition had in fact always assumed that in the realm of the natural law, it was not only possible but indispensable to reach knowledge of moral norms on the basis of purely rational arguments. And this is exactly what "autonomous morality" is supposed to be: the autonomy of a "human and natural" morality and a rational insight, as opposed to revelation. There would be a corresponding need for discursive strategies of argument to justify the rectitude of actions in every situation.

The confused concept of autonomy put forward by A. Auer, as I tried to show,[52] leads not only to unclarity about the ethical grounding of norms but also to a conception of practical reason that, as I wrote, did not take sufficient account of anthropological points of reference. Or, to put it another way, the proponents of autonomous morality held that the traditional modes of proof based on recourse to the "nature of man" or the "will of God" are no longer possible, and that the one and only model of justification possible is the "teleological" one. This involves the weighing in each situation of the premoral goods and evils that can foreseeably result from concrete actions, something that must nevertheless (as Klaus Demmer says in his criticism) in every case be responsible to "governing anthropological models."[53]

But I believe that this critique avoids the deeper problem: the "weighing of goods" as such is not the problem, since this is quite legitimate and is really a basic method of practical reason at the level of prudence. Probably no critic of teleological ethics will maintain that concrete action is completely predetermined by a rigid system of moral norms—such moral norms must be rightly applied in concrete judgments about actions.

Such a way of thinking corresponds, rather, to "rule utilitarianism" or to what I call "norm utilitarianism."[54] This is the tradition to which teleological ethics is more indebted than its proponents care to admit: in fact, the "teleological" establishment of norms is one component of this doctrine, which is in rivalry with an ethics of virtue.

The issue is not the "weighing of goods" as such, but rather the area of the "absolute limits" of such weighing, or the determination of the area within which the weighing is permissible. This has to do with the uncrossable boundary around the area of fundamental goods that are constitutive of human identity, or "humanity" itself. In this region there must be completely unconditional prohibitions in order for man, as moral subject, not to put himself at his own disposal, and this pertains as well to the concept and significance of "morality" in general.[55]

If I may be permitted to use an example of a recent event: the French collaborator with the Nazis Paul Touvier argued before a panel of judges that with his order of June 28, 1944, to have seven Jews shot, he and the military chief of Lyons, Victor de Bourmont, prevented the killing of 100 Jews, as wished by the Gestapo chief of Lyons, Werner Knab. Thus Touvier claimed to have rescued ninety-three Jews. A liberal newspaper found this argument "in bad taste," and the judges were not won over in the least.[56]

Such cases of "weighing of goods" have always been used as examples by the opponents of teleological ethics. The question is not whether someone could not also conclude, by the method of weighing goods, that the "right way to act" would be simply to refuse to obey the command, or to collaborate at all. The problem of teleological ethics consists precisely in its readiness to "weigh" goods at all in such a situation, instead of thinking as follows: these people are innocent; they have done nothing to deserve punishment, nor have they been judged according to the law. Therefore, the only "right" (and, of course, also "good") answer to such a situation is "I cannot do that," even if one sees in advance that in this way a much greater number of people will die.

It is a fundamental perversion of moral discourse if someone must in principle and always look to the consequences and "weigh" them. The method cannot serve to clarify at any given moment whether a definite behavior is "in itself" objectively permissible or otherwise. In this connection, teleological ethicists typically bring up the classic "exceptional" or "borderline" cases.[57] The opponents of teleological ethics have come up with good arguments to overcome the problem, which is scarcely treated in this context by teleologists.[58]

But the really decisive point, in my view, is to show that the question of the "absolute limits," or of the "intrinsically evil action," becomes intelligible only in the context of a virtue ethics.[59] There is need for an ethical theory in which the "rectitude of striving" or "willing" is brought into connection with the choosing of concretely describable ways of behaving. This is the very idea of a virtue ethics. For the rest, E. Gillen agreed with my critique of "autonomous morality," saying that the inadequacy of "autonomous morality" consists in the fact that "the actually right action can scarcely be mediated to the ethical subject who wants to behave rightly and wants to realize himself in his action as a good or bad person."[60] Nevertheless, it is astounding to see that, for Gillen, my view (essentially the view of a "virtue ethics") that an intrinsece malum must "always be understood in relation to an ethical context" cannot be distinguished in praxis from the view of teleological ethicists (who support a "norm ethics") who "formulate well-grounded exceptions, in order to ward off an absolutistic and legalistic morality."[61]

But my theory of the "ethical context" is not "a theory of well-grounded exceptions" designed "to ward off" the logic of "an absolutistic and legalistic morality." It was never developed according to such a logic to begin with, and thus does not need to be "protected" from one. The idea of an "ethical context" reflects the fact that moral norms in no way constitute morality but only bring morality to expression in linguistic form. Norms reflect "human action" in detail, action that is always intentional.[62] Intentional actions never take place on the physical level in respect to which teleological ethicists establish norms.[63] Intentional actions are defined and are describable only in an intentional context, and this is what I describe as an "ethical context." Speech acts thus relate to the context of "justice of communication." Only in this context can it be indicated what a "lie" is, and how a prohibitive norm can be formulated and held to be "exceptionless." Then we no longer need a theory of "exceptions"; rather, it becomes clearer wherein really consists the corresponding moral good (or virtue), to which wrong behavior is opposed as morally evil.[64] In any case, it will then no longer be possible to permit a few favorite "well-grounded" exceptions, for example, the killing of unborn children "for a sufficiently grave reason."

### *Practical Reason, Conscience, Prudence, and Virtue Ethics*

As I have already mentioned, some critics appear to have missed the fact that the position represented in *Natural Law and Practical Reason* is that of a virtue ethics. This is an ethical theory that understands the perfection of practical reason to consist in the *habitus* that Aristotle calls *phronesis* and Thomas Aquinas calls *prudentia*: the virtue of prudence. I believe that only from this perspective can one adequately grasp the connection between practical reason as *lex naturalis* and the concrete, moral "ought."

Perhaps this aspect is not treated in this book as fully as it should be, since the theme, after all, is the natural law. The misunderstanding that easily arose from this was twofold: First, it was assumed that the book represented the view that a concrete judgment of action takes place simply through an application of the universal precepts of the natural law to the concrete situation—which is the task of the conscience. Second, it was assumed that I held the view that someone can derive the concrete determination of what is called for here and now from the general principles of the natural law, without any further mediation by experience. In other words, that it was a mere "theology of conclusions," or purely deductive and derivative ethics, according to which the concretizing of what is morally required was already "given" in the principles.[65]

Both reproaches arise from a considerable misunderstanding. Paradoxically, this is caused by the fact that these critics appear to be reasoning from a position that I fundamentally reject: namely, from the position of a "norm ethics"—from an ethical theory, that is, that does not conceive the normative as coming from "striving" and its rational fulfillment in moral virtue, but rather begins with the concept of the (normative) rule, in accordance with which striving is directed and on the basis of which it can then be judged (indeed, "morally" judged). Such rules would then, of course, have to be mediated with what is required by the concrete circumstances. Ethics then becomes a discourse about the "collision" of goods and duties.[66] But in no way whatsoever am I dreaming of a revival of casuistry.[67]

I have already pointed out, in my answer to S. Ernst, that the critics have missed the fundamental difference between reason's grasping of principles, on the one hand, and prudence, on the other.[68] Concrete action is not regulated by universal principles, and thus cannot simply be "derived" from them. Universal principles are always insufficient with relation to what is required *here and now.* The practical completion of practical reason is to be seen only in prudence, which is oriented toward particulars: what needs to be done concretely, here and now.[69]

Now this twofold reproach becomes completely problematic when it is formulated as it is by E. Schockenhoff, on the basis of an assumption that I wanted to maintain that the conscience is responsible for every concretization of what is required by the natural law. I am then supposed to limit this "concretization" to the mere "application" of universal commands of the natural law, and in the same breath, of course, I am thought to have reduced the conscience to the mere explicative and confirmative "instance" of a "pregiven" complex of norms. And thus Schockenhoff actually claims I hold that the "practical reason only has the task of 'reading off' the moral 'ought,' " in each instance, from its higher principles and of transforming this into a prescriptive judgment that is related to a concrete case.[70] In another context Schockenhoff describes my position as follows: "According to this understanding, the moral law meets man as something "already given" and "achieved," to which man must obediently submit; the conscience only has the function of recognizing the moral law and relating its demands to the moral subject" (*Das umstrittene Gewissen,* p. 107). This is indeed a strange reduction of my position.

First, the moral law (as precepts of the practical reason) does not "confront" man as something "pregiven and ready-made," in the sense of some naturally given thing, objectively there for human knowing; rather (as I wrote, making use of a phrase of T. Styczén), it is something noetically indispensable, the cognitive positing of which, however, is the task of the subject (see chapter 4, section "Personal Autonomy," subsection "Constitutive Autonomy"). The essential point is that the natural law is itself a work of the practical reason of the human being; it is, according to the concise formula of St. Thomas, the "light of understanding" that has been planted in us by God at our creation: through it, we know what we should do and avoid."[71] Only in the conscience does the natural law emerge as a command that may not be modified, as a "voice of truth." This presumes a differentiation between the principle-grasping reason (natural law) on the one side, and the judgment of the conscience on the other; but from this it cannot be concluded, as Schockenhoff attempts to conclude, that according to my view, the conscience fulfills its task of concretizing moral obligation simply by "transforming" the precepts of the natural law into a concrete judgment of action.

Such a conclusion is off the mark because, in my understanding, (1) judgments of conscience are not action judgments; and (2) the task of concretizing the "ought" contained in the principles of the natural law, and the task of "prolonging" it to concrete, situationally determined action, is really not the task of the conscience. Consequently, such concretizing is not being implied when it is said that the conscience has merely the function of "applying" the natural law to concrete action. Of course, this is ultimately a terminological problem, and it is never worthwhile to quibble about words only. But in a Thomistic context, the judgment of the conscience will be distinguished from the actual judgment of action, which Thomas calls the *iudicium electionis*: this is the really practical, concrete judgment, which, embedded in striving and affectivity, preceptively determines action *hic et nunc*. This is the judgment with which we really act (whereas the conscience is a judgment that someone can follow or not follow). This truly practical judgment is not at all a mere "application" of generally valid norms to single cases. Action judgments simply do not arise in this way.

In constructing a moral philosophy of Thomistic orientation, the function of the conscience must be clearly distinguished from that of the "choosing judgment" (*iudicium electionis*): not, to be sure, as two different faculties, but as two distinguishable ways in which the activity of the practical reason takes place. And this means (taking the reasoning one step further) that *prudence* must be distinguished from *conscience*.[72] Prudence, again, is the virtuous fulfillment of the choosing judgment (*iudicium electionis*); it is the virtue of the commanding or elective function of the practical reason,[73] and this takes place, in fact, on the level of the determination of the concrete *operabile*. On the universal level of the principles—the level of the *lex naturalis*—such a virtue is not needed, although it must be recalled that even these principles can be "lost"—can become difficult or impossible to see—through vice. This teaching is also found within the Aristotelian tradition. The perfection of the practical reason in its primary function of grasping principles, as the *lex naturalis*, is fulfilled in the immediate "choosing judgment" (*iudicium electionis*), which needs to be completed through (moral) virtue. This is how the judgment of action becomes a judgment of prudence. Of utmost importance here is the central Aristotelian concept (taken over by Thomas) of moral virtue as *hexis prohairetikê*, or *habitus electivus*.[74]

The conscience, by contrast, has another function: it is the reflective monitor of choosing and doing. Conscience "applies," in the mode of reflection, or moral knowing (general norms), to an action about to be done, to an action in the process of being done, or to an action already done, or to suggestions of the practical reason concerning all these, with the purpose of approving or prohibiting, urging on or restraining. The conscience judges the particular from the point of view of the universal, and it comes to the fore with all its weight when it *prohibits* the doing of what the practical reason judges, in its direction of actions, to be a plausible path, a possible way of acting, or a demand of the moment. The prudent man, in the ideal sense, would really need no conscience, since his conscience would never have to present itself (in its urgings, warnings, or prohibitions) as something *divergent* from the judgment of prudence.

But this does not mean that the conscience presents itself only negatively, as prohibitive. It also speaks in an affirmative, positively requesting way, but the positively formulated norm always remains behind the demand to do something concrete. It only provides a framework within which action can take place, and that must be further concretized. In a negative judgment (the validation of a prohibitive norm), on the other hand, the conscience is capable of making a particular determination by saying that something is not to be done *in any situation at all*. A universal negative, with its unconditionality, can reach the particular by saying, "This can never be done!"—that is, in every particular case this action must be omitted. Here is the line I cannot cross. But it must be repeated that this "application" of the universal to action takes place reflectively. Structurally speaking, it is a "supplementary" examination, and thus does not replace the real *iudicium electionis.* This latter function, as the fruit of a previous deliberation (*deliberatio*), will in any case often turn out differently as a result of a judgment of the conscience.

The actual *iudicium electionis* runs a different course from the act of the conscience. It arises from another kind of *applicatio* (see *II–II,* q. 47, a. 4, *applicatio rectae rationis ad opus*), which does not have the character of a subsumption of the particular under the universal, but entails, rather, a discovery of the means to the attainment of a given goal (the goals of the virtues are conceptually correlated with the principles or precepts of the natural law, while prudence, as the practical reason oriented toward the particular, directs concrete action toward these goals). Now this is precisely something that cannot happen through mere deduction from the universal (the principle); it happens, rather, through a *newer* and *deeper* grasp of the principle on the basis of *concrete experience,* which is itself cognitively guided by the principle.[75] Only in this way do we really understand completely what the principles contain. Moral knowing, like theoretical knowing, runs in two directions: from principles to particulars, and from particulars back to the principles.[76] Without a grasp of the principles and of situations, principles can become neither apparent nor usable. In a certain sense, the knowledge of a principle—of the universal—really begins with the concrete.

I cannot lightly shrug off the accusation that I am proposing an ethical theory according to which concrete moral guidance is simply "derived" from general norms, and that thereby moral action is reduced to the "fulfillment" of norms. With Thomas, things are not so simple,[77] and yet we still do not have to grasp at an interpretation that holds that every "principle" is dissolved into an "option" through the mediation of human empirical reasoning! For this is exactly the tendency of certain emphases of "autonomous morality." The communication of human knowledge leads all too easily into a "morality of experts," which ends with silencing the practical reason and the true moral autonomy of the individual.[78] Despite all the empirical knowledge of the human sciences, despite behavioral research, psychology, and the findings of the social sciences, the very point of ethics remains the ordering of the "empirical," the evaluation of it, and the overcoming of its "pressures," right at the horizon of the morally binding. For moral obligation is fundamentally not restricted to the empirically given—nor the "purely natural"—but rather always exceeds it for the sake of the human good. In this sense, the ethical reason cannot be reduced to another, merely empirical given. And yet, in order for this transcendence to remain practical and realistic, knowledge of the human sciences can offer indispensable help.

Practical reason, as I see it, is reason embedded in striving and providing a guide for action. Beginning with the principles of the *lex naturalis,* it becomes more and more concrete until the *iudicium electionis* is reached, whose habitual perfection is known as the virtue of prudence. Concretized practical reason, which meets what in particular is to be done, here and now, is practical reason in the stage of its highest perfection. This is because the job of practical reason is not to *know* but to *act*; and actions, unlike knowing, are always *particular.* This particular is in each case also the explication of some universal aimed at in principle, and when it departs from this, and moves out of itself, a reflective judgment can make this known and, at the same time, "intervene" in the process of the practical reason as a "higher voice" by warning or prohibiting. This "voice" is what we call the conscience. It is a judgment that applies the universal to the particular. But to maintain that this would require an ethics that reduces human action to the application of universal norms, and thereby slights the value of the conscience, is to overlook the entire teaching about the connection of practical principles with judgments about actions (*iudicia electionis*), as well as the related concept of moral virtue as an "elective habit" (*habitus electivus*); it means overlooking the fundamental theory of the practical reason, and especially its character as a prudence ethics and not a conscience ethics, which would take its starting point in the phenomena of laws and norms. This is why it is so important to understand that the doctrine of the natural law is not, fundamentally, a doctrine about a "law" (standing "over" man), but rather a doctrine about man's practical reason—and its principles.

## A Few Precisions, Corrections, and Supplements to the 1987 Text

Every author is indebted to his critics, because for the most part criticism is partly caused by lack of precision in the criticized author's logic or method of exposition. Many disagreements can help in the filling of gaps and in the discovery of obscurities in one's argument. Even though an author may not be convinced that his position is wrong, he can certainly be encouraged to think things over again, to arrive at some new insights, and to try to develop his argument further.

Something like this took place even while I was engaged in the writing of *Natur als Grundlage der Moral.* The book is the documentation of a process of reflection, and this explains why many important aspects came to be expressed only in the final chapter, and these ideas became the subjects of subsequent works.

In what follows, I would like to point out some of the passages in the book where the ideas have been more fully developed in other publications. At the same time, I can refer to some important contributions to the problems by other scholars (see the Bibliographical Supplement).

### *Chapter 7, Section "The Concept of Moral Action and the Proper Subject of Ethics," Subsection, "The Proper Subject Matter of Ethics"*[79]

The definition here of "the proper subject matter of ethics" is too little developed in terms of action theory. In this connection, a more exact analysis of so-called "intentional actions" would be especially helpful. This way, I could more clearly ground the central connection between the "rectitude of actions" and "good action in the context of virtue"—and in particular, the inner connection of "striving" and "action"—so that the "rectitude of actions" can always be described in terms of the "rectitude of a striving/willing," which would in turn make questionable the distinction between "good" and "right" with regard to actions. The direct connection could then be seen between "the rectitude of action" and the "goodness of the person."[80]

### *Chapter 8, Section "The Naturalistic (Physicalistic) Basis of Teleological Ethics"*

The style of argument used against teleological ethics is "metacritical," that is, I tried to uncover *immanent* contradictions within the position. With regard to the position as such, this kind of criticism can be very efficient, at least for those who take self-contradiction as a sign (or at least a preliminary sign that may later be refuted) of the falsity of the doctrine. But such criticism is not absolutely convincing for those who have already adopted the position of "teleological ethics" for pragmatic reasons or, as they may put it, for "pastoral" reasons. Their hope, of course, is that this will be a "more human morality," where the criterion of "humanness" is not the *truth* of the ethical doctrine, but its capacity to arrive at certain desirable results. In this case, it is the capacity to establish exceptions from absolute prohibitions and to keep such unhappy thoughts as "never" away from the conscience.

In *La prospettiva della morale* I take a different course, which I had prepared in other writings, and I criticize teleological ethics on the basis of a special, fully established position of virtue ethics.[81] This is a more constructive kind of criticism, for it shows a way out of the dilemma. But it appears to be successful only if someone is willing to free himself from the traditional perspective of norm ethics, while at the same time opening oneself to the possibility of the existence of so-called "actions that are evil in themselves" (and for the contemporary moral theologian this will cost a certain amount of "acceptance" and popularity).

### *Chapter 9, Section "Physicalism and the Naturalistic Fallacy in the 'Weighing of Goods' "*

The lack of action-theory analysis in my criticism of F. Böckle caused a few obscurities (especially, the subsection " 'Values' and 'Goods' " of the above section). I am trying to establish here (not quite correctly) that "human life" is a moral good (as distinct from mere "physical integrity"). The obscurity arises from the fact that "human life" also (and "physical integrity, too, for that matter) emerges only as moral good in the perspective of praxis, that is, as the subject of a choosing or intending will. My argument here (and in the subsection "The Derivation of Moral Claims from Premoral Goods" of the above section) was essentially concerned with showing something I believe is still quite valid. Using the example of Böckle, I tried to show that, according to the logic of his position, every "willing adoption of a position" (*willentliche Stellungnahme*) toward "life" remains in principle on the premoral level, and thus the perspective of praxis is completely lost.[82] But I think my later, more fully action-theoretical argument, is clearer and more complete.

*Chapter 9, Section "The Hidden Deontologism of Teleological Ethics," Subsection "The Problem of Reconstructing a Hierarchy of Actions and Moral Values"*

Here, too, the concept of action is not sufficiently clear. The concept "intentional action"—as employed in the later chapter dealing with the special problems of the *voluntarium indirectum* and the *intrinsece malum*—could have been used here as well, to improve the clarity of the presentation. But the purpose of this section was to show that even this ordering of concretely describable modes of acting (*Veritatis Splendor* now speaks of "modes of behavior") and moral qualification ("morally good"—"morally bad") can only be grounded in the framework of an ethics of virtue; that is, in the framework of an ethics where the point of departure lies in the "basic fact" of intentional actions, and finally, from what I have later come to call "basic action," or "intentional basic action," drawing on the teminology of Danto.[83]

In this matter the decisive point is made in a passage of *Natural Law and Practical Reason* (chapter 7, section "Concluding Remarks") is "Every action is essentially a willing." This is precisely what grounds the "moral perspective" in all its dimensions, even those ultimates concerned with striving for happiness, for what all of us always want is the fulfilling of our desire (which follows from the very nature of willing). Now this fulfillment is what we ultimately call "happiness" (*Glück*) or, as classically stated, "blessedness" (*Glückseligkeit*).[84] A thorough treatment of the action-theory side of the Aristotelian tradition, especially the connection between the Aristotelian doctrine of the virtues and the Thomistic concept of the *lex naturalis* as a teaching on practical principles, can be found in my study *Praktische Vernunft und Vernünftigkeit der Praxis* (1994).[85]

*Chapter 10, The Objectivity of Human Action: The Object of Action and the Practical Reason*

The analysis of the "object" as the "basic content" of intentional actions is treated systematically and in detail in *La prospettiva della morale,* ch. III, where there is also a discussion of the "absolute prohibitions" (killing and lying). "Killing" is grounded as an absolute prohibition, without recourse to the category of the "innocent" (which is restricted to the context of justice).[86]

*Chapter 12, Section "The Problem of the Contingency of the Matter of Actions," First Three Subsections*

For this theme, the distinction made in *La prospettiva della morale* between "practical principles" and "moral norms" would have been useful in order to clarify some points (above all, concerning the question of exceptions, dispensation, and *epieíkeia* with regard to the natural law, see subsection "Exceptions, Dispensations, *Epieíkeia*"). Also compare chapter 12, note 23, where the same distinction is already hinted at. It would have been helpful here to fill out the picture somewhat: the question is differently posed, depending on whether negatively or positively formulated norms are at issue. "Norms valid without exception" are, strictly speaking, formulated only negatively, as prohibitive norms.[87]

*Chapter 13, "Some Philosophical Conclusions and Prospects for Moral Theology" Points 8 and 9, concerning the proper subject matter of Christian morality,*[88] have been treated anew and in more detail, beginning with the question of whether there is such a thing as a specifically Christian humanism.

Martin Rhonheimer
March 23, 1995

## NOTES

1. M. Rhonheimer, *Praktische Vernunft und Vernünftigkeit der Praxis: Handlungstheorie bei Thomas von Aquin in ihrer Entstehung aus dem Problemkontext der Aristotelischen Ethik* (Berlin, 1994).

2. See M. Rhonheimer, *Sexualität und Verantwortung. Empfängnisverhütung als ethisches Problem* (Vienna, 1995).

3. In A. Kenny, ed. Aquinas. *A Collection of Critical Essays.* (London, 1969), pp. 340–382.

4. Especially his *Natural Law and Natural Rights* (Oxford, 1980) and *Fundamentals of Ethics* (Oxford and New York, 1983).

5. See, for example, the works of T. Styczén cited in the Bibliography.

6. Let me recall here my gratitude (as expressed in the Foreword of the original edition) to Wolfgang Kluxen, not only for his reading of my manuscript, encouragement, and constructive criticism, but also for his personal efforts to find financial support for publication. In this connection I would also like to thank the Union of German Dioceses (the German Bishops' Conference), the Archdiocese of Cologne (Cardinal Höffner), and the Lindenthal Institute.

7. Against this, F. Furger ("Moraltheologie nach dem Konzil," *Schweizerische Kirchenzeitung* 43 [1987]: 668) wrote, "Despite the abundant notes, exact references are lacking to the monstrosities mentioned in the Foreword, supposed to have been put forward by Catholic moral theologians." As I said, the references are all there in the book (naturally not in the Foreword as well). I am grateful to this reviewer for confirmation that the statements in question can in fact be called "monstrosities."

8. One concrete illustration of this is the statement by F. Scholz about the "nonproportionality" of the measures taken by the Third Reich to kill Jews. The statement is quoted with reference on p. 371 of the German edition (part II, ch. 7.1.9, n. 127 [in the present English edition, chapter 11, n. 29]), and the quotation is made from a very well-known book of Scholz. In regard to this statement as given in the Foreword, K. Demmer (in his review in *Gregorianum* 70 [1989]: 166), said, "It would be interesting to know which Catholic moral theologian seriously represented that position."

9. "Moraltheologie nach dem Konzil," p. 668. Furger is Director for Christian Social Sciences at the University of Münster.

10. My answers to Furger's criticisms are in the *Schweizerische Kirchenzeitung* 46 (1987): 720.

11. *Zeitschrift für Katholische Theologie* 2 (1989): 211–216; see 213.

12. A more thorough treatment of this question can be found in my book *La prospettiva della morale* (Rome, 1994), especially ch. III, sec. 5e. See also M. Rhonheimer, "Zur Begründung sittlicher Normen aus der Natur. Grundsätzliche Erwägungen und Exemplifizierung am Beispiel der I.v.F.," in J. Bonelli, ed., *Der Mensch als Mittel und Maßstab der Medizin* (Vienna, 1992), pp. 49–94.

13. *Doctor Communis* 42 (1989): 167–174.
14. Ibid., p. 167.
15. See esp. chs. 38–45 of this encyclical as well as my commentary, "L' uomo, un progetto di Dio. La fondazione teonomica dell'autonomia morale secondo l'Enciclica *Veritatis Splendor*" in *L'Osservatore Romano,* Nov. 5–6, 1993, pp. 1, 4. In more detail, my "Sittliche Autonomie und theonomie gemäß der Enzyklika *Veritatis Splendor,*" *Forum Katholische Theologie,* 10,4 (1994): 241–268; in Spanish, "Autonomia y teonomia moral según la encíclica *Veritatis Splendor,*" in G. del Pozo Abejón, ed., *Commentarios a la Veritatis Splendor* (Madrid, 1994), pp. 543–578.
16. Among other things, Elders reproaches me for speaking of the "intellect naturel," a concept never used by Thomas. (I speak of the "natural reason" or *ratio naturalis,* a concept one finds quite frequently in Thomas). He then accuses me of "intuitionism," because I believe that the *first* principle of the practical reason cannot be proven, since it is immediately evident (*per se notum,* as Thomas says of it). This in fact is "intellectual intuition," the existence of which was expressly disputed by Kant. Elders further chides me for using the expression "teleological" ethics to describe the proportionalist and consequentialist schools of the "weighing of goods," since in reality only Aristotelian and Thomistic ethics deserve this name! His conclusion is that I am denying "teleology" in morality, and along with it the fundamental desire for happiness. I do recognize that *Natur als Grundlage der Moral* scarcely dealt with the question of happiness, but this was a necessary result of having to focus on one theme.
17. *Ordenskorrespondenz,* no. 3 (1988): 373–374.
18. In a review entitled "Wonach richtet sich das Gewissen?" *Die neue Ordnung* no. 2 (1988): 52–156.
19. See also R. Spaemann, *Das Natürliche und das Vernünftige: Aufsätze zur Anthropologie* (Munich, 1987), and *Glück und Wohlwollen. Versuch über Ethik* (Stuttgart, 1989).
20. Utz, "Wonach richtet sich das Gewissen?," p. 155.
21. In this connection see the valuable qualification given in the *Catechism of the Catholic Church,* para. 1955 (cited in *Veritatis Splendor,* 42), where it is explained that the natural law is called *natural* "not in reference to the nature of irrational beings, but because reason which decrees it properly belongs to human nature."
22. An exchange of letters between us and a personal and very friendly conversation have done nothing to change this situation.
23. In my judgment it seems that this was not sufficiently realized by V. Hildebrandt, *Virtutis non est virtus. Ein scholastischer Lehrsatz zur naturgemässen Bestimmung vernünftigen Handelns in seiner Vorgeschichte*

(Frankfurt 1989), esp. pp. 187–224. His criticism of my position appears rather hastily conceived and superficial.

24. So, for example, the review of F. A. Bednarski in *Angelicum* 64 (1987): 664–667. See also the very thorough review by C. Vansteenkiste in *Rassegna della Letteratura Tomistica,* 23 (1990).

25. See Léonard's account in *Studia Moralia* 26, 2, pp. 291–300, and also A. Léonard, *Le fondement de la morale. Essai d'ethique philosophique* (Paris, 1991).

26. *Forum Katholische Theologie* 4, 2 (1988): 152–154.

27. *Salesianum* 50, 2 (1988): 453–454.

28. See G. Abbà, *Felicità, vita buona e virtù. Saggio di filosofia morale* (Rome, 1989), p. 183.

29. See the review of G. Simon Harak, S.J. in *Theological Studies* (June, 1988): 358–359.

30. And this is true not only of Catholic authors: See the thoroughgoing, critical, but just review by the evangelical social ethicist Martin Honecker: "Paradigmenwechsel in der katholischen Moraltheologie," in *Theologische Rundschau* 56 (1991): 437–445.

31. This is maintained by K. W. Merks, "Autonome Moral," in D. Mieth, ed., *Moraltheologie in Abseits? Antwort auf die Enzyklika "Veritatis Splendor* (Freiburg im Breisgau, 1994), pp. 46–68, at p. 61.

32. G. Wieland, "Secundum naturam vivere. Über das Verhältnis von Natur und Sittlichkeit," in B. Fraling, ed., *Natur im ethischen Argument* (Freiburg i. Ue./Freiburg im Breisgau, 1990), pp. 13–32, esp. pp. 21–26.

33. See, for instance, J. Römelt, "Der neue Streit um den Naturbegriff," *Theologie der Gegenwart* 31 (1988): 187–192; L. Honnefelder, "Natur als Handlungsprinzip: die Relevanz der Natur für die Ethik, in L. Honnefelder, ed., *Natur als Gegenstand der Wissenschaften* (Freiburg and Munich, 1992), pp. 151–183. Recently K. Hedwig also appears to take Wieland's view to be the most accurate to date: see K. Hedwig, "Über die Theorie der Praxis bei Thomas von Aquin," *Philosophisches Jahrbuch* 99 (1992): 245–261. The position can also be found as a textbook doctrine in A. Anzenbacher, *Einführung in die Ethik* (Düsseldorf, 1992), pp. 87ff.

34. I still do not understand why the person responsible for organizing the—closed—session rejected the petition made by some of his colleagues to invite me to it, even though, as I was afterwards informed, the session appeared to have been dominated by discussion about my book.

35. This reproach of "derivation" was also taken up by S. Ernst: see his "Hat die autonome und teleologische Ethik die Objektivität sitt-

lichen Handeln vergessen? Marginalien zu M. Rhonheimer's Buch Natur als Grundlage der Moral," *Theologie und Glaube* 78 (1988): 80–89. My answer to this appeared under the title, " 'Natur als Grundlage der Moral': Nichts als Spiegelfechterei? Anmerkungen zu Stephan Ernsts Marginalien," *Theologie und Glaube* 79 (1989): 69–83 (and a rebuttal by S. Ernst can be found in the same issue at pp. 84–87).

36. Wieland, "Secundum naturam vivere," p. 25. This reviewer formulates two questions that he handles separately. The first question is whether the activity of reason that orders the natural inclinations is itself ever once bound, in its turn, to material normative givens which emerge from "nature," or whether the reason carries out its ordering solely on the basis of the structure of practical reasonableness? The second question is whether the natural inclinations are not already *bona humana* simply because of their being included in human nature, or must they not rather become so only through the ordering and integrating activity of the reason? In my view, the answer to both questions depends on the same consideration, so I will take the liberty of answering both at the same time.

37. L. Honnefelder, "Die Begründbarkeit des Ethischen und die Einheit der Menschheit," in G. W. Humold, W. Korff, eds., *Die Welt für morgen. Ethische Herausforderungen im Anspruch der Zukunft* (Munich, 1986), p. 320.

38. This is why I write in chapter 2, section "The Constitution of the Natural Law Through the *Ratio Naturalis,*" subsection "The Spontaneous Comprehension of Fundamental Human Values" (p. 79 of the original German ed.), that the natural reason "does not lord it over these inclinations: it can neither bring them into existence nor even become "free" of their dynamism without completely forfeiting the possibility of a fundamental and specifically human practical knowledge."

39. The demonstration of this plurality, by the way, is precisely the theme of the text of Thomas under discussion here: *I–II,* q. 94, a. 2. Thomas's doctrine on the necessary "branching-out" of the first principle according to the contents of particular actions has been recognized of late by Böckle, to an unusual length, in a passage full of vague formulations: "Was bedeutet Natur in der Moraltheologie?" in F. Böckle, ed., *Der umstrittene Naturbegriff. Person-Natur-Sexualität in der kirchlichen Morallehre* (Düsseldorf, 1987), pp. 45–68, esp. pp. 54–58.

40. I do understand and share, however, Wieland's concern not to confuse the distinction between human praxis and events; but this distinction is available only when practical reason "remains capable of putting itself expressly into relationship with what it depends upon" (Wieland, "Secundum naturam vivere," p. 23). I will not go further at

this stage into the relationship between the *lex aeterna* and the *lex naturalis,* which is first touched on here, but what he says applies as well to the relationship of reason to nature. The question is, what does it mean "to relate oneself to nature in a practical perspective" (p. 25). Does it mean insofar as the nature that we ourselves are is implied, meaning the "natural tendencies" of the self? Would not a "practical perspective" be fundamentally constituted only through such a tendency? Is not practical reason practical for just this reason, that it is "embedded" in the striving dynamic of the natural inclination?

41. *I–II,* q. 91, a. 3, ad 2um. Wieland took note of the Latin pronoun *ei* that had been omitted in a footnote quoting St. Thomas; this was not an intentional omission, just a misprint. My argument is based on the correct text, as quoted later in the book (p. 237 of the German edition, n. 122 [ch. 6, section "The Extension of the Natural Law," subsection "Another Look at *I–II,* q. 94, a. 2" note 74]).

42. If Thomas speaks in *I–II,* q. 91, a. 3, ad 2um about *Principia ei* [sc. *rationi*] *naturaliter indita,* he surely does not mean as Wieland suggests, an a priori content of the reason in the sense of "innate ideas." Rather, he is referring to the principles mentioned in q. 94, a. 2. In that passage he says of them that they are understood *naturaliter* as bona, and thus to be "carried out in action." *Even a natural habitus* is never an a priori for Thomas, but is something we must acquire, even naturally (through a *cognitio* or apprehension), that is, with a natural spontaneity, from which the individual cannot escape.

43. This is treated in more detail in my later book, *La prospettiva della morale,* V. 1, 239–248. On this horizon, then, "practical reasonableness" (as Finnis has so convincingly argued) is itself a human good. Wieland also discusses the difference between the anthropological-existential constitution of the *bonum humanum* ("Secundum naturam vivere," p. 24) and its practical constitution. In this matter he is at least partly correct.

44. For this point Wieland refers to Kluxen's article "Menschliche Natur und Ethos," *Münchener Theologische Zeitschrift* 23 (1972): 1–17, esp. 3–11.

45. Ibid. Kluxen, pp. 5 ff., and Kluxen's *Ethik des Ethos,* (Freiburg and Munich, 1974), esp. pp. 27ff.

46. This point also seemed unclear to W. Korff, according to whom the *naturales inclinationes* are not "mere material of the acting reason," but really "free the reason from arbitrariness"; see W. Korff, "Der Rückgriff auf die Natur. Eine Rekonstruktion der thomasischen Lehre vom natürlichen Gesetz," *Philosophisches Jahrbuch* 94 (1987): 285–296, esp. p. 289; see also Korff's *Wie kann der Mensch glücken? Perspektiven der Ethik* (München, 1985).

47. This is the point of my repeated statement—noted but not fully appreciated by Wieland—that the reason does not effect an ordering *of*, but rather *in* the natural inclinations.

48. See also R. Spaemann, *Das Natürliche und das Vernünftige, Aufsätze zur Anthropologie* (Munich, 1987).

49. Kluxen, "Menschliche Natur und Ethos," p. 15.

50. See his review in *Gregorianum* 70 (1989): 166–167.

51. This was the view also of S. Ernst in his "Hat die autonome und teleologische Ethick. . . ."

52. I have been defended in this by E. Gillen, *Wie Christen ethisch handeln und denken. Zur Debatte um die Autonomie der Sittlichkeit im Kontext katholischer Theologie* (Würzburg, 1989), p. 93. The author of this comprehensive dissertation (with a preface by Franz Böckle) is of the opinion that I had, finally, not sufficiently taken into account "autonomous morality" in its simplicity. On the other hand, he (correctly) classifies my position as belonging to "autonomous morality" in the sense of holding up the possibility of an establishment of moral norms independently of faith, in the realm of "natural morality" (this sense of "autonomous morality" is favorably used also in *Veritatis Splendor*, 74–75).

53. K. Demmer, *Moraltheologische Methodenlehre* (Freiburg i. Ue and Freiburg im Breisgau, 1989), p. 144, note 58.

54. See *La prospettiva della morale*, pp. 275ff.

55. See also M. Rhonheimer, "Menschliches Handeln und seine Moralität. Zur Begründung sittlicher Normen," in M. Rhonheimer, A. Laun, and T. Goritschewa, *Ethos und Menschenbild. Zur Überwindung der Krise der Moral* (St. Ottilien, 1989), pp. 45–114.

56. See also M. Rhonheimer, "Intentional Actions and the Meaning of Object: A Reply to Richard McCormick," *The Thomist* 59, 2 (1995); see also the case of the physicians (reported by R. Spaemann, "Nochmals: Deontologische oder teleologische Moralbegründung?," *Herder Korrespondenz* 37 [1983]: 80) who cooperated in the Nazi euthanasia program in order to save lives, but who were later convicted by the Federal German court. On this also see M. Rhonheimer, "Ethik–Handeln–Sittlichkeit. Zur sittlichen Dimension menschlichen Tuns," in J. Bonelli, ed., *Der Mensch als Mitte und Maßstab der Medezin* (Vienna, 1992), pp. 137–174, esp. pp. 161f.

57. J. Gründel used this method in his critique; see J. Gründel, "Spannungsfelder der Moraltheologie," in *Zur Debatte* (January/February 1989): 15f. Also similar are the final arguments of S. Ernst in his rebuttal to my reply, *Theologie und Glaube* 79 (1989):84–87. And B. Häring reacted in the same way to the Encyclical *Veritatis Splendor*: see B. Häring, "A Distrust That Wounds," *The Tablet* (Oct. 23, 1993): 1378–1379.

58. The way the otherwise very subtle Demmer reacts to this is very symptomatic (see the review cited in note 46 above): "The author employs an expanded critique of teleological norm justification. It is not a new one." With that remark, his reply is finished. S. Ernst (see note 35 above) has this remark about the chapters in which I begin the extensive critique of autonomous and teleological morality: "The criticisms of autonomous and teleological morality are familiar, so that we only need refer to what I have already said. . . ." An exception here is W. Wolbert, who always brings in concrete opposing arguments, even though these arguments are not completely convincing in my view. *Cf.* now W. Wolbert, *Vom Nutzen der Gerechtigkeit. Zur Diskussion um Utilitarismus und teleologische Theorie [Studien zur theologischen Ethik,* 44], (Freiburg i. Ue/ Freiburg i. B, 1992) e.g. p. 72.

59. See also M. Rhonheimer, " 'Ethics of Norms' and the Lost Virtues: Searching the Roots of the Crisis of Ethical Reasoning," *Anthropotes* 9, n. 2 (1993): 231–243; and also " 'Intrinsically Evil Acts' and the Moral Viewpoint: Clarifying a Central Teaching of *Veritatis Splendor,*" in *The Thomist,* 58,1 (1994): 1–39.

60. Gillen, *Wie Christen ethisch handeln und denken,* p. 113.

61. Ibid., p. 110; Gillen refers here to p. 370 of the German original (where this point is treated in part II, ch. 9.3).

62. For a more detailed treatment of the difference between "practical principles" and "moral norms," with respect to the analysis of "norms" as a linguistic expression of the normative content of intentional actions, see *La prospettiva della morale,* esp. V.3.

63. This is shown clearly and significantly in B. Häring's reaction to *Veritatis Splendor* (see note 57). Häring maintains that the *Catechism of the Catholic Church* teaches that there are "exceptions" to negative norms: "For example, the prohibition against killing can be set aside in cases of self-defense, exaction of the death penalty, and even just wars" (p. 1378). Häring complains in this article that the Pope does not take moral theologians like himself seriously, but he himself fails to consider any position that tries to solve the problems he mentions in any manner other than the proportionalistic one. The problem is that Häring does not relate the prohibition of killing to actions that can be described as intentional actions, and therefore holds that this is a matter of "exceptions."

64. See also *La prospettiva della morale,* V.3d).

65. See E. Schockenhoff, *Das umstrittene Gewissen. Eine theologische Grundlegung* (Mainz, 1990), esp. pp. 80ff.; and S. Ernst, "Hat die autonome und teleologische Ethik . . . ," p. 86.

66. See also *La prospettiva della morale,* p. 275ff; 297ff. The difference between a "striving" ethics and a "rule" ethics ("moral philosophy")

has recently been clearly worked out (although from quite a different point of view) in H. Krämer, *Integrative Ethik* (Frankfurt, 1992); Krämer tries to attain a synthesis of both, and conceives a "striving" ethics as "postteleological," but again, that is no longer an ethics of virtue.

67. Unfortunately, in this respect thinking runs too much in terms of alternatives that are by no means necessary: so M. Honecker, "Paradigmenwechsel in der katholischen Moraltheologie," *Theologische Rundschau* 56 (1991): 437–445. The article assumes that my position leads to a traditional norm ethics; I think that this need not occur, provided the components of virtue ethics and prudence are kept in mind.

68. Rhonheimer, "Natur als Grundlage der Moral: Nichts als Spiegelfechterei?," pp. 77ff.

69. See, in more detail, Rhonheimer, *Praktische Vernunft und Vernünftigkeit der Praxis,* pp. 361, 575.

70. Schockenhoff, *Das umstrittene Gewissen,* pp. 80. The same criticism has been made of A. Laun, *Das Gewissen. Oberste Norm sittlichen Handelns* (Innsbruck, 1984), a book to which I owe many valuable insights.

71. *In Duo Praecepta,* Prologus, no. 1129. This very expression, like the one of Leo XIII mentioned before, was taken up by the encyclical *Veritatis Splendor.* See also the works cited in note 15.

72. See now the detailed treatment in my *Praktische Vernunft und Vernünftigkeit der Praxis,* pp. 383ff.

73. On this see A. Rodríguez Luño, *La scelta etica. Il rapporto fra libertà et virtù* (Milan, 1988).

74. See my *Praktische Vernunft und Vernünftigkeit der Praxis,* pp. 62ff. It is curious to observe that E. Schockenhoff's wide-ranging study on the Thomistic doctrine of virtue does not once mention this concept of moral virtue, so central to both Aristotle and Thomas; see E. Schockenhoff, *Bonum hominis. Die anthropologischen und theologischen Grundlagen der Tugendethik bei Thomas von Aquin* (Mainz, 1987), esp. pp. 246ff., 282. Schockenhoff takes as central the definition of virtue as presented in *Nichomachean Ethics* II, 5, 1106a 15–23, which is valid for virtue *in general,* but is not specific for *ethical* virtue (see *Praktische Vernunft und Vernünftigkeit der Praxis,* p. 66).

75. On this see *Praktische Vernunft und Vernünftigkeit der Praxis,* pp. 575, 581ff.

76. See also the remarks of A. MacIntyre, *Whose Justice? Which Rationality?* (Notre Dame, Indiana, 1988) pp. 174ff.

77. See the interesting work by C. Schröer, *Praktische Vernunft bei Thomas von Aquin* (Stuttgart, 1995), p. 201.

78. Some remarks on this can be found in my "Sittliche Autonomie und Theonomie . . . , p. 266.

79. Supplements to my discussion about contraception (in chapter 2, section "*Excursus*: The Natural Law and Contraception") can be found in note 15 and in the Bibliographical Supplement.

80. On this see my article, " 'Intrinsically Evil Acts' and the Moral Viewpoint," as well as *La prospettiva della morale,* esp. chs. III and V.

81. See also the following articles: "Menschliches Handeln und seine Moralität"; "Ethik–Handeln—Sittlichkeit" (the first edition of this article was "Gut und böse oder richtig und falsch—was unterscheidet das Sittliche?" in H. Thomas, ed., *Ethik der Leistung* [Herford, 1988], pp. 47–75); " 'Ethics of Norms' and the Lost Virtues"; " 'Intrinsically Evil Acts' and the Moral Viewpoint."

82. This is also why W. Wolbert's criticism does not completely grasp my critique of Böckle (see W. Wolbert, "Naturalismus in der Ethik. Zum Vorwurf des 'naturalistischen Fehlschlusses,' " *Theologie und Glaube* 3 [1989]: 243–267, esp. 259–263), because for Wolbert, too, the whole matter is left "in brackets": it is not possible to say of any goods or values that they are only "premoral" or "nonmoral" goods, and at the same time be *practically disposed* in relation to them. "Practical disposition" always includes "willingly taking a position." In every act of the will, however, the "willed good" appears in the dimension of the ethical, something that teleological ethicists also admit.

83. See *La prospettiva della morale,* III, 2.

84. See Schockenhoff, *Bonum hominis*; H. Kleber, *Glück als Lebensziel. Untersuchungen zur Philosophie des Glücks bei Thomas von Aquin* (Münster, 1988).

85. Also important for the concept of action is J. M. Finnis, "Object and Intention in Moral Judgments According to Aquinas," *The Thomist* 55 (1991): 1–27.

86. More precise treatment of this can be found in my "Intentional Actions and the Meaning of Object: A Reply to Richard McCormick," *The Thomist,* 59, 2 (1995).

87. See J. M. Finnis, *Moral Absolutes: Tradition, Revision, and Truth* (Washington, D.C., 1991) pp. 91, 104.

88. M. Rhonheimer, "Über die Existenz einer spezifisch christlichen Moral des Humanums," *Internationale katholische Zeitschrift "Communio"* 23, 4(1994): 360–372.

# BIBLIOGRAPHY

Abba, G. *Lex et virtus: Studi sull'evoluzione della dottrina morale di san Tommaso d'Aquino*. Rome, 1983.

Allan, D. J. "Aristotle's Account of the Origin of Moral Principles." In *Articles on Aristotle. II. Ethics and Politics*. Ed. J. Barnes, M. Schofield, and R. Sorabji. New York, 1977. Originally published in *Actes du XIème Congrès international de Philosophie*, 12 (1953), 120–27.

———. "The Practical Syllogism." In *Autour d'Aristote*. Festschrift for A. Mansion. Louvain, 1955. Pp. 325–40.

Ando, T. *Aristotle's Theory of Practical Cognition*. 3rd ed. The Hague, 1971.

Anscombe, G. E. M. *Intention*. Oxford, 1958.

———. "Thought and Action in Aristotle." In *Articles on Aristotle. II. Ethics and Politics*. Ed. J. Barnes, M. Schofield, and R. Sorabji. New York, 1977. Pp. 61–71.

———. "Modern Moral Philosophy." In *The Collected Philosophical Papers of G. E. M. Anscombe. III. Ethics, Religion, and Politics*. Oxford, 1981. Pp. 26–42. Originally published in *Philosophy*, 33 (1958).

———. "War and Murder." In *The Collected Philosophical Papers of G. E. M. Anscombe. III. Ethics, Religion, and Politics*. Oxford, 1981. Pp. 51–61. Originally published in *Nuclear Weapons: A Catholic Response*. Ed. W. Stein. London and New York, 1961.

Armstrong, R. A. *Primary and Secondary Precepts in Thomistic Natural Law Teaching*. The Hague, 1966.

Arntz, J. T. C. "Die Entwicklung des naturrechtlichen Denkens innerhalb des Thomismus." In *Das Naturrecht im Disput*. Ed. F. Böckle. Düsseldorf, 1966. Pp. 87–120.

———. "Prima principia propria." In *Thomas von Aquino: Interpretation und Rezeption*. Ed. W. P. Eckert. Mainz, 1974. Pp. 3–15.

Ashmore, R. B., Jr. "Aquinas and Ethical Naturalism." *The New Scholasticism*, 49 (1975), 76–86.

Aubenque, P. *La prudence chez Aristote*. Paris, 1963.

Aubert, J.-M. *Loi de Dieu, lois des hommes*. Tournai, 1964.

———. "L'universalité et l'immutabilité du droit naturel." In *The Ethics of St. Thomas Aquinas: Proceedings of the Third Symposium of St. Thomas Aquinas' Philosophy, Rolduc, 1983*. Ed. L. J. Elders and K. Hedwig. Studi Tomistici 25. Vatican City, 1984. Pp. 143–60.

———. "Y a-t-il des normes morales universelles?" In *Universalité et permanence des Lois morales*. Ed. S. Pinckaers and C. J. Pinto de Oliveira. Études d'éthique chrétienne 16. Fribourg and Paris, 1986. Pp. 314–29.

Auer, A. *Autonome Moral und christlicher Glaube*. 2nd ed. Düsseldorf, 1984.

———. "Die Autonomie des Sittlichen nach Thomas von Aquin." In *Christlich glauben und handeln—Fragen einer fundamentalen Moraltheologie in der Diskussion*. Festschrift for J. Fuchs. Ed. K. Demmer and B. Schüller. Düsseldorf, 1977. Pp. 31–54.

———. "Hat die autonome Moral eine Chance in der Kirche?" In *Moral begünden/Moral verkünden*. Ed. G. Virt. Innsbruck and Vienna, 1985. Pp. 9–30.

Bajda, J. "Verantwortete Elternschaft und Antikonzeption: Eine moraltheologische Analyse." In *Elternschaft und Menschenwürde: Zur Problematik der Empfängnisregelung*. Ed. E. Wenisch. Vallendar and Schonönstatt, 1984. Pp. 243–60.

Belmans, T. G. *Le sens objectif de l'agir humain: Pour relire la morale conjugale de Saint Thomas*. Studi Tomistici 8. Vatican City, 1980. German translation: *Der objektive Sinn des menschlichen Handelns: Zur Ehemoral des hl. Thomas*. Vallendar, 1984.

Bien, G. "Die menschlichen Meinungen und das Gute: Die Lösung des Normproblems in der aristotelischen Ethik." In *Rehabilitierung der praktischen Philosophie* I. Ed. M. Riedel. Freiburg, 1972. Pp. 345–71.

Böckle, F. *Das Naturrecht im Disput*. Düsseldorf, 1966.

———. *Grundbegriffe der Moral*. 8th ed. Aschaffenburg, 1966.

———. "Natur als Norm in der Moraltheologie." In *Naturgesetz und christliche Ethik*. Ed. F. Henrich. Munich, 1970. Pp. 75–90.

———. "Natürliches Gesetz als göttliches Gesetz in der Moraltheologie." In *Naturrecht in der Kritik*. Ed. F. Böckle and E.-W. Böckenförde. Mainz, 1973. Pp. 165–88.

———. "Theonome Rationalität als Prinzip der Normbegründung bei Thomas von Aquin und Gabriel Vazquez." In *L'Agire morale: Atti del Congresso Internazaionale, Roma–Napoli, 17/24 Aprile 1974*. Ed. M. Zalba. Tommaso d'Aquino nel suo settimo centenario 5. Naples, 1974. Pp. 213–27.

———. "Werteinsicht und Normbegründung." *Concilium*, 12 (1976), 615–17.

———. *Fundamental Moral Theology*. Trans. N. D. Smith. New York, 1980. Originally published as *Fundamentelmoral*, Munich, 1977.

Bourke, V. J. *St. Thomas and the Greek Moralists*. Milwaukee, 1947.

———. "Right Reason as the Basis for Moral Action." In *L'Agire morale: Atti del Congresso Internazaionale, Roma–Napoli, 17/24 Aprile 1974*. Ed. M. Zalba. Tommaso d'Aquino nel suo settimo centenario 5. Naples, 1974. Pp. 122–27.

———. "Right Reason in Contemporary Ethics." *The Thomist*, 38 (1974), 106–24.

Boyle, J. M. " 'Praeter Intentionem' in Aquinas." *The Thomist*, 42 (1978), 649–65.

———. "Toward Understanding the Principle of Double Effect." *Ethics*, 90 (July 1980), 527–38.

Bujo, B. *Moralautonomie und Normfindung bei Thomas von Aquin*. Paderborn, 1979.

Caffarra, C. "Die Unmoral der Empfängnisverhütung." In *Elternschaft und Menschenwürde: Zur Problematik der Empfängnisregelung*. Ed. E. Wenisch. Vallendar and Schonönstatt, 1984. Pp. 261–73.

Caldera, R. T. *Le Jugement par Inclination chez saint Thomas d'Aquin*. Diss. Freiburg Switzerland, University Library, 1974.

Capone, D. "Oggettività dell'ordine morale nel giudizio di coscienza in situation." In *Universalité et permanence des Lois morales*. Ed. S. Pinckaers and C. J. Pinto de Oliveira. Études d'éthique chrétienne 16. Fribourg and Paris, 1986. Pp. 389–407.

Cathrein, V. "Quo sensu secundum S. Thomam ratio sit regula actuum humanorum?" *Gregorianum*, 5 (1924), 584ff.

Composta, D. *Natura e ragione: Studio sulle inclinazioni naturali in rapporto al diritto naturale*. Zurich, 1971.

———. "Nuove impostazioni della teologia morale." In *Universalité et permanence des Lois morales*. Ed. S. Pinckaers and C. J. Pinto de Oliveira. Études d'éthique chrétienne 16. Fribourg and Paris, 1986. Pp. 258–76.

Cooper, J. M. *Reason and Human Good in Aristotle*. Cambridge, Mass., 1975.

Crowe, F. E. "Universal Norms and the Concrete "operabile" in St. Thomas Aquinas." *Sciences Ecclésiastiques*, 7 (1955), 115–49, 257–91.

Crowe, M. B. *The Changing Profile of the Natural Law*. The Hague, 1977.

Curran, C. E. *Themes in Fundamental Moral Theology*. Notre Dame and London, 1977.

Curran, C. E., and R. A. McCormick, eds. *Readings in Moral Theology* I. New York, 1979.

De Broglie, G. "La Doctrine de saint Thomas sur le fondement communautaire de la chasteté." In *L'Agire morale: Atti del Congresso Internazaionale, Roma–Napoli, 17/24 Aprile 1974*. Ed. M. Zalba. Tommaso d'Aquino nel suo settimo centenario 5. Naples, 1974. Pp. 297–307.

De Finance, J. *Grundlegung der Ethik*. Freiburg, 1968.

———. "Autonomie et Théonomie." In *L'Agire morale: Atti del Congresso Internazaionale, Roma–Napoli, 17/24 Aprile 1974*. Ed. M. Zalba. Tommaso d'Aquino nel suo settimo centenario 5. Naples, 1974. Pp. 239–60.

Delhaye, P. " 'Droit naturel' et Théologie morale: Perspectives actuelles." *Revue théologique de Louvain* (1975), 137–64.

Demmer, K., and B. Schüller, eds. *Christlich glauben und handeln—Fragen einer fundamentalen Moraltheologie in der Diskussion*. Festschrift for J. Fuchs. Düsseldorf, 1977.

Donagan, A. "The Scholastic Theory of Moral Law in the Modern World." In *Aquinas: A Collection of Critical Essays*. Ed. A. Kenny. London, 1962. Pp. 325–39.

Door, D. J. "K. Rahner's Formal Existential Ethics." *The Irish Theological Quarterly*, 36 (1969), 211–29.

Dupré, L. "Situation Ethics and Objective Morality." *Theological Studies*, 28 (1967), 245–57.

Elders, L. J., and K. Hedwig, eds. *The Ethics of St. Thomas Aquinas: Proceedings of the Third Symposium of St. Thomas Aquinas'*

*Philosophy, Rolduc, 1983*. Studi Tomistici 25. Vatican City, 1984.

Elter, P. "Norma honestatis ad mentem Divi Thomae." *Gregorianum*, 8 (1927), 337ff.

Endres, J. "Anteil der Klugheit am Erkennen des konkret Wahren und am Wollen des wahrhaft Guten." *Studia Moralia*, 1 (1963), 223–63.

Engberg-Pedersen, T. *Aristotle's Theory of Moral Insight*. Oxford, 1983.

Ermecke, G. "Das Naturrecht in Disput." *Theol. Revue*, 4 (1969), 267–74.

———. "Zur Christlichkeit und Geschichtlichkeit der 'Moral in der Krise.' " *Münchener Theologische Zeitschrift*, 21 (1970), 297–312.

———. "Das Problem der Universalität oder Allgemeingültigkeit sittlicher Normen innerweltlicher Lebensgestaltung." *Münchener Theologische Zeitschrift*, 24 (1973), 1–24.

Ernst, W. "Universalität sittlicher Normen—heutige Tendenzen." In *Sittliche Normen: Zum Problem ihrer allgemeinen und unwandelbaren Geltung*. Ed. W. Kerber. Düsseldorf, 1982. Pp. 58–73.

Esser, G. "Intuition in Thomistic Moral Philosophy." *Proceedings of the American Catholic Philosophical Association*, 31 (1957), 156–77.

Fabro, C. *Participation et causalité selon S. Thomas d'Aquin*. Louvain and Paris, 1961.

———. *Percezione e pensiero*. 2nd ed. Brescia, 1962.

Fay, C. "Human Evolution: A Challenge to Thomistic Ethics." *International Philosophical Quarterly*, 2 (1960), 50–80.

Finnis, J., and Grisez, G. "The Basic Principles of Natural Law: A Reply to Ralph McInerny." *The American Journal of Jurisprudence and Legal Philosophy*, 26 (1981), 21–31.

Finnis, J. M. *Natural Law and Natural Rights*. Oxford, 1980.

———. *Fundamentals of Ethics*. Oxford and New York, 1983.

———. "*Humanae Vitae*: Its Background and Aftermath." *International Review of Natural Family Planning*, 4 (1980), 141–53.

———. "Practical Reasoning, Human Goods, and the End of Man." *Proceedings of the American Catholic Philosophical Association*, 58 (1984), 23–36.

———. "Personal Integrity, Sexual Morality, and Responsible Parenthood." *Anthropos*, 1 (1985), 43–55.

Frankena, W. K. "The Naturalistic Fallacy." In *Theories of Ethics*. Ed. P. Foot. Oxford, 1967. Pp. 50–63.

Fuchs, J. *Theologia Moralis Generalis*. Rome, 1960.

———. " '*Operatio*' et '*operatum*' in dictamine conscientiae." *Thomistica Morum Principia* II. Rome, 1961. Pp. 71–79.

———. "Biologie und Ehemoral." *Gregorianum*, 2 (1962), 225–53.

———. *Natural Law: A Theological Investigation*. Trans. H. Reckter, S.J., and John Dowling. New York, 1965. Originally published as *Lex naturae: Zur Theologie des Naturrechts*, Düsseldorf, 1955.

———. *Moral und Moraltheologie nach dem Konzil*. Freiburg, 1967.

———. "Gibt es eine spezifisch christliche Moral?" *Stimmen der Zeit*, 2 (1970), 99–112.

———. "Der Absolutheitscharakter sittlicher Handlungsnormen." In *Testimonium Veritati*. Ed. H. Wolter. Frankfurter Theologische Studien 7. Frankfurg, 1971. Pp. 211–40.

———. "Autonome Moral und Glaubensethik." In *Ethik im Kontext des Glaubens: Probleme, Grundsätze, Methode*. Ed. D. Mieth and F. Compagnoni. Fribourg–Freiburg–Vienna, 1978. Pp. 46–74.

———. " 'Intrinsece malum': Überlegungen zu einem umstrittenen Begriff." In *Sittliche Normen: Zum Problem ihrer allgemeinen und unwandelbaren Geltung*. Ed. W. Kerber. Düsseldorf, 1981. Pp. 74–91.

———. "Das Gottesbild und die Moral innerweltlichen Handelns: *Stimmen der Zeit*, 202 (1984), 363–82.

Furger, F. *Gewissen und Klugheit in der katholischen Moraltheologie der letzten Jahrzehnte*. Lucerne and Stuttgart, 1965.

———. " 'Kenosis' und das Christliche einer christlichen Ethik: Eine christologische Rückfrage." In *Christlich glauben und handeln—Fragen einer fundamentalen Moraltheologie in der Diskussion*. Festschrift for J. Fuchs. Ed. K. Demmer and B. Schüller. Düsseldorf, 1977. Pp. 96–111.

———. "Zur Begründung eines christlichen Ethos: Forschungstendenzen in der katholischen Moraltheologie." *Theologische Berichte* IV. Zurich, 1974. Pp. 11–87.

———. *Was Ethik begründet: Deontologie oder Teleologie—Hintergrund und Tragweite einer moraltheologischen Auseinandersetzung.* Einsiedeln, 1981.
Garcia de Haro, R. "I concetti fondamentali della Morale." *Anthropos*, 1 (1985), 95–108.
Gauthier R. A., and J. Y. Jolif. *L'Ethique à Nicomaque: Introduction, Traduction, et Commentaire.* 2 vols. 2nd ed. Louvain and Paris, 1970.
Geach, P. "The Moral Law and the Law of God." In *God and the Soul.* London, 1969. Pp. 117–29.
Gilson, É. *L'être et l'essence.* 2nd ed. Paris, 1972.
Grisez, G. "The Logic of Moral Judgement." *Proceedings of the American Catholic Philosophical Association*, 36 (1962), 67–76.
———. "A New Formulation of a Natural-Law Argument Against Contraception." *The Thomist*, 30 (1966), 343–61.
———. "The First Principle of Practical Reason." In *Aquinas: A Collection of Critical Essays.* Ed. A. Kenny. London, 1969. Pp. 340–82.
———. "Dualism and the New Morality." In *L'Agire morale: Atti del Congresso Internazaionale, Roma–Napoli, 17/24 Aprile 1974.* Ed. M. Zalba. Tommaso d'Aquino nel suo settimo centenario 5. Naples, 1974. Pp. 323–30.
———. "Choice and Consequentialism." *Proceedings of the American Catholic Philosophical Association*, 51 (1977), 144–52.
———. "Against Consequentialism." *The American Journal of Jurisprudence and Legal Philosophy*, 23 (1978), 21–72.
———. *The Way of the Lord Jesus.* I. *Christian Moral Principles.* Chicago, 1983.
———. "Moral Absolutes: A Critique of the View of Josef Fuchs, S.J." *Anthropos*, 2 (1985), 155–201.
Gründel, J. "Naturrecht." In *Sacramentum Mundi* III. Freiburg, 1969. Pp. 707–19.
———. *Aktuelle Themen der Moraltheologie.* Munich, 1971.
———. *Ethik ohne Normen.* Freiburg, 1970.
Häring, B. *Das Gesetz Christi.* 6th ed. 3 vols. Freiburg, 1961.
Hardie, W. F. R. *Aristotle's Ethical Theory.* 2nd ed. Oxford, 1980.
Hedwig, K. "Circa particularia: Kontingenz, Klugheit, und Notwendigkeit im Aufbau des ethischen Aktes bei Thomas von Aquin." In *The Ethics of St. Thomas Aquinas: Proceedings of the*

*Third Symposium of St. Thomas Aquinas' Philosophy, Rolduc, 1983*. Ed. L. J. Elders and K. Hedwig. Studi Tomistici 25. Vatican City, 1984. Pp. 161–87.

Hilpert, K. *Ethik und Rationalität: Untersuchungen zum Autonomieproblem und zu seiner Bedeutung für die theologische Ethik*. Düsseldorf, 1980.

Höffe, O. *Sittlich-politische Diskurse*. Frankfurt, 1981.

Hörmann, K. "Die Prägung des sittlichen Wollens durch das Objekt nach Thomas von Aquin." In *Moral zwischen Anspruch und Verantwortung*. Ed. F. Böckle and F. Groner. Düsseldorf, 1964. Pp. 233–51.

———. "Das Objekt als Quelle der Sittlichkeit." In *The Ethics of St. Thomas Aquinas: Proceedings of the Third Symposium of St. Thomas Aquinas' Philosophy, Rolduc, 1983*. Ed. L. J. Elders and K. Hedwig. Studi Tomistici 25. Vatican City, 1984. Pp. 118–32.

Huftier, M. "Conscience individuelle et règle morale." *Esprit et Vie*, 85 (1975), 465–76, 481–90.

Inciarte, F. "Theoretische und praktische Wahrheit." In *Rehabilitierung der praktischen Philosophie* II. Ed. M. Reidel. Freiburg, 1974. Pp. 155–70.

———. "Autonomie und Theonomie des Gewissens." *Theologisches*, 126–127 (1980), 3817–25, 3885–90.

———. "Theonomie, Autonomie, und das Problem der politischen Macht." *Theologische Revue*, 78, No. 2 (1982), 89–102.

Irwin, T. H. "First Principles in Aristotle's Ethics." *Midwest Studies in Philosophy: Studies in Ethical Theory*, 3 (1978), 252–72.

———. "Aristotle on Reason, Desire, and Virtue." *The Journal of Philosophy*, 72 (1975), 567–78.

Jannsens, L. "Ontic Evil and Moral Evil." *Louvain Studies*, 4 (1972), 115–56.

John Paul II. *Mann und Frau schuf er: Grundfragen menschlicher Sexualität*. Munich–Zurich–Vienna, 1981.

———. *Original Unity of Man and Woman: Catechesis on the Book of Genesis*. Ed. Donald Wuerl. Boston, 1981.

———. *Communio personarum*. II. *Die Erlösung des Leibes und die Sakramentalität der Ehe, Katechesen 1981–1984*. Ed. N. and R. Martin. Vallendar, 1984.

———. *Communio personarum. I. Die menschliche Liebe, Katechesen 1979–1981.* Ed. N. and R. Martin. Vallendar, 1985.

———. *The Theology of Marriage and Celibacy: Catechesis on Marriage and Celibacy in the Light of the Resurrection of the Body.* Ed. Donald Wuerl. Boston, 1986.

Jonas, H. *The Gnostic Religion.* 2nd ed. Boston, 1963.

Juros, H., and T. Styczen. "Methodologische Ansätze ethischen Denkens und ihre Folgen für die Theologische Ethik: Bericht über Ethik in Polen." *Theologische Berichte* IV. Zurich, 1974. Pp. 89–108.

Kalinowski, G. *Le problème de la Vérité en Morale et en Droit.* Lyons, 1967.

Kelly, Geffrey, ed. *Karl Rahner: Theologian of the Graced Search for Meaning.* The Making of Modern Theology 8. Minneapolis, 1992.

Kenny, A. *Will, Freedom and Power.* Oxford, 1975.

———. *The Aristotelian Ethics: A Study of the Relationship between the Eudemian and Nichomachean Ethics of Aristotle.* Oxford, 1978.

Kerber, W., ed. *Sittliche Normen: Zum Problem ihrer allgemeinen und unwandelbaren Geltung.* Düsseldorf, 1981.

Kluxen, W. "Menschliche Natur und Ethos." *Münchener Theologische Zeitschrift,* 23 (1972), 1–17.

———. *Philosophische Ethik bei Thomas von Aquin* (1964). 2nd ed. Hamburg, 1980.

Knauer, P. "Das rechtverstandene Prinzip der Doppelwirkung als Grundnorm jeder Gewissensentscheidung." *Theologie und Glaube,* 57 (1967), 107–33. Translated as "The Hermeneutic Function of the Principle of Double Effect." Natural Law Forum, 12 (1967), 132–62. Repr. in *Readings in Moral Theology* I. Ed. C. E. Curran and R. A. McCormick. New York, 1979. Pp. 1–39.

Korff, W. *Norm und Sittlichkeit.* Mainz, 1973.

———. *Theologische Ethik.* Freiburg, 1975.

———. "Natur oder Vernunft als Kriterium?" *Concilium,* 17 (1981), 831–36.

Kuhn, H. "Wissenschaft der Praxis und praktische Wissenschaft." In *Werden und Handeln.* (Festschrift for V. e. Freiherr von Gebsattel). Ed. E. Wisenhütter. Stuttgart, 1963. Pp. 157–90.

Lambertino, A. "Eudemonologia tomista e critica kantiana all'eudemonismo." In *L'Agire morale: Atti del Congresso Internazaionale, Roma–Napoli, 17/24 Aprile 1974*. Ed. M. Zalba. Tommaso d'Aquino nel suo settimo centenario 5. Naples, 1974. Pp. 261–69.

Laun, A. *Die naturrechtliche Begründung der Ethik in der neueren katholischen Moraltheologie*. Vienna, 1973.

———. "Theologische Normenbegründung in der moraltheologischen Diskussion." *Theologisch-Praktische Quartalschrift*, 126 (1978), 162–70.

———. *Das Gewissen: Oberste Norm sittlichen Handelns*. Innsbruck, 1984.

Lawler, R., O.F.M. Cap., J. M. Boyle, and W. E. May. *Catholic Sexual Ethics: A Summary, Explanation, and Defense*. Huntington, Ind., 1985.

Lehu, L. *La Raison: Règle de la moralité d'après Saint Thomas*. Paris, 1930.

Lottin, O. *Le droit naturel chez Saint Thomas et ses prédécesseurs*. Bruges, 1931.

———. *Psychologie et morale au XIIme siècle*. Gembloux, 1942ff.

———. "La Valeur des formules de Saint Thomas d'Aquin concernant la Loi naturelle." In *Mélanges Joseph Maréchal* II. Brussells, 1950. Pp. 355–77.

———. "Aristote et la connexion des vertus." In *Autour d'Aristote*. Festschrift for A. Mansion. Louvain, 1955. Pp. 343–64.

Lotz, J. B. "Philosophische Bemerkungen zum Finden und Gelten sittlicher Normen." In *Christlich glauben und handeln—Fragen einer fundamentalen Moraltheologie in der Diskussion*. Festschrift for J. Fuchs. Ed. K. Demmer and B. Schüller. Düsseldorf, 1977. Pp. 147–70.

Manser, G. M. *Das Naturrecht in thomistischer Beleuchtung*. Fribourg, 1944.

Maritain, Jacques. *An Essay on Christian Philosophy*. Trans. E. Flannery. New York, 1955. Originally published as *Essai sur la philosophie chrétienne*, 1935.

———. *An Introduction to the Basic Problems of Moral Philosophy*. Trans. Cornelia Borgerhoff, Petersham, Mass., 1990. Originally published as *Neuf leçons sur les notions premières de la philosophie morale*. Paris, 1951.

Marmy, E., ed. *Mensch und Gemeinschaft in christlicher Schau: Dokumente*. Freiburg, 1945.

Mausbach, J., and G. Ermecke. *Katholische Moraltheologie*. I. *Die allgemeine Moral*. 9th ed. Münster, 1959.

McCormick, R. A. "Notes on Moral Theology." *Theological Studies*, 28 (1967), 749–800; 36 1975), 77–129; 40 (1979), 59–112.

———. "Neuere Überlegungen zur Unveränderlichkeit sittlicher Normen." In *Sittliche Normen: Zum Problem ihrer allgemeinen und unwandelbaren Geltung*. Ed. W. Kerber. Düsseldorf, 1982. Pp. 46–57.

McInerny, R. M. "Truth in Ethics: Historicity and Natural Law." *Proceedings of the American Catholic Philosophical Association*, 43 (1969), 71–82.

———. "Prudence and Conscience." *The Thomist*, 38 (1974), 291–305.

———. "Naturalism and Thomistic Ethics." *The Thomist*, 40 (1976), 222–42.

———. "The Principles of Natural Law." *American Journal of Jurisprudence*, 25 (1980), 1–15.

———. *Ethica Thomistica: The Moral Philosophy of Thomas Aquinas*. Washington, D.C., 1982.

———. "On Knowing Natural Law." In *The Ethics of St. Thomas Aquinas: Proceedings of the Third Symposium of St. Thomas Aquinas' Philosophy, Rolduc, 1983*. Ed. L. J. Elders and K. Hedwig. Studi Tomistici 25. Vatican City, 1984. Pp. 133–42.

Merks, K. W. *Theologische Grundlegung der sittlichen Autonomie: Strukturmomente eines "autonomen" Normbegründungsverständnisses im lex-Traktat der "Summa Theologiae" des Thomas von Aquin*. Düsseldorf, 1978.

Messner, J. *Das Naturrecht*. 6th ed. Innsbruck–Vienna–Munich, 1966.

Michelakis, E. M. *Aristotle's Theory of Practical Principles*. Athens, 1961.

Mieth, D., and F. Compagnoni, eds. *Ethik im Kontext des Glaubens: Probleme, Grundsätze, Methoden*. Fribourg–Freiburg–Vienna, 1978.

Milhaven, J. G., and Casey, D. J. "Introduction to the Theological Background of the New Morality." *Theological Studies*, 28 (1967), 213–44.

Monan, J. D. *Moral Knowledge and Its Methodology in Aristotle.* Oxford, 1968.

Morisset, B. "Le syllogisme prudentiel." *Laval théologique et philosophique.* 19, No. 1 (1963), 62–92.

Morisset, P. "Prudence et fin selon Saint Thomas." *Sciences ecclésiastiques,* 15 (1963), 73–98, 439–58.

Naus, J. E. *The Nature of the Practical Intellect According to Saint Thomas Aquinas.* Rome, 1959.

Nicolas, M. J. "L'Idée de nature dans la pensée de Saint Thomas d'Aquin." *Revue Thomiste* (1974), 533–90.

Oehler, K. "Thomas von Aquin als Interpret der aristotelischen Ethik." *Philosophische Rundschau,* 5 (1957), 135–52.

Oeing-Hanhoff, L. "Thomas von Aquin und die Situation des Thomismus heute." *Philosophisches Jahrbuch,* 70 (1962), 17–33.

———. "Der Mensch: Natur oder Geschichte? Die Grundlagen und Kriterien sittlicher Normen im Licht der philosophischen Tradition." In *Naturgesetz und christliche Ethik: Zur wissenschaftlichen Diskussion nach "Humanae Vitae."* Ed. F. Henrich. Munich, 1970. Pp. 13–47.

Pesch, O. H. *Das Gesetz: Kommentary zu I–II,* qq. 90–105 (*Summa Theologica, Duetsche Thomas-Ausgabe* 13. Band). Heidelberg/Graz, Vienna, and Cologne, 1977.

Pieper, Josef. *Living the Truth.* Trans. Stella Lange. San Francisco, 1989. Originally published as Die Wirklichkeit und das Gute. 7th ed. Munich, 1963.

Pinckaers, S. "Eudämonismus und sittliche Verbindlichkeit in der Ethik des heiligen Thomas." In *Sein und Ethos.* Ed. P. Engelhardt. Mainz, 1963. Pp. 267–305.

———. *Le renouveau de la morale: Études pour une morale fidèle à ses sources et à sa mission présente.* Tournai, 1964.

———. "La nature de la moralité casuistique et morale thomiste." In St. Thomas Aquinas. *Somme Théologique, Les actes humains.* II. *Renseignements techniques.* Paris and Tournai, 1966. Pp. 215–73.

———. "Le problème de l'Intrinsece malum': Esquisse historique." In *Universalité et permanence des Lois morales.* Ed. S. Pinckaers and C. J. Pinto de Oliveira. Études d'éthique chrétienne 16. Fribourg and Paris, 1986. Pp. 277–90.

———. *Les sources de la morale chrétienne: Sa méthode, son contenu, son histoire*. Études d'éthique chrétienne/Studien zur theologischen Ethik 14. Fribourg and Paris, 1985.

Pinckaers, S., and C. J. Pinto de Oliveira, eds. *Universalité et permanence des Lois morales*. Études d'éthique chrétienne 16. Fribourg and Paris, 1986.

Pohlmann, R. "Autonomie." In *Historisches Wörterbuch der Philosophie* I. Ed. J. Ritter. Basel, 1971. Cols. 701–19.

Rahner, K. "Bemerkungen über das naturgesetz und seine Erkennbarkeit." *Orientierung*, 19 (1955), 239–43.

———. "Über das Verhältnis des Naturgesetzes zur übernatürlichen Gnadenordnung." *Orientierung*, 20 (1956), 8–11.

———. "Über das Verhältnis von Natur und Gnade." *Schriften zur Theologie* I. Einsideln, 1956. Pp, 323–45.

———. "Über die Frage einer formalen Existentialethik." *Schriften zur Theologie* II. Einsiedeln, 1956. Pp. 227–46.

———. "Das 'Gebot' der Liebe unter den anderen Geboten." *Schriften zur Theologie* V. Einsiedeln, 1962. Pp. 494–517.

———. *A Rahner Reader*. Ed. Gerald A. McCool. New York, 1975.

Reiner, H. "Wesen und Grund der sittlichen Verbindlichkeit (*obligatio*) bei Thomas von Aquin." In *Sein und Ethos*. Ed. P. Engelhardt. Mainz, 1963. Pp. 236–66.

Rhonheimer, M. "Die Entdeckung der Familie." In J. M. Fontes, B. Hassenstein, N. Lobkowicz, and M. Rhonheimer. *Familie: Feindbild und Leitbild*. Cologne, 1977. Pp. 11–44.

———. *Familie und Selbstverwirklichung*. Cologne, 1979.

———. "Sozialphilosophie und Familie: Gedanken zur humanen Grundfunktion der Familie." In *Familie: Herausforderung der Zukunft (Symposium an der Universität Freiburg Schweiz von 26–28.11.1981)*. Ed. B. Schnyder. Fribourg, 1982. Pp. 113–40.

———. "Die praktische Vernunft als Gegenstand philosophischer Ethik: Vorbereitende Überlegungen für eine 'Rekonstruktion' der Lehre von Naturgesetz bei Thomas von Aquin." *Forum Katholische Theologie*, 2 (1986), 97–119.

Rodriguez Luño, A. "Sulla recezione del modello filosofico utilitaristico da parte di alcuni teologi moralisti." *Anthropos*, 2 (1985), 203–13.

Rommen, H. *Die ewige Wiederkehr des Naturrechts*. Munich, 1947.

Rotter, H. "Subjektivität und objektivität des sittlichen Anspruchs." *Christlich glauben und handeln—Fragen einer fundamentalen Moraltheologie in der Diskussion.* Festschrift for J. Fuchs. Ed. K. Demmer and B. Schüller. Düsseldorf, 1977. Pp. 195–207.

———. "Tendenzen in der heutigen Moraltheologie." *Stimmen der Zeit,* 4 (1970), 259–68.

———. *Christliches Handeln: Seine Begründung und Eigenart.* Graz–Vienna–Cologne, 1977.

———. "Zwölf Thesen zur heilsgeschichtlichen Begründung der Moral." In *Heilsgeschichte und ethische Normen.* Ed. H. Rotter. Quaestiones Disputatae 99. Freiburg, 1984. Pp. 99–122.

Schelauske, H. D. *Naturrechtsdiskussion in Deutschland.* Cologne, 1968.

Scholz, F. "Objekt und Umstände, Wesenwirkungen und Nebeneffekte: Zur Möglichkeit und Unmöglichkeit indirekten Handelns." In *Christlich glauben und handeln—Fragen einer fundamentalen Moraltheologie in der Diskussion.* Festschrift for J. Fuchs. Ed. K. Demmer and B. Schüller. Düsseldorf, 1977. Pp. 243–60.

———. *Wege, Unwege, und Auswege der Moraltheologie: Ein Plädoyer für begründete Ausnahmen.* Munich, 1976.

———. "Durch ethische Grenzsituationen aufgeworfene Normprobleme." *Theologisch-Praktische Quartalschrift,* 123 (1975), 341–55.

Schüller, B. "Zur theologischen Diskussion über die lex naturalis." *Theologie und Philosophie,* 4 (1966), 481–503.

———. "Die Bedeutung des natürlichen Sittengesetzes für den Christen." In *Herausforderung und Kritik der Moraltheologie.* Ed. G. Teichtweier and W. Dreier. Würzburg, 1971. Pp. 105–30.

———. "Direkte Tötung—indirekte Tötung." *Theologie und Philosophie,* 47 (1972), 341–57. Translated as "Direct Killing/Indirect Killing." In *Readings in Moral Theology* I. Ed. C. E. Curran and R. A. McCormick. New York, 1979. Pp. 138–57.

———. "Neuere Beiträge zum Thema 'Begründung sittlicher Normen.' " *Theologische Berichte,* 4 (1974), 109–81.

———. *Die Begründung sittlicher Urteile: Typen ethischer Argumentation in der Moraltheologie.* 2nd rev. and enl. ed. Düsseldorf, 1980.

———. "Eine autonome Moral, was ist das?" *Theol. Revue,* 78, No. 2 (1982), 103–105.

Scola, A. *La fondazione della legge naturale nello "Scriptum super Sententiis" di san Tommaso d'Aquino.* Freiburg, 1982.

———. "Antropologia, etica, e scienza." *Anthropos*, 2 (1985), 215–26.

Seidl. H. *Der Begriff des Intellekts (noûs) bei Aristoteles im philosophischen Zusammenhang seiner Hauptschriften*. Meisenheim am Glan, 1971.

———. "Natürliche Sittlichkeit und metaphysische Voraussetzung in der Ethik des Aristoteles und Thomas von Aquin." In *The Ethics of St. Thomas Aquinas: Proceedings of the Third Symposium of St. Thomas Aquinas' Philosophy, Rolduc, 1983*. Ed. L. J. Elders and K. Hedwig. Studi Tomistici 25. Vatican City, 1984. Pp. 95–117.

Seifert, J. *Was ist und was motiviert eine sittliche Handlung?* Salzburg and Munich, 1976.

———. "Der Unterschied zwischen natürlicher Empfängnisregelung und künstlicher Empäangnisverhütung." In *Elternschaft und Menschwürde: Zur Problematik der Empfängnisregelung*. Ed. E. Wenisch. Vallendar and Schönstatt, 1984. Pp. 191–242.

———. "Gott und die Sittlichkeit innerweltlichen Handelns: Kritische philosophische Reflexionen über den Einfluß anthropomorpher und agnostischer Gottesvorstellungen auf Ethik und Moraltheologie." *Forum Katholische Theologie*, 1 (1985), 27–47.

———. "Absolute Moral Obligations Towards Finite Goods as Foundation of Intrinsically Right and Wrong Actions: A Critique of Consequentialist 'Teleological Ethics'—Destruction of Ethics Through Moral Theology?" *Anthropos*, 1 (1985), 57–94.

Sorabji, R. "Aristotle and the Rôle of Intellect in Virtue." *Proceedings of the Aristotelian Society*, N.S. 74 (1973–74), 107–29.

Spaemann, R. "Die Aktualität des Naturrechts." In *Naturrecht in der Kritik*. Ed. F. Böckle and E.-W. Böckenförde. Mainz, 1973. Pp. 262–76.

———. "Natur." In *Handbuch philosophischer Grundbegriffe* III. Ed. H. Krings, H. M. Baumgartner, and C. Wild. Pp. 956–69.

———. "Wovon handelt die Moraltheologie?" *Internationale Katholische Zeitschrift* (1977), 289–311.

———. "Naturteleologie und Handlung." *Zeitschrift für philosophische Forschung*, 32 (1978), 478–93.

———. "Über die Unmöglichkeit einer universalteleologischen Ethik." *Philosophisches Jahrbuch*, 88 (1981), 70–89.

Stallmach, J. "Das Problem sittlicher Eigengesetzlichkeit des Individuums in der philosophischen Ethik." *Theologie und Philosophie*, 42 (1967), 22–50.

Styczen, T. "Autonome Ethik mit einem christlichen 'Proprium' als methodologisches Problem." In *Ethik im Kontext des Glaubens: Probleme, Grundsätze, Methode*. Ed. D. Mieth and F. Compagnoni. Fribourg–Freiburg–Vienna, 1978. Pp. 75–100.

———. "Zur Frage einer unabhängigen Ethik." In K. Wojtyla, A. Szostek, and T. Styczen. *Der Streit um den Menschen: Personaler Anspruch des Sittlichen*. Ed. J. Cardinal Höffner. Kevelaer, 1979. Pp. 113–75.

———. "Das Gewissen—Quelle der Freiheit oder der Knechtung?" *Archiv für Religionspsychologie*, 17 (1986), 130–47.

———. "Die Wahrheit öber den Menschen als Schutz gegen einen Antipersonalismus in der Ethik." *Communio*, 12 (1983).

———. "Das problem der Allgemeingültigkeit ethischer Normen in epistemologischer Sicht." In *Universalité et permanence des Lois morales*. Ed. S. Pinckaers and C. J. Pinto de Oliveira. Études d'éthique chrétienne 16. Fribourg and Paris, 1986. Pp. 239–57.

Tettamanzi, D. "L'oggettività dell'ordine moral nel giudizio di coscienza in situazione." In *Universalité et permanence des Lois morales*. Ed. S. Pinckaers and C. J. Pinto de Oliveira. Études d'éthique chrétienne 16. Fribourg and Paris, 1986. Pp. 362–88.

Tonneau, J. "Le volontaire in *esse naturae* et in *esse moris*." *Thomistica Morum Principia*. Rome, 1960. Pp. 196–203.

———. *Absolut et obligation en Morale*. Montreal and Paris, 1965.

Urdanoz, T. "La moral y su valor objetivo: Nueva moralidad y Moral de Santo Tomás." *Angelicum*, 52 (1975), 179–227.

Vanni Rovighi, S. "C'è un'etica filosofica in S. Tommaso D'Aquino?" *Rivista di Filosofia Neo-Scolastica*, 2–4 (1974), 653–70.

Veatch, H. B. "Are There Non-Moral Goods?" *The New Scholasticism*, 52 (1978), 471–99.

Voegeli. E. *The New Science of Politics*. Chicago and London, 1952.

Von Hildebrand, Dietrich, *Ethics*. Chicago, 1953.

Walgrave, J. H. "The Personal Aspect of St. Thomas' Ethics." In *The Ethics of St. Thomas Aquinas: Proceedings of the Third Symposium of St. Thomas Aquinas' Philosophy, Rolduc, 1983*. Ed. L. J.

Elders and K. Hedwig. Studi Tomistici 25. Vatican City, 1984. Pp. 202–25.

Wallace, W. A. *The Role of Demonstration in Moral Theory*. Washington, D.C., 1962.

———. "Existential Ethics: A Thomistic Appraisal." *The Thomist*, 27 (1963), 493–515.

Walsh, J. J., and H. L. Shapiro, ed. *Aristotle's Ethics: Issues and Interpretations*. Belmont, Calif., 1967.

Welzel, H. *Naturrecht und materiale Gerechtigkeit*. 4th ed. Göttingen, 1980.

Wenisch, E., ed. *Elternschaft und Menschenwürde: Zur Problematik der Empfängnisregelung*. Vallendar and Schonönstatt, 1984.

Wieland, G. *Ethica-Scientia practica: Die Anfänge der philosophischen Ethik im 13. Jahrhundert*. Beiträge zur Geschichte der Philosophie und Theologie des Mittelalters 21, N. S. Münster 1981.

Wittmann, M. *Die Ethik des hl. Thomas von Aquin*. Munich, 1933.

Wojtyla, K. *The Acting Person*. Trans. Andrzej Potocki. Analecta Husserliana 10. Boston and London, 1979.

———. "The Person: Subject and Community." *Review of Metaphysics*, 33 (1979), 273–308.

———. *Love and Responsibility*. Trans. H. J. Willetts. New York, 1981.

———. *Lubliner Vorlesungen*. Ed. J. Stroynowski. Stuttgart, 1981.

———. "The Problem of the Will in the Analysis of the Ethical Act." In K. Wojtyla. *Person and Community: Selected Essays*. Trans. Theresa Sandok, O.S.M. New York, 1993. Pp. 3–22.

Yartz, F. J. "Order and Right Reason in Aquinas' Ethics." *Mediaeval Studies*, 37 (1975), 407–18.

Zalba, M., ed. *L'Agire morale: Atti del Congresso Internazaionale, Roma–Napoli, 17/24 Aprile 1974*. Tommaso d'Aquino nel suo settimo centenario 5. Naples, 1974.

# BIBLIOGRAPHICAL SUPPLEMENT


Abba, G. *Felicità, vita buona, e virtù: Saggio di filosofia morale*. Rome, 1989.

Anzenbacher, A. *Einführung in die Ethik*. Düsseldorf, 1992.

Böckle, F. "Was bedeutet 'Natur' in der Moraltheologie?" *Der unstrittene Naturbegriff: Person–Natur–Sexualität in der kirchlichen Morallehre*. Düsseldorf, 1981. Pp. 45–68.

Bruch, R. "Das sittliche Naturgesetz als Gottes- und Menschenwerk bei Thomas von Aquin." *Zeitschrift für Katholische Theologie*, 109 (1987), 204–311.

Cessario, R. *The Moral Virtues and Theological Ethics*. Notre Dame, Ind., 1991.

———. "The Examined Life." Italian translation: *Le virtù*. Manuali di Teologia Cattolica 19. Milan, 1994.

Elders, L. J., and K. Hedwig. *Lex et Libertas: Freedom and Law According to St. Thomas Aquinas*. Studi Tomistici 30. Vatican City, 1987.

Ernst, S. "Hat die autonome und teleologische Ethik die Objektivität sittlichen Handeln vergessen? Martinalien zu M. Rhonheimers Buch *Natur als Grundlage der Moral*." *Theologie und Glaube*, 79 (1989), 840–87.

———. "Erwiderung auf die Replik von M. Rhonheimer zu meiner Rezension seines Buches *Natur als Grundlage der Moral*. *Theologie und Glaube*, 79 (1989), 80–89.

Finnis, J., J. Boyle, and G. Grisez. *Nuclear Deterrence, Morality and Realism*. Oxford, 1987.

Finnis, J. M. "Object and Intention in Moral Judgements According to Aquinas." *The Thomist*, 55 (1991), 1–27.

———. *Moral Absolutes: Tradition, Revision and Truth*. Washington, D.C., 1991.

———. "Reason, Relativism, and Christian Ethics." *Anthropotes*, 9 (1993), 211–30.

Furger, F. *Einführung in die Moraltheologie*. Darmstadt, 1988.

Furger, F., K. Arntz, P. Schallenberg, and T. Schwartz. *Ethische Theorie praktisch: Der Fundamentaltheologische Ansatz in sozialethischer Entfaltung*. Münster, 1991.

Gillen, E. *Wie Christen ethisch handeln und denken: Zur Debatte um die Autonomie der Sittlichkeit im Kontext katholischer Theologie*. Würzburg, 1989.

Grisez, G. *The Way of the Lord Jesus*. II. *Living a Christian Life*. Quincy, Ill., 1993.

Grisez, G., J. Boyle, and J. Finnis. "Practical Principles, Moral Truth, and Ultimate Ends." *The American Journal of Jurisprudence*, 32 (1987), 99–151.

Hedwig, K. "Über die Theorie der Praxis bei Thomas von Aquin." *Philosophisches Jahrbuch*, 99 (1992), 245–61.

Hildebrandt, V. *Virtutis non est virtus: Ein scholastischer Lehrsatz zur naturgemässen Bestimmung vernünftigen Handelns in seiner Vorgeschichte*. Europäische Hochschulschriften, Series 20, Vol. 277. Frankfurt, 1989.

Hittinger, R. *A Critique of the New Natural Law Theory*. Notre Dame, Ind., 1987.

Honecker, M. "Paradigmenwechsel in der katholischen Moraltheologie." *Theologische Rundschau*, 56 (1991), 437–45.

Honnefelder, L. "Die Begründbarkeit des Ethischen und die Einheit der Menschheit." In *Die Welt für morgen: Ethische Herausforderungen im Anspruch der Zukunft*. Ed. G. W. Hunold and W. Korff. Munich, 1986. Pp. 315–27.

———. "Wahrheit und Sittlichkeit: Zur Bedeutung der Wahrheit in der Ethik." In *Wahrheit in Einheit und Vielheit*. Ed. E. Corteh. Düsseldorf, 1987. Pp. 147–69.

———. "Natur als Handlungsprincip: Die Relevanz der Natur für die Ethik." In *Natur als Gegenstand der Wissenschaften*. Ed. L. Honnefelder. Grenzfragen 19. Freiburg and Munich, 1992. Pp. 151–83.

Honnefelder, L., ed. *Sittliche Lebensform und praktische Vernunft*. Paderborn, 1992.

Höver, G. *Sittlich handeln im Medium der Ziet: Ansätze zur handlungstheoretischen Neuorientierung der Moraltheologie*. Würzburg, 1988.

———. "Autonomie (II. Theologisch-ethisch)." *Lexikon für Theologie und Kirche*. 3rd ed. Freiburg, 1993. 1:1296–97.

Kerber. W., ed. *Das Absolute in der Ethik*. Fragen einer neuer Weltkultur 7. Munich, 1991.

Kleber, Hermann. *Glück als Lebenziel: Untersuchungen zur Philosophie des Glücks bei Thomas von Aquin*. Beiträge zur Geschichte der Philosophie und Theologie des Mittelalters 13, N.S. Münster, 1988.

Korff, W. *Wie kann der Mensch glücken? Perspektiven der Ethik*. Munich, 1985.

———. "Der Rückgriff auf die Natur: Eine Rekonstruktion der thomanischen Lehre von natürlichen Gesetz." *Philosophisches Jahrbuch*, 94 (1987), 285–96.

Laun, A. *Aktuelle Probleme der Moraltheologie*. Vienna, 1991.

———. *Fragen der Moraltheologie heute*. Vienna, 1992.

Léonard, A. *Le fondement de la morale: Essai d'éthique philosophique*. Paris, 1991.

MacIntyre, A. *After Virtue: A Study in Moral Theory*. 2nd ed. Notre Dame, Ind., 1984.

———. *Whose Justice? Which Rationality?* Notre Dame, Ind., 1988.

———. *Three Rival Versions of Moral Enquiry*. Notre Dame, Ind., 1990.

May, W. *Moral Absolutes: Catholic Tradition, Current Trends, and the Truth*. Milwaukee, 1989.

McInerny, R. *Aquinas on Human Action: A Theory of Practice*. Washington, D.C., 1992.

———. *The Question of Christian Ethics*. Washington, D.C., 1993.

Melina, L. *La conoscenza morale: Linee di riflessione sistematica sul commento di S. Tommaso all'Etica Nichomachea*. Rome, 1988.

Mertens, G., W. Kluxen, and P. Mikat., eds. *Markierungen der Humanität: Sozialethische Herausforderungen auf dem Weg in ein neues Jahrtausend*. Paderborn, 1992.

Mieth, D., ed. *Moraltheologie im Abseits? Antwort auf die Enzyklika "Veritatis splendor."* Freiburg, 1994.

Niesters, T. *Akzidentien der Praxis: Thomas von Aquins Lehre von den Umständen menschlichen Handelns*. Freiburg and Munich, 1992.

Piegsa, J. "Autonomie des Sittlichen: Ein Einblick in den Diskussionsstand." *Forum Katholische Theologie*, 4 (1988), 143–48.

Pinckaers, S. *Ce qu'on ne peut jamais faire: La question des actes in-*

*trinsèquement mauvais—Histoire et discussion*. Fribourg and Paris, 1986.

Pozo Abejón, G. del, ed. *Comentarios a la "Veritatis Splendor."* Madrid, 1994.

Rhonheimer, M. *Praktische Vernunft und Vernünftigkeit der Praxis: Handlungstheorie bei Thomas von Aquin in ihrer Entstehung aus dem Problemkontext der Aristotelischen Ethik*. Berlin, 1994.

———. *La prospettiva della morale: Fondamenti dell'etica filosofica*. Rome, 1994.

———. "Gut und böse oder richtig und falsch—was unterscheidet das Sittliche?" In *Ethik der Leistung (Lindenthal-Colloquium, 1987)*. Ed. Hans Thomas. Herford, 1988. Pp. 47–75.

———. *Natur als Grundlage der Moral*: Nichts als Spiegelfechterei? Anmerkungen zur Stephan Ernsts 'Marginalien.' " *Theologie und Glaube*, 79 (1989), 69–83.

———. "Contraception, Sexual Behavior, and Natural Law: Philosophical Foundation of the Norm of *Humanae Vitae*." *The Linacre Quarterly*, 56, No. 2 (1989), 20–57.

———. "Der anspruchsvolle Weg zum Glück." *Rheinischer Merkur/Christ und Welt*, 29 (1989), 22.

———. "Menschliches Handeln und seine Moralität: Zur Begründung sittlicher Normen." In *Ethos und Menschenbild: Zur Überwindung der Krise der Moral*. Ed. M. Rhonheimer, A. Laun, and T. Goritschewa. Sinn und Sendung 2. St. Ottilien, 1989. Pp. 45–114.

———. "Zur Begründung sittlicher Normen aus der Natur: Grundsätzliche Erwägungen und Exemplifizierung am Beispiel de I.v.f." In *Der Mensch als Mitte und Maßstab der Medizin*. Ed. J. Bonelli. Medizin und Ethik 1. Vienna, 1992. Pp. 49–94.

———. "Ethik—Handeln—Sittlichkeit: Zur sittlichen Dimension menschlichen Tuns." In *Der Mensch als Mitte und Maßstab der Medizin*. Ed. J. Bonelli. Medizin und Ethik 1. Vienna, 1992. Pp. 137–74.

———. "Die Instrumentalisierung des menschlichen Lebens: Ethische Erwägungen zur In-Vitro-Fertilisierung." In *Fortpflanzungsmedizin und Lebensschutz*. Ed. F. Bydlinski and T. Mayer-Maly. Veröffentlichungen des Internationalen Forschungszentrums für Grundfragen der Wissenschaften Salzburg 55 N.S. Innsbruck and Vienna, 1992. Pp. 41–64.

———. "L'uomo, un progetto di Dio: La fondazione teonomica dell'autonomia morale secondo l'Enciclica 'Veritatis Splendor.' " *L'Osservatore Romano*, November 5–6, 1993, pp. 1 and 4.
———. " 'Ethics of Norms' and the Lost Virtues: Searching the Roots of the crisis of Ethical Reasoning." *Anthropotes*, 9 No. 2 (1993), 231–43.
———. " 'Intrinsically Evil Acts' and the Moral Viewpoint: Clarifying a Central Teaching of *Veritatis splendor.*" *The Thomist*, 58, No. 1 (1994), 1–39.
———. "Über die Existenz spezifisch christlichen Moral des Humanums." *Communio*, 23, No. 4 (1994), 360–72.
———. *Sexulität und Verantwortung: Empfängnisverhütung als ethisches Problem.* IMABE-Studie 3. Vienna, 1995.
———. "Sittliche Autonomie und Theonomie gemäss der Enzyklika 'Veritatis splendor.' *Forum Katholische Theologie*, 10, No. 4 (1994), 241–68.
———. "Intentional Actions and the Meaning of Object: A Reply to Richard McCormick." *The Thomist*, 59, No. 2 (1995).
Rodríguez Luño, A. *La scelta etica: Il rapporto fra libertà e virtù.* Milan, 1988.
———. *Etica general.* Pamplona, 1991.
———. "El acto moral y la existencia de una moralidad intrínseca absoluta." In *Comentarios a la "Veritatis splendor."* Ed. G. del Pozo Abejón. Madrid, 1994. 693–712.
Römelt, J. "Der neue Streit um den Naturbegriff." *Theologie der Gegenwart*, 31 (1988), 187–92.
Sala, G. B. "Das Gesetz oder das Gute? Zum Ursprung und Sinn des Formalismus in der Ethik Kants." *Gregorianum*, 71 (1990), 67–95, 315–52.
———. *Gewissensentscheidung: Philosophisch-theologische Analyse von Gewissen und sittlichem Wissen.* Innsbruck and Vienna, 1993.
Schallenberg, P. *Naturrecht und Sozialtheologie: Die Entwicklung des theonomen Naturrechts der späten Neuscholastik im deutschen Sprachraum (1900–1960).* Münster, 1993.
Schockenhoff, E. *Bonum hominis: Die anthropologischen und theologischen Grundlagen der Tugendethik des Thomas von Aquin.* Mainz, 1987.

Schröer, C. *Praktische Vernunft bei Thomas von Aquin.* Stuttgart, Berlin, and Cologne, 1995.

Schüller, B. *Pluralismus in der Ethik: Zum Stil wissenschaftlicher Kontroversen.* Münster, 1988.

———. "Naturrecht und Naturgesetz." In *Grundlagen und Probleme der heutigen Moraltheologie.* Ed. W. Ernst. Würzburg, 1989. Pp. 61–74.

Seidl, H. *Sittengesetz und Freiheit: Erörterungen zur Allgemeinen Ethik.* Schriftenreihe der Gustav-Siewerth-Akademie 7. Weilheim and Bierbronnen, 1992.

Spaemann, R. *Das Natürliche und das Vernünftige: Aufsätze zur Anthropologie.* Munich, 1987.

Stanke, G. *Die Lehre von den "Quellen der Moralität": Darstellung und Diskussion der neuscholastischen Aussagen und neuerer Ansätze.* Regensburg, 1984.

Szostek, A. *Natur–Vernunft–Freiheit: Philosophische Analyse der Konzeption "schöpferischer Vernunft" in zeitgenössischer Moraltheologie.* Frankfurt, 1992.

Virt, G. *Epikie–verantwortlicher Umgang mit Normen: Eine historisch-systematische Untersuchung zu Aristoteles, Thomas von Aquin, und Franz Suarez.* Mainz, 1983.

Wieland G. "Secundum naturam vivere. Über das Verhältnis von Natur und Sittlichkeit." In *Natur im ethischen Argument.* Ed. B. Fraling. Freiburg, 1990. Pp. 13–32.

Wolbert, Werner. "Naturalismus in der Ethik: Zum Worwurf des 'naturalistischen Fehlschlusses.' " *Theologie und Glaube,* 3 (1989), 243–67.

———. "Wege und Umwege einer ethischen Normierungstheorie." In *Grundlagen und Probleme der heutigen Moraltheologie.* Ed. W. Ernst. Würzburg, 1989. Pp. 75–93.

———. *Vom Nutzen der Gerechtigkeit: Zur Diskussion um Utilitarismus und teleologische Theorie.* Studien zur theologischen Ethik 44. Freiburg, 1992.

# INDEX


Abelard, Peter, 93
abortion, 334, 359, 458, 497, 510, 542
*actus:*
  *actus debitus,* 68–70, 74–75, 138–39
  *actus exterior,* 77, 418
  *actus humanus,* 75–78, 410–37 *passim*
  *actus imperatus,* 68–70, 418–19, 425, 453
anthropology, 34–38, 95–103, 212–14, 234–36, 388
anthropomorphism, 217–24
Augustine, St., 15, 262, 330, 457, 545
autonomy:
  competence, 199–204
  constitutive, 199–204
  of ethics from metaphysics, 35, 208–11
  functional, 197–99
  of moral insight, xvii–xviii, 14, 282–83, 303–304*n*69
  of the moral order from the natural order, 64, 206–208
  and participation, 142, 217–24, 234–51, 319
  personal, 38, 96, 137, 195–97, 206–11, 273–74, 320, 335–36, 534

Baius, M., 327
Bentham, Jeremy, 353–59 *passim*
birth control, 104–105, 373
Boethius, 252*n*6
Bonaventure, St., 444*n*25
*bonum rationis* (good of the reason), 69, 75, 83, 251, 320, 328, 333, 357, 420

Cajetan, 60, 467
casuistry, 308–10, 471
*causa prima/secunda,* 65, 98, 222, 236, 243, 258
Cicero, 377–78*n*3
consequences, 359, 361–65, 385–86, 395, 459–60, 541–44
consequentialism. *See* ethics: teleological
contraception, 3, 109–38 *passim,* 211, 362
  as an intrinsic evil, 362–63, 475–83

Damascene, St. John, 237
Decalogue, 260, 281, 382, 480–83, 511
deontology. *See* ethics: deontological
Descartes, René, 124, 464
(Pseudo-) Dionysius, 262
dualism, xiii, xvi, 6, 82, 88, 94–95, 102, 208–209, 371, 536–39
  of nature and reason, 13, 43*n*4, 182–83
Duns Scotus, Bl. John, 347*n*44

ethics:
deontological, 320, 359–61
eudaimonistic, 55*n*62, 212, 353
existential, 143–44
of love, 385, 391–93
normative, 308, 335–36
of salvation, 325–26, 399
teleological, xiii, 50*n*42, 64, 88, 90, 123, 145*n*1, 179, 216, 259, 319, 351–404 *passim*, 426, 459, 480, 502–503, 512, 540–44, 570–74
euthanasia, 497, 510
exceptions, 460, 474, 480, 497, 506, 515–16, 527
experience:
moral or practical, xiv, 14–22, 71, 124, 209, 351, 494
reflective, of the self, 30, 34–36, 40–41, 139, 202–203, 493–94

*finis:*
debitus (right end), 67, 138–39, 245, 506
*naturalis* (natural end), 81, 100, 416, 426, 429, 431–36 (esp. 435), 476, 486*n*16
*operis/operantis* (end of the deed/end of the doer), 91–92, 188, 310, 319, 383, 415, 430–36 *passim*, 437, 467, 486*n*16
freedom, 21, 29, 66, 78, 96, 120–22, 143, 184, 196, 213–14, 218–20, 223–24, 240, 436, 449*n*45, 527
fundamental option, 539, 551

God:
as creator, 26, 65–66, 99, 217–18, 238–39
as moral law-giver, 68, 217–18, 224, 286, 321, 537–38

Hume, David, 43–44*n*4

*inclinationes naturales* (natural inclinations), 28, 74, 117, 246–47, 259, 272, 284–85, 356–57, 536, 562–70
to the conservation of one's own being, 75, 82, 95
to the joining of male and female, 75, 95, 96–97, 104, 118, 119, 124
to knowing and loving God, 238
to knowledge of the truth, 75, 95
to life according to reason, 80, 89–90, 319
to living in community with others, 75, 95
to the proper (*proprius*) act and end, 67, 75, 83, 95, 104, 107, 246
to the right (*debitus*) act and end, 67, 70, 72–73, 75, 83, 95, 138–39, 249, 422–23, 492
as "seeds (*semina*) of the virtues," 85–87, 104, 250, 272, 405–406*n*7
as "sub-human" or indifferent material of actions, 81–82, 107–108, 152*n*29, 159*n*61, 284–85, 538–39
intrinsic evil (*intrinsece malum*), 308, 362, 390, 404, 475–83 *passim*, 495, 510

Kant, Immanuel, 64, 196, 205, 212–16 *passim*, 379–80
Killing (*see also* "abortion"):
in capital punishment, 481–82
in a just war, 481–82

in self-defense, 461, 480–81, 487*n*20

lying, 266, 334, 359, 370–71, 420, 452–58 *passim*

magisterium, 110, 211, 372–73, 547
and autonomy of moral insight, 296*n*41, 303–304*n*69, 321
marriage, 17, 75, 95–98, 112, 341*n*21, 506
love and marriage, 110, 113–14, 362, 369, 372, 423
marriage and biological or physiological laws, 5, 104–105, 115, 135–38
Mill, John Stuart, 43*n*4, 352, 356
Moore, G. E., 43*n*4, 484*n*8, 554*n*5
*mutatio materiae* ("change of matter"), 501–505, 507–11, 517

naturalistic fallacy, 6, 43–44*n*4, 287, 342*n*26, 351, 364–65, 375–77, 403, 422–23, 540–41
natural law:
as constituted by the reason (*aliquid per rationem constitutum*), 42, 63–64, 67–68, 80, 138–45 *passim*
as participation of the eternal law, 60, 64–68, 138–43, 224–28, 428, 535, 545–47
as an order of being (neo-scholastic "essentialist" misinterpretation), 7, 15–20, 42, 66, 140, 559–62
natural reason. *See* reason: natural

"ought," 14, 38, 59, 183, 185, 187, 196, 214–16, 365, 549–50

Plato, 55*n*64, 215, 255*n*21, 248, 262, 312–13, 325, 357, 388, 540
popes:
Leo XIII, 11–12, 140, 523
John Paul II, 134, 162*n*75, 164*nn*80 & 81, 166*n*88
Paul VI, 553
Pius XII, 166*n*87, 367, 440*n*10
procreation, 97–98, 100–101, 109–38 *passim*, 341*n*21, 363, 368–69, 382, 413, 416–17, 423–24, 431, 434–35
*proportio (debita) ad rationem* ("right proportion according to reason"), 29, 80, 87, 90, 307, 421–22, 427
proportionalism. *See* ethics: teleological
prudence (*recta ratio agibilium*), 32, 38, 40, 85, 93, 145–47*n*1, 157*n*53, 193*n*5, 196, 225, 274, 280, 281–82, 322, 331–33, 392, 493, 512, 525–27, 574–79

Rahner, Karl, 141, 143–44, 152*n*30, 326–27, 350*n*57, 437
reason:
as "creative" of the moral order, xviii, 3, 6, 42, 70, 211–12, 217, 220–28 *passim*, 286, 535
discursive reason and intellection, 268–71, 284–86
natural reason (*ratio naturalis*), 13, 28, 40–41, 57*n*73, 64, 68–72, 81, 93, 107, 136, 138–40, 208, 228, 244, 257–

306 *passim*, 315, 403, 436, 494, 516, 526, 534, 567
as an organ that merely "reads off" (*Ableseorgan*), 7, 42, 70, 183, 247
practical (as dist. from theoretical), 24–27, 33–35, 208, 319, 497
*reditio completa* ("complete return" of the human intellect on itself in reflection), 29, 35, 285

sexuality, 99–100, 110–11, 117–35 *passim*, 369–71, 414
sin, 174*n*20, 486*n*18, 546, 551
original sin, 174*n*120, 340*n*17, 488*n*23, 546, 551–53
Suarez, Francisco, 43*n*4
syllogism, practical, 145–47*n*1, 153*n*34

teleological ethics. *See* ethics: teleological
Ten Commandments. *See* Decalogue
tendencies, natural. *See* inclinations, natural
theft, 402–403, 423, 502, 505, 513–14

Ulpian, 162–63*n*77
Utilitarianism, 6, 55*n*62, 64, 89, 212–13, 351–59 *passim*, 396, 404

virtue, 142–45, 215–16, 231*n*22, 388–89, 574–79

will (*voluntas*), 15, 86, 91–93, 117, 316, 328, 333, 415, 418, 430–31, 457, 466–67, 492, 502, 524, 541, 546

# ABOUT THE AUTHOR

MARTIN RHONHEIMER studied history, philosophy, political science, and theology in Zürich and Rome and holds a doctorate in philosophy from the University of Zürich. He was ordained a Roman Catholic priest in 1983 and currently serves as professor of ethics and political philosophy at the Philosophical Faculty of the Pontifical University of the Holy Cross (Pontificio Ateneo della Santa Croce) in Rome. His books include *Politisierung und Legitimitätsentzug*, *Familie und Selbstverwirklichung*, *La prospettiva della morale*, *Praktische Vernunft und Vernünftigkeit der Praxis*, and *Sexualität und Verantwortung*, and he has published a wide range of articles in German, Italian, English, and Spanish scholarly reviews and journals.